Peterson's®

MASTER THE DSST® EXAMS, VOLUME II

THE ULTIMATE GUIDE TO MASTERING THE DSST® EXAMS

About Peterson's

Peterson's® has been your trusted educational publisher for over 50 years. It's a milestone we're quite proud of, as we continue to offer the most accurate, dependable, high-quality educational content in the field, providing you with everything you need to succeed. No matter where you are on your academic or professional path, you can rely on Peterson's publications and its online information at www.petersons.com for the most up-to-date education exploration data, expert test-prep tools, and the highest quality career success resources—everything you need to achieve your education goals.

For more information about Peterson's range of educational products, contact Peterson's, 8740 Lucent Blvd., Suite 400 Highlands Ranch, CO 80129, 800-338-3282 Ext. 54229; or find us online at www.petersons.com.

ISBN-13: 978-0-7689-4186-9

Printed in the United States of America
10 9 8 7 6 5 4 3 2 1   19 18

First Edition

www.petersonspublishing.com/publishingupdates

Check out our website at www.petersonspublishing.com/publishingupdates to see if there is any new information regarding the test and any revisions or corrections to the content of this book. We've made sure the information in this book is accurate and up-to-date; however, the test format or content may have changed since the time of publication.

Prometric™

Prometric, the DSST® program provider, has reviewed the contents of *Master the DSST® Exams, Volume II* and found this study guide to be an excellent reflection of the content of the respective DSST tests. However, passing the sample tests provided in any study material does not guarantee you will pass the actual tests.

Contents

Contents

Before You Begin

HOW THIS BOOK IS ORGANIZED

Peterson's *Master the DSST ® Exams, Volume II* provides diagnostic tests, subject-matter reviews, and post-tests for twelve DSST exams. The following table provides a summary of the information covered in each chapter.

Chapter 1: Principles of Advanced Composition	Elements of effective writing, reading and writing arguments and using secondary sources. This exam was newly created January 2017 and includes content reviewed by the American Council on Education (ACE).
Chapter 2: Math for Liberal Arts	Real number systems, sets and logic, metric system, conversions and geometry, algebra, graphs and functions, linear systems and inequalities, exponents and logarithms. This exam was newly created January 2017 and includes content reviewed by the American Council on Education (ACE).
Chapter 3: Principles of Public Speaking	Principles of Public Speaking, audience analysis, purposes of speeches, structure/organization, content/supporting materials, research, language and style, delivery, communication apprehension, listening and feedback, criticism and evaluation. Record an impromptu persuasive speech that will be scored.
Chapter 4: Organizational Behavior	Scientific approaches, research designs, data collection methods, individual processes and characteristics, interpersonal and group processes, organizational processes, change and development processes.

Chapter 5: Human Resource Management	Training and development, performance appraisals, compensation issues, security issues, personnel legislation and regulation, labor relations and current issues.
Chapter 6: Technical Writing	Theory & practice of technical writing, purpose, content, organizational patterns of common types of technical documents, elements of various technical reports, technical editing.
Chapter 7: Principles of Statistics	Principles and concepts underlying higher-order statistics, continuous and discrete distributions, use of predictive statistics using the linear model and confidence intervals.
Chapter 8: Criminal Justice	Criminal behavior, police, the court system, sentencing issues, adult prison systems and juvenile correction alternatives.
Chapter 9: Environmental Science	Ecological concepts (ecosystems, global ecology, food chains and webs), environmental impacts, environmental management & conservation, and political processes & the future.
Chapter 10: Fundamentals of Cybersecurity	This examination includes content related to major topics in cybersecurity including application and systems security, implementing authentication and authorization technologies, compliance, security pertaining to networks and physical environments, and vulnerability management.
Chapter 11: Introduction to Law Enforcement	Overview of the U.S. criminal justice system, police systems in the U.S., police organization, management & issues; and U.S. law and precedents.
Chapter 12: The Civil War and Reconstruction	The Civil War from pre-secession (1861) through Reconstruction.

Each chapter of the book is organized in the same manner:

- **Diagnostic Test**—Twenty questions, followed by an answer key and explanations
- **Assessment Grid**—a chart designed to help you identify areas you need to focus on based on your test results
- **Subject-Matter Review**—General overview of the exam subject, followed by a review of the relevant topics and terminology covered on the exam
- **Post-Test**—Sixty questions, followed by an answer key and explanations

The purpose of the diagnostic test is to help you figure out what you know . . . or don't know. The twenty multiple-choice questions are similar to the ones found on the DSST exam, and they should provide you with a good idea of what to expect. Once you take the diagnostic test, check your answers to see how you did. Included with each correct answer is a brief explanation regarding why a specific answer is correct and, in many cases, why other options are incorrect. Use the assessment grid to identify the questions you miss so that you can spend more time reviewing that information later. As with any exam, knowing your weak spots greatly improves your chances of success.

Following the diagnostic test in each chapter is a subject matter review. The review summarizes the various topics covered on the DSST exam. Key terms are defined; important concepts are explained; and, when appropriate, examples are provided. As you read the review, some of the information may seem familiar while other information may seem foreign. Again, take note of the unfamiliar because that will most likely cause you problems on the actual exam. If you need more information about a topic than what the review provides, refer to one of the textbooks recommended for the test.

After studying the subject-matter review, you should be ready for the post-test. The post-test for each chapter contains sixty multiple-choice items, and it will serve as a dry run for the real DSST exam. Take the time to answer all of the questions because they are similar to those found on the DSST exam for that particular subject. As with the diagnostic test, post-test answers and explanations are at the end of each chapter.

SPECIAL STUDY FEATURES

Peterson's *Master the DSST® Exams, Volume II* is designed to be as user-friendly as it is complete. To this end, it includes two features to make your preparation more efficient.

Overview

Each chapter begins with a bulleted overview listing the topics covered in the chapter. This overview will allow you to quickly target the areas in which you are most interested and need to review.

Summing It Up

Each review chapter ends with a point-by-point summary that captures the most important information in the chapter. The summaries offer a convenient way to review key points.

EXPAND YOUR DSST® TEST PREP ARSENAL

Peterson's *Master the DSST® Exams, Volume II* is the second of a two-volume set designed to give you the most comprehensive test prep resource available for the DSST exams. Peterson's *Master the DSST® Exams, Volume I* features the same effective test preparation strategies provided in this publication for twelve additional DSST exams: Ethics in America, General Anthropology, Health and Human Development, Computing and Information Technology, Introduction to Business, Introduction to World Religions, Management Information Systems, Money and Banking, Personal Finance, Principles of Supervision, History of the Soviet Union, and Substance Abuse.

YOU'RE WELL ON YOUR WAY TO SUCCESS

You've made the decision to take a DSST exam and earn college credit for your life experiences. Peterson's *Master the DSST® Exams, Volume II* will help prepare you for the steps you'll need to achieve your goal—scoring high on the exam!

GIVE US YOUR FEEDBACK

Peterson's publishes a full line of resources to help guide you through the exam process. Peterson's publications can be found at college libraries and career centers and at your local bookstore or library.

Publishing Department
Peterson's
8740 Lucent Blvd., Suite 400
Highlands Ranch, CO 80129

About DSST®

OVERVIEW

- **What is DSST®?**
- **Why Take a DSST® Exam?**
- **DSST® Test centers**
- **How to Register for a DSST® Exam**
- **Preparing for a DSST® Exam**
- **Test Day**

WHAT IS DSST®?

The DSST program provides the opportunity for people to earn college credit for what they have learned outside of the traditional classroom. Accepted or administered at over 1,900 colleges and universities nationwide and approved by the American Council on Education (ACE), the DSST program enables people to use the knowledge they have acquired outside the classroom to accomplish their educational and professional goals.

WHY TAKE A DSST® EXAM?

Previously known as DANTES Subject Standardized Tests, DSST exams offer a way for you to save both time and money in your quest for a college education. Why enroll in a college course in a subject you already understand? For over 30 years, the DSST program has offered the perfect solution for people who are knowledgeable in a specific subject and who want to save both time and money. A passing score on a DSST exam provides physical evidence to universities of proficiency in a specific subject. Over 1,900 accredited and respected colleges and universities across the nation award undergraduate credit for passing scores on DSST exams. With the DSST program, individuals can shave months off the time it takes to earn a degree.

The DSST program offers numerous advantages for people in all stages of their educational development:

- Adult learners
- College students
- Military personnel

Adult learners desiring college degrees face unique circumstances—demanding work schedules, family responsibilities, and tight budgets. Yet adult learners also have years of valuable work experience that can be applied toward a degree through the DSST program. For example, adult learners with on-the-job experience in business and management might be able to skip the Business 101 courses if they earn passing marks on DSST exams such as Introduction to Business and Principles of Supervision.

Adult learners can put their prior learning into action and move forward with more advanced course work. Adults who have never enrolled in a college course may feel a little uncertain about their abilities. If this describes your situation, then sign up for a DSST exam and see how you do. A passing score may be the boost you need to realize your dream of earning a degree. With family and work commitments, adult learners often feel they lack the time to attend college. The DSST program enables adult learners the unique opportunity to work toward college degrees without the time constraints of semester-long course work. DSST exams take 2 hours or less to complete. In one weekend, you could earn credit for multiple college courses.

The DSST exams also benefit students who are already enrolled in a college or university. With college tuition costs on the rise, most students face financial challenges. The fee for each DSST exam starts at $80 plus administration fees charged by some testing facilities—significantly less than the $750 average cost of a 3-hour college class. Maximize tuition assistance by taking DSST exams for introductory or mandatory course work. Once you earn a passing score on a DSST exam, you are free to move on to higher-level course work in that subject matter, take desired electives, or focus on courses in a chosen major.

Not only do college students and adult learners profit from DSST exams, but military personnel reap the benefits as well. If you are a member of the armed services at home or abroad, you can initiate your post-military career by taking DSST exams in areas with which you have experience. Military personnel can gain credit anywhere in the world, thanks to the fact that almost all of the tests are available through the Internet at designated testing locations. DSST testing facilities are located at over 500 military installations, so service members on active duty can get a jump-start on a post-military career with the DSST program. As an additional incentive, DANTES (Defense Activity for Non-Traditional Education Support) provides funding for DSST test fees for eligible members of the military.

Over thirty subject-matter tests are available in the fields of Business, Humanities, Math, Physical Science, Social Sciences, and Technology.

Available DSST® Exams	
Business	**Social Sciences**
Business Ethics and Society Business Mathematics Computing and Information Technology Human Resource Management Introduction to Business Management Information Systems Money and Banking Organizational Behavior Personal Finance Principles of Finance Principles of Supervision	A History of the Vietnam War Art of the Western World Criminal Justice Foundations of Education Fundamentals of Counseling General Anthropology History of the Soviet Union Human/Cultural Geography Introduction to Law Enforcement Lifespan Developmental Psychology Substance Abuse Civil War and Reconstruction
Humanities	**Physical Science**
Ethics in America History of the Soviet Union Introduction to World Religions Math for Liberal Arts Principles of Public Speaking Principles of Advanced English Composition	Astronomy Environmental Science Health and Human Development Principles of Physical Science I
Math	**Technology**
Fundamentals of College Algebra Math for Liberal Arts Principles of Statistics	Computing and Information Technology Fundamentals of Cybersecurity Technical Writing

As you can see from the table, the DSST program covers a wide variety of subjects. However, it is important to ask two questions before registering for a DSST exam.

1. Which universities or colleges award credit for passing DSST exams?

2. Which DSST exams are the most relevant to my desired degree and my experience?

Knowing which universities offer DSST credit is important. In all likelihood, a college in your area awards credit for DSST exams, but find out before taking an exam by contacting the university directly. Then review the list of DSST exams to determine which ones are most relevant to the degree you are seeking and to your base of knowledge. Schedule an appointment with your college adviser to determine which exams best fit your degree program and which college courses the DSST exams can replace. Advisers should also be able to tell you the minimum score required on the DSST exam to receive university credit.

DSST® TEST CENTERS

You can find DSST testing locations in community colleges and universities across the country. Contact your local college or university to find out if the school administers DSST exams, or check the DSST website (www.getcollegecredit.com) for a location near you. Keep in mind that some universities and colleges administer DSST exams only to enrolled students. DSST testing is available to men and women in the armed services at over 500 military installations around the world.

HOW TO REGISTER FOR A DSST® EXAM

Once you have located a nearby DSST testing facility, you need to contact the testing center to find out the exam administration schedule. Many centers are set up to administer tests via the Internet, while others use printed materials. Almost all DSST exams are available as online tests, but the method used depends on the testing center. The cost for each DSST exam starts at $80, and many testing locations charge a fee to cover their costs for administering the tests. Credit cards are the only accepted payment method for taking online DSST exams. Credit card, certified check, and money order are acceptable payment methods for paper-and-pencil tests.

Test-takers are allotted two score reports—one mailed to them and another mailed to a designated college or university, if requested. Online tests generate unofficial scores at the end of the test session, while individuals taking paper tests must wait four to six weeks for score reports.

PREPARING FOR A DSST® EXAM

Even though you are knowledgeable in a certain subject matter, you should still prepare for the test to ensure you achieve the highest score possible. The first step in studying for a DSST exam is to find out what will be on the specific test you have chosen. Information regarding test content is located on the DSST fact sheets, which can be downloaded at no cost from **www.getcollegecredit.com**. Each fact sheet outlines the topics covered on a subject-matter test, as well as the approximate percentage assigned to each topic. For example, questions on the Principles of Supervision exam are distributed in the following way: 20 percent on the roles and responsibilities of the supervisor, 30 percent on organizational environment, and 50 percent on management functions.

In addition to the breakdown of topics on a DSST exam, the fact sheet also lists recommended reference materials. If you do not own the recommended books, then check college bookstores. Avoid paying high prices for new textbooks by looking online for used textbooks. Don't panic if you are unable to locate a specific textbook listed on the fact sheet; the textbooks are merely recommendations. Instead, search for comparable books used in university courses on the specific subject. Current editions are ideal, and it is a good idea to use at least two references when studying for a DSST exam. Of course, the subject matter provided in this book will be a sufficient review for most test-takers. However, if you need additional information, then it is a good idea to have some of the reference materials at your disposal when preparing for a DSST exam.

Fact sheets include other useful information in addition to a list of reference materials and topics. Each fact sheet includes subject-specific sample questions like those you will encounter on the DSST exam. The sample questions provide an idea of the types of questions you can expect on the exam.

Test questions are multiple choice with one correct answer and three incorrect choices. The fact sheet also includes information about the number of credit hours that ACE has recommended be awarded by colleges for a passing DSST exam score. However, you should keep in mind that not all universities and colleges adhere to the ACE recommendation for DSST credit hours. Some institutions require DSST exam scores higher than the minimum score recommended by ACE. Once you have acquired appropriate reference materials and you have the outline provided on the fact sheet, you are ready to start studying, which is where this book can help.

TEST DAY

After reviewing the material and taking practice tests, you are finally ready to take your DSST exam. Follow these tips for a successful test day experience.

1. **Arrive on time.** Not only is it courteous to arrive on time to the DSST testing facility, but it also allows plenty of time for you to take care of check-in procedures and settle into your surroundings.

2. **Bring identification.** DSST test facilities require that candidates bring a valid government-issued identification card with a current photo and signature. Acceptable forms of identification include a current driver's license, passport, military identification card, or state-issued identification card. Individuals who fail to bring proper identification to the DSST testing facility will not be allowed to take an exam.

3. **Bring the right supplies.** If your exam requires the use of a calculator, you may bring a calculator that meets the specifications. For paper-based exams, you may also bring No. 2 pencils with an eraser and black ballpoint pens. Regardless of the exam methodology, you are NOT allowed to bring reference or study materials, scratch paper, or electronics such as cell phones, personal handheld devices, cameras, alarm wrist watches, or tape recorders to the testing center.

4. **Take the test.** During the exam, take the time to read each question-and-answer option carefully. Eliminate the choices you know are incorrect to narrow the number of potential answers. If a question completely stumps you, take an educated guess and move on—remember that DSSTs are timed; you will have 2 hours to take the exam.

With the proper preparation, DSST exams will save you both time and money. So join the thousands of people who have already reaped the benefits of DSST exams and move closer than ever to your college degree.

Principles of Advanced English Composition

OVERVIEW

- **Test Answer Sheets**
- **Principles of Advanced English Composition Diagnostic Test**
- **Answer Key and Explanations**
- **Diagnostic Test Assessment Grid**
- **Types of Writing**
- **Elements of Effective Writing**
- **Reading and Writing Arguments**
- **Using Secondary Sources**
- **Summing It Up**
- **Principles of Advanced English Composition Post-test**
- **Answer Key and Explanations**

Using effective techniques for writing compositions is a key skill to learn for your academic career—and often your professional career, as well. Writing is one of the main ways we express ourselves. Having a proper grasp of the different and most effective ways to express ideas and using sources to back up our ideas and claims makes us strong communicators.

The DSST Principles of Advanced English Composition exam will test your ability to identify all of those skills and elements necessary for writing the kind of high-level composition you would be expected to produce at this stage of your education.

You have probably taken composition exams in the past, and most of them likely required you to write an original composition of your own. The DSST Principles of Advanced English Composition exam is very different from those exams. Like all DSST exams, this test is exclusively in the multiple-choice format. The exam consists of 64 questions; you will have two hours to complete the questions. That means you will be expected to identify the principles of composition without actually having to put them to use.

Chapter 1

DIAGNOSTIC TEST ANSWER SHEET

1. Ⓐ Ⓑ Ⓒ Ⓓ   5. Ⓐ Ⓑ Ⓒ Ⓓ   9. Ⓐ Ⓑ Ⓒ Ⓓ   13. Ⓐ Ⓑ Ⓒ Ⓓ   17. Ⓐ Ⓑ Ⓒ Ⓓ

2. Ⓐ Ⓑ Ⓒ Ⓓ   6. Ⓐ Ⓑ Ⓒ Ⓓ   10. Ⓐ Ⓑ Ⓒ Ⓓ   14. Ⓐ Ⓑ Ⓒ Ⓓ   18. Ⓐ Ⓑ Ⓒ Ⓓ

3. Ⓐ Ⓑ Ⓒ Ⓓ   7. Ⓐ Ⓑ Ⓒ Ⓓ   11. Ⓐ Ⓑ Ⓒ Ⓓ   15. Ⓐ Ⓑ Ⓒ Ⓓ   19. Ⓐ Ⓑ Ⓒ Ⓓ

4. Ⓐ Ⓑ Ⓒ Ⓓ   8. Ⓐ Ⓑ Ⓒ Ⓓ   12. Ⓐ Ⓑ Ⓒ Ⓓ   16. Ⓐ Ⓑ Ⓒ Ⓓ   20. Ⓐ Ⓑ Ⓒ Ⓓ

POST-TEST ANSWER SHEET

1. Ⓐ Ⓑ Ⓒ Ⓓ   13. Ⓐ Ⓑ Ⓒ Ⓓ   25. Ⓐ Ⓑ Ⓒ Ⓓ   37. Ⓐ Ⓑ Ⓒ Ⓓ   49. Ⓐ Ⓑ Ⓒ Ⓓ

2. Ⓐ Ⓑ Ⓒ Ⓓ   14. Ⓐ Ⓑ Ⓒ Ⓓ   26. Ⓐ Ⓑ Ⓒ Ⓓ   38. Ⓐ Ⓑ Ⓒ Ⓓ   50. Ⓐ Ⓑ Ⓒ Ⓓ

3. Ⓐ Ⓑ Ⓒ Ⓓ   15. Ⓐ Ⓑ Ⓒ Ⓓ   27. Ⓐ Ⓑ Ⓒ Ⓓ   39. Ⓐ Ⓑ Ⓒ Ⓓ   51. Ⓐ Ⓑ Ⓒ Ⓓ

4. Ⓐ Ⓑ Ⓒ Ⓓ   16. Ⓐ Ⓑ Ⓒ Ⓓ   28. Ⓐ Ⓑ Ⓒ Ⓓ   40. Ⓐ Ⓑ Ⓒ Ⓓ   52. Ⓐ Ⓑ Ⓒ Ⓓ

5. Ⓐ Ⓑ Ⓒ Ⓓ   17. Ⓐ Ⓑ Ⓒ Ⓓ   29. Ⓐ Ⓑ Ⓒ Ⓓ   41. Ⓐ Ⓑ Ⓒ Ⓓ   53. Ⓐ Ⓑ Ⓒ Ⓓ

6. Ⓐ Ⓑ Ⓒ Ⓓ   18. Ⓐ Ⓑ Ⓒ Ⓓ   30. Ⓐ Ⓑ Ⓒ Ⓓ   42. Ⓐ Ⓑ Ⓒ Ⓓ   54. Ⓐ Ⓑ Ⓒ Ⓓ

7. Ⓐ Ⓑ Ⓒ Ⓓ   19. Ⓐ Ⓑ Ⓒ Ⓓ   31. Ⓐ Ⓑ Ⓒ Ⓓ   43. Ⓐ Ⓑ Ⓒ Ⓓ   55. Ⓐ Ⓑ Ⓒ Ⓓ

8. Ⓐ Ⓑ Ⓒ Ⓓ   20. Ⓐ Ⓑ Ⓒ Ⓓ   32. Ⓐ Ⓑ Ⓒ Ⓓ   44. Ⓐ Ⓑ Ⓒ Ⓓ   56. Ⓐ Ⓑ Ⓒ Ⓓ

9. Ⓐ Ⓑ Ⓒ Ⓓ   21. Ⓐ Ⓑ Ⓒ Ⓓ   33. Ⓐ Ⓑ Ⓒ Ⓓ   45. Ⓐ Ⓑ Ⓒ Ⓓ   57. Ⓐ Ⓑ Ⓒ Ⓓ

10. Ⓐ Ⓑ Ⓒ Ⓓ   22. Ⓐ Ⓑ Ⓒ Ⓓ   34. Ⓐ Ⓑ Ⓒ Ⓓ   46. Ⓐ Ⓑ Ⓒ Ⓓ   58. Ⓐ Ⓑ Ⓒ Ⓓ

11. Ⓐ Ⓑ Ⓒ Ⓓ   23. Ⓐ Ⓑ Ⓒ Ⓓ   35. Ⓐ Ⓑ Ⓒ Ⓓ   47. Ⓐ Ⓑ Ⓒ Ⓓ   59. Ⓐ Ⓑ Ⓒ Ⓓ

12. Ⓐ Ⓑ Ⓒ Ⓓ   24. Ⓐ Ⓑ Ⓒ Ⓓ   36. Ⓐ Ⓑ Ⓒ Ⓓ   48. Ⓐ Ⓑ Ⓒ Ⓓ   60. Ⓐ Ⓑ Ⓒ Ⓓ

answer sheet

PRINCIPLES OF ADVANCED ENGLISH COMPOSITION DIAGNOSTIC TEST

> **Directions:** Carefully read each of the following 20 questions. Choose the best answer to each question and fill in the corresponding circle on the answer sheet. The Answer Key and Explanations can be found following this Diagnostic Test.

1. The term for writing that captures the personality of an individual is _____ writing.
   - A. informative
   - B. argumentative
   - C. narrative
   - D. critical

2. Which of the following is an example of a secondary source?
   - A. Biography
   - B. Autobiography
   - C. Interview
   - D. Diary

3. A paper written for an audience of college professors should be written in a style that is
   - A. colloquial.
   - B. emotive.
   - C. academic.
   - D. simplistic.

4. The term for the element of an argument that clearly states the author's opinion on an issue is the
   - A. thesis.
   - B. background.
   - C. evidence.
   - D. conclusion.

5. The author of an argument strengthens her or his opinion by
   - A. ensuring that the opinion is shared by many other people.
   - B. stating that opinion clearly and concisely.
   - C. insulting anyone who disagrees with that opinion.
   - D. including claims that support that opinion.

6. A weak argument does NOT
   - A. make assumptions based on the author's personal prejudices.
   - B. include clear connections between reasons and claims.
   - C. explicitly indicate the reasons why the author makes certain claims.
   - D. indicate the author's personal experiences at all.

7. When deciding on a topic for an informative essay assignment, it is MOST helpful to read
   - A. nonfiction books or articles related to the assigned topic.
   - B. fiction to get a better idea of how to tell an effective story.
   - C. poorly written essays to understand what not to do.
   - D. magazine articles about as many different topics as possible.

8. The MOST appropriate source for writing an essay on aviation pioneers the Wright Brothers is
   A. a history of aviation.
   B. a pamphlet from the National Air and Space Museum.
   C. a biography of the Wright Brothers.
   D. a newspaper article about the Wright Brothers' first flight.

9. The term for jotting down as many ideas as a writer can think of about an essay topic is
   A. freewriting.
   B. brainstorming.
   C. questioning.
   D. hypothesizing.

10. Which of the following sources would be LEAST relevant to an essay on the history of silent film?
    A. A magazine article about silent films that no longer exist
    B. A biography of a famous silent filmmaker
    C. A history of recording audio for film
    D. Film reviews from a current newspaper

11. The term for the way an argument appeals to a reader's emotions is
    A. syllogism.
    B. ethos.
    C. logos.
    D. pathos.

12. The MOST effective method for structuring a paragraph in the body of an essay is to
    A. end the paragraph with a transitional sentence that leads into the next paragraph.
    B. begin the paragraph by restating the main thesis of the essay.
    C. end the paragraph by summarizing the main findings of the entire essay.
    D. begin the paragraph with a new topic that is not directly related to the main topic.

13. A logical syllogism
    A. cannot have more than two premises.
    B. only has one true conclusion.
    C. has several true conclusions.
    D. does not require a believable premise.

14. A paraphrase
    A. directly repeats the words of another person.
    B. simplifies the meaning of a long piece of writing into a simple statement.
    C. clarifies a person's meaning or opinion by using different words.
    D. contrasts one person's opinions with opposing ideas.

15. APA documentation style should be used in a manuscript about
    A. literature.
    B. philosophy.
    C. communications.
    D. social sciences.

16. The thesis statement of a composition should appear in the
    A. first paragraph.
    B. third paragraph.
    C. fourth paragraph.
    D. final paragraph.

17. In MLA in-text citation style, the page number from which the quote was cited must appear
    A. within parentheses.
    B. in the text of the sentence.
    C. within brackets.
    D. in a footnote.

18. The main points of an argument support the argument's
    A. counterclaims.
    B. thesis.
    C. evidence.
    D. reasons.

19. Mind mapping is MOST effective when performed right after
    A. outlining.
    B. brainstorming.
    C. clustering.
    D. freewriting.

20. When an author intends to show that an authority supports his or her point, it is MOST effective to use a
    A. paraphrase.
    B. quotation.
    C. summary.
    D. counterargument.

diagnostic test

ANSWER KEY AND EXPLANATIONS

1. C	5. D	9. B	13. B	17. A
2. A	6. B	10. D	14. C	18. B
3. C	7. A	11. D	15. D	19. B
4. A	8. C	12. A	16. A	20. B

1. **The correct answer is C.** Writing that captures the personality of an individual is a narrative composition. Choice A is incorrect because informative writing conveys information rather than the nuances of an individual's personality. Choice B is incorrect because argumentative writing argues in favor of or against a particular issue. Choice D is incorrect because critical writing involves considering evidence in order to draw a conclusion.

2. **The correct answer is A.** A secondary source discusses a historical event or issue at a later period and is written by someone who was not directly involved in the events described, such as a biography. Choices B, C, and D are all primary sources because autobiographies, interviews, and diaries involve the perspective of individuals directly involved in the events these sources discuss.

3. **The correct answer is C.** An audience of college professors is a highly educated audience, and the best style for a paper directed at such an audience is academic. Choice A, colloquial, indicates an informal style that resembles everyday speech, which is not the best style for an audience of college professors. Choice B, emotive, suggests writing that conveys heightened emotions, which is not necessarily the best style for an audience of college professors. Choice D, simplistic, suggests writing with brief sentences geared toward young or uneducated people.

4. **The correct answer is A.** The author of an argument states his or her essential opinion on the issue to be discussed in a thesis statement. Choice B is incorrect because background refers to a brief description of past events that lead into the thesis statement. Choice C, evidence, is the details that support the thesis. Choice D, conclusion, wraps up the argument with a final, summarizing statement.

5. **The correct answer is D.** A strong argument is supported by convincing claims. Choice A is not the best answer because a majority opinion is not necessary if the author supports her or his argument with strong supporting claims. Choice B is incorrect because it merely describes a way to state an opinion, not how to make that opinion strong. Choice C does not describe an effective way to strengthen the main opinion in an argumentative piece of writing.

6. **The correct answer is B.** A strong argument includes warrants, which are statements that connect reasons to claims. A weak argument will fail to include warrants. Choice A is incorrect because making assumptions based on personal prejudices is not a strong way to build an argument. Choice C is not the best answer because warrants do not have to be explicit; they can also be implicit. Choice D is not the best answer because an argument does not have to contain personal author stories—just opinions and evidence to back them up.

7. **The correct answer is A.** Reading various nonfiction works related to the assigned topic is one effective way to come up with ideas for your own informative essay before you begin writing it. Choice B is not the best answer because fiction is written in a very different style from that of most informative essays. Choice C is not a very sensible prewriting strategy. The strategy described in choice D lacks focus and might make it very difficult to select a topic before writing an informative essay.

8. **The correct answer is C.** The best and most thorough of these secondary sources would be a biography of the Wright Brothers. Choice A may be a good source, but since it is not specifically focused on the Wright Brothers, it is less likely to contain an abundance of information on them than a biography specifically about that topic would. Choice B is incorrect because a pamphlet is unlikely to contain more than a brief blurb about any topic. Choice D might be a good source too, but a single newspaper article will contain far less information than a full-length biography.

9. **The correct answer is B.** The term for this prewriting strategy is brainstorming. Freewriting is a bit different because it involves writing nonstop about a single topic for 5 to 10 minutes, so choice A is not the best answer. Choice C, questioning, involves asking questions related to a topic, not jotting down every idea related to it. Hypothesizing involves formulating a preliminary thesis, so choice D is not correct.

10. **The correct answer is D.** Since silent films are extremely rare today, film reviews from a current newspaper are very unlikely to contain any information related to the history of silent films. Choices A and B are likely to contain information very relevant to an essay about the history of silent films.

Choice C is related to sound in film, and is likely to contain some information about the transition from the silent film era to the sound era.

11. **The correct answer is D.** An appeal to the emotions is known as pathos. Choice A, syllogism, is when the conclusion of an argument is built on two or more premises. Choice B, ethos, is an appeal to a reader's sense of ethics. Choice C, logos, is an appeal to a reader's sense of logic.

12. **The correct answer is A.** Choice A describes the most effective way to structure a paragraph in the body of an essay. Choice B might not necessarily be effective and could cause the essay to become tiresomely repetitive. Choice C describes a way to structure a concluding paragraph, not a body paragraph. The method described in choice D would result in a paragraph that is irrelevant to the overall essay.

13. **The correct answer is B.** A logical syllogism can only have one true conclusion. This fact eliminates choice C. However, a logical syllogism can have several premises, so choice A is incorrect. It does require believable premises, so choice D is wrong.

14. **The correct answer is C.** Only choice C describes what a paraphrase does. Choice A describes a quotation. Choice B describes a summary. Choice D describes a counterargument.

15. **The correct answer is D.** APA, or American Psychological Association, citation style is used in papers about social sciences. MLA, or Modern Language Association, style would be more appropriate when citing the sources described in choices A, B, and C.

16. **The correct answer is A.** The thesis statement explicitly states the purpose of a composition, and it should appear early in the composition. It should certainly be

stated before the third or fourth paragraphs, so choices B and C are not the best answers. The final paragraph is the place for the concluding statement, not the thesis, so choice D is wrong.

17. **The correct answer is A.** According to MLA in-text citation style, the page number from which the quote was cited must appear within parentheses. Choices B and C violate MLA style. Any information included in a footnote is not considered to be in-text, so choice D is incorrect.

18. **The correct answer is B.** The main points of an argument support the argument's thesis. Counterclaims disagree with an argument's claims, so choice A is incorrect. Evidence is used to support claims, it is not what the main points support, so choice C is incorrect as well. A reason explains why a writer makes a claim, so choice D is incorrect.

19. **The correct answer is B.** Mind mapping is a method of organizing ideas generated during a brainstorming session, so it is most effective to perform this method right after brainstorming. Choice A is not correct because mind mapping is not directly related to outlining. Choice C is incorrect because clustering is a similar process to mind mapping. Choice D is incorrect because freewriting would more logically be performed after mind mapping, not before it.

20. **The correct answer is B.** A direct quotation is the most effective way to indicate that an authority shares an author's point. Changing the authority's wording by paraphrasing or summarizing may imply that the author is trying to manipulate the authority's intentions, so choices A and C are not the best answers. A counterargument would oppose the author's point, so choice D is incorrect.

DIAGNOSTIC TEST ASSESSMENT GRID

Now that you've completed the diagnostic test and read through the answer explanations, you can use your results to target your studying. Find the question numbers from the diagnostic test that you answered incorrectly and highlight or circle them below. Then focus extra attention on the sections within the chapter dealing with those topics.

Principles of Advanced English Composition		
Content Area	Topic	Question #
Types of Writing	• Narrative • Informative • Argumentative and persuasive • Critical response	1
Elements of Effective Writing	• Audience and purpose analysis • Prewriting strategies and content generation • Drafting • Revising and editing	3, 7, 9, 12, 16, 19
Reading and Writing Arguments	• Identifying elements of arguments • Analyzing arguments • Identifying key terms • Warrants and assumptions	4, 5, 6, 11, 13, 18
Using Secondary Sources	• Finding sources • Evaluating sources • Using sources • Citing and documenting	2, 8, 10, 14, 15, 17, 20

GET THE FACTS

To see the DSST® Principles of Advanced Composition Fact Sheet, go to *http://getcollegecredit. com/exam_fact_sheets* and click on the **Humanities** tab. Scroll down and click the **Principles of Advanced English Composition** link. Here you will find suggestions for further study material and the ACE college credit recommendations for passing the test.

TYPES OF WRITING

Does a composition tell a story or make a case for a particular point of view? Does it seek to inform or analyze? Every piece of writing has a particular purpose, and the type of writing used is intrinsically tied to that purpose.

There are four main types of essay writing, and you will be expected to identify each one based on its unique characteristics.

NARRATIVE

Narrative writing essentially tells a story. That story may be a work of fiction, such as a short story or novel, but it does not have to be. In fact there are several forms of nonfictional narratives, including:

- The **autobiography** or **memoir**, which tells the author's own personal story
- The **biography**, which tells the story of a person other than the author
- The **personal essay**, which tells a short form story about the author's own experiences
- The **news article**, which tells the story of a current event in a way that intends to capture the tone of the event (for example, the excitement of a rally or the sadness of a tragedy)
- A **history**, which tells the story of an important event from the past

Nonfiction narratives can be distinguished from informative writing because narratives utilize all the elements that any story uses: setting, people, and theme. Narrative writing does not merely seek to convey facts and details; it intends to bring those facts and details to life in the way that any great novelist brings a fictional story to life: with descriptive and imaginative writing. For example, a history textbook is a piece of informative writing and a biography is a piece of narrative writing. Any general American history textbook worth its salt will contain details about Abraham Lincoln, one of the United States' most significant presidents. The textbook will give details about Lincoln's actions and accomplishments in a straightforward manner, presenting the facts without really attempting to give the reader a detailed picture of what the man was like. A biography, however, will attempt to vividly illustrate President Lincoln as a living, breathing person, giving readers a clear sense of what the man was like by describing his personality and interests, as well as details of his life that may not be directly relevant to his actions and accomplishments.

Narrative writing can also be identified by its structure. It tends to be organized sequentially. In other words, events are described as they happened and not according to other organizational structures such as problem/solution, compare/contrast, or cause/effect.

Because narrative writing seeks to both entertain and inform readers, its voice tends to be richer than that of an informative piece of writing. Narrative writing conveys mood as well as information. For example, if the story is a suspenseful one, the narration utilizes suspenseful tone. Despite its tonal and structural similarities to the fictional narrative, a nonfictional narrative must still adhere to the conventions of all nonfictional writing. It must be factual, well researched, and properly cited and documented.

INFORMATIVE

Unlike a narrative, informative writing is concerned with conveying information—it does so without the creative flourishes of narrative writing. "Just the facts" is the motto of any informative composition, and teaching is its purpose. Informative writing tends to adopt an authoritative style without being too concerned with conveying a particular mood. Creativity is much less important than ensuring that facts and details are clear and easy to grasp.

Informative compositions are mainly concerned with helping the reader grasp an unfamiliar event, concept, process, or idea. Types of informative writing include:

- Summaries
- Instructions
- Encyclopedia articles
- Textbooks
- News reports that intend to convey facts and details only
- How-to articles
- Comparisons

Informative writing can be organized sequentially, but it might also use problem/solution, compare/contrast, or cause/effect structure, so it is easiest to identify by its straightforward style. An informative piece will usually include a **thesis statement** identifying the piece's purpose or main idea in the first paragraph. Evidence and details that support that thesis follow while the concluding paragraph reinforces or sums up the purpose or main idea.

Unlike persuasive writing (which we'll get to next), informative writing is not concerned with gaining the reader's trust and acceptance. In other words, an informative composition is generally accepted as fact, though that acceptance can be undermined by sloppiness, which is why facts alone do not guarantee that an informative composition is effective. As is the case for all writing types, it must be well written, organized, cited, and documented.

ARGUMENTATIVE AND PERSUASIVE

Have you ever felt particularly passionate about an issue and tried to make a case for your point of view? Well, then you have basically done what writers of argumentative or persuasive compositions do. The word "argumentative" tends to have negative connotations, bringing to mind an angry person who likes to fight and contradict for the sake of contradicting. Actually, adopting an angry tone often is not what a writer wants to do when composing an argumentative piece of writing, because the

NOTE

Neutrality is the key to informative writing. It merely presents the topic without taking a position on that topic.

ALERT

The thesis statement identifies the main idea of a composition clearly and usually appears in the first paragraph.

real function of such writing is not to fight or contradict, but to persuade. Consequently, there are a number of approaches to writing argumentative compositions, and choosing the right one often depends on the kind of audience the author wants to reach.

Types of arguments include:

- The **Aristotelian argument**, which presents a case for the purpose of persuasion
- The **Toulmin argument**, which establishes a claim and argues in favor or against it
- The **Rogerian argument**, which considers two or more options and argues in favor of the strongest one
- **Debate**, which shows both sides of an issue but favors one particular position over the other
- **Satire**, which uses humor to argue a point; a satire pretends to argue in favor of the point of view with which the writer does not agree in order to present that point of view as foolish

An argument can be written in a friendly and familiar style for, say, an audience of young readers, or it can be written using technical language for a very specific audience of educated adults. It may appeal to a reader's sense of right and wrong or logic. It may also play on the reader's emotions or intellect.

One of the keys to building a strong argument is identifying both the pros and cons of an issue. The issue will generally be clarified in the thesis statement while the body paragraphs may use a point/counterpoint structure to deal with the pros and cons of that issue. However, an argumentative composition may also utilize other organizational structures, such as problem/solution, compare/contrast, or cause/effect. Therefore, the best way to identify an argumentative composition is to figure out the piece's purpose. If the author is trying to persuade you to share his or her point of view, the piece is argumentative.

CRITICAL RESPONSE

When a piece of writing conveys the author's reactions without necessarily trying to persuade the reader to do or think something, that piece is most likely a critical response. A critical response is more analytical than expressly persuasive in nature. Nevertheless, the ultimate effect of a critical response may be persuasion, even though this is not its specific purpose. For example, after reading an analysis of a movie that identifies the movie's numerous weak points, you may decide to steer clear of that movie even if that is not the writer's express intention. But a good critical response is actually written from a perspective of objectivity. It evaluates a work on the work's own merit, using well-researched evidence to support its conclusions.

Essentially, a critical response has two main functions: summarizing and analyzing.

Summarizing may involve identifying a work's:

- Purpose
- Main ideas
- Supporting evidence
- Arguments
- Organizational structure

Analyzing may involve evaluating whether or not a work:

ALERT

The use of personal pronouns—I, my, me, myself—are clues that a piece of writing is narrative or argumentative. Informative and critical compositions usually are not written from a personal perspective.

- Achieves its purpose
- Provides strong evidence
- Is well organized
- Has artistic merit
- Is original
- Is sufficiently creative or imaginative

Because a critical response should be objective, it tends to avoid personal statements such as "I think" and "I believe." A formal tone also helps to establish a sense of objectivity. Such objective methods are clues that the piece in question is critical rather than argumentative.

ELEMENTS OF EFFECTIVE WRITING

NOTE

Thirty-two percent of the questions on the DSST Principles of Advanced English Composition exam are devoted to elements of effective writing.

After you decide on the kind of composition you want to write, you must then figure out the very best way to achieve your purpose. Consider the kinds of people you want to read your composition and how to reach those readers. Then, generate ideas for your composition and organize those ideas in a sensible manner.

There are a number of elements of effective writing, and each needs to be carefully considered during the writing process.

AUDIENCE AND PURPOSE ANALYSIS

Every piece of writing must have a purpose. Think about the types of compositions we've already discussed—each one has a general purpose.

Type of Writing	Purpose
Narrative	To inform and entertain
Informative	To provide knowledge, explain a process or function, describe a concept, define an idea, etc.
Argumentative/Persuasive	To persuade
Critical Response	To summarize and analyze

In order to achieve these purposes, writers must consider the audiences they intend to reach. The writer of an informative composition who intends to publish in a science journal has a very different audience from that of an elementary school teacher writing a humorous narrative about his first year on the job. Knowing one's audience is a vital key to informing, entertaining, or persuading through writing. It will help determine the language, tone, and kinds of details to include in the composition.

The language one uses when writing can either reach or alienate a particular audience. Therefore, it is crucial to identify the tone of a composition before deciding if its language is appropriate:

- **Colloquial language** is informal, everyday speech that may include common expressions or slang. It is useful for appealing to a young audience, an uneducated audience, or an audience of friends. However, it might be less effective when used for an educated or unfamiliar audience.

- **Emotive language** can be even trickier. Using words that express strong emotions can be effective when writing narratives or particularly heated arguments, but it is entirely inappropriate for informative or critical response pieces.

- **Academic language** is very formal and utilizes high-level vocabulary and expressions. Academic language is very appropriate when writing for an audience of scholars but will certainly alienate an uneducated audience.

- **Technical jargon** can also be appealing or alienating depending on the audience. Technical jargon is words and terms specific to a particular field. For example, a professional computer programmer will know that "content migration" is the movement of data from one computer system to another, but a first-year computing student might be baffled by such a term.

In general, there are certain language choices that remain valid for almost all purposes and audiences. For example, it is always very wise to use **inclusive language**. Inclusive language is not directed toward people of one particular gender, race, religion, orientation, or culture, and it should be used unless the audience specifically comprises a particular gender, race, religion, orientation, or culture.

On the other hand, sexist, racist, and homophobic language is always inappropriate. Such language can be clearly hostile to a certain gender, race, or orientation, but it may also be more causally insensitive, ignorant, or patronizing. For example, making the assumption that an audience of doctors consists only of men is sexist.

The kind of language a writer uses helps to establish a particular **tone**. The two essential tones are **formal** and **informal**. Academic language and technical jargon might establish a formal tone, while colloquial and emotive language would be more effective for setting an informal tone. The tone a writer decides to use depends on both the type of writing (for example, one would not use an informal tone in a critical response) and the audience.

Deciding on which tone to use may depend on analyzing the audience in question. Audience analysis begins with asking some essential questions:

- What are the characteristics of my audience?
- What is the age range of my audience?
- What language does my audience speak?
- What is the education level of my audience?
- Do the people in my audience share particular beliefs or values?
- Do all the people in my audience study or work in the same field?
- Will my audience be receptive to humor, emotive language, colloquial language, etc.?

Answering these questions should help a writer decide upon a particular tone. For example, answering the question "What is the age range of my audience?" may lead a writer to use an informal tone after deciding that audience is too young to respond well to a formal tone. If the answer to the question

TIP

Slang is extremely informal language, and it should generally be used very sparingly in composition both because it is not considered "proper" language and because many slang expressions are only used by certain groups of people. Misjudging an audience can result in using a slang expression for an audience that does not understand the expression's meaning.

TIP

The type of publication often determines the type of audience. For example, scholarly journals are aimed at a highly educated audience while entertainment magazines are not.

"Do all the people in my audience study or work in the same field?" is "yes," the writer may decide that technical jargon is appropriate.

PREWRITING STRATEGIES AND CONTENT GENERATION

Once a writer has figured out the purpose of, and audience for, a piece of writing, it is time to really get to work. That does not mean it's time to start pounding the keyboard just yet, because a lot needs to be done before the actual drafting process can begin. This preparatory work is known as **prewriting**, and there are an abundance of prewriting strategies to ensure a composition is well thought out, organized, and structured.

Thinking, Reading, Analyzing, and Discussion

Generating ideas for the topic of a composition is the very first step of the prewriting process. As obvious as it may seem, that process begins with something we do constantly: **thinking**.

Thinking is the most basic way to generate topic ideas for a composition. It may happen in the shower in the morning, in the car while driving home from work, waiting in line at the grocery store—you get the idea. Basically, thinking up an idea for a composition can happen anywhere and anytime. A well-prepared writer keeps a pen and paper handy at all times to capture those ideas before they slip away.

Another way to come up with ideas is **reading**. Selecting relevant reading material can be very helpful when deciding on the right topic for a particular assignment. For example, if the assignment is "write an essay about a current event," reading newspapers and news magazines is the ideal way to generate topic ideas. If a writer wants to get published in a science journal, she or he might start cracking biology texts and journals or even the science section of today's paper to see if any articles inspire topic ideas.

Analyzing the world around us can also be a valuable method for generating topic ideas. For example, observing the way people in one's family interact may generate a topic for a sociology journal article. Examining recent temperature trends may be a springboard for an article about climate change. Start by asking questions: Why are they acting that way? Why did that happen? What will happen next? And so on.

This first step of the prewriting process does not have to be performed alone. Holding **discussions** with other people can also generate topic ideas. Talking to a family member, friend, peer, or colleague may lead to interesting ideas that can be explored further in a composition. Perhaps the person will bring up a point with which you disagree—leading to an argumentative essay. Or maybe a friend will recommend a novel that can be the topic of a critical response. You never know what ideas may bob to the surface while thinking, reading, analyzing, and discussing.

TIP

Thinking, reading, analyzing, and discussion may involve taking a few notes, but these prewriting techniques do not involve a great deal of writing. They are essentially performed in the writer's head.

Invention Techniques

Thinking, reading, analyzing, and discussing can help to generate some general ideas for composition topics. The next step in the prewriting process is to whittle those general ideas down to more specific ones. This step involves more active processes than simply allowing your mind to wander or having a talk with a friend that may lead to topic ideas. Now is the time to get out that pen and paper or sit down in front of the computer, because the following invention techniques involve quite a bit of writing.

Brainstorming is kind of like a more active form of thinking. It involves jotting down every idea that comes to mind about a particular idea or subject. Allow the ideas to flood into your mind and write them all down, regardless of each idea's merit. The ideas may come in the form of single words, phrases, or sentences, but it is important not to get too bogged down with the mechanics of writing. Don't worry about the particular phrasing, grammatical correctness, or even spelling of these ideas. Just get them all down as they surface, because one or more might prove significant in homing in on the right topic.

For example, the results of a brainstorming session about the influential pop band The Beatles may look something like this.

popularized the band format
first band to write most of its own songs
used instruments from other cultures
wrote complex songs
changed the way other bands made records
used recording studio creatively
helped make albums a cultural force
changed the way young people thought about politics
starred in movies
used classical, avant garde, and world music influences
played guitars
wore suits
revolutionized hair styles and fashions
were funny
are still popular today
had lots of hit songs
made songs used in commercials

NOTE
You will not be asked to perform any prewriting techniques on the DSST, but you will be asked to identify those techniques.

Notice that not all of these entries are necessarily well written. Notice that there are strong ideas and weak ones. Once again, brainstorming is not about judging or perfecting ideas; it's just a technique for generating as many ideas as possible.

Freewriting is another strong technique for generating ideas, but it is more specific than brainstorming. In fact, it is often helpful to use ideas generated while brainstorming as a springboard for freewriting. Freewriting involves writing about one particular idea for a brief period of time. The technique begins with setting a timer for five to ten minutes, then spending that time developing the selected idea through writing. Write constantly for those five to ten minutes, again paying no attention to the mechanics of proper writing and not wasting time correcting such errors. The important thing is to keep writing, even if you can only write things like "That's all I can think of!" (which may be clues that the selected idea is not the right one or that a lot of research will be necessary to develop that particular idea into a complete composition).

Here's an example of freewriting by the same writer who generated that brainstorming list about The Beatles.

> The Beatles were one of the most popular and culturally influential bands of all time. They changed the way other bands made music by writing complex songs which they wrote on their own and by using the recording studio creatively. They were one of the first bands to use classical, world music, and avant garde influences in their pop songs. They made the band format really popular at a time when most artists were solo or group singers who didn't play their own instruments. The Beatles influenced other things as well. They changed the way men could wear their hair by wearing their own hair long and they changed fashion with their iconic collarless jackets and Cuban-heeled boots and ... that's all I can think of!

ALERT

Thinking is always the first step of the prewriting process. Brainstorming, freewriting, questioning, and hypothesizing cannot be performed without thinking of a topic to brainstorm, freewrite, ask questions, or hypothesize about first.

Obviously this is not a great piece of writing and would not be acceptable as a finished composition. However, it does formulate the ideas from the brainstorming list in a more sensible way, discards the least effective ideas, and can be developed into a fine essay with a great deal of organization and development. Basically, it is a very good example of freewriting.

Asking questions is useful during the analysis process we discussed before. However, **questioning** can also be performed in a more active way as an invention technique. Instead of merely thinking of questions that may generate ideas, write them down in list form. Don't worry about answering the questions just yet, and of course, don't worry about whether or not they are phrased or spelled perfectly. Just write down as many questions as you can think of during a particular period of time to see if they lead anywhere interesting. Answering the most provocative question might be the research foundation of a very interesting composition.

Here are some examples.

> What made The Beatles so significant?
>
> Why did people like their music so much?
>
> Why do people still listen to their music?
>
> What did The Beatles change?
>
> Why were they different from other bands?
>
> How did The Beatles work differently from other bands?
>
> What was special about them beside music?

Ideas generated while brainstorming, freewriting, and questioning may lead to the formulation of a preliminary main idea or main purpose for a composition. Drafting such an early thesis is an invention technique known as **hypothesizing**. Forming a hypothesis is considering that a particular idea may be true or have some sort of merit. That initial hypothesis may turn out to be wrong or it may lead to a dead end, but that is the nature of forming hypotheses. A hypothesis that raises numerous questions or seems as though it could be supported with evidence may grow into a good thesis.

Organizing Ideas

Invention techniques can be extremely helpful in generating ideas for a composition. However, developing topics and details are not the only concerns of the prewriting process. The organization of a composition can also be decided before actual drafting ever takes place. Figuring out the best way to organize information while prewriting can ensure that the drafting process goes as smoothly as possible.

Mind Mapping (Clustering)

One way to organize while prewriting is by using a technique called **mind mapping**. Also known as **clustering**, mind mapping involves creating a visual representation of all the ideas generated during the brainstorming process. To create a mind map, a writer reviews the ideas he or she jotted down while brainstorming, hunts for the strongest ideas, and considers whether or not they can be grouped into categories or subcategories.

Next, the writer draws a circle in the center of a piece of paper and writes the composition's main purpose inside the circle. For example, that purpose can be "Argue in favor of universal health care." The writer then writes down the most basic relevant ideas generated during brainstorming around that circle and connects them to the circle with lines. According to our universal health care example, these ideas might include the following.

> good for economy
>
> assists the underprivileged
>
> reduces number of uninsured people

The most effective time to begin mind mapping is after brainstorming.

Then the ideas can get more specific. For example, around "good for the economy," the writer might cluster ideas such as the following:

> maintains global competitiveness
>
> employer-based insurance is bad for business
>
> strain on national debt is relatively small
>
> keeps healthy people in workforce

Our example mind map might look something like this:

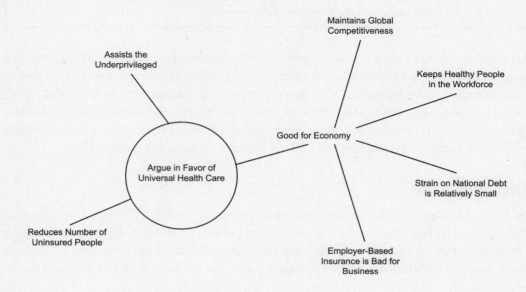

So how does this assist with the organization of a composition? Well, the innermost circle provides the basis of the thesis statement that belongs in the opening paragraph of the composition. Moving outward from the inner circle, the next group of ideas (assists the underprivileged, good for economy, reduces number of uninsured people) provides the sub-claims that support the thesis' main claim—they are the main ideas of each paragraph in the body of the composition. The outermost ideas (maintains global competitiveness, employer-based insurance is bad for business, strain on national debt is relatively small, keeps healthy people in workforce) are the details that support the sub-claim that universal health care is good for the economy.

Remember that a writer does not have to use particular ideas just because they are used in a mind map. Much like the ideas generated during brainstorming, the particulars of a mind map are simply possible details. If they do not help develop the topic well, they can be discarded. So, a mind map can help to organize a composition *and* weed out weak ideas.

Outlining

A mind map is a fine way to figure out how to organize a composition, but it is not an outline in itself. After creating a mind map, the ideas it contains can be organized in a way that better resembles how those ideas will actually appear in the composition. The outline for our argument in favor of universal health care may look something like this:

I. Introduction

    A. Background details on universal health care

    B. Preview of composition's main points

    C. Thesis: Argument in favor of universal health care

II. Body

    A. Paragraph 1

        1. Topic sentence indicating that universal health care is good for the economy

        2. Evidence that universal health care maintains global competitiveness

        3. Evidence that employer-based insurance is bad for business

        4. Evidence that universal health care keeps healthy people in workforce

    B. Paragraph 2

        1. Topic sentence indicating that universal health care assists the underprivileged

        2. Evidence that universal health care makes insurance more affordable

        3. Evidence that universal health care makes insurance available for the unemployed

        4. Evidence that universal health care makes medicine more affordable

    C. Paragraph 3

        1. Topic sentence indicating that universal health care can help save lives

        2. Evidence that universal health care requires everyone to have health insurance

        3. Evidence that more people are treated for potentially fatal ailments when they can afford health care and medicine

        4. Evidence that people will seek treatment if they are confident that they will be able to pay for treatment

III. Conclusion

    A. Summarize main points

    B. Concluding statement

After completing an outline, a writer can clearly see how ideas will develop in the completed composition. If one idea does not flow well into the next, the outline can be reorganized to best support the thesis. If the outline indicates that the composition can be more thorough—perhaps a sub-claim

TIP

While outlining, a writer might begin to see patterns that will lead to an organizational method for the composition, such as cause/effect, problem/solution, or comparison/contrast.

could use some additional supporting evidence—it can also be developed further. Once the outline is sturdy, it is time to put it to use in the next step of the composing process.

Notice that the writer of this particular outline has also refined his ideas a bit since making the mind map. Refining ideas is important to do throughout the prewriting process. Writers should never feel locked into particular ideas when better ones arise.

CREATING YOUR DRAFT

After planning out ideas and organizational approaches during the prewriting process, the next task is to begin drafting. Drafting is the beginning of the actual writing phase. While drafting, the writer translates the thesis and details generated during prewriting into a well-structured composition according to the outline. The drafting phase is when writers really need to start thinking about the organization of the composition as a whole as well as the structure of individual paragraphs.

Decide on an Organizational Structure

An outline only indicates the most basic way information is structured in a composition—there are finer connections between ideas to be made. Perhaps presenting ideas sequentially is the best format. Or, maybe stating arguments against the thesis before countering those arguments is the most engaging approach.

There are a number of standard ways to organize a paper:

- **Cause/Effect:** explains processes and follows up with the results of those processes (appropriate for informative and argumentative writing)
- **Compare/Contrast:** describes similarities and/or differences among ideas (appropriate for informative and argumentative writing)
- **Description:** explains the characteristics of a topic (appropriate for critical responses and informative writing)
- **Division/Classification:** groups ideas into categories (appropriate for informative writing)
- **Problem/Solution:** presents a problem and explains how to solve that problem (appropriate for narrative, informative, and argumentative writing)
- **Process:** presents information step by step (appropriate for informative writing)
- **Sequential Order:** presents information in the order in which it occurred (appropriate for narrative and informative writing)

Using transitional words and phrases is an effective way to clarify the selected organizational pattern. Certain transitions are most appropriate for particular patterns.

TIP

Deciding on an organizational pattern can lead to choosing the type of writing, since certain patterns are more appropriate for particular types of writing than others.

Organizational Patterns	Examples of Common Transitions
Cause/Effect	because, since, therefore, as a result, consequently, etc.
Compare/Contrast	*To compare*: similarly, comparatively, just as, in the same way, correspondingly, likewise, etc. *To contrast*: however, but, conversely, in contrast, on the contrary, yet, on the other hand, nevertheless, in spite of, rather, instead, etc.
Description	above, below, inside, outside, beside, etc.
Division/Classification	the first type, the second variety, the third group, the fourth kind, etc.
Problem/Solution	because, obviously, evidently, furthermore, in fact, in any case, since, for the same reason, etc.
Process	step one, step two, first, second, third, next, finally, as soon as, by the time, etc.
Sequential Order	first, next, then, later, meanwhile, the following year, etc.

Designing Paragraphs

After figuring out the most effective overall organizational pattern for a composition, it is then necessary to think about how each paragraph of the composition should be structured. There are certain basic guidelines for organizing the paragraphs in any effective composition.

The thesis statement is the focal point of any introductory paragraph. However, starting off by stating a thesis bluntly is not necessarily the best way to ease into a composition. Before getting to the thesis, it is effective to first capture the reader's interest. That catchy opening line is known as "the hook."

Strong ways of hooking the reader's interest include asking a provocative question…

Example: *What is the most popular form of communication?*

…or making a provocative statement:

Example: *There is no living creature quite like the fascinating chameleon.*

…or including a provocative quotation:

Example: *"Darkness cannot drive out darkness: only light can do that."*

—Dr. Martin Luther King, Jr.

…or relaying a provocative statistic:

Example: *Ninety-one percent of adults with Internet access use social media on a regular basis.*

As you can see, the key word here is "provocative." A writer wants to provoke the reader to continue reading with a hook of some sort. Another way to hook readers is to compose opening lines that:

- Express an interesting anecdote (example: *"When I was a child I had a most incredible experience…"*)
- Set a vivid scene (example: *"The date was December 7, 1941; the place was Pearl Harbor, Hawaii."*)

TIP

Voice is another consideration during the drafting process. The voice a writer uses is how he or she imparts information to the reader. This involves both point of view (first person, second person, third person) and style (informal or formal).

TIP

A well-structured paragraph fits perfectly into a particular spot in a composition because of the way it develops the thesis and uses transitions. It cannot just be moved anywhere in the composition.

- Define an interesting term (example: *"To troll is to intentionally attempt to cause discord in the comments of a web page or on an Internet forum."*)
- Convey an interesting fact (example: *"The vast majority of Americans recognize Barack Obama as the 44th President of the United States, but many are not aware that he is also a Grammy winner."*)
- Reveal a common misconception (example: *"It is commonly believed that medieval Europeans thought the Earth was flat. However…"*)

After hooking the reader's interest, *then* you can lead into a thesis statement, preview the main claims of the paragraphs that follow, or provide background information related to the thesis in the opening paragraph.

Next, follow the body paragraphs that support the thesis. A well-structured body paragraph:

1. Begins by identifying the main point of the paragraph
2. Follows with relevant evidence to support that point
3. Ends with a transitional sentence leading into the next paragraph

Finally, a composition ends with its concluding paragraph. A concluding paragraph is not as concerned with introducing new ideas and evidence as the composition's other paragraphs. The concluding paragraph merely intends to tie up the composition neatly. It does so by:

- Restating the thesis
- Summarizing the main points of the composition
- Leaving the reader with some "food for thought," such as:
  - Asking a final provocative question (example: *"The question is: will history repeat itself?"*)
  - Calling for an action (example: *"Consequently, it is now more important than ever to support truth-based journalism."*)
  - Imparting a warning (example: *"If we are not careful, the future of the United States may be a very bleak one."*)
  - Painting a picture with words (example: *"Those violent, vivid paint splatters constitute no childish mess; they comprise the revolutionary vision of influential artist Jackson Pollock."*)

TIP

Transitional sentences indicate that a piece of writing is moving from one idea to another.

REVISING AND EDITING

The first draft of a composition usually isn't quite perfect. There may be grammatical or mechanical mistakes. Ideas might not flow together as well as they could. Certain details may be a bit too off topic. Such problems are fixed during the revising and editing phase. While these terms are sometimes used interchangeably, they actually each have their own particular tasks.

Revision involves examining and improving the content of a composition. Things to look out for while revising include the strength of the composition's ideas, word choice, organization, voice, sentences, and thoroughness.

While examining these elements, it is helpful for a writer to ask him or herself some tough questions.

Element	Potential Questions
Ideas	• Should any of my ideas be deleted because they detract from the topic? • Should any of my ideas be deleted because they are too off topic or otherwise irrelevant? • Is my evidence relevant and reliable?
Word Choice	• Are the words I use sufficiently descriptive and imaginative? • Do I overuse any words or phrases, and if so, what is the best way to replace them? • Are my verbs weak or strong? • Do I use the passive voice? If so, how can I reword these phrases actively? • Are my word choices vague or precise?
Organization	• Does my opening sentence hook the reader's interest effectively? • Is my thesis statement clear? • Are each of my body paragraphs focused on a particular topic? • Are there smooth transitions between sentences and paragraphs? • Does my concluding paragraph wrap up the composition effectively?
Voice	• Is my voice consistent? • Are any sentences too formal for an overall informal tone or too informal for an overall formal tone? • Does my point of view ever shift?
Sentences	• Do I use a variety of sentence styles (complex, compound, compound-complex) to prevent my writing from becoming repetitious?
Thoroughness	• Do my ideas develop my topic sufficiently? • Is there supporting evidence for each of my claims? • Can I add any other details that might strengthen my main points or sub-claims?

TIP

Sometimes it is difficult for a writer to objectively evaluate his or her own work. In such cases, it is often helpful to ask another person to read and offer helpful criticism.

If the answer to any of these questions is "No," then some revision needs to take place.

In the passive voice, action is performed by a subject rather than the subject performing the action actively. For example:

> **Passive voice:** *The kite was pulled by the child.* (less effective)

> **Active voice:** *The child pulled the kite.* (more effective)

Editing is a bit different from revision. Also known as proofreading, editing involves reviewing a composition to ensure that it maintains English conventions.

While editing, a writer should search for and correct errors in:

- Spelling
- Grammar
- Word usage
- Capitalization
- Punctuation

Failing to revise and edit a composition can really undermine that composition's purpose. This can be especially problematic when trying to actually persuade readers to believe or think something with an argumentative composition.

READING AND WRITING ARGUMENTS

NOTE

Thirty-two percent of the questions on the DSST Principles of Advanced English Composition exam are devoted to reading and writing arguments.

While narratives describe events in a straightforward, usually sequential manner, and informative pieces have no loftier goals than to impart information to readers, argumentative pieces tend to be a bit more complex. They can be organized in a number of ways and utilize various kinds of evidence to support their theses. Good argument writers create strong links between those pieces of evidence and the piece's main points. Consequently, identifying and analyzing can be an involved process.

IDENTIFYING ELEMENTS OF ARGUMENTS

A well-organized and thought-out argument consists of several key elements: a thesis, main points, and support of claims. Without these elements an argument can collapse like a poorly constructed building.

Thesis (Main Claim)

The **thesis**, or main claim, is the foundation of an argument. It is the central point the writer is trying to make; the thing that the writer is trying to persuade readers to believe. Perhaps the writer is trying to convince readers that recycling is good for the environment. The thesis of that writer's argument would express this main claim in a clear, complete, declarative sentence, such as "Everyone should recycle."

Of course, that is an extremely simple example, and a thesis can be a bit more complexly worded (for example, "It is imperative that all global citizens recycle for the sake of the natural environment we all share."), but it must maintain complete clarity. After all, readers will be hard to persuade if they are not sure about what they are being persuaded to believe.

Because the thesis statement is so integral to the meaning and purpose of an argument, it is usually stated early in the piece—usually in the first paragraph, but it may appear in the second or even third paragraph if the writer spends the first paragraph or two providing background information.

If the thesis statement is obscured by a great deal of background information, there may be ways to identify it beyond the piece itself. An **abstract** is a summary often included with scholarly papers and journal articles; it will lay out the thesis clearly. If the argument is in the form of a book, the copy (text) on its jacket may state its thesis. Key words such as "In this book, the author argues that…" or "The author explains how…" may signal the thesis statement. The headline of an editorial or other form of article may also clarify the article's thesis in very simple terms. For example, an editorial with a title such as "Now is the Time to Get Out and Recycle" can be translated into a simple thesis statement such as "Everyone should recycle."

Main Points (Sub-Claims)

An argument is not built on a thesis alone. More specific ideas are required to get deeper into the issue the thesis states in a general manner. These ideas are the argument's main points or **sub-claims**.

Main points are like mini-theses. Just as the thesis sums up the purpose of an argument as a whole, main points may sum up the purposes of each body paragraph in the argument.

Let's go back to our original thesis example: "Everyone should recycle." That is a fine purpose for an argument as a whole, but it is too general to stand on its own. Why should everyone recycle? The answers to that question are the argument's main points.

For example:

1. The main point of the first body paragraph of our composition about recycling may be "Recycling reduces pollution."

2. The main point of the second paragraph may be "Recycling conserves materials."

3. The third paragraph may be "Recycling saves money."

Developing and explaining these main points will build a strong case for the idea that everyone should recycle.

Locating and identifying the main points of an argument is very similar to identifying the argument's thesis statement. Like the thesis, the main points are expressed in declarative statements. They will often appear in the first sentence of a paragraph, but they may be delayed by a bit of background information. Abstracts, book jacket copy, and headlines may provide clues to the main points. For example, a headline reading "Now Is the Time to Get Out and Recycle for the Sake of Our Environment and Our Wallets!" tips the reader off that the thesis ("Everyone should recycle") will be supported with main points about how recycling reduces pollution and saves money.

The thesis statement of an argument may even indicate its main points.

Take this example:

> *Everyone should recycle because it reduces pollution, conserves materials, and saves money.*

As you may have noticed, this thesis statement is more detailed than the simplistic one that merely stated, "Everyone should recycle." You may have also noticed that this statement includes both the thesis ("Everyone should recycle…") and the main points ("…because it reduces pollution, conserves materials, and saves money."). Words and phrases that indicate a cause/effect relationship such as

The main points of an argument are usually found in the topic sentence of each paragraph.

It is important to not confuse supporting details or evidence for main points. Remember that a paragraph's main claim will capture the purpose of the paragraph as a whole, while supporting details and evidence provide reasons for those main points.

because, therefore, so, as a result of, and *consequently* may be clues that a thesis statement does more than just state the thesis.

Claims Support

As we've already indicated, main points are distinct from the details and evidence that support those main points. Just as stating that "Everyone should recycle" is not sufficiently persuasive on its own, stating "Recycling reduces pollution" may not be entirely persuasive either. After all, how does recycling reduce pollution? How does the writer know that recycling reduces pollution? Answering these questions provides the support for the main and sub-claims a strong argument needs—it gives the reasons for making those claims.

There are a number of ways to support claims in an argument. **Examples** are the most basic forms of support. They may be gleaned from reliable sources or personal experiences. For example:

> *I know that recycling helps save money because when my company started recycling paper instead of constantly buying new supplies, it reduced our monthly expenditures by nearly one quarter.*

This is a fair personal example to use to support the claim that everyone should recycle because it saves money. However, examples need to be made carefully, because they will weaken an argument if they are not built on strong logic or reasoning.

Another form of claims support is **statistics**, which is numerical data. Statistics may be collected through polls, studies, public records, or other methods of data collection. They may come in the form of specific numbers (for example: "In 2015, U.S. paper mills used 30.9 tons of recycled paper.") or percentages (for example: "In 2015, use of recycled paper at U.S. mills increased by 1.2% from the previous year.").

Statistics are usually used sparingly because arguments that get bogged down in numbers might risk losing the reader's interest. Nevertheless, surprising statistics can provide rather dramatic support for an argument.

Expert opinions can also provide convincing support for claims. Unlike examples and statistics, expert opinions tend to be a bit less concrete, depending more on the standing of the expert than the gist of the opinions themselves. For example:

> *Shara Reese, the superintendent of our city's department of sanitation, agrees that "everyone should recycle."*

Taken on its own, Reese's statement is no more convincing the original thesis statement that "Everyone should recycle." It is Reese's authority as "superintendent of our city's department of sanitation" that makes this sentence a supportive piece of evidence. Ideally, expert opinions will be more detailed and convincing than this particular example, but such opinions will still depend on the authority or expertise of the person providing the opinion.

As you may have noticed, there are strong signifiers for at least two of these forms of claims support. Statistics are easy to spot in an argument because of their numerical nature. Expert opinions are easy to spot because they often appear as quotations, or at least reference the experts who provided them. Examples may be tougher to identify, but they should still be clear because of the specific role they play: to support the main points of an argument.

> **TIP**
>
> Relevance is key to choosing the right expert to quote when relying on expert opinions. For example, an expert in the field of medicine might not be the best expert to quote when supporting the idea that everyone should recycle.

ANALYZING ARGUMENTS

An argument may contain everything it needs—a thesis, main points, supporting details—but it will not be a strong argument if its elements are not well selected and convincingly presented. Arguments must be analyzed to determine their efficacy; there are a number of key elements to study in order to see if one is sound and strong.

The most essential element of an argument is the evidence used to support it. Without convincing evidence, the most skillfully worded and organized argument in the world will not hold water. Determining whether or not the evidence of an argument is sound will determine whether or not the argument, itself, is sound.

LOGIC

When looking at an argument, you must first consider whether or not the logic behind the argument is reliable. An argument must be based on sound logical approaches—it must be grounded on a strong premise, which is the argument's essential intention, and reach a conclusion with evidence used to support it. There are a number of ways to reach a logical conclusion.

The simplest method for reaching a logical conclusion is the **syllogism**. Devised by the philosopher Aristotle, a syllogism uses two or more essential premises to reach a conclusion. The major premise makes a statement about something general. The minor premise is more specific. The conclusion draws the two premises together logically.

For example:

- **Major premise:** All birds lay eggs.
- **Minor premise:** Pigeons are birds.
- **Conclusion:** Pigeons lay eggs.

This particular syllogism is also an example of **inductive reasoning** because it is based on the assumption that the premises of the argument are strong enough to validate the conclusion. It involves a movement from specific evidence to a general conclusion. **Deductive reasoning**, however, begins with a general conclusion before considering the evidence that might support it. In other words, deductive reasoning makes a hypothesis or a prediction by working backwards from conclusion to evidence.

Here's an example of deductive reasoning:

- Pigeons lay eggs.
- Pigeons are birds.
- Therefore, birds lay eggs.

An **enthymeme** is an abbreviated syllogism that omits the details most obvious to readers.

For example:

- Pigeons are birds.
- So pigeons lay eggs.

NOTE
A syllogism may have more than two premises.

This enthymeme makes the fair assumption that the reader already understands that all birds lay eggs, though it is still an incomplete argument since it omits details. In other words, it is not as strong of a logical statement as a syllogism. However, even syllogisms can be flawed because an enthymeme or syllogism built on false premises will lead to a false conclusion.

Take this example:

- **Major premise:** All animals with two eyes lay eggs.
- **Minor premise:** Pigeons have two eyes.
- **Conclusion:** Therefore, pigeons lay eggs.

Every element of a syllogism must be true for its logic to hold water. The minor premise and conclusion of this particular syllogism are both true, but the premise that "all animals with two eyes lay eggs" is false, otherwise every person you know who has two eyes would have hatched out of an egg.

There are a number of other forms of flawed reasoning known as **logical fallacies**.

TIP

The individual parts of a logical fallacy may be true, but it is still a fallacy if the parts do not connect logically.

Fallacy	Description	Example
Ad hominem	An unfair attack against a person with a differing opinion	"You only think humans cause climate change because you're a wimp!"
Begging the question	When the conclusion is assumed within the premise of an argument	"Ghosts are real because I'm pretty sure I've seen ghosts."
Circular reasoning	When the conclusion is the reason for an argument.	Shakespeare is a great playwright because his plays are excellent.
False analogy	A comparison between two essentially unlike things	"Steven Spielberg is like a god because he made some good movies."
False cause	Using a false cause as the reason for a particular effect	"Young people gravitate toward crime because of the terrible music they listen to."
False dilemma (either/or fallacy)	Presenting an alternative as if it is the only possible one	"We are either going to recycle plastic bottles or the environment is doomed."
False equivalence	The presentation of two unlike, opposing arguments as if they are similar	"He may have assaulted someone, but she told a lie, so they are just as bad as each other."
Equivocation	A conclusion based on the misinterpretation of words with more than one meaning or through misused language	"A feather is light so it cannot be dark."
Hasty generalization	A conclusion reached without sufficient evidence	"He has a strange expression on his face, so he is clearly a criminal."

Fallacy	Description	Example
Incomplete comparison	A comparison that is missing one of the items being compared	"This book is better."
Moral equivalence	A comparison between something bad and something significantly worse	"Watching that awful movie is like dying a slow, painful death."
Oversimplification	Omitting information to make an issue seem simpler than it is	"I don't know anyone who has suffered because of global warming, so global warming clearly is not that big of a problem."
Post hoc, ergo propter hoc	Latin: after this, therefore on account of it. A false correlation between cause and effect	"After I brushed my teeth, I slipped on the rug, so clearly brushing my teeth caused me to slip."
Slippery slope	The assumption that one action will naturally lead to a negative consequence	"If we allow all people to vote, soon we'll be allowing dogs to vote."

To analyze the quality of the logic of an argument, it is helpful to test its evidence against these fallacies. An abundance of evidence based on logical fallacies will severely damage the quality of an argument—even if some of the argument's logic is sound.

ANECDOTES

Sometimes writers enrich their arguments with short narratives. Such stories are known as **anecdotes**, and they may lend an emotional texture to an argument or illustrate an important point the writer intends to make. For example, an article about the importance of universal health care might begin with a tragic story about someone who suffered because he could not afford health insurance. Such an anecdote would not only illustrate the importance of universal health care, but it will also connect with the reader because of its emotional component. Stirring readers' emotions and empathies is an effective way to persuade them to share a particular point of view. However, anecdotes should contain concrete details to serve the argument in a meaningful manner rather than merely manipulate the reader's emotions.

While logic is not crucial in the anecdote itself, anecdotes must be selected logically. Merely telling an entertaining story will not enrich an argument if the anecdote has nothing to do with the overall argument. So it is important to analyze the anecdote for relevance. For example, a sad story about someone who suffers because he cannot afford health insurance would be a disingenuous way to begin an argument in favor of a particular medicine.

Anecdotes must also have some basis in reality to serve an argument. Watch out for anecdotes that begin with statements such as, "I once heard that…" or "I'm not sure if this is true, but…" because no matter how emotionally stirring the anecdote that follows may be, it is meaningless if it is not verifiable. Therefore, it may be necessary to also state the source of the anecdote explicitly.

TIP

Anecdotes often appear at the very beginning of an argument. They can be very effective in hooking a reader's interest and getting them on the writer's side before the thesis statement has even been introduced. An anecdote might also be an effective way to bring an argument to a powerful conclusion.

The DSST Principles of Advanced English Composition exam is mainly concerned with the use of secondary sources.

SOURCES

Sources are the texts from which evidence is gathered. They may be print sources such as books, newspaper editorials, and magazine articles; online sources such as websites and databases; or multimedia sources such as audio or video interviews. There are also primary and secondary sources.

- A **primary source** comprises firsthand accounts and evidence, such as an interview, memoir, autobiography, speech, experiment, or eyewitness account.

- A **secondary source** is composed by someone who did not personally experience the events the source describes, such as a textbook, biography, objective journalistic article, or research paper.

Using sources of any sort serves two essential functions when writing a composition:

1. Sources provide the ideas and information that develop a thesis and expand the author's understanding of the topic.

2. Sources provide the evidence that supports the thesis.

Sources are also necessary for:

- Showing that an argument is not based solely on personal opinions

- Indicating that evidence was culled from a variety of high-quality reading material

- Revealing the process by which an argument was built

- Proving that a writer is capable of blending ideas from a variety of material into a single argument

- Providing readers with the names of texts they may want to read to further their understanding of the topic

- Allowing readers to evaluate the quality of an argument's evidence by reviewing the texts that provide its evidence

Different sources may serve different purposes, and deciding the role of each source is something writers may do during the drafting process. Doing so involves asking some key questions and allowing the answers to dictate how the sources are used in the composition.

Correctly citing sources is essential for avoiding plagiarism, the stealing of ideas.

If "yes" is the answer to:	Then:
Did a source provide background information?	Use it to provide background in the introductory paragraph(s) of your argument.
Did a source raise any compelling or provocative questions?	Use it to express those questions before answering them yourself (possibly with information culled from other sources).
Did a source composed by an authority support your claims or conclusions?	Quote it to strengthen your argument with an expert opinion.
Did a source provide context for an issue?	Use it to provide context in your argument.
Did a source provide supporting evidence for a particular claim?	Use it to support your claim.

If "yes" is the answer to:	Then:
Did a source refute any of your conclusions?	Refer to it as a counterargument and explain how it strengthened your conclusions.
Did a source make you think differently about your main points which led you to revise your argument?	Explain how it resulted in your shift of position.

When analyzing how sources are used in an argument, make sure that sources are used logically and persuasively. Using sources as irrelevant filler or failing to link the argument's claims and the source clearly are significant flaws. A source must also introduce new and relevant information rather than merely repeat claims that have already been well supported in the argument. Furthermore, the argument as a whole cannot rely too exclusively on the findings of sources or the writer risks repeating the ideas of others without contributing anything original of her/his own. In other words, sources are vital to the strength of an argument, but they must still be used carefully and sparingly.

KEY TERMS

Throughout our discussion of arguments, we have learned a variety of key terms such as:

- **Thesis:** the main idea of an argument
- **Syllogism:** using two essential premises to reach a conclusion
- **Enthymeme:** a conclusion expressed in a single sentence that omits obvious details
- **Logical fallacy:** a type of flawed reasoning
- **Premise:** the idea upon which a conclusion is reached
- **Inductive reasoning:** the assumption that the premises are strong enough to validate the conclusion
- **Deductive reasoning:** reasoning that begins with a general conclusion before considering the evidence that supports it

However, there are several other key terms to consider when constructing or analyzing an argument. Most essentially, there is the term **rhetoric**, which refers to the art of persuasion. Rhetoric involves all of the skills already described, such as careful use of language to reach a particular audience, as well as the effective use of evidence, valid logic, anecdotes, and supporting sources to build a persuasive argument.

A **rhetorical triangle** is the relationship between audience, message, and writer. When writers identify their audiences, it is easier to construct the particular message to reach that particular audience. The writer must consider how likely an audience is to understand the message and respond well to it, as well as figure out if a particular audience is likelier to be led by logic or emotional responses. The message (thesis) must be sufficiently developed and well supported for a particular audience, while the writer must be credible and authoritative.

The way the writer persuades the audience to share her or his point of view on an issue constitutes the **appeal** in an argument. There are three main kinds of appeals:

- **Logos:** an appeal to logic (for example, a conclusion based on a syllogism)

NOTE

Expect to have to identify key terms on the DSST Principles of Advanced English Composition exam.

- **Pathos:** an appeal to emotions (for example, a touching anecdote)
- **Ethos:** an appeal to ethics (for example, an argument against an injustice)

In analyzing an argument, it is effective to understand the kinds of appeals a writer uses. An over-reliance on pathos can undermine the overall effect of the argument and indicate that the writer may have spent so much time working on the audience's emotions because of a lack of evidence. However, an argument that relies too much on logos risks causing the audience to simply not care enough to be persuaded by the message. A skillful balance of logos, pathos, and ethos is the key to conveying a message effectively. Of course, the claims and reasons that comprise the argument must also be well connected.

WARRANTS/ASSUMPTIONS

British philosopher Stephen Toulmin is the father of the concept of warrants in an argument. **Warrants** are the statements that bridge the gaps between facts and conclusions.

For example:

> **Fact:** *Margot went to a loud concert last night without wearing earplugs.*
>
> **Conclusion:** *Margot's ears are probably ringing this morning.*

This assumption is missing a warrant to connect its reason and claim. That warrant might look something like this:

> **Warrant:** *People who attend loud concerts without wearing earplugs may find that their ears ring the following day.*

Warrants are important in arguments because they help the audience determine whether or not a claim is effectively supported. Warrants can be explicitly stated or implicitly suggested.

An example of an **explicit warrant** might be a mother telling her child, "If you want to go to the park today, you will clean up your room."

An **implicit warrant** might be something like a mother telling her child, "I'd clean up your room if I were you," because its wording implies there will be negative consequences if the child does not clean up his room without specifying what those consequences are.

Implicit warrants may be difficult to identify in an argument. In such cases, it is necessary to find the reasoning behind a claim. Furthermore, warrants should not be accepted as valid simply because they are present. Like all evidence, they require support; whether or not they are acceptable may also depend on the particular audience. For example, an audience of vegetarians may take issue with the warrant that it is morally acceptable to eat animals because people are intellectually superior to animals. So the rhetorical triangle must be considered when analyzing how warrants are used in an argument.

TIP

The term "assumption" is often used in place of "warrant," and the two terms are indeed accepted as synonyms.

TIP

A warrant most often appears in an argument at a point where the writer thinks the reader might not accept the argument because it clarifies the connection between reasons and claims.

USING SECONDARY SOURCES

In the previous section of this lesson, we introduced the importance of using secondary sources as evidence. Because of the crucial role they play in effective compositions, secondary sources require additional consideration. After all, how does a writer make sure that the sources she or he uses are appropriate, relevant, and credible? What are the various types of secondary sources available? How are they used to summarize, paraphrase, and quote, and what is the proper way to cite and document sources to avoid charges of plagiarism? These are some of the issues we'll discuss in the following section.

FINDING SOURCES

Before evaluating or using secondary sources, a writer must first find them. Sources may be found in physical locations such as libraries, bookstores, newspaper stands, or one's own personal bookshelf, but they may also be discovered in the virtual environment of the Internet. The fact that anyone can publish anything he or she wants to on the Internet has made finding the right sources a lot trickier than it used to be.

Before even worrying about whether or not a source is valid, a writer must consider whether or not it is appropriate for the task at hand. Just because a source is thematically connected to a topic does not mean it will contain information that will support the composition's specific thesis. Examining inappropriate sources can waste valuable research time, particularly when writing a composition on a tight deadline. It is crucial to figure out which sources may be most appropriate before even cracking them open.

First, it is important for a writer to decide where she or he will hunt for sources. Sometimes the composition assignment itself will answer this question, perhaps directing the writer to a particular credible online database or text. Perhaps the assignment will ban online sources outright. Often writers will have to use their own judgment when seeking sources.

Online is the easiest place to start since it affords one a vast variety of sources without ever having to leave one's seat. However, the unreliability of much of the information on the Internet can make finding sources online problematic. That means it is best to start with websites that have some sort of official affiliation. While any person with a computer and a smidgeon of know-how can set up a .com site and fill it with any kind of wild information he or she can conceive, sites with other domain designations may prove to be more reliable.

These generally reliable websites will end with the following domain designations:

Domain Designation	Indicates
.edu	A website affiliated with an educational institution
.gov	A website affiliated with the U.S. government
.org	A website affiliated with an official organization

TIP

Thirty-two percent of the questions on the DSST Principles of Advanced English Composition Exam are devoted to using secondary sources.

TIP

Remember that a secondary source is one composed by someone who did not personally experience the events the source describes.

TIP

Online versions of print sources, such as newspapers and magazines, may end with the .com domain designation, but they are generally as credible as their print equivalents.

Writers must still be careful, though, because even sites with these designations may prove to contain erroneous information—but that is also true of any source.

A writer definitely should not rely on certain online sources during the research process. Much like .com websites, blogs and Internet forums are often unmediated and can be littered with errors and outright lies. The online encyclopedia Wikipedia is extremely popular, but its "wiki" prefix indicates that it can be written, edited, and updated by anyone with computer access, so its information should be taken with a grain of salt. However, while sources such as blogs, forums, and wiki sites should never be used as the final word in research, they may prove to be valuable springboards for gathering evidence—writers just need to make sure that they double-check the information culled from such sites with more reliable sources. Most Wikipedia entries even include links to the sources from which their information was supplied.

Meanwhile, traditional print texts are available anywhere books, newspapers, and magazines are found. Before the Internet age, the local library was the most popular spot to begin a research project, and libraries still prove to be rich sources of relevant materials while also offering Internet access.

Types of Sources

Once writers decide where to start looking for sources, they must think about the types of sources they plan to seek out. There are a wide variety of potential sources.

Print Source	Purpose	Primary or Secondary Source?
Biographies	Provide narratives of particular people's lives	Secondary
Autobiographies, diaries, and memoirs	Provide narratives of writers' own lives and experiences	Primary
Textbooks, histories, and encyclopedias	Provide straight information about any conceivable topic	Secondary
Newspapers and magazines	Provide information and opinions about current events	• Reports are secondary sources • Editorials and interviews are primary sources
Academic journals	Relay information about recent studies and research in a variety of fields, such as science and sociology	• Studies written by those who performed them are primary sources • Reports on studies performed by others are secondary sources

Trade journals	Relay recent information about businesses	• Studies written by those who performed them are primary sources • Reports on studies performed by others are secondary sources
Government reports	Reveal recent data related to population, tax policy, the national debt, and other matters of national importance	Primary

Although they should be evaluated carefully, online sources are also abundant and varied. These days there are online versions of numerous print sources, such as the websites of newspapers, magazines, and journals, as well as eBooks and online postings of government reports. However, there are also several sources unique to the Internet:

- **Websites:** pages and series of pages usually devoted to a particular topic or affiliated with a particular institution, business, publication, etc.
- **Databases:** extensive archives of online books, articles, reports, etc.
- **Blogs:** online journals or magazines often administered and written entirely by a single individual; may include a comments section to allow feedback from readers
- **Forums:** online gathering spots for individuals to discuss various topics

Some sources are not text-based at all. Such multimedia sources include audio and video reports and interviews that appear on television news and magazine programs, radio programs, and websites such as YouTube.

EVALUATING SOURCES

Sources may be in print, web, video, or audio, and there are good and not-so-good materials in every form. The secret for separating the best sources from the ones that should be avoided is evaluation. A writer must always consider the relevance and credibility of sources before relying on them.

Relevance

The issue of relevance is whether or not a particular source is right for a particular assignment. The source may be perfectly reliable, but if it isn't relevant to the assignment at hand, it won't be helpful and might even muddy a composition's vision with irrelevant information.

Assessing relevance begins with a simple and essential question: What is my composition about? A writer should try to be as specific as possible when answering that question, because answering it with "My composition is about Amelia Earhart." will not lead to as relevant information as answering it with "My composition is an informative piece about Amelia Earhart's solo flight across the Atlantic Ocean."

TIP

Sometimes sources are not captured for posterity in text, video, or audio form at all. For example, a town hall meeting may be a source for a news report or a concert may be a source for a critical response composition.

NOTE

Questions about appropriate sources may ask you to identify the most or least relevant credible source for a specific hypothetical topic.

TIP

One way to evaluate the relevance of a source is to skim its text or check its index for terms related to the composition for which it is to be used.

A writer should be equally specific when searching for sources. For example, a magazine about flying aircraft *may* include details about Amelia Earhart, but a biography about her would be a better place to begin research. More general sources can be considered, since such sources may actually enrich a topic with interesting details that cannot be gleaned from the most obvious sources—but only after examining the most relevant sources first.

The date a book or article was published will also be of interest when assessing relevance. Publication date is not much of an issue when writing a composition about a historical figure such as Amelia Earhart, since knowledge of the details of her life probably has not changed that much over the years, but the date will be crucial when writing about a more fluctuating topic. For example, an article published in a science magazine from 2002 will not be of great value when writing an argument about the importance of technology in today's society.

Furthermore, as we learn more about the truth, facts may change. For example, scientists believed that the number of genes an organism had was related to the complexity of that organism, but this was disproved when the human genome project was completed in 2003. Therefore, a source published before 2003 might lead someone writing a composition about genes down the wrong path.

Not only are facts in flux, but the ways we look at the world are changing, too. Pluto was once considered to be a planet, but in 2006, scientists officially settled on what defines a planet and Pluto was demoted to planetoid, or dwarf planet. Scientists did not learn anything significantly new about Pluto itself that they didn't already know; they just started looking at it differently through the lens of a new definition. So a pre-2006 source that refers to Pluto as a planet might cause problems if used to write a composition about the dwarf today.

The kind of piece a source is may also determine its relevance. For example, when researching a strictly informative composition, a writer might decide to avoid overly opinionated sources such as critiques and editorials, although such sources may still be relevant depending on the assignment. So it is always important to pay close attention to the assignment. Some assignments may even specify the types of sources that are allowed, such as an assignment that demands only online sources be used. The assignment may be even more specific than that, such as one that specifies that *only* qualitative research may be used, *no* qualitative statistics or experimental findings are allowed, or *only* scholarly sources, such as articles in academic journals, may be used.

Credibility

Another significant matter to consider when selecting sources is credibility. Will the source contain accurate information? A blog about the 2016 election may be relevant to a composition about the election, but blogs are generally not thought of as credible sources since anyone with Internet access can set up a blog and write whatever he or she wants to on it. Traditional print sources are often good places to start the research process because of their relative reliability. Since traditional print sources need to pass through a publishing process of acceptance and editing, the least reliable ones tend to get weeded out before they are ever published. However, even print sources have their issues. The fact that they are more difficult to update than online sources means that they are more likely to go out of date quicker. Also, the increasing commonness of self-publishing means that many print sources have not even passed through any kind of editorial process.

One must also consider that tabloid papers that contain fantastical or exaggerated information are both traditional print sources *and* are wholly unreliable. Print sources focused on a single philosophy or point of view may prove to be unreliable if they omit or manipulate details to further a particular political, cultural, or social agenda. So assessing credibility also depends on having some understanding of the kinds of materials out there, and exercising a good degree of critical thinking. If a source seems like it contains bogus information, it may very well contain bogus information. In such instances, seeking out other sources to find out whether or not they support the information in the original source is necessary. If particular details appear in one source only, it is entirely possible that that source is incorrect. Complicating matters further, errors sometimes get reprinted from source to source, ending up being accepted as fact even though they are not truthful.

The bottom line is that writers can never trust their sources entirely. Even sources widely accepted as credible, such as *The New York Times*, print errors. However, by eliminating the least reliable sources, writers have a better chance of using only credible ones. Such unreliable sources include:

- .com websites
- Blogs
- Sensationalistic tabloids
- Self-published writings
- Writings by authors or publishers affiliated with fringe organizations (hate groups, cults, etc.)
- Any writings that reveal an unacceptable level of bias (ones motivated by or infused with racism, sexism, homophobia, ageism, or any other form of prejudice)
- Research papers based on insufficient experimentation or data
- Advertisements (including seemingly traditional journalistic articles with the unstated purpose of selling something or pushing a particular special interest)
- Any writings lacking attribution
- Any technical writings by someone outside the given field (a medical article not written by a doctor, etc.)
- Any writings that commit logical fallacies
- Any writings littered with spelling, punctuation, grammatical, and other forms of mechanical errors
- Any writings that contain abusive language or are otherwise not written at an adult level
- Hearsay and gossip
- Testimonials
- Predictions

The best defense against unreliable sources is to credit all sources thoroughly. This is not only a necessary method for avoiding plagiarism but also a way to indicate that a certain idea or opinion can be attributed to a particular source rather than the writer of the composition in which it is used. This also allows the reader to get in on the assessing by deciding for her or himself whether or not the source in question is credible.

TIP

When assessing credibility, it is also helpful to think about the purpose of a source. If the purpose is to entertain rather than inform, then that particular publication may not be the best source. Anything satirical should be avoided outright.

TIP

Summaries should always add something meaningful to a composition. Before summarizing, a writer should ask him or herself if the summary is actually adding something meaningful to the composition. If the answer is "no," then the summary should be avoided.

USING SOURCES

After hunting down the most relevant and credible sources, a writer must then decide the best way to use them. The three primary ways to use sources are summarizing, paraphrasing, and quoting. Each method also has its own particular purposes.

Summarizing Information

When a writer gathers information from a source and relays that information in his or her own words, that writer is summarizing. Summarizing is most useful when a writer wants to incorporate the ideas in a source into her or his own composition, but:

- Prefers to restate the information in original language
- Can restate the information more clearly than the source states it
- Can restate the information in fewer words than the source uses
- Is afraid that she or he has been overusing quotations and paraphrases and wants to use sources in a more varied way

Summaries must always be shorter than the relevant passages in the source text—otherwise they aren't doing their jobs. For example, take a look at this paragraph from a source called *Principles of Public Health* by Thomas D. Tuttle:

> These bodies of ours are built somewhat like automobiles. An automobile is made up of a framework, wheels, body, gasoline tank, engine, and steering-gear. The human body has much the same form of construction. We have a frame, which is made of the bones of the body. We have arms and legs, which correspond to the wheels of the automobile. We have many little pockets in our bodies in which fat is stored, and these little pockets answer to the gasoline tank of the automobile. We have an engine which, like the automobile engine, is made up of many parts; and we have a head or brain, that plays the same part as the steering-gear of the automobile.
>
> The automobile has a tank in which is carried the gasoline necessary to develop power for the machine. If the gasoline gives out, the engine will not run, and before the owner starts on a trip, he is always careful to see that the tank is well filled. In the same way, if we do not provide new fat for the pockets in our bodies in which the fat is stored, our supply will soon give out and our bodies will refuse to work, just as the engine of the automobile will refuse to work when the gasoline is used up

That is a lot of information and rewording it in another two paragraphs wouldn't be much of a summary. The solution is to pick out the most important and relevant details and restate them in a sentence or two. For example:

> The human body is constructed to facilitate its functioning and survival. Thomas D. Tuttle likens this construction to that of an automobile, noting how bones are similar to an auto's frame, the limbs function similarly to wheels, fat fuels the body as gasoline fuels a car, and the brain steers the human machine as a steering wheel directs a car.

TIP

A writer does not have to work the source into a paraphrase or quotation explicitly. In-text citation can also be used to achieve proper attribution.

This summary expresses the same information as the source paragraphs and with about one-quarter of the text. Notice how it also refers to the source text directly. Even though the writer of the summary did not use the same wording as the source text, she still had to cite that text because the ideas are the same.

Because summarizing involves reusing information, it should be used sparingly, particularly in arguments. An argument mainly expresses the ideas and opinions of the writer, not merely regurgitates those of sources, and overusing summaries will undermine the thesis by making it seem repetitive and unoriginal. Summaries should be used to provide a bit of background on a topic or illustrate or support evidence. They should not constitute the bulk of the argument. They also should not necessarily stand on their own—summaries may require additional analysis from the writer.

Let's look at our previous summary again and see how the writer builds on it with her own ideas about Tuttle's comparison between human bodies and automobiles.

> The human body is constructed to facilitate its functioning and survival. Thomas D. Tuttle likens this construction to that of an automobile, noting how bones are similar to an auto's frame, the limbs function similarly to wheels, fat fuels the body as gasoline fuels a car, and the brain steers us as a steering wheel directs a car. While a bit simplistic and glib, Tuttle's comparison draws attention to the provocative concept of the human body as ingenious machine rather than mere organic matter.

Because sources are so integral to writing informative compositions, it is important for a writer to be wary of crossing the line from using details and summarizing to avoid plagiarism. **Plagiarism** is the illegal and unethical practice of passing off the words and ideas of another as one's own and must be avoided at all costs. If the writer of our summary had tried to pass off that comparison between human bodies and automobiles as her own without crediting Thomas D. Tuttle as she did, the writer would have been guilty of plagiarism.

Paraphrasing Information

Paraphrasing is a bit similar to summarizing. In both methods, writers do not repeat the specific language used in a source. Paraphrasing uses the composition writer's own words and must be phrased in a way that credits the source. However, it does not use as much of the source as a summary does, and doesn't even have to be shorter than the source material. It merely rewords it. Basically, the key element of the word "paraphrase" is "phrase," because paraphrases reword just a single phrase or sentence from a source.

Let's take another look at Thomas D. Tuttle's *Principles of Public Health*, but this time we're only going to look at a single sentence from the excerpt:

> *These bodies of ours are built somewhat like automobiles.*

Here's one way to paraphrase this line:

> *To paraphrase Thomas D. Tuttle, human bodies are pretty similar to automobiles.*

TIP

When taking notes during the research process, paraphrasing instead of direct quoting can help avoid direct quoting without proper attribution (plagiarism) in the composition's final draft.

Notice how the composition writer cites Tuttle as the author of this idea but restates the idea in original language. Perhaps the writer decided not to quote Tuttle directly because Tuttle's wording did not completely fit the style and tone of the composition. Perhaps the composition does not use first person phrases such as "These bodies of ours," so the writer decided to paraphrase the quotation in the third person to avoid slipping into the first person.

Like summarizing, paraphrasing is also a way to simplify the main idea of the source material being paraphrased. More broadly, paraphrasing is yet another way to vary the use of sources in a composition. If a writer has gone to the summarizing or quoting well a few times too often, she or he may decide to paraphrase instead.

Using Quotations

The simplest way to use a source is a direct quotation. This way, the composition writer does not have to think about how to condense information or rephrase language in the source text; he or she simply pulls words from the source, places them within quotation marks, and cites the source.

Here's that line from *Principles of Public Health* again:

> *These bodies of ours are built somewhat like automobiles.*

And now the quotation as it might appear in a composition:

TIP

Depending on the documentation style being used, it may be necessary to cite the particular paragraph of a source that provided the material for a quotation or even a paraphrase.

> *As Thomas D. Tuttle wrote, "These bodies of ours are built somewhat like automobiles."*

As simple as quoting may seem, it should be done with as much care as a writer uses when summarizing and paraphrasing. Because quotations repeat the language of others, they must be used extra sparingly for the sake of originality. There are also limits on how much a writer can quote from a particular text without committing plagiarism. Proper citation will not rescue a composition that basically consists of nothing but quotations from a couple of sources.

Quotations must also be punctuated with care. Only the source's original punctuation should be included within the quotation marks.

Take a look at this quotation:

> *Why did Thomas D. Tuttle write, "These bodies of ours are built somewhat like automobiles?"*

This quotation contains an error because Tuttle's original statement was not a question. Therefore, the composition writer's question mark must be placed outside of the quotation.

> *Why did Thomas D. Tuttle write, "These bodies of ours are built somewhat like automobiles"?*

That's much better.

If a writer intends to quote a selection of text that is too wordy or contains details irrelevant to the composition in which it is to be quoted, ellipses can be used to cut out the unnecessary language without violating the conventions of quoting. Here's another excerpt from *Principles of Public Health*.

> *If the gasoline gives out, the engine will not run, and before the owner starts on a trip, he is always careful to see that the tank is well filled. In the same way, if we do not provide new fat for the pockets in our bodies in which the fat is stored, our supply will soon give out and our bodies will refuse to work, just as the engine of the automobile will refuse to work when the gasoline is used up.*

These lengthy lines can be condensed within a quotation a bit like this:

> *As Tuttle wrote, "If the gasoline gives out, the engine will not run… In the same way, if we do not provide new fat for the pockets in our bodies in which the fat is stored, our supply will soon give out and our bodies will refuse to work…*

Notice that the writer used ellipses to indicate both words cut out of the middle of the quotation and at the end since the writer has not quoted a completed sentence ending in terminal punctuation (period, question mark, or exclamation mark). Had the composition writer decided to use the rest of that final sentence ("…just as the engine of the automobile will refuse to work when the gasoline is used up."), a second ellipsis would not have been necessary.

Although quotations must be handled with care, they should not be avoided since they can really strengthen a composition if used effectively. A direct quote shows the reader that the composition writer is not trying to manipulate the meaning of a source with inauthentic rewording. If the original quote is particularly well phrased or eloquent, the mere repetition of that fine language can really spruce up a composition. Also, when quoting someone who is a well-regarded authority on the topic of the composition, it is wisest not to try to "improve" that authority's wording. To quote a common sentiment, "Don't mess with the classics."

CITING AND DOCUMENTING

While discussing the use of sources, we've tried to emphasize the importance of proper attribution and citation to avoid the crime of plagiarism, avoid violating the conventions of using sources, and simply give credit where credit is due. This involves citing sources that have been summarized, quoted, and paraphrased within the text and documenting all sources used in a "works cited" page at the end of the composition. In this section, we will discuss the various styles of, and methods for, proper citing and documenting.

NOTE

Some questions on the DSST Principles of Advanced English Composition exam may ask you to identify the circumstances under which a writer might decide to summarize, paraphrase, or quote a source in a composition.

NOTE

Although there are a number of documentation styles, the DSST Principles of Advanced English Composition exam is only concerned with three styles: MLA, APA, and CMS.

Choosing a Documentation Style

First of all, a writer has to settle on a documentation style and use it consistently throughout her or his composition. An assignment will often state the kind of citation method required, but this may not always be the case. If a particular documentation style is not specified in the assignment, the writer must consider the nature of the assignment to select the right style. The three most common documentation styles are MLA, APA, and CMS. Each style has its own purposes and particularities.

MLA Style

Modern Language Association or MLA style is one of the most popular and versatile documentation styles. It is most commonly used in papers on the humanities, as well as literary research compositions, so it will be handy when writing about the following:

- Literature
- Art
- Communications
- Film
- Linguistics
- Music
- Theater
- Religion
- Philosophy

APA Style

APA is short for the American Psychological Association, and based on that organization's name, you may be able to figure out the kinds of topics that require APA citation and documentation style. APA style is most commonly used in articles about psychology, as well as with other social sciences:

- Business
- Criminology
- Education
- Linguistics
- Journalism
- Politics
- Sociology
- International matters

TIP

More than one documentation style may be appropriate for certain topics, but only one documentation style must be used throughout a single composition.

CMS Style

Finally there's the Chicago Manual of Style or CMS documentation and citation approach. The topics for which a writer would choose CMS style bridge the divide between the topics appropriate for the MLA and APA styles. Like MLA style, CMS style is used for topics in the humanities, and like APA style, it is also used for topics in the social sciences. So a writer may choose CMS style when writing about the following:

- Anthropology
- Art History
- Business
- Computer science
- Education
- History
- International matters
- World cultures
- Music
- Philosophy
- Religion
- Theater

Using Style Manuals

After selecting the appropriate documentation style for a particular composition, you must then get familiar with all the particulars of that style. This can be a very involved process—those particulars will not only depend on the style used, but also on the publication being documented. For example, the way you document a book in MLA style will not be the same the way you document a newspaper or website according to MLA standards.

When writing a composition, it makes the most sense to simply refer to the MLA, APA, or CMS standards online or in print to ensure all citations and documentations are correct. However, that will not be an option when answering questions about citation and documentation on the DSST Principles of Advanced English Composition exam, so you will need to remembers as many of the particulars about the three types of styles as possible when taking the test.

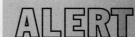

ALERT

Style manuals are sometimes updated with new documentation and citation methods. Be sure to always refer to the latest edition of a style guide

MLA

Let's begin with MLA style, which depends on the essential elements in any documentation. Each element in the citation should be formatted as follows:

Placement of Element	Element	Particulars
1st	Author or authors' name(s)	Last name first, then a comma, then first name and middle name or middle initial if used in source. The names of additional authors are cited with first name first, middle name next, and last name last. Always end with period.
2nd	Source's title	• Article titles in quotation marks. • Book, periodical, and website titles in italics. End with period unless documentation indicating collection or edition follows, in which case a comma follows.
3rd	Collection's title	If source came from a collection, periodical containing a number of articles, or anthology, italicize name of collection and follow with a comma.
4th	Additional contributors	If an editor, translator, illustrator, or other contributor aside from the author is cited as a main contributor on the title page, that person needs to be included in documentation. First name first, middle name next, and last name last followed by a comma.
5th	Edition	If a source is a particular edition (cited as **ed.**), comes from a particular volume (cited as **vol.**), or has a particular number (cited as **no.**), that must be cited next followed by a comma.
6th	Publisher's name	Name of publisher followed by a comma.
7th	Publication date	Publication date followed by a period if no page numbers are documented. Ends with a comma if page numbers are documented
8th	Page number(s) or web address documented	• Single physical page numbers are documented with **p.** and the particular page used. Ends with a period. • Multiple pages are documented with **pp.** and the range of page numbers are separated with a hyphen. Ends with a period. • Websites are documented with the complete web address. Ends with a period.

Here are some samples of documentations using MLA style:

A book with a single author:

> Lord, Walter. *A Night to Remember*. 5th ed., Bantam Books, 1997, pp. 50-67.

A book with multiple authors and contributors:

> Pim, Keiron, and Jack Horner. *Dinosaurs: The Grand Tour*. Illustrated by Fabio Pastori. The Experiment Publications, 2014, p. 124.

A magazine article with a single author:

> Collis, Clark. "How to Get Away with Murder on the Orient Express." *Entertainment Weekly*, no. 1465, May 12, 2017, pp. 5-7.

An article with a single author on a website:

> Amster-Burton, Matthew. "The saucy comforts of Taiwanese turkey rice." *The AV Club*, http://www.avclub.com/article/saucy-comforts-taiwanese-turkey-rice-254431. May 9, 2017.

APA

Now let's consider how sources are documented according to APA style. As you will see, APA style has certain similarities but also significant differences to the way sources are documented in MLA style.

Placement of Element	Element	Particulars
1st	Author or authors' name(s)	For all authors, last name first, then a comma, followed by first and middle initial. End with period.
2nd	Publication date	Placed within parentheses. Year first; month and day follow. End with period.
3rd	Source's title	• Article titles are not formatted. • Book, periodical, and website titles in italics End with period unless documentation indicating collection or edition follows, in which case a comma follows.
4th	Collection's title	If source came from a collection, periodical containing a number of articles, or anthology, italicize name of collection and follow with a comma.

ALERT

Style manuals are sometimes updated with new documentation and citation methods. Be sure to always refer to the latest edition of a style guide.

TIP

Documentation appears alphabetically by author's last name on a "works cited" page at the end of a composition.

Placement of Element	Element	Particulars
5th	Edition	• If a source is a book that is a particular edition (cited as **ed.**), or comes from a particular volume (cited as **Vol.**), that must be cited within parentheses before the period after the title. • If a source is a magazine, volume is documented after collection title followed by number of the edition in parentheses. Ends with a comma.
6th	Location	Location where published followed by a colon.
7th	Publisher's name	Name of publisher. Ends with a period.
8th	Page numbers	For multiple pages, the range of page numbers are separated with a hyphen. Ends with a period.
9th	Date accessed and web address (Internet source only)	Date accessed follows month/day/year format. Full web address follows. Web documentation includes *Retrieved* and *from*. Ends with a period.

Here are some samples of documentations using APA style:

A book with a single author:

> Kurlansky, M. (2004). *1968*. New York, NY: Ballantine Books.

A book with multiple authors:

> Strunk, W. & White, E. B. (2000). *The Elements of Style* (4th ed.). Needham Heights, MA: Longman Publishers.

A journal article with multiple authors:

> Dale, S. E. & Sheets, K. S (2017, April). 3 Critical Management Areas that Demand Attention. *Journal of Financial Planning*, 30(4), p. 24.

An article with a single author on a website:

> McLeod, S. (2015). Cognitive Psychology. Retrieved May 10, 2017, from https://www.simplypsychology.org/cognitive.html.

CMS

Finally, let's review CMS documentation style.

Placement of Element	Element	Particulars
1st	Author or authors' name(s)	First name first, middle name next, and last name last for all authors. A comma follows.
2nd	Source's title	• Book titles are italicized. A period follows. • Article titles are placed within quotation marks. A comma follows.
3rd	Collection's title and volume	If source came from a collection, periodical containing a number of articles, or anthology, italicize name of collection. If source has a volume number, include number with no further formatting. Follow with a comma.
4th	Additional contributors	If an editor, translator, illustrator, or other contributor aside from the author is cited as a main contributor on the title page, that person needs to be included in documentation. First name first, middle name next, and last name last.
5th	Location (book only)	Location where published followed by a colon. Placed within same parentheses as publisher's name and publication date.
6th	Publisher's name (book only)	Name of publisher followed by a comma. Placed within same parentheses as location and publication date.
7th	Publication date	Publication date is placed within the same parentheses as location and publication name. Comma placed outside of parentheses for book documentation. Colon follows for periodical documentation. For web address, indicate last date modified with **last modified** or date accessed with **Accessed.**
8th	Page numbers	For multiple pages, the range of page numbers is separated with a hyphen. Ends with a period.
9th	Web address (Internet source only)	Full web address. Ends with a period.

NOTE

The "works cited" page of a composition is the equivalent of a bibliography and sometimes these terms are used interchangeably, so the DSST Principles of Advanced English Composition exam may use the term "bibliography" instead of "works cited" page.

Here are some samples of documentations using CMS style:

A book with a single author:

> Thor Heyerdahl, *Kon-Tiki.* (New York: Perma Books, 1953), 200-201.

A book with multiple authors and contributors:

Abdul Weisel and Miriam Julian, *An Introduction to Computing.* trans. Gertrude Evers (Chicago: Contemporary Press, 2011), 308.

A magazine article with a single author:

Jennifer Klein, "An Inauspicious Debut," *Theatrical Times* 801 (February, 2015): 49.

An article with a single author on a website:

Carl Engelking, "City Dwellers and Hunter-Gatherers Have Similar Sleep Habits," Discover Magazine.com, last modified October 15, 2015, http://blogs.discovermagazine.com/d-brief/2015/10/15/preindustrial-sleep-habits/#.

In-Text Citations

While documentation appears at the end of a composition on the "works cited" page, citation appears within the text when a quotation, paraphrase, or summary requires immediate attribution. The good news is that since citation appears within the text, it tends to be much simpler than documentation. Nevertheless, there are still a number of styles to learn since the MLA, APA, and CMS methods each have their own citation styles.

MLA

According to MLA style, in-text citations will vary depending on how they are used and the number of sources by a single author used.

If a composition uses only one source by an author, and the author's name is explicitly stated in the composition, nothing more than the page number of the information cited within parentheses is necessary.

For example:

> *According to Williamson, "technology is a necessary evil" (210).*

However, if the author's name is not stated explicitly, her or his name must appear within the parentheses. For example:

> *One should always remember that, "technology is a necessary evil" (Williamson 210).*

If different authors share the same name, then first initials are required. For example:

> *One should always remember that, "technology is a necessary evil" (B. Williamson 210).*

TIP
All works cited in-text must also be documented on the works cited page.

TIP
According to MLA style, the last name of the author and the page or pages from which the citation was pulled must be included within the text of a composition.

If the author of a source is unknown, or more than one source by a single author is used, then the title of the source should be used in place of his or her name.

As for her second novel, it has been called "a very worthy successor" ("Exceptions to the Sophomore Slump" 12).

In-text citations for websites require only the author's name, or if that is not included on the web page, the title of the article or site:

This was certainly "an exceptionally peculiar situation." (contemporarycriticism.com).

APA

APA in-text citation style is quite similar to that of MLA style, but it requires the publication date within parentheses and **p.** or **pp.** before the page number or numbers from which the information cited was pulled. For example, that quotation about technology we used earlier would look like this in APA style:

According to Williamson (2008), "technology is a necessary evil" (p. 210).

If the author is not explicitly named, then the author's last name is required, and all pertinent information appears within the same parentheses.

One should always remember that, "technology is a necessary evil" (Williamson, 2008, p. 210).

In-text citations for websites are basically identical to the MLA style aside from the fact that they also require the publication date. For example:

This was certainly "an exceptionally peculiar situation" (contemporarycriticism.org, 2017).

Citations of web pages without dates need to indicate this with the abbreviation **n.d.** For example:

This was a "breakthrough of monumental proportions" (nowscience.edu, n.d.).

CMS

Like MLA style, CMS in-text citation does not require **p.** or **pp.** to indicate page numbers. Like APA style, it does require the publication date.

According to Williamson (2008), "technology is a necessary evil" (210).

When the author is not stated explicitly in the text, citation is again similar to that of APA style, but there is no comma between the author's name and the date as well as the absence of **p.** or **pp.**

One should always remember that, "technology is a necessary evil" (Williamson 2008, 210).

In-text citations for websites require only the name of the article:

His performance has been called "a true marvel" ("Review: Our Town at the Community Theater").

Choosing and using citation and documentation styles correctly also helps a composition to have a certain professional polish that may make its central argument or purpose more convincing. After all, every element in a composition from the style in which it is written to the way it uses sources to the ways it is cited and documented should all be working toward making it an effective piece of narration, information, persuasion, or criticism.

TIP

According to both APA and CMS style, the last name of the author, the year the source was published, and the page or pages from which the citation was pulled must be included within the text of a composition.

SUMMING IT UP

- The DSST Principles of Advanced English Composition exam consists only of multiple-choice questions about types and elements of **writing, writing strategies, elements of arguments,** and **sources.**

- The DSST Principles of Advanced English Composition exam consists of 64 questions. Test takers have two hours to complete the questions.

- Around four percent of the questions on the DSST Principles of Advanced English Composition exam are devoted to identifying four types of writing: **narrative, informative, argumentative/persuasive,** and **critical response compositions.**

- Thirty-two percent of the questions on the DSST Principles of Advanced English Composition exam are devoted to elements of **effective** writing.

- Each type of writing has its own **purpose** and is intended for a particular **audience.**

- Knowing a composition's purpose and audience helps writers to decide the kind of **language, tone,** and **style** to use.

- Before beginning a draft, writers use **prewriting strategies** such as reading, thinking, analyzing, and discussing to generate topics for their compositions.

- **Invention techniques** such as brainstorming, freewriting, questioning, and hypothesizing help writers to generate more specific ideas to develop their main topics.

- To **organize** ideas in their compositions, writers use such strategies as mind mapping (also known as clustering) and outlining.

- There are a number of patterns that can be used to organize ideas in a composition, such as **cause/effect, compare/contrast, description, division/classification, problem/solution, process,** and **sequential order.**

- Using a **"hook"** to snare the reader's interest is an effective technique for beginning a composition.

- Each body paragraph of a composition should include a **main point, supporting evidence,** and a **transitional sentence** that leads to the next paragraph.

- The **concluding** paragraph of a composition should restate the thesis, summarize the main points, and/or leave the reader with something to think about.

- **Revision** involves examining and improving the content of a composition.

- **Editing** involves reviewing a composition to ensure that it maintains English conventions, such as correct spelling, grammar, word usage, capitalization, and punctuation.

- Thirty-two percent of the questions on the DSST Principles of Advanced English Composition exam are devoted to reading and writing arguments.

- The **thesis,** or main claim, is the central point the writer is trying to make or the thing that the writer is trying to persuade readers to believe.

- **Main claims,** or sometimes called **sub-claims,** are the more specific claims that support the relatively general claim in the thesis.

- **Claims support** is the evidence that supports the main claims.

- **Expert opinions** are ideas or quotations expressed by authorities on topics related to a composition's thesis. They are used as evidence to support the main claims.

- A composition must be built on sound **logic** and may include such methods for reaching logical conclusions as syllogisms, inductive reasoning, deductive reasoning, and enthymemes.

- A **logical fallacy** is when a conclusion is drawn using flawed logic. There are a number of types of logical fallacies.

- An **anecdote** is a short story used as supporting evidence. Anecdotes are used to lend an emotional texture to an argument or illustrate an important point the writer intends to make.

- **Sources** are the texts from which evidence is gathered.

- A **secondary source** is composed by someone who did not personally experience the events the source describes, such as a textbook, biography, objective journalistic article, or research paper.

- **Rhetoric** is the art of persuasion.

- A **rhetorical triangle** is the relationship between audience, message, and writer.

- **Appeals** are the ways the writer persuades the audience to share her or his point of view.

- Major appeals include **logos** (an appeal to logic), **pathos** (an appeal to emotions), and **ethos** (an appeal to ethics).

- **Warrants**, or **assumptions**, are the statements that connect facts to conclusions.

- Thirty-two percent of the questions on the DSST Principles of Advanced English Composition exam are devoted to using secondary sources.

- Finding secondary sources involves searching in locations such as libraries, bookstores, newspaper stands, or the Internet.

- **Print sources** include biographies, autobiographies, textbooks, encyclopedias, newspapers, magazines, academic journals, trade journals, and government reports.

- **Internet sources** include websites, databases, blogs, and forums.

- All sources must be evaluated for **relevance** and **credibility**.

- Sources can be used for the purposes of **summarizing** (relaying information from a source in one's own words), **paraphrasing** (relaying the gist of a quotation in one's own words), and **quoting** (repeating a quotation word-for-word).

- Summaries, paraphrases, and quotations must be properly **cited** and **documented** to avoid **plagiarism**, which is the illegal and unethical practice of passing off the words and ideas of another as one's own.

- The three main citation and documentation styles are **MLA** (Modern Language Association), **APA** (American Psychological Association), and **CMS** (Chicago Manual of Style). Each style has its own very specific conventions.

- MLA style is mainly used in compositions on the **humanities** and **literature**.

- APA style is mainly used in compositions on the **social sciences**.

- CMS style is used in compositions on both the humanities and the social sciences.

- **Documentation** is included on the "works cited" page at the end of a composition.

- **Citation** is included within the text of a composition.

PRINCIPLES OF ADVANCED ENGLISH COMPOSITION POST-TEST

Directions: Carefully read each of the following 60 questions. Choose the best answer to each question and fill in the corresponding circle on the answer sheet. The Answer Key and Explanations can be found following this post-test.

1. Which of the following would be LEAST effective in a speech written for an audience of high school students?
   A. Idiomatic expressions
   B. Technical jargon
   C. Contemporary slang
   D. Inclusive language

2. The concluding statement of an essay should appear in the
   A. first paragraph.
   B. second paragraph.
   C. third paragraph.
   D. final paragraph.

3. The term for a composition that conveys details about a nonfictional topic in a neutral manner is _____ writing.
   A. critical
   B. argumentative
   C. narrative
   D. informative

4. The first step of the prewriting process is
   A. thinking.
   B. freewriting.
   C. brainstorming.
   D. questioning.

5. When a writer is determining the relevance of a source, it is typically effective to
   A. find out how recently the source was published.
   B. research how much material the author of the source has published.
   C. see if the source includes a number of images.
   D. ensure that the source is a book and not just an article.

6. The role of freewriting is to
   A. organize paragraphs.
   B. outline important details.
   C. establish a purpose.
   D. generate ideas.

7. A writer should paraphrase when
   A. a quotation shows that its source supports a particular idea.
   B. a quotation presents an argument that can be critiqued.
   C. the idea of a quotation is more important than its specific wording.
   D. using a quotation would result in plagiarism.

8. A well-structured paragraph in a composition should
   A. explain the main purpose of the composition as a whole.
   B. make a point and offer support for that point.
   C. work well if placed anywhere in the composition.
   D. only include one piece of evidence.

9. Why does a writer include a thesis statement in a composition?
   A. To clarify the main claim of the composition
   B. To persuade readers to share a particular opinion
   C. To support the main claim of the composition
   D. To indicate that the composition is well organized

10. The best way to indicate that a paragraph is introducing a new idea is to
    A. begin the paragraph with a new thesis statement.
    B. number all the paragraphs in the piece of writing.
    C. explicitly state that the paragraph will introduce a new idea.
    D. end the previous paragraph with a transitional sentence.

11. A composition about computers written for an audience of computer experts should be written in a(n) _____ style.
    A. friendly
    B. academic
    C. technical
    D. emotional

12. Which of the following shows the correct way to use CMS documentation on the "works cited" page of a composition?
    A. Lisa McManus, *An Introduction to Medical Science* (New York: Brewer Books, 2017).
    B. Lisa McManus, *An Introduction to Medical Science* (New York: Brewer Books, 2017), 77-89.
    C. Lisa McManus, *An Introduction to Medical Science* (New York: Brewer Books), 77-89.
    D. McManus, Lisa, *An Introduction to Medical Science* (New York: Brewer Books, 2017), 77-89.

13. A strong argument uses sources as evidence to
    A. show that it is not just based on personal opinion.
    B. prove that the writer is well read.
    C. indicate the popularity of its opinions.
    D. make it seem less critical.

14. The term for grouping ideas visually during the prewriting process is
    A. freewriting.
    B. mind mapping.
    C. outlining.
    D. brainstorming.

15. Clues to the main claim of an article can often be found in its
    A. footnotes.
    B. evidence.
    C. supporting details.
    D. headline.

16. Which of the following would NOT be a flaw in an argument?
    A. A personal attack
    B. An example that refutes an argument
    C. A claim identical to its own conclusion
    D. A comparison between two things that do not correspond

17. A writer should improve word choice while
    A. drafting.
    B. revising.
    C. outlining.
    D. brainstorming.

18. CMS citation style is MOST appropriate in an article on
    A. journalism.
    B. linguistics.
    C. the arts.
    D. psychology.

19. The term for a short story used to enrich an argument is
    A. assumption.
    B. summary.
    C. logic.
    D. anecdote.

20. The role of editing is to
   A. correct errors in grammar, usage, and spelling.
   B. clarify ideas, add variety, and develop the topic.
   C. express ideas in an organized fashion.
   D. generate and decide on ideas for a topic.

21. An author would use a quotation when a source
   A. uses distinctive phrasing.
   B. states an essential truth.
   C. is written by a well-educated person.
   D. uses complex wording.

22. Which of the following is the BEST evidence that an argument may be unreliable?
   A. The author includes numerous quotations from an expert on the topic being argued.
   B. The author uses information found on a blog as evidence to support the argument.
   C. The author fails to name anyone else who agrees with his or her argument.
   D. The author does not end each point with citation of the sources he or she used.

23. An author should summarize a text when
   A. making an original argument.
   B. explaining why a text is important.
   C. providing background on a topic.
   D. providing evidence to support a claim.

24. A writer interested in hooking a reader's interest might use which method?
   A. Organizing paragraphs in chronological order
   B. Using cause and effect structure
   C. Ending an essay with a summary
   D. Beginning an essay with a question

25. Which of the following shows the correct way to use MLA in-text citation?
   A. Mashima warns that "climate change is very real and we ignore it at our own risk" (63).
   B. Mashima warns that "climate change is very real and we ignore it at our own risk" (Mashima 63).
   C. Mashima (63) warns that "climate change is very real and we ignore it at our own risk."
   D. Mashima warns that climate change is very real and we ignore it at our own risk (63).

26. The most relevant secondary source for a research paper on World War II is
   A. a novel set during World War II.
   B. a history textbook about World War II.
   C. an interview with a veteran of World War II.
   D. a newspaper article published during World War II.

27. Citing evidence in an argument can help the reader to
   A. know how the author became a writer.
   B. figure out whether or not an argument is original.
   C. understand the process by which the author reached a conclusion.
   D. decide whether or not the author of the argument is an authority.

28. Using statistics, examples, and expert opinions are all examples of
   A. prewriting strategies.
   B. elements of a thesis.
   C. editing techniques.
   D. ways to support a claim.

post-test

29. What is a warrant in an argument?
    A. A connecting statement between a reason and a claim
    B. A conclusion based on personal bias
    C. A series of statements intended to persuade readers to accept a conclusion
    D. A judgment determined by reasoning

30. One purpose of an anecdote in an argument is to
    A. appeal to a reader's sense of logic.
    B. make an emotional connection with the reader.
    C. generate ideas for the argument.
    D. summarize the main idea of the argument.

31. A summary
    A. condenses the most important details in a composition.
    B. defines key terms in a composition.
    C. states the main idea of a composition.
    D. may reorder the main ideas in a composition.

32. The term for the way an argument with a conclusion built on two or more premises is
    A. logos.
    B. ethos.
    C. syllogism.
    D. pathos.

33. In APA style, in-text citations that follow quotations for which the author is not explicitly named require
    A. the full name of the author and the title of the source.
    B. the author's last name and a paragraph number.
    C. the publication date and a page number.
    D. the author's last name, the publication date, and a page number.

34. Multimedia sources include
    A. books and newspapers.
    B. radio and television broadcasts.
    C. academic and trade journals.
    D. websites and blogs.

35. The main points of an article are most often found in
    A. the thesis statement.
    B. the concluding statement.
    C. the topic sentence of each paragraph.
    D. the transitional sentences between paragraphs.

36. The wording of a quotation should be
    A. clearer than the wording used in the source to avoid plagiarism.
    B. identical to the wording used in the source.
    C. more succinct than the wording used in the source.
    D. expanded so that it is more detailed than the wording in the source.

37. A summary should focus on
    A. several key terms.
    B. all the details in a source.
    C. the tone of the source.
    D. a single main idea.

38. During the prewriting process, hypothesizing involves
    A. searching for ideas in books and online.
    B. drafting a preliminary thesis.
    C. figuring out how ideas are connected.
    D. creating an inventory of personal interests.

39. Mind mapping involves organizing ideas generated while
    A. outlining.
    B. freewriting.
    C. brainstorming.
    D. clustering.

40. Thinking, analyzing, and discussing a topic or topics are examples of
    A. outlining techniques.
    B. brainstorming ideas.
    C. prewriting strategies.
    D. paraphrasing.

41. A thesis must be phrased as
    A. an interrogative sentence.
    B. an exclamatory sentence.
    C. an imperative sentence.
    D. a declarative sentence.

42. The term for a piece of writing that makes a case in favor of or against a particular issue is _____ writing.
    A. narrative
    B. informative
    C. critical
    D. argumentative

43. Cause/effect, problem/solution, and comparison/contrast are all examples of
    A. mind mapping strategies.
    B. freewriting techniques.
    C. summarization approaches.
    D. organizational methods.

44. Another term for "main point" is
    A. sub-claim.
    B. main claim.
    C. thesis.
    D. headline.

45. Numerical information used to support a claim is called
    A. statistics.
    B. data.
    C. an opinion.
    D. an example.

46. What is true about most contemporary newspapers?
    A. They can only be found in print.
    B. They are not as reliable as trade journals.
    C. They can be found in print or online.
    D. They are not as reliable as blogs.

47. The term for a general persuasive method is
    A. pathos.
    B. inductive reasoning.
    C. argument.
    D. appeal.

48. A writer often uses a warrant in an argument at a point when the writer
    A. introduces the argument's main claim.
    B. thinks the reader might not accept the argument.
    C. reaches the conclusion of the argument.
    D. wants to recapture the reader's attention.

49. Circular reasoning, false equivalences, and hasty generalizations are all examples of
    A. philosophical logic.
    B. narratives.
    C. logical fallacies.
    D. incomplete comparisons.

50. While freewriting, a writer should NOT
    A. time the activity.
    B. write without stopping.
    C. correct errors.
    D. write about a single idea only.

51. The term for beginning an argument with a conclusion before moving to the premises on which that conclusion was built is
    A. inductive reasoning
    B. deductive reasoning.
    C. reaching a conclusion.
    D. making an appeal.

post-test

52. When paraphrasing, it is crucial to
    A. attribute the source of the ideas presented.
    B. use the same phrasing that the original source uses.
    C. place the entire paraphrase within quotation marks.
    D. place the subject of the paraphrase within quotation marks.

53. What is the MOST appropriate secondary source for a paper about baroque music?
    A. An "introduction to music" textbook
    B. The Wikipedia page for baroque music
    C. An encyclopedia entry for baroque music
    D. An original letter written by a baroque composer

54. A website with the domain designation ____ is LEAST likely to be credible.
    A. .edu
    B. .gov
    C. .org
    D. .com

55. MLA documentation style should be used in a manuscript about
    A. anthropology.
    B. education.
    C. religion.
    D. criminology.

56. An argument that makes the assumption that one act will inevitably lead to another commits the logical fallacy known as
    A. slippery slope.
    B. post hoc, ergo propter hoc.
    C. a fallacy of composition.
    D. moral equivalence.

57. According to APA citation style, the title of a journal article should be
    A. italicized.
    B. underlined.
    C. placed within quotation marks.
    D. unformatted.

58. The most relevant source for an article on a march to raise climate change awareness would MOST LIKELY be found in
    A. a biology journal.
    B. a chemistry textbook.
    C. a newspaper.
    D. an entertainment magazine.

59. Cause/effect order is the most appropriate way to organize
    A. a personal narrative.
    B. a biography.
    C. an argument.
    D. a history.

60. When deciding on a specific topic for an informative text about current population trends, it is MOST helpful to read
    A. government reports.
    B. encyclopedia articles.
    C. old current events reports.
    D. biographies.

ANSWER KEY AND EXPLANATIONS

1. B	13. A	25. A	37. D	49. C
2. D	14. B	26. B	38. B	50. C
3. D	15. D	27. C	39. C	51. B
4. A	16. B	28. D	40. C	52. A
5. A	17. B	29. A	41. D	53. C
6. D	18. C	30. B	42. D	54. D
7. C	19. D	31. A	43. D	55. C
8. B	20. A	32. C	44. A	56. A
9. A	21. A	33. D	45. A	57. D
10. D	22. B	34. B	46. C	58. C
11. C	23. C	35. C	47. D	59. C
12. B	24. D	36. B	48. B	60. A

1. **The correct answer is B.** An audience of high school students is likely to respond to informal, nontechnical speech, so technical jargon would be least appropriate for this particular audience. Choices A, idiomatic expressions, and C, contemporary slang, are informal styles of speech that would be more appropriate when addressing high school students than technical jargon would be. Choice D, inclusive language, is language that does not exclude anyone based on their gender, race, culture, or abilities and is perfectly appropriate to use when addressing high school students.

2. **The correct answer is D.** The concluding statement must appear near the conclusion of the essay. A concluding statement would never appear in the first paragraph, so choice A is incorrect. It would not likely appear as early as the second or third paragraphs, so choices B and C are not the best answers.

3. **The correct answer is D.** Writing that conveys details about a nonfictional topic in a neutral manner is informative writing. Choice A is incorrect because critical writing involves considering evidence in order to

draw a conclusion. Choice B is incorrect because argumentative writing argues in favor of or against a particular issue. A story that explains the experiences of a character is narrative writing, so choice C is incorrect.

4. **The correct answer is A.** The very first step of the prewriting process is simply thinking in order to determine a basic topic to explore further. Choices B, C, and D cannot be correct because a writer cannot freewrite, brainstorm, or question before thinking of a basic topic to freewrite about, brainstorm about, or question.

5. **The correct answer is A.** Typically, the more recently a source was published, the more relevant it will be because older sources may contain outdated information. Whether or not an author has published a lot of material has no bearing on whether or not a source is relevant, so choice B is incorrect. The number of images a source contains is similarly irrelevant, so choice C can be eliminated as well. Choice D would only be a factor if the assignment specifies that articles cannot be used as sources, so it is not the best answer choice.

6. **The correct answer is D.** Freewriting is a prewriting technique used to generate ideas for a particular piece of writing. It is not used for organization or outlining, so choices A and B are incorrect. Freewriting can only be performed after a writer has established the purpose of the piece of writing, so choice C is incorrect.

7. **The correct answer is C.** Only choice C describes a reason to paraphrase instead of directly quote. Choices A and B are reasons to quote directly, not paraphrase. Choice D is not the best answer since a correctly cited quotation should never result in plagiarism.

8. **The correct answer is B.** A well-structured paragraph in a composition makes a point and offers strong evidence to support that point. Choice A describes the best way to construct a strong thesis statement, not a strong paragraph. A well-structured paragraph fits perfectly into a particular spot in a composition because of the way it develops the thesis and uses transitions, so choice C is incorrect. A well-structured paragraph can and often should include more than one piece of supporting evidence, so choice D is not correct.

9. **The correct answer is A.** A thesis statement clarifies and specifies the main claim of any piece of writing. Its main purpose is not persuasive in nature, so choice B is not the best answer. Evidence supports the main claim—the thesis statement does not—so choice C is incorrect. A strong thesis statement may be a clue that a composition is well organized, but this is not really the essential purpose of a thesis statement, so choice D is not the best answer.

10. **The correct answer is D.** Transitional sentences indicate that a piece of writing is moving from one idea to another. Any piece of writing has only one thesis statement, so choice A is incorrect. Choice B would not really help to organize the paragraphs in a piece of writing in any meaningful way. Choice C describes a lazy and clumsy way to indicate that a paragraph introduces a new idea, so it is not the best answer.

11. **The correct answer is C.** An audience of computer experts would mostly likely be familiar with technical language as it applies to computers, so choice C is the best answer. Writing such a composition in a friendly style would be less important, so choice A is not the best answer. An academic style is most appropriate for educators or scholars, so choice B is not the best answer either. A composition about computers is not likely to be particularly emotional, so choice D is not the most logical answer.

12. **The correct answer is B.** Only choice B shows the correct way to cite a book with a single author on the "works cited" page of a composition according to the Chicago Manual of Style. Choice A is incorrect because it fails to indicate the pages of the source cited. Choice C fails to indicate the year the source was published. Choice D is incorrect because it places the author's last name before her first name, which violates CMS citation particulars.

13. **The correct answer is A.** One reason evidence is crucial to an argument is that evidence shows that the argument's main thrust is not merely based on the writer's personal opinions. Whether or not the author is well read in general is not important, so choice B is not the best answer. An argument does not have to express popular opinions in order to be strong, so choice C is not the best answer either. A strong argument can be very critical, so choice D is not correct.

14. **The correct answer is B.** Grouping ideas visually during the prewriting process is known as mind mapping. The other answer choices describe different prewriting

strategies. Choice A, freewriting, involves writing about a single topic for a short period of time to generate ideas. Choice C, outlining, involves organizing information. Choice D, brainstorming, involves listing all ideas that pop into one's mind during the process.

15. **The correct answer is D.** The headline or title of an article will often provide valuable clues to its main claim. Footnotes tend to be incidental details that have little to do with the main claim, so choice A is incorrect. Choices B and C describe elements that support the main claim, and they are not the best elements for determining what those main claims are.

16. **The correct answer is B.** Each answer choice describes a logical fallacy except for choice B, which is a perfectly logical way to build an argument. Choice A is known as an ad hominem fallacy. Choice C describes circular reasoning. Choice D is known as a false equivalence.

17. **The correct answer is B.** The improving of word choice should be performed during the revision stage of the writing process. Choice A, drafting, choice C, outlining, and choice D, brainstorming, are all performed before the revision phase.

18. **The correct answer is C.** Chicago Manual of Style citation is the most appropriate way to use citation in an article on the arts. APA, or American Psychological Association, style is more appropriate for articles on journalism (choice A), linguistics (choice B), or psychology (choice D).

19. **The correct answer is D.** A short story used to enrich an argument is called an anecdote. An assumption is a statement that links facts and conclusions, so choice A is incorrect. A summary condenses a long story or block of information, so choice B is incorrect. Logic

is the sensible structure of an argument, so choice C is incorrect.

20. **The correct answer is A.** The main purpose of editing is to correct errors in grammar, usage, and spelling. Choice B lists tasks that should be performed while revising. Choice C is done during the drafting phase. Choice D describes prewriting.

21. **The correct answer is A.** Whether or not to use a quotation often depends on the wording of the quotation, and choice A is the only answer that takes this matter into account. The fact that a source states an essential truth is not necessarily a reason to quote it word for word, so choice B is not the best answer. The education level of the source's author is not really a factor either, so choice C is not the best answer. Complex wording might actually be a reason to paraphrase instead of quote, so choice D is incorrect.

22. **The correct answer is B.** A blog is generally considered an unreliable source. Choice A is incorrect because quoting experts is actually a strong way to support an argument. Choice C in not the best answer because an argument does not need to be shared by many people to be effective. Choice D is not the best answer either since not every point in an argument requires a citation.

23. **The correct answer is C.** Summaries should be used sparingly, but one appropriate use for them is to provide background details on a topic. Summarizing is not appropriate when a writer presents his or her own ideas, as when making an original argument (choice A) or explaining why a text is important (choice B). Evidence should not be a summary, so choice D is incorrect.

24. **The correct answer is D.** A writer should hook the reader's interest early in a piece of writing, and one way to do this is with a

provocative question. Choices A and B refer to the overall structure of the piece, and neither would necessarily hook the reader's interest in and of themselves. Choice C refers to the very end of an essay, and summarizing is not a particularly interest-hooking method in any event.

25. **The correct answer is A.** Only choice A shows the correct way to use MLA in-text citation for a quotation that uses the author's name in the sentence itself. Choice B is incorrect because it repeats the author's name unnecessarily. Choice C is incorrect because it misplaces the page number on which the quotation originally appeared. Choice D is incorrect because it fails to use quotation marks.

26. **The correct answer is B.** A history textbook is a secondary source and the most appropriate secondary source to use when researching a paper on World War II. Choice A is incorrect because a novel is not a reliable source of historical facts. An interview is a primary source, so choice C is incorrect. An article published during World War II might not necessarily contain any information about the war, so choice D is not the best answer.

27. **The correct answer is C.** Evidence can help a reader understand how the author of an argument reached a particular conclusion. Evidence will not necessarily tell the reader anything about the author's personal life, so choice A is not the best answer. Evidence may not express ideas identical to those of the author's argument, so choice B is not the best answer either. Evidence says more about the authority of the source of the evidence than the author of the argument the evidence supports, so choice D is wrong.

28. **The correct answer is D.** Using statistics, examples, and expert opinions are all ways to support a claim. They are not prewriting

strategies (choice A), elements of a thesis (choice B), or editing techniques (choice C).

29. **The correct answer is A.** Only choice A correctly defines what a warrant in an argument is. Choice B is the definition of a prejudice. Choice C is the definition of an argument. Choice D is the definition of a conclusion.

30. **The correct answer is B.** Anecdotes are often used in arguments to appeal to the reader's emotions. They are not usually used for purposes of logic, so choice A is not the best answer. Prewriting techniques, not anecdotes, are used to generate ideas for an argument, so choice C is incorrect. Anecdotes are not used to summarize the main idea of an argument either, so choice D can be eliminated.

31. **The correct answer is A.** A summary condenses the most important details in a composition. Choice B describes something more like a glossary than a summary. Choice C describes a thesis statement, not a summary. Choice D does not describe a function of a summary.

32. **The correct answer is C.** A syllogism is when the conclusion of an argument is built on two premises. Choice A, logos, is an appeal to readers' sense of logic. Choice B, ethos, is an appeal to readers' sense of ethics. An appeal to the emotions is known as pathos, so choice D is incorrect.

33. **The correct answer is D.** In APA style, in-text citations that follow quotations for which the author is not explicitly named require the author's last name, the publication date, and a page number. Choices A and B do not describe an APA style in-text citation format. Choice C describes how to use in-text citation when the author's name is explicitly stated.

34. **The correct answer is B.** Radio and television broadcasts are known as multimedia

sources. Books and newspapers (choice A) and academic and trade journals (choice C) are traditional print sources. Websites and blogs (choice D) are Internet sources.

35. **The correct answer is C.** The main points are the sub-claims that support the main claim, and they are often explicitly stated in the topic sentences of each paragraph. The main points support the thesis statement, they are not the thesis itself, so choice A is wrong. They would not appear in the concluding statement either, so choice B is not correct. The transitional statements between paragraphs may hint at the main points, but they are less likely to state them explicitly than the topic sentences of each paragraph are, so choice D is not the best answer.

36. **The correct answer is B.** A quotation uses the same exact wording as is used in the source from which it is taken. Choice A describes a paraphrase. Choice C describes a summary. Choice D describes an elaboration.

37. **The correct answer is D.** The purpose of a summary is to reduce the main idea of a longer piece to a single, succinct statement. Choice A is incorrect because a summary should focus on a source's main idea, not its key terms. Choice B is incorrect because a summary should be focused on a single idea, not all of the ideas in a source. Choice C is incorrect because a summary is focused on the main idea of a source, not the source's tone.

38. **The correct answer is B.** Hypothesizing involves drafting a preliminary thesis. Choice A describes research, not hypothesizing. Choice C describes something that should be performed during the outlining process. Choice D describes something that may be performed during the brainstorming process.

39. **The correct answer is C.** Mind mapping involves organizing ideas generated while brainstorming visually. Ideas are not generated during outlining, so choice A is incorrect. Ideas are generated while freewriting, but the process generates additional ideas based on those generated while mind mapping, so mind mapping must be performed first. Therefore, choice B is not the best answer. Clustering is just another name for mind mapping, so choice D is incorrect.

40. **The correct answer is C.** Thinking, analyzing, and discussing a topic are all strategies that may be performed during the prewriting process. They are not outlining techniques (choice A), brainstorming ideas (choice B), or paraphrasing (choice D).

41. **The correct answer is D.** A thesis must be phrased as a complete declarative sentence. An interrogative sentence is a question, and a thesis statement should never be expressed as a question, so choice A is incorrect. An exclamatory sentence expresses extreme emotion and ends with an exclamation mark. While a thesis statement could be expressed as an exclamatory sentence under the right circumstances, it does not have to be expressed this way, so choice B is not the best answer. An imperative sentence expresses a command, and a thesis statement must never express a command, so choice C is incorrect.

42. **The correct answer is D.** Argumentative writing makes a case in favor of or against a particular issue. Choice A is incorrect because a story that explains the experiences of a character is narrative writing. Writing that conveys details about a nonfictional topic in a neutral manner is informative writing, so choice B is incorrect. Critical writing involves considering evidence in order to draw a conclusion, so choice C is incorrect.

43. **The correct answer is D.** Cause/effect, problem/solution, and comparison/contrast are all examples of organizational methods. They are not examples of mind mapping strategies (choice A), freewriting techniques (choice B), or summarization approaches (choice C).

44. **The correct answer is A.** Another term for "main point" is "sub-claim." Sub-claims support the main claims, so choice B is incorrect. The main claim is the thesis, so choice C is incorrect as well. The headline of an article may provide clues to the article's main points, but "headline" is not a synonym for "main claim," so choice D is incorrect.

45. **The correct answer is A.** Numerical information used to support a claim is known as statistics. Statistics are a form of data, but data does not have to be numerical, so choice B is not the best answer. Statistics may reflect opinions, but opinions, themselves, are not numerical, so choice C is incorrect. Examples do not have to be numerical either, so choice D is wrong.

46. **The correct answer is C.** Most contemporary newspapers can be found both in print and online. Therefore, choice A is incorrect. Choice B is not the best answer because newspapers are often as reliable as any other valid sources, such as trade journals. Choice D is incorrect because newspapers are generally more reliable sources than blogs.

47. **The correct answer is D.** The persuasive method used in an argument is known as its appeal. Pathos is a specific kind of appeal— an appeal to readers' emotions—it is not a synonym for a general persuasive method, so choice A is incorrect. Inductive reasoning is a specific approach to making a logical appeal, so choice B is incorrect. Persuasive methods are used while making arguments; they are not arguments in themselves, so choice C is not correct.

48. **The correct answer is B.** A warrant most often appears in an argument at a point at which the writer thinks the reader might not accept the argument because it clarifies the connection between reasons and claims. Choice A is the point at which the writer would most likely state the thesis, not use a warrant. Choice C is the point at which the writer would most likely state the concluding sentence, not use a warrant. A warrant is meant to strengthen the main claim, not recapture a reader's flagging interest, so choice D is not the best answer.

49. **The correct answer is C.** Circular reasoning, false equivalences, and hasty generalizations are all examples of logical fallacies, which are types of poor reasoning. Philosophical logic is a sound method of logic, so choice A is incorrect. A narrative is not a form of logic at all, so choice B does not make sense. An incomplete comparison is a type of logical fallacy; "incomplete comparison" is not a synonym for "logical fallacy," so choice D is incorrect.

50. **The correct answer is C.** The process of freewriting involves writing without stopping (choice B) about a single topic only (choice D) during a specific time frame (choice A). However, one should never waste time correcting errors while freewriting.

51. **The correct answer is B.** Deductive reasoning involves beginning an argument with a conclusion before moving to the premises on which that conclusion was built. Inductive reasoning involves presenting evidence before reaching a conclusion, so choice A is incorrect. Reaching a conclusion is part of the deductive reasoning process, but it is not the name for the process as a whole, so choice C is incorrect. Making an appeal involves using various methods for reaching a particular audience, so choice D is incorrect.

52. **The correct answer is A.** Although in-text citation formatting may not be necessary when paraphrasing, it is still crucial to attribute the source of the paraphrase's ideas. Choice B describes a quotation, not a paraphrase. A paraphrase only needs quotation marks when part of the paraphrase is a direct quotation, and that is not what choices C or D describe.

53. **The correct answer is C.** Encyclopedias are generally reliable sources, and an encyclopedia entry about baroque music is specifically focused on the paper's main topic, so choice C is the best source among the answer choices. An "introduction to music" textbook might not necessarily contain any information about baroque music at all, so choice A is not the best answer. Anyone can update Wikipedia regardless of the person's expertise, so choice B does not describe the most reliable source. An original letter written by a baroque composer may not necessarily contain any usable information about baroque music. Furthermore, a letter is a primary source, not a secondary one, so choice D is incorrect.

54. **The correct answer is D.** Anyone can publish a website with the domain designation .com, so a website with such a domain designation is least likely to be credible. The .edu designation indicates the website of an educational institution, so choice A is not the best answer. Seeing .gov at the end of a URL indicates a government website, so choice B is not the best answer either. Likewise, .org is an indicator of a website belonging to an official organization, which may be unreliable but will likely be more credible than a .com address that could be set up by any person at all.

55. **The correct answer is C.** Citations in a manuscript about religion should use MLA style. CMS style is more appropriate in manuscripts about anthropology (choice A). APA style is ideal for a manuscript about education (choice B) or criminology (choice D).

56. **The correct answer is A.** The assumption that one act will inevitably lead to another commits the logical fallacy known as slippery slope. Post hoc, ergo propter hoc (choice B) confuses a sequential relationship with a cause/effect one. A fallacy of composition (choice C) is the assumption that what is true of a part is also true of the whole. Moral equivalence (choice D) compares something bad with something significantly worse.

57. **The correct answer is D.** According to APA citation style, the title of an article page requires no special formatting. Using italics (choice A), underlining (choice B), or bolding (choice C) instead of placing quotation marks violates APA style for journal article citation.

58. **The correct answer is C.** Of all the sources in these answer choices, a newspaper article is the most likely to contain information on a march to raise climate change awareness. This topic would most likely be reported in a newspaper since such a march is a current event and newspapers report on current events. While climate change is a scientific topic, an article on a march to raise climate change awareness will not necessarily involve a great deal of the kind of scientific information found in a biology journal (choice A) or a chemistry textbook (choice B). Since a march to raise climate change awareness does not necessarily have a strong connection to the entertainment world, choice D is not the best answer.

59. **The correct answer is C.** Cause/effect structure is the most appropriate way to organize an argument. Sequential order is more appropriate for a personal narrative (choice A), biography (B), or history (choice D).

60. **The correct answer is A.** Of the answer choices, government reports are most likely to contain the kind of statistics that would inspire an informative composition about population trends. Encyclopedia articles (choice B) and biographies (choice D) are irrelevant to the topic of current population trends. Old current events reports are no longer relevant, so choice C is not the best answer.

Math for Liberal Arts

OVERVIEW

- **Math for Liberal Arts Diagnostic Test**
- **Answer Key and Explanations**
- **Diagnostic Test Assessment Grid**
- **Real Number Systems**
- **Sets and Logic**
- **Metric System, Conversions, and Geometry**
- **Algebra, Graphs, and Functions**
- **Linear Systems and Inequalities**
- **Exponents, Logarithms, and Financial Literacy**
- **Counting, Probability Theory, and Statistics**
- **Summing It Up**
- **Math for Liberal Arts Post-test**
- **Answer Key and Explanations**

The information tested on the DSST® Math for Liberal Arts exam touches on several different areas of mathematics, some of which may be very familiar to you and others that may be new concepts for you. The topics covered include many levels of math. First, you'll find familiar basics like arithmetic and real numbers, percentages, measurement, and elementary geometric concepts. Then, tougher questions build on that, asking about basic algebra, elementary functions, and the rules of probability—be prepared to encounter word problems involving rates, work completed, and solving systems of equations. Finally, you'll have to tackle less familiar topics such as elements of set theory and logic and basic financial mathematics—these are equally as important on the exam and may take you longer to master. They, too, have interesting applications that range from determining the validity of an argument to computing your monthly payment for an installment loan on a house or boat purchase. The math on this exam is the math you can use to navigate your everyday life.

Chapter 2

DIAGNOSTIC TEST ANSWER SHEET

1. Ⓐ Ⓑ Ⓒ Ⓓ   5. Ⓐ Ⓑ Ⓒ Ⓓ   9. Ⓐ Ⓑ Ⓒ Ⓓ   13. Ⓐ Ⓑ Ⓒ Ⓓ   17. Ⓐ Ⓑ Ⓒ Ⓓ
2. Ⓐ Ⓑ Ⓒ Ⓓ   6. Ⓐ Ⓑ Ⓒ Ⓓ   10. Ⓐ Ⓑ Ⓒ Ⓓ   14. Ⓐ Ⓑ Ⓒ Ⓓ   18. Ⓐ Ⓑ Ⓒ Ⓓ
3. Ⓐ Ⓑ Ⓒ Ⓓ   7. Ⓐ Ⓑ Ⓒ Ⓓ   11. Ⓐ Ⓑ Ⓒ Ⓓ   15. Ⓐ Ⓑ Ⓒ Ⓓ   19. Ⓐ Ⓑ Ⓒ Ⓓ
4. Ⓐ Ⓑ Ⓒ Ⓓ   8. Ⓐ Ⓑ Ⓒ Ⓓ   12. Ⓐ Ⓑ Ⓒ Ⓓ   16. Ⓐ Ⓑ Ⓒ Ⓓ   20. Ⓐ Ⓑ Ⓒ Ⓓ

POST-TEST ANSWER SHEET

1. Ⓐ Ⓑ Ⓒ Ⓓ   13. Ⓐ Ⓑ Ⓒ Ⓓ   25. Ⓐ Ⓑ Ⓒ Ⓓ   37. Ⓐ Ⓑ Ⓒ Ⓓ   49. Ⓐ Ⓑ Ⓒ Ⓓ
2. Ⓐ Ⓑ Ⓒ Ⓓ   14. Ⓐ Ⓑ Ⓒ Ⓓ   26. Ⓐ Ⓑ Ⓒ Ⓓ   38. Ⓐ Ⓑ Ⓒ Ⓓ   50. Ⓐ Ⓑ Ⓒ Ⓓ
3. Ⓐ Ⓑ Ⓒ Ⓓ   15. Ⓐ Ⓑ Ⓒ Ⓓ   27. Ⓐ Ⓑ Ⓒ Ⓓ   39. Ⓐ Ⓑ Ⓒ Ⓓ   51. Ⓐ Ⓑ Ⓒ Ⓓ
4. Ⓐ Ⓑ Ⓒ Ⓓ   16. Ⓐ Ⓑ Ⓒ Ⓓ   28. Ⓐ Ⓑ Ⓒ Ⓓ   40. Ⓐ Ⓑ Ⓒ Ⓓ   52. Ⓐ Ⓑ Ⓒ Ⓓ
5. Ⓐ Ⓑ Ⓒ Ⓓ   17. Ⓐ Ⓑ Ⓒ Ⓓ   29. Ⓐ Ⓑ Ⓒ Ⓓ   41. Ⓐ Ⓑ Ⓒ Ⓓ   53. Ⓐ Ⓑ Ⓒ Ⓓ
6. Ⓐ Ⓑ Ⓒ Ⓓ   18. Ⓐ Ⓑ Ⓒ Ⓓ   30. Ⓐ Ⓑ Ⓒ Ⓓ   42. Ⓐ Ⓑ Ⓒ Ⓓ   54. Ⓐ Ⓑ Ⓒ Ⓓ
7. Ⓐ Ⓑ Ⓒ Ⓓ   19. Ⓐ Ⓑ Ⓒ Ⓓ   31. Ⓐ Ⓑ Ⓒ Ⓓ   43. Ⓐ Ⓑ Ⓒ Ⓓ   55. Ⓐ Ⓑ Ⓒ Ⓓ
8. Ⓐ Ⓑ Ⓒ Ⓓ   20. Ⓐ Ⓑ Ⓒ Ⓓ   32. Ⓐ Ⓑ Ⓒ Ⓓ   44. Ⓐ Ⓑ Ⓒ Ⓓ   56. Ⓐ Ⓑ Ⓒ Ⓓ
9. Ⓐ Ⓑ Ⓒ Ⓓ   21. Ⓐ Ⓑ Ⓒ Ⓓ   33. Ⓐ Ⓑ Ⓒ Ⓓ   45. Ⓐ Ⓑ Ⓒ Ⓓ   57. Ⓐ Ⓑ Ⓒ Ⓓ
10. Ⓐ Ⓑ Ⓒ Ⓓ   22. Ⓐ Ⓑ Ⓒ Ⓓ   34. Ⓐ Ⓑ Ⓒ Ⓓ   46. Ⓐ Ⓑ Ⓒ Ⓓ   58. Ⓐ Ⓑ Ⓒ Ⓓ
11. Ⓐ Ⓑ Ⓒ Ⓓ   23. Ⓐ Ⓑ Ⓒ Ⓓ   35. Ⓐ Ⓑ Ⓒ Ⓓ   47. Ⓐ Ⓑ Ⓒ Ⓓ   59. Ⓐ Ⓑ Ⓒ Ⓓ
12. Ⓐ Ⓑ Ⓒ Ⓓ   24. Ⓐ Ⓑ Ⓒ Ⓓ   36. Ⓐ Ⓑ Ⓒ Ⓓ   48. Ⓐ Ⓑ Ⓒ Ⓓ   60. Ⓐ Ⓑ Ⓒ Ⓓ

answer sheet

MATH FOR LIBERAL ARTS DIAGNOSTIC TEST

Directions: Carefully read each of the following 20 questions. Choose the best answer to each question and fill in the corresponding circle on the answer sheet. The Answer Key and Explanations can be found following this Diagnostic Test.

1. Write the following compound statement symbolically: "If I go to my personal trainer, then I will not overeat."

   Let p represent "The food is delicious."

   Let q represent "I will overeat."

   Let s represent "I will go to my personal trainer."

   A. $q \Rightarrow s$
   B. $s \Rightarrow \sim q$
   C. $\sim(q \Rightarrow s)$
   D. $p \wedge q$

2. $\log\left(\dfrac{z}{1,000}\right) = \underline{\hspace{2cm}}$

   A. $3\log z$
   B. $\log(z - 1,000)$
   C. $3 + \log z$
   D. $-3 + \log z$

3. 8.48 m = $\underline{\hspace{2cm}}$ cm
   A. 0.0848
   B. 0.848
   C. 84.8
   D. 848

4. High school students who complete advanced course work in American History are invited to take an exam that will earn them college credit. The exam is scored on a scale of 1 to 5. The following represents the score distribution for a certain state.

Score	Percentage of Students Earning This Score
5	0.40
4	0.20
3	0.08
2	0.20
1	0.12

   What is the mean exam score for this state?
   A. 4.00
   B. 3.56
   C. 3.20
   D. 3.00

5. What is the quotient of 6.9×10^7 and 2.3×10^3 expressed using scientific notation?
   A. 3×10^3
   B. 3×10^4
   C. $3,000$
   D. $30,000$

6. What is the value of the expression $4y - 3y^2x$ when $x = 2$ and $y = -4$?

    A. 272

    B. 80

    C. −80

    D. −112

7. The Junior Tennis League hosts an annual tournament in early summer. Eighty individuals are invited to participate in the tournament based on their rankings that year. After each round of matches, half of the individuals are eliminated. Which equation represents the number of individuals, I, that remain after m matches?

    A. $I = 80(1.5)^m$

    B. $I = 80(0.5)^m$

    C. $I = 80(m)^{0.5}$

    D. $I = 80(-0.5)^m$

8. If the probability of being selected for a paid internship is $\frac{1}{5}$, what are the odds of not being selected for the internship?

    A. 4:5

    B. 4:1

    C. 1:4

    D. 5:4

9. A survey conducted at a local gym shows that 70% of its patrons do aerobic exercise daily, 20% do strength-training exercises daily, and 10% do both daily. If a patron is selected at random, what is the probability that he or she does aerobic exercise or strength-training exercises daily?

    A. 0.08

    B. 0.10

    C. 0.80

    D. 0.90

10. The computing center at a university has purchased a new high-level server for $25,000. The value of the server, y, x years after its purchase is modeled by the linear function graphed below:

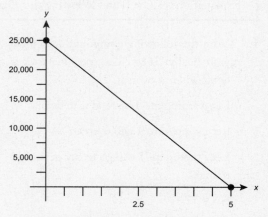

    Determine the equation of this line and use it to predict the value of the server 2 years after purchase.

    A. $y = -25,000x + 25,000$; value 2 years after purchase is −$25,000

    B. $y = -5,000x + 25,000$; value 2 years after purchase is $15,000

    C. $y = 5,000x - 25,000$; value 2 years after purchase is $15,000

    D. $y = 25,000x + 5$; value 2 years after purchase is $15,000

11. Let p be the statement "The street is slippery" and q be the statement "The trees are losing their leaves." Which of the following is the truth table for the compound statement "The street is slippery or the trees are losing their leaves"?

A.

p	q	$p \vee q$
T	T	F
T	F	T
F	T	T
F	F	F

B.

p	q	$p \wedge q$
T	T	T
T	F	F
F	T	F
F	F	F

C.

p	q	$p \vee q$
T	T	T
T	F	T
F	T	T
F	F	F

D.

p	q	$p \wedge q$
T	T	T
T	F	F
F	T	F
F	F	T

12. The volume of a cylindrical container is 32π cubic centimeters. If the height of the container is 2 centimeters, what is the diameter of its base?

A. 2 centimeters

B. 4 centimeters

C. 8 centimeters

D. 16 centimeters

13. If X and Y are sets, which of the following Venn diagram correctly illustrates the set $X \cup Y$?

A.

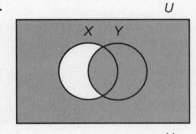

B.

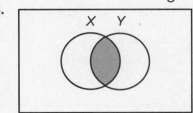

C.

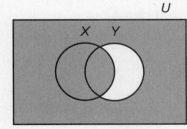

D.

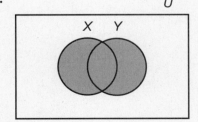

14. Erica invested \$4,500 in a money market account that earns 3% interest compounded annually. She allowed the interest earned to be rolled into the account at the end of each year, but made no additional withdrawals from or deposits into this account. Which of these expressions can be used to determine the value of the account at the end of 4 years?

   A. $4,500(1 + 0.03)^4$ dollars

   B. $4,500(1 + 0.04)^3$ dollars

   C. $4,500(1 + 0.3)^4$ dollars

   D. $4,500(1 + 0.4)^3$ dollars

15. To which of the following systems of inequalities is this the solution set?

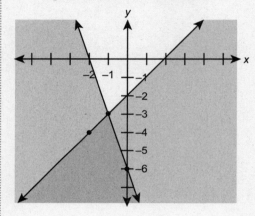

   A. $\begin{cases} y \geq x + 3 \\ y \leq 2x - 6 \end{cases}$

   B. $\begin{cases} y \leq x - 2 \\ y \leq -3x - 6 \end{cases}$

   C. $\begin{cases} y \geq x - 2 \\ y \leq -3x - 6 \end{cases}$

   D. $\begin{cases} y \leq x + 3 \\ y \geq 2x - 6 \end{cases}$

16. Three identical circular chips, one side of which is red and the other black, are tossed 80 times. The number of red sides is counted for each of these tosses, and the results of the experiment are recorded below. Based on this experiment, what is the probability that *at most* two red chips occur?

Number of Red Sides Occurring for a Toss	Frequency
0	10
1	8
2	12
3	50

   A. $\dfrac{1}{8}$

   B. $\dfrac{5}{8}$

   C. $\dfrac{3}{8}$

   D. $\dfrac{3}{20}$

17. What is the equivalent base-10 numeral for 10010000_2?

   A. 20,020,000

   B. 288

   C. 144

   D. 4

18. The set $A = \{x : x$ is a multiple of 3 that is larger than 5 and smaller than 20\} has _____ elements.

   A. 3

   B. 5

   C. 6,280

   D. infinitely many

19. Jeffrey takes out a small student loan of $1,000 for 18 months at 11.5% APR to pay for books for a year. What is the finance charge?

A. $60.75

B. $93.50

C. $1,060.75

D. $1,093.50

20. Which of the following expressions is used to convert 90 kilometers per hour to meters per minute?

A. $\dfrac{90 \text{ km}}{1 \text{ hr}} \times \dfrac{1{,}000 \text{ m}}{1 \text{ km}} \times \dfrac{1 \text{ hr}}{60 \text{ min}}$

B. $\dfrac{90 \text{ km}}{1 \text{ hr}} \times \dfrac{1{,}000 \text{ m}}{1 \text{ km}} \times \dfrac{60 \text{ min}}{1 \text{ hr}}$

C. $\dfrac{90 \text{ km}}{1 \text{ hr}} \times \dfrac{1 \text{ km}}{1{,}000 \text{ m}} \times \dfrac{60 \text{ min}}{1 \text{ hr}}$

D. $\dfrac{90 \text{ km}}{1 \text{ hr}} \times \dfrac{1 \text{ km}}{1{,}000 \text{ m}} \times \dfrac{1 \text{ hr}}{60 \text{ min}}$

diagnostic test

ANSWER KEY AND EXPLANATIONS

1. B	**5.** B	**9.** C	**13.** D	**17.** C
2. D	**6.** D	**10.** B	**14.** A	**18.** B
3. D	**7.** B	**11.** C	**15.** B	**19.** B
4. B	**8.** B	**12.** C	**16.** C	**20.** A

1. **The correct answer is B.** The given statement is a conditional (if-then statement). The hypothesis is s and the conclusion is the negation of q, or $\sim q$. So, symbolically, this statement can be written as $s \Rightarrow \sim q$.

   Choice A is equivalent to "If I will overeat, then I will go to my personal trainer." In choice C, $\sim (q \Rightarrow s) \equiv \sim (\sim q \vee s) \equiv q \wedge \sim s$, which is the statement "I will overeat and I will not go to my personal trainer." Choice D is equivalent to "The food is delicious and I will overeat."

2. **The correct answer is D.** Use the logarithm property governing quotients and simplify to get $\log\left(\frac{z}{1000}\right) = \log z - \log 1{,}000 = \log$

   $z - 3 = -3 + \log z$.

   Choice A is incorrect because the logarithm of a quotient is the difference of the logarithms of the inputs, not their product. Choice B is incorrect because the logarithm of a quotient is the difference of the logarithms of the input, not the logarithm of the difference of the inputs. Choice C is incorrect because the logarithm of a quotient is not the sum of the logarithms of the inputs.

3. **The correct answer is D.** Since 1 m = 100 cm, it follows that 8.48 m = 8.48(100) cm = 848 cm. Choices A and B moved the decimal point in the wrong direction, while Choice C did not move the decimal point enough places to the right.

4. **The correct answer is B.** To compute the mean, multiply each score by the percentage of students receiving that score, and then sum the products: 5(0.40) + 4(0.20) + 3(0.08) + 2(0.20) + 1(0.12) = 3.56. Choice A is the median score. Choice C is the result of an arithmetic error. Choice D is the middle score that students can earn, but based on the percentages provided, it is not the (arithmetic) mean score.

5. **The correct answer is B.** Divide the decimal parts and the powers of ten separately:

   $$\frac{6.9 \times 10^7}{2.3 \times 10^3} = \frac{6.9}{2.3} \times \frac{10^7}{10^3}$$

   $$= 3 \times 10^{7-3} = 3 \times 10^4$$

   Choices C and D are not expressed using scientific notation and choice A is one power of 10 off from the correct quotient.

6. **The correct answer is D.** Substitute $x = 2$ and $y = -4$ into the expression and simplify using the order of operations:

   $4(-4) - 3(-4)^2(2) = -16 - 3(16)(2) = -16 - 96 = -112$

   Choice A is the result of an arithmetic error. Choices B and C are the results of sign errors arising when computing products of integers with different signs.

7. **The correct answer is B.** Before the first match, there are 80 individuals. Following the first match, there are half as many individuals in the match, namely 80(0.5).

After the second match, there are half of this number, namely $80(0.5)(0.5) = 80(0.5)^2$. So, after m matches, the number of individuals who remain in the tournament is $80(0.5)^m$. Choice A has the number of individuals who remain in the tournament *increasing* the more matches that are played. Choice C has m and 0.5 interchanged. Choice D yields a negative number of individuals for any odd number of matches played.

8. **The correct answer is B.** Let A be the event "being selected for the internship." We are given that $P(A) = \frac{1}{5}$. So, the probability of *not* being selected for the internship is $P(\text{not } A) = \frac{4}{5}$. The odds of *not* being selected for the internship are:

$$\frac{P(\text{not } A)}{1 - P(\text{not } A)} = \frac{\frac{4}{5}}{1 - \frac{4}{5}} = \frac{\frac{4}{5}}{\frac{1}{5}} = \frac{4}{1},$$

which can be written as 4:1. Choice A is the probability of not winning the race incorrectly written in the form of an odds ratio. Choice C is nearly correct, but written backwards. Choice D is the reciprocal of the probability of not winning the race incorrectly written in the form of an odds ratio.

9. **The correct answer is C.** Let A be the event "patron does aerobic exercise daily" and B be the event "patron does strength-training exercises daily." Then, $A \cap B$ is the event "patron does both types of exercise daily" and $A \cup B$ is the event "patron does aerobic exercise *or* strength-training exercise daily." Using the addition formula yields

$P(A \cup B) = P(A) + P(B) - P(A \cap B) =$
$0.70 + 0.20 - 0.10 = 0.80$

Choice A is wrong because of an arithmetic error made when working with decimals.

Choice B is wrong because this is the probability that the patron does *both* types of exercise daily, not *either type*. Choice D is wrong because you must subtract the probability that the patron does *both* types of exercise daily when applying the addition formula.

10. **The correct answer is B.** The y-intercept, apparent from the graph, is 25,000. The slope of the line is $\frac{25,000 - 0}{0 - 5} = -5,000$. The equation of the line is $y = -5,000x + 25,000$. Using this line with $x = 2$ yields the value after 2 years as \$15,000. Choice A is wrong because the slope of the line is $-5,000$ not $-25,000$. Choices C and D cannot be correct because their slopes are positive, but the graph of the line is decreasing and so has a negative slope.

11. **The correct answer is C.** The given statement is a disjunction ("or") statement. So, this immediately eliminates choice B. Of choices A, C, and D, choice C is correct because only one statement needs to be true for the "or" statement to be true. The only way for the "or" statement to be false is for both statements to be false. This is the case with the truth table in choice C.

12. **The correct answer is C.** Let r be the radius, h the height, and V the volume of the cylinder. Substituting the given information into the volume formula $V = \pi r^2 h$ yields the equation $32\pi = \pi r^2 (2)$. This is equivalent to $r^2 = 16$, so that $r = 4$. As such, the diameter is 8 inches. Choice A is the height, not the radius. Choice B is the radius. Choice D is twice the diameter.

13. **The correct answer is D.** The union of two sets X and Y is the set of elements that belong to either X or Y or to both. The portion shaded in the Venn diagram in choice D shows this set. Choice A is incorrect because it shows the union of

Y and the complement of X. Choice B is incorrect because it shows the intersection of X and Y. Choice C is incorrect because it shows the union of X and the complement of Y.

14. **The correct answer is A.** The account starts at $4,500. After one year, 3% interest is earned, which results in the account being worth $4,500 + $4,500(0.03) = $4,500(1 + 0.03) at the end of one year. This amount is now invested in the account and earns 3% interest at the end of the second year. This results in the account being worth:

    $4,500(1 + 0.03) + [$4,500(1 + 0.03)](0.03) = $4,500(1 + 0.03){1 + 0.03} = $4,500 (1 + 0.03)^2.

    Continuing this process for the third and then fourth years yields the value of the account at the end of four years being $4,500(1 + 0.03)^4.

    Choice B is incorrect because it has the 3 and 4 reversed in the formula. Choice C is incorrect because it has the interest rate as 30%, not 3%. In choice D, the 3 and 4 are reversed and involves an error when converting the interest rate to a decimal.

15. **The correct answer is B.** First, find the equations of both lines. The slope of the line that is rising from left to right is $m = \frac{-3 - (-4)}{-1 - (-2)} = 1$. Using the point-slope formula with the point $(-2, -4)$ yields the equation $y - (-4) = 1(x - (-2))$, which is equivalent to $y = x - 2$. Since the region *below* this line is shaded, one inequality of the system must be $y \leq x - 2$. The slope of the other line is $m = \frac{-3 - (-6)}{-1 - 0} = 3$. Since the y-intercept is -6, the equation of this line is $y = -3x - 6$. Since the region *below* this line is shaded, one inequality of the system must be $y \leq -3x - 6$. Thus, the system of inequalities for which the shaded region is the solution set is given by choice B. The

answer in choices A and D have the wrong equations of both lines. The answer in choice C has both inequality signs reversed.

16. **The correct answer is C.** The event "*at most* 2 red chips" is satisfied if there are 0 red chips, 1 red chip, or 2 red chips on a toss. Adding those entries and dividing by 80 total tosses yields $\frac{30}{80} = \frac{3}{8}$. Choice A is the probability of getting 0 red chips. Choice B is the probability of getting more than 2 red chips. Choice D is the probability of getting exactly 2 red chips.

17. **The correct answer is C.** Using the place-value chart for base 2 shows that

2^7	1
2^6	0
2^5	0
2^4	1
2^3	0
2^2	0
2^1	0
2^0	0

So, the base–10 equivalent of 10010000_2 is $2^7 + 2^4 = 144$. Choice A is equivalent to the product of 1001000 and 2; this is not how you convert a base–2 numeral to a base–10 numeral. Choice B is equivalent to 100100000_2 (one extra zero at the end of the numeral). Choice D is equivalent to 100_2.

18. **The correct answer is B.** The multiples of 3 that are larger than 5 but smaller than 20 are 6, 9, 12, 15, and 18. Therefore, there are 5 elements in the set. Choice A is incorrect since it just counts the 3, 5, and 20 as elements. Choice C is incorrect since it counts 3 along with the other elements (but 3 is not in the set since it is smaller than 5). Finally, choice D is incorrect since there are finitely many numbers with these properties.

19. **The correct answer is B.** Using the formula

$$R = \frac{A \times i}{\left(1 - \frac{1}{(1+i)^n}\right)}$$, where A is the amount

of the loan, R is the monthly payment, i is the monthly interest rate (= APR/12), and n is the total number of payments, with A = \$1,000, $i = \frac{0.115}{12}$, and n = 18 yields

$$R = \frac{1,000 \times \frac{0.115}{12}}{\left(1 - \frac{1}{(1+\frac{0.115}{12})^{18}}\right)} \approx 60.75 \cdot$$

So, the total amount Jeffrey pays is \$60.75(18) = \$1,093.50. So, the total finance charge is \$1,093.50 − \$1,000 = \$93.50. Choice A is the monthly payment. Choice C is the original loan amount plus a monthly payment. Choice D is the total amount paid.

20. **The correct answer is A.** Two units need to be converted: km to m and hours to minutes. So, the end result must have m in the numerator (with km canceling) and min in the denominator (with hours canceling). This is given by the following:

$$\frac{90 \text{ km}}{1 \text{ hr}} \times \frac{1,000 \text{ m}}{1 \text{ km}} \times \frac{1 \text{ hr}}{60 \text{ min}}$$

Choice B is wrong because "hours" does not cancel. Choice C is wrong because neither "km" nor "hours" cancel. Choice D is wrong because "km" does not cancel.

DIAGNOSTIC TEST ASSESSMENT GRID

Now that you've completed the diagnostic test and read through the answer explanations, you can use your results to target your studying. Find the question numbers from the diagnostic test that you answered incorrectly and highlight or circle them below. Then focus extra attention on the sections within the chapter dealing with those topics.

Math for Liberal Arts		
Content Area	**Topic**	**Question #**
Real Number Systems	<ul><li>Real numbers: natural numbers, integers, rational numbers, irrational numbers, the real number line</li><li>Operations with real numbers and their properties (including the distributive properties)</li><li>Prime and composite numbers, divisibility rules, prime factors of composite numbers</li><li>Systems of numeration: place value or positional value numeration, Base 10 expanded forms, base 2 numbers, conversion between base 10 and base 2, (including roman numerals)</li><li>Rules of exponents including rational exponents</li><li>Scientific notation</li></ul>	5, 17
Sets and Logic	<ul><li>The nature of sets</li><li>Subsets and set operation</li><li>Using Venn diagrams</li><li>Infinite sets</li><li>Simple and compound statements</li><li>Truth value</li><li>Types of statements</li><li>Logical arguments</li></ul>	1, 11, 13, 18

Math for Liberal Arts (continued)		
Content Area	**Topic**	**Question #**
Metric System, conversions, and geometry	• Introduction to metrics and U.S. customary unit systems • Conversions between metric and U.S. customary unit systems, including dimensional analysis • Properties of lines and angles • Perimeter and area of 2-D geometric objects • Area, surface area, and volume of 3-D solid objects	3, 12, 20
Algebra, graphs, and Functions	• Order of operations • Simplifying expressions; equations with one variable; proportion problems • Evaluation of formulas • Graphs of linear equations in the rectangular coordinate system • Functions including polynomials (not to include rational, exponential and logarithmic functions)	6, 10
Linear Systems and Inequalities	• Solving linear equations including applications and systems • The rectangular coordinate system and linear equations in two variables • Graphing and solving linear inequalities • Graphing and solving systems of inequalities	15

Math for Liberal Arts (continued)		
Content Area	Topic	Question #
Exponents, logarithms including financial literacy	• Properties of logarithms • Logarithmic and exponential Functions • Simple interest • Compound interest • Installment buying • Student loans and home buying • Investing in stocks and bonds	2, 7, 14, 19
Counting, Probability Theory, and Statistics	• Fundamentals of probability including the counting principle • Permutations and combinations • Events involving not and or • Odds and conditional probability • Mean, median, and mode • Range, variance, and standard deviation • Graphical representation (including bar graph, pie chart, histogram, line graph, scatterplots, etc.)	4, 8, 9, 16

GET THE FACTS

To see the DSST® Math for Liberal Arts Fact Sheet, go to *http://getcollegecredit.com/exam_fact_sheets* and click on the **Math** tab. Scroll down and click the **Math for Liberal Arts** link.

Around 11 percent
of the questions
on the DSST
Math for Liberal
Arts exam are
devoted to real
number systems.

REAL NUMBER SYSTEMS

In this section, we'll review the basic arithmetic and properties of real numbers, along with two other commonly used numeration systems. The information covered by real number systems will serve you well when approaching every math problem on your exam—it is the foundation of even the most complex problems.

REAL NUMBERS

Natural Numbers

The set of **natural numbers** consists of the numbers 1, 2, 3, 4… The result when at least two natural numbers are multiplied is called a **product** and each number in the list being multiplied is a **factor** or **divisor**. A natural number is a **multiple** of each of its factors.

- For instance, in the expression $2 \times 5 \times 7 = 70$, 70 is the product; 2, 5, and 7 are factors of 70; and 70 is a multiple of 2, 5, and 7.

A natural number other than 1 is **prime** if it can only be written as a product of itself and 1; otherwise, it is **composite**.

Every composite number can be written as a product of prime numbers; the product is the **prime factorization** of the number.

- For instance, $56 = 2 \times 2 \times 2 \times 7$, or more succinctly, $56 = 2^3 \times 7$.

The following divisibility rules are useful when determining factors of a natural number.

Natural Number	A natural number n is divisible by the number in the left column if…
2	The number n ends in 0, 2, 4, 6, or 8.
3	The digit sum of n (i.e., the sum of all digits in the numeral n) is divisible by 3.
4	The last two numbers of n, taken as a number in and of itself, is divisible by 4.
5	The number n ends in 0 or 5.
6	The number n is divisible by both 2 and 3.
9	The digit sum of n is divisible by 9.
10	The number n ends in 0.

For instance, 459 is divisible by 3 because the digit sum (4 + 5 + 9 = 18) is divisible by 3. The **greatest common factor (GCF)** of two natural numbers x and y is the *largest* natural number that is a factor of both x and y, while the **least common multiple (LCM)** of x and y is the *smallest* natural number that is a multiple of both x and y.

- For instance, the GCF of 32 and 56 is 8 and the LCM is 224.

Integers

The set of integers is comprised of the natural numbers, their negatives, and 0: $\{\ldots, -3, -2, -1, 0, 1, 2, 3\ldots\}$.

The following rules and terminology are useful when working with integers:

- $-(-a) = a$, for any integer a.
- $a - (-b) = a + b$, for any integers a, b.
- A product of two negative integers is positive.
- A product of one positive and one negative integer is negative.
- An integer is *even* if it is a multiple of 2, while it is *odd* if it is not a multiple of 2. Any even number can be written as $2n$, where n is an integer, and an odd number can be written as $2n + 1$, where n is an integer.

Exponent Rules

If b and n are natural numbers, then $b^n = \underbrace{b \times \ldots \times b}_{n \text{ times}}$.

Suppose that a, b, m, and n are all real numbers. The following properties hold:

Example 1: $b^m b^n = b^{m+n}$

Example 2: $\dfrac{b^m}{b^n} = b^{m-n}$

Example 3: $(ab)^m = a^m b^m$

Example 4: $\left(\dfrac{a}{b}\right)^m = \dfrac{a^m}{b^m}$

Example 5: $\left(b^m\right)^n = b^{m \cdot n}$

Example 6: $b^0 = 1$, provided b is not zero

Example 7: $b^{-n} = \dfrac{1}{b^n}$

Example 8: $\dfrac{1}{b^{-n}} = b$

The following are some examples that demonstrate how these properties can be used to simplify various expressions involving exponents. They apply not only to arithmetic expressions, but also to algebraic expressions: the latter are discussed more thoroughly later in this chapter.

$$\frac{2}{5 \cdot \underbrace{3^{-2}}_{(E8)}} = \frac{2 \cdot 3^2}{5} = \frac{2 \cdot 9}{5} = \frac{18}{5}$$

$$\left(\frac{3}{2x^{-3}}\right)^2 \underset{(E8)}{=} \left(\frac{3x^3}{2}\right)^2 \underset{(E4)}{=} \frac{(3x^3)^2}{2^2} \underset{(E3)}{=} \frac{3^2(x^3)^2}{2^2} \underset{(E5)}{=} \frac{9x^6}{4}$$

$$\left(\frac{4x^{-3}y^{-1}z}{2x^{-1}yz^{-3}}\right)^{-2} \underset{(E7),\,(E8)}{=} \left(\frac{4xzz^3}{2x^3yy}\right)^{-2} \underset{(E1)}{=} \left(\frac{4z^4}{2x^2y^2}\right)^{-2} \underset{(E4),\,(E3)}{=} \frac{4^{-2}z^{-8}}{2^{-2}x^{-4}y^{-4}} \underset{(E7),\,(E8)}{=} \frac{2^2x^4y^4}{4^2z^8} = \frac{4x^4y^4}{16z^8} = \frac{x^4y^4}{4z^8}$$

Rational Numbers and Irrational Numbers

A **rational number** is a quotient of two integers, denoted by $\frac{a}{b}$, where $b \neq 0$. Such a fraction is **simplified** if a and b do not share common factors. If $a \neq 0$, the **reciprocal** of $\frac{a}{b}$ can be computed by flipping the fraction over to get $\frac{b}{a}$. To get the reciprocal of a mixed number, first convert it to an improper fraction (one with a numerator greater than its denominator) and flip *that* fraction over.

The arithmetic rules for working with fractions are as follows:

Arithmetic Operation	Rule (in symbols)	What To Do (in words)
Cancellation Property	$\frac{a \cdot c}{b \cdot c} = \frac{a}{b}$	Factors common to numerator and denominator can be canceled.
Sum/Difference (same denominator)	$\frac{a}{b} \pm \frac{c}{b} = \frac{a \pm c}{b}$	Just add or subtract the numerators.
Sum/Difference (different denominators)	$\frac{a}{b} \pm \frac{c}{d} = \frac{ad \pm cb}{bd}$	First get a common denominator. Apply it to the fractions and then add the numerators.
Multiply by −1	$-\frac{a}{b} = \frac{-a}{b} = \frac{a}{-b}$	You can multiply either the numerator or denominator by −1, but NOT both.
Product	$\frac{a}{b} \cdot \frac{c}{d} = \frac{ac}{bd}$	Multiply numerators and denominators, though it is better to simplify first.
Quotient	$\frac{a}{b} \div \frac{c}{d} = \frac{a}{b} \cdot \frac{d}{c} = \frac{ad}{bc}$	Convert to a multiplication problem, and then multiply as above.

When performing arithmetic operations involving fractions, simplifying all fractions *first* will lead to smaller numbers which makes working out your calculations easier.

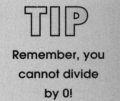

TIP

Remember, you cannot divide by 0!

TIP

The complex fraction $\dfrac{\frac{a}{b}}{\frac{c}{d}}$ means $\frac{a}{b} \div \frac{c}{d}$.

OPERATIONS WITH REAL NUMBERS AND THEIR PROPERTIES

As the name implies, an **irrational number** is a real number that is not rational. Some common examples are square roots of prime numbers, π, and e. Irrational numbers can be formed by performing arithmetic combinations of pairs of rational and irrational numbers:

- The sum of two positive irrational numbers is a positive irrational number.

- The sum of two negative irrational numbers is a negative irrational number.

- The product of a nonzero rational number and an irrational number is an irrational number.

- The sum or difference of a rational number and an irrational number is an irrational number.

The sets of rational numbers and irrational numbers both possess the so-called **density property**. This means that between *any* two rational (or irrational) numbers, there is another rational number and an irrational number. In fact, there are *infinitely many!* This can be counterintuitive, especially when the two rational (or irrational) numbers are very close together.

For instance, what is a rational number between $\frac{1}{10,000}$ and $\frac{1}{10,001}$? Using the fact that sums and quotients of rational numbers are again rational, the arithmetic average of these two numbers is a rational number halfway between them: $\dfrac{\frac{1}{10,000} + \frac{1}{10,001}}{2} = \dfrac{\frac{20,001}{100,010,000}}{2} = \dfrac{20,001}{200,020,000}$.

The following properties apply *for all* real numbers a, b, and c:

Property Name	Rule (In Symbols)	What To Do (In Words)
Commutative	$a + b = b + a$ $a \times b = b \times a$	The order in which real numbers are added or multiplied does not affect the outcome.
Associative	$(a + b) + c = a + (b + c)$ $(a \cdot b) \cdot c = a \cdot (b \cdot c)$	The way terms of a sum or a product comprised of more than two terms are grouped does not affect the outcome.
Distributive	$a \cdot (b + c) = a \cdot b + a \cdot c$	To multiply a sum by a real number, multiply each term of the sum by the number and add the results.
Identity	$a + 0 = 0 + a = a$ $a \cdot 1 = 1 \cdot a = a$	If you add 0 to a real number or multiply it by 1, the result is the same real number.
Zero Factor Property	If $a \cdot b = 0$, then either $a = 0$ or $b = 0$, or both $= 0$.	If a product of real numbers is zero, then at least one of the factors must be zero.

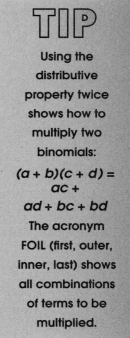

TIP

Using the distributive property twice shows how to multiply two binomials:

$(a + b)(c + d) = ac + ad + bc + bd$

The acronym FOIL (first, outer, inner, last) shows all combinations of terms to be multiplied.

DECIMALS

Decimals are comprised of numerals appearing before and after a decimal point, each which represents a multiple of a power of 10. A place-value chart is useful when interpreting a decimal.

For example, 3,320.4461 is interpreted as follows:

10^4	10^3	10^2	10^1	10^0	.	10^{-1}	10^{-2}	10^{-3}	10^{-4}	10^{-5}
	3	3	2	0	.	4	4	6	1	

$3,320.4461 = (3 \times 10^3) + (3 \times 10^2) + (2 \times 10^1) + (0 \times 10^0) +$
$(4 \times 10^{-1}) + (4 \times 10^{-2}) + (6 \times 10^{-3}) + (1 \times 10^{-4})$

To convert 3,320.4461 to a fraction, note the following:

$$(4 \times 10^{-1}) + (4 \times 10^{-2}) + (6 \times 10^{-3}) + (1 \times 10^{-4}) = \frac{4}{10} + \frac{4}{100} + \frac{6}{1,000} + \frac{1}{10,000} = \frac{4,461}{10,000}$$

As such, 3,320.4461 is equal to the mixed number $3,320\frac{4,461}{10,000}$, which is subsequently equal to the improper fraction $\frac{33,204,461}{10,000}$. As in this case, representing a decimal as a fraction will not always be in its simplest form, but it is nonetheless the fraction equivalent to the decimal. Likewise, any rational number can be converted into a decimal by dividing its numerator by its denominator. Such decimals will either terminate or repeat. Irrational numbers, like $\sqrt{5}$, π, and e, have decimal representations that neither terminate nor repeat—meaning it is impossible to list all the digits of such a decimal.

The arithmetic of decimals is the same as for natural numbers, with the additional step of correctly positioning the decimal point. The following are some rules of thumb to apply when working with decimals:

- When *adding or subtracting* decimals, line up the decimal points and add or subtract as you would natural numbers, keeping the decimal point in the same position.

- When *multiplying* decimals, first multiply the numbers as you would natural numbers. To determine the position of the decimal point, count the number of digits present after the decimal point in all numbers being multiplied and move that many steps to the left. Start at the end of the product and place the decimal point in the correct position.

SCIENTIFIC NOTATION

Real numbers that cannot be conveniently written in decimal form are expressed using scientific notation: this is the form $m \times 10^n$, where m is a decimal with a single nonzero digit appearing before the decimal point and n is an integer. The following are some basic rules for working with scientific notation:

- To convert from scientific notation to decimal form, remove the "$\times 10^n$" portion by shifting the decimal point n places to the right (if $n > 0$) or n places to the left (if $n < 0$).

- To convert from decimal form to scientific notation, move the decimal point n places (to the left if there is more than a single digit before the decimal point, or to the right if there are no nonzero digits appearing before the decimal point). Then, append "$\times 10^n$" to the right of the decimal. The exponent n will be negative if the decimal point was moved to the right n places, and will be positive if it was moved to the left n places.

Suppose m$_2$ $x = m_1 \times 10^{n_1}$ and $y = m_2 \times 10^{n_2}$. Then, using the laws of exponents and the commutative and associative properties of real numbers, we can multiply and divide real numbers expressed in scientific notation as follows:

$$x \bullet y = \left(m_1 \times 10^{n_1}\right) \bullet \left(m_2 \times 10^{n_2}\right) = \left(m_1 \bullet m_2\right) \times \left(10^{n_1} \times 10^{n_2}\right) = \left(m_1 \bullet m_2\right) \times 10^{n_1+n_2}$$

$$\frac{x}{y} = \frac{m_1 \times 10^{n_1}}{m_2 \times 10^{n_2}} = \left(\frac{m_1}{m_2}\right) \times \left(\frac{10^{n_1}}{10^{n_2}}\right) = \left(\frac{m_1}{m_2}\right) \times 10^{n_1-n_2}$$

These products and quotients may need to be further converted to scientific notation form if the portion before the decimal point corresponding to $m_1 \bullet m_2$ and $\frac{m_1}{m_2}$ consists of anything but one digit.

WORKING WITH PERCENTAGES

A **percent** is used to express the number of parts of a whole. For instance, 34 percent means "34 parts of 100," which can be expressed as the fraction $\frac{34}{100}$, as the decimal 0.34, or using the notation 34%. All three representations are equivalent. To go from decimal form to percent form, you simply move the decimal point two units to the right and affix the % sign; to convert in the opposite manner, move the decimal point two units to the left, insert a decimal point and drop the % sign.

The following are basic scenarios that arise when working with percentages.

Question: What percent of x is y?

Answer: Divide x by y.

Question: Compute x % of y.

Answer: Convert x % to a decimal and multiply by y.

Question: x is y % of what number z?

Answer: Convert y % to a decimal, multiply by z, and set this equal to x. Now, solve for z.

THE REAL NUMBER LINE AND ORDERING

The **real number line** is a convenient way of illustrating the relative position of real numbers with respect to 0. This leads to the notion of **ordering**. What does it mean for a real number p to be *less than* a real number q, written $p < q$? Pictorially, q would be further to the right along the real number line than p. We also say that q is *greater than p*.

For instance:

$$-2 < -\frac{3}{5}$$

$$3.234 \le 3.235$$

$$\pi \ge 3.14$$

$$0 > -0.0002$$

The following are some important properties involving inequalities of real numbers:

Rule (in symbols)	What To Do (in words)
If $0 < a < 1$, then $a^2 < a$.	Squaring a real number between 0 and 1 results in a smaller real number.
If $0 < a < b$, then $-b < -a < 0$.	If a and b are both positive and a is less than b, then the reverse inequality is true of the negatives of a and b.
If $a < b$ and $c < d$, then $a + c < b + d$.	If you add the left sides and right sides of inequalities involving the same sign, then the sums satisfy the same inequality.

Other Numeration Systems

Different numeration systems have been designed for specific purposes, while others arose as different civilizations' means of communicating numeracy. The base 2 (binary) system and Roman numerals are two well-known examples.

The familiar base 10 system involves expressing real numbers using powers of 10, and allows for digits 0, 1, 2, 3, 4, 5, 6, 7, 8, and 9 to occupy any space in the place-value system. Similarly, base 2 involves expressing real numbers using powers of 2, and allows for digits 0 or 1 to occupy any space in its place-value system.

Focusing only on expressing whole numbers in base 2, the place-value chart is as follows:

...	2^7	2^6	2^5	2^4	2^3	2^2	2^1	2^0

We insert a subscript "2" to the right of a number expressed in base 2. The absence of such a subscript means that the number is in base 10, by default.

For example, $110{,}001_2$ means:

$$110{,}001_2 = (1 \times 2^0) + (0 \times 2^1) + (0 \times 2^2) + (0 \times 2^3) + (1 \times 2^4) + (1 \times 2^5)$$

The corresponding base 10 number can be deciphered by expanding the right side as:

$$1 + 0 + 0 + 0 + 16 + 32 = 49.$$

How is a base 10 number converted to a base 2 number? The strategy is to find the largest power of 2 that divides into the given number *once*. If there is a remainder, repeat this procedure and insert zeros in the positions of the place-value chart down to the one for which that power of 2 divides into the remainder once; otherwise, fill in all positions in the place-value chart to its right with zeros.

Let's work through converting 49 to the base 2 number from the previous example:

- The largest power of 2 that divides into 49 *once* is 2^5, or 32. So, put a 1 in that position in the place-value chart and repeat the process on the remainder $49 - 32 = 17$.

- The largest power of 2 that divides into 17 *once* is 2^4, or 16. So, put a 1 in that position in the place-value chart and repeat the process on the remainder $17 - 16 = 1$.

- The largest power of 2 that divides into 1 once is 2^0, or 1. So, put a 0 in the position in the place-value chart corresponding to $2^3, 2^2$, and 2^1, and a 1 in the position corresponding to 2^0.

You were likely introduced to Roman numerals in grade school. If you have watched a movie, maybe you have paid attention to the production company screen on which the production date of the movie is listed—there, you will see a sequence of Ms, Cs, Ls, Ds, Xs, Vs, and Is. This sequence is a Roman numeral. The fact that this represents a *number* is perhaps strange since the digits are letters rather than numerals. But, each letter stands for a certain natural number:

- I = 1
- V = 5
- X = 10
- L = 50
- C = 100
- D = 500
- M = 1,000

The Roman numeral system is not a place-value system like base 2 or base 10. Rather, Roman numerals are formed by listing groups of these symbols from left to right, starting with the symbol with the largest value. To determine the base 10 number corresponding to a Roman numeral, interpret the value of each natural grouping of symbols from left to right and add them. For example, CCCXII consists of 3 hundreds, 1 ten, and 2 ones; so, its base 10 equivalent is 312.

You will never find more than three of the same symbol written consecutively in a Roman numeral. Rather, subtraction is used in the following manner:

- An I appearing directly before a V or an X means to subtract 1 from the value of that symbol. For example, IV is used instead of writing IIII to mean 4.

- An X appearing directly before an L or a C means to subtract 10 from the value of that symbol. For example, XC is used instead of LXXXX to mean 90.

- A C appearing directly before a D or an M means to subtract 100 from the value of that symbol. For example, CM is used instead of DCCCC to mean 900.

Around 16 percent of the questions on the DSST Math for Liberal Arts exam will test your knowledge of sets and logic.

SETS AND LOGIC

Logic and sets form the foundation of mathematics. In this section, we'll review the basic terminology, symbolism, and mechanics of both.

SIMPLE LOGICAL STATEMENTS

A **statement** is a declarative sentence that is *either* true *or* false. It cannot be neither true nor false and it cannot be both true and false. This is known as the **Law of the Excluded Middle**.

The following are examples of statements:

- Lyndon Johnson was the 36th president of the United States.
- Andrew Wiles did not prove Fermat's Last Theorem.

An **open sentence** is any declarative sentence that contains one or more variables. An open sentence is not a statement, but becomes a statement when all the variables are assigned values.

Consider a typical example from algebra: $x - 1 = 2$. Here, x is a **variable**: it is a symbol that stands for a specific, but as-of-yet unspecified, real number. This sentence becomes a statement if we specify for what number x stands. The result is a true statement if x stands for 3, and a false statement if x stands for any other number.

An open sentence such as $x + 3 = 5$ or $x + y > 0$ can be made into a statement by assigning numerical values to the variable(s) x and y. But, there are other ways to convert open sentences into statements. We could ask whether there is some value of the variable for which the statement is true, or whether it is true for all possible values of the variable. This is called **quantifying** the open sentence. We do this by prefixing expressions with phrases such as "for every x," "there is an x such that," "for every x there is a y such that." The phrase "for every x" is called a **universal quantifier**. For instance, the sentence, "For each real number x, $x + 3 = 5$" is a statement which happens to be false, while the statement, "There is an integer x, such that $x + 3 = 5$," happens to be true.

NEGATION

The truth of any statement is denied by asserting the truth of its **negation**. Formally, given any statement p, the *negation of p*, denoted $\sim p$ (and read "not p"), is a statement that is true whenever p is false and false whenever p is true. For example, we deny the truth of the assertion, "Today is Monday" by asserting "Today is not Monday." Equivalently, we can write, "It is not true that today is Monday" or "It is not the case that today is Monday." A mathematical example is: "If p is the statement '$4 + 5 < 10$,' then the negation $\sim p$ is '$4 + 5 \geq 10$.'"

Sometimes, forming the negation of a statement is more complicated. For example, consider the statement, "It rained every day this week." The negation of this statement is **not** "It did not rain every day this week." To negate this statement, it is sufficient that there be only *one* day of the week on which it did not rain. That is, the negation is, "There was a day this week on which it did not rain." The negation of the mathematical statement, "There is a real number that satisfies the equation $x^2 - 2 = 0$." is the statement, "For all real numbers x, $x^2 - 2 \neq 0$."

COMPOUND LOGICAL STATEMENTS AND TRUTH TABLES

Suppose we have several statements, denoted by $p, q, r \ldots$ We can combine these into more complex statements by means of certain words such as *and, or, if ... then* called **logical connectives**. Since the result is a statement, it must be either true or false and its truth value depends only on the truth values of the constituent statements, not their specific content. Such statements are called **compound statements**.

The logical connective *or* is denoted by the symbol $\vee$. That is, "p or q" is denoted $p \vee q$ and is called the **disjunction** of p and q. The statement $p \vee q$ is true whenever at least one of p, q is true; it is false only when both are false. These truth values are summarized in the following **truth table**. We use T for "true" and F for "false":

p	q	$p \vee q$
T	T	T
T	F	T
F	T	T
F	F	F

For example, the disjunction "2 is even or 3 is even" is true because one of the statements is true while the other is false. The disjunction "2 is even or 3 is odd" is true because both statements are true. The disjunction, "2 is odd or 3 is even" is false because both statements are false.

The logical connective *and* is denoted by the symbol $\wedge$. That is "p and q" is denoted $p \wedge q$ and called the **conjunction** of p and q. The compound statement $p \wedge q$ is true whenever both p, q are true; it is false otherwise. These truth values are summarized as follows:

p	q	$p \wedge q$
T	T	T
T	F	F
F	T	F
F	F	F

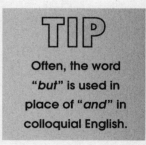

TIP

Often, the word "*but*" is used in place of "*and*" in colloquial English.

LOGICALLY EQUIVALENT STATEMENTS

Often, a statement can be expressed in different, yet equivalent, ways. As a simple example, consider the two statements, "Today is hot and humid." and "Today is humid and hot." If we denote the statement "Today is hot" by p and "Today is humid" by q, the first sentence is translated symbolically as $p \wedge q$, while the second is interpreted as $q \wedge p$. Clearly, if one is true so is the other, and vice versa. Such statements are said to be **logically equivalent**. More precisely, two compound statements involving one or more constituents $p, q, r \ldots$ are logically equivalent provided they have the same truth value for every possible truth assignment to their constituent parts.

Some of the most important and useful logical equivalences are those concerning the negations of compound statements. Sensibly, $\sim(\sim P)$ is logically equivalent to P; this is called the **Law of the Double Negative**. In words, this is the same as saying that two "nots" in a row cancel each other.

CONDITIONALS AND BICONDITIONALS

Another important class of mathematical assertions are those of the form "if p, then q." Statements of this form are called **conditionals** or **implications**. Such statements are denoted "$p \Rightarrow q$" and we say p *implies* q. The statement p is called the **hypothesis** and the statement q is called the **conclusion**. The commonly accepted meaning of such a statement is that the truth of p assures the truth of q. Thus, the statement would be false if we had p true and q false. However, if the conditional is to be a statement in the technical sense we defined above, it must have a truth value when p is false. The truth values are summarized as follows:

p	q	$p \Rightarrow q$
T	T	T
T	F	F
F	T	T
T	F	T

The convention that $p \Rightarrow q$ is true when p is false may seem a bit strange. To make this plausible, consider the statement, "If it rains tomorrow, then I will take you to the movies." Clearly, if it rains and I take you to the movies you will agree that I told the truth when I made the statement. Also, if it rains and I do not take you to the movies, I lied. The issue is: if it does not rain, did I tell the truth or lie? In real life one might say, it does not matter. But, to be precise we are committed to assigning a truth value. And, it does not make sense to say that we *lied* in making our assertion in the case that it does not rain. So, we must have told the truth.

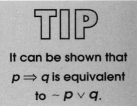

TIP

It can be shown that $p \Rightarrow q$ is equivalent to $\sim p \vee q$.

How do we form the negation of a conditional? Since an implication is only false when p is true and q is false, its negation is only true under those circumstances. So, the negation is only true if both p and $\sim q$ are true. But this is the same as the conjunction $p \wedge \sim q$. Thus, $\sim(p \Rightarrow q)$ is logically equivalent to the conjunction $p \wedge \sim q$.

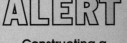

ALERT

Constructing a truth table for such a statement is a common exam question.

We can form more complex statements by using more than one logical connective. For example, we could write $p \Rightarrow (q \wedge r)$. From our discussion, this statement would be true whenever p is false. It would also be true if all three statements p, q, and r are true. But, it would be false if p is true and either q or r is false (since in such case, the entire conclusion is false).

A statement of the form "p if and only if q" is called a **biconditional statement** and is denoted "p　q." It is true when p and q have the same truth values and is otherwise false:

p	q	$p \Leftrightarrow q$
T	T	T
T	F	F
F	T	F
F	F	T

By constructing a truth table, you can show that $(p \Leftrightarrow q)$ is logically equivalent to the conjunction $((p \Rightarrow q) \wedge (q \Rightarrow p))$.

DE MORGAN'S LAWS

How do we negate a disjunction or conjunction? Let us start with an example. The negation of the statement, "Today is hot and humid." is "It is not true that today is hot and humid." This statement is true provided the original statement is false, and vice versa. The original statement is true if it is both hot and humid, and false if either weather condition does not hold. Therefore, the negation as written above is logically equivalent to "Today is not hot or today is not humid."

Symbolically, to negate a conjunction we proceed as follows:

Original statement: $p \wedge q$

Negation: $\sim (p \wedge q)$

Equivalent form: $\sim p \vee \sim q$

The general rule to remember here is that when you negate an "and" statement you get an "or" statement. This rule is one of **De Morgan's laws**. What about negating a disjunction? The rule is similar and results in the second of De Morgan's laws:

Original statement: $p \vee q$

Negation: $\sim (p \vee q)$

Equivalent form: $\sim p \wedge \sim q$

CONTRAPOSITIVE AND CONVERSE STATEMENTS

We now consider two implications related to the conditional "$p \Rightarrow q$", namely the **contrapositive** and the **converse**. Given the conditional $p \Rightarrow q$, the contrapositive is the conditional $\sim q \Rightarrow \sim p$, and the converse is the conditional $q \Rightarrow p$.

For instance:

Conditional: If Chicago is in Illinois, then Baltimore is in Maryland.

Contrapositive: If Baltimore is not in Maryland, then Chicago is not in Illinois.

Converse: If Baltimore is in Maryland, then Chicago is in Illinois.

All three statements are true.

Here's another, more mathematical, example:

> **Conditional:** If triangles A and B are congruent, then they are similar.
>
> **Contrapositive:** If triangles A and B are not similar, then they are not congruent.
>
> **Converse:** If triangles A and B are similar, then they are congruent.

In this case, the original statement and its contrapositive are true, but the converse is not.

These examples illustrate the logical relationship among these statements. Namely, a conditional and its contrapositive are logically equivalent, but this relationship does not hold when considering the converse. That is, a conditional and its converse are not logically equivalent.

VALID LOGICAL ARGUMENTS AND EULER DIAGRAMS

How does one prove an assertion? As we have seen, a statement of the form $p \Rightarrow q$ is true if it is impossible for p to be true and q to be false. So, we can start the proof by assuming p is, in fact, true and try to show that q must also be true. Note that if we could find a statement r such that we know—from prior knowledge or by definition—that $p \Rightarrow r$ is true, then we could conclude that r must be true. If we *also* know that $r \Rightarrow q$ is true, then we could infer that q must be true. Symbolically, $[(p \Rightarrow r) \wedge (r \Rightarrow q)]$ is logically equivalent to $p \Rightarrow q$. This stringing together of implications is the main method used for constructing a valid logical argument.

The following **syllogism** (that is, a collection of statements followed by a conclusion) illustrates this method:

> All blankets are soft.
>
> All soft things are comfortable.
>
> Thus, all blankets are comfortable.

We say the syllogism is **valid** if whenever the syllogism is true, the conclusion is true.

A pictorial way of determining if a syllogism is valid is by using an **Euler diagram**. Let's construct one for the above example. Here, we have two sets of objects: "Blankets" and "Things that are soft." Sensibly, the first set is entirely included within the second, a fact that we illustrate as follows:

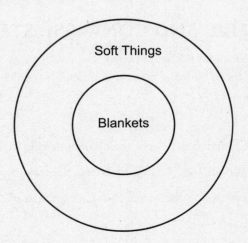

Consider the following jazzed-up syllogism:

> All blankets are soft.
>
> All soft things are comfortable.
>
> The wool jacket is not comfortable.
>
> Thus, the wool jacket is not a blanket.

Sometimes, it is difficult to parse the relationship among premises without using a diagram. This time, we have the same two sets, but we additionally have an object that does not belong to the set "Things that are soft." As such, the Euler diagram for this syllogism is as follows:

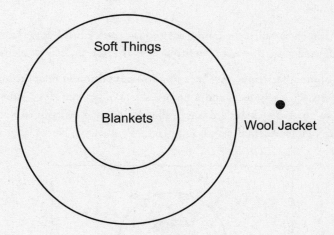

From this diagram, the object "wool jacket" does not belong to the set "blankets" and so, the conclusion is true. Hence, the syllogism is valid.

THE NATURE OF SETS AND SET-BUILDER NOTATION

Let's informally think of a **set** as a collection of objects. The objects that make up a set can be numbers, words, shapes, sets, or other symbols that are referred to as **elements** (or *members*) of the set. Sets are usually labeled using uppercase Latin letters (e.g., A, B, C) and the elements of a given set by lowercase Latin letters (e.g., a, b, c).

Some sets can be displayed by explicitly listing all of its members and enclosing this list of elements within braces { }. For example, if A denotes the set whose members are 1, 2, and 3, we would write $A = \{1, 2, 3\}$. When the number of members of a set becomes rather large, it can be cumbersome (or even impossible) to list all of them explicitly. In such case we need an alternate way, commonly referred to as **set-builder notation**, to describe the set. Precisely, if $P(x)$ is an open sentence and if A is the set of all those objects satisfying $P(x)$, then we write $A = \{x : P(x)\}$, or equivalently $A = \left\{ x \mid P(x) \right\}$, and read this is "$A$ is the set of all x such that $P(x)$ is true." Consider the following examples:

- Let $P(x)$ be the open sentence, "x is a positive integer less than 21 and x is divisible by 5." Observe that 5, 10, 15, and 20 are the only elements of the set $A = \{x : P(x)\}$. Since the number of elements is small, it is more convenient to write $A = \{5, 10, 15, 20\}$.

- Let $P(x)$ be the open sentence. "x is an integer and x is a multiple of 3." If $C = \{x : P(x)\}$ then, $C = \{x :$ There exists an integer k such that $x = 3k\}$. Equivalently, $C = \{0, \pm 3, \pm 6, \dots\}$.

SET MEMBERSHIP AND CONTAINMENT

All elements under consideration in a discussion must come from *some* tacitly understood **universal set** U—this is an underlying set that contains all possible elements that any of our sets in the discussion can ever contain.

A set that has no members is called the **empty set** and is denoted by $\emptyset$. If A is a nonempty set and x is an element of A, we denote this fact by writing $x \in A$, read as, "x is an element of A."

We use this notion of **membership** to give meaning to a **containment** relationship that sometimes exists between two sets. Precisely, let A and B be two sets. We say that A is a **subset** of B and write $A \subseteq B$ if $x \in A \implies x \in B$. A standard way of illustrating such containment is by drawing a so-called **Venn diagram** (which resembles an Euler diagram), as shown here:

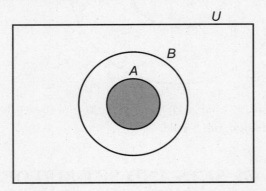

If $A \subseteq B$ and $B \subseteq A$, then we say A is *equal* to B, denoted by $A = B$. If $A \subseteq B$ and $A \neq B$, then A is called a **proper subset** of B.

SET OPERATIONS

Just as several different arithmetic operations can be performed on real numbers, there are also operations, listed below, that can be performed on sets to produce another set.

Set Operation	Set (in symbols)	Set (in words)	Venn Diagram
Complement A^c	$\begin{Bmatrix} x: x \in U \\ \text{and } x \notin A \end{Bmatrix}$	All members of the universal set that are not in A.	
Union $A \cup B$	$\begin{Bmatrix} x \in U: x \in A \\ \text{or } x \in B \end{Bmatrix}$	All members of the universal set that are in A, B, or both.	
Intersection $A \cap B$	$\begin{Bmatrix} x \in U: x \in A \\ \text{and } x \in B \end{Bmatrix}$	All members of the universal set that are in both A and B.	

If $A \cap B = \varnothing$, then A and B are said to be **disjointed**.

INTERPRETING VENN DIAGRAMS

Venn diagrams are useful aids when visualizing complicated relationships. A single diagram can contain a lot of information about how various sets are related. For instance, consider the Venn diagram shown here:

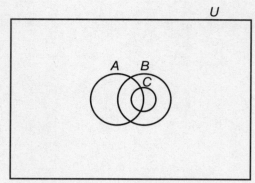

The following statements can be made concerning sets A, B, and C, and their elements:

- Every element of C belongs to B.
- Some elements of B are in A.
- Not every member of C is in A and B.
- If an object is not in B, then it cannot be in C.

If the sets A, B, and C are described in context, then these mathematical statements also take on contextual meaning. Suppose we take as the universal set the set of all senior students in High School X, and that we impose the following context on sets A, B, and C:

- A is the set of all students who play sports.
- B is the set of all students who plan to attend college next year.
- C is the set of all students taking AP classes.

Then, the mathematical statement, "Every element of C belongs to B." is interpreted as "Every student taking AP classes intends to attend college next year." Likewise, the mathematical statement, "Not every member of C is in A and B." is interpreted as "Not every student taking AP classes both plays sports and plans to attend college next year."

METRIC SYSTEM, CONVERSIONS, AND GEOMETRY

On the DSST exam, you will need to be familiar with basic conversions involving the U.S. customary unit system and metric system, as well as mathematical and applied problems involving elementary geometry. This section will review the major concepts you should know before test day.

NOTE

Around 12 percent of the questions on the DSST Math for Liberal Arts exam cover the metric system, conversions, and geometry.

U.S. CUSTOMARY UNIT SYSTEM AND METRIC SYSTEM

Different units of measurement are used to quantify different types of quantities, like time, speed, liquid measures, length, area, and volume. Below are some common units of measure expressed in equivalent ways.

Type of quantity being measured	Units of measure and their conversions
Time	1 minute = 60 seconds
	1 hour = 60 minutes = 3,600 seconds
	1 day = 24 hours = 1,440 minutes = 86,400 seconds
Weight	1 pound = 16 ounces
	1 ton = 2,000 pounds
Liquid Measure	1 gallon = 4 quarts = 8 pints = 16 cups
	1 quart = 2 pints = 4 cups
	1 pint = 2 cups
Length	1 foot = 12 inches
	1 yard = 3 feet = 36 inches
	1 mile = 1,760 yards = 5,280 feet
Area	1 square foot = $(12 \text{ inches})^2 = 12^2$ square inches
	1 square yard = $(3 \text{ feet})^2 = 3^2$ square feet
	1 square mile = $(5,280 \text{ feet})^2 = 5,280^2$ square feet
Volume	1 cubic foot = $(12 \text{ inches})^3 = 12^3$ cubic inches
	1 cubic yard = $(3 \text{ feet})^3 = 3^3$ cubic feet

The **metric system** is based on powers of 10 and applies to units of length, area, volume, and liquid measure. The basic unit of length measure is the *meter* (m). This unit is squared and cubed to get the units of measure for area and volume, respectively; the unit names are *square meters* (m^2) and *cubic meters* (m^3), respectively. The unit used for measuring volumes of liquid is the *liter* (L), which is defined by $1L = 1 \text{ dm}^3$, and the unit used for measuring weight is the *gram* (g). The following is a list of commonly used prefixes and their associated powers of 10:

NOTE

The abbreviated notation ft.² means *square feet* and ft.³ means *cubic feet*. The same exponentiation notation is used for all units.

Prefix	Abbreviation	Power of 10
mega	M	10^6
kilo	k	10^3
hecto	h	10^2
deca	da	10^1
---	*base unit*	10^0
deci	d	10^{-1}
centi	c	10^{-2}
milli	m	10^{-3}
micro	μ	10^{-6}

UNIT CONVERSIONS

TIP

In the metric system, when converting from a smaller unit to a larger unit, move the decimal point to the left the appropriate number of places; when converting from a larger to a smaller unit, move it to the right.

Knowing how to convert from one unit to another is important when trying to solve problems in which similar quantities are expressed using different units.

Let's start with the metric system. Since the metric system is based on powers of 10, converting units expressed in the metric system is simply a matter of appropriately moving the decimal point. For example, 300 cm = 3 m because 1 cm = 10^{-2} m; therefore, multiplying both sides by 300 yields the result. Likewise, 400 dm = 40 m since 1 dm = 10^{-1} m. In both cases, note that the conversion simply involved moving the decimal point to the *left* the number of places indicated by the power without the negative sign (2 and 1, respectively). This is always true when converting a unit lower on the table to one higher up. The exact opposite is true if you are converting a unit higher on the table to one lower. For instance, 2 km = 200 hm because 1 km = 100 hm.

Performing conversions of units of area or volume also are simple matters of moving the decimal point. But the number of places the decimal point is moved for area conversions is now double what it was for length conversions, and triple for volume conversions. The reason is that the units themselves are squared and cubed to get units of area and volume measure, respectively. For instance, since 1 cm = 10^{-2} m, it follows that 1 cm^2 = (1 cm)^2 = (10^{-2} m)^2 = 10^{-4} m^2. So, to convert from square centimeters to square meters, the decimal point must be moved to the left *four* units, not two as it was for length measure. The same reasoning works for volume unit conversions.

Converting units in the U.S. customary system is slightly more involved only because the units are not based on powers of 10. Here, the key is to set up products of fractions that show the original units canceling and the new units remaining in the final product. For example, to convert 3.5 feet to inches, we use the conversion factor 1 foot = 12 inches in the following computation:

$$3.5 \text{ feet} = \frac{3.5 \text{ feet}}{1} \times \frac{12 \text{ inches}}{1 \text{ foot}} = \frac{3.5 \text{ feet}}{1} \times \frac{12 \text{ inches}}{1 \text{ foot}} = (3.5) \cdot (12) \text{ inches} = 42 \text{ inches}$$

This works because the fraction $\frac{12 \text{ inches}}{1 \text{ foot}} = 1$.

Converting units of speed involves making *two* conversions—one for the numerator and one for the denominator. For example, to convert 85 miles per hour to *feet per minute*, we use the conversion factors 1 mile = 5,280 feet and 1 hour = 60 minutes and perform the following computation:

$$\frac{85 \text{ miles}}{1 \text{ hour}} = \frac{85 \text{ miles}}{1 \text{ hour}} \times \frac{5,280 \text{ feet}}{1 \text{ mile}} \times \frac{1 \text{ hour}}{60 \text{ minutes}} = \frac{85 \times 5,280}{60} \text{ feet per minute}$$

You can also convert between the metric and U.S. customary systems, but you need to use established conversion factors (like 1 m ≈ 3.28 feet) to do so.

NOTE

In such case, you would be given the necessary conversion factors on the exam.

BASIC NOTIONS IN GEOMETRY

You have encountered the terms *point, line, line segment, ray,* and *angle* throughout your education. We will focus on the terminology that is likely less familiar in this short section.

Angles are classified according to their "size" measured using **degrees**. The notation $m(\angle A)$ is used to denote the measure of angle A. The following is some basic angle terminology:

Term	Definition
Acute Angle	An angle with measure between 0 and 90 degrees.
Right Angle	An angle with measure of 90 degrees.
Obtuse Angle	An angle with measure between 90 and 180 degrees.
Complementary Angles	Two angles with measures that sum to 90 degrees.
Supplementary Angles	Two angles with measures that sum to 180 degrees.
Congruent Angles	Two angles with the same measure.

The relationships between pairs of angles are also important to recognize. We've identified these relationships in the following diagram.

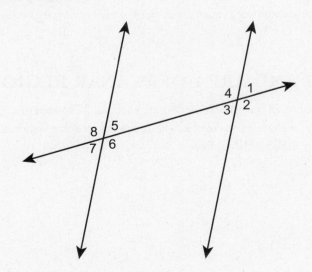

Term	Examples from Diagram
Vertical Angles	∠2 and ∠4; ∠6 and ∠8
Adjacent Angles	∠3 and ∠4; ∠7 and ∠8
Corresponding Angles	∠4 and ∠8; ∠3 and ∠7
Alternate Interior Angles	∠4 and ∠6; ∠3 and ∠5

TRIANGLES AND QUADRILATERALS

The Pythagorean theorem ONLY works for right triangles!

Two important rules that all triangles obey are the Triangle Sum Rule and Triangle Inequality. **Triangle Inequality** says that the sum of the lengths of any two sides of a triangle must be strictly larger than the length of the third side. It is impossible to construct a triangle that does not satisfy *both* conditions. The **Triangle Sum Rule** says that the sum of the measures of the three angles in any triangle must be 180°.

The **Pythagorean theorem** relates the lengths of the sides of *right* triangles. For the right triangle shown below, the sides with lengths a and b are called legs and the side opposite the right angle is the **hypotenuse**; the hypotenuse is the longest side of a right triangle. The Pythagorean theorem says that $a^2 + b^2 = c^2$.

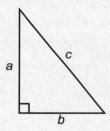

NOTE

Often, questions involving the Pythagorean theorem are asked in a real-world context in which you must compute the height of a tree, length of a bridge, etc., when you have information about two other sides of a triangle.

Quadrilaterals are figures in the plane with four sides, each of which is a line segment. There are several common quadrilaterals (e.g., square, rectangle, parallelogram) that arise in solving practical problems.

PERIMETER AND AREA OF PLANAR REGIONS

The **perimeter** of a region in the plane is the "distance around." The **area** of a region in the plane is the number of *unit squares* needed to cover it. The following are some standard perimeter and area formulas with which you should be familiar.

Region	Illustration	Perimeter Formula	Area Formula
Square		$P = 4s$	$A = s^2$
Rectangle		$P = 2l + 2w$	$A = l \times w$
Circle		Since the diameter d is $2r$, there are two common expressions for this formula: $P = 2\pi r = \pi d$	$A = \pi r^2$
Arc of a Circle		$P = \left(\dfrac{\theta}{180°} \right) \cdot \pi$	$A = \left(\dfrac{\theta}{360°} \right) \cdot \pi r^2$
Triangle		Sum the three lengths of the triangle.	$A = \dfrac{1}{2} b \cdot h$

Do NOT include *h* in the perimeter of a triangle unless it is an actual leg of the triangle.

Questions involving perimeter and area will be somewhat more complicated than merely applying these formulas. In fact, questions often involve concepts from multiple categories. For instance, you might be asked to determine a formula for the area of a new rectangle formed by reducing the width and length of a different rectangle by a certain percentage. In such case, you need to know about area formulas and how to work with percentages.

Other common questions will ask you to compute the perimeter or area of a geometric figure that is comprised of smaller, identifiable shapes, such as the one pictured below:

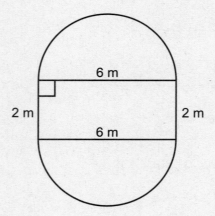

This figure is composed of two congruent semicircles whose radii are 3 m (since the diameter is 6 m) and a rectangle. The area of each semicircle is $\frac{1}{2}\pi(3\text{ m})^2 = \frac{9}{2}\pi\text{ m}^2$ and the area of the rectangle is $(2\text{ m})(6\text{ m}) = 12\text{ m}^2$. So, the area enclosed by the figure is $2\left(\frac{9}{2}\pi\text{ m}^2\right) + 12\text{m}^2 = (9\pi + 12)\text{m}^2$.

For the perimeter, do NOT include the sides with lengths 6 m since they are inside the figure. The perimeter is the distance *around* the figure! So, the lengths of the two semicircles and two short sides of the rectangle are all that are used. The length of each semicircle is $\frac{1}{2}(2\pi \cdot 3\text{m}) = 3\pi\text{ m}$. So, the perimeter is 3π m + 3π m + 2(2 m) = $(6\pi + 4)$ m.

SURFACE AREA AND VOLUME OF SOLIDS

Two measures of interest for three-dimensional solids are **surface area** and **volume**. Conceptually, to compute the surface area of a solid, the solid is dissected and flattened out so that it can be visualized as a combination of recognizable figures whose areas can be computed using known formulas. The volume of a solid in space is the number of *unit cubes* needed to fill it. The following are formulas for the surface area and volume of some common solids:

Solid	Illustration	Surface Area Formula	Volume Formula
Cube		$SA = 6e^2$	$V = e^3$
Rectangular Prism		$SA = 2(lw + lh + wh)$	$V = lwh$

Solid	Illustration	Surface Area Formula	Volume Formula
Circular Cone		$SA = \pi r^2 + \pi r \sqrt{r^2 + h^2}$	$V = \frac{1}{3}\pi r^2 h$
Circular Cylinder		$SA = 2\pi r^2 + 2\pi rh$	$V = \pi r^2 h$
Sphere		$SA = 4\pi r^2$	$V = \frac{4}{3}\pi r^3$

As with problems concerning the area of planar regions, common questions concerning volume and surface area will involve decomposing a more complicated solid into smaller solids whose surface area and volume are easily computed using known formulas. Other types of problems will involve a crossover to algebra. For example, if a spherical balloon has surface area 36π square centimeters, what is its volume? Determining the volume of a sphere requires that you have the radius, and this information is readily attainable from the surface area formula. Indeed, solving the equation $4\pi r^2 = 36\pi$ for r yields $r = 3$ cm. As such, the volume of the sphere is $\frac{4}{3}\pi(3 \text{ cm})^3 = \frac{4}{3}\pi \cdot 27 = 36\pi$ cm^3.

ALGEBRA, GRAPHS, AND FUNCTIONS

The subject of algebra is vast, as you may recall from your high school course! The DSST exam focuses deeply on a handful of the topics you learned, rather than requiring you to know every nuance and every technique you studied.

ORDER OF OPERATIONS AND ALGEBRAIC EXPRESSIONS

Often, you need to simplify an arithmetic expression involving all types of real numbers and operations. You must use the following rules that tell us the **order of operations**:

- **Step 1:** Simplify all expressions contained within parentheses.
- **Step 2:** Simplify all expressions involving exponents.
- **Step 3:** Perform all multiplication and division as it arises from left to right.
- **Step 4:** Perform all addition and subtraction as it arises from left to right.

If there are multiple groupings, apply the same steps *within* each grouping.

When evaluating algebraic expressions for specific values of the variables, simply substitute the values in for the variables and simplify the resulting arithmetic expression using the arithmetic rules involving integers, fractions, and decimals, together with the order of operations. For example, to evaluate the algebraic expression $1 - x^3(2x - y^2)$ when $x = -2$ and $y = 3$, substitute these values into the expression and simplify:

$$1 - (-2)^3 (2(-2) - (3)^2) = 1 - (-2)^3 (-4 - 9)$$

$$= 1 - (-2)^3 (-13)$$

$$= 1 - (-8)(-13)$$

$$= 1 - 104$$

$$= -103$$

EVALUATING AND MANIPULATING FORMULAS

Formulas relating two or more quantities arise in nearly all fields of study and in everyday life. Whether it's converting degrees Fahrenheit to degrees Celsius using the formula $C = \frac{5}{9}(F - 32)$ or determining the height of a baseball struck at a certain height above home plate with a certain speed using the well-known physics formula $s = \frac{1}{2}g t^2 + v_0 t + s_0$, you have likely encountered *some* formula for *some* reason. You will need to manipulate and evaluate formulas on the DSST exam. Typically, a description of the context of a formula will be given and you will be asked to determine the value of one of the variables given the values of the others.

For instance, suppose the temperature of a computer lab is 12 degrees Celsius and you're asked to determine the temperature in degrees Fahrenheit. This requires substituting $C = 12$ into $C = \frac{5}{9}(F - 32)$ and solving for F:

$$C = \frac{5}{9}(F - 32)$$

$$12 = \frac{5}{9}(F - 32)$$

$$12 \cdot \frac{9}{5} = F - 32$$

$$12 \cdot \frac{9}{5} + 32 = F$$

$$53.6 = F$$

Sometimes, rather than being given values for the other variables, you will be asked to solve a formula for a specific variable. This sort of algebraic manipulation uses the properties of fractions and integers, the order of operations, and the notion of **balancing an equation**. For example, you might be asked to solve the area formula for a trapezoid $A = \frac{1}{2}h(a + b)$, where the bases have lengths a and b and the height is h, for b. There are two ways to proceed which yield different looking, yet equivalent, results:

$$A = \frac{1}{2}h(a + b) \qquad\qquad\qquad A = \frac{1}{2}h(a + b)$$

$$2A = h(a + b) \qquad\qquad\qquad\qquad 2A = h(a + b)$$

$$2A = ha + hb \qquad\qquad\qquad\qquad \frac{2A}{h} = a + b$$

$$2A - ha = hb \qquad\qquad\qquad\qquad \frac{2A}{h} - a = b$$

$$\frac{2A - ha}{h} = b$$

APPLICATIONS OF LINEAR EQUATIONS

Setting up linear equations to solve applied problems is an important skill to master. Many word problems will require you to use linear equations—some examples might ask about rates, mixtures, time, cost, or work. Below is a sampling of these problems, along with a discussion of how to best set up the linear equation to solve them.

Problem: Tom scored 12, 7, 5, and 6 goals in each of his first four hockey games at a weekend tournament. How many goals does he need in the fifth game so that his average is 8 goals per game for the first five games?

Set-up: Let x be the number of goals scored in the fifth game. The average number of goals for 5 games is computed by summing the goals scored in the five games and dividing the sum by 5. Since this average is supposed to be 8, we arrive at this equation:

$$\frac{12 + 7 + 5 + 6 + x}{5} = 8$$

$$12 + 7 + 5 + 6 + x = 40$$

$$30 + x = 40$$

$$x = 10$$

Tom must score 10 goals in his fifth game for an average of 8 goals per game.

Problem: The Eagle Coffee and Tea Company makes a tea blend of chai tea worth $2.50 per kilogram and Darjeeling worth $2.00 per kilogram. How many kilograms of each should be used to produce a 20-kilogram tea blend with a total value of $46.00?

Set-up: Let x be the number of kilograms of chai tea used. Then, there are $(20 - x)$ kilograms of Darjeeling tea used. Multiply each by the corresponding cost per kilogram, sum the two costs and set the sum equal to $46 to get the equation:

$$2.50x + 2.00(20 - x) = 46$$

$$2.5x + 40 - 2x = 46$$

$$0.5x = 6$$

$$x = 12$$

So the company uses 12 kilograms of chai tea and 8 kilograms of Darjeeling tea.

Problem: A 10% salt solution is to be mixed with a 20% salt solution to obtain 100 gallons of an 18% salt solution. How many gallons of each original solution should be used to form the mixture?

Set-up: Let x be the number of gallons of 10% salt solution. Then, there are $(100 - x)$ gallons of 20% salt solution. Multiply each by the corresponding concentration—doing so gives the amount of salt in each of these two mixtures. Sum these quantities and set the sum equal to the amount of salt in 100 gallons of 18% solution to get the equation:

$$0.10x + 0.20(100 - x) = 0.18(100)$$

$$0.10x + 20 - 0.20x = 18$$

$$-0.10x = -2$$

$$x = 20$$

So the final answer is 10 grams of 10% salt solution and 90 grams of 20% salt solution.

Problem: A train traveled from Newark to St. Louis in 20 hours. It returned from St. Louis to Newark along the same route in 15 hours since its average speed was 25 miles per hour faster on the return trip. Find the distance from Newark to St. Louis.

Set-up: Let x be the rate (in mph) of the trip from Newark to St. Louis. Then, the rate of the reverse trip is $(x + 25)$ mph. Using distance = rate × time, an expression for the distance of the Newark to St. Louis trip is $20x$ and an expression for the distance traveled for the reverse trip is $15(x + 25)$. Since the same route is used, the distances traveled for both trips are the same. So, equate these expressions to get the equation:

$$20x = 15(x + 25)$$

$$20x = 15x + 375$$

$$5x = 375$$

$$x = 75$$

Keep in mind that order matters when writing down a ratio _a:b_.

RATIOS AND PROPORTIONS

A **ratio** is a comparison of one positive quantity x to another positive quantity y expressed as a fraction $\frac{x}{y}$ or using the notation $x{:}y$ (read "x to y"). For instance, if there are 4 girls to every 3 boys in a class, we say that the ratio of girls to boys is 4:3, or 4 to 3. The order in which a ratio is expressed is important because of the representation as a fraction. We could alternatively describe the above example using the ratio "3 boys for every 4 girls" and say the ratio of boys to girls is 3:4—this conveys the same information. However, since $\frac{3}{4} \neq \frac{4}{3}$, the two ratios are not equal.

A **proportion** is an equation relating two ratios; it is expressed by equating two fractions, say $\frac{a}{b} = \frac{c}{d}$. Proportions are formulated when one ratio is known and one of the two quantities in an equivalent ratio is unknown. They arise when changing units of measure and similar triangles, just to name a couple.

Let's look at a sample problem.

> **Problem:** Suppose there are 2 hockey sticks for every 5 pucks in the storage locker room. If the last count was 60 pucks, how many hockey sticks are in the storage room?

> **Set-up:** Let h denote the number of hockey sticks in the storage room.
> Set up the proportion:

$$\frac{2}{5} = \frac{h}{60}$$

$$5h = 120$$

$$h = 24$$

APPLICATIONS INVOLVING GRAPHS OF EQUATIONS IN TWO VARIABLES

The **graph of an equation of two variables** is the collection of all ordered pairs (x,y) in the xy-coordinate plane that satisfy the equation—that is, when the respective values for x and y are substituted into the equation, the result is a true statement. You should be able to interpret a graph in a context and use it to answer questions in that context.

Consider the following scenario.

A tool salesperson earns $42,000 as an annual base salary and earns commission as indicated in the following graph:

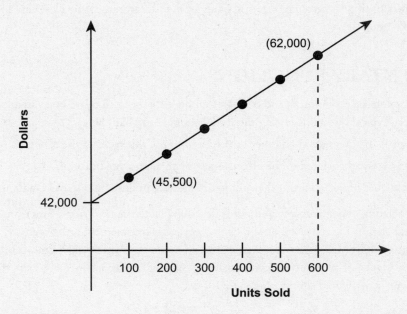

You might be asked how many units the salesperson must sell to earn an annual salary of $62,000. From the graph, it is evident he or she must sell 600 tools.

The graph might not be linear in nature, but you should be able to interpret parts of the graph in context and extract information. For instance, the following graph represents the height of a rock above the ground after it has been thrown by a hiker.

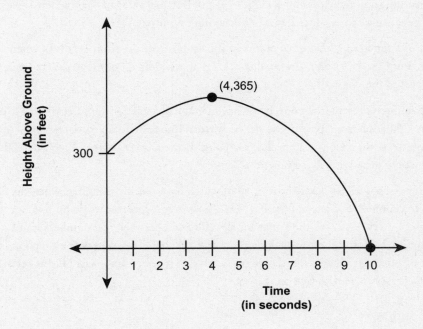

It is evident from the graph that the rock was thrown starting at a height of 300 feet above the ground, that the maximum height above the ground the rock achieves is 365 feet, and that it traveled for 10 seconds before hitting the ground. You will likely have to interpret graphs like these for questions on the DSST exam.

ELEMENTARY FUNCTIONS

Physicists, biologists, economists, and others often have the need to relate one variable to another in their work. Typical questions testing these skills might look like these:

- How is the pressure in an inner tube related to the thickness of the tubing?
- How is weight related to the effectiveness of an allergy medication?
- How does projected profit depend on the number of units sold to early-adopters?

The notion relating one quantity to another is described mathematically by a **function**. A function f is a rule that assigns to each element x in one set A exactly one element y, denoted $f(x)$, in another set B. When working with functions, we need to compute the **functional value** $f(x)$ for different inputs. For instance, if we want to compute the functional value when $x = -2$ for the function $f(x) = x^3 + 2x - 5$, we would simply plug in -2 for x:

$$f(-2) = (-2)^3 + 2(-2) - 5 = -8 - 4 - 5 = -17$$

You may be asked to perform such a computation for any number of functions, including those with an expression involving multiple powers, the square root, or absolute value of the input. In all cases, the way you compute the functional value is the same: substitute the given value in for the variable and simplify the resulting arithmetic expression using the rules of arithmetic. The set of points that you *can* plug in for the input is called the **domain**. For example, for the function $f(x) = \sqrt{1-x}$, you can substitute any value of x for which $1 - x \geq 0$. But, any value of x for which $1 - x < 0$ would result in a negative radicand, which yields a meaningless output.

The graph of a function is the set of points in the xy-plane of the form $(x, f(x))$, where x belongs to the domain of the function f. An x-value belongs to the domain of f if an ordered pair with that x-value is part of the graph of f.

But not all graphs represent functions. If you have a graph of a relationship, an easy way to determine if it defines a function is to apply the so-called **vertical line test**. To do so, determine if any vertical line that intersects the graph in *more than one* point. If the answer is "yes," then the relationship is NOT a function; otherwise, it is a function.

Graphs can possess various characteristics, all of which have specific meanings when the function is described in a context. For one, a function $f(x)$ equals zero whenever its graph touches the x-axis. If the graph of $y = f(x)$ is *above* the x-axis for all values of x between real numbers a and b, then the corresponding y-values at these x-values are positive. In such case, we say the function is **positive** on this set of x-values. Likewise, if the graph of $y = f(x)$ is *below* the x-axis on this set of x-values, the function is said to be **negative** on this set.

Next, as you move from left to right throughout a portion of the *x*-axis and you inspect the shape of the graph of a function, one of three things must happen:

- The graph climbs upward.
- The graph declines downward.
- Or the points remain on the same horizontal line.

A function is said to be **increasing** if the graph climbs upward from left to right, and **decreasing** if the graph declines downward from left to right. A function is **constant** if the points lie on a horizontal line.

For example, the **value function** (that is, how much the company is worth if it were to be purchased) for a new upstart financial consultation company is graphed below:

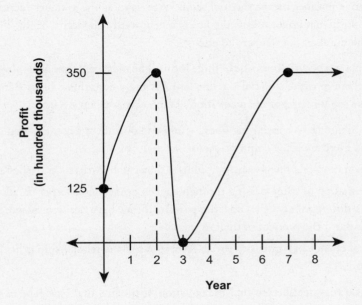

Some contextual observations are as follows:

- The value of the company increased considerably during the first two years, but then fell precipitously the next year until it was worthless. Thereafter, its value increased during the next 4 years and leveled off.
- The maximum worth of the company is $350,000.

LINEAR SYSTEMS AND INEQUALITIES

As a continuation of the previous section, let's now delve a bit deeper and focus on graphing and solving linear equations and systems of linear equations and inequalities.

GRAPHS OF LINEAR EQUATIONS

First, we'll explore the graphs of linear functions in detail. A key concept to understand is that associated with every line is a **slope**. Suppose two points (x_1, y_1) and (x_2, y_2), with $x_1 \neq x_2$, lie on a line.

The **slope**, m, of the line is defined as $m = \dfrac{y_2 - y_1}{x_2 - x_1}$. This number is an indication of the steepness of the line. A negative number means the line slants downward as the x-values increase from left to right, whereas a positive number means the line slants upward from left to right. The larger the absolute value of the number, the steeper the line.

The equation of a line can be written in one of three forms. The most common is the **slope-intercept** form $y = mx + b$, where m is the slope of the line and b is the y-coordinate of its y-intercept. The latter is true because the y-intercept of an equation's graph occurs when $x = 0$.

There are a variety of questions concerning lines, within and outside of a context, that can be asked on the DSST exam. Here are some common scenarios:

- Find the equation of a line given two points—they can be written or part of a graph.
- Find the equation of a line passing through a given point that is either parallel or perpendicular to a different line. (Two lines are **parallel** if they have the same slope; two lines are **perpendicular** if the product of their slopes is −1.)
- Find rate of change of a quantity y with respect to x if the relationship is linear and given by a graph.

For example, suppose you are asked to find the equation of the line that has slope $m = 2$ and that passes through the point $(3,10)$. What would you do? Well, since we want $(3,10)$ to lie on the line, we can use any other point (x,y), which is also on the line, and use the slope formula to deduce that $\dfrac{y - 10}{x - 3} = 2$. Now, solve for y:

$$\frac{y - 10}{x - 3} = 2$$

$$(x - 3)\frac{y - 10}{x - 3} = 2(x - 3)$$

$$y - 10 = 2(x - 3)$$

$$y - 10 = 2x - 6$$

$$y = 2x + 4$$

SOLVING LINEAR EQUATIONS

Solving linear equations involves simplifying various expressions using the order of operations, together with the distributive property of multiplication, to isolate the variable on one side of the equation. You must balance both sides of the equations. The same basic strategy is also used to solve linear inequalities, with the one additional feature: the inequality sign is switched whenever both sides of the inequality are multiplied by a negative real number. Also, the **solution set** of an inequality (that is, the set of real numbers that satisfies the inequality) contains infinitely many values, whereas a linear equation has *one* solution.

Consider the following:

$$\frac{\frac{1}{2}x - 4}{3} = \frac{x + 8}{5}$$

$$15 \cdot \left(\frac{\frac{1}{2}x - 4}{3}\right) = 15 \cdot \frac{x + 8}{5}$$

$$5 \cdot \left(\frac{1}{2}x - 4\right) = 3(x + 8)$$

$$\frac{5}{2}x - 20 = 3x + 24$$

$$2 \cdot \left(\frac{5}{2}x - 20\right) = 2 \cdot (3x + 24)$$

$$5x - 40 = 6x + 48$$

$$5x - 88 = 6x$$

$$-88 = x$$

$$\frac{\frac{1}{2}x - 4}{3} < \frac{x + 8}{5}$$

$$15 \cdot \left(\frac{\frac{1}{2}x - 4}{3}\right) < 15 \cdot \frac{x + 8}{5}$$

$$5 \cdot \left(\frac{1}{2}x - 4\right) < 3(x + 8)$$

$$\frac{5}{2}x - 20 < 3x + 24$$

$$2 \cdot \left(\frac{5}{2}x - 20\right) < 2 \cdot (3x + 24)$$

$$5x - 40 < 6x + 48$$

$$5x - 88 < 6x$$

$$-88 < x$$

SYSTEMS OF LINEAR EQUATIONS

Two or more equations considered simultaneously form a **system** of equations. Consider the system:

$$\begin{cases} 3x - 2y = 2 \\ x + 2y = -2 \end{cases}$$

Since the point $(0, -1)$ satisfies both equations in the system, we say that $(0, -1)$ is a **solution** of the system. On the other hand, the ordered pair $(2,2)$ is NOT a solution of the given system because it does not satisfy BOTH equations.

There are three methods for solving such systems: elimination, substitution, and graphing.

Elimination	Substitution	Graphing
Strategy: Multiply one or both equations, if needed, by appropriate numbers so that upon doing so and adding the equations results in one variable being canceled. Solve for the other variable, and then plug it back into either equation to find the value of the second variable.	**Strategy:** Solve one of the equations for a variable. Substitute this expression for that same variable in the other equation. This yields a linear equation in one variable. Solve it. Then, plug the solution into the expression used for substitution to find the value of the second variable.	**Strategy:** Put each equation in slope-intercept form and graph them. There are three possibilities: • There is one intersection point that is the solution of the system. • There are NO intersection points, so the lines are **parallel**. There is no solution in this case. • The lines are identical. In such case, every point on the line is a solution of the system.
Solution: $$\begin{cases} 3x - 2y = 2 \\ x + 2y = -2 \end{cases}$$ Add the equations to get $4x = 0$. So, $x = 0$. Now, substitute this back into either equation, say the first one, to get $3(0) - 2y = 2$. So, $y = -1$. Thus, the solution of the system is $(0, -1)$.	**Solution:** $$\begin{cases} 3x - 2y = 2 \\ x + 2y = -2 \end{cases}$$ Solve the second equation for x: $x = -2 - 2y$. Substitute this expression into the first equation: $3(-2 - 2y) - 2y = 2$ Solve for y: $-6 - 6y - 2y = 2$ $-8y = 8$ $y = -1$ Plug this into $x = -2 - 2y$ to see that $x = 0$. Thus, the solution of the system is $(0, -1)$.	**Solution:** $$\begin{cases} 3x - 2y = 2 \\ x + 2y = -2 \end{cases}$$ The equations are: $y = \dfrac{3}{2}x - 1, \quad y = -\dfrac{1}{2}x - 1$ The graphs are the lines as follows: The intersection point is $(0, -1)$, which is the solution of the system.

Systems of linear equations are used to solve real-world problems like those modeled using single linear equations. Let's walk through how to set up several such problems.

Problem: Tickets to a production of *The Color Purple* at a local university cost $6 for general admission or $3 with a student I.D. If 225 people paid to see a performance and $1,071 was collected, how many of each type of admission were sold?

Set-up: Let x be the number of general admission tickets sold and y the number of student tickets sold. Create two linear equations involving x and y. First, since there are 225 tickets sold all told, we know that $x + y = 225$. Next, multiply the number of each type of ticket by its price, sum the two dollar amounts, and equate it to the total collected, $1,071. Doing so yields the second equation $6x + 3y = 1,071$. So, the system is as follows:

$$\begin{cases} x + y = 225 \\ 6x + 3y = 1,071 \end{cases}$$

Problem: Traveling for 3 hours into a steady head wind, a plane makes a trip of 1,450 miles. The pilot determines that flying with the same wind for 2 hours, she could make a trip of 1,150 miles. What is the speed of the plane in the absence of wind and what is the speed of the wind?

Set-up: Let x be the speed of the plane in the absence of wind and y be the speed of the wind. A head wind reduces the plane's speed, while a tail wind (or traveling *with* the wind) increases the plane's speed. Using distance equals rate *times* time, the equation for the trip *into* the wind is $1,450 = 3(x - y)$ and the equation for the trip *with* the wind is $1,150 = 2(x + y)$. So, the system is

$$\begin{cases} 1,450 = 3(x \quad y) \\ 1,150 = 2(x + y) \end{cases}$$

LINEAR INEQUALITIES IN TWO VARIABLES

Just as the nature of the solution set for a linear equation in one variable differed from the nature of the solution set of a linear inequality in one variable—a linear equation has one solution while a linear inequality has infinitely many solutions—the nature of the set of points that satisfy a linear equation in two variables is different from the solution set of a linear inequality in two variables.

To determine the solution set of a linear inequality in two variables, start by graphing the line. If the inequality symbol is < or >, the boundary line will be dotted; if the inequality symbol is ≤ or ≥, the boundary line will be solid. Then, the only extra step is to choose a point either above or below the line and see if it satisfies the inequality. If it does, then shade the entire region containing that point on that side of the line; otherwise, shade the entire region on the other side of the line.

Consider the following examples:

Sketch the Solution Set of $y + x > 4$	Sketch the Solution Set of $y + x \leq 4$
Graph the related linear equation $y + x = 4$. The slope-intercept form is $y = -x + 4$. The slope is -1 and the y-intercept is 4.	This time, since the inequality sign includes "equals," the points on the line will satisfy the inequality and so, the line is solid.
Since the inequality sign is strict, the points on the line do not satisfy the inequality and so are not included in the solution set. To denote this fact, the line is dotted.	The other change is the side of the line that is shaded. The inequality can be written equivalently as $y \geq -x + 4$. Since y is *greater than or equal to* the right side, you now shade above the line instead of below it.
Replacing the equals sign by the original "<" sign gives the equivalent inequality $y < -x + 4$. Since y is *less than* the right side, shade below the line.	So, the solution set is as follows:
So, the solution set is as follows:	

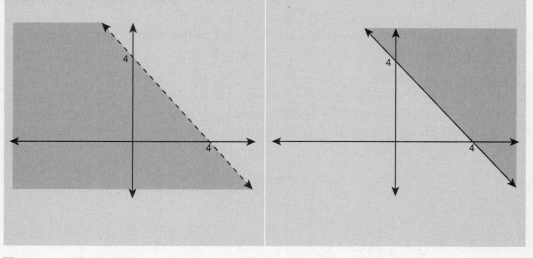

These types of inequalities are used to model certain real-world scenarios. For instance, suppose you have two part-time jobs. One job pays $35 per hour and the other pays $50 per hour. To determine the various combinations of the numbers of hours you would need work at each job to earn more than $4,000, you would need to set up a linear inequality. To this end, let x be the number of hours worked at the first job and let y be the number of hours worked at the second job. The inequality would be $35x + 50y > 4,000$.

SYSTEMS OF LINEAR INEQUALITIES

Lastly, we consider solving a system comprised of two such linear inequalities. Doing so is simply a matter of sketching the solution set of each inequality separately, but on the same set of axes. The overlap of the two regions is where both inequalities hold simultaneously and so, is the solution of the system.

Suppose we want to solve the system

$$\begin{cases} 3x - 2y > 2 \\ x + 2y \le -2 \end{cases}$$

First, sketch the graphs of the corresponding lines $3x - 2y = 2$ (dotted) and $x + 2y = -2$ (solid) on the same set of axes:

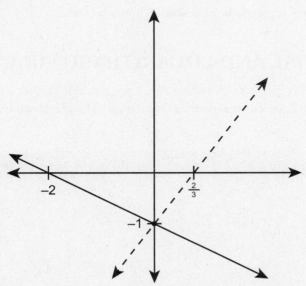

Since the point $(0,0)$ lies on neither line, use it as a test point for determining the solution set for each separate inequality. For the first one, substituting $(0,0)$ into the inequality yields $0 > 2$, a false statement. So, shade on the side of the line that does *not* include $(0,0)$. Similarly, substituting $(0,0)$ into the second inequality yields $0 \le -2$, a false statement. So, shade on the side of the line that does *not* include $(0,0)$. The solution set of the system of inequalities is the intersection of the two shaded areas, as shown here:

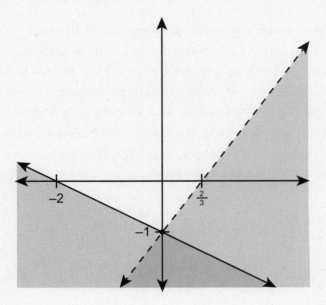

EXPONENTS, LOGARITHMS, AND FINANCIAL LITERACY

Exponential and logarithmic functions arise when modeling important phenomena, such as half-life of radioactive substances, population dynamics, savings account value when interest is compounded continuously, and the measurement of seismic activity. We review the basics of these functions and their main applications, especially to basic finance, in this section.

EXPONENTIAL AND LOGARITHMIC FUNCTIONS

Functions of the form $f(x) = A \cdot b^x$, where A is a nonzero real number and b is a positive real number not equal to 1, are called **exponential functions**. The graphs are broken down into two cases depending on b:

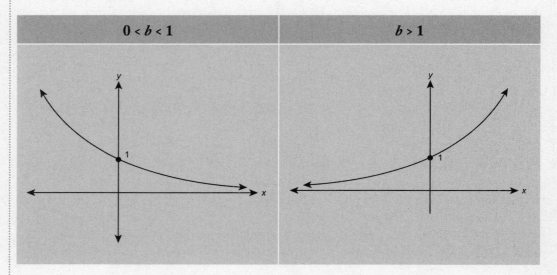

The following are some general observations about exponential functions:

- If $0 < b < 1$, the graph of $y = b^x$ gets very close to the x-axis as the x-values move to the right, and the y-values grow very rapidly as the x-values move to the left.

- If $b > 1$, the graph of $y = b^x$ gets very close to the x-axis as the x-values move to the left, and the y-values grow very rapidly as the x-values move to the right.

- If $b > 0$, then $b^x > 0$, for any value of x. Consequently, the equation $b^x = 0$ has no solutions.

- A common value for b is the irrational number e, which is approximately 2.71828… This value arises in many business applications.

The inverse function (that is, the function obtained by reflecting a given function's graph over the $y = x$ line) of $f(x) = b^x$, $b > 1$, is a function called a **logarithmic function**, which we denote as $g(x) = \log_b x$, where the **base** $b > 1$. The graph looks like this:

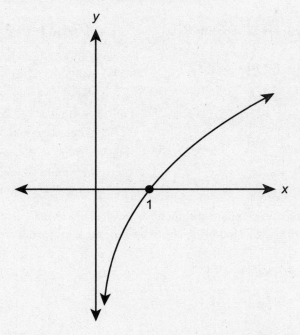

The following are some general observations about logarithmic functions, for any $b > 1$:

- The domain of $g(x) = \log_b x$ is the set of all positive x-values.

- The graph of $y = \log_b x$ plunges sharply as the x-values decrease toward zero, and it grows very slowly as the x-values move to the right.

- If the base b is taken to be the irrational number e, then $\log_b$ is typically written as ln, which stands for **natural logarithm**.

Since $f(x) = b^x$ and $g(x) = \log_b x$ are inverses, the following relationships hold, which are useful when solving equations involving them:

$$\log_b(b^x) = x, \text{ for any real number } x$$

$$b^{\log_b(x)} = x, \text{ for all } x > 0$$

LOGARITHMS AND THEIR PROPERTIES

The inverse relationship between exponentials and logarithms gives rise to the following:

$$\log_a b = c \text{ whenever } a^c = b$$

When simplifying expressions involving logarithms, think of $\log_a b$ in the following sense: "To what power must a be raised to get b?" For instance, to simplify $\log_3 9$, identify $a = 3$ and $b = 9$. So, we would ask the question, "To what power must 3 be raised to get 9?" The answer is 2. Similarly, $\log_2 1 = 0$ because $2^0 = 1$.

This also works for fractional exponents. For example, $\log_9 27 = \dfrac{3}{2}$ because $9^{\frac{3}{2}} = \left(\sqrt{9}\right)^3 = 3^3 = 27$.

There are three main properties used to simplify logarithmic expressions:

Logarithmic Property (in symbols)	Verbal Interpretation
$\log_a M \cdot N = \log_a M + \log_a N$	The logarithm of a product is the sum of the logarithms of the individual factors.
$\log_a \dfrac{M}{N} = \log_a M - \log_a N$	The logarithm of a quotient is the difference of the logarithms of the dividend and divisor (i.e., numerator and denominator).
$\log_a (M^n) = n \log_a M$	The logarithm of the power of a quantity is the power times the logarithm of just the quantity (without the power).

These properties are used to combine arithmetic expressions involving logarithms with the same base into a single logarithm. The following illustrates how these properties are used:

$$\log_7 \frac{2}{49} - \log_7 \frac{2}{7} = \log_7 \left(\frac{2}{49} \div \frac{2}{7}\right)$$

$$= \log_7 \left(\frac{2}{49} \cdot \frac{7}{2}\right)$$

$$= \log_7 \frac{1}{7}$$

$$= -1$$

$$3 \log_4 \frac{2}{3} + \log_4 27 = \log_4 \left(\frac{2}{3}\right)^3 + \log_4 27$$

$$= \log_4 \frac{8}{27} + \log_4 27$$

$$= \log_4 \left(\frac{8}{27} \cdot 27\right)$$

$$= \log_4 8$$

$$= \frac{3}{2}$$

The rules can also be used to expand the logarithm of complicated expressions involving powers, products, and quotients, as follows:

$$\log_3 \frac{x^2 \sqrt{2x-1}}{(2x+1)^{\frac{3}{2}}} = \log_3 \left(x^2 \sqrt{2x-1}\right) - \log_3 (2x+1)^{\frac{3}{2}}$$

$$= \log_3 \left(x^2\right) + \log_3 \underbrace{\left(\sqrt{2x-1}\right)}_{(2x-1)^{1/2}} - \log_3 (2x+1)^{\frac{3}{2}}$$

$$= 2 \log_3 x + \frac{1}{2} \log_3 (2x-1) - \frac{3}{2} \log_3 (2x+1)$$

Beware of common mistakes involving logarithms!

$$\log_a (M + N) \neq \log_a M + \log_a N$$

$$\log_a (M - N) \neq \log_a M - \log_a N$$

$$\log_a (M + N) \neq \log_a M \cdot \log_a N$$

$$\log_a (M - N) \neq \frac{\log_a M}{\log_a N}$$

The properties are very useful when solving equations involving logarithms. For instance, to solve the equation $\log (x + 2) = 2 + \log (x - 3)$, proceed as follows:

$$\log (x + 2) = 2 + \log (x - 3)$$

$$\log (x + 2) - \log (x - 3) = 2$$

$$\log \left(\frac{x + 2}{x - 3} \right) = 2$$

$$\frac{x + 2}{x - 3} = 10^2$$

$$x + 2 = 100 (x - 3)$$

$$x + 2 = 100x - 300$$

$$302 = 99x$$

$$x = \frac{302}{99}$$

TIP

You must always verify that the *x*-values you arrive at actually satisfy the original equation.

SIMPLE AND COMPOUND INTEREST WITH INVESTMENT APPLICATIONS

When you open a savings account, the two most natural questions to ask are:

- What is the interest rate?
- How often do you compute the interest?

If the interest is computed once at the end of the year, then the interest is characterized as **simple interest**, while it is called **compound interest** if it is computed multiple times per year. The formula for computing such interest is as follows:

$V = A \left(1 + \frac{r}{n} \right)^{nt}$, where V is the future value of the account after t years, A is the amount deposited into the account, r is the annual interest rate, n is the number of times per year interest is computed (4 if quarterly, 12 if monthly, 52 if weekly, etc.), and t is the number of years you continue to reinvest the amount in the account. If $n = 1$ (that is, the simple interest case), then the **interest earned**, I, after t years is given by the formula $I = Art$.

The following are some typical problems involving simple and compound interest:

Problem	Solution
If you deposit $8,000 into a savings account paying 3% annual interest compounded weekly, what will be the value of the account after 5 years?	Use $V = A\left(1+\dfrac{r}{n}\right)^{nt}$ with $A = 8{,}000$, $r = 0.03$, $n = 52$, and $t = 5$. Solve for V. $$V = \$8{,}000\left(1+\frac{0.03}{52}\right)^{52(5)} = \$9{,}294.27$$
What amount of money would you need to deposit in an account today at 4% interest compounded quarterly to have $14,500 in the account after 8 years?	Use $V = A\left(1+\dfrac{r}{n}\right)^{nt}$ with $V = 14{,}500$, $r = 0.04$, $n = 4$, and $t = 8$. Solve for A. $$\$14{,}500 = A\left(1+\frac{0.04}{4}\right)^{4(8)}$$ $$\$14{,}500 \approx A\left(1.37494\right)$$ $$\$10{,}545.90 = A$$
If you deposit $10,000 into an account paying 4% annual interest compounded daily, how many years will it take until the value of the account is $13,500?	Use $V = A\left(1+\dfrac{r}{n}\right)^{nt}$ with $A = 10{,}000$, $r = 0.04$, $n = 365$, and $V = 13{,}500$. Solve for t. $$\$13{,}500 = 10{,}000\left(1+\frac{0.04}{365}\right)^{365t}$$ $$1.35 = \left(1.00011\right)^{365t}$$ $$\log 1.35 = \log\left(1.00011\right)^{365t}$$ $$\log 1.35 = \left(365t\right)\log\left(1.00011\right)$$ $$\frac{\log 1.35}{365\log\left(1.00011\right)} = t$$ $$7.475 \text{ years} \approx t$$

INSTALLMENT BUYING, STUDENT LOANS, AND HOME BUYING

Whenever you take out a loan—whether it is to pay for school, a car, or a house—a critical question is determining the monthly payment of the loan to ensure you have the means to pay it off. This might seem daunting, but the calculation is not bad at all once you are familiar with the financial jargon. Let us review that first and then jump into the computations.

The **cash price** is the amount of the item (school, house, car, etc.) for which you need the loan. The amount you borrow is the **financed amount** and the amount you pay up-front is the **down payment**. Observe that:

$$\text{Financed amount} = \text{cash price} - \text{down payment}$$

You make a down payment as well as fixed monthly payments for a certain number of months. The sum of these is the amount you pay all told and is called the **total installment price**. The total interest that you pay once all is said and done is the **finance charge**. Observe that:

$$\text{Finance charge} = \text{total installment price} - \text{cash price}$$

The formula $A = \left(1 - \dfrac{1}{(1+i)^n}\right) \times \dfrac{R}{i}$, where A is the amount of the loan, R is the monthly payment, i is the monthly interest rate (= annual interest rate divided by 12), and n is the total number of payments, is used to determine the amount of the loan.

The following is a typical problem involving installment buying:

Problem	Solution
Suppose you purchase a car for $19,500 with a $2,000 down payment at a monthly interest rate of 1.35% for 60 months. What is the monthly payment and what are the total finance charges?	First, use $A = \left(1 - \dfrac{1}{(1+i)^n}\right) \times \dfrac{R}{i}$ with $A = \$19,500 - \$2,000 = \$17,500$, $i = 0.0135$, and $n = 60$. Solve for R: $$A = \left(1 - \frac{1}{(1+i)^n}\right) \times \frac{R}{i}$$ $$17,500 = \left(1 - \frac{1}{(1+0.0135)^{60}}\right) \times \frac{R}{0.0135}$$ $$17,500 \approx 40.94R$$ $$R \approx \$427.46$$ Next, note that the total installment price is ($427.46)(60) + ($2,000) = $27,647.60. Hence, the finance charge is $27,647.60 − $19,500 = $8,147.60.

TIP

Around 20 percent of the questions on the DSST Math for Liberal Arts exam will test your knowledge of counting, probability theory, and statistics.

COUNTING, PROBABILITY THEORY, AND STATISTICS

This final section is devoted to reviewing some concepts of elementary probability and basic statistics.

PERMUTATIONS AND COMBINATIONS

There are two systematic ways of counting: permutations and combinations. To begin, a **permutation** of a set of objects is an arrangement of those objects in which each object is used only once and the order in which they are arranged matters. For example, if you have objects labeled A, B, C, and D, both ABCD and DACB are permutations of these objects. Any ordering of the letters produces another permutation. The number of ways to arrange n objects in such a manner is $n!$, where $n! = n \times (n-1) \times (n-2) \times \ldots \times 3 \times 2 \times 1$. (For example, $5! = 5 \times 4 \times 3 \times 2 \times 1$.) Sometimes, we want to only arrange a subset of the objects in set; that is, what if we had n letters but we only wanted to arrange k ($< n$) of them? This is "a permutation of n objects taken k at a time." The number of such arrangements is $P(n, k) = \dfrac{n!}{(n-k)!}$.

The order in which objects are arranged is not always relevant, like when forming a committee of 4 people from a group of 10 people in which all committee members are equally influential in the work being performed, or when simply selecting 4 cards randomly from a standard deck of 52 cards. To determine the number of such selections, we use a **combination**. The "number of combinations of n objects taken k at a time" in which order does NOT matter is computed using the formula $C(n, k) = \dfrac{n!}{k!(n-k)!}$.

For example, let's say a couple wants to try new recipes part of the Paleo diet. They have gathered 15 recipes and want to make 3 for the upcoming week. They like them all equally well so they put them in a box and choose 3 randomly. The number of ways they can make such a selection is $C(15,3)$, since the order in which the recipes are arranged is not relevant.

FUNDAMENTALS OF PROBABILITY

The notion of **chance** pervades real-life. The likelihood of rain, the chance you will win the lottery, how likely is it for a receiver to score a touchdown, etc., are all applications of probability. Addressing these questions requires we establish a method for measuring likelihood. To begin, let us introduce some terminology.

An **outcome** is the result of a single trial of a probability experiment. The collection of all outcomes of an experiment is a set called the **sample space S**. For instance, if you roll an eight-sided die (with faces labeled 1, 2, 3, 4, 5, 6, 7, and 8) and record the number of the face on which it comes to rest, the outcomes of the experiment are simply the labels on the faces. So, $S = \{1, 2, 3, 4, 5, 6, 7, 8\}$. An **event** is a subset of the sample space and is usually described by one or more conditions. For instance, the event E that "the die lands on an odd number" is the subset $E = \{1, 3, 5, 7\}$.

The **probability** of an event E, denoted $P(E)$, is a number between 0 and 1, inclusive, that measures the percent chance of the occurrence of event E. How is this number computed? For most experiments you will encounter, each outcome in the sample space is *equally likely*. So, if the sample space contains N outcomes, then the probability of any *one* of them occurring is $\frac{1}{N}$. More generally, if

event E contains k elements, then $P(E) = \dfrac{\text{Number of outcomes in } A}{\text{Number of possible outcomes}} = \dfrac{k}{N}$.

Let's revisit the Paleo diet example. Suppose 4 of the recipes contain quinoa and the couple wants to know the probability that the 3 recipes they select at random all contain quinoa. To compute this probability, first note that the total number of possible outcomes is $C(15,3)$. Also, there are $C(4,3)$ ways of selecting 3 recipes from the 4 quinoa recipes in the collection. Combining these two pieces of information, we conclude:

$$P(\text{all 3 recipes contain quinoa}) = \frac{C(4,3)}{C(15,3)}$$

Sometimes, data from an experiment, like the results of a survey, is in the form of **frequencies**. For instance, say you ask 400 randomly chosen people a series of 10 questions for which each question has 7 possible outcomes. For each question, you would tabulate the frequencies, or number of responses, for each of the 7 choices and divide each by the total number of responses, or 400; the decimals obtained are called **relative frequencies**. They can be used to make educated guesses about how the entire population from which the respondents were chosen would answer such questions.

You have likely heard the question, "What are the *odds* of that event happening?" While it is intuitive that this should be related to computing the probability of the event happening, the manner the **odds** of an event occurring is reported is different. Specifically, the odds of event E occurring $= \dfrac{P(E)}{1 - P(E)}$.

So, this is really the ratio, "probability that E occurs *to* probability that E does not occur." As such, the odds of E occurring are often written as $P(E) : (1 - P(E))$. Referring to the Paleo diet example, the odds that all three recipes chosen contain quinoa are $\dfrac{C(4,3)}{C(15,3)} : 1 - \dfrac{C(4,3)}{C(15,3)}$.

COMPOUND EVENTS

Suppose E and F are events of a probability experiment. Three common **compound events** that can be formed using E and F are as follows:

Event	Description (In Words)
Complement of E	All outcomes NOT in E
E or F	All outcomes in E or in F or in both
E and F	All outcomes in common to E and F

Two events are **mutually exclusive** if they do not share any outcomes.

When computing the probability of the event E or F, we must make certain not to count the outcomes common to both E and F twice. The **addition formula** comes to the rescue:

$$P(E \text{ or } F) = P(E) + P(F) - P(E \text{ and } F)$$

When E and F are mutually exclusive, $P(E \text{ and } F) = 0$ and so this formula simplifies to $P(E \text{ or } F) = P(E) + P(F)$.

For instance, suppose a children's cereal manufacturer has decided to include two different types of special codes in some of the boxes of cereal it produces for the next three months. The codes can be redeemed online for special prizes. One type of code is included in 10% of all boxes of cereal produced and the second type of code is included in 0.5% of all boxes of cereal produced. Finally, 0.003% of the cereal boxes include *both* types of codes. If a box of cereal is purchased, what is the probability that the box will include at least one type of code?

To answer this question, first note that the event "box contains at least one type of code" represents the event that the box contains the first type of code, the second type of code, or BOTH. So, P("box contains at least one type of code") = P(contains first code OR second code).

Applying the addition rule yields:

$$P(\text{first code OR second code}) = P(\text{first code}) + P(\text{second code}) - P(\text{first AND second code}) = 0.10 + 0.05 - 0.003 = 0.147$$

CONDITIONAL PROBABILITY

Suppose that when computing the probability of an event, you are given an extra piece of information that enables you to restrict your attention to a portion of the sample space. This would impact the probability calculation because the number of possible outcomes has been reduced. A probability like this, where you are given an extra piece of information, is known as a **conditional probability**.

This type of problem occurs on the DSST exam in the form of using a so-called **two-way table**. For example, the table below shows the distribution by gender of 200 voters polled and their answers to the question, "Do you prefer a candidate for mayor who prioritizes education reform primarily, or one who prioritizes controlling urban violence?"

	Preference of Candidate's Top Priority		
	Education Reform	Controlling Urban Violence	TOTAL
Male	45	30	75
Female	60	65	125
TOTAL	105	95	200

Suppose a voter is selected at random from this sample. Depending on the nature of the event for which the probability is sought, the data is used in different ways.

The following are some common questions that can be asked:

Problem	Solution
What is the probability that the voter is male and prefers a candidate who prioritizes controlling urban violence?	**Identify the event:** "male AND urban violence" **Compute probability:** Use only one cell in the table: the one with the entry "30." The probability is $\frac{30}{200} = 0.15$.
What is the probability that the voter is either female or prefers a candidate who prioritizes education?	**Identify the event:** "female OR education" **Compute the probability:** This time, you must use the addition formula: P(female OR education) = P(female) + P(education) − P(female AND education). Using the second row yields P(female) = $\frac{125}{200}$. Using the first column yields P(education) = $\frac{105}{200}$ Using the second cell in the first column yields P(female AND education) = $\frac{60}{200}$ So, P(female OR education) = $\frac{125}{200} + \frac{105}{200} - \frac{60}{200} = \frac{170}{200} = 0.85$.
What is the probability that the voter prefers a candidate who priorities controlling urban violence *given that* the voter is male?	**Identify the event:** This requires computing a conditional probability. The key phrase that tells us this is "given that." **Compute the probability:** The "given that" portion, namely "voter is male," tells us to restrict our attention to the first row of the table. This means we only have 75 outcomes to consider rather than the whole 200. Next, *of these* 75, the number preferring a candidate who prioritizes controlling urban violence is 30. So, the probability is $\frac{30}{75} = 0.4$.

TIP

Be very careful to use the "given that" information to restrict your attention in the table to the appropriate row or column.

TIP

If zero is among the values you included in the sum, you MUST include that value (however many times it occurs) in the total count by which you divide; otherwise, you haven't accounted for its effect on the average.

DESCRIPTIVE STATISTICS

Once data is collected, the next step is to understand the information it conveys. A first line of attack in this regard is using **descriptive statistics**. This includes a set of measures that tell us something about the data.

The **mean** of a numerical data set is the usual arithmetic average of the data values. Just sum the values and divide by *the total number of values* you added.

This measure gives a good idea about the **center** of the data set when there are no **extreme values**, or values that are vastly different from the bulk of the data. But, in a data set like {20, 20, 20, 20, 90}, it is reasonable to think that the "average value" should be 20 since 4 of the 5 values are 20; however, the arithmetic average, or mean, is 34, which is not a good descriptor of the center of this data set! For such a situation, we need a different way of computing "average" or center.

The **median** is another way of computing the center of a data set that is not impacted by the effects of extreme values. To compute the median, arrange the values in the data set from smallest to largest. If there is an odd number of data values, then the median is the data value in the middle of the set. For instance, if there are 29 data values arranged in numerical order, the median is the value in the 15th position (obtained by dividing 29 by 2 and adding 1 to the whole part). If there is an even number of data values, then the median is the arithmetic average of the "middle two" values. For instance, if there are 40 data values arranged in numerical order, then median is the average of the values in the 20th and 21th positions. By definition, half of the data values lie to the left of the median and half lie to its right.

The mean and median are only defined for data sets of numerical values. If the data is **qualitative** in nature (e.g., favorite novel, movie genre preference), then there is no average value. But, we *can* determine which value occurs most often in a data set; this is called the **mode**. For instance, the mode of the data set {horror, comedy, comedy, drama, comedy, horror} is comedy. There can be two values that occur the same number of times and for which this is the greatest frequency; such a data set is **bimodal**. For example, the modes of the data set {7, 9, 7, 7, 2, 4, 9, 9, 3, 4} are 7 and 9. If all values of a data set occur the same number of times, then there is *no mode*.

The above three measures provide no indication as to how the data is **spread out**. For instance, the data sets {20, 20, 20, 20, 20, 20} and {16, 16, 16, 24, 24, 24} both have a mean of 20, but are *very* different. To distinguish between such data sets, there are two commonly used **measures of variability**: standard deviation and interquartile range.

The **standard deviation**, *s*, is generally used for data sets for which the mean is a good description of its center. This is a measure of the *typical distance* between data values and the mean. The formula for the standard deviation for a data set containing *n* data values is as follows:

$$s = \sqrt{\frac{\sum (x - \text{mean})^2}{n-1}}$$

Here, x represents a data value. You will not need to compute this for a complicated data set, but you should know that the larger the s value, the more spread out the data.

The **interquartile range**, IQR, is generally used with data sets for which the median best describes the center. This is a measure of the spread of the middle 50% of the data set. To compute the IQR, we must determine the **quartiles,** or data values in the 25th, 50th, and 75th positions in the data set whose values have been arranged from least to greatest. The 2nd quartile is the median. To find the 1st quartile, divide the number of values in the data set by 4. The resulting number is the position of the 1st quartile; to get the value, locate the data value with the position at the *whole* portion of this quotient. The position of the 3rd quartile is obtained by multiplying the position of the 1st quartile by 3; its value is determined in a manner like the 1st quartile.

Finally, the **range** of a data set gives an idea of the overall span of the data values. It is computed by subtracting the smallest data value from the largest one.

VISUAL STATISTICS

There are many different types of graphs used to visualize a data set. Let's briefly explore each one below.

A **bar graph** (or **frequency histogram**) is arguably the most basic way of visualizing data; bars of different heights are used to display the frequency of a collection of categories. A **relative frequency histogram** is obtained from a bar graph by simply dividing each bar height by the sum of *all* bar heights of which the graph is composed. So, the height of each bar now represents the percentage of the whole that the bar contributes. Hence, each bar height can be interpreted as the probability that the category would be chosen if a choice were made at random. Whenever the shape of the histogram peaks in the middle and falls symmetrically to the left and right, the mean and median are approximately equal. When it is not symmetric, the mean is pulled toward the tail of the histogram since outliers affect it.

For example, suppose there are 6 candidates vying for the position of student government treasurer. At the beginning of the campaigning period, 50 students are randomly chosen and asked to indicate their top candidate based on information available at that moment in time.

The results are as follows:

Frequency		Relative Frequency	
Candidate	Frequency	Candidate	Frequency
A	6	A	0.12
B	11	B	0.22
C	2	C	0.04
D	8	D	0.16
E	15	E	0.30
F	8	F	0.16

Relative Frequency Histogram

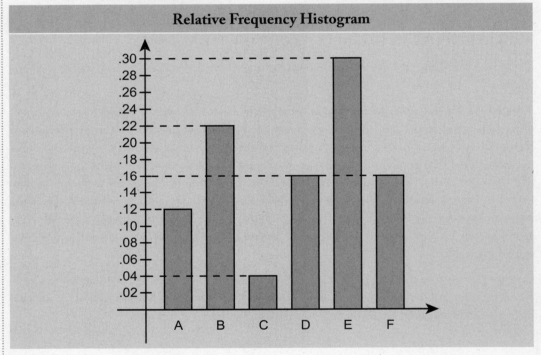

Some questions that could be asked are as follows:

- What is the probability that a randomly selected student favors candidate A? (Answer: 0.12)

- What is the probability that a randomly selected student favors either candidate B or D? (Answer: 0.22 + 0.16 = 0.48)

- What is the probability that a randomly selected student does not favor candidate E? (Answer: 1 – 0.30 = 0.70)

A **pie chart** is a circular graph that is divided into pie-shaped wedges, each representing a percentage of the entire circle. Interpreting the relative frequencies in the above example as percentages, we can form a pie chart to illustrate the data as follows:

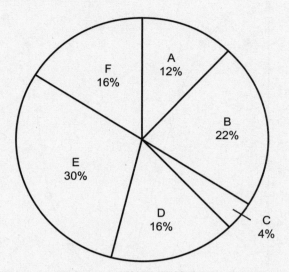

A **dot plot** is a quickly formed bar graph useful for displaying and visualizing small data sets. You decide on a scale and then put a dot above each value along the x-axis; multiple occurrences of values in a data set are represented by stacked dots above that value on the x-axis. For instance, consider the following example:

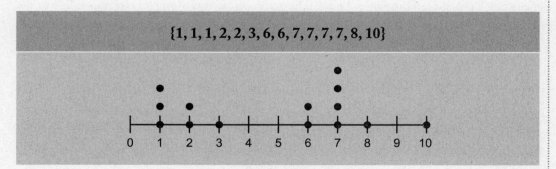

A **line graph** is a graph that consists of a sequence of data points, typically generated in some order dictated by the numerical scale along the x-axis (e.g., time, length, weight, cost), connected by straight line segments. A **trend** is sought in the ebb and flow of the data point heights as a function of the x-axis variable.

For example, a small company logs the number of bags of deer corn (in hundreds) it sells monthly. Its findings are illustrated in the following line graph:

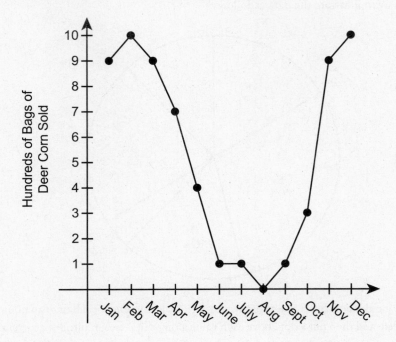

A **box plot** is a way to visualize a numerical data set using five statistics: minimum value, 1st quartile, median, 3rd quartile, and maximum value. The graph consists of two points corresponding to the smallest and largest values in the data set, and three vertical line segments corresponding to the quartiles and median. A box is constructed with the quartiles as two parallel sides, and horizontal line segments are drawn from these two sides to the minimum and maximum values.

For instance, consider the following example:

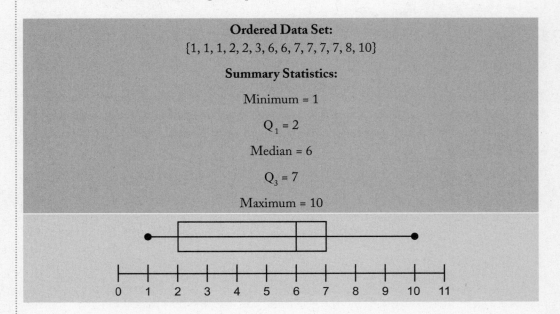

Ordered Data Set:
{1, 1, 1, 2, 2, 3, 6, 6, 7, 7, 7, 7, 8, 10}

Summary Statistics:

Minimum = 1

$Q_1 = 2$

Median = 6

$Q_3 = 7$

Maximum = 10

Rather than eyeballing them, outliers in a data set can be detected using the IQR. Here, IQR = 7 − 2 = 5. An **outlier** is a data value that is *less than* $Q_1 − 1.5 \times IQR$ or *larger than* $Q_3 + 1.5 \times IQR$. For the above example, any value less than 2 − 1.5(5) = −5.5 or greater than 7 + 1.5(5) = 14.5 is an outlier. So, there are no outliers present.

A **scatterplot** is a way of representing data sets consisting of ordered pairs (x, y) on a coordinate plane in order to find the relationship between x and y. The more tightly packed the points are in a scatterplot, the stronger the relationship. If the data points rise from left to right, we say the relationship is *positive,* while if they fall from left to right, we say the trend is *negative.* For example, medical records for a large sample of patients from the past year who were seen for complications due to influenza were used to determine if there might be a relationship between the duration of the flu symptoms and the patient's weight.

The following is a scatterplot illustrating this data:

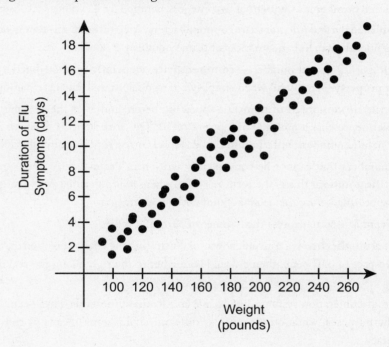

Judging from the data, it is reasonable to suspect there is a relationship between weight and duration of flu symptoms—the higher the weight, the longer it seems to take for the flu symptoms to dissipate.

SUMMING IT UP

- The set of **natural numbers** consists of the numbers 1, 2, 3, 4 … A natural number other than 1 is **prime** if it can only be written as a product of itself and 1; otherwise, it is **composite.** The **GCF** of two natural numbers x and y is the *largest* natural number that is a factor of both x and y; the **LCM** of x and y is the *smallest* natural number that is a multiple of both x and y.

- The set of integers is $\{\dots, -3, -2, -1, 0, 1, 2, 3\dots\}$. An even number can be written as $2n$, where n is an integer; an odd number can be written as $2n + 1$, where n is an integer.

- If b and n are natural numbers, then $b^n = \underbrace{b \times \dots \times b}_{n \text{ times}}$. Suppose that $a, b, m,$ and n are all real numbers. There are several rules governing how to work with expressions with exponents.

- A **rational number** is a quotient of two integers, denoted by $\frac{a}{b}$, where $b \neq 0$. Such a fraction is **simplified** if a and b do not share common factors. An **irrational number** is a real number that is not rational, like square roots of prime numbers, π, and e.

- The properties of real numbers—**commutativity**, **associativity**, **distributivity**, and **zero factor property**—are useful when simplifying expressions and solving equations.

- Decimals are comprised of numerals appearing before and after the decimal point, each of which represents a multiple of a power of 10. The arithmetic of decimals is the same as for natural numbers with the additional step of correctly positioning the decimal point.

- Real numbers that cannot be conveniently written in decimal form are expressed using **scientific notation**: this is the form $m \times 10^n$, where m is a decimal with a single nonzero digit appearing before the decimal point and n is an integer.

- A **percent** is used to express the number of *parts* of a *whole*.

- The **real number line** is a convenient way of illustrating the relative position of real numbers with respect to 0. If $p < q$, then q would be further to the right along the real number line than p.

- Different numeration systems, like **base 2** and **Roman numerals**, have been designed for specific purposes, while others arose as different civilizations' means of communicating numeracy.

- A **logical** statement is a declarative sentence that is *either* true *or* false. It cannot be neither true nor false and it cannot be both true and false. An **open sentence** is any declarative sentence that contains one or more variables. We could ask whether there is some value of the variable for which the statement is true, or whether it is true for all possible values of the variable. This is called **quantifying** the open sentence.

- The truth of any statement is denied by asserting the truth of its **negation**.

- Complex statements can be formed by connecting statements by means of certain words such as *and, or, if … then* called **logical connectives.** Such statements are called **compound statements**.

- The **disjunction** $p \lor q$ is true whenever *at least one* of p, q is true; it is false only when both are false.

- The **conjunction** $p \wedge q$ is true whenever *both* p, q are true; it is false otherwise.

- Compound statements involving one or more constituents $p, q, r \ldots$, are **logically equivalent** provided they have the same truth value for every possible truth assignment to their constituent parts.

- An assertion of the form "if p, then q" (denoted $p \Rightarrow q$) is an **implication**. The statement p is called the **hypothesis** and the statement q is called the **conclusion**. The negation of an implication, $\sim (p \Rightarrow q)$, is logically equivalent to $p \Rightarrow \sim q$.

- A statement of the form "p if and only if q" is called a **biconditional** and is denoted "$p \Leftrightarrow q$."

- **De Morgan's laws** are used to negate disjunctions and conjunctions.

- Given the conditional $p \Rightarrow q$, the **contrapositive** is the conditional $\sim q \Rightarrow \sim p$, and the **converse** is the conditional $q \Rightarrow p$.

- **Proving** a statement is often done by stringing together implications and using the fact that $[(p \Rightarrow r) \wedge (r \Rightarrow q)]$ is logically equivalent to $p \Rightarrow q$.

- A **syllogism** is a collection of statements followed by a conclusion. It is **valid** if whenever the syllogism is true, the conclusion is true. A pictorial way of determining if a syllogism is valid is by using an **Euler diagram**.

- A **set** is a collection of objects, or **elements**. If $P(x)$ is an open sentence and if A is the set of all objects satisfying $P(x)$, then using **set-builder notation**, we write $A = \{x: P(x)\}$.

- An underlying set that contains all possible elements that any of our sets in the discussion can contain is the **universal set**. A is a **subset** of B and written as $A \subseteq B$ if $x \in A \Rightarrow x \in B$.

- The **complement** of a set A is $\{x: x \in U \text{ and } x \notin A\}$.

- The **union** $A \cup B$ is the set $\{x \in U: x \in A \text{ or } x \in B\}$.

- The **intersection** $A \cap B$ is the set $\{x \in U: x \in A \text{ and } x \in B\}$.

- Different **units of measurement** are used to quantify different types of quantities, like time, speed, liquid measures, length, area, and volume. The **metric system** is based on powers of 10.

- Performing conversions of units of length, area, or volume in the metric system are simple matters of moving the decimal point. **Converting units** in the U.S. customary system is slightly more involved only because the units are not based on powers of 10. The key is to set up products of fractions that show the original units canceling and the new units remaining in the final product.

- The triangle **inequality** says that the sum of the lengths of any two sides of a triangle must be strictly larger than the length of the third side. It is impossible to construct a triangle that does not satisfy *both* conditions.

- The **triangle sum rule** says that the sum of the measures of the three angles in any triangle must be 180º.

- If the legs of a right triangle are a and b and the **hypotenuse** (side opposite the right angle) is c, then the **Pythagorean theorem** says $a^2 + b^2 = c^2$.

- The **perimeter** of a region in the plane is the "distance around."

- The **area** of a region in the plane is the number of *unit squares* needed to cover it.

- To compute the **surface area** of a solid, the solid is dissected and flattened out so that it can be visualized as a combination of recognizable figures whose areas can be computed using known formulas.

- The **volume** of a solid in space is the number of *unit cubes* needed to fill it.

- A set of rules called the **order of operations** is used to simplify an arithmetic expression involving all types of real numbers and operations.

- A **ratio** is a comparison of a positive quantity x to another positive quantity y expressed as a fraction $\frac{x}{y}$ or using the notation $x : y$.

- A **proportion** is an equation relating two ratios; it is expressed by equating two fractions.

- The **graph of an equation of two variables** is the collection of all ordered pairs (x, y) in the xy-coordinate plane that satisfy the equation; that is, when the respective values for x and y are substituted into the equation, the result is a true statement.

- A **function** f is a rule that assigns to each element x in one set A exactly one element y, denoted $f(x)$, in another set B. To compute the functional value, substitute the given value in for the variable and simplify the resulting arithmetic expression using the rules of arithmetic.

- The **slope**, m, of the line is defined to be $m = \frac{y_2 - y_1}{x_2 - x_1}$ and is an indication of the steepness of the line. The **slope-intercept form** of the equation of a line is $y = mx + b$, where m is the slope of the line and b is the y-coordinate of its y-intercept.

- **Solving linear equations** involves simplifying various expressions using the order of operations, together with the distributive property of multiplication, to isolate the variable on one side of the equation. You must **balance** both sides of the equations.

- Two or more equations considered simultaneously form a **system** of equations. The methods of **elimination**, **substitution**, and **graphing** can be used to solve systems.

- To determine the solution set of a **linear inequality in two variables**, start by graphing the line (dotted if the inequality sign is > or <, and solid otherwise). Choose a point either above or below the line and see if it satisfies the inequality. If it does, then shade the entire region containing that point on that side of the line; otherwise, shade the entire region on the other side.

- Solving a **system of two linear inequalities in two variables** involves sketching the solution set of each inequality separately, but on the same set of axes. The overlap of the two regions is where both inequalities hold simultaneously and so, is the solution of the system.

- Functions of the form $f(x) = A \cdot b^x$, where A is a nonzero real number and b is a positive real number not equal to 1, are called **exponential functions**. The **inverse function** (that is, the function obtained by reflecting a given function's graph over the $y = x$ line) of $f(x) = b^x$, $b > 1$, is a function called a **logarithmic function**, denoted as $g(x) = \log_b x$, where b is the **base**.

- $\log_a b = c$ whenever $a^c = b$. There are three main **logarithm rules** used for simplifying expressions involving the logarithms of powers, products, and quotients.

- When you open a savings account that earns interest, if the interest is computed once at the end of the year, then the interest is characterized as **simple interest**, while it is called **compound interest** if it is computed multiple times per year.

- When taking out a loan, the **cash price** is the amount of the item for which you need the loan. The amount you borrow is the **financed amount** and the amount you pay upfront is the **down payment**. You make a down payment, as well as fixed monthly payments for a certain number of months. The sum of these is the amount you pay all told and is called the **total installment price**.

- A **permutation** of a set of objects is an arrangement of those objects in which each object is used only once and the order in which they are arranged matters. The number of distinct ways in which k of n letters can be arranged in order is $P(n, k) = \dfrac{n!}{(n-k)!}$.

- The number of **combinations of n objects taken k at a time** where order does not matter is $C(n, k) = \dfrac{n!}{k!(n-k)!}$.

- An **outcome** is the result of a single trial of a probability experiment. The collection of all outcomes of an experiment is a set called the **sample space** S. An **event** is a subset of the sample space and is usually described by one or more conditions. The **probability** of an event E, denoted $P(E)$, is a number between 0 and 1, inclusive, that measures the percent chance of the occurrence of event E.

- The **addition formula** is $P(E \text{ or } F) = P(E) + P(F) - P(E \text{ and } F)$.

- Suppose that when computing the probability of an event, you are given an extra piece of information that enables you to restrict your attention to a portion of the sample space. A probability like this is a **conditional probability**.

- The **mean** of a numerical data set is the usual arithmetic average of the data values. The **median** of a data set is a number for which half of the data values lie to its left and half lie to its right. The **mode** is the value in a data set that occurs most frequently. There can be two values that occur the same number of times and for which this is the greatest frequency; such a data set is **bimodal**.

- The **standard deviation** is a measure of the *typical distance* between data values and the mean.

- The **interquartile range (IQR)** is the difference of the 1st and 3rd quartiles.

- A **relative frequency histogram** is obtained from a bar graph by simply dividing each bar height by the sum of *all* bar heights of which the graph is composed.

- A **pie chart** is a circular graph that is divided into pie-shaped wedges, each of which represents a percentage of the entire circle.

- A **dot plot** is a useful for displaying and visualizing small data sets.

- A **line graph** is a graph that consists of a sequence of data points, typically generated in some order dictated by the numerical scale along the x-axis (e.g., time, length, weight, cost), connected by straight line segments.

- A **box plot** is a way to visualize a numerical data set using five statistics: minimum value, 1st quartile, median, 3rd quartile, and maximum value. An **outlier** is a data value that *is less than $Q_1 - 1.5{*}IQR$ or larger than $Q_3 + 1.5{*}IQR$*.

- A **scatterplot** is a way of representing data sets consisting of ordered pairs (x, y) on a coordinate plane. The more tightly packed the points are in a scatterplot, the stronger the relationship. If the data points rise from left to right, we say the relationship is **positive**; if they fall from left to right, we say the trend is **negative**.

MATH FOR LIBERAL ARTS POST-TEST

Directions: Carefully read each of the following 60 questions. Choose the best answer to each question and fill in the corresponding circle on the answer sheet. The Answer Key and Explanations can be found following this post-test.

1. Determine the GCF and LCM of the set of whole numbers {171, 54, 12}.
   A. GCF = 1; LCM = 2,052
   B. GCF = 2; LCM = 360
   C. GCF = 3; LCM = 360
   D. GCF = 3; LCM = 2,052

2. What is one-fourth of 2^6?
   A. 1^4
   B. 2^4
   C. 2^3
   D. 2^8

3. An Olympic diver performs a dive from a 20-foot high springboard; the parabola below illustrates the trajectory of her dive:

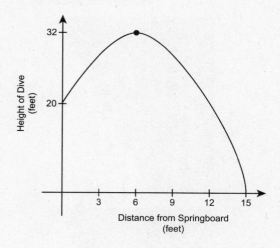

   What is the maximum height of the dive?
   A. 6 feet
   B. 15 feet
   C. 20 feet
   D. 32 feet

4. Which Euler diagram accurately depicts the following syllogism:

   Some investments are risky.

   College education is an investment.

   Therefore, college education is risky.

   A.
   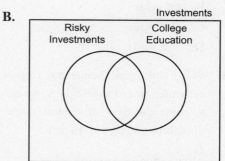

   B.
   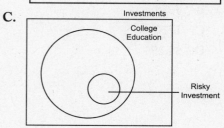

   C.
   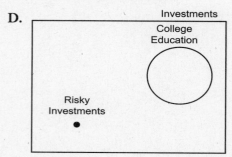

   D.

5. Suppose that ln 3 = *a* and ln 7 = *b*. Which of the following is equal to ln 63?
   A. 2*a* + 2*b*
   B. 4*b*
   C. 2*ab*
   D. 2*a* + *b*

6. The winner of a semi-annual raffle will receive a paid vacation to the Turks and Caicos Islands. If 10,000 raffle tickets were sold and Henry purchased 40 tickets, what are the odds against him winning the vacation?
   A. 40 to 10,000
   B. 10,000 to 40
   C. 40 to 9,960
   D. 9,960 to 40

7. What is the distance, in yards, around a circle with a diameter 18 feet?
   A. 3π yards
   B. 6π yards
   C. 18π yards
   D. 36π yards

8. What is the cost (before tax) to purchase carpeting, priced at $8.50 per square yard, to cover the floor of a guest room with dimensions 15 feet by 18 feet?
   A. $33
   B. $255
   C. $270
   D. $2,295

9. Which of the following is the solution set of the linear inequality 4*x* < 6 + 2*y*?

   A.

   B.

   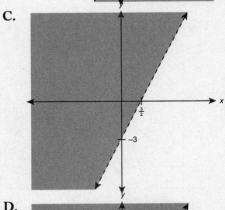

   C.

   D.

   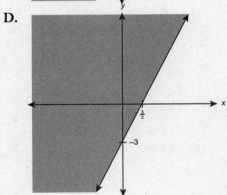

10. To which of the following is the expression
$\dfrac{-12z^3x^9}{3x^3z^3}$ equivalent?

    A. $-9x^6$

    B. $-4x^6$

    C. $-9x^3$

    D. $-4x^3z$

11. Which property of real numbers does the following illustrate?

    $2.3(1.2) - 2.3(3.4) = 2.3(1.2 - 3.4)$

    A. Distributive property

    B. Commutative property

    C. Associative property

    D. Identity

12. What is the range of the data set {4, 4, 4, 17, 26, 26, 26}?

    A. 4

    B. 17

    C. 22

    D. 26

13. In a fantasy novel, a sorcerer found a magic stone whose powers decreased in intensity every day. The table below shows the percent-strength of the magic retained by the stone at midnight on several successive days:

Day	Percent-strength of Magic Retained by Stone
1	100%
2	50%
3	25%
4	12.5%

What is the approximate percent-strength of magic retained in the stone on day 7?

    A. 0.0078%

    B. 0.78%

    C. 1.56%

    D. 3.125%

14. What is the product of (4.6×10^3), (6.0×10^{-2}), and (2.0×10^5), expressed using scientific notation?

    A. 5.52×10^7

    B. 5.52×10^{10}

    C. 55,200,000

    D. 552,000,000

15. Gina bought her spouse a new watch for his birthday. It comes in a box whose dimensions are 2 inches by 3 inches by 4 inches. How many square inches of wrapping paper does she need to wrap the entire box?

    A. 9

    B. 24

    C. 26

    D. 52

16. Find a rational number and an irrational number between $\dfrac{1}{31}$ and $\dfrac{1}{32}$.

    A. Rational number = $\dfrac{63}{1,984}$; irrational number = $\dfrac{1}{10\pi}$

    B. Rational number = $\dfrac{1}{33}$; irrational number = $\dfrac{1}{10e}$

    C. Rational number = $\dfrac{63}{992}$; irrational number = $\dfrac{1}{\pi}$

    D. Rational number = $\dfrac{1}{30}$; irrational number = $\dfrac{1}{\sqrt{31}}$

post-test

17. You have invested a certain amount of money in an account that pays 6% interest compounded monthly. Three years later, your investment was worth $31,000. Which of the following equations is used to describe this investment?

A. $V = 31,000(1 + 0.0005)^{36}$

B. $V = 31,000(1 + 0.05)^{12}$

C. $V = \dfrac{31,000}{(1 + 0.05)^{12}}$

D. $V = \dfrac{31,000}{(1 + 0.005)^{36}}$

18. What type of triangle would have two angles with measures 20° and 80°?

A. Equilateral

B. Scalene

C. Right

D. Isosceles

19. To which of the following equations is $\log_4 z = 2$ equivalent?

A. $z^2 = 4$

B. $2^4 = z$

C. $4^2 = z$

D. $4^z = 2$

20. Consider the Venn diagram pictured below—assume no region is empty:

Which of the following statements is **false**?

A. All members of the set B are also members of set A.

B. Set B and set C are disjoint.

C. Set B is a subset of $A \cup C$.

D. $A \cap C = \varnothing$.

21. Nicole's quiz scores in trigonometry are: 97, 90, 69, 85, 78, 76, 76, 63, 81, 94, 89

Which of the following expresses an accurate relationship between pairs of measures of central tendency?

A. median = mean

B. mode > median

C. mean > mode

D. median > mean

22. Express the following as a decimal: $5 \times 10^3 + 9 \times 10^0 + 6 \times 10^{-2} + 8 \times 10^{-3}$.

A. 5,009.068

B. 5,900.068

C. 5,090.68

D. 5,009.68

23. To which of the following sets is $\{x|\ x$ is an integer multiple of 4$\}$ equivalent?

A. $\{0, 4, 8, 12, \ldots\}$

B. $\{4, 8, 12, \ldots\}$

C. $\{\ldots, -12, -8, -4, 0, 4, 8, 12, \ldots\}$

D. $\{\ldots, -12, -8, -4, 4, 8, 12, \ldots\}$

24. The faces of a fair 6-sided die are labeled as A, C, ←, →, ↑, and ↓. If the die is rolled once, which of the following outcomes is the *least* likely to occur?

A. Rolling an arrow

B. Rolling an A or C

C. Not rolling an arrow

D. Rolling an arrow pointing left

25. Which statement could be inserted in the blank so that the conclusion to the following symbolic argument is valid?

$$p \Rightarrow q$$
$$q \Rightarrow r$$
$$\boxed{}$$

   A. $q \Rightarrow p$

   B. $p \Rightarrow r$

   C. p

   D. $\sim p$

26. A common velocity formula is $v = \frac{1}{2}g\,t^2$, where v is velocity, t is time, and g is gravity. Which of the following correctly expresses g in terms of v and t?

   A. $g = \frac{2v}{t^2}$

   B. $g = 2vt^2$

   C. $g = \frac{2v}{t}$

   D. $g = \frac{v}{2t^2}$

27. How many different four-letter arrangements are possible using the letters S, P, R, I, N, G if each letter can be used only once?

   A. 15

   B. 24

   C. 360

   D. 720

28. Michelle is purchasing a time-share condominium for $100,000. She can secure a loan for 95% of the purchase price at 8% interest for a 25-year term. What would be the amount of her monthly payments under these terms?

   A. $557.40

   B. $586.73

   C. $733.23

   D. $771.82

29. Lucas jogged 150 meters in 1.5 minutes. What is his speed in meters per hour?

   A. 6 meters per hour

   B. 60 meters per hour

   C. 100 meters per hour

   D. 6,000 meters per hour

post-test

30. The gas tank of an SUV holds 18 gallons of gasoline. When pulling a horse trailer, the SUV travels 100 miles on 3 gallons of gas. Assuming the gas tank is full at the start of the trip, which of the following graphs represents the amount of gas in the tank as a function of the number of miles traveled?

A.

B.

C.

D.

31. The value of a jeep purchased for $20,000 decreases at a rate of 12% annually. What is the value of the car at the end of three years, rounded to the nearest dollar?

A. $28,099

B. $17,600

C. $13,629

D. $12,800

32. An upstart cupcake company conducts a survey at a local mall to determine 300 shoppers' preferences for pistachio, lemon, and chocolate chip cupcakes. The number of shoppers who indicate they like each type of cupcake are indicated in the following Venn diagram:

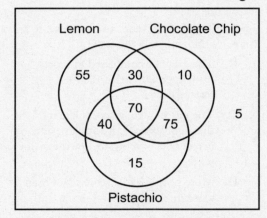

How many shoppers like chocolate chip or pistachio cupcakes, but not lemon?

A. 100

B. 105

C. 240

D. 245

33. Which of the following correctly completes this truth table?

p	q	$\sim p$	$\sim q$	$\sim p \vee \sim q$
T	T			
T	F			
F	T			
F	F			

A.

p	q	$\sim p$	$\sim q$	$\sim p \vee \sim q$
T	T	F	F	F
T	F	F	F	T
F	T	T	T	T
F	F	T	F	T

B.

p	q	$\sim p$	$\sim q$	$\sim p \vee \sim q$
T	T	F	F	F
T	F	F	T	T
F	T	T	F	T
F	F	T	T	T

C.

p	q	$\sim p$	$\sim q$	$\sim p \vee \sim q$
T	T	F	F	T
T	F	F	T	F
F	T	T	F	F
F	F	T	T	F

D.

p	q	$\sim p$	$\sim q$	$\sim p \vee \sim q$
T	T	F	F	F
T	F	F	T	F
F	T	T	F	F
F	F	T	T	T

34. If 1 inch = 2.54 cm, convert 18 cm to inches to the nearest hundredth.
    A. 0.14 inches
    B. 0.39 inches
    C. 7.09 inches
    D. 45.72 inches

35. A high school booster club recorded the number of tickets sold for each home basketball game for the current season. The box plot shown below represents the data for the number of tickets sold for each game:

    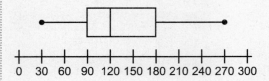

    Which conclusion can be made using this graph?
    A. The second quartile is 180.
    B. The range of tickets sales is 90 to 180.
    C. The mean number of tickets sold per game is 120.
    D. Twenty-five percent of ticket sales fell between 30 and 90.

36. Peter has gathered 42 medium-sized rocks to use alongside of a walkway. In this group, the number of bluish-gray rocks is three more than twice the number of brown rocks. How many bluish-gray rocks does he have?
    A. 13
    B. 26
    C. 29
    D. 36

37. The following line graph shows a distribution of test scores on a college mathematics placement exam.

    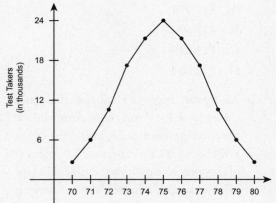

    Which of these statements is true based on the graph?
    A. The median score and mean score are approximately the same.
    B. The graph is comprised of scores from approximately 20,000 test-takers.
    C. The percentage of scores larger than a given score is the same as the percentage of scores below that same score.
    D. More people had a score of 78 than a score of 72.

38. The length of a rectangular room is 5 inches less than three times the width of the room, w. Which expression below is equal to the area of the room?
    A. $3w - 5$ square inches
    B. $3w^2 - 5w$ square inches
    C. $3w^2$ square inches
    D. $3w^2 - 5$ square inches

39. What is the base-ten decimal equivalent of the Roman number MMI?

   A. 21

   B. 101

   C. 201

   D. 2,001

40. To pay a loan, Allison must make 360 monthly payments of $500 at an 8.5% annual interest rate. To the nearest dollar, what was the original amount of the loan?

   A. $2,550

   B. $15,300

   C. $65,027

   D. $70,588.24

41. The probability that it will rain on Tuesday is $\frac{3}{5}$. The probability that it will rain on both Tuesday and Thursday is $\frac{3}{10}$. The probability that it rains on either Tuesday or Thursday is $\frac{4}{5}$. What is the probability that it will rain on Thursday?

   A. $\frac{1}{5}$

   B. $\frac{1}{2}$

   C. $\frac{1}{10}$

   D. $\frac{2}{5}$

42. Based on this tabulated information, which of the following formulas describes this function?

x	$F(x)$
-2	30
-1	10
0	$\frac{10}{3}$
1	$\frac{10}{9}$
2	$\frac{10}{27}$

   A. $F(x) = 10 \cdot 3^{-x}$

   B. $F(x) = \frac{10}{3} \cdot 3^{x}$

   C. $F(x) = 10 \cdot \left(\frac{1}{3}\right)^{-x}$

   D. $F(x) = 10 \cdot 3^{-1-x}$

43. Suppose that A dollars are invested in a money market account that pays i% interest compounded quarterly. What is the value, V, of the account at the end of 10 years?

   A. $V = A\left(1 + \frac{100i}{4}\right)^{40}$

   B. $V = A\left(\frac{1+i}{4}\right)^{40}$

   C. $V = A\left(1 + \frac{i}{400}\right)^{40}$

   D. $V = A\left(1 + \frac{i}{4}\right)^{40}$

44. What is the negation of the following statement:

    "Mario is not older than 25 and Patricia is older than 25."

    A. Mario is older than 25 or Patricia is not older than 25.

    B. Mario is older than 25 or Patricia is not younger than 25.

    C. Mario is older than 25, but Patricia is not older than 25.

    D. It is not true that Mario is older than 25 or Patricia is not older than 25.

45. Which of these scenarios describes a negative correlation?

    A. The number of quarts of oil purchased and the total amount paid for the oil

    B. The amount of gasoline remaining in a truck's tank and the price of gasoline per gallon

    C. The size of a truck and the number of gallons of gasoline its tank holds

    D. The number of miles driven and the time until the next oil change

46. Teri placed a ladder against the side of her house to clean the rain gutters, as shown below:

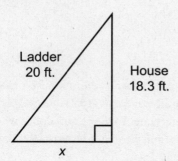

    Which of the following is the correct expression for x?

    A. $x = 20^2 - 18.3^2$

    B. $x = 20 - 18.3$

    C. $x = \sqrt{20^2 + 18.3^2}$

    D. $x = \sqrt{20^2 - 18.3^2}$

47. Suppose that $2,000 was invested at 4% simple interest for 8 years. Which value of r would be substituted into the formula $I = Art$?

    A. 0.04

    B. 4

    C. 8

    D. 2,000

48. If $a + ay = b + y$, determine the value of a if $b = -\frac{1}{2}$ and $y = \frac{1}{3}$?

    A. $-\frac{1}{8}$

    B. $-\frac{1}{2}$

    C. $-\frac{3}{2}$

    D. $\frac{7}{6}$

49. A tree farm owner examines the relationship between the price he charges for his spruce trees and the number of spruce trees sold weekly. He records this information for one year and calculates the average number of trees sold weekly for each of five different prices. This information is tabulated below:

Price of Spruce Tree	Number Sold Weekly
$50	14
$100	9
$150	15
$200	11
$250	6

Which scatterplot represents this data?

A.

C.

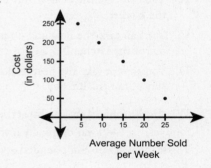

B.

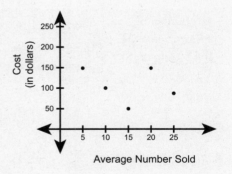

D.

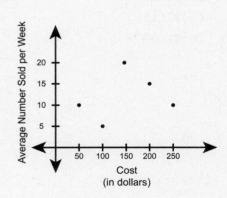

50. What is the equation of the line passing through the points (1,4) and (–2, 2)?

   A. $y - 1 = \frac{2}{3}(x - 4)$

   B. $y + 1 = \frac{2}{3}(x + 4)$

   C. $y - 2 = \frac{2}{3}(x + 2)$

   D. $y + 2 = \frac{3}{2}(x - 2)$

51. Which of the following statements is equivalent to the statement, "If you cannot take the heat, stay out of the kitchen?"

   A. You can take the heat, but stay out of the kitchen.

   B. You can take the heat or stay out of the kitchen.

   C. You can take the heat and do not stay out of the kitchen.

   D. You cannot take the heat or do not stay out of the kitchen.

52. What is the value of an account at the end of four years if $480 was originally invested at a 10% interest rate compounded quarterly?

   A. $320.12

   B. $529.83

   C. $712.56

   D. $1,047.78

53. Consider the following Venn diagram—assume all regions are nonempty:

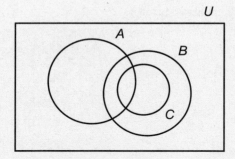

Which one of the following statements is **true**?

   A. No element of the set C is a member of the universal set U.

   B. Any element that is a member of the universal set U is also a member of the set A.

   C. Some elements of the set A are also elements of the set B.

   D. Set B is a subset of set C.

54. The following measurements regarding time and the amount of accumulated snow were taken by a weather aficionado during a storm:

Number of Hours Since the Beginning of the Storm	Number of Inches of Snow Accumulation
0.5	0.75
1	1.50
1.5	2.25
2	3.00
2.5	3.75

What is true about the rate of change of accumulation with respect to time?

   A. It is positive.

   B. It is negative.

   C. It is zero.

   D. It is undefined.

55. Suppose U is a universal set for all sets arising in this problem. Which of the following statements is **false**?

A. For any set, $A \cap A^c = \varnothing$.

B. The set of real numbers is an infinite set.

C. If $A = \{0, 1, 2, 3, 4, 5, \ldots, 19\}$, then A contains 20 elements.

D. If $B = \{x \mid x$ is an even integer$\}$ and $C = \{y \mid y$ is a multiple of 3$\}$, then B and C are disjoint.

56. Josh invests $1,800 on his 25th birthday in a savings account that earns 7% compounded annually. What will be the value of the account on his 65th birthday? Round your answer to the nearest dollar.

A. $18,974

B. $26,954

C. $50,400

D. $72,000

57. Which equation represents a line perpendicular to the y-axis?

A. $y = 3$

B. $x = 6$

C. $y = x$

D. $y = -x$

58. Farrah uses the substitution method to solve the following system of linear equations:

$$\begin{cases} 3x + 2y = -3 \\ 2x - y = 5 \end{cases}$$

To which of the following equations in one variable does the system reduce as a result?

A. $3\left(y + \dfrac{5}{2}\right) + 2y = -3$

B. $3\left(\dfrac{5}{2} - y\right) + 2y = -3$

C. $3x + 2(5 - 2x) = -3$

D. $3x + 2(2x - 5) = -3$

59. If $2,600 is invested in an account that pays 3% simple interest for 5 months, what value of t is substituted into the equation $I = Art$ to compute the interest earned?

A. 0.03

B. 0.05

C. $\dfrac{5}{12}$

D. 5

60. A set C contains 22 elements and a set D contains 35 elements. If $C \cup D$ contains 40 elements, then how many elements does $C \cap D$ contain?

A. 13

B. 17

C. 18

D. 22

ANSWER KEY AND EXPLANATIONS

1. D	**13.** C	**25.** B	**37.** A	**49.** A
2. B	**14.** A	**26.** A	**38.** B	**50.** C
3. D	**15.** D	**27.** C	**39.** D	**51.** B
4. B	**16.** A	**28.** C	**40.** C	**52.** C
5. D	**17.** D	**29.** D	**41.** B	**53.** C
6. D	**18.** D	**30.** B	**42.** D	**54.** A
7. B	**19.** C	**31.** C	**43.** C	**55.** D
8. B	**20.** D	**32.** A	**44.** A	**56.** B
9. C	**21.** C	**33.** B	**45.** D	**57.** A
10. B	**22.** A	**34.** C	**46.** D	**58.** D
11. A	**23.** C	**35.** D	**47.** A	**59.** C
12. C	**24.** D	**36.** C	**48.** A	**60.** B

1. **The correct answer is D.** The largest whole number that divides evenly into all three numbers is 3; this is the GCF. The least common multiple is the product $2^2 \times 3^3 \times 19 = 2,052$. Choice A is wrong because the only way the GCF of three numbers is 1 is if they share no common factors, but, 3 divides evenly into all three. Choice B is wrong because 2 does not divide evenly into 171. Choice C is wrong because the LCM is not 360.

2. **The correct answer is B.** Use the exponent rules:

$$\frac{2^6}{4} = \frac{2^6}{2^2} = 2^{6-2} = 2^4$$

Choice A is wrong because it divides the bases, which is not part of the exponent rule used to simplify quotients of powers of the same base. Choice C is wrong because the powers must be subtracted not divided. Choice D is wrong because you need to subtract the exponents, not add them.

3. **The correct answer is D.** The height of the dive is the y-coordinate of a point on the parabola. The largest that value ever gets is at the vertex, which has a y-coordinate of 32 feet. Choice A is wrong because this is the distance the diver is from the springboard when she achieves the maximum height of her dive (the x-coordinate of the vertex). Choice B is wrong because this is how far she is when she hits the water; so, it is the maximum distance traveled from the springboard. Choice C is the height of the springboard.

4. **The correct answer is B.** The set "Risky Investments" is a subset of the universal set "Investments." The set "College Education" can be risky or not risky, depending on the school, if the major is marketable, etc. So, it should intersect, but not be entirely contained within, the set "Risky Investments." This is shown in the Euler diagram in choice B. Choice A is wrong because a college education may not be risky if the major is very marketable and one has a full scholarship, for instance. Choice C is wrong because not every risky investment deals with getting a college education; for

instance, investing in an upstart company would be a risky investment. Choice D is wrong because "Risky Investments" should be a set, not a single point, since there are a variety of them.

5. **The correct answer is D.** Use the logarithm properties:

$\ln 63 = \ln(3^2 \times 7) = \ln(3^2) + \ln 7 = 2\ln 3 + \ln 7 = 2a + b$

Choice A is equal to $\ln 441$, choice B is equal to $\ln 7^4$, and choice C is equal to $2(\ln 3)(\ln 7)$.

6. **The correct answer is D.** Let A be the event "winning the vacation." Then, A^C is the event "not winning the vacation." The odds of A^C occurring are $P(A^C)$ to $1 - P(A^C)$. Since

$P(A^C) = \dfrac{9,960}{10,000}$ and $1 - P(A^C) = \dfrac{40}{10,000}$,

the odds are $\dfrac{9,960}{10,000}$ to $\dfrac{40}{10,000}$. An equivalent way of expressing the ratio is as the fraction $\dfrac{\frac{9,960}{10,000}}{\frac{40}{10,000}} = \dfrac{9.960}{40}$, which is equivalent to "9,960 to 40." Choice A is wrong because you must subtract 40 from 10,000, and the ratio is written in the wrong order. Choice B is wrong because you must subtract 40 from 10,000. Choice C is wrong because it is expressed in the wrong order.

7. **The correct answer is B.** The radius of the circle is 9 feet. This is equivalent to 3 yards. So, the circumference (in yards) is $2\pi(3 \text{ yards}) = 6\pi$ yards. Choice A is wrong because you need to multiply by 2 in the circumference formula. Choice C is wrong because you did not convert the diameter to yards. Choice D is wrong because you used the diameter, as originally expressed in feet, instead of the radius expressed in yards.

8. **The correct answer is B.** First, convert the dimensions to yards. So, the room is 5 yards by 6 yards. The area is 30 square yards. So,

multiply this by \$8.50 (the cost per square yard) to get the pre-tax price: \$8.50(30) = \$255. Choice A is wrong because you simply added the width to the length; this is not related to the area. Choice C is wrong because this is the area in square feet. Choice D is wrong because you did not convert feet to yards before computing the price.

9. **The correct answer is C.** First, the equation of the corresponding line in slope-intercept form is $y = 2x - 3$. Graph it on the xy-plane as a *dotted* line since the inequality is strict. Next, since $(0,0)$ satisfies the inequality, shade the side of the line containing it–namely above it. Choices B and D are wrong because the line is solid, but should be dashed; and the shaded region is wrong in choice B. Choice A is wrong because the wrong side of the line is shaded.

10. **The correct answer is B.** Use the exponent rules as follows:

$$\frac{-12z^3x^9}{3x^3z^3} = \frac{-12}{3} \cdot \frac{x^9}{x^3} \cdot \frac{z^3}{z^3}$$
$$= -4 \cdot x^{9-3} \cdot 1$$
$$= -4x^6$$

Choice A is wrong because you added the coefficients instead of dividing them. Choice C is wrong because you added the coefficients instead of dividing them, and you divided the powers of x when you should have subtracted them. Choice D is wrong because you divided the powers of x when you should have subtracted them, and the z-terms should cancel completely.

11. **The correct answer is A.** The distributive property tells us how to multiply a quantity by a sum or difference; that is precisely what is displayed in the given equation. The answer in choice B governs the order in which real numbers are added or multiplied. The answer in choice C governs the way terms of a sum or product are grouped. The answer in choice

D says that if you add 0 to a real number or multiply it by 1, you get the same number back.

12. **The correct answer is C.** The range of a data set is the difference between the maximum and minimum values. Here, this difference is $26 - 4 = 22$. Choice A is the minimum of the data set. Choice B is the median of the data set. Choice D is the maximum of the data set.

13. **The correct answer is C.** Each cell is $\frac{1}{2}$ the value of the one directly above it. So, to get the percent-strength for Day 5, divide the percent-strength for Day 4 by 2 to get 6.25%. Then divide again to find that the percent-strength for Day 6 is 3.125%. And finally, divide once more to get 1.56% as the percent-strength for Day 7. Choice A is the result of an incorrect calculation of the percent-strength for Day 8. Choice B is the percent-strength for Day 8. Choice D is the percent-strength for Day 6.

14. **The correct answer is A.** Multiply by grouping the decimal parts together and the powers of ten together (which is valid by the associativity and commutativity properties):

$(4.6 \times 10^3) \times (6.0 \times 10^{-2}) \times (2.0 \times 10^5) = (4.6 \times 6.0 \times 2.0) \times (10^3 \times 10^{-2} \times 10^5) = 55.2 \times 10^6 = 5.52 \times 10^7$

Choice B is wrong because you inadvertently used 2 in place of the exponent –2 when computing the power of 10. Choice C is not expressed using scientific notation, even though the result is equivalent. Choice D is not expressed using scientific notation and the power of 10 used to find this value is wrong.

15. **The correct answer is D.** Compute the surface area of the box by doubling the area of the three distinct faces. Doing so yields $2(2 \cdot 3) + 2(2 \cdot 4) + 2(3 \cdot 4) = 52$ square inches. This is the amount of wrapping paper Gina needs. Choice A is simply the sum of the three given dimensions, which is not related to the surface area. Choice B is the volume. Choice C is half the surface area; do not forget to double the area of each of the three distinct faces.

16. **The correct answer is A.** The average of $\frac{1}{31}$ and $\frac{1}{32}$ is $\frac{63}{1,984}$. This is a rational number halfway between $\frac{1}{31}$ and $\frac{1}{32}$. Also, $10\pi = 10(3.14) = 31.4$. Hence, $31 < 10\pi < 32$, their reciprocals satisfy the reverse inequality: $\frac{1}{31}$. The fraction $\frac{1}{10\pi}$ is a quotient of a nonzero rational number and an irrational number. So, it must be irrational, as needed. Choice B is wrong because $\frac{1}{33}$ is not between $\frac{1}{31}$ and $\frac{1}{32}$. Choices C and D are wrong because neither of the given numbers in each answer is between $\frac{1}{31}$ and $\frac{1}{32}$.

17. **The correct answer is D.** Use the formula $V = A\left(1 + \frac{r}{n}\right)^{nt}$ with $V = 31,000$, $r = 0.06$, $n = 12$, and $t = 3$. The amount of the original investment is A:

$$31,000 = A\left(1 + \frac{0.06}{12}\right)^{12(3)}$$
$$= A(1 + 0.005)^{36}$$

Solve for A to get $A = \frac{31,000}{(1 + 0.005)^{36}}$. Choice A is wrong because you mistakenly interchanged the meaning of A and V in the compound interest formula. Choice B is incorrect because you mistakenly interchanged the meaning of A and V in the compound interest formula, and you divided 0.06 by 12 incorrectly. Choice C is wrong because you divided 0.06 by 12 incorrectly.

18. **The correct answer is D.** The sum of the three angles of a triangle is 180 degrees. So, the measure of the missing angle is 180 − (20 + 80) = 80 degrees. Since two angles are congruent, the triangle is isosceles. Choice A would require all three angles to be 60 degrees. Choice B would require all three angles to be different, but two of them have angles of 80 degrees. Choice C requires one of the angles to have measure 90 degrees, which is not the case.

19. **The correct answer is C.** Use the fact that $\log_b x = y$ is equivalent to $b^y = x$ to see that the given equation is equivalent to $4^2 = z$. Choice A has the z and 4 interchanged. Choice B would be equivalent to $\log_2 z = 4$. Choice D has the z and 2 interchanged.

20. **The correct answer is D.** Since all regions are assumed to be nonempty and there is an overlapping region of sets A and C, their intersection cannot be empty. Choice A is a true statement because the circle representing set B is entirely included inside of the circle representing set A. Choice B is true because the circles representing sets B and C do not overlap. Choice C is true because the circle representing set B is entirely inside the region that is comprised of sets A and C.

21. **The correct answer is C.** First, arrange the data in numerical order:

    63, 69, 76, 76, 78, 81, 85, 89, 90, 94, 97

    The mode is the most frequently occurring value: 76. The median is the middle value, which is the one in the 6th position: 81. The mean is the sum of the values divided by 11: approximately 81.6. So, it is evident that the only true statement of those listed is choice C.

22. **The correct answer is A.** Using the standard base-10 place-value chart, this arithmetic expression is equal to 5,009.068. All other choices are the result of misinterpreting the

relationship between the power of 10 and the position of its multiple in the place-value chart.

23. **The correct answer is C.** An *integer* multiple of 4 has the form $4n$, where n is any integer. You must include the natural numbers, zero, and the negatives of the natural numbers. The only set that includes all these possibilities for n is the one in choice C. Choice A does not account for negative multiples of 4. Choice B does not account for 0 or negative multiples of 4. Choice D neglects to include 0.

24. **The correct answer is D.** Since the die is fair, it is equally likely for the die to land on any of the six faces. Observe that P(an arrow) = $\frac{4}{6}$, P(rolling an A or C) = $\frac{2}{6}$, P(not rolling an arrow) = $\frac{2}{6}$, and P(rolling an arrow pointing left) = $\frac{1}{6}$. So, this last event is the least likely to occur.

25. **The correct answer is B.** By stringing together the two conditionals using statement q as a common link, the only logical conclusion one can make from these two statements is that $p \Rightarrow r$. There is not enough information to conclude any of the other statements.

26. **The correct answer is A.** Solve for g as follows:

$$v = \frac{1}{2} g t^2$$
$$2v = g t^2$$
$$\frac{2v}{t^2} = g$$
$$g = \frac{2v}{t^2}$$

In choice B, you should have divided by t^2. In choice C, you forgot to square t. In choice D, you should have interchanged the position of 2.

27. **The correct answer is C.** This question requires that we determine the number of permutations of 6 letters taken 4 at a time—order matters here since we are forming "words." This number is $\frac{6!}{(6-4)!} = \frac{6!}{2!} = 6 \times 5 \times 4 \times 3 = 360$. Choice A is the number of combinations of 6 letters taken 4 at a time, but order matters here. Choice B is just the product of the number of letters from which to choose and the 4 you *want* to choose; it has nothing to do with the number of permutations. Choice D is the number of ways to arrange 6 distinct objects in order; you did not take 4 of them to arrange.

28. **The correct answer is C.** Use the formula
$$A = \left(1 - \frac{1}{(1+i)^n}\right) \times \frac{R}{i} \text{ with } A =$$
$100,000(0.95) = 95,000$, $i = 0.08/12$, and $n = 25(12) = 300$. You want to determine the value of R:
$$95,000 = \left(1 - \frac{1}{\left(1 + \frac{0.08}{12}\right)^{300}}\right) \times \frac{R}{\left(\frac{0.08}{12}\right)}$$
$$733.23 \approx R$$

So, the monthly payment is $733.23. In choice A, you mistakenly used a *plus* instead of the *minus* in the formula $A = \left(1 - \frac{1}{(1+i)^n}\right) \times \frac{R}{i}$. In choice B, you mistakenly used a *plus* instead of the *minus* in the formula $A = \left(1 - \frac{1}{(1+i)^n}\right) \times \frac{R}{i}$, and used $A = 100,000$ instead of 95,000. In choice D, you used $A = 100,000$ instead of 95,000.

29. **The correct answer is D.** Use the fact that 1 hour = 60 minutes to perform the following unit conversion:

$$\frac{150 \text{ meters}}{1.5 \text{ minutes}} = \frac{150 \text{ meters}}{1.5 \text{ minutes}} \times \frac{60 \text{ minutes}}{1 \text{ hour}}$$
$$= 6,000 \text{ meters per hour}$$

Choices A and B are off by power(s) of 10, likely due to an arithmetic error. In choice C, you assumed there are 10 minutes in an hour rather than 60.

30. **The correct answer is B.** As the distance traveled increases, the amount of gasoline remaining in the tank decreases. So, the line describing this relationship should have a negative slope, meaning it slants downward from left to right. This eliminates choices C and D. Both lines in choices A and B have the correct y-intercept of 18 gallons. The x-intercept should be 600 gallons since this is the number of miles the SUV can travel before it runs out of gas. So, choice A is not correct.

31. **The correct answer is C.** Use the formula
$$V = A\left(1 + \frac{r}{n}\right)^{nt} \text{ with } A = 20,000, r = -0.12$$
(negative since the value is decreasing), $n = 1$ (since the decrease is annual), and $t = 3$. The value of the jeep, V, at the end of 3 years is $V = \$20,000\left(1 + \frac{-0.12}{1}\right)^{1(3)}$,
$$= \$20,000(0.88)^3$$
$$= \$13,629.40$$

which we round to $13,629. In choice A, you used $r = 0.12$ instead of -0.12, but this means the value is increasing with time. Choice B is the value at the end of 1 year, not 3. Choice D is wrong because you incorrectly computed the parenthetical quantity in $V = A\left(1 + \frac{r}{n}\right)^{nt}$.

32. **The correct answer is A.** Add the numbers in the three regions in the sets representing chocolate chip cupcakes and pistachio cupcakes that do *not* overlap the region representing lemon cupcakes: 10 + 15 + 75 = 100. The answer in choice B includes the

5 shoppers who liked none of these three types of cupcakes. The answer in choice C does not exclude the shoppers who like lemon cupcakes from the total. The answer in choice D does not exclude the shoppers who like lemon cupcakes from the total, and included the 5 shoppers who liked none of these three types of cupcakes.

33. **The correct answer is B.** This is the correct truth table because it uses the facts that the truth value of the negation of a statement is the opposite of the truth value of the statement itself. The truth value of a disjunction is true if at least one of the statement used to form it is true and is false if both are false. In choice A, you did not solve for the negation of q correctly. Choice C has the last column wrong; these are the truth values for the negation of the given disjunction. Choice D is the truth table for the conjunction $\sim p \wedge \sim q$.

34. **The correct answer is C.** Convert the units as follows:

$$18\,\text{cm} = 18\,\cancel{\text{cm}} \times \frac{1\,\text{inch}}{2.54\,\cancel{\text{cm}}} \approx 7.09\,\text{inches}$$

In choice A, you divided in the wrong order. Choice B is the number of inches in 1 cm, not 18 cm. In choice C, you multiplied instead of dividing when converting the units.

35. **The correct answer is D.** The first quartile is represented by the vertical line segment at 90. So, 25% of the data lie between the minimum value 30 and 90. Choice A is wrong because the second quartile is 120 and the third quartile is 180. The answer in choice B would be used to get the inter-quartile range, not the range. Choice C is wrong because we can only deduce that the median is 120; since the data set is skewed, evidenced by that fact that the median is not in the middle of the box, it is likely that the mean is not 120.

36. **The correct answer is C.** Let x be the number of brown rocks. Then, there are $3 + 2x$ bluish-gray rocks. Summing these gives 42: $x + (3 + 2x) = 42$. Solve for x:

$$3x + 3 = 42$$
$$3x = 39$$
$$x = 13$$

So, there are $(3 + 2(13)) = 29$ bluish-gray rocks. Choice A is the number of brown rocks. In choice B, you forgot to add 3; this assumes the number of bluish-gray rocks is twice the number of brown rocks. In choice D, you solved $3x = 39$ by subtracting 3 from both sides instead of dividing by 3.

37. **The correct answer is A.** Since the shape of the graph is symmetric, the median and mean scores are approximately the same. In choice B, you did not compute the total number of test-takers correctly; you should add the y-coordinates of all the points on the line graph. Choice C is wrong because this is only ever true for the 2nd quartile or median, not for *every* score. Choice D is wrong since the y-coordinates of the points for which $x = 72$ and $x = 78$ are the same.

38. **The correct answer is B.** Let w be the width of the room. Then, the length is $3w - 5$. The area is the product of width and length, namely $w(3w - 5) = 3w^2 - 5w$ square inches. Choice A is the length only. The answer in choice C assumes the length is three times the width, not 5 less than this quantity. In choice D, you did not use the distributive property when multiplying $w(3w - 5)$.

39. **The correct answer is D.** In Roman numerals, M stands for 1,000 and I stands for 1. There are two Ms, giving 2,000. Adding 1 to this number yields 2,001. The answer in choice A mistakenly equates M to 10 instead of 1,000. The answer in choice B mistakenly equates M to 50 instead of

1,000. The answer in choice C mistakenly equates M to 100 instead of 1,000.

40. **The correct answer is C.** Use the formula $A = \left(1 - \dfrac{1}{(1+i)^n}\right) \times \dfrac{R}{i}$ with $i = \dfrac{0.085}{12}$, $n = 360$, and $R = \$500$. The value of A is the total amount of the loan:

$$A = \left(1 - \frac{1}{\left(1 + \frac{0.085}{12}\right)^{360}}\right) \times \left(\frac{\$500}{\left(\frac{0.085}{12}\right)}\right) = \$65,631$$

Choice A is the result of using the simple interest formula, which does not apply to this scenario. Choice B is the product of n, R, and i, which is not the correct formula. Choice D is just the $\dfrac{R}{i}$ portion of the formula $A = \left(1 - \dfrac{1}{(1+i)^n}\right) \times \dfrac{R}{i}$.

41. **The correct answer is B.** Use the addition formula:

P (rain on Tues. or rain on Thurs.) $= P$ (rain on Tues.) $+ P$ (rain on Thurs.) $- P$ (rain on Tues. and rain on Thurs.)

Substituting the given information into this formula yields the following:

$$\frac{4}{5} = \frac{3}{5} + \text{P(rains on Thurs)} - \frac{3}{10}$$

Now, solve for P (rains on Thurs.) to obtain P (rains on Thurs.) $= \dfrac{4}{5} - \dfrac{3}{5} + \dfrac{3}{10} = \dfrac{1}{2}$.

Choice A is wrong because you did not subtract P (rain on Tues. and rain on Thurs.), as required by the addition formula. Choices C and D are the results of arithmetic errors involving fractions.

42. **The correct answer is D.** Substituting the x-values in the left column of the table into each of the functions reveals that choice D gives the correct formula. All other choices have an exponent or base of the exponential portion of the formula wrong.

43. **The correct answer is C.** Use the formula $V = A\left(1 + \dfrac{r}{n}\right)^{nt}$ with $r = \dfrac{i}{100}$ (which is the correct conversion of i %), $n = 4$, and $t = 10$ to get

$$V = A\left(1 + \frac{\frac{i}{100}}{4}\right)^{4(10)} = A\left(1 + \frac{i}{400}\right)^{40}.$$

The answer in choice A has 100 in the numerator of the fraction, but it should be in the denominator. Choice B is the result of incorrectly dividing the 1 in the parentheses by n, and converts i% to a fraction incorrectly. Choice D is the result of converting i% to a fraction incorrectly.

44. **The correct answer is A.** Symbolically, the given statement is the conjunction $(\sim p) \wedge q$, where p is the statement, "Mario is older than 25." and q is the statement, "Patricia is older than 25." Use De Morgan's laws, together with the Law of the Double Negative, to form the negation:

$$\sim\left[(\sim p) \wedge q\right] \equiv \left[\sim(\sim p)\right] \vee (\sim q)$$
$$\equiv p \vee (\sim q)$$

This is equivalent to the disjunction, "Mario is older than 25 or Patricia is not older than 25."

Choice B should have the word "younger" replaced by "older." Choice C is wrong because the word "but" is semantically equivalent to an "and." Choice D is equivalent to the given statement, not its negation.

45. **The correct answer is D.** As the number of miles driven increases, the number of miles until the next oil change decreases. This describes a negative correlation. Choice A does not describe a negative correlation since as you buy more oil, the total amount paid will increase regardless of the price. The answer in choice B would likely have neither a negative nor a positive correlation.

Choice C describes what is probably a positive relationship between two variables since the larger the truck, the larger the gas tank (though it may not be linear).

46. **The correct answer is D.** Use the Pythagorean theorem with legs having lengths 18.3 and x and hypotenuse being 20: $x^2 + 18.3^2 = 20^2$. Solve for x as follows:

$$x^2 = 20^2 - 18.3^2$$
$$x = \sqrt{20^2 - 18.3^2}$$

Choice A needs to have a radical of the right side. Choice B is the result of incorrectly saying the radical of a difference is the difference of the radicals. Choice C should have a minus instead of a plus inside the radicand.

47. **The correct answer is A.** In the formula, r is the interest rate expressed as a decimal. Since 4% = 0.04, r must be 0.04. Choice B did not convert 4% to a decimal. Choice C is the value of t. Choice D is the value of A.

48. **The correct answer is A.** Substitute the given values of b and y into the equation and solve for a, as follows:

$$a + a\left(\frac{1}{3}\right) = -\frac{1}{2} + \frac{1}{3}$$
$$\frac{4}{3}a = -\frac{1}{6}$$
$$a = -\frac{1}{6} \cdot \frac{3}{4}$$
$$a = -\frac{1}{8}$$

In choice B, the coefficients of the a-terms are not added correctly; the coefficient of a should be $\frac{4}{3}$, not $\frac{1}{3}$. In choice C, the coefficient of a is subtracted from both sides rather than dividing by it when solving for a. Choice D is the result of multiplying both sides of the equation by the coefficient of a rather than dividing by it when solving for a.

49. **The correct answer is A.** Plotting the points given in the table by identifying the values in the first column as x-values and the values in the second column as the y-values yields the scatterplot in choice A. None of the other scatterplots plot the points correctly.

50. **The correct answer is C.** The slope of the line is $m = \frac{4-2}{1-(-2)} = \frac{2}{3}$. Using the point $(-2,2)$, the equation of the line using point-slope form is $y - 2 = \frac{2}{3}(x - (-2))$, which simplifies to $y - 2 = \frac{2}{3}(x + 2)$. Choice A is the result of interchanging the x- and y-values of the point $(1,4)$ when writing the equation in point-slope form. Choice B is the result of interchanging the x- and y-values of the point $(1,4)$ when writing the equation in point-slope form; they should have been subtracted from x and y in the equation, respectively, rather than added. Choice D has the wrong slope (it should be the reciprocal) and interchanges the x- and y-values of the point $(-2,2)$ when writing the equation in point-slope form.

51. **The correct answer is B.** Let p be the statement, "You can take the heat." and q be the statement, "Stay out of the kitchen." The given conditional can be written symbolically as $(\sim p) \Rightarrow q$. But, this is equivalent to $p \vee q$. In words, this is equivalent to, "You can take the heat or you stay out of the kitchen." Choices A and C are conjunctions, but the conditional is equivalent to a disjunction. Choice D should have both statements of which the disjunction is comprised be replaced by their negations.

52. **The correct answer is C.** Use the formula $V = A\left(1 + \frac{r}{n}\right)^{nt}$ with A = \$480, r = 0.10, n = 4, and t = 4 to obtain

$$V = \$480\left(1 + \frac{0.10}{4}\right)^{4(4)}$$
$$= \$480(1.025)^{16}$$
$$= \$712.56$$

Choice A is the result of subtracting instead of adding $\frac{r}{n}$ in the formula $V = A\left(1 + \frac{r}{n}\right)^{nt}$. Choice B is the result of using the wrong exponent in the formula $V = A\left(1 + \frac{r}{n}\right)^{nt}$. Choice D is the result of using $n = 2$ instead of 4.

53. **The correct answer is C.** Since all regions are assumed to be nonempty and the circles representing sets A and B overlap, then some elements of A are also elements of B. Choice A is wrong because the universal set contains all sets within a given discussion. Choice B means that the universal set U is a subset of A, but the opposite is true. (This can only happen if $A = U$.) Choice D has the relationship backwards; set C is a subset of B.

54. **The correct answer is A.** Note that the values in the right column increase by 0.75 for every increase by 0.5 in the left column. This implies the relationship is linear. Moreover, since the values are increasing, the rate of change is positive. As such, all other choices are not viable.

55. **The correct answer is D.** Sets B and C have *infinitely many* elements in common; all multiples of 6 belong to both. Choice A is true since an object cannot both be inside and not inside a set. Choice B is true since, for instance, the set of natural numbers belongs to the set of real numbers and there are clearly infinitely many natural numbers since there is no end to counting. Choice C is true as can be seen by simply counting the elements.

56. **The correct answer is B.** Use the formula $V = A\left(1 + \frac{r}{n}\right)^{nt}$ with $A = \$1,800$, $r = 0.07$, $n = 1$, and $t = 40$ to obtain

$$V = \$1,800\left(1 + \frac{0.07}{1}\right)^{1(40)} = \$1,800(1.07)^{40}$$
$$= \$26,954.$$

Choice A is the result of incorrectly using $r = 0.4$ and $t = 7$. Choice C is the product of 1,800, 40, and 0.7. Choice D is the product of $\$1,800$ and 40, which is not how you compute the value of an account at the end of 40 years.

57. **The correct answer is A.** A line perpendicular to the y-axis must be horizontal. Horizontal lines have equations of the form $y = a$, where a is a real number. The only choice that satisfies this condition is $y = 3$. Choice B is parallel to the y-axis. Choices C and D are diagonal lines through the origin, neither of which intersects the y-axis in a ninety-degree angle.

58. **The correct answer is D.** Solve the second equation for y to get $y = 2x - 5$. Substitute this in for y in the first equation to get $3x + 2(2x - 5) = -3$. Choice A should have the y inside the parentheses being divided by 2. Choice B has the wrong expression inside the parentheses; it should be a sum and the y should be divided by 2. Choice C has the difference inside the parentheses written in the wrong order.

59. **The correct answer is C.** In this formula, t represents the number of *years* of the investment. Be careful—the given number of *months* is 5. This is $\frac{5}{12}$ of a year. Choice A is the interest rate and so, is the value of r, not t. Choice B is equal to $\frac{5}{100}$, but this is the wrong conversion of months to years; divide 5 by 12, not 100. Choice D is expressed in months, not years, as the formula requires.

60. **The correct answer is B.** Of the total 57 elements that comprise sets C and D, 17 must be in common since otherwise, their union would have more than 40 elements. Choice A is the difference of the number of elements in C and D. Choice C would imply that $C \cup D$ contains 39 elements, not 40. Choice D would imply that C is a subset of D, which is not assumed; moreover, $C \cup D$ would not include 40 elements in such case.

Principles of Public Speaking

OVERVIEW

- **Test Answer Sheets**
- **Principles of Public Speaking Diagnostic Test**
- **Answer Key and Explanations**
- **Diagnostic Test Assessment Grid**
- **Ethical, Social, and Theoretical Considerations of Public Speaking**
- **Audience Analysis and Adaptation**
- **Speech Topics and Purposes**
- **Research and Content**
- **Organizing Your Speech**
- **Language and Style**
- **Delivering Your Speech**
- **Summing It Up**
- **Principles of Public Speaking Post-test**
- **Answer Key and Explanations**

The DSST® Principles of Public Speaking two-part exam is unique. Part 1 of the exam contains 100 questions, to be answered in 2 hours, and it consists of multiple-choice questions covering audience analysis, purposes of speeches, structure and organization, content and supporting materials, research, language and style, delivery, communication apprehension, listening and feedback, and criticism and evaluation. Part 2 requires you to record an impromptu persuasive speech that will be scored by a faculty member who teaches public speaking at an accredited college or university. The person scoring your speech will use a scoring rubric containing these five elements: structure and organization, delivery, content and supporting material, effect and persuasiveness, and language and style.

Chapter 3

DIAGNOSTIC TEST ANSWER SHEET

1. Ⓐ Ⓑ Ⓒ Ⓓ   5. Ⓐ Ⓑ Ⓒ Ⓓ   9. Ⓐ Ⓑ Ⓒ Ⓓ   13. Ⓐ Ⓑ Ⓒ Ⓓ   17. Ⓐ Ⓑ Ⓒ Ⓓ
2. Ⓐ Ⓑ Ⓒ Ⓓ   6. Ⓐ Ⓑ Ⓒ Ⓓ   10. Ⓐ Ⓑ Ⓒ Ⓓ   14. Ⓐ Ⓑ Ⓒ Ⓓ   18. Ⓐ Ⓑ Ⓒ Ⓓ
3. Ⓐ Ⓑ Ⓒ Ⓓ   7. Ⓐ Ⓑ Ⓒ Ⓓ   11. Ⓐ Ⓑ Ⓒ Ⓓ   15. Ⓐ Ⓑ Ⓒ Ⓓ   19. Ⓐ Ⓑ Ⓒ Ⓓ
4. Ⓐ Ⓑ Ⓒ Ⓓ   8. Ⓐ Ⓑ Ⓒ Ⓓ   12. Ⓐ Ⓑ Ⓒ Ⓓ   16. Ⓐ Ⓑ Ⓒ Ⓓ   20. Ⓐ Ⓑ Ⓒ Ⓓ

POST-TEST ANSWER SHEET

1. Ⓐ Ⓑ Ⓒ Ⓓ   13. Ⓐ Ⓑ Ⓒ Ⓓ   25. Ⓐ Ⓑ Ⓒ Ⓓ   37. Ⓐ Ⓑ Ⓒ Ⓓ   49. Ⓐ Ⓑ Ⓒ Ⓓ
2. Ⓐ Ⓑ Ⓒ Ⓓ   14. Ⓐ Ⓑ Ⓒ Ⓓ   26. Ⓐ Ⓑ Ⓒ Ⓓ   38. Ⓐ Ⓑ Ⓒ Ⓓ   50. Ⓐ Ⓑ Ⓒ Ⓓ
3. Ⓐ Ⓑ Ⓒ Ⓓ   15. Ⓐ Ⓑ Ⓒ Ⓓ   27. Ⓐ Ⓑ Ⓒ Ⓓ   39. Ⓐ Ⓑ Ⓒ Ⓓ   51. Ⓐ Ⓑ Ⓒ Ⓓ
4. Ⓐ Ⓑ Ⓒ Ⓓ   16. Ⓐ Ⓑ Ⓒ Ⓓ   28. Ⓐ Ⓑ Ⓒ Ⓓ   40. Ⓐ Ⓑ Ⓒ Ⓓ   52. Ⓐ Ⓑ Ⓒ Ⓓ
5. Ⓐ Ⓑ Ⓒ Ⓓ   17. Ⓐ Ⓑ Ⓒ Ⓓ   29. Ⓐ Ⓑ Ⓒ Ⓓ   41. Ⓐ Ⓑ Ⓒ Ⓓ   53. Ⓐ Ⓑ Ⓒ Ⓓ
6. Ⓐ Ⓑ Ⓒ Ⓓ   18. Ⓐ Ⓑ Ⓒ Ⓓ   30. Ⓐ Ⓑ Ⓒ Ⓓ   42. Ⓐ Ⓑ Ⓒ Ⓓ   54. Ⓐ Ⓑ Ⓒ Ⓓ
7. Ⓐ Ⓑ Ⓒ Ⓓ   19. Ⓐ Ⓑ Ⓒ Ⓓ   31. Ⓐ Ⓑ Ⓒ Ⓓ   43. Ⓐ Ⓑ Ⓒ Ⓓ   55. Ⓐ Ⓑ Ⓒ Ⓓ
8. Ⓐ Ⓑ Ⓒ Ⓓ   20. Ⓐ Ⓑ Ⓒ Ⓓ   32. Ⓐ Ⓑ Ⓒ Ⓓ   44. Ⓐ Ⓑ Ⓒ Ⓓ   56. Ⓐ Ⓑ Ⓒ Ⓓ
9. Ⓐ Ⓑ Ⓒ Ⓓ   21. Ⓐ Ⓑ Ⓒ Ⓓ   33. Ⓐ Ⓑ Ⓒ Ⓓ   45. Ⓐ Ⓑ Ⓒ Ⓓ   57. Ⓐ Ⓑ Ⓒ Ⓓ
10. Ⓐ Ⓑ Ⓒ Ⓓ   22. Ⓐ Ⓑ Ⓒ Ⓓ   34. Ⓐ Ⓑ Ⓒ Ⓓ   46. Ⓐ Ⓑ Ⓒ Ⓓ   58. Ⓐ Ⓑ Ⓒ Ⓓ
11. Ⓐ Ⓑ Ⓒ Ⓓ   23. Ⓐ Ⓑ Ⓒ Ⓓ   35. Ⓐ Ⓑ Ⓒ Ⓓ   47. Ⓐ Ⓑ Ⓒ Ⓓ   59. Ⓐ Ⓑ Ⓒ Ⓓ
12. Ⓐ Ⓑ Ⓒ Ⓓ   24. Ⓐ Ⓑ Ⓒ Ⓓ   36. Ⓐ Ⓑ Ⓒ Ⓓ   48. Ⓐ Ⓑ Ⓒ Ⓓ   60. Ⓐ Ⓑ Ⓒ Ⓓ

answer sheet

PRINCIPLES OF PUBLIC SPEAKING DIAGNOSTIC TEST

Directions: Carefully read each of the following 20 questions. Choose the best answer to each question and fill in the corresponding circle on the answer sheet. The Answer Key and Explanations can be found following this Diagnostic Test.

1. When writing your speech, which of the following would be a good way to narrow or focus a topic choice?
   A. Topoi
   B. Brainstorming
   C. A tree diagram
   D. Surveys

2. In the U.S., the First Amendment ensures that speech is
   A. always protected, regardless of content.
   B. not all protected all of the time.
   C. protected if it's not broadcast.
   D. never protected.

3. Which of the following might be used as a narrative for supporting material?
   A. An example of how MP3 music files sound compared to MP4 files
   B. A story about how the Dodge brothers came to found their automobile company
   C. The opinion of a musician about a new recording technique
   D. A startling quotation meant to break the ice when beginning a speech

4. Which of the following is NOT a tool used in audience analysis?
   A. Demographic analysis
   B. Linguistics
   C. Questionnaires
   D. Situational analysis

5. In an interview, asking a closed question is a good way to
   A. get the interviewee to open up about his or her feelings and values.
   B. find out how the interviewee felt about his or her childhood.
   C. elicit brief, one- or two-word answers to questions about basic facts.
   D. communicate to the interviewee the fact that you're running short of time.

6. A gazetteer is a
   A. dictionary of foreign terms.
   B. broadsheet containing population data.
   C. geographical dictionary.
   D. dictionary of research terms.

7. The main points of a speech should be constructed as
   A. compound sentences.
   B. infinitive statements.
   C. parallel statements.
   D. rhetorical questions.

8. When using expert testimony from a person who may not be familiar to the audience, it's important to
   A. make the competence of the individual clear to the audience.
   B. place the source's name on the whiteboard, PowerPoint slide, or other display.
   C. discard that testimony, since the audience has no idea who the person is.
   D. challenge the testimony to show that you're unbiased.

9. In which of the following is the danger of stereotyping most likely?
   A. Questionnaires
   B. Direct observation
   C. Situational analysis
   D. Psychological analysis

10. Global plagiarism is the act of
    A. stealing from the speech of someone who lives far away.
    B. stealing an entire speech and presenting it as your own.
    C. using someone else's ideas in your speech.
    D. using parts of multiple speeches and combining them into one speech for which you take credit.

11. A good persuasive speech requires
    A. facts, evidence, and other supporting materials.
    B. that the writer agree with the position he or she takes in a speech.
    C. a strongly held opinion.
    D. familiarity with the topic.

12. The purpose of audience analysis is to
    A. help you memorize your speech.
    B. allow you to adapt your speech to your listener.
    C. improve the logic of your argument.
    D. determine the listeners' attitudes.

13. Which of the following do you NOT need to do when preparing for an interview?
    A. Determine the purpose of the interview.
    B. Write out intelligent and meaningful questions ahead of time.
    C. Select the specific goal of the speech.
    D. Choose an individual to interview and arrange an appointment.

14. The most effective speeches are written with what in mind?
    A. A specific audience
    B. A general audience
    C. The presenter's field of expertise
    D. The goal of the speech

15. Which type of argument is being used in the following statement: "Fever and a rash indicate an allergic reaction."?
    A. Argument from causation
    B. Argument from example
    C. Argument from analogy
    D. Argument from sign

16. What is one advantage of a manuscript speech?
    A. Eye contact is maintained.
    B. It's easy to respond to audience feedback.
    C. It may sound awkward or stilted.
    D. Timing can be controlled.

17. The introduction should
    A. make up about 20 percent of the entire speech.
    B. include a rhetorical question.
    C. gain the attention of the audience.
    D. clarify what listeners should do in response to the speech.

18. An informative speech attempts to
    A. persuade a listener.
    B. amuse a listener.
    C. explain something to a listener.
    D. convince a listener of something.

19. Because people listening to a speech are normally unable to follow along with a written copy, it's best to
    A. keep the language simple, and use only short words.
    B. use connectives and many concrete and familiar words.
    C. use as many abstract words as possible.
    D. keep the speech brief so as not to confuse listeners.

20. Adding sounds to words where they do not belong is a problem associated with
    A. articulation.
    B. pronunciation.
    C. pauses.
    D. proxemics.

diagnostic test

ANSWER KEY AND EXPLANATIONS

1. C	**5.** C	**9.** B	**13.** C	**17.** C
2. B	**6.** C	**10.** B	**14.** A	**18.** C
3. B	**7.** C	**11.** A	**15.** D	**19.** B
4. B	**8.** A	**12.** B	**16.** D	**20.** A

1. **The correct answer is C.** All four options are good tools for topic selection, but only a tree diagram is specifically meant to help you narrow your choice of topic.

2. **The correct answer is B.** Not all speech is protected all the time. Speech that is untrue, inflammatory, or seen as a danger to the community may be proscribed. Whether the speech is broadcast, printed, or spoken is irrelevant.

3. **The correct answer is B.** A narrative is a *story*. Examples (choice A) and opinions (choice C) often make good supporting material, but only choice B describes a story. A startling quotation (choice D) sometimes makes a good opening for a speech, but it's not normally supporting material, nor is it a story.

4. **The correct answer is B.** Linguistics is the study of language. Knowledge of language might play a part in crafting your speech, but it is not an audience analysis tool, as are the other three options.

5. **The correct answer is C.** The point of a closed question (*In what year were you born? In what state?*) is to elicit brief answers to basic questions. You would use *open* questions (*How do you feel about what's happened in the state politically?*) to get the interviewee to open up about his or her feelings or values (choice A) or childhood (choice B). You would never ask questions designed to

hurry the interviewee along because you're running out of time.

6. **The correct answer is C.** A gazetteer is a geographic dictionary. It is generally used with a map or atlas and presents information about the social and geographical makeup of a region or country.

7. **The correct answer is C.** Main points of a speech should be written in a parallel grammatical structure: each statement should be phrased in a similar way. Infinitive statements (choice B) are appropriate for specific purpose statements. Rhetorical questions (choice D) are often used in introductions to encourage listeners to consider a concept or an idea. Although writing a main point as a compound sentence (choice A) is acceptable, it's not required, and it does not necessarily imply parallelism.

8. **The correct answer is A.** Since your audience has not heard of this person, it's important to make sure they realize that the expert knows his or her subject. You might do this by citing the person's experience or educational background. You may choose to display the expert's name (choice B), but that's not as important as showing that he or she is competent to comment on this subject. You certainly wouldn't want to discard the expert's opinion (choice C) or challenge it (choice D).

9. **The correct answer is B.** It's possible to stereotype based on any of these, if you're willing to make the leap in logic. But the one that's *most* likely to lead to stereotyping is direct observation: it would be easy to make

judgments based on what you see when you *look at* (observe) your audience, and those judgments may be flawed, based on what you assume about what you see.

10. **The correct answer is B.** Global plagiarism is the act of stealing the entirety of another's work. Where your source lives (choice A) is irrelevant, and stealing the source's words or ideas is plagiarism in one form or another. Using someone else's ideas (choice C) is known as *incremental plagiarism*. Using multiple parts of multiple speeches verbatim (choice D) is known as *patchwork plagiarism*.

11. **The correct answer is A.** A persuasive speech cannot be effective unless its claims are supported by evidence—facts, examples, statistics, etc. It's not necessary to *agree* (choice B) with a position to argue it; in fact, arguing against (or for) a position in which you do (or do not) believe is excellent training in rhetoric, speechmaking, or debate. Similarly, you need not hold a strong opinion (choice C) or be familiar with the topic (choice D) in order to argue for or against something— although in the case of choice D, you will probably have to gain some familiarity with the topic through your research.

12. **The correct answer is B.** The purpose of audience analysis is to help you adapt your speech, modifying it so that it's effective with a specific audience. Analyzing your audience (choice A) would have little bearing on helping you memorize your speech, nor would it necessarily affect the logic of your argument (choice C). As a part of your analysis, you may wish to determine the attitudes of your listeners (choice D), but the *purpose* of that determination of attitude would be to help you adapt the speech.

13. **The correct answer is C.** You *may* have selected the specific goal of the speech, but it's not absolutely necessary to have done so; in fact, you may be interviewing as part of a process to *help* you select that goal. However, you do need to decide on the purpose of the interview, write out your questions, and arrange/schedule the interview ahead of time.

14. **The correct answer is A.** The best speeches are ones that are tailored to a particular audience. The goal (choice D) is definitely important, but a clear goal may still result in an ineffective speech if the speech is not audience-centered.

15. **The correct answer is D.** An argument from sign cites information that signals a claim. A fever and a rash typically accompany allergic reactions, so they are signs of an allergic reaction. The rash and fever did not *cause* the allergic reaction, so choice A is incorrect. An argument from example (choice B), supports a claim with examples, while an argument from analogy (choice C) supports a claim with a comparable situation.

16. **The correct answer is D.** With a manuscript speech, it's easy to control the timing, because you can deliver the exact same speech during practice until you get the timing where you want it; if you need a speech of exactly four minutes, you can write and practice it so that it takes exactly that long to deliver. Eye contact (choice A) is very desirable, and the inability to maintain eye contact is a *disadvantage* of reading from a manuscript. Similarly, it's very difficult to respond to feedback (choice B) when reading a speech. The fact that it may sound awkward (choice C) is a *disadvantage* of reading a speech from a prepared manuscript.

17. **The correct answer is C.** The introduction needs to grab the attention of your listeners. It generally makes up about 10 percent of the speech, not 20 percent (choice A). It may or may not include a rhetorical question (choice B), though that is one good approach. It usually does not clarify what the listeners

should do in response to the speech (choice D), because they've not yet heard the speech.

18. **The correct answer is C.** An informative speech *explains*. While the new information could persuade your listeners to act or think in a certain way (choice A)—and while the speech may be somewhat amusing (choice B)— the primary purpose of an informative speech is to inform, not to amuse or persuade.

19. **The correct answer is B.** Effective speeches tend to use concrete words that refer to tangible objects because they're easy to visualize. It's also good to use connectives as a way of making sure the audience is following along as you move from one idea, point, or topic to another. It's not necessary to use simple language (choice A), unless your audience (perhaps you're speaking to elementary school students) requires it. Using abstract words (choice C) tends to make it *more* difficult to understand, which is why concrete terms are recommended. You may wish to keep your speech brief (choice D), but that's a function of the topic and your audience analysis, not because the audience cannot follow along with a written copy.

20. **The correct answer is A.** Adding sounds where they do not belong is an articulation problem; a speaker might say ath-a-lete instead of ath-lete, for example. Errors in accentuation and the pronunciation of silent sounds are pronunciation problems (choice B). Filled and unfilled pauses (choice C) are typical of many speeches, but do not involve adding sounds to words. Proxemics (choice D) refers to how space is used by a speaker during a presentation

answers diagnostic test

DIAGNOSTIC TEST ASSESSMENT GRID

Now that you've completed the diagnostic test and read through the answer explanations, you can use your results to target your studying. Find the question numbers from the diagnostic test that you answered incorrectly and highlight or circle them below. Then focus extra attention on the sections within the chapter dealing with those topics.

Principles of Public Speaking	
Content Area	**Question #**
Ethical, Social, and Theoretical Considerations	2, 10
Audience Analysis, Adaptation, and Effect	4, 9, 12, 14
Topics and Purposes of Speeches	1, 18
Structure/Organization	7, 15, 17
Content/Supporting Materials	3, 5, 8, 13
Research	6, 11
Language and Style	19
Delivery	16, 20

GET THE FACTS

To see the DSST® Public Speaking Fact Sheet, go to *http://getcollegecredit.com/exam_fact_sheets* and click on the **Humanities** tab. Scroll down and click the **Public Speaking** link. Here you will find suggestions for further study material and the ACE college credit recommendations for passing the test.

ETHICAL, SOCIAL, AND THEORETICAL CONSIDERATIONS OF PUBLIC SPEAKING

Public speaking is simply one aspect of what's known more generally as *communication skills*. Knowing how to deliver a speech is not just a theoretical or intellectual exercise; it's very practical, and knowing how to speak in public will serve you well not only in your academic career, but also at work, at home, and with friends and colleagues.

Many students fear public speaking, but you don't have to: If you have a well-crafted speech and you've practiced delivering that speech, you have little to worry about. It's all about confidence, and if your speech is solid and you know some of the "tricks of the trade," you will have the confidence you need to deliver it effectively. This chapter will help you develop both your skills and your confidence.

The good news is that if you've ever taken a writing or rhetoric course, you already know much of what you'll need to craft a good speech. Many of the same skills and methods used to create a good story or fashion a cohesive argument on paper are exactly the same ones you will use to create an entertaining or persuasive speech; it's just that rather than a paper or essay as the final product, this time the final product will be a speech. So, many of the topics discussed here may look very familiar to you; if so, consider this a brush-up and an opportunity to learn how to use those skills in a new way.

ETHICS IN PUBLIC SPEAKING

We may not always stop to realize it, but there is an ethical component to speaking in public. In other words, when delivering a speech (as when writing a paper), there are issues of morality and fairness to consider, and those issues are present at every stage of the process—from selecting your topic to researching your speech, and from analyzing your audience to delivering the speech.

In the U.S., the First Amendment protects freedom of speech, but both law and common sense have long determined that not *all* speech is protected all the time; after all, some of that speech might be unfair, some might be untrue, some might be harmful, and the goals of some forms of speech may run counter to the goals of the society in which you live.

When the Greek philosopher Aristotle considered the speaker's role in public speaking, he referred to the concept of *ethos*, by which he meant the *character and credibility* of the speaker. In our terms, what he meant was that there are certain moral considerations to a speech—or any communication: Are the goals of the speech ethically sound? Is the subject matter appropriate for the audience? Is the information accurate and appropriately cited? If you can answer all of these questions in the affirmative, then both your speech and the person delivering the speech are considered credible; Aristotle would have said that the requirements of ethos have been met. If you are instead delivering a speech that evokes strong feelings for an immoral purpose (consider Hitler's use of hatred toward Jews to encourage German support of his actions, or the use of name-calling to degrade people based on their ethnicity, sexual orientation, or religion) then your ethos is suspect; you have subverted the tools we're discussing here. Aristotle would have said that your ethos—and therefore your credibility—are lacking.

Plagiarism

Perhaps the most obvious form of unethical speechwriting is plagiarism: the theft of another person's words or ideas. This can occur in any of three ways:

1. *Global plagiarism* occurs when an entire speech is stolen from a source, and the speaker presents the work as his or her own.

2. *Patchwork plagiarism* involves stealing from a number of sources, rather than from a single source. A speaker might copy word for word from *multiple* sources and then combine them into a single speech, for which he takes full credit.

3. *Incremental plagiarism* is subtler and sometimes difficult to recognize. Instead of stealing (and keep in mind that plagiarism is indeed a form of theft) sections of another's work verbatim, the speechwriter incorporates direct quotations in a speech or paraphrases the unique *ideas* of another person without giving proper credit. Both are considered plagiarism unless the original source is cited during the speech. (How can you know when an idea is uniquely yours or whether it came from elsewhere? It's not always easy to tell, but when in doubt, *cite*. The citation doesn't have to be complicated or clumsy; simply insert a quick reference into your speech—something like, "*As Dr. Olen Davis noted in a recent Stanford University study*, chimpanzees raised in a non-nurturing environment seem to become non-nurturers themselves, showing little affection for their offspring." In this example, the italicized portion is your citation.)

The bottom line is that any form of plagiarism is ethically unacceptable. It's a form of thievery; by taking credit for others' words or ideas, you're denying them credit (and sometimes payment) for what is rightfully theirs.

AUDIENCE ANALYSIS AND ADAPTATION

Imagine a conversation between two experienced photographers:

> Photographer 1: Well, it's a good setup, but I'm not sure the depth of field is going to work; I'd really like to see some circles of confusion behind those highlights. Otherwise, we'll be going all F/64 school—I don't think that'd work here.

> Photographer 2: Wouldn't you think that sort of bokeh would *detract*? Maybe distract the viewer?

> Photographer 1: No, I wouldn't worry about that. As long as we're following the rule of thirds, the viewer will look where we want him to. I'm a bit more worried about the lighting—you know, the inverse square law. I'd want to be careful about keeping the background correctly exposed without blowing out the highlights in her face. Maybe a balloon reflector off to one side? That kind of catchlight might also add some nice highlights in the eyes, too.

> Photographer 2: I think that'd help a lot! And if we start at F/2.8 and then bracket as we close down, we can shoot reciprocals; that should get us some we can use.

That conversation would make little sense to anyone who is not familiar with photography and with photographic technique. Of course, these two (theoretical) people understand one another; they're both familiar with the terminology and the shorthand—they're each an appropriate audience for what the other is saying.

Audience knowledge of a subject plays a major role in the language and terminology used in a speech. *Your* audience may not be familiar with your subject, so you need to learn about your audience and then tailor your speech to fit that audience.

In fact, your speech should be largely audience-centered: crafted specifically for your audience. In other words, the audience is your *primary* consideration when writing and delivering a speech. You don't want to be speaking over their heads; the audience might not understand you. But you also don't want to "dumb it down" too much; that would be insulting—not to mention boring. You need to understand your audience, identify with them, and get them on your side. This is known as *audience identification*, the process of forming a bond with listeners. You can do that by acquiring information about the audience's background and attitudes, and that knowledge will help you adapt your speech.

Speakers can learn about listeners in a number of ways:

- Direct observation
- Questionnaires
- Demographic audience analysis
- Situational audience analysis
- Psychological audience analysis

DIRECT OBSERVATION

Direct observation of your audience is the simplest, most straightforward way to gather information about your listeners: *look* at them. You can make inferences about them as people, about their economic status, and about their interests—all based largely on their clothing and appearance. But watch out, because there's a danger here; it's very easy to stereotype people based on their appearances, the way they speak, etc.

QUESTIONNAIRES

Depending on the situation, you may be able to gather information about your audience through a questionnaire. Questionnaires distributed via e-mail prior to a speech can help a speaker determine the attitudes and knowledge base of audience members regarding a particular topic; this method is often used for classroom speeches.

DEMOGRAPHIC ANALYSIS

A demographic analysis lets you learn about listeners based on demographic factors, including age, gender, religion, sexual orientation, ethnicity, economic status, occupation, education, and organizational membership.

Using a demographic analysis, it can be easy to stereotype, so watch out for that. On the other hand, this sort of analysis *does* allow us to make certain types of assumptions. For example, the age of audience members can have a significant impact on many aspects of a speech. An older audience would most likely be more interested in a speech about estate planning than about dating issues. In addition to guiding the speech topic, age also affects the information presented in the speech. An older audience would most likely understand historical references to World War II or the Great Depression, while a younger audience may require additional background information.

SITUATIONAL ANALYSIS

A situational analysis considers the characteristics of a particular audience, such as size, physical setting, occasion, and time. The size of an audience affects speech delivery; a small audience can be addressed informally, while a large audience requires more structure. Moreover, a large audience prevents a speaker from assessing how listeners are responding to a speech because of the distance between the speaker and each audience member. Flexibility during speech presentation is essential to adapting to audience size, which may be unknown until moments before the speech begins. The setting of a speech may be a classroom, a crowded auditorium, or a large dining hall, and unpleasant settings require speakers to remain energetic in order to hold the interest of listeners.

The time and occasion of a speech are important situational factor to consider. The tone and content of a pep-rally speech is very different from that of a presentation to stockholders. Time is another situational factor and refers to both the time of day and the length of the speech. Speakers often find listeners attentive in the morning and tired late in the afternoon, which is a consideration when determining the length of a speech. (Experts speaking at conventions, for example, always dread being assigned the 4:00 p.m. slot; the audience is tired and ready to head out to dinner. Speakers with the most clout—i.e., the best reputations and who are the most powerful draw—are usually assigned something close to the 10:00 a.m. slot. At that time, listeners tend to be focused and alert; they just had breakfast and have not yet started thinking about lunch; the day is young, so they're not yet tired. Think about your own experience taking that late afternoon/early evening class; it was often difficult to concentrate, wasn't it?)

PSYCHOLOGICAL ANALYSIS

A psychological analysis seeks to determine whether audiences are willing to listen to the speaker, whether they view your topic or thesis in a favorable or unfavorable light, and whether they're knowledgeable about the topic.

The answer to each of these will affect how you write and deliver your speech. If the audience is interested and there voluntarily (they may even have *paid* to attend), you should have little trouble. But if they were *forced* to attend (perhaps it's a class or work requirement), then you have to work to *make* them more willing. Use humor or startling examples to get their attention. Reward them for their attendance—let them know that you are aware of and appreciate their sacrifice. Do this *first*, before getting to the main topic of your speech. Show your audience how your topic relates to them and to their needs. In all of these cases, what you've done is connected with your audience and given them a good reason to listen.

ADAPTATION

All of this analysis is simply to allow you to *adapt* your message to make it appropriate for a specific audience. Audience adaptation occurs when preparing the speech *and* when presenting the speech. During the speechwriting process, the information gained from the audience analysis directs topic selection, determines examples to use, and guides the phrasing of introductions and conclusions. Audience adaptation is an important part of creating an audience-centered speech—one that is crafted for your specific audience and which takes their knowledge and attitudes into account. Every stage of the speechmaking process should consider audience response to the message. During the writing phase, a speaker modifies a speech to make it as coherent and appropriate as possible for the given audience. During speech presentations, effective speakers make adaptations based on audience feedback. For example, a speaker who presents a concept and notices confused looks on the faces of many listeners may review the idea again or rephrase the information in a different way. (This is one reason to make frequent eye contact during a speech; it helps you gather real-time feedback about how your message is being received. We'll address eye contact in more depth later.) Successful public speakers use audience analysis to adapt to audiences both before and during speeches.

SPEECH TOPICS AND PURPOSES

As with writing a paper, there are three possible purposes of a speech:

- To inform
- To persuade
- To entertain

An *informative* speech seeks to increase audience awareness and understanding of a subject. This kind of speech does not try to persuade listeners to respond or act, but a *persuasive* speech does exactly that: you're trying to change your listeners' attitudes, beliefs, or behaviors. The main purpose of an *entertaining* speech is, not surprisingly, simply to use humor and cleverness to amuse.

Note that these purposes can sometimes overlap. It is very possible to use humor and wit as a way of changing someone's beliefs or persuading them to take some action. It's equally possible to inform listeners in an entertaining fashion, while at the same time hoping to persuade them. Still, it helps to think of the purpose of your speech as predominantly informative, persuasive, or entertaining—while keeping in mind the possibility of some overlap.

Of course, every speech needs a topic, and there are many ways to generate topic ideas. Sometimes, as when an instructor or supervisor *assigns* you a topic (*Joanne, would you address the Board of Directors at the next meeting and explain to them how our supply chain works?*), you simply have no real choice of topic.

SOURCES OF TOPICS

Usually, though, you'll need to come up with a topic and there are plenty of possible sources. You might start by looking at *surveys*, such as the Gallup Poll; those can provide you with topic ideas related to current issues, trends, or problems. Newspapers and magazines, such as *Time*, *Newsweek*, and *Forbes*, can provide information about current events and issues about which people are concerned.

Brainstorming is another topic-selection tool, one that works especially well when there are two or more people involved. You simply throw out ideas, preferably as quickly as possible, while someone jots them down in a notepad or on a marker board. The only rule is that there's no such thing as a bad idea—*everything* gets written down, even if it sounds silly at first; sometimes these "silly" ideas lead to good ones, and sometimes the silly one turns out not to be silly at all.

A *tree diagram* can also help you generate a topic, and it's an especially good way to help you *focus* on or narrow a topic. You simply write a topic idea on a "branch," and then repeatedly divide that first topic into smaller and smaller parts until you arrive at a manageable topic. You can do the same thing by placing topics into "bubbles" and then drawing more bubbles off of that main one, and then more off of those smaller bubbles, etc. This approach is sometimes called **mind mapping**. If you were going to speak about motorcycles, for example, you might realize right away that "motorcycles" is much too broad a topic for a brief speech; you could write an entire book—or several books—about motorcycles. But you might be able to narrow that topic by using a tree diagram or mind map. If you did, you might end up with the much more manageable motorcycle-related topic of "helmets" in this fashion: Motorcycles-->Safety-->Safety Gear-->Helmets. If you know (or would like to learn) about motorcycle helmets, you can certainly deliver a focused 5- or 10-minute speech on that topic much more easily than trying to cram everything there is to know about motorcycles into one speech.

A fourth way to generate topic ideas is to use *topoi*. This method is based on ancient rhetorical techniques (back to Aristotle again) and involves asking and answering questions in order to generate topic ideas by stimulating creative thinking. The word "topoi" comes from "topos," and means a collection of stock topics used in rhetoric as subjects for argument. It has since come to mean generating topics in a broader sense. Ask yourself some questions about your general subject area: *Who? What? Why? When? Where? How? So?* For example, if we start with drug addiction as our main subject, we might ask these questions: Who is the addict? What does addiction really mean? Why did that person become an addict? When did it happen? Where did it happen? How did he or she become addicted? What does it mean; that is, *so*? (i.e., Who cares? Should I care?)

You can see how this sort of dialog can lead to some very penetrating questions, which can in turn lead to excellent topic ideas.

Of course, after you develop a list of topics, all possible speech subjects should be evaluated to determine which one is most appropriate:

- Topics should be interesting to the speaker; otherwise, your lack of enthusiasm will be apparent to listeners.
- Topics should be interesting and useful to the audience, which can be determined through an audience analysis.
- Topics should be ethically appropriate.
- Topics should be appropriate for the specific occasion, which means that the speech should meet audience expectations, be relevant, and be narrow in scope.

In general, topics that are interesting and appropriate for the speaker, the audience, and the occasion make the most effective speeches.

GENERAL PURPOSE, SPECIFIC PURPOSE, AND GOALS

Once you've established a topic and a general purpose (to persuade, inform, or entertain—or some combination of these), it's time to think about the *specific* purpose of your speech, your exact goal. What are you trying to *do* with this speech, exactly? It helps to have a specific purpose statement that focuses on one clear idea, and which can be stated in a brief infinitive phrase—that is, "to," followed by a verb: "to explain how a recycling plant works," "to inform listeners about their choices in the upcoming election," "to persuade my audience to stop texting while driving." Specific purpose statements guide the direction of the speech, and they serve as one of the most critical early steps of the speechmaking process.

The specific purpose statement leads into the thesis statement, which is the central idea or theme of the speech. Does this sound familiar? It should; it's exactly the same way you might write an essay or paper, by using a thesis statement to explain to your reader—in this case, listener—what you want your audience to learn.

Just as in writing an essay, the thesis statement of an informative speech should be neutral, while the thesis statement of a persuasive speech should express a clear opinion. Here are two examples:

- There are three primary causes of heart disease. (thesis statement for an informative speech)
- All high school athletes should be drug-tested. (thesis statement for a persuasive speech)

The formation of the specific statement of purpose occurs early in the speechwriting process, but the thesis statement typically develops only after you've researched and analyzed the topic. A well-written thesis statement helps develop main ideas for a speech, and it focuses audience attention.

For informative speeches, the thesis is most often stated early in the presentation. For persuasive speeches, the time to introduce your thesis statement depends on the audience: If an audience analysis has determined that listeners are neutral or positive toward the speech topic, then clearly stating the thesis early in the presentation is appropriate. If the audience of a persuasive speech is most likely hostile to the speaker's position, then arguments and evidence should be provided *before* gradually presenting the thesis.

RESEARCH AND CONTENT

In some ways, this is the most difficult part of writing a speech (or a paper). We're used to "arguing" off the top of our heads; we know what we think, and we want the listener to think that way too. If we don't have enough information to convince them, we simply get *louder*. Pretty soon, what started out as a rational discussion or argument turns ugly. It's no longer an argument, it's a fight.

Speech topics require research and planning; that's why this is the difficult part—we may not be used to doing research, to having to come up with facts and examples, to finding *evidence* to convince our listeners. You generally can't simply use the force of your strongly held opinion to make someone believe as you do. Of course, if the speech topic is an area familiar to the writer, then life stories and personal experiences make excellent additions to any presentation. However, most speeches cannot rely solely on the expertise of the speaker, so supplemental information needs to be gathered.

One more thing to note about research: If you're doing it right, you will always end up with *too much* information. There will be data, quotes, facts, and general information that you simply don't need. Of course, you won't know that until you begin writing your speech. But you will find that if you've done the "legwork" (i.e., the research), writing the speech will be fairly straightforward. If you run into trouble while writing, it will almost always be because you didn't do enough research. So, too much information is exactly what you want; you don't have to use it, of course, but if it's not there, you'll miss it.

LIBRARY VERSUS THE INTERNET

It's the Internet age. To find information, we rely on digital devices and on data stored on servers many thousands of miles away. And we have at hand millions of websites and blogs and online news media that we can use when we seek information.

And yet, for a number of reasons, the library remains the primary place to go when we need information, partly because the library houses both types of information sources, print and electronic. Also, the print information in a library (especially in the research sections) tends to be *vetted*; it's usually evaluated and scrutinized prior to making it into print. There's nothing magic about this. It's just that printing things costs a lot of money, and people—read: publishers and printers—usually want to make sure that what they're about to publish meets certain standards. Thus, print content in a library tends to have been checked over pretty thoroughly. This is not always the case with online sources. But more about that shortly.

Even in the digital age, you can find a number of excellent sources at your local (or school) library:

- Books
- Periodical databases
- Newspapers
- Encyclopedias
- Government publications
- Quotation books
- Biographical aids
- Atlases and gazetteers

If the topic of a speech has been a significant issue for at least six months, then it is highly likely that information can be located in a book. Information regarding more recent issues and topics will be found in periodicals: magazines and professional journals that are published on a regular basis. Periodical databases can help you locate particular articles from magazines and journals and typically provide abstracts, or summaries, of each article. General databases, such as *Reader's Guide to Periodical Literature* and LexisNexis, include popular magazines as well as major academic journals. For topics not covered in general periodicals, search special databases, such as ERIC (the Educational Research Information Center). Libraries keep copies of current issues of local newspapers, and they keep back issues on microfilm or in digital form. LexisNexis and ProQuest are useful tools for locating articles from national and international newspapers. When information is needed about contemporary individuals, biographical aids, such as *Who's Who in America*, can be useful. Atlases, which are books of maps, and gazetteers, which are geographical dictionaries, are resources for facts about places around the world. Another excellent resource for facts about places around the world is the *World Factbook*, published—oddly enough—by the Central Intelligence Agency (CIA). The *World Factbook* used to be published only as an actual printed book, but it is now available online (see ***https://www.cia.gov/library/publications/the-world-factbook***).

Which brings us to the Internet. In addition to the library, the Internet plays a significant role in modern research, but the accuracy of information is sometimes a concern. The wealth of information available on the Internet is extensive, but unlike libraries, the Internet lacks quality-control mechanisms. The reality is that, while it takes money and skill and a certain level of investment to print a book or newspaper, just about anyone can publish anything he or she wants on the World Wide Web, basically at no cost. There are no barriers to entry there, as there are in traditional publishing. In many ways this is good: The Internet has democratized information; unfortunately, it's also democratized misinformation.

There are search engines of course, including Google, DuckDuckGo, and Yahoo, and they can help you find almost anything you would like to find. (And many things you may not want to find.) But these search engines merely *index* Web pages, they do not *evaluate* those pages. Instead, that evaluation is up to you. Wikipedia is an interesting experiment in the democratization of information: Anyone can write a Wikipedia article, and anyone can edit those articles. The site can definitely contain biased or erroneous information, but errors tend over time to get weeded out by others who come along and improve or remove the questionable data. As a result, Wikipedia is not a bad place to start your research; just don't rely on it exclusively. And be sure to check out the references listed at the bottom of any articles in which you're interested; those usually point to excellent source materials.

CONDUCTING INTERVIEWS

Research interviews are another useful tool for gathering information for speeches. Depending on the topic, college professors, business professionals, physicians, psychologists, and engineers can all offer expertise, information, and opinions that may prove useful and interesting.

In order for an interview to be successful, you'll need to:

- Determine the purpose of the interview
- Write out questions that are intelligent and meaningful
- Choose an individual to interview and arrange an appointment

During an interview, it is important to remain flexible and attentive. Follow-up questions help gain additional information from primary questions, which are prepared in advance. Open questions (*Why did you become a police officer?*) are broad questions designed to discover the interviewee's values and perspectives, and they tend to elicit long, rambling answers. These are questions to which it is impossible to give one- or two-word answers. Let the interviewee talk; sometimes he or she will get off on a tangent that turns out to be interesting and useful. Obviously, you don't have to use everything the interviewee says, so you're free to pick and choose. But keep in mind that you can't selectively use quotes taken out of context to advance your own agenda or bolster your own opinion; doing so would be unethical. In contrast, closed questions (*Where were you born?*) elicit brief answers. Being appropriately dressed, arriving on time, and maintaining the purpose of the interview all show respect for the interviewee's time. Taking accurate notes or recording the interview ensures that the information gathered will not be lost and that your recollection of the conversation will be accurate.

Here's an important interviewing trick. When your interview is finished, after you've thanked the interviewee for his or her time, ask one last follow-up question: *Is there anyone else knowledgeable about this topic that you would recommend I call or e-mail?* You will almost always end your interview with another source of information, and when you call or email that person, you can explain, "so-and-so suggested I speak with you." Having one expert recommend another expert is a gift of sorts; you didn't have to go search out another source, and your new source has already been vetted by the expert who recommended him or her.

CONTENT AND SUPPORTING MATERIALS

As we've discussed, effective speeches require evidence to validate and explain opinions and issues. The evidence comes in the form of supporting materials—content that is incorporated into a speech that provides information, maintains listener interest, and asserts persuasive evidence. Supporting materials include examples, narratives, testimonies, statistics, and quotations. Most of these types of supporting materials are fairly obvious, but let's break them down, just for the sake of clarity:

- *Narratives* are stories told to illustrate a concept or point. Narratives help illustrate abstract ideas, and they come in three basic types: explanatory, exemplary, and persuasive. As suggested by the names, explanatory narratives explain events, exemplary narratives are examples of excellence (such as rags-to-riches stories about famous people), and persuasive narratives attempt to change beliefs or attitudes. An anecdote is a brief story that is usually humorous.

- *Examples* are brief, specific instances used to illustrate a point. If the example is long enough and you tell a story about it, it becomes a narrative. Be sure to distinguish between real and hypothetical (imaginary) examples, so as not to confuse or mislead your audience.

- *Testimonies* are the opinions of experts (or, in some cases, eyewitnesses) that support a speaker's claim. Testimonies add substance to a speech. Although personal testimonies can be incorporated into a speech, listeners are generally more persuaded by expert testimonies. When using expert testimonies, it is important to make the competence of the individual clear to the audience, especially if the person's name is unknown to most listeners. The testimony's unbiased nature should be emphasized so that the information will have a significant impact on the audience. Testimonies should also be recent in order to be most effective.

- *Statistics* are verifiable numerical data used to clarify or make a point. The fact that the data is verifiable is important; otherwise, people could just make up numbers to "prove" whatever they wanted you to believe. You can use statistics to illustrate points in informative speeches; in persuasive speeches, statistics serve to provide the basis of claims and arguments. Be sure to use only recent statistics, and only from reliable (and perhaps multiple) sources. Finally, don't overuse them. Nothing will make your listeners' eyes glaze over more quickly than an overwhelming amount of data; the use of only a few interesting numbers is far more effective.

- Quotations are verbatim explanations or opinions used in a speech. Naturally, you would cite the source of the quotation: *As British statesman Winston Churchill once said, "In politics when you are in doubt what to do, do nothing ... when you are in doubt what to say, say what you really think."* As with statistics (or really, any supporting material), it's best not to overuse quotations or to use quotations that are too lengthy.

EVALUATING SUPPORTING MATERIAL

Remember: If you're doing a good job of research, you're going to end up with more information than you can use in this one speech. And that's okay; better too much information than not enough.

So how will you evaluate this material? You can start by subjecting the information to a four-pronged test, asking these questions:

- Is the information relevant and significant?
- Is it easily understood?
- Is it striking and/or unique?
- Is it credible, ethical, and accurate?

If you're using the Internet for research, you might consider using what some teachers call the CRAAP test. When you look at a website, ask these questions:

- **Currency:** Is the material current? When was it published or posted? Has it been recently updated? Do the links work, or have they gone dead?

- **Relevance:** Does the information relate to the topic? Who is the intended audience? Is that audience similar to yours in terms of the level or scope of the information? Could you comfortably cite this material in a research paper?

- **Authority:** What is the source of this information? Can you determine who is the author? The publisher? What are the author's credentials? Is there contact information on the site? Could you contact the writer or publisher if you wanted to? Does the URL reveal anything about the author or publication? (For instance, a .com or .biz address is commercial, .org is usually a nonprofit organization, .edu is an educational institution, .gov is a government-sponsored website.)

- **Accuracy:** Can you tell if the information is reliable, correct, and truthful? Is there evidence to support the author's contentions? Could you verify that information using another source—or even from personal knowledge?

- **Purpose:** Why is this information there in the first place? Is the site trying to inform? To sell? To entertain? To persuade? Is the information objective and impartial, or can you spot ideological, religious, personal, or other biases?

Remember, the Internet is an excellent source of information, but much of it has not been verified to the degree that, say, a professional journal has been verified. Always double-check anything you find on the Internet—after all, people can put anything they want on a website or blog.

PERSUASIVE APPEALS

Writers and public speakers must support their assertions with what Aristotle referred to as extrinsic or intrinsic proofs. *Extrinsic* proofs support claims with objective evidence, such as laws and confessions.

Intrinsic proofs, also known as artistic proofs, are based on the speaker's character and credibility, the emotional nature of the issue, and the logic of the argument to persuade listeners.

Aristotle referred to three kinds of persuasive appeals, or intrinsic proofs, used in public speaking:

Types of Persuasive Appeals	
Logos	The appeal to reason or logic
Ethos	An appeal based on a speaker's moral character and knowledge
Pathos	The appeal to emotion

Logical proof, or *logos*, takes place when a speaker attempts to persuade an audience with rational evidence and arguments. In order for logical proof to be effective, evidence and supporting materials closely connect to the arguments presented in a speech.

In modern society, *ethos* is referred to as source or speaker credibility. Credible speakers are viewed as knowledgeable about the speech topic, trustworthy, friendly, poised, believable, and energetic.

Emotional proof, or *pathos*, involves the use of emotional appeals to persuade an audience. Public speakers may evoke negative emotions from listeners, such as fear, guilt, shame, anger, and sadness. When tapping into negative emotions, the goal is to convince listeners that the proposal presented in the speech will reduce such feelings. For example, a speech aimed at convincing teenagers to stop smoking might include cancer and heart disease statistics in an attempt to arouse fear and ultimately the elimination of a harmful habit. Speeches may also arouse positive emotions, such as joy, pride, relief, hope, and compassion. For example, a speaker who is trying to encourage the audience to volunteer with the Red Cross might describe the feelings of pride associated with assisting hurricane and tornado victims.

There are four common types of argument. One can argue from *example*, from *analogy*, from *causation*, and from *sign*. Let's look briefly at each of these.

- **Example:** Draws a conclusion from one or more instances or examples. *I like the paintings of Monet, Renoir, and Cassatt. I like Impressionist art.*

- **Analogy:** Illustrates similarities between two things or events. *David likes Bach, Beethoven, and Brahms. I know Kate likes Bach and Beethoven, so she will probably like Brahms.* The speaker assumes that because David likes Brahms and the others, Kate will also like all three.

- **Causation:** Draws a conclusion that an event that occurs first is responsible for a later event. *Interest rates have fallen, so home sales will probably increase.* (This type of logic can lead to the false-cause or *post hoc* fallacy, discussed below.)

- **Sign:** Uses an observable symptom or indicator as proof of a claim. *The Republican candidate will be elected. She has more campaign workers and yard signs in the community.* Or consider this one: *That streetlight is out. I'll bet those kids next door have been out shooting their pellet guns again!*

Even without knowing the names of these forms of arguments, you will tend to use one or more of them in a persuasive speech. However, when arguing, be sure to avoid the common fallacies or errors that occur in public speeches. Those are *hasty generalizations*, *false-cause fallacies*, *invalid analogies*, and *ad hominem attacks*. Here's a brief explanation of each:

- Hasty generalizations occur when a speaker jumps to a conclusion without sufficient evidence.

- False-cause (or *post hoc ergo propter hoc*; or simply *post hoc*) fallacies occur when a speaker makes the invalid assumption that one event causes another event, when in fact the events may have been coincidental. Or, as others have said more succinctly, "Correlation does not imply causation."

- Invalid analogies occur when a speaker compares two events or things that are in fact not alike.

- Ad hominem refers to the fallacy of attacking (or praising) the character or integrity of the person making the argument rather than dealing with the actual issue being discussed.

ORGANIZING YOUR SPEECH

It doesn't matter how much effort you've put into research or how perceptive or logical your argument is if you end up presenting the speech in a confusing, disorganized fashion. You may have some excellent points to make, but if the speech isn't structured well, your audience will be unable to appreciate them, and will be confused—especially when you move from one point to another.

The process of organizing a speech takes time, but it's time well spent. Making the effort to organize and structure your speech will help you see which points need additional development and which ones need trimming. Organized speeches, whether they are informative or persuasive, are easier for audiences to follow and to remember. Your credibility will also be increased, because audience members are more likely to view an organized individual as competent.

MAIN POINTS

You need to organize the body of your speech even before you write the introduction or conclusion— or at least before you finalize your introduction and conclusion. After all, the process of organizing and reorganizing the body of the speech may suggest to you a different, more effective introduction or conclusion.

Use your thesis statement as a guide or starting point for developing the main points of your speech, the two to five points that will appear in the body of your speech. Why limit yourself to five main points? You're delivering a brief speech, not a dissertation; more points may make a speech too confusing for listeners. Keep in mind that:

- Main points should be relevant and interesting to the audience. Don't go off on a tangent, especially not a tangent that's interesting only to you.

- Main points should be worded in a parallel style. Parallel statements help listeners understand and follow a speech more easily than points constructed in different grammatical styles. If your first main point is phrased as an imperative (e.g., *Never go grocery shopping when hungry.*), then your remaining points should *also* be phrased as imperatives (e.g., *Always walk the store in a clockwise direction, because the stores expect you to walk counterclockwise and they arrange their most tempting goods so that you encounter them first.*).

- Main points should also be distinct, which means there should be no overlap among them. If you combine points, you diminish their impact and confuse the listener. So, you should probably avoid saying *Speed and style are the main reasons the Corvette consistently wins awards*. It's more effective to break out the points, saying *Speed is one of the main reasons the Corvette consistently wins awards*. Then explain why that is so, and then move on to your next point: *Style also plays a large role in the success of the Corvette*. and then go on to explain why that is so. (Of course, you can combine your points as part of a brief introduction or during a recap near the end of the speech, as a way to review.)

After the main points have been determined, information and supporting materials need to be structured in a strategic organizational pattern. Strategic organization refers to arranging a speech in a specific way in order to achieve a specific result with a specific audience. (That's a large number of "specifics" at one time, but keep in mind that this is what you're trying to do; you want to tailor your speech, and the organization of that speech, to a very specific audience. That's why we refer to audience-centeredness as an important component of speechwriting.)

ORGANIZATIONAL PATTERNS

The best organizational pattern for a speech depends on the topic, purpose, and audience. There are six types of organizational patterns used most often in public speaking:

- Topical
- Temporal
- Spatial
- Problem-solution
- Cause-effect
- Motivated sequence

The *topical* pattern of speech organization is useful when a topic is easily subdivided, such as the five branches of the U.S. military. The main points of a topical speech are parts of a whole. Topical order works well with both informational and persuasive speeches, so it is a commonly used pattern.

With the *temporal* or *chronological* pattern of organization, the main points follow a timeline: first one thing happens, then another, and then another, and so on until the end. Temporal patterns are most often used in informative speeches. For example, a temporal pattern might be appropriate for a speech about the construction of Mount Rushmore, with the main points following the creation of the monument from the first carving until its completion. Temporal patterns are also useful when explaining a process, such as how photosynthesis works or how to change a flat tire, assemble a bicycle, or download a music file.

Spatial order is a type of speech structure in which main points are organized in a directional pattern—top to bottom, left to right, east to west, or inside to outside. Speeches about the layout of a university or the skeletal structure of the human body would be suitable for spatial order. Spatial order is another organizational pattern that is most appropriate for informative speeches. Note that the fact that you're moving top to bottom or east to west is important; there has to be a logic to your movement. You don't want to be skipping all over the place, first describing the front of the university's main office and then skipping to the basement in the chemistry lab, then jumping over to the orange grove that's part of the agriculture department, and then back to the university's main building, and so on. If it's not a spatial sequence that the listener can envision easily, the audience will be confused.

The *problem-solution* pattern is common in persuasive speeches when a speaker wants to convey the existence of a problem and then provide a solution that will mitigate or eliminate the problem. In the problem-solution structure, the first main point focuses on the existence of the problem, and the second main point offers a solution to the problem. Keep in mind that the structure can get a bit complicated, because there are often multiple problems contributing to the main one, so your solution(s) would have to address each of those.

Causal order, or the *cause-effect* pattern, organizes main points to illustrate a cause-effect relationship. The causal order calls for dividing a speech into two main points, similar to the problem-solution pattern. A speech about teenage drug use might be appropriate for a cause-effect organization. Effects of illicit drug use by adolescents would follow the potential causes. However, causal order lends itself to some flexibility—either the causes or the effects can be presented first, depending on which order is more appropriate for the topic. For example, perhaps it would be more impactful if you began your speech talking about the *effects* of drug use and *then* move into the causes. Causal order is used in both persuasive and informative speeches.

The *motivated sequence* is an organizational pattern developed in the 1930s by Alan H. Monroe, a communications professor. Monroe created the pattern for sales presentations, but it has since been found useful in all types of persuasive and informative speeches. When you think about it, this makes perfect sense: You want to get the audience on your side; you want them to buy into what you're saying. What better approach than something that was originally designed as a sales tool?

Motivated sequence is useful when a speaker wants listeners to respond in a positive way, so it is often employed in political speeches and advertisements. Rather than structuring a speech in three parts—introduction, body, and conclusion—as is typical of most speeches, the motivated sequence divides a speech into *five* steps:

1. Step 1: Gain attention from listeners.
2. Step 2: Establish a need or a problem.
3. Step 3: Satisfy the need by offering a solution.
4. Step 4: Visualize the need of being satisfied in the future.
5. Step 5: Ask for action from the audience to ensure the need is satisfied.

INTRODUCTIONS

When writing a speech, many students find themselves staring at a blank computer screen or pad of paper, wondering, "Where do I start?! I have no idea how to begin." If that's you, then the answer is simple: *Don't* begin. Or at least, don't begin at the beginning. You've done your research, you have some idea of the main points you want to make; don't worry yet about how to begin (or end) your speech, just start in the middle, with the body. Thinking about the points you're making will almost always provide you with that introduction (or conclusion) that you need.

Now, that said, sooner or later you *do* have to come up with a decent introduction and conclusion, and there are many proven approaches that you can use to find a good way to begin or end your speech.

The introduction of a speech serves a number of critical functions:

- Gain the attention and interest of the audience
- Preview the topic of the speech
- Establish speaker credibility and a connection with listeners

Speech introductions are typically about 10 percent of the entire speech, so a speech that is 500 words in length needs an introduction that is 40–60 words. Creativity is the key to a good introduction, and there are six primary types of introductions commonly used by public speakers:

Types of Introductions	
Startling statement	A shocking statement that relates to the speech topic
Rhetorical question	A question relevant to the topic that listeners answer mentally rather than vocally
Story	An interesting story related to the main point of the speech
Personal reference	An illustration of the way(s) in which the speech topic is relevant to audience members
Quotation	An attention-getting or thought-provoking quotation
Suspense	Wording that leaves the audience uncertain about the topic and raises listener curiosity

Keep in mind that introductions are only valuable if they directly relate to the speech topic. Irrelevant stories, quotations, or statements may initially intrigue listeners, but if the introduction fails to connect to the subject of the speech, listeners may become annoyed or confused. Establishing credibility and goodwill with listeners is critical during the introduction. An audience needs to perceive that a speaker is qualified to discuss a topic (i.e., that he or she is credible) and has the best interests of listeners in mind.

EFFECTIVE CONCLUSIONS

The conclusion of your speech may be the thing that leaves the most lasting impression with your listeners. Thus, good speakers take the time to construct memorable conclusions. Your conclusion should do three things:

- *Alert the audience that the speech is ending.* There's nothing worse than an abrupt end to a speech. The audience is confused and has no idea what just happened. Is it over? Should they applaud? Wait—what was the point?! Are we supposed to leave now? It's important to provide your audience with signals that the speech is ending. Phrases such as *in conclusion* and *to summarize,* are obvious cues that a speaker is preparing to stop. Experienced speakers use their voices and bodies to indicate the conclusion of a speech. Dramatic gestures, stepping away from the podium, pausing, and changing vocal pitch signal the end of a speech. A speaker who utilizes a *crescendo ending* builds a speech to a powerful and intense conclusion. In contrast, a *dissolve ending* evokes emotions by fading gradually to one final dramatic statement.

- *Summarize the speech.* This is your chance to recap your main points and reinforce your thesis or central idea. One way to do this is to (briefly) restate your main points; another is to recast those main ideas into a single statement.

- *Clarify what listeners should think or do as a response to the speech.* When you finish a speech, you're seeking a specific response—what's called the *anticipated response*. Especially with persuasive speeches, you want your listeners to act or think in a certain way; with informative speeches, you want your audience to *remember* certain things—what to do in case of a fire, how to reboot their computers, how to react if they happen upon a bear while on a camping trip. Your conclusion should make these anticipated responses clear to your listener, clarifying what you wish them to think or do as a result of having heard your speech. Some might phrase this as a call to action, and your conclusion may literally invoke such a call: *Now, don't forget—next week during the School Board meeting, we need to show up in strength and make our views known!* Or, *Now that you know how to keep your pets safe and healthy, be sure to visit your vet and pick up some Acme Not-On-My-Dog-You-Don't flea and tick spray.*

LANGUAGE AND STYLE

The introduction, body, and conclusion of a speech are only effective if they flow well together and if the language used is appropriate for the audience, so effective public speakers address issues of language and style.

LINKING WITH CONNECTIVES

The various elements of your speech can only flow well together if ideas are *connected*—i.e., linked in such a way that your listener can follow them. Linking various ideas within a speech—that is, transitioning from one idea to another—is accomplished by using words and phrases known as connectives.

Connectives help listeners understand the relationship between one concept and another, and a speech without connectives lacks flow and confuses listeners. There are four types of connectives commonly used in public speaking:

1. Transitions
2. Signposts
3. Internal previews
4. Internal summaries

Transitions are words or phrases that indicate when a speaker is moving from one point to another, and they're most commonly included when a speaker is shifting from the introduction to the body, from the body to the conclusion, and between main points in the speech. In the following example, the connectives are underlined.

> <u>Now that we have looked at</u> what nanotechnology is, let's see how it is used.

Signposts are a second type of connective used in speeches. Signposts consist of brief statements that indicate to listeners where the speaker is in the speech, in the same way that signposts on a road tell you where you are on a highway. Sometimes, signposts are numerical, as in the following example.

> *The second reason to protect your skin with sunscreen is to prevent the development of melanoma.*

Many speakers also use questions as signposts because questions invite listeners to think about the answer and become more attentive.

> *So, why do teenagers begin smoking when they are aware of all of these health risks?*

In addition to alerting audiences to the speaker's location in a speech, signposts are also useful as a way of signaling that an important point is coming up.

> *Foremost, you need to remember that…*
>
> *Make sure that you keep this in mind…*
>
> *This is a critical point…*

Internal previews are another type of connective used in the body of public speeches. As the name suggests, an internal preview is a statement that tells the audience what's coming up, that is, what to expect next. Internal previews differ from transitions and signposts because they are more detailed.

> *In discussing the effects of World War II on Japan, we'll first look at the economic consequences of the war and then at the cultural impact.*

Although internal previews are not necessary for every main point, they are useful when an audience may need assistance grasping concepts presented in a speech.

The fourth connective is an *internal summary*, a quick review of the points that a speaker has just made. Internal summaries are especially useful when a speaker has finished discussing a complicated or especially significant point. Before moving on to the next point, the speaker will provide a statement in the form of an internal summary to remind an audience of what has just been presented.

> *As we've seen, the path leading to World War I was complex and confusing, with many seemingly random events contributing to its outbreak. But the events that followed the war were even more tumultuous.*

Effectively used connectives help speakers form coherent speeches that are easy for listeners to understand. Most speakers use a combination of different connectives to unify the main points presented in a speech.

MAKING THE MOST OF YOUR WORDS

Words matter. They can be very powerful and very helpful or, if misused, very hurtful. You know this from your interactions with friends, colleagues, and loved ones. While it's important to utilize such things as connectives in your speech to join your ideas and to help the listener move from one topic to another, those ideas will lose their impact if presented via poorly chosen, ineffective words. If you want your speech to be informative or persuasive—or both—choosing the most effective words can increase the clarity and impact of a speech. This makes vocabulary a powerful tool for the speechmaker. Your vocabulary will grow as you read and write, but there's nothing wrong with turning to a dictionary or thesaurus to find the exact word you're looking for.

Words have two kinds of meaning. The denotative meaning of a word is its literal and objective meaning found in a dictionary. For example, the dictionary definition of the noun *government* means "a branch of the ruling authority of a state or nation." The connotative meaning of a word is subjective and variable. Therefore, the connotative meaning of the word *government* includes the feelings and emotions that the word suggests—the associations your listener brings to the word, and these will vary within an audience. Some audience members may think of democracy or beneficial services that the government provides. Others may associate government with bureaucracy, politics, and overspending. Effective public speakers choose words that are less likely to set off intense reactions, and they are aware of and sensitive to a word's denotation and connotation. It's interesting to note that some connotations are cultural; in western societies, the color white is associated with purity, but in some eastern countries, white is associated with death and mourning.

Using language clearly and specifically is essential to an effective speech because listeners do not have the benefit of following along with a written copy. In contrast with most written language, oral style includes the use of familiar words, connectives, and references to the speaker, such as *in my opinion*, or *it seems to me*. Public speakers are also likely to use concrete words rather than abstract words. Concrete words refer to tangible objects that are easy to visualize, such as *flat tire, beagle*, and *digital camera*. Abstract words, such as *science, entertainment*, and *technology*, refer to ideas or concepts that conjure up different images for different people. Abstract words are typically more ambiguous than concrete words. Although the use of abstract words cannot (and should not) be completely avoided, speeches dominated by concrete words are typically clearer for the audience.

While concrete words serve to improve the clarity of a speech, they can also be used effectively with imagery. Imagery refers to vivid language included in a speech that creates mental images of experiences, objects, or concepts. Concrete words establish sights, sounds, and emotions that draw listeners into a speech, while similes and metaphors bring life and creativity to a speech.

Similes make direct comparisons between two unlike things using *like* or *as*:

> *When the storm approached, the clouds swirled in the sky like cotton candy being twisted onto a stick.* (The clouds aren't really cotton candy, but in some ways, they are *like* cotton candy.)

Metaphors compare two dissimilar things without the use of *like* or *as*:

> *The air in the crowded stadium was thick with anticipation while everyone waited for the concert to begin.* (Anticipation doesn't really make air thick, but it can *feel* thick. Note the lack of the words *like* or *as*.)

So, a combination of concrete words and vivid language (the latter often created by using metaphor and simile), can help create an effective speech.

Language used in a speech should not only be vivid and clear, but it should also be appropriate for the occasion, the audience, the topic, and the speaker. First, public speakers must adapt their language to the occasion. For example, a teacher's presentation to a small group of coworkers would be less formal than one given to the school board. Second, appropriate language avoids jargon, slang, or technical words unless the audience is familiar with such terms. Specialized vocabulary, such as medical or computer terms, is only appropriate if the audience understands it; otherwise, specialized words should be replaced with terms that are more general. Third, the speech topic also determines the appropriateness of language. A speech about how to build a birdhouse calls for straightforward language, but a speech about the art of Renoir may require imagery to convey an appreciation of his paintings. Finally, language should be appropriate to the speaker. Effective speakers convey a particular style through the language they employ. Studying the styles of other speakers may help you develop an awareness of language used in public speeches.

DELIVERING YOUR SPEECH

Most people are very nervous about speaking in public. They're not as concerned with the content and organization of the speech—two aspects that we've already covered—as they are with the actual delivery. The idea of standing up there in front of people and delivering a speech is, for many people, frightening. Luckily, there are some tips and tricks to make it easier and, as with most things, a bit of time and practice can help you become a polished speechmaker.

Of course, not everyone is the same and speakers vary in terms of how they present a speech; what works for one person may not work for another.

TYPES OF SPEECHES

There are basically four methods of speech delivery: impromptu, from a manuscript, from memory, and extemporaneous.

Impromptu speeches are ones that involve little or no specific preparation. Suddenly, you're simply asked (or required) to speak on a topic. This can happen in a class, of course, but it can also happen on the job: *Bob, I know we haven't really had a chance to talk about this, but would you mind standing up and letting our visitors know a bit about the history of our company?* Something similar can also happen during a job interview: *So, tell us about a time you failed at something, but then learned something from that failure.* The key here is to maintain eye contact, respond to feedback, and organize your thoughts. The disadvantages, obviously, are that you haven't been able to do any research, nor do you have the time to concentrate on style and language.

In speaking *from a manuscript,* what you're really doing is reading a speech that you've previously written out. The advantages here are that you can control the presentation time—especially useful for televised or timed speeches. Also, reading from a manuscript means that you needn't worry about forgetting words or ideas. However, reading from a manuscript can prevent you from sounding natural (reading a speech usually sounds stilted or awkward), maintaining eye contact, and responding to audience feedback.

As with a manuscript speech, a *memorized* speech allows you to control the timing and wording and, since you're not reading, you may be able to maintain eye contact with the audience. An obvious disadvantage is that it's possible to forget entire sections of a speech, or to flub a word or phrase and then get flustered as you try to figure out where you left off.

The *extemporaneous* speech is the most common method of speech delivery. An extemporaneous speech is researched and planned, but the precise wording of the speech is not written out. Instead, speakers refer to brief notes or an outline to remember the ideas they wish to present and the order to follow. A set of three-by-five index cards can help you here. (Hint: Number the cards. That way if you drop them or they get shuffled around somehow, it'll be easy to restore order quickly.)

Here's a handy recap in the form of a table:

Methods of Speech Delivery	
Speaking impromptu	Speech involves/allows little or no specific or immediate preparation
Speaking from a manuscript	Entire speech is written out and read
Speaking from memory	Entire speech is written out and memorized
Speaking extemporaneously	Speech is prepared and presented from a basic set of notes or an outline (this is the most common method of presentation)

PHYSICAL ASPECTS OF SPEECH PRESENTATION

Now that you've given some thought to the organization, content, and type of speech you're giving, it's time to consider the physical aspects of a speech: voice, articulation, and bodily movements.

Since your voice conveys the words and ideas of a speech, it's important to understand the four main elements of that voice—pitch, volume, rate, and quality.

Pitch is the relative highness or lowness of your voice. People tend to speak at a pitch that's natural for them, but it's important to vary the pitch a bit in order to emphasize specific words and phrases. Doing so can help you communicate your ideas more effectively. Speaking with no variation at all results in what's known as *monotone*. The voice simply drones on and on, with no variations to set words, phrases, and ideas apart. No one wants to listen to a speaker who speaks in a monotone; there's a reason we call boring things monotonous.

Volume, naturally enough, refers to the loudness or intensity of the speaker's voice. Sometimes volume is a problem. A speaker's voice might fade off at the end of a sentence, or she might speak too loudly. For that matter, many people habitually speak too softly.

Rate is the speed at which a person talks. Most people speak an average of about 150 words per minute; if you speak too slowly, then you lose your listeners' attention. On the other hand, if your speech is too fast, then the audience can't keep up; after all, they can't process new information if they're still trying to sort out the information from the previous sentence.

The *quality* of someone's voice can sometimes be hard to judge, since it's often a subjective measure. Nonetheless, we know that clear, pleasant tones are desirable in a public speaker. You don't want your voice to sound harsh, raspy, or nasal.

There are a few additional elements related to speech delivery, including articulation and pronunciation. *Articulation* refers to the movement of the tongue, palate, teeth, lips, jaw, and vocal cords to produce sounds. *Pronunciation* refers to the production of syllables in a word based upon accepted standards. For example, in the word *dictionary*, articulation refers to how each of the ten letters and their sounds are shaped—d-i-c-t-i-o-n-a-r-y. Pronunciation of the word refers to how the sounds are grouped and accented—dik'-shuh-ner-ee.

Some speakers have trouble with articulation and pronunciation, but most of these problems can be resolved with a bit of practice. Some people leave off a sound or a syllable in a word. Perhaps they say *comp-ny* instead of *comp-a-ny*. That's an error of omission. Some speakers will substitute one sound for another; that's an error of substitution, and it may often involve substituting *d* for *t* or *th*; they'll say *beder* instead of *better*. On the other hand, some speakers commit errors of addition instead, adding unnecessary sounds to words, such as saying *ath-a-lete* instead of *ath-lete*. Pronunciation errors typically involve accenting words incorrectly and pronouncing silent sounds. For example, some people pronounce the *t* in the word *often* in the mistaken belief that by doing so, they're somehow being super-correct—i.e., even more correct than usual. Linguists call this a hypercorrection.

Pauses are another tool utilized by public speakers, and they can both help and hurt your speech. A filled pause is one that the speaker fills with utterances such as *ah*, *well*, and *um*. Avoid filled pauses; they make you sound tentative or unprepared. On the other hand, brief unfilled pauses (maybe a second or two in length) can be a very effective rhetorical tool. They are appropriate at the beginning of a speech or at transitional moments as a type of connective, used to indicate that one thought has ended and that another is about to begin.

BODY LANGUAGE

Language is not just verbal, of course. In addition to the words we use—and the tone we use when uttering those words—we also communicate with our bodies. Nonverbal bodily actions, such as eye contact, facial expressions, gestures, and movements, convey information to an audience.

By far the most important nonverbal form of communication is appropriate eye contact with listeners. Speakers who do not make eye contact with an audience are often perceived as aloof, uncaring, and less credible than speakers who maintain eye contact. Facial expressions can also be effective; they are understood universally, and they can be used to convey emotions, including anger, fear, boredom, and excitement. Gesturing with your hands, arms, and fingers can help emphasize points. We've all seen people who step up to a podium or lectern and then deliver a speech while standing completely still. That comes off as wooden and stilted; it's uncomfortable for listeners and it tends to decrease your perceived credibility. Instead, a good speaker uses movement of the entire body to emphasize points and to help listeners remain attentive. If the surroundings allow it, you can even move from behind the podium, perhaps stepping to the edge of the stage or platform, and addressing the audience more or less directly. This increases the connection between speaker and audience, and that connection serves to increase your perceived credibility.

SUMMING IT UP

- **Ethics** is the area of philosophy that concerns issues of morality and fairness. Public speakers have to make ethical choices at every stage of the speechmaking process, from selecting a topic to presenting the final message. One of the most unethical public speaking actions is plagiarism—when writers or speakers present the ideas or words of other people as their own.

- **Audience-centeredness** is making the audience the primary consideration during the entire speechmaking process. **Audience identification** is the process of forming a bond with listeners by pointing out common beliefs, experiences, and goals. **Audience analysis** is the process of acquiring information about an audience in order to adapt a speech. Speakers learn about listeners through direct observation, questionnaires, demographic audience analysis, and situational audience analysis.

- The three main types of speech are informative, persuasive, and entertaining. An **informative** speech increases audience awareness and knowledge about a specific subject. A **persuasive** speech is designed to change the attitudes, behaviors, feelings, and beliefs of listeners. The purpose of an **entertaining** speech is to use humor and cleverness to amuse the audience.

- You can generate ideas for potential speech topics by **brainstorming** and by checking surveys, newspapers, and magazines. A **tree diagram** or **mind map** limits a speech topic and helps focus your speech by repeatedly dividing a topic into smaller parts. The **topoi** method involves asking and answering questions to generate topic ideas.

- In addition to the library, the **Internet** serves a significant role in modern research. While there is a wealth of information available on the Internet, the accuracy of that information can be suspect because, unlike libraries, the Internet lacks quality-control mechanisms.

- **Research interviews** are useful for gathering information for speeches. **Follow-up questions** help gain additional information from primary questions, which are prepared in advance. **Open questions** are broad questions designed to discover an interviewee's values and perspectives, while closed questions tend to elicit brief answers. Always end your interview by asking your subject if he or she can recommend someone else to whom you can speak.

- In a speech, **supporting material** is content that provides information, maintains listener interest, and asserts persuasive evidence. Supporting materials include examples, narratives, testimonies, and statistics.

- **Extrinsic proofs** support claims with objective evidence, such as laws and confessions. **Intrinsic** or **artistic proofs** are based on the speaker's character and credibility, the emotional nature of the issue, and the logic of the argument. Aristotle referred to three kinds of persuasive appeals, or intrinsic proofs, used in public speaking: **logos, ethos**, and **pathos**.

- Arguing from **example**, from **analogy**, from **causation**, and from **sign** are the common types of arguments. The four most common types of fallacies in public speeches are **hasty generalization, false cause** (also called *post hoc*), **invalid analogy**, and **ad hominem**.

- The **thesis statement** is the starting point for developing the main points of the body of a speech. Most speeches include two to five main points. Main points should be relevant and interesting to the audience and worded in a parallel format. Main points should be distinct, with no overlap among them.

- The six most common types of organizational patterns used in public speaking are **topical, temporal, spatial, problem-solution, causal,** and **motivated**.

- The **introduction** to a speech helps gain the audience's interest and preview the topic, and it establishes speaker credibility and a connection with listeners. Types of introductions include **startling statements, rhetorical questions, stories, personal references, quotations,** and **suspense**.

- The **conclusion** of a speech alerts the audience that the speech is ending, summarizes the speech, and clarifies what listeners should think or do in response to the speech.

- **Connectives** help listeners understand the relationship between one concept and another. The four most common types of connectives are **transitions, signposts, internal previews,** and **internal summaries**.

- Words have two basic kinds of meaning. The **denotative** meaning of a word is its literal and objective meaning. The **connotative** meaning of a word is subjective and variable, and it carries a certain amount of (positive or negative) emotional weight.

- The four basic methods of speech delivery are **impromptu, from a manuscript, from memory,** and **extemporaneous**. The latter of these is the most common.

- The **physical aspects** of speech presentation include voice, articulation, and bodily movements. Public speakers need to be aware of voice pitch, volume, rate, quality, articulation, and pronunciation. Common speaking errors include errors of omission, errors of substitution, errors of addition, and pronunciation errors.

- **Nonverbal bodily actions,** including eye contact, facial expressions, gestures, and movements, convey information to an audience. The most important and effective nonverbal form of communication is appropriate eye contact with listeners.

PRINCIPLES OF PUBLIC SPEAKING POST-TEST

post-test

Directions: Carefully read each of the following 60 questions. Choose the best answer to each question and fill in the corresponding circle on the answer sheet. The Answer Key and Explanations can be found following this post-test.

1. Which of the following is NOT an element of situational analysis?
   A. Audience size
   B. Occasion
   C. Time of day
   D. Sexual orientation of the audience

2. It's not always easy to tell whether an idea is yours or whether you got it—or part of it—from another source. So, when in doubt, the speechwriter should
   A. cite the likely source.
   B. avoid using the idea.
   C. get the other person's permission.
   D. bury the reference in the middle of the speech.

3. Successful public speakers use audience analysis to adapt to audiences
   A. before a speech.
   B. after a speech.
   C. during a speech.
   D. before and during a speech.

4. Stealing from a number of sources and combining their exact words into a single speech without citing those sources is known as
   A. research.
   B. patchwork plagiarism.
   C. incremental plagiarism.
   D. global plagiarism.

5. When crafting a speech, your primary consideration should be
   A. your main topic.
   B. effective language.
   C. the purpose of your speech.
   D. your audience.

6. Aristotle's term, ethos, refers mainly to
   A. the style of the speaker.
   B. the role of the speaker as arbitrator.
   C. character of the speaker.
   D. the goal of a speech.

7. If your subject rambles when you've asked an open question, you should
   A. close down that avenue and steer the subject back to the question at hand.
   B. let him or her ramble, to see if interesting facts arise or if new questions come up.
   C. remind the subject of the goal(s) of the interview.
   D. turn off your recorder or stop taking notes, since this sort of thing is off the record.

8. Ethical considerations are present
   A. only in persuasive speeches.
   B. only in informative speeches.
   C. in all speeches.
   D. only in speeches delivered via mass media.

9. A tree diagram or mind map is a good tool for helping the speechwriter
   A. determine what the audience would like to hear about.
   B. focus on a narrow topic that can be addressed in a brief speech
   C. correct mistakes in logic prior to delivering the speech.
   D. judge the socioeconomic background of the audience.

10. A demographic analysis is a useful tool, but potentially dangerous because it can lead to
    A. an excessively long speech.
    B. awkward sentences.
    C. direct observation
    D. stereotyping.

11. Topoi is
    A. the use of a question-and-answer dialog to generate possible topic ideas for a speech.
    B. a method of determining whether a topic is appropriate for a specific audience.
    C. a way to narrow the focus of a speech during topic selection.
    D. a rhetorical device that Aristotle recommended to encourage audience interest during a speech.

12. In a persuasive speech given to an audience that is largely positive or neutral toward the topic, a thesis statement
    A. should occur toward the end of the speech.
    B. should occur toward the beginning of the speech.
    C. is largely unnecessary, since the audience already agrees with you.
    D. should point out flaws in an opponent's argument.

13. During speechwriting, information gained from an audience analysis can help you
    A. select a topic and examples.
    B. recap or rephrase if the audience looks confused.
    C. modify your volume and tone of voice.
    D. adapt to audience feedback.

14. The thesis statement of an informative speech should be what sort of statement?
    A. informative
    B. an opinion
    C. brief
    D. neutral

15. If the topic of the speech is an area familiar to you, then you
    A. can rely on using just stories and personal experiences from your own life.
    B. should find another topic, because you're too close to this one to be objective.
    C. still need to find, evaluate, and cite additional sources for your arguments.
    D. can rely on the expertise of the speaker as your main source.

16. Which of the following is NOT a component of a demographic analysis?
    A. age of the audience
    B. religion
    C. occupation
    D. view of your topic

17. Public speakers must adapt their language to
    A. the time of day.
    B. the length of the speech.
    C. the type of topic.
    D. the formality of the occasion.

18. Which of the following is NOT a useful audience analysis tool?
    A. Direct observation
    B. Situational analysis
    C. Adaptation
    D. Questionnaires

19. Which of the following topics would make a good choice for an informative speech?
    A. Assembling a unicycle
    B. Why you should quit smoking
    C. Stop abortion now
    D. Funny stories my grandfather told me

20. If you visit a speech venue ahead of time to check out the stage, lighting, audio, etc., which of the following are you undertaking?
    A. Demographic analysis
    B. Situational analysis
    C. Psychological analysis
    D. Questionnaire-based analysis

21. If you do a good job of researching, you
    A. should end up using all of your research material.
    B. will always end up with extra material that you will not use.
    C. will make an excellent argument in your speech.
    D. will find that too much material will confuse you as you write.

22. A questionnaire is an audience-analysis tool most commonly used in which of these situations?
    A. A classroom speech
    B. An address to a large group
    C. An impromptu speech
    D. A job interview

23. Which of the following is a story told to illustrate a concept or a point?
    A. A narrative
    B. An example
    C. A set of statistics
    D. An expert opinion

24. The CIA's *World Factbook* is
    A. known for having a biased presentation that favors democratic governments.
    B. an excellent source for information about countries around the world.
    C. no longer available, having gone out of print.
    D. now out of date, since it's not regularly revised.

25. You might ask your interviewee an open question
    A. to elicit brief, one- or two-word answers to questions about basic facts.
    B. so that you'll have time to make notes of everything he or she says.
    C. as a way of discovering your interviewee's values and perspectives.
    D. if you want to keep the interview strictly on topic.

26. Which of the following speech organization patterns was first developed as a model for sales presentations?
    A. Pro-and-con
    B. Cause-effect
    C. Statement of reasons
    D. Motivated sequence

27. If an example is long enough, it eventually becomes
    A. boring.
    B. a narrative.
    C. irrelevant.
    D. a testimony.

28. Which of the following would be most appropriate in a speech conclusion?
    A. Introducing a new idea
    B. Telling an old joke
    C. Listing credentials
    D. Restating the thesis

post-test

29. For some, research is the most difficult part of writing a speech, because
    A. there are few legitimate sources one can consult.
    B. it requires taking the time to find authoritative evidence to support claims.
    C. the audience can object to the sources used in the research.
    D. it requires citing the sources used in the speech.

30. Although personal testimonies can be incorporated into a speech, listeners are generally more persuaded by what sort of testimony?
    A. Recent
    B. Expert
    C. Statistical
    D. Emotional

31. An emotional proof is known as
    A. logos.
    B. ethos.
    C. pathos.
    D. credibility.

32. When examining material from the Internet, you should subject it to the CRAAP test, which is used as a way to determine whether the information is
    A. available for publication.
    B. credible.
    C. enjoyable.
    D. entertaining.

33. Which of the following is a function of speech introductions?
    A. Explaining your visual aids
    B. Establishing your credibility
    C. Summarizing the main points of your speech
    D. Indicating how listeners should respond

34. Speechwriters and researchers use the CRAAP test to
    A. practice their speeches in front of a mirror.
    B. find out if information has already been published.
    C. determine the validity of information found on the Internet.
    D. help evaluate the logic of their arguments.

35. A persuasive appeal based on a speaker's moral character, knowledge, and credibility is known as
    A. proof.
    B. ethos.
    C. logos.
    D. pathos.

36. If one delivers a speech that evokes strong feelings for an immoral purpose, Aristotle would have said that which of the following aspects of the speech was questionable?
    A. Logos
    B. Ethos
    C. Pathos
    D. Unity

37. Which of the following is another term for literal and objective word meanings?
    A. Connotative
    B. Emotional
    C. Denotative
    D. Imagery

38. As your interview concludes, what's the one last question you should always ask your interviewee?

- **A.** "Will you have time for another interview later?"
- **B.** "May I check with you if I have follow-up questions?"
- **C.** "Is there anyone else you would recommend I speak with about this topic?"
- **D.** "Is there anything else you would like my audience to know about you?"

39. A speech that describes a place or an object using a directional pattern would be said to be using what form of organization?

- **A.** Causal
- **B.** Temporal
- **C.** *Post hoc*
- **D.** Spatial

40. Which of the following is most likely to prove useful in determining whether your audience will respond favorably to an informative speech about modern fashion trends?

- **A.** Situational analysis
- **B.** Psychological analysis
- **C.** Demographic analysis
- **D.** Direct observation

41. If your first main point is phrased as an imperative, then your remaining points should also be phrased as imperatives. If your first point is a question, then your remaining points should also be phrased as questions. This practice is an example of what?

- **A.** Infinitives
- **B.** Parallel style
- **C.** Relevance
- **D.** Strategic organization

42. During an interview, the purpose of a follow-up question is to

- **A.** help gain additional information after you've asked the primary questions.
- **B.** throw your interviewee off-guard so that he or she might accidentally reveal important information.
- **C.** ensure that the interviewee is being truthful in his or her answers.
- **D.** gain information about the interviewee's background.

43. A speaker who develops a speech to a powerful and intense conclusion is most likely using which of the following?

- **A.** Motivated sequence
- **B.** Crescendo ending
- **C.** Dramatic gestures
- **D.** Dissolve ending

44. Transitions and signposts are examples of which of the following?

- **A.** References
- **B.** Connectives
- **C.** Internal summaries
- **D.** Supporting materials

45. The topical pattern of organization is useful when the topic

- **A.** can be easily subdivided.
- **B.** occurs along a timeline.
- **C.** is especially controversial.
- **D.** is difficult to understand.

46. Which of the following is an example of plagiarism?

- **A.** Using and acknowledging statistics from a government agency
- **B.** Changing key words from a speech found in the public domain
- **C.** Paraphrasing information and citing the source
- **D.** Crediting unique ideas to the original source

47. What is one advantage of a manuscript speech?
    A. Eye contact is maintained.
    B. It's easy to respond to audience feedback.
    C. It may sound awkward or stilted.
    D. Timing can be controlled.

48. Incremental plagiarism is sometimes difficult to recognize because it does NOT involve
    A. stealing someone's ideas.
    B. using someone else's words verbatim.
    C. a subjective judgment.
    D. a citation in your speech.

49. The main purpose of a psychological analysis of your audience is to
    A. assure you of your listeners' sanity.
    B. find out your listeners' backgrounds.
    C. determine if your audience views your topic favorably or unfavorably.
    D. determine your listeners' political preferences.

50. An informative speech discussing the three branches of the federal government would most likely be arranged in which one of the following patterns?
    A. Temporal
    B. Topical
    C. Spatial
    D. Causal

51. A word's connotation can depend upon
    A. the tone of voice used.
    B. the denotation of the word.
    C. the culture in which the word is used.
    D. the listeners' reactions to the speech.

52. An impromptu speech is one that is
    A. delivered with little or no preparation.
    B. read from a prepared manuscript.
    C. delivered from notes or an outline.
    D. memorized.

53. A speech body that includes statements beginning with *the first cause*, *the second cause*, and *the third cause* is using which of the following?
    A. Supporting materials
    B. Causal order
    C. Signposts
    D. Spatial order

54. The most important nonverbal form of communication is
    A. eye contact.
    B. gestures.
    C. movement.
    D. facial expression.

55. When you evaluate support material, you seek to ensure that the information is
    A. striking and humorous.
    B. accurate and completely objective.
    C. credible and relevant.
    D. objective and entertaining.

56. A figurative comparison that uses "like" or "as" is called what?
    A. Metaphor
    B. Jargon
    C. Simile
    D. Gesture

57. A speaker who pronounces the *t* in *often* is exhibiting what sort of problem?
    A. Articulation
    B. Pronunciation
    C. Pauses
    D. Proxemics

58. If you were to use the phrase, "Next we'll be talking about . . ." as a way of alerting your audience of an upcoming point, you would be using which of the following?

A. Transition

B. Signpost

C. Follow-up

D. Internal preview

59. Which of the following is the most common method of speech delivery?

A. Memorized

B. Manuscript

C. Extemporaneous

D. Impromptu

60. It's a good idea to record (or take notes during) your interview so that

A. the subject knows that he or she must be honest.

B. you can selectively use quotes to advance the agenda you have in mind.

C. you can be sure of getting accurate quotes and keeping your facts straight.

D. you can share your notes with others before writing the speech.

post-test

ANSWER KEY AND EXPLANATIONS

1. D	13. A	25. C	37. C	49. C
2. A	14. D	26. D	38. C	50. B
3. D	15. C	27. B	39. D	51. C
4. B	16. D	28. D	40. C	52. A
5. D	17. D	29. B	41. B	53. C
6. C	18. C	30. B	42. A	54. A
7. B	19. A	31. C	43. B	55. C
8. C	20. B	32. B	44. B	56. C
9. B	21. B	33. B	45. A	57. B
10. D	22. A	34. C	46. B	58. D
11. A	23. A	35. D	47. D	59. C
12. B	24. B	36. B	48. B	60. C

1. **The correct answer is D.** The sexual orientation of your audience may affect how you write and deliver your speech, but it is not a part of a situational analysis, which looks at the environment in which a speech is given: size of venue, size of audience, time of day, type of occasion, etc.

2. **The correct answer is A.** When in doubt, always cite the source. It's simple enough to do, so there's no need to avoid using the idea (choice B), and it's not always possible to get permission (choice C). Including the reference in the middle of the speech without a citation (choice D) would be plagiarism.

3. **The correct answer is D.** The purpose of audience analysis is to help you adapt your speech to the specific audience. Before you give the speech, you adapt your writing to fit the audience. During the speech, you adapt to your audience in many ways, including by recapping or reviewing when you notice confusion, or by livening things up if you see that the audience is getting bored. Adapting *after* the speech (choice B) doesn't do you much good—unless you happen to be scheduled to give a similar speech to a similar audience in the near future.

4. **The correct answer is B.** When you steal from multiple sources and use their words verbatim, that's called *patchwork plagiarism*. Research (choice A) is how you find ideas and information, although you must cite the sources of those ideas and that information. Incremental plagiarism (choice C) involves stealing another's ideas, while global plagiarism (choice D) is stealing large pieces (or all) of another's work verbatim.

5. **The correct answer is D.** A speech should always be crafted around the audience. Your topic, language, and purpose are certainly important, but nothing is more important than the audience—they should be your primary consideration.

6. **The correct answer is C.** Ethos refers to the character and credibility of the speaker, not to his or her style or role. The goal of a speech may of course be ethical or unethical, but Aristotle was speaking mainly of the speaker's character and credibility.

answers post-test

7. **The correct answer is B.** The point of an open question is to *let* the subject ramble so that you can uncover new facts, come up with new questions, and find out what he or she thinks. Thus, you would never shut down (choice A) that kind of response, nor would you remind your subject of the goals of the interview (choice C). You would not stop recording or taking notes, because this type of response is *not* off the record (choice D) unless you and your subject agree beforehand that it is.

8. **The correct answer is C.** Ethical considerations are always present in all speeches, and in all phases of speechwriting.

9. **The correct answer is B.** A tree diagram (also known as a mind map) is an excellent tool for helping you focus on a narrow topic that you can address in a limited amount of time. The other choices are all useful things to accomplish before writing the speech, but none are specifically meant to help you narrow a topic.

10. **The correct answer is D.** A demographic analysis allows you to make assumptions about your audience based on the member's religious affiliations, age, sexual orientation, ethnicity, etc. This can be useful, but whenever you make assumptions, you have to be careful to avoid stereotyping. This sort of analysis would normally have no effect on the length of your speech nor on whether it is delivered awkwardly. Direct observation (choice C) is another audience analysis tool, and it too can lead to stereotyping.

11. **The correct answer is A.** Topoi, used by Aristotle and others as a rhetorical tool to encourage creative thinking, is used today to help develop topic idea for speeches and other types of writing.

12. **The correct answer is B.** If you're giving a speech to a group that already agrees with your main point(s), there's no reason not to state the thesis early in the speech and then go on with your examples and evidence. You might want to place the thesis statement at the end of the speech (choice A) if the audience tends to disagree with your statement, so that you can first present arguments and examples that prove your point and then follow up with the thesis statement. A thesis statement should be present in all speeches, so that the audience can grasp your point(s). You could very well point out flaws in an opponent's argument (choice D), but that would be done in the body of the speech, not in the thesis statement.

13. **The correct answer is A.** While writing your speech, your analysis of the audience can guide you as you select a topic and also as you choose examples to use to illustrate that topic. The other three options are indeed adaptations you might want to make, but they'd be made during the delivery of the speech, not as it was being written.

14. **The correct answer is D.** A thesis statement for an informative speech should be neutral; you're not writing a persuasive speech, so there's really no place for an opinion (choice B) in the statement, although the information in the body of the speech could eventually lead to an opinion on the part of the listener.) The body of the speech will be informative (choice A), but the thesis statement need not be. Similarly, a thesis statement could indeed be brief (choice C), but there's nothing that says it absolutely has to be.

15. **The correct answer is C.** If you're familiar with a topic, that can help you in your speech, and you can certainly use life stories and personal experiences as supplements to your research, but you'll still need to find other expert opinions and examples for your arguments.

16. **The correct answer is D.** A demographic analysis includes such things as age, gender, religion, sexual orientation, ethnicity, economic status, occupation, education, and organizational membership. It does not include the audience's view of your topic, which is a component of a psychological analysis, not a demographic one.

17. **The correct answer is D.** The formality of the occasion has a great effect on the language used by the speaker. Neither of time of day (choice A) nor the length of the speech (choice B) would affect the speaker's choice of language. The type of topic (choice C) should have little effect on the language used; the topic could be something formal or something lighthearted, but it's the formality of the occasion that should have the greatest effect.

18. **The correct answer is C.** Adaptation is the *purpose* of the analysis; the rest of the choices are all tools used in that analysis.

19. **The correct answer is A.** There could certainly be an informational element to all of these, but the only one whose purpose is purely informational—that is, explanatory—is the one about assembling a unicycle. "How to…" speeches are almost always primarily informative, as are speeches that explain how a process works. Choices B and C would be appropriate for persuasive speeches, and telling funny stories (choice D) might be a good approach if you were writing a speech meant to be amusing.

20. **The correct answer is B.** A situational analysis is an examination of the environment in which the speech will be given; it includes everything from time of day to lighting, and from the size of the venue to the type of audio equipment used. A demographic analysis (choice A) seeks to understand your listeners' backgrounds and values, while a psychological analysis

(choice C) is aimed at determining whether the audience views your topic favorably or unfavorably. Questionnaires (choice D) can be very effective, but their use is limited, and that sort of tool would have nothing to do with visiting the setting of a speech beforehand.

21. **The correct answer is B.** If you're doing a thorough job of researching, you'll generally end up with too much information—some of it will remain unused. But that's okay, because it allows you to pick and choose the best, most convincing evidence and ignore the rest. Conversely, if you skimp on the research, you're likely have trouble with the writing, and then end up going back to do more research. It's better to do all of the legwork ahead of time. Of course, doing good research is no guarantee that your argument will be strong (choice C); that depends on how well you use that research and how effectively you write the speech.

22. **The correct answer is A.** A questionnaire is an excellent audience-analysis tool to use when preparing for a classroom speech: your fellow students could answer it at home and send (or bring) in their answers, and the group is small enough to make analyzing their answers feasible. It would be difficult to use a questionnaire with a large group (choice B), and in a job interview or impromptu speech (choices C and D), you would have no time to prepare (and get responses to) a questionnaire.

23. **The correct answer is A.** All of these could be useful in a speech, but a narrative is by definition a story.

24. **The correct answer is B.** The *World Factbook* is an extensive work that lists facts about places around the world. The *Factbook* does not display any biases (choice A); it's strictly an objective listing of information, including population, location, economy, and other

data about just about every country in the world. The *Factbook* is still available in print (choice C), though it's more accessible (and less expensive) to view it online. The *Factbook* is not out of date (choice D), it's actually quite current; one advantage of publishing it on the Internet is that it's easy to update.

25. **The correct answer is C.** The point of an open question is to allow your subject to ramble a bit, to talk about his or her thoughts, values, and ideas. It's definitely not a way to elicit brief answers (choice A) or to ensure that you'll have time to take notes. (You should be taking notes regardless.) In response to an open question, your interviewee may ramble a bit—or a lot; it's not a way to keep the interview strictly on topic (choice D), but it is a good way to come up with new and unanticipated facts or questions, or to find out about your subject's values and ideas.

26. **The correct answer is D.** Alan Monroe developed the motivated sequence pattern as a technique for giving sales presentations. Since then, the pattern has been used in political speeches and advertisements. The statement of reasons pattern is a persuasive speech structure, but it was not initially developed for sales presentations. Choices A and B are both useful for informative and persuasive speeches, but neither was created for the purpose of sales presentations. The statement of reasons pattern (choice C) is used in persuasive speeches and recommends that you place the weakest reason in the middle of your list of reasons, the second-strongest first, and your strongest reason last, so that it leaves the biggest impression.

27. **The correct answer is B.** An example, if it's long enough, eventually becomes a story of its own—that is, a narrative. It need not be boring (choice A), even if it's long, and it may not become irrelevant (choice C). A testimony (choice D) is an opinion.

28. **The correct answer is D.** Restating the thesis, or central idea, of the speech is appropriate in a conclusion because it reminds the audience about the specific purpose of the presentation. Introducing a new idea is a common mistake because the focus of the conclusion should be on concepts already developed in the speech. Telling a joke (choice B) is inappropriate for most speech conclusions, and speaker credentials (choice C) should be established during the introduction.

29. **The correct answer is B.** If you're giving a speech that requires evidence (and most do), then you'll have to take the time and make the effort to find that evidence and ensure that it's legitimate. There are actually many legitimate sources (choice A) available, though it can take some time and effort to locate and assess them. The audience is unlikely to object to your sources (choice C), especially if you've done a good job of researching your topic, and citing your sources within the speech (choice D) is neither difficult nor time-consuming.

30. **The correct answer is B.** The most effective form of testimony is that given by experts in the field being discussed. That testimony may be recent (choice A), or it may have been given in an article that's a few years old—the important thing is that it is the relevant opinion of someone regarded as an expert. Statistics (choice C) are good, when used in moderation, but they're not a form of testimony. An emotional opinion (choice D) may be useful, but what's important is that the opinion, emotional or not, comes from an expert.

31. **The correct answer is C.** Pathos is an appeal to emotion, and it could evoke either positive or negative emotion in order to make its point. Logos (choice A) is an appeal to logic, while ethos (choice B) is an appeal

to credibility. Credibility itself (choice D) is a sought-after attribute, but is not itself a type of emotional proof.

32. **The correct answer is B.** You need to determine that the information you wish to use is credible, that is, believable and accurate. It's already been published (choice A), and you can legally use portions of it as long as you cite the source. It doesn't really matter whether the material is enjoyable (choice C) or entertaining (choice D).

33. **The correct answer is B.** Establishing speaker credibility is one of the primary functions of a speech introduction. Visual aids (choice A) may be used in an introduction to gain listener attention, but explaining them is not the purpose of an introduction. Choices C and D are functions best left to the conclusion of a speech.

34. **The correct answer is C.** The CRAAP test is used to determine the validity and accuracy of information found on the Internet. The test has nothing to do with practicing speeches (choice A), finding out whether the information has been published (choice B), or evaluating logic (choice D).

35. **The correct answer is B.** An appeal based on the speaker's character is known as ethos. All persuasive appeals are known as what Aristotle called *intrinsic proofs*. Logos and pathos (choices C and D) are, respectively, appeals to logic and emotion.

36. **The correct answer is B.** Ethos refers to the character and credibility of the speaker. If the goals of the speech were immoral, Aristotle would have said that the character and credibility of the speaker were questionable. Logos (choice A) refers to logic, while pathos (choice C) refers to emotion. Unity (choice D) is not something with which Aristotle dealt in this context.

37. **The correct answer is C.** Denotative meanings are those that are literal and objective; these are the meanings found in the dictionary. Connotative meanings (choice A) are those suggested by word associations. Emotional meanings (choice B) would be the same as connotative, given that there is an emotional association, whether positive or negative. Imagery (choice D) is vivid language that creates word images for an audience,

38. **The correct answer is C.** These are all excellent questions to ask your subject near the end of the interview, but the very last thing you should ask is whether he or she can recommend another person as a source of information.

39. **The correct answer is D.** A directional pattern (north, west; up, down; forward, back) is known as spatial. It is useful for describing places and objects in an organized, understandable fashion. Causal (choice A) and temporal (choice B) are other organizational patterns. A *post hoc* argument is a logical fallacy, not an organizational pattern.

40. **The correct answer is C.** A demographic analysis lets you learn about listeners based on things such as age, gender, religion, sexual orientation, ethnicity, etc. These are likely to tell you whether the audience would be interested in fashion trends. A situational analysis (choice A) would tell you about the environment in which you'll be delivering the speech, but it wouldn't tell you anything about the listeners' preferences. A psychological analysis (choice B) is generally used to determine whether the audience views your topic favorably or unfavorably, but that analysis is normally used when preparing for a persuasive speech. Direct observation (choice D) might be a tempting answer, since you might assume that you could gauge your listeners' interest

answers post-test

in fashion by what they're wearing, but that might not always be true.

41. **The correct answer is B.** Using the same phrasal structure as you make each main point is known as *parallelism*. Parallel statements help listeners understand and follow a speech more easily than points constructed in different grammatical styles. You might choose to use infinitives (choice A), but that doesn't necessarily imply parallelism. Neither relevance (choice C) nor strategic organization (choice D) has anything to do with using parallel grammatical structures.

42. **The correct answer is A.** The point of a follow-up is to gain additional information related to a primary question. In most interviews, there's no need to attempt to throw your subject off-guard (choice B) or to ensure that he or she is being truthful (choice C). If you're using a follow-up to ask about your subject's background, then your technique is weak, because asking about his or her background should be a primary question.

43. **The correct answer is B.** A crescendo ending is characterized by building toward a powerful and intense conclusion. A motivated sequence (choice A) is a type of persuasive pattern. Some speakers use dramatic gestures (choice C) to signal conclusions, and those gestures might accompany a crescendo ending. A dissolve ending (choice D) is emotional, but it fades gradually to a dramatic statement.

44. **The correct answer is B.** Connectives are words and phrases that link ideas in speeches. Transitions, internal summaries, and signposts are types of connectives, so choice C is incorrect. Supporting materials (choice D) support ideas but do not connect them.

45. **The correct answer is A.** A topical pattern is used when dividing your speech into main parts that align with the parts of the subject being discussed: the five branches of the service, eight systems that make up an automobile, the three types of motorcycle helmets, etc. This way, the main points of your speech can correspond with the main parts of a whole. A temporal pattern is one that occurs along a timeline (choice B). The subject may or may not be especially controversial (choice C) or difficult to understand (choice D).

46. **The correct answer is B.** Even though the material is in the public domain, that doesn't mean you can use it without giving credit. Nor can you simply change a few words and call it your own work. The other choices are all ethical ways to use the material.

47. **The correct answer is D.** With a manuscript speech, it's easy to control the timing, because you can deliver the exact same speech during practice until you get the timing where you want it; if you need a speech of exactly four minutes, you can write and practice it so that it takes exactly that long to deliver. Eye contact (choice A) is very desirable, and the inability to maintain eye contact is a disadvantage of reading from a manuscript. Similarly, it's very difficult to respond to feedback (choice B) when reading a speech. The fact that it may sound awkward (choice C) is a disadvantage of reading a speech from a prepared manuscript.

48. **The correct answer is B.** Incremental plagiarism involves the use of someone else's ideas, rather than his or her actual words. It is sometimes subjective, and it does require that you cite in your speech the source of the ideas.

49. **The correct answer is C.** A psychological analysis is used to determine how willing your audience is to listen to the speaker. Generally, this comes down to whether they're knowledgeable about the subject and

whether they view the topic in a favorable or unfavorable light. In spite of the name, the analysis doesn't actually tell you anything about the listeners' sanity (choice A), nor does it address their backgrounds (choice B). A psychological analysis normally wouldn't tell you about the audience's political preferences (choice D).

50. **The correct answer is B.** Topical patterns are useful for speeches in which the topic is easily subdivided, so in this case, each main point would address one branch of the government. Choices A, C, and D are useful patterns for other types of speeches, but less appropriate for a speech describing parts of a whole.

51. **The correct answer is C.** Connotative meanings (positive or negative associations with the word) can depend on the culture in which the word is used; for example, not all cultures view the color white as a symbol of purity and the color black as a symbol of evil. The tone of voice (choice A) would have no effect on a word's connotation, and the denotation of the word (choice B) is the dictionary meaning—the opposite of connotation. The listeners may react to the use of a word, but that reaction would not affect the word's connotations.

52. **The correct answer is A.** An impromptu speech is one delivered with little or no warning or preparation—you're given a subject and required to deliver a speech right then and there. Speaking from a manuscript (choice B) involves reading a speech you've previously written out. Delivering a speech from notes (choice C) is known as extemporaneous speech, while one you've memorized (choice D) is simply known as speaking from memory.

53. **The correct answer is C.** Signposts are connectives that help audiences keep track of points in a speech. Supporting materials (choice A) are materials that help prove a point. Choices B and D refer to organizational patterns used in speeches, not to types of connectives. Supporting materials are the examples, narratives, and statistics included in a speech.

54. **The correct answer is A.** Eye contact is the most important and most effective form of body language for a speaker. All of the other choices are important aspects of nonverbal communication, but none are as effective as appropriate eye contact.

55. **The correct answer is C.** You need to make sure that your material is relevant and credible. The information should be striking or unique (choice A), but it need not be humorous. While it should be accurate, it need not be completely objective (choice B); after all, you may be using an opinion piece as support material—any facts it contains should be credible, but the piece is not likely to be completely objective. The material may not be at all entertaining (choice D), and that's okay.

56. **The correct answer is C.** A comparison that uses "like" or "as" (*I was as hungry as a horse!*) is called a simile. A metaphor (choice A) is a comparison that does not use "like" or "as." Jargon (choice B) is specialized, technical language—sometimes referred to as "shop talk." A gesture (choice D) is a nonverbal communication involving movement of the hands.

57. **The correct answer is B.** Pronouncing an unpronounced letter in a word is a pronunciation problem. A typical articulation problem (choice A) might be adding a sound where one does not belong. Filled and unfilled pauses (choice C) are typical of many speeches but do not involve adding sounds to words. Proxemics (choice D) refers to how space is used by a speaker during a presentation.

58. **The correct answer is D.** An internal preview alerts the audience about the next main point to be presented. Transitional words or phrases (choice A), are connectives that help a speaker move from one point to another, but they do not indicate the subject of the next point. Signposts (choice B) tell listeners where a speaker is in a speech and do not indicate the next point. A follow-up (choice C) is a type of question that occurs in response to an interviewee's answer to a previous question.

59. **The correct answer is C.** An extemporaneous speech is the most common type; it tends to allow eye contact as well as response to feedback, and if you lose your place, you can glance at your notes or outline. A memorized speech (choice A) may let you maintain eye contact and control the timing, but it's easy to get flustered and lose your place or forget parts of the speech. A manuscript speech (choice B) is read to the audience, which can sound awkward and stilted. An impromptu speech (choice D) is delivered with little or no preparation; this is fairly common in speech or debate classes, or on the job, but rare elsewhere.

60. **The correct answer is C.** Recording your interview is a way to help make sure that your facts, recollections, and quotes are accurate. We assume that the subject knows enough to be honest (choice A), and if he or she were dishonest, taking notes would probably not change that. You should never selectively use quotes out of context (choice B) in order to advance your own agenda, and there's normally no need to share your notes with others (choice D), unless this happens to be a group project.

Organizational Behavior

OVERVIEW

- Test Answer Sheets
- Organizational Behavior Diagnostic Test
- Answer Key and Explanations
- Diagnostic Test Assessment Grid
- Organizational Behavior Overview
- Individual Processes and Characteristics
- Interpersonal and Group Processes
- Organizational Processes and Characteristics
- Change and Development Processes
- Summing It Up
- Organizational Behavior Post-test
- Answer Key and Explanations

The DSST® Organizational Behavior exam covers the field and study of organizational behavior, individual processes, interpersonal and group processes, organizational processes and characteristics, and change and development processes.

Chapter 4

DIAGNOSTIC TEST ANSWER SHEET

1. Ⓐ Ⓑ Ⓒ Ⓓ   5. Ⓐ Ⓑ Ⓒ Ⓓ   9. Ⓐ Ⓑ Ⓒ Ⓓ   13. Ⓐ Ⓑ Ⓒ Ⓓ   17. Ⓐ Ⓑ Ⓒ Ⓓ

2. Ⓐ Ⓑ Ⓒ Ⓓ   6. Ⓐ Ⓑ Ⓒ Ⓓ   10. Ⓐ Ⓑ Ⓒ Ⓓ   14. Ⓐ Ⓑ Ⓒ Ⓓ   18. Ⓐ Ⓑ Ⓒ Ⓓ

3. Ⓐ Ⓑ Ⓒ Ⓓ   7. Ⓐ Ⓑ Ⓒ Ⓓ   11. Ⓐ Ⓑ Ⓒ Ⓓ   15. Ⓐ Ⓑ Ⓒ Ⓓ   19. Ⓐ Ⓑ Ⓒ Ⓓ

4. Ⓐ Ⓑ Ⓒ Ⓓ   8. Ⓐ Ⓑ Ⓒ Ⓓ   12. Ⓐ Ⓑ Ⓒ Ⓓ   16. Ⓐ Ⓑ Ⓒ Ⓓ   20. Ⓐ Ⓑ Ⓒ Ⓓ

POST-TEST ANSWER SHEET

1. Ⓐ Ⓑ Ⓒ Ⓓ   13. Ⓐ Ⓑ Ⓒ Ⓓ   25. Ⓐ Ⓑ Ⓒ Ⓓ   37. Ⓐ Ⓑ Ⓒ Ⓓ   49. Ⓐ Ⓑ Ⓒ Ⓓ

2. Ⓐ Ⓑ Ⓒ Ⓓ   14. Ⓐ Ⓑ Ⓒ Ⓓ   26. Ⓐ Ⓑ Ⓒ Ⓓ   38. Ⓐ Ⓑ Ⓒ Ⓓ   50. Ⓐ Ⓑ Ⓒ Ⓓ

3. Ⓐ Ⓑ Ⓒ Ⓓ   15. Ⓐ Ⓑ Ⓒ Ⓓ   27. Ⓐ Ⓑ Ⓒ Ⓓ   39. Ⓐ Ⓑ Ⓒ Ⓓ   51. Ⓐ Ⓑ Ⓒ Ⓓ

4. Ⓐ Ⓑ Ⓒ Ⓓ   16. Ⓐ Ⓑ Ⓒ Ⓓ   28. Ⓐ Ⓑ Ⓒ Ⓓ   40. Ⓐ Ⓑ Ⓒ Ⓓ   52. Ⓐ Ⓑ Ⓒ Ⓓ

5. Ⓐ Ⓑ Ⓒ Ⓓ   17. Ⓐ Ⓑ Ⓒ Ⓓ   29. Ⓐ Ⓑ Ⓒ Ⓓ   41. Ⓐ Ⓑ Ⓒ Ⓓ   53. Ⓐ Ⓑ Ⓒ Ⓓ

6. Ⓐ Ⓑ Ⓒ Ⓓ   18. Ⓐ Ⓑ Ⓒ Ⓓ   30. Ⓐ Ⓑ Ⓒ Ⓓ   42. Ⓐ Ⓑ Ⓒ Ⓓ   54. Ⓐ Ⓑ Ⓒ Ⓓ

7. Ⓐ Ⓑ Ⓒ Ⓓ   19. Ⓐ Ⓑ Ⓒ Ⓓ   31. Ⓐ Ⓑ Ⓒ Ⓓ   43. Ⓐ Ⓑ Ⓒ Ⓓ   55. Ⓐ Ⓑ Ⓒ Ⓓ

8. Ⓐ Ⓑ Ⓒ Ⓓ   20. Ⓐ Ⓑ Ⓒ Ⓓ   32. Ⓐ Ⓑ Ⓒ Ⓓ   44. Ⓐ Ⓑ Ⓒ Ⓓ   56. Ⓐ Ⓑ Ⓒ Ⓓ

9. Ⓐ Ⓑ Ⓒ Ⓓ   21. Ⓐ Ⓑ Ⓒ Ⓓ   33. Ⓐ Ⓑ Ⓒ Ⓓ   45. Ⓐ Ⓑ Ⓒ Ⓓ   57. Ⓐ Ⓑ Ⓒ Ⓓ

10. Ⓐ Ⓑ Ⓒ Ⓓ   22. Ⓐ Ⓑ Ⓒ Ⓓ   34. Ⓐ Ⓑ Ⓒ Ⓓ   46. Ⓐ Ⓑ Ⓒ Ⓓ   58. Ⓐ Ⓑ Ⓒ Ⓓ

11. Ⓐ Ⓑ Ⓒ Ⓓ   23. Ⓐ Ⓑ Ⓒ Ⓓ   35. Ⓐ Ⓑ Ⓒ Ⓓ   47. Ⓐ Ⓑ Ⓒ Ⓓ   59. Ⓐ Ⓑ Ⓒ Ⓓ

12. Ⓐ Ⓑ Ⓒ Ⓓ   24. Ⓐ Ⓑ Ⓒ Ⓓ   36. Ⓐ Ⓑ Ⓒ Ⓓ   48. Ⓐ Ⓑ Ⓒ Ⓓ   60. Ⓐ Ⓑ Ⓒ Ⓓ

ORGANIZATIONAL BEHAVIOR DIAGNOSTIC TEST

> **Directions:** Carefully read each of the following 20 questions. Choose the best answer to each question and fill in the corresponding circle on the answer sheet. The Answer Key and Explanations can be found following this Diagnostic Test.

1. Jenna regularly attends gatherings at a local restaurant arranged by the professional marketing organization to which she belongs. Jenna hopes to develop contacts with people outside her firm in case she ever needs to find a new job. Which of the following best describes Jenna's activities?
   - **A.** Illegitimate political behavior
   - **B.** Legitimate political behavior
   - **C.** Integrative bargaining
   - **D.** Risk aversion

2. Which of the following people first identified the ten roles of managers?
   - **A.** Kurt Lewin
   - **B.** Henri Fayol
   - **C.** Henry Mintzberg
   - **D.** Abraham Maslow

3. Which type of small-group network depends on a central figure to convey the group's communications?
   - **A.** Single-channel
   - **B.** All-channel
   - **C.** Wheel
   - **D.** Chain

4. The sales manager at Hoffman Car Dealership is concerned because of the dealership's low sales numbers over the last quarter. The sales manager blames the problem on the laziness of his sales team instead of on price incentives offered by competitors. Which of the following best explains the sales manager's beliefs?
   - **A.** Fundamental attribution error
   - **B.** Overconfidence bias
   - **C.** Self-serving bias
   - **D.** Contrast effect

5. Which of the following involves a sender purposely manipulating information so the receiver will view it favorably?
   - **A.** Selective perceiving
   - **B.** Monitoring
   - **C.** Disseminating
   - **D.** Filtering

6. Which employee personality trait has the most consistent correlation with organizational success?
   - **A.** Openness to new ideas
   - **B.** Conscientiousness
   - **C.** Agreeableness
   - **D.** Extraversion

7. Which of the following is not part of systematic study?
   A. Observing relationships
   B. Drawing conclusions based on evidence
   C. Using intuition to come to conclusions
   D. Identifying causes and effects

8. An employee states, "My pay is too low." Which attitude component is the employee most likely expressing?
   A. Emotional
   B. Cognition
   C. Behavior
   D. Affect

9. Which of the following are the three categories of primary causes of work stressors?
   A. Environmental factors, organizational factors, and employee factors
   B. Organizational factors, personal factors, and culture factors
   C. Organizational factors, personal factors, and environmental factors
   D. Employee factors, culture factors, and environmental factors

10. Which model of learning asserts that the consequences of actions shape voluntary behavior?
    A. Observational learning
    B. Classical conditioning
    C. Situational learning
    D. Operant conditioning

11. Which organizational design approach is most likely to generate confusion regarding authority?
    A. Bureaucracy
    B. Matrix
    C. Product
    D. Simple

12. Which of the following represents the highest level of Maslow's hierarchy of needs?
    A. Achievement
    B. Friendship
    C. Security
    D. Shelter

13. Which of the following is the decision-making model that assumes that decision makers have all available information, can identify relevant options, and can choose the most logical and sensible option?
    A. Bounded rationality
    B. Intuitive decision-making
    C. Rational decision-making
    D. Informed decision-making

14. What is one way to overcome resistance to organizational change?
    A. Provide employees with little information about the change
    B. Stimulate a culture of innovation
    C. Restricting group norms
    D. Asking employees to change their habits

15. Which of the following is NOT one of the causes of organization-wide resistance?
    A. Personal stressors
    B. Having to change habits
    C. Worrying about security
    D. Fear of the unknown

16. In the norming stage of group development, members are more likely to
    A. accomplish a specific task.
    B. establish a formal hierarchy.
    C. form close relationships.
    D. experience conflict.

17. Which term refers to making planned changes by improving the effectiveness of an organization through research, technology, and training?
    A. Effectiveness strategizing
    B. Organizational development
    C. Job design
    D. Organizational design

18. Which of the following statements best describes the transformational leadership theory?
    A. Leaders exhibit accuracy in decision-making.
    B. Leaders possess unique risk-taking behaviors.
    C. Leaders have specific personality traits.
    D. Leaders provide organizational vision.

19. Lewin's three-step model primarily addresses how organizations can
    A. minimize conflicts.
    B. implement changes.
    C. motivate workers.
    D. develop leaders.

20. A star quarterback has endorsement contracts with numerous firms, including an electronics manufacturer, a soft drink company, and a sports drink company. Advertisers are most likely hoping that the football star has
    A. referent power.
    B. coercive power.
    C. legitimate power.
    D. expert power.

diagnostic test

ANSWER KEY AND EXPLANATIONS

1. B	5. D	9. C	13. C	17. B
2. C	6. B	10. D	14. B	18. D
3. C	7. C	11. B	15. A	19. B
4. A	8. B	12. A	16. C	20. A

1. **The correct answer is B.** Legitimate political behavior includes networking, so choice B is correct. Choice A is incorrect because Jenna is not involved in activities that would harm her employer. Choices C and D are irrelevant to Jenna's activities.

2. **The correct answer is C.** Henry Mintzberg is an academic who conducted research on management roles and identified ten of them. Choice A is incorrect because Kurt Lewin developed an organizational change model. Choice B is incorrect because Henri Fayol identified six functions of management and fourteen principles of management. Choice D is incorrect because Abraham Maslow developed the theory of a hierarchy of needs.

3. **The correct answer is C.** A wheel network depends on one leader to relay information. Choice A is not a type of small-group network. Choice B is incorrect because all members communicate with one another in an all-channel network. Chain networks follow hierarchies for communication, so choice D is incorrect.

4. **The correct answer is A.** Fundamental attribution error is the tendency to underestimate the power of external factors and overestimate the power of internal factors. Choice B is incorrect because overconfidence bias involves being too optimistic. Choice C is incorrect because a self-serving bias involves attributing failures to external factors. Contrast effect involves making comparisons between people, so choice D is incorrect.

5. **The correct answer is D.** Filtering occurs when a sender manipulates information, so choice D is correct. Selective perception involves hearing what you want to hear, so choice A is incorrect. Choice B is not a type of communication barrier. Dissemination involves sharing information, but not necessarily manipulating it, so choice C is incorrect.

6. **The correct answer is B.** The most important and consistent trait for both individual and organizational success is conscientiousness, so choice B is correct. Openness, agreeableness, and extraversion are not as strongly related to organizational success, so choices A, C, and D are incorrect.

7. **The correct answer is C.** Systematic study involves using the best scientific evidence to inform managerial decisions. This means research should involve observing relationships, drawing conclusions based on evidence, and identifying causes and effects. Therefore, choices A, B, and D are incorrect. Choice C is correct because relying on intuition is not part of the scientific method of systematic study.

8. **The correct answer is B.** Attitudes develop from three components: cognition, affect, and behavior. The cognitive component is an opinion, such as "My pay is too low." Emotions and feelings are the affective component, so choices A and D are incorrect.

The behavioral component is the individual's intention to behave, so choice C is incorrect.

9. **The correct answer is C.** The causes of work stressors are categorized as environmental factors, organizational factors, and personal factors. Therefore, choice C is the only option that contains all three of these categories. Choices A, B, and D contain some of these categories but also include other concepts that are not primary categories of work stressors. Therefore, these choices are incorrect.

10. **The correct answer is D.** The operant conditioning model made famous by B.F. Skinner linked behavior with consequences, so choice D is correct. Choice A is incorrect because observational learning asserts that people learn by imitating behaviors observed in other people. Choice B is incorrect because Pavlov linked associations with responses. Choice C is not a model of learning.

11. **The correct answer is B.** The matrix structure is more likely to cause employees confusion because of its dual line of command. Chain of command is clear in a bureaucracy and simple structures, so choices A and D are incorrect. Departments organized by product are not likely to trigger leadership confusion, so choice C is incorrect.

12. **The correct answer is A.** Choice A is correct because achievement falls in the category of ego, which is near the top of Maslow's hierarchy of needs. Choices B, C, and D are incorrect because all are lower than achievement on Maslow's hierarchy.

13. **The correct answer is C.** Choice A is incorrect because bounded rationality accounts for some of the assumptions that aren't visible in the real world and assumes that decision makers search for solutions that are sufficient rather than ideal. Choice D is incorrect because it is not one of the decision-making models. Choice B is incorrect because intuitive decision-making involves making a decision based on a hunch.

14. **The correct answer is B.** Choices A, C, and D are incorrect because providing employees with little information about organizational change, restricting group norms, and asking employees to change their habits can all increase resistance to organizational change by posing threats to individuals. Therefore, choice B is the best answer.

15. **The correct answer is A.** Having to change habits, worrying about security, and fearing economic changes and the unknown are common sources of individuals' resistance to organizational change. Therefore, choice A is the best answer.

16. **The correct answer is C.** During the norming stage, members form close relationships and develop common expectations of member behavior. Choice A occurs in the performing stage. A hierarchy forms during the storming stage, so choice B is incorrect. Conflict occurs in the storming stage, so choice D is incorrect.

17. **The correct answer is B.** Effectiveness strategizing is not an organizational behavior term, so choice A is incorrect. Choice C refers to how an employee's job is structured and is incorrect. Choice D refers to the way in which the organization is structured. Therefore, choice B is the correct answer.

18. **The correct answer is D.** The transformational leadership theory asserts that leaders convey visionary goals to followers. Choices A and B are not necessarily linked to the transformational leadership theory. Trait theories focus on personal qualities, so choice C is incorrect.

19. **The correct answer is B.** Choice B is correct because Lewin's model describes the process of implementing organizational changes. Conflicts, motivation, and leadership are not addressed by Lewin's model, so choices A, C, and D are incorrect.

20. **The correct answer is A.** Referent power stems from identifying with a person who has desirable personality traits and resources. Coercive power relies on the fear of negative results, so choice B is incorrect. Legitimate power refers to the formal authority to control, so choice C is incorrect. Although the star quarterback is a football expert, he is not necessarily an expert on electronics or soda, so choice D is incorrect.

answers diagnostic test

DIAGNOSTIC TEST ASSESSMENT GRID

Now that you've completed the diagnostic test and read through the answer explanations, you can use your results to target your studying. Find the question numbers from the diagnostic test that you answered incorrectly and highlight or circle them below. Then focus extra attention on the sections within the chapter dealing with those topics.

Organizational Behavior		
Content Area	**Topic**	**Question #**
Organizational Behavior Overview	• The field of organizational behavior • The study of organizational behavior	2, 7
Individual Processes and Characteristics	• Perceptual processes • Personality • Attitudes and emotions • Learning processes • Motivation • Work stress	4, 6, 8, 9, 10, 12
Interpersonal and Group Processes	• Group dynamics • Group behavior and conflict • Leadership and influences • Power and politics • Communication processes	1, 3, 5, 16, 18, 20
Organizational Processes and Characteristics	• Organizational decision-making • Organization structure and design • Organization culture	11, 13, 14
Change and Development Processes	• Basic processes • Concepts of change • Applications and techniques of change and development	15, 17, 19

GET THE FACTS

To see the DSST® Organizational Behavior Fact Sheet, go to *http://getcollegecredit.com/exam_fact_sheets* and click on the **Business** tab. Scroll down and click the **Organizational Behavior** link. Here you will find suggestions for further study material and the ACE college credit recommendations for passing the test.

ORGANIZATIONAL BEHAVIOR OVERVIEW

Historically, business schools and corporations have focused on developing managers with effective technical skills and have given very little attention to improving the interpersonal skills of managers. However, modern businesses are realizing that managers need people skills on a daily basis to retain high-performing workers, handle employee conflicts, improve workplace productivity, and enhance both worker and firm performance. Organizational behavior addresses these essential managerial skills. Around 10 percent of the questions on your DSST exam will cover general questions about organizational behavior.

THE FIELD OF ORGANIZATIONAL BEHAVIOR

Organizational behavior is a relatively new field of study that emerged during the 1980s as businesses began to realize the connection between organizational performance and employee behavior. Organizational behavior is a field of study that involves analyzing the effect that individuals, groups, and structure have on an organization's performance.

While the field of organizational behavior only developed within the last three or four decades, the study of management began much earlier. Henri Fayol, an early twentieth-century French businessman, developed the first theory of management. According to Fayol, professional management involved the functions of planning, organizing, commanding, coordinating, and controlling. Fayolism has since been condensed to planning, organizing, leading, and controlling.

In the 1960s, Canadian academic Henry Mintzberg studied five executives for two weeks to determine what they did as managers. Mintzberg identified ten roles that can be categorized as interpersonal, informational, or decisional, but the roles and their associated behaviors are highly interconnected.

Mintzberg's Management Roles	
Interpersonal	• *Figurehead:* performs routine duties as symbolic leader • *Leader:* motivates and directs workers • *Liaison:* maintains a network of outside contacts
Informational	• *Monitor:* receives information • *Disseminator:* transmits information to organization members • *Spokesperson:* transmits information to outsiders
Decisional	• *Entrepreneur:* initiates projects and searches for opportunities • *Disturbance Handler:* takes corrective action when problems occur • *Resource Allocator:* makes or approves organizational decisions • *Negotiator:* represents the organization at significant negotiations

The underlying purpose of studying managers has been to improve the performance and effectiveness of an organization, so it was a natural progression that led to the field of organizational behavior. By understanding the impact that individuals, groups, and structures have on organizational performance, firms can function more effectively.

THE STUDY OF ORGANIZATIONAL BEHAVIOR

Although organizational behavior benefits numerous settings, it is primarily intended to help managers handle workplace situations such as employee motivation, absenteeism, turnover, and productivity. The following table provides an overview of core topics studied at each level of an organization.

Types of Organizational Behavior	
Individual	Perceptual processes, personality, attitudes, learning processes, motivation, and work stress
Group	Dynamics, conflict, leadership, power, politics, and communication processes
Structure	Decision-making processes, organizational structure, organizational design, and change processes

Although some managers may have a knack for "reading" people, such attempts at predicting or interpreting behavior often lead to false assumptions. Managers improve their chances of making accurate predictions by balancing personal intuition with research derived from systematic study.

Systematic study involves observing relationships, identifying causes and effects, and drawing conclusions based on evidence. The most commonly used research design methods are as follows:

- Case studies
- Field surveys
- Laboratory experiments
- Field experiments
- Aggregate quantitative reviews

Psychology, social psychology, sociology, and anthropology are the fields of study that provide the primary research contributions. Evidence-based management is a growing trend resulting from the vast body of research now available. Rather than relying on hunches and intuition, adherents of evidence-based management rely on the best scientific evidence to make managerial decisions.

INDIVIDUAL PROCESSES AND CHARACTERISTICS

Because individual employees have a significant impact on an organization's performance, understanding individual processes is important in the field of organizational behavior. Perceptions, personalities, attitudes, learning processes, motivations, and stress factors will be discussed in the following sections. A high number of questions (around 30 percent) on your DSST exam will test your knowledge of individual processes and characteristics.

PERCEPTUAL PROCESSES

Behavior is based on individual perceptions of the world, so understanding perceptual processes is essential in the study of organizational behavior. Perceptions are how individuals organize and interpret what they experience, which may differ significantly from reality. In the workplace, for example, one employee may perceive a firm's benefits package as exceptional, while another employee may perceive the same compensation as mediocre. In another situation, one coworker may be perceived as loud and obnoxious by some, but perceived as a leader by other individuals.

Three key factors explain why employees frequently have such different perceptions:

1. The perceiver
2. The target
3. The situation

An individual perceiver's attitudes, motives, interests, experiences, and expectations influence personal perceptions. The target or object being perceived has certain distinguishing characteristics that influence perceptions either positively or negatively. For example, a young worker may be perceived as having poor work habits, while a defense attorney may be perceived as unethical. The situation or context also plays a role in perception. A female employee who wears a short skirt to work may be viewed as unprofessional, but if she wears the same skirt to a party, the perceptions would most likely change.

Although perceptions may seem to occur automatically, people are actually employing various techniques when making judgments. These techniques are useful because they speed up the perception process, but they may also act as barriers to accurate perceptions. Understanding the methods and their associated problems will enhance the accuracy of the perception process.

Methods of Perception		
Method	**Description**	**Problem**
Selective Perception	Interpreting only selected observations of a person based on personal interests, experiences, and attitudes	Quick, narrow interpretations lead to unfounded conclusions.
Halo Effect	Drawing general impressions of a person based on one characteristic	Single traits influence broad conclusions.
Contrast Effects	Evaluating a person's characteristics by making comparisons to another person	Misperceptions occur because individuals are not evaluated in isolation.
Stereotyping	Judging a person based on group association	Generalizations are often unfair and untrue.

The perceptions people develop about one another are known as person perceptions. Scientists have attempted to explain the different ways that judgments are made through attribution theory. According to attribution theory, people try to explain the behavior of others based on internal attributes or external attributes. Behaviors that occur because of internal attributes are under the control of an individual, whereas externally caused behaviors are out of the individual's control. For example, a manager who attributes an employee's tardiness to laziness is making an internal attribution. If the manager attributes the employee's tardiness to bad traffic, she is making an external attribution. Determining whether a person's behavior is caused by internal or external factors depends on the factors of the following:

- **Distinctiveness:** Does the person behave differently in different situations? If the late employee also fails to complete tasks on time, then the behavior would be judged as an internal attribute. However, if the employee typically performs well, then an external attribution would most likely be made.

- **Consensus:** Does everyone behave similarly when faced with a similar situation? If numerous employees are also late, then the behavior shows consensus and would be attributed to external causes.

- **Consistency:** Does the person behave similarly over a period of time? If the late employee is regularly late, then the behavior would most likely be internally attributed.

Research shows that attributions are often distorted by fundamental attribution errors and self-serving biases. The fundamental attribution error is the tendency to place more value on internal factors than external ones. The tendency of individuals to attribute successes to internal causes and failures to external causes is known as a self-serving bias.

PERSONALITY

In the field of organizational behavior, personality refers to an individual's pattern of reactions in terms of behavior, thoughts, and actions that tend to remain stable over time and across situations. Research indicates that personality traits are determined by a combination of genetic and environmental factors. Characteristics that an individual exhibits in many situations are considered personality traits. Two primary tools are used to identify and classify personality traits: **the Myers-Briggs Type Indicator (MBTI)** and the **Big Five model**.

More recent research has also begun to evaluate other personality traits that could have an influence on individual and organizational outcomes. Such findings are early, but some of these traits are proactivity, adaptability, and emotional intelligence. Since research on these traits is still new, the MBTI and Big Five model are still the main tools for assessing personality in organizational behavior research.

The MBTI, which consists of 100 questions, is the most frequently used personality-assessment tool. Individuals are identified as one of sixteen personality types identified by a four-letter combination. The MBTI test results determine which four of the following eight characteristics best describes a person:

1. **Extraverted or Introverted:** Extraverts are outgoing and sociable, while introverts are quiet and shy.

2. **Sensing or Intuitive:** Sensing individuals are practical and detail-oriented, whereas intuitive individuals focus on future possibilities.

3. **Thinking or Feeling:** Thinking individuals solve problems with logic, whereas feeling individuals depend on emotions.

4. **Judging or Perceiving:** Judging individuals prefer control in an orderly world, whereas perceiving individuals are adaptable and spontaneous.

The MBTI is used by many large organizations, and it serves as a useful tool for career guidance. However, the MBTI is based on questionable evidence and is not recommended as a selection assessment.

In contrast, the Big Five model is supported by a large body of evidence regarding the tool's five personality traits:

1. **Extraversion:** comfort level with relations

2. **Agreeableness:** tendency to defer to others

3. **Conscientiousness:** measure of reliability

4. **Emotional stability:** ability to handle stress

5. **Openness to experience:** range of interests and creativity

Studies have indicated a strong connection between the personality dimensions of the Big Five model and job performance. The most important and consistent trait for both individual and organizational success is conscientiousness. The following table indicates the link between high scores in each of the five traits and any positive or negative work behaviors.

Influence of Big Five Traits on Job Performance	
Trait	**Significance**
Extraversion	• Higher job satisfaction, better interpersonal skills, and higher job performance • More impulsive and more likely to be absent and partake in risky behaviors
Agreeableness	• More compliant, better likeability, and higher job performance • Lower levels of career success and negotiation skills
Conscientiousness	• Better organization, better attention to detail, more persistence, and higher job performance • Lower ability to adapt to change and think creatively
Emotional Stability	• Lower stress levels, higher job satisfaction, and less negative thinking
Openness	• More adaptable to change, more creative, and enhanced leadership • More susceptible to workplace accidents

ATTITUDES AND EMOTIONS

In the field of organizational behavior, positive or negative evaluations of objects, people, or events are referred to as attitudes. Attitudes develop from three components:

1. Cognition
2. Affect
3. Behavior

The cognitive component is an opinion, such as, "My boss is unfair." The affective and emotional component is a feeling, such as, "I'm angry about how much work I have to do on the weekend." The behavioral component is the individual's intention to behave, such as, "I'm going to look for a better job that requires less overtime."

Attitudes are typically connected to values, which are the convictions that a person has about what is right, wrong, or desirable. Values serve as the basis for understanding people's attitudes and motivations. The Rokeach Value Survey, developed by the social psychologist Milton Rokeach, presents a philosophical basis for the association of values with beliefs and attitudes. According to the Rokeach Value Survey, values can be divided into two types: terminal values and instrumental values. Terminal values are goals that an individual would like to accomplish during a lifetime, such as prosperity, equality, family security, happiness, and wisdom. Instrumental values are the means to achieving terminal values, and they are exhibited through behaviors such as hard work, truthfulness, sincerity, dependability, and honesty. Studies indicate that individuals holding similar positions have similar values and vice versa. Such information is important in organizations, as conflicts may arise because executives and hourly workers, for example, have different values.

Research shows that job attitudes are influenced by several factors: job characteristics, emotions, the social environment, leadership, and organizational policies and practices. Job attitudes are such a large area of research within organizational behavior because they have the ability to impact a variety of outcomes including job performance, creativity, withdrawal behaviors, counterproductive work, extra-role helping behaviors, and organizational performance.

Although everyone holds many different attitudes, organizational behaviorists primarily focus on the following key employee attitudes.

Key Employee Attitudes	
Job satisfaction	Positive or negative feelings about a job based on evaluations of the job's characteristics
Job involvement	The extent to which employees identify and care about their job
Organizational commitment	The extent to which employees identify with the goals of an organization and want to continue as members
Perceived organizational support	The extent to which employees believe an organization cares for their well-being and values their work
Employee engagement	An employee's job-related involvement, satisfaction, and enthusiasm

Managers benefit from a strong understanding of employee attitudes, because satisfied and committed workers are more productive and less likely to quit.

While employee attitudes tend to be more stable over time, affect and emotion are shorter in duration and are triggered by specific events or stimuli. According to the Circumplex Model of Affect, emotions can be defined according to where they fall on two dimensions: energy (from low to high) and pleasantness (from low to high). For example, an emotion with high energy and low pleasantness is nervousness. An emotion with low negative affectivity and low energy would be calmness.

Emotions are important because positive emotions tend to be associated with better outcomes for individuals and organizations (improved work performance, better supervisor evaluations, effective decision-making, creativity, and fewer intentions to leave the organization, for example). Research also shows that emotions are contagious and can be transferred from one person to the rest of a work group. Therefore, it is important to maintain positive emotions in the workplace as negative emotions can cause a downward spiral.

One developing area of research examines emotional labor, or how employees manage their emotions in the workplace to align with social norms. Surface acting occurs when employees outwardly display emotions that they do not feel. Deep acting occurs when employees actually work to change how they feel so that the emotions they are displaying are also felt. Research suggests that displaying emotions that are incongruent with how one feels can increase work stress.

LEARNING PROCESSES

Understanding the basics of the learning process benefits managers, because not all employees will learn information or skills in the same manner. Learning is an active and purposeful process that occurs through experiences and results in permanent behavior changes. Numerous factors influence an individual's learning process, especially in an employment setting, including interest, motivation, experience, memory, ability, context, environment, perception, and maturity.

Psychological studies have led to three basic learning models.

Models of Learning	
Classical conditioning	A behaviorist model associated with Ivan Pavlov's well-known experiment. Pavlov triggered a dog's salivary response after an association was made between the smell of food and a ringing bell.
Operant conditioning	A behaviorist model made famous by B.F. Skinner, who linked behavior with consequences. This model asserts that the consequences of actions shape voluntary behavior.
Observational learning	A social learning theory commonly associated with Albert Bandura's Bobo Doll Experiment. The model asserts that people learn by imitating behaviors observed in other people without the need for direct reinforcement. Observational learning requires attention, motor skills, motivation, and memory.

Reinforcement theory, which stems from B.F. Skinner's work, asserts that consequences influence behavior. In an organization, reinforcement theory is implemented by rewarding desirable employee behavior and punishing unwanted behavior. In psychological terms, a reinforcer, which can be either positive or negative, is anything that increases the probability of a specific response. The following provides a description of the four types of reinforcers and work-related examples.

Reinforcement Methods		
Type of Reinforcer	**Description**	**Example**
Positive reinforcement	Providing a positive response for a desired behavior	Providing a salesperson with a bonus for exceeding a sales quota
Negative reinforcement	Withholding a negative consequence to increase a desired behavior	Eliminating an undesirable area from a salesperson's territory after the salesperson increases sales in other areas
Punishment	Giving an undesirable consequence to decrease a behavior	Suspending a salesperson for breaking a company policy
Extinction	Removing a reward to decrease a behavior	Eliminating praise for an employee's good work, which may unintentionally lower the desirable behavior

In addition to understanding the different types of reinforcers, effective managers should also understand the schedule of reinforcement. Reinforcers can either be implemented on a continuous schedule or an intermittent schedule. A manager who gives an employee a raise after every successful project is following a continuous schedule.

Continuous schedules are either on a *fixed ratio* or a *fixed interval*. A fixed ratio schedule applies reinforcement after a specific number of behavioral occurrences, whereas a fixed interval schedule applies a reinforcer after a set amount of time.

Intermittent schedules are ones that don't reinforce every instance of desired behavior and are either a *variable ratio* or a *variable interval*. Variable ratio schedules apply reinforcers after a variable number of responses, such as giving an employee a bonus after a varying number of desired behaviors occur. Variable interval schedules apply reinforcers after varying periods of time.

According to research, continuous reinforcement is the most effective way to change employee behaviors, but the method is not practical in an organization because not every behavior is observed. Therefore, intermittent schedules are more common in businesses.

MOTIVATION

Surveys have found that most U.S. workers are not enthusiastic about their jobs, so motivation is a serious concern for organizations. Motivation refers to the processes guiding an individual's intensity level, focus, and persistence. Businesses benefit from motivated employees who work hard to accomplish organizational goals, so motivation is a heavily studied topic in the field of organizational behavior. The following table summarizes the most common theories of motivation.

Motivation Theories	
Maslow's Hierarchy of Needs Theory	Every individual has a hierarchy of five needs: 1. Physiological 2. Safety 3. Social 4. Esteem 5. Self-actualization The higher-order needs of social, esteem, and self-actualization are satisfied internally, and the lower-order needs of physiological and safety are satisfied externally, such as through salary and tenure.
Herzberg's Two-Factor Theory	Two components on separate continuums motivate employees. Hygiene factors, such as company policies, supervision, work conditions, and salaries, lead to dissatisfaction. Motivators, such as recognition, responsibility, achievement, and advancement, lead to satisfaction.
Alderfer's ERG Theory	Individuals have three needs: 1. Existence 2. Relatedness 3. Growth Safety and physical comfort are the lowest level of existence needs. Relatedness needs involve a sense of identity in society. Growth needs are the highest level, where individuals feel a sense of accomplishment and fulfillment.
McClelland's Theory of Needs	Employee motivation is influenced by the need for achievement, power, and affiliation.
Goal-Setting Theory	Specific and challenging goals combined with feedback lead to higher levels of employee productivity.

Motivation Theories (continued)	
Equity Theory	Employees derive motivation and job satisfaction by comparing their inputs, such as effort, and outcomes, such as income, with those of others. Employees then respond to eliminate any inequities.
Victor Vroom's Expectancy Theory	Employees are motivated to work hard when they believe their efforts will result in desirable outcomes, such as a good performance appraisal leading to a salary increase.

The motivation theories described in the previous table vary in their validity and usefulness. The needs theories of Maslow, Herzberg, Alderfer, and McClelland aren't generally considered valid tools for explaining employee motivation, although some research indicates a connection between achievement and productivity associated with McClelland's theory. Research related to goal-setting theory indicates that employees are motivated by specific and difficult goals, especially when they receive feedback on their progress. However, goal-setting theory fails to address issues of absenteeism, turnover, and job satisfaction. In regards to equity theory, some workers are sensitive to pay inequities while others are tolerant, so it does not provide consistently accurate predictions. Expectancy theory is one of the most supported explanations of employee motivation because of the strong connection between effort, performance, and reward.

Job design is another managerial tool for motivating employees. Studies in job design indicate that how the elements of a job are organized can increase or decrease employee efforts. **Job rotation** and **job enrichment** are the two primary methods of redesigning a job. Job rotation involves periodically shifting a worker from one task to another, a technique that reduces boredom in highly routine jobs. Job enrichment increases an employee's responsibility and provides variety through vertical job expansion. For example, instead of having an assembly worker perform one task in the manufacturing process, the worker could assemble an entire unit.

Alternative work arrangements are another tool for motivating employees. Flextime, job sharing, and telecommuting are popular options among firms. Flextime offers flexible work hours for employees, such as 6:00 a.m. until 3:00 p.m. instead of the typical 8:00 a.m. to 5:00 p.m. Job sharing splits one 40-hour job between two or more individuals, which is a popular option for working mothers and retirees. Telecommuting, or working from home at least part of the week, is increasingly popular, especially for employees who spend the bulk of their workday on the computer or the phone.

An increasing number of firms are implementing reward systems through variable-pay programs to motivate workers. The following list describes the different types of variable-pay programs.

- **Piece-rate pay:** Workers receive a fixed sum for each unit produced.
- **Merit-based pay:** Compensation is based on performance appraisal ratings.
- **Bonuses:** Employees are rewarded for recent rather than historical performance.

- **Skill-based pay:** Pay levels are based on the number of skills an employee has or the number of jobs an employee can perform.
- **Profit-sharing plan:** An organization-wide plan, rather than an individual pay plan, which distributes cash or stock options based on a firm's profitability.
- **Gainsharing plan:** A group incentive plan that distributes money based on improvements in group productivity.
- **Employee stock ownership plan:** A benefits plan that enables employees to obtain company stock.

Research indicates that variable-pay programs are effective tools for motivating employees and improving productivity levels. Profit-sharing plans are linked to higher levels of profitability, while gainsharing plans typically improve both worker productivity and attitude. Piece-rate plans have also been found to increase employee productivity.

Motivation theories have a number of implications for managers. Effective managers are sensitive to the individual differences of employees, so they establish individual goals, rewards, and punishments. Allowing employees to participate in setting work goals and solving productivity problems is more likely to generate motivation than dictating goals and solutions. In addition, rewards should be linked to performance, and workers should clearly understand the connection. A weak relationship between rewards and performance leads to job dissatisfaction, turnover, and absenteeism.

WORK STRESS

Stress occurs when an individual faces a real or perceived mental, physical, or social demand associated with an important and uncertain outcome. Work stress is an important area of study because approximately one third of people report that work is very stressful. Although stress typically has negative connotations, in certain situations it can be a positive condition that increases performance levels. Two types of stressors are associated with employment: challenge stressors and hindrance stressors. **Challenge stressors** are linked to workload, deadlines, and pressure to complete tasks. **Hindrance stressors** prevent individuals from reaching their goal, such as bureaucracy and office politics.

The primary causes of stress can be divided into three categories: environmental factors, organizational factors, and personal factors. **Environmental factors** include economic uncertainty and changes in technology. Task and role demands are examples of **organizational factors**, whereas family problems are **personal factors** influencing stress. Individuals handle stress differently based on their perceptions, job experience, and social support network. Work stress can result in short-term consequences, such as disturbed mood, that can then turn into long-term issues, such as lost workdays. Common consequences of work stress include headaches, high blood pressure, anxiety, depression, decreased job satisfaction, absenteeism, and lower productivity.

So how can employees and organizations minimize work stress? Individuals can exercise regularly, manage their time more effectively, and talk to friends, family, and coworkers about their problems. Organization-wide strategies for reducing employee stress include improved job placement methods, effective training programs, realistic goal setting, improved communication systems, and corporate wellness programs.

INTERPERSONAL AND GROUP PROCESSES

Given that working with other people is an essential and frequent activity for managers, understanding both interpersonal and group processes is beneficial. The following section addresses group dynamics, group behavior, leadership, power, politics, and the communication process. Questions about interpersonal and group processes will make up about 30 percent of your exam.

GROUP DYNAMICS

A group consists of at least two individuals who interact to achieve certain objectives. Security, status, self-esteem, affiliation, power, and goal achievement are common reasons that people join groups.

- **Formal groups** are designated by an organization to complete specific tasks or projects, such as a sales team.
- **Informal groups** develop naturally in the workplace for the purpose of social interaction, such as workers from different departments who gather for lunch regularly.

In addition to being designated as formal or informal, groups can be classified as command, task, interest, or friendship groups. Both command and task groups are formal, while interest and friendship groups are informal. Members of a command group report to the same manager. Each member of a task group plays a different role in completing a specific task for the organization. Interest groups develop when workers share a common concern, such as improving worker safety. Friendship groups are social alliances that form at work and often continue outside of the workplace.

Groups typically develop in the same manner. The following table describes each stage of the group development process.

Group Development Stages	
Stage 1: Forming	Uncertainty among members about acceptable behaviors and group structure. Stage is complete when members feel a part of the group.
Stage 2: Storming	Characterized by intragroup conflict regarding constraints on individuality and group leadership. Stage ends with clarified hierarchy.
Stage 3: Norming	Members form close relationships and develop common expectations of member behavior.
Stage 4: Performing	Working to achieve a specific task. It's the final stage for permanent work groups.
Stage 5: Adjourning	Preparing to disband and complete tasks if group is temporary.

Just as most groups form in the same manner, groups also have common characteristics that influence member behaviors. Roles, norms, status, size, and cohesiveness are the key properties found in groups. Group members have specific roles or expected behavior patterns based on their position in a group. For example, a manager is expected to provide leadership, whereas an employee is expected to follow directions. Norms are the acceptable behavior standards shared by group members. Performance norms indicate how hard group members should work, while appearance norms provide cues about appropriate work attire. Status refers to a group member's rank and is primarily determined by power, degree of contribution, and personal characteristics.

Group performance is significantly influenced by the group's size. Research indicates that smaller groups complete tasks more quickly than larger groups and that employees work more effectively in smaller groups. Cohesiveness refers to how well members work together and how motivated they are to remain in the group. Because cohesiveness influences productivity, managers should strive to do the following:

- Form smaller groups
- Encourage goal agreement
- Stimulate competition with other groups
- Provide rewards to the group rather than to individual members

GROUP BEHAVIOR AND CONFLICT

No matter how cohesive and productive a group or an organization may be, conflicts are bound to occur. Over the years, the attitudes about workplace conflicts have changed. During the 1930s and 1940s, advocates of the traditional view of conflict asserted that conflict must be avoided because it is harmful. However, conflict can't always be avoided, which led to the interactionist view of conflict. The interactionist school views conflict as a positive activity in some cases that should be encouraged to improve group performance.

The interactionist view realizes that not all conflicts are beneficial, and it separates conflict into two main categories: functional and dysfunctional. **Functional conflicts** benefit group goals, whereas **dysfunctional conflicts** obstruct group performance. Functional and dysfunctional conflicts are distinguished by conflict type: task, process, and relationship:

- Task conflicts are associated with work goals.
- Process conflicts stem from how work is accomplished. Low degrees of task and process conflicts can be productive if they stimulate new ideas and solutions.
- Relationship conflicts stem from personality clashes between group members, and such conflicts are nearly always dysfunctional.

Conflicts typically follow a five-stage process as indicated in the following table.

Stage 1: Potential opposition or incompatibility	Conditions create opportunities for conflicts to occur. Conditions include: • communication problems • task structure • personal variables
Stage 2: Cognition and personalization	Conflict issues are defined and parties determine what a conflict is about. Emotions play a role in shaping conflict perceptions.
Stage 3: Intentions	Decisions are made to act in a certain way. The main intentions for handling conflict are: • competing • collaborating • avoiding • accommodating • compromising
Stage 4: Behavior	Conflict becomes visible through statements, actions, and reactions by both parties.
Stage 5: Outcomes	Consequences result from the actions and reactions.

The fourth stage of the conflict process is the step for conflict management. Conflict management involves using resolution and stimulation methods to manage conflict levels.

Conflict-resolution methods include the following:

- Problem-solving sessions
- Expanding resources
- Compromising
- Withdrawing from the conflict

Conflict-stimulation methods include realigning work groups and changing rules.

LEADERSHIP AND INFLUENCES

All groups require a leader to create plans, inspire members, establish organizational structures, and achieve goals and visions. Firms benefit from understanding what makes a good leader because such knowledge improves individual, group, and organizational performance.

The following table provides an overview of the various models of leadership that have been developed to identify leadership skills:

Models of Leadership	
Trait Theories	Personal qualities and characteristics of leaders differ from those of non-leaders.
Behavioral Theories	Behaviors of effective leaders differ from behaviors of ineffective leaders.
Contingency Theories	Situational variables determine whether specific leader traits and behaviors are effective or not according to the Fiedler contingency model.
Leader-Member Exchange Theory (LMX)	Leaders develop personal relationships with some members of a group, but not others. In-group subordinates exhibit better performance and job satisfaction.
Charismatic Leadership Theory	Effective leaders inspire subordinates by articulating a vision, taking risks, and perceiving the needs of others.
Transformational Leadership Theory	Leaders inspire followers by providing vision, communicating high expectations, solving problems, and giving personal attention.

Although early trait theory studies failed to isolate specific leadership traits, later research was more successful when traits were categorized alongside the Big Five personality framework. Extraversion, conscientiousness, and openness to experience are traits that have been strongly linked to effective leadership.

Behavioral theories, which suggest that leaders can be developed, focus primarily on two aspects of leadership: initiating structure and consideration. **Initiating structure** refers to the extent that leaders define their roles and the roles of employees. For example, a leader with a high degree of initiating structure assigns subordinates to specific tasks and stresses the importance of deadlines. **Consideration** relates to job relationships and the extent to which a leader helps group members, treats subordinates fairly, and shows appreciation. Studies indicate that leaders with high consideration receive more respect, and leaders with high levels of initiating structure experience high levels of group productivity.

Studies indicate that aspects of the Fiedler contingency model are valid. The Fiedler model includes eight categories, but only three categories are supported by evidence. Critics of the contingency model find the questionnaire and variables confusing and participants' scores unreliable. The Fiedler model is the most well-known contingency theory, but others include the situational leadership theory, path-goal theory, and leader-participation theory.

- **Situational leadership theory** asserts that the best action of a leader depends on the degree that followers are willing and able to complete a task.

- **Path-goal theory** asserts that it is the job of the leader to help followers accomplish goals by providing the necessary information, support, and resources. Leadership style is determined by subordinate preference and task structure.

- **Leader-participation theory** asserts that the way in which leaders make decisions is equally important to the decision itself. The decision tree for this model includes a set of twelve contingency variables, eight problem types, and five leadership styles, which can be too cumbersome for real-world managers.

The leader-member exchange theory is relatively supported by research. Studies show that leaders and followers are clearly different, with differences that are not random. Research also verifies that in-group members perform better and experience greater job satisfaction than out-group members, which is not necessarily surprising. Studies have also shown that the relationship between leaders and followers is even stronger when employees have higher levels of autonomy and control over their job performance.

Many experts believe that charismatic and transformational leadership styles are virtually the same or have only minor differences. In most cases, charismatic and transformational leadership theories are supported with evidence. Such leaders are more effective in some situations and settings than others. Charismatic or transformational leaders are most effective when interacting closely with employees, so such leaders may be more effective in small firms rather than large organizations.

While the extensive amount of leadership research may be overwhelming, managers can take the most relevant information and apply it in a business setting. The following list provides an overview of leadership implications for managers:

- Traits such as extraversion, conscientiousness, and openness to experience are typically associated with strong leaders.

- Consider the situation before assigning a leader as some leaders are task-oriented and others are people-oriented.

- Leaders who show they believe in group members by investing time and resources will most likely be rewarded with productive and satisfied employees.

- Leaders with vision, charisma, and clear communication skills are the most effective.

- Effective leaders develop relationships with group members and show that they can be trusted.

POWER AND POLITICS

Power refers to the ability that one person has to influence the behavior of another person, and in organizations, power and politics are natural and unavoidable. Effective managers understand how power functions in an organization. Power in an organization is either personal or formal.

Personal power stems from the characteristics of an individual. The two sources of personal power are expertise and the respect of others. **Formal power** is derived from an individual's position in an organization. Sources of formal power are the ability to coerce, the ability to reward, and the formal authority to control. The following table provides an overview of the different sources of power:

Sources of Power		
Source	**Type**	**Description**
Expert power	Personal	Based on expertise, special skills, or knowledge. Physicians, tax accountants, economists, and computer specialists have power due to their expertise.
Referent power	Personal	Based on identification with an individual who possesses desirable resources or traits, such as charisma, beauty, and likability. Individuals who are admired have power over those who want to be like them. Celebrities have referent power, which is why they are commonly used to endorse products.
Coercive power	Formal	Based on an individual's fear of negative consequences for failing to obey. In the workplace, an individual who wields coercive power may have the ability to suspend, dismiss, or demote an employee. More subtle forms of coercive power involve embarrassing an individual or withholding valuable data or information.
Reward power	Formal	Based on an individual's ability to bestow valuable rewards or benefits, such as bonuses, raises, promotions, work assignments, sales territories, and work shifts.
Legitimate power	Formal	Based on an individual's position in an organization's hierarchy. Considered the most common source of power in the workplace, given its broad scope. Individuals comply with those who hold a higher rank in an organization.

Research indicates that personal sources of power are more effective than formal sources of power. Managers who exhibit expert and referent power are more likely to have satisfied employees who are committed to an organization. Coercive power has been shown to have the opposite effect: Employees are dissatisfied with their jobs and lack commitment if their manager uses negative consequences as a control method.

Although political behavior is not a formal job requirement, office politics is a reality that cannot be avoided in most organizations. Individuals with effective political skills are able to use their power sources to influence outcomes in the workplace. Within organizations, political behavior is either legitimate or illegitimate. **Legitimate** actions involve complaining to a supervisor, developing business contacts through networking, and bypassing the chain of command. **Illegitimate** actions exceed normal organizational behavior by violating implied rules of business conduct. Sabotage and whistleblowing are examples of illegitimate political behavior. Most organizational political behavior is categorized as legitimate.

According to researchers, a number of factors, both individual and organizational, determine the political environment in an organization. The following factors characterize individuals who are more likely to engage in political behaviors:

- expect to succeed
- perceive job alternatives because of skills, reputation, or job market
- believe they can control their environment
- show sensitivity to social cues and conformity
- exhibit Machiavellian personality (manipulative and power hungry)

Organizational factors play an even greater role than individual factors in the degree to which political behaviors occur. Some organizational cultures foster politicking more than others, especially if a firm is experiencing financial difficulties or significant changes. An organizational culture characterized by minimal trust, unclear roles, and ambiguous performance evaluation systems will typically experience a high degree of political activity. A culture with low levels of trust has a higher level of political behavior and a greater likelihood of experiencing illegitimate political behavior. The following list includes the organizational factors that influence political behavior:

- low trust
- unclear employee roles
- subjective performance appraisal systems
- pressures for high performance
- political senior managers

For many people, organizational politics are a negative aspect of the job, especially if they don't understand the dynamics of political behavior. Employees who are threatened by organizational politics experience decreased job satisfaction, increased stress, increased turnover rates, and lower performance ratings. However, politically astute individuals are more likely to view politics as an opportunity, and they are more likely to receive higher performance evaluations, more raises, and better promotions than those lacking political skills.

COMMUNICATION PROCESSES

Clear communication, defined as the transfer and understanding of meaning, is an essential element to organizational success and serves four key functions:

1. Controlling behavior
2. Fostering motivation
3. Expressing emotion
4. Providing information

Communication is a process that requires a message, a sender, and a receiver as depicted below.

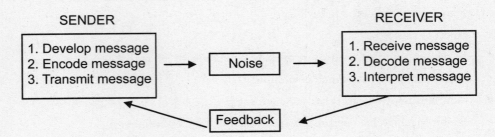

Senders initiate messages by encoding an idea through speaking, writing, gesturing, or making a facial expression. The message passes through a channel determined by the sender. Formal channels are established by an organization to transmit messages and usually follow a chain of command, while informal channels occur spontaneously. The message is directed at the receiver who must decode and interpret the message.

Communication barriers in the form of noise stand between the sender and receiver and can distort message clarity. Comprehension difficulties, cultural differences, and information overload are common noise problems. The feedback loop is the final aspect of the communication process. Feedback serves to determine whether the receiver understood the message.

Group members in an organization use oral, written, and nonverbal communication to transfer meaning.

Interpersonal Communication Methods	
Oral	The vast majority of organizational communication occurs orally through such activities as speeches, one-on-one conversations, and group discussions. Quickness and immediate feedback are the advantages. Message distortions may occur if a message passes between multiple people.
Written	Memos, letters, e-mails, instant messages, and newsletters are used by organizations to convey written messages. Written communication provides both parties with a record of the message for future reference. Typically, they are more logical and clear because the sender is required to consider the message in advance. Disadvantages include the time-consuming nature of written communication and the lack of immediate feedback.
Nonverbal	Oral messages include nonverbal messages, such as body movement, tone of voice, facial expression, and physical distance between sender and receiver. Such communications provide additional meaning to a message.

Nonverbal communication involves various activities, and each one conveys a different meaning. Body language expresses how much individuals like each other and the status between the sender and receiver. For example, a sender and receiver that like and respect each other are more likely to stand close to each other. Senders that feel their status is higher than the receiver's may appear more casual, or if they feel their status is lower, they may act more formal to show deference. The most appropriate physical distance between sender and receiver often depends on cultural norms.

In addition to understanding aspects of interpersonal communication, managers should be aware that communication networks, both formal and informal, exist within organizations. The three primary types of formal small-group networks include the chain, wheel, and all-channel networks.

1. **Chain networks** follow a formal chain of command and are characterized by high accuracy, moderate speed, and member satisfaction.

2. **Wheel networks** depend on a central individual or leader to convey information and are characterized by high accuracy and speed, but low member satisfaction.

3. **All-channel networks** allow all members to participate in communication with no single individual taking a leadership position. These networks are characterized by high speed, high member satisfaction, and moderate accuracy.

The grapevine is an informal communication network that involves word-of-mouth message conveyance. Research indicates that nearly 75 percent of all employees in a firm first learn about information through the grapevine. Studies also show that approximately 75 percent of the information flowing through a grapevine is accurate. Organizational grapevines typically have the following three key characteristics:

1. Management does not control communications in the grapevine.

2. Most employees find grapevine messages more believable than messages conveyed by upper management.

3. Grapevines benefit those within the network.

Although managers cannot eliminate rumors that spread through the grapevine, they can reduce negative consequences by providing information to employees, explaining decisions, and maintaining open communication channels.

Effective communication is often distorted in an organization by a variety of barriers. The following table provides an overview of barriers:

Communication Barriers	
Filtering	Sender manipulates information so the receiver will view it more positively, such as telling someone what he or she wants to hear rather than the truth.
Selective Perception	This is the tendency to process messages based on personal interests, experiences, and attitudes.
Information overload	Receivers select, ignore, or forget information when individuals receive more messages than they can process.

Communication Barriers (continued)	
Emotions	Receivers experiencing extreme emotions, such as anger or excitement, may not interpret messages objectively.
Language	Word meanings can vary depending on the context of the communication and the experiences of the sender and receiver. Lack of language uniformity can hinder communication.
Silence	Withholding communication is a common problem in organizations. Employees fail to report operational problems, misconduct, and harassment, which prevent management from correcting problems.
Communication apprehension	Tension and social anxiety about communicating orally and/or in writing affects 5 to 20 percent of individuals.
Gender differences	Men and women often communicate differently and for different purposes. Many men communicate to establish status and power, whereas many women communicate to provide support and connections.
Politically correct communication	Concerns about being inoffensive can prevent meaningful and accurate communication.

ORGANIZATIONAL PROCESSES AND CHARACTERISTICS

As with individuals and groups, organizations have unique processes and characteristics. The following section discusses decision-making, organizational structure, and organizational design. You will find that about 15 percent of the questions you see on test day will cover organizational processes and characteristics.

ORGANIZATIONAL DECISION-MAKING

When faced with two or more alternatives, organizations, groups, and individuals must make decisions. Building new facilities, expanding services, and downsizing are examples of decisions faced by organizations. Making a decision involves interpreting information and evaluating the strengths and weaknesses of the various alternatives, which can be accomplished through three methods:

1. Rational decision-making
2. Bounded rationality
3. Intuitive decision-making

The rational decision-making model assumes that decision makers have all the available information, can identify the relevant options, and can choose the most logical and sensible option. The model involves the following six steps:

1. Define the problem.
2. Identify the decision criteria.
3. Allocate weights to the criteria.
4. Develop the alternatives.
5. Evaluate the alternatives.
6. Select the best alternative.

The rational decision-making model may involve too many assumptions that aren't viable in the real world. Bounded rationality accounts for some of these realities. Economist Herbert Simon first presented the theory of bounded rationality in 1982. According to Simon, individuals are faced with the following three inescapable limitations when making decisions:

1. Only limited information about possible alternatives is available.
2. Individuals have a limited capacity to evaluate available information.
3. Only a limited amount of time is available for making decisions.

As a result, most decision makers search for solutions that are sufficient rather than ideal.

Making a decision based on a hunch exemplifies the intuitive decision-making model. Intuitive decisions occur quickly and typically rely on emotion and experience rather than quantifiable evidence. Current studies suggest that intuition can enhance rational decision-making, but it should not necessarily replace rational evaluations, especially on an organization-wide level where numerous intuitive perspectives would be unlikely to agree.

Within organizations, decisions are made by both individuals and groups. Managers benefit from knowing when it is more or less advantageous to have a decision made by a group or an individual. Groups offer a diversity of viewpoints, knowledge, and creativity that benefits the decision-making process. Moreover, decisions made by a group are more likely to be accepted and implemented by group members. However, group decision-making is a time-consuming process that involves conformity pressures, conflicts, and ambiguous responsibilities. In contrast, individuals make decisions quickly and efficiently with clear accountability for the final results.

ORGANIZATIONAL STRUCTURE AND DESIGN

In organizations, tasks must be divided, grouped, and coordinated for the greatest efficiency, which is the purpose of having an organizational structure. **Organizational structure** involves six essential elements, as seen in the following table.

Elements of Organizational Structure	
Work specialization	The division of labor established by Henry Ford. Activities are divided into separate jobs and steps with individuals specializing in one task instead of the entire process, which can improve productivity in some industries, but decrease employee satisfaction in others.
Departmentalization	Departmentalization is grouping jobs to coordinate common tasks. Activities are grouped by function, product, service, geography, process, and/or customer.
Chain of command	Chain of command is an unbroken line of authority that reaches from the highest to the lowest levels of an organization for the purpose of clarifying authority and responsibility.
Span of control	Span of control refers to the number of employees that a manager can effectively and efficiently oversee, so it determines the number of levels and managers in an organization. A narrow span of control allows for close supervision, but wider spans are more cost-effective and efficient.
Centralization/decentralization	Centralization/decentralization refers to the degree that decision-making is concentrated at the top of an organization's hierarchy. Top managers in centralized organizations make most decisions that are implemented by lower-level managers. Decentralized organizations assign decision-making authority to lower-level managers. Decentralization quickens problem-solving, lessens employee alienation, and allows for greater employee input.

Elements of Organizational Structure (continued)	
Formalization	Formalization is the extent to which jobs are governed by rules and procedures. For examples, sales representatives may have more flexibility to perform their tasks than assembly-line workers who must follow specific guidelines.

Organizational design primarily consists of three classic structures; however, additional designs have been developed in recent years to account for changes in the business world. The simple structure, the bureaucracy, and the matrix structure are the most commonly implemented designs, while the virtual organization and the boundaryless organization designs are relatively new options.

Organizational Designs	
Design Type	**Characteristics**
Simple structure	<ul><li>Considered a flat structure with only 2 to 3 vertical levels, minimal departmentalization, wide spans of control, centralized authority, and minimal formalization</li><li>Most commonly used in small businesses run by owner-managers who employ fewer than 50 people</li></ul>
Bureaucracy	<ul><li>Relies on standardized work processes, specialization, highly formalized rules, centralized authority, narrow spans of control, minimal innovation, chain-of-command decision-making</li></ul>
Matrix structure	<ul><li>Establishes a dual chain of command and combines functional and product departmentalization</li><li>Can cause confusion and power struggles, but can maximize activity coordination, improve the flow of information, and achieve economies of scale</li><li>Commonly used in advertising agencies, hospitals, universities, construction firms, and government agencies</li></ul>

Organizational Designs (continued)	
Virtual organization	• Major business functions are outsourced by a small, core organization; highly centralized with minimal if any departmentalization; minimizes bureaucratic costs and long-term risks and maximizes flexibility • Limited by unclear responsibilities, slow response time, and intermittent communication • Common in the film industry
Boundaryless organization	• Idea spurred by former GE chairman Jack Welch, who wanted to eliminate hierarchies, replace functional departments with multidisciplinary teams, and implement limitless spans of control • Used to some degree at 3M, Hewlett-Packard, and AT&T

ORGANIZATION CULTURE

Organizational culture consists of an organizations values, ideologies, and beliefs and how these are translated to employees through socialization, practices, and organizational policies and procedures. Culture has the ability to impact the employee experience. Culture research was introduced to the field of organizational behavior in 1979 by Pettigrew in an effort to incorporate concepts from anthropology.

Researchers of organizational culture focus on things like the language, myths, stories, and history within an organization and how this impacts organizational effectiveness. In addition to these organizational artifacts leading to the development of organizational culture, leadership is also a signal of the organization's culture. For example, employees learn what the organization values by observing what leadership prioritizes and devotes resources to. Currently, there is a lack of research that demonstrates a clear linkage between organizational culture and performance. This is due to the fact that culture is difficult to study since it is hard to measure and it varies so greatly across different organizations. Researchers do agree, though, that culture can be leveraged in times of organizational change. By establishing a culture that appreciates innovation, organizational change tends to be met with less resistance.

CHANGE AND DEVELOPMENT PROCESSES

The final section addresses organizational change and organizational development and the forces and processes involved with change. Around 15 percent of the questions on your DSST exam will cover the topics in this section.

BASIC PROCESSES

Given the unstable nature of economies, consumers, competitors, and markets, successful organizations must be willing to make changes when necessary. The changing workforce, technology advancements, major economic shifts, competition, social trends, and global politics pressure organizations into making changes and being flexible.

Organizations making plans to change typically turn to one of four approaches, as seen in the following table.

Processes of Change	
Lewin's Three-step Model	1. *Unfreeze:* Ensure that employees are ready for change. 2. *Change:* Implement the desired change. 3. *Refreeze:* Ensure that changes are permanent.
Kotter's Eight-step Plan	1. Establish a sense of urgency for change. 2. Create a guiding coalition. 3. Develop a vision and strategy. 4. Convey the vision. 5. Empower and encourage others to act on the vision. 6. Plan for, create, and reward advances toward vision. 7. Reassess changes and make necessary adjustments. 8. Reinforce changes by linking them to success.
Action research	Changes based on systematically collected and analyzed data. The five steps are: 1. Diagnosis 2. Analysis 3. Feedback 4. Action 5. Evaluation
Organizational development	Systematic effort to improve an organization's effectiveness and adaptability by changing the attitudes, beliefs, and values of employees through long-term training programs.

CONCEPTS OF CHANGE

Change threatens both individuals and the organization. Resistance to organizational changes can be especially harmful at a time when an organization critically needs the support and loyalty of employees. Common sources of resistance among individuals include having to change habits, worrying about security, and fearing economic changes and the unknown. In addition, individuals often process only selected information by ignoring information that challenges the security of their environment. Organization-wide resistance occurs through regulations, processes, restrictive group norms, and threats to specialized groups and power relationships.

Organizational culture plays a significant role in the change and development process. Organizations can overcome resistance by stimulating a culture of innovation, encouraging experimentation, and promoting training and development opportunities for employees. Moreover, a strong corporate culture fosters employee loyalty, which is necessary during times of major upheaval.

APPLICATIONS AND TECHNIQUES OF CHANGE AND DEVELOPMENT

Organizational development refers to making planned changes by improving the effectiveness of an organization through research, technology, and training. The primary values underlying organizational development methods include respecting individuals, establishing a trusting and supportive environment, de-emphasizing hierarchical control and authority, openly confronting problems, and encouraging participation in decision-making.

The following list describes organizational development methods and approaches to implementing change.

- Sensitivity training or T-groups attempt to change behavior through unstructured group interactions. Early attempts were chaotic and have been replaced by alternative methods such as diversity training, executive coaching, and team-building exercises, which are more structured.

- Survey feedback assesses attitudes and perceptions of organizational members. Data is analyzed for discrepancies, and members then gather for discussions and problem-solving.

- Process consultation involves hiring an outside consultant to help managers identify processes that need improvement, such as workflow and communication.

- Team building involves interactive group activities to improve trust and communication among team members.

- Intergroup development attempts to alter the attitudes, stereotypes, and perceptions that group members may have towards one another. Most intergroup development sessions focus on differences between departments and occupations, such as between manufacturing and financial divisions in a firm.

- Appreciative inquiry involves the identification of unique strengths in an organization and building on these qualities to improve performance.

- The sociotechnical or structural approach to redesigning organizations focuses on meeting the needs of a changing external environment. Sociotechnical refers to the relationship between people and structure in an organization.

SUMMING IT UP

- In addition to having effective **technical skills,** managers need to develop **people skills** in order to retain high-performing workers, handle employee conflicts, improve workplace productivity, and enhance both worker and firm performance. The study of organizational behavior provides the basis for these essential **managerial skills.**

- Early important theorists in the study of management are **Henri Fayol,** who developed the first management theory identifying five (now condensed to four) functions of managers and **Henry Mintzberg,** who identified 10 roles of managers categorized as **interpersonal, informational,** and **decisional.**

- **Evidence-based management** relies on observing relationships, identifying causes and effects, and drawing conclusions based on evident.

- **Perceptions** are how individuals organize and interpret what they experience, which may differ significantly from reality and one another's perceptions.

- Three key factors explain why employees frequently have such different perceptions: (1) the **perceiver,** (2) the **target,** and (3) the **situation.** An individual perceiver's attitudes, motives, interests, experiences, and expectations influence personal perceptions. The target or object being perceived has certain distinguishing characteristics that influence perceptions either positively or negatively.

- The methods of perceptions are **selective perception,** the **halo effect, contract effects,** and **stereotyping.**

- According to **attribution theory,** people try to explain the behavior of others based on internal attributes or external attributes. Behaviors because of internal attributes are under the control of an individual, whereas externally caused behaviors are out of the individual's control.

- Determining whether behavior is caused by **internal** or **external** factors depends on the factors of distinctiveness, consensus, and consistency.

- **The Big Five** model is supported by a large body of evidence to support the tool's five personality traits (extraversion, agreeableness, conscientiousness, emotional stability, openness to experiences) and their connection to job performance.

- **Attitudes** develop from three components: (1) cognition, (2) affect, and (3) behavior. Organizational behaviorists primarily focus on job satisfaction, job involvement, organizational commitment, perceived organizational support, and employee engagement.

- **Emotions** fall on two dimensions: energy (from low to high) and pleasantness (from low to high). Positive emotions tend to be associated with better outcomes for individuals and organizations. Research also shows that emotions are contagious.

- Research suggests that displaying emotions that are incongruent with how one feels can increase work stress.

- According to the Rokeach Value Survey, values can be divided into **terminal** values and **instrumental** values.

- **Learning** is an active and purposeful process that occurs through experiences and results in permanent behavior changes. The models of learning are classical conditioning, operant conditioning, and observational conditioning.

- **Reinforcement methods of learning** that operate in the workplace are positive reinforcement, negative reinforcement, punishment, and extinction.

- Reinforcers can either be implemented on a **continuous** schedule or an **intermittent** schedule.

- **Continuous schedules** are either fixed ratio or fixed interval. A fixed ratio schedule applies reinforcement after a specific number of behavioral occurrences, whereas a fixed interval schedule applies a reinforcer after a set amount of time.

- **Intermittent schedules** are ones that don't reinforce every instance of desired behavior and are either a variable ratio or a variable interval. Variable ratio schedules apply reinforcers after a variable number of responses. Variable interval schedules apply reinforcers after varying periods of time.

- The most common **motivation theories** are Maslow's hierarchy of needs, Herzberg's two-factor theory, **Alderfer's ERG theory, McClelland's theory of needs, goal-setting, equity**, and **Victor Vroom's expectancy theory**. Of these, the first four aren't considered valid for employee motivation, but the other three have some merit, especially the expectancy theory.

- **Job design** (job rotation and job enrichment) as well as alternative work arrangements (flextime, job sharing, and telecommuting) are motivational tools used by companies. Variable-pay programs (piece-rate, merit-based, bonuses, skill-based, profit-sharing, gainsharing, and employee stock ownership) are also popular ways to motivate employees.

- Two types of **stressors** are associated with employment: challenge stressors and hindrance stressors. The primary causes of stress can be divided into three categories: (1) environmental factors, (2) organizational factors, and (3) personal factors.

- Groups are **formal** or **informal**, and **command, task, interest**, or **friendship**.

- Groups typically **develop** in the same way: forming, storming, norming, performing, and adjourning, if temporary.

- Groups have common characteristics that influence member behaviors and those key properties are **roles, norms, status, size**, and **cohesiveness**. Research indicates that smaller groups complete tasks more quickly than larger groups and that employees work more effectively in smaller rather than in larger groups.

- **Interactionists** believe that, in some cases, conflict can be beneficial to the group. Conflict may be functional or dysfunctional. Functional and dysfunctional conflicts are distinguished by conflict type: task, process, and relationship.

- The **conflict process** has five stages: (1) potential opposition or incompatibility, (2) cognition and personalization, (3) intentions, (4) behavior, and (5) outcomes. The fourth stage is the time for conflict resolution or conflict stimulation.

- Research into leadership styles has produced six major models or theories that identify leadership skills: (1) **trait**, (2) **behavioral**, (3) **contingency**, (4) **leader-member exchange** (LMX), (5) **charismatic**, and (6) **transformational**.

- **Power** in an organization is either **personal** or **formal**. The sources of personal power are expert power and referent power. The sources of formal power are coercive power, reward power, and legitimate power. Political power in an organization may be either legitimate or illegitimate.

- **Clear communication**—the transfer and understanding of meaning—is an essential element to organizational success and serves four key functions: (1) controlling behavior, (2) fostering motivation, (3) expressing emotion, and (4) providing information.

- **Communication** is a process that requires a **message**, a **sender**, and a **receiver**.

- **Barriers** to effective communication include filtering, selective perception, information overload, emotions, language, silence, communication apprehension, gender differences, and politically correct communication.

- Making a decision involves interpreting information and evaluating the strengths and weaknesses of the various alternatives, which can be accomplished through three methods: (1) **rational decision-making**, (2) **bounded rationality**, and (3) **intuitive decision-making**.

- **Organizational structure** involves six essential elements: (1) work specialization, (2) departmentalization, (3) chain of command, (4) span of control, (5) centralization and decentralization, and (6) formalization.

- **Organizational design** may be simple, bureaucracy, matrix, virtual, or boundaryless.

- **Organizational culture** consists of an organization's values, ideologies, and beliefs and how these are translated to employees. Culture impacts employees' experiences at work and can be used to improve reactions to organizational change.

- Organizations making plans to **change** typically turn to one of four approaches: (1) Kurt Lewin's three-step model, (2) John Kotter's eight-step plan, (3) action research, and (4) organizational development.

- Common sources of **resistance** among individuals include having to change habits, worrying about security, and fearing economic changes and the unknown. Organization-wide resistance occurs through regulations, processes, restrictive group norms, and threats to specialized groups and power relationships.

- The **primary values** underlying organizational development methods include respecting individuals, establishing a trusting and supportive environment, de-emphasizing hierarchical control and authority, openly confronting problems, and encouraging participation in decision-making.

ORGANIZATIONAL BEHAVIOR POST-TEST

Directions: Carefully read each of the following 60 questions. Choose the best answer to each question and fill in the corresponding circle on the answer sheet. The Answer Key and Explanations can be found following this post-test.

1. Juanita, a new employee, wears stylish clothes and always looks polished. Her coworkers assume she is frivolous and unintelligent, even though they have not spoken to her yet. Which of the following most likely describes the perception method used by Juanita's coworkers?
   A. Selective perception
   B. Contrast effect
   C. Stereotyping
   D. Halo effect

2. Which of the following statements best summarizes goal-setting theory?
   A. Establish simple goals to improve employee job satisfaction.
   B. Address employee goals for self-identity by giving them autonomy.
   C. Set challenging goals for employees and provide them with feedback.
   D. Allow employees to set their own goals and eliminate performance appraisals.

3. The first theory of management was developed by
   A. John Kotter.
   B. Henri Fayol.
   C. Kurt Lewin.
   D. Henry Mintzberg.

4. Which of the following is NOT a commonly used research design method in the field of organizational behavior?
   A. Asking a manager for their opinions
   B. Field experiments
   C. Aggregate quantitative reviews
   D. Case studies

5. Catherine, a pharmaceutical sales representative, dramatically increased her sales numbers in two out of her three assigned sales territories. Catherine's manager responds by assigning the third territory, which is considered undesirable, to another sales representative and giving another territory to Catherine. Which of the following methods is most likely being used by Catherine's manager?
   A. Negative reinforcement
   B. Positive reinforcement
   C. Punishment
   D. Extinction

6. What is the most common type of reinforcement schedule used by businesses?
   A. Continuous schedule
   B. Fixed ratio schedule
   C. Intermittent schedule
   D. Fixed interval schedule

7. Which of the following is a type of personal power?
   A. Expert power
   B. Reward power
   C. Coercive power
   D. Legitimate power

8. Which theory asserts that employees are motivated to work hard when they believe they will be rewarded?
   A. ERG theory
   B. Expectancy theory
   C. Goal-setting theory
   D. Path-goal theory

9. What is the most common source of power in the workplace?
   A. Expert power
   B. Reward power
   C. Coercive power
   D. Legitimate power

10. Which of the following is most critical to action research?
    A. Employee attitudes
    B. Organizational culture
    C. Data analysis
    D. Training

11. Which of the following is most likely to encourage a high degree of political behavior within an organization?
    A. Pressures to excel
    B. Union involvement in human resources
    C. Over-structured employee roles
    D. Objective performance appraisal systems

12. Greg, a sales manager, reaches a deal with his firm's CEO to implement flexible scheduling for the sales department. Greg is most likely acting as a
    A. liaison.
    B. negotiator.
    C. figurehead.
    D. disseminator.

13. Members of a command group are more likely to
    A. work in different departments.
    B. belong to the same union.
    C. share the same manager.
    D. interact socially.

14. Which of the following is an example of an environmental factor that can cause work stress?
    A. Task demands
    B. Family problems
    C. Role demands
    D. Changes in technology

15. According to the path-goal theory, leadership style is determined by
    A. leader characteristics.
    B. reward immediacy.
    C. group relationships.
    D. task structure.

16. According to LMX theory research, the relationship between managers and employees grows stronger when
    A. employees have greater autonomy.
    B. managers are open to new experiences.
    C. employees are assigned challenging tasks.
    D. managers have charisma and long-term vision.

17. What is an advantage of oral communication?
    A. Expresses emotions clearly
    B. Provides immediate feedback
    C. Minimizes common noise problems
    D. Allows for logical message formation

18. Group hierarchy is most likely established during which stage of group development?
    A. Norming
    B. Forming
    C. Storming
    D. Performing

19. Which of the following is NOT a benefit of group decision-making over individual decision-making?
    A. Diversity of viewpoints
    B. Quicker decisions
    C. Higher degree of acceptance by others
    D. Diversity of knowledge

20. What is the primary criticism of the Fiedler model?
    A. Vague connections between leader behaviors and traits
    B. Confusion regarding the questionnaire and variables
    C. Inadequate support from psychological assessments
    D. Failure to isolate specific leadership characteristics

21. Which of the following is NOT a field that contributes to organizational behavior?
    A. Psychology
    B. Anthropology
    C. Geology
    D. Sociology

22. Which decision-making method assumes that individuals face limitations on information and time when making decisions?
    A. Intuitive decision-making
    B. Rational decision-making
    C. Bounded rationality
    D. Work specialization

23. When employees display emotions that they are not actually feeling, this is called
    A. surface acting.
    B. the affective circumplex model.
    C. deep acting.
    D. emotional contagion.

24. Performance norms primarily indicate
    A. the way that group members should communicate.
    B. how group members are expected to behave.
    C. how hard group members should work.
    D. the roles that group members should play.

25. A firm that groups jobs by product is most likely using which element of organizational structure?
    A. Formalization
    B. Departmentalization
    C. Work specialization
    D. Centralization

26. Which of the following is the most commonly used personality-assessment tool?
    A. Myers-Briggs Type Indicator
    B. Sentence completion test
    C. Thematic apperception test
    D. Big Five model

27. Which aspect of organizational structure was first established by Henry Ford?
    A. Departmentalization
    B. Span of control
    C. Work specialization
    D. Formalization

28. Which of the following is NOT a driver of employee culture?
    A. Organizational policies
    B. Leadership
    C. A competitor's products and services
    D. Myths

29. Which of the following statements best summarizes Mintzberg's study?
    A. Some management roles are more important than others.
    B. The leadership role is most directly connected to success.
    C. Most management roles are decision-oriented.
    D. All roles of management are interrelated.

30. Which of the following is a major feature of a bureaucratic organization?
    A. Dual chains of command
    B. Standardized work processes
    C. Minimal departmentalization
    D. Decentralized authority

31. Which of the following activities is least likely to occur at a firm implementing an organizational development strategy?
    A. Distributing surveys to work units
    B. Hiring an outside process consultant
    C. Developing new job specifications
    D. Planning team-building activities

32. According to the interactionist view of conflict, which of the following is most likely a dysfunctional conflict?
    A. Personality clashes
    B. Different work objectives
    C. Communication breakdowns
    D. Unclear work assignment procedures

33. Which type of stressor is linked to workload, deadlines, and pressure to complete tasks?
    A. Challenge stressors
    B. Task stressors
    C. Hindrance stressors
    D. Emotional stressors

34. Which term refers to the extent to which employees care about their jobs?
    A. Job satisfaction
    B. Job involvement
    C. Employee engagement
    D. Employee commitment

35. During the cognition stage of the conflict process, which of the following statements describes what is most likely to occur?
    A. Conditions create conflict opportunities.
    B. Emotions shape conflict perceptions.
    C. Conflicts are actively avoided.
    D. Conflicts become visible.

36. From which field did organizational culture research originate from?
    A. Sociology
    B. Social psychology
    C. Psychology
    D. Anthropology

37. Which of the following involves basing managerial decisions on a systematic study of the best available research?
    A. Evidence-based management
    B. Analytical management
    C. Strategic management
    D. Rational management

38. Which of the following is NOT one of the primary values underlying organizational development methods?
    A. Emphasizing hierarchical control and authority
    B. Respecting individuals
    C. Openly confronting problems
    D. Encouraging participation in decision-making.

39. John, a sales manager, is interviewing job candidates. The first three applicants are clearly unqualified for the position. He offers the position to the last interviewee, who lacks sales experience, but has a better personality for the job than the other candidates. Which of the following has most likely occurred?
    A. Halo effect
    B. Stereotyping
    C. Contrast effect
    D. Selective perception

40. Which term refers to identifying and building on an organization's unique strengths during the process of organizational change?
    A. Process consultation
    B. Appreciative inquiry
    C. Intergroup development
    D. SWOT analysis

41. For which of the following scenarios is employee loyalty particularly beneficial?
    A. When employees experience stress
    B. During organizational change
    C. When employees are low in motivation
    D. When making group decisions

42. Which of the following approaches to implementing change is described by the identification of unique strengths in and organization and building on these qualities to improve performance?
    A. Sensitivity training
    B. Process consultation
    C. Appreciative inquiry
    D. Team building

43. Which of the following is a conflict-stimulation method?
    A. Realigning work groups
    B. Holding problem-solving sessions
    C. Developing joint compromises
    D. Expanding group resources

44. All of the following factors help determine whether a person's behavior is caused by internal or external issues EXCEPT
    A. consensus.
    B. personality.
    C. consistency.
    D. distinctiveness.

45. The transformational leadership theory is most similar to which of the following?
    A. LMX theory
    B. Contingency theory
    C. Behavioral theory
    D. Charismatic leadership theory

46. Which of the following is asserted by the interactionist school of thought?
    A. Conflict can improve group performance.
    B. Conflict always harms group productivity.
    C. Conflict can be minimized by strong leadership.
    D. Conflict benefits small groups but not large ones.

47. Which process of change is the systematic effort to improve an organization's effectiveness and adaptability by changing the attitudes, beliefs, and values of employees through long-term training programs?
    A. Action research
    B. Kotter's eight-step plan
    C. Lewin's three-step model
    D. Organizational development

48. Feeling anxious about making an oral presentation at work is an example of a/an
    A. illegitimate job behavior.
    B. communication barrier.
    C. nonverbal cue.
    D. chain network.

49. Raj has been especially helpful to his manager over the last few weeks by working long hours to complete an important project. However, Raj's manager has not exhibited any appreciation for Raj's hard work, and Raj's motivation has diminished. Which type of reinforcement method has most likely been used by Raj's manager?
    A. Positive reinforcement
    B. Negative reinforcement
    C. Punishment
    D. Extinction

50. Which of the following is NOT a key function of communication in an organization?
    A. Increasing performance
    B. Controlling behavior
    C. Expressing emotion
    D. Fostering motivation

51. According to the Big Five model, a worker with which personality trait is more likely to have a workplace accident?
    A. Extraversion
    B. Agreeableness
    C. Emotional stability
    D. Openness to experience

52. According to the bounded rationality model of decision-making, which of the following is NOT one of the limitations individuals have when making a decision?
    A. Individuals have a limited capacity to evaluate available information
    B. Individuals are often indecisive
    C. Only limited information about possible alternatives is available
    D. Only a limited amount of time is available for making decisions

53. Which of the following is most likely a true statement about groups?
    A. Competition within a group is detrimental to productivity.
    B. Small groups complete tasks more quickly than large groups.
    C. Employers stimulate productivity by rewarding individuals rather than entire groups.
    D. Employees work more productively and cohesively in large groups than in small groups.

54. Which of the following consists of an organization's values, ideologies, and beliefs and how these are translated to employees through socialization, practices, and policies?
    A. Leadership style
    B. Organizational design
    C. Organizational structure
    D. Organizational culture

55. Ludi received a bonus after six months of working at ION Electronics. She received an additional bonus seven months later and another bonus twelve months later. Assuming that Ludi's bonuses don't correspond to specific accomplishments, which type of reinforcement schedule is most likely being used by Ludi's employer?
    A. Continuous schedule
    B. Variable interval schedule
    C. Fixed ratio schedule
    D. Variable ratio schedule

56. The purpose of the third step in Kurt Lewin's model is to
    A. ensure that organizational change is permanent.
    B. prepare employees for organizational changes.
    C. implement desired organizational changes.
    D. develop an organizational change plan.

57. Which of the following is NOT a way for employees and organizations to minimize work stress?
    A. Using effective training programs
    B. Job reassignment
    C. Regular exercise
    D. Realistic goal setting

58. An employee with a high degree of agreeableness is most likely to have
    A. lower levels of job performance.
    B. better negotiation skills.
    C. lower levels of career success.
    D. more detail-oriented skills.

59. What is the primary benefit of job rotation?
    A. Expanding work teams
    B. Minimizing employee boredom
    C. Appealing to working mothers
    D. Increasing an employee's responsibilities

60. Which of the following is a terminal value according to the Rokeach Value Survey?
    A. Honesty
    B. Sincerity
    C. Equality
    D. Dependability

post-test

ANSWER KEY AND EXPLANATIONS

1. D	13. C	25. B	37. A	49. D
2. C	14. D	26. A	38. A	50. A
3. B	15. D	27. C	39. C	51. D
4. A	16. A	28. C	40. B	52. B
5. A	17. B	29. D	41. B	53. B
6. C	18. C	30. B	42. C	54. D
7. A	19. B	31. C	43. A	55. B
8. B	20. B	32. A	44. B	56. A
9. D	21. C	33. A	45. D	57. B
10. C	22. C	34. B	46. A	58. C
11. A	23. A	35. B	47. D	59. B
12. B	24. C	36. D	48. B	60. C

1. **The correct answer is D.** Drawing general impressions of a person based on one characteristic, such as appearance, suggests the halo effect. Selective interpretation occurs when people perceive only what interests them, so choice A is incorrect. Contrast effect involves making comparisons, so choice B is incorrect. Stereotyping is judging based on group association, such as an ethnic group, so choice C is incorrect.

2. **The correct answer is C.** Research related to goal-setting theory indicates that employees are motivated by specific and difficult goals, especially when they receive feedback on their progress. Choice A is incorrect because goals should be challenging. Choices B and D are not relevant to goal-setting theory.

3. **The correct answer is B.** Fayol established the first theory of management, so choice B is correct. Choices A and C are incorrect because Kotter and Lewin developed organizational change theories. Mintzberg followed Fayol by identifying ten roles of managers, so choice D is incorrect.

4. **The correct answer is A.** Research design methods that are most commonly used in organizational behavior research are case studies, field surveys, laboratory experiments, field experiments, and aggregate quantitative reviews. Therefore, choices B, C, and D are incorrect. Choice A is correct because asking managers for their opinions is not a systematic method of study.

5. **The correct answer is A.** Negative reinforcement involves withholding a negative consequence—the undesirable territory—to increase a desired behavior, Catherine's high sales. A bonus is a type of positive reinforcement, so choice B is incorrect. A suspension is an example of punishment, so choice C is incorrect. Extinction removes a reward to decrease behavior, so choice D is incorrect.

6. **The correct answer is C.** Intermittent schedules are most common in businesses. Continuous reinforcement is the most effective way to change employee behaviors, but it is impractical, so choice A is incorrect. Fixed ratio and fixed interval are types of continuous reinforcement, so choices B and D are incorrect.

7. **The correct answer is A.** Expert power is a personal power that is based on an individual's expertise or knowledge. Choice B, reward power; choice C, coercive power; and choice D, legitimate power, are formal powers that stem from an individual's position in an organization.

8. **The correct answer is B.** Expectancy theory is one of the most supported explanations of employee motivation because of the strong connection between effort, performance, and reward. ERG theory asserts that individuals need existence, relatedness, and growth, so choice A is incorrect. Goal-setting theory doesn't link effort with rewards, so choice C is incorrect. Choice D, path-goal theory, is a leadership theory.

9. **The correct answer is D.** Legitimate power stems from an individual's position in a firm and is the most common source of power because of its broad scope. Expert power, choice A; reward power, choice B; and coercive power, choice C, are less common in work environments.

10. **The correct answer is C.** With action research, organizational changes are based on systematically collected and analyzed data. Employee attitudes, organizational culture, and training are less relevant, so choices A, B, and D are incorrect.

11. **The correct answer is A.** A culture that pressures employees to excel is more likely to foster political behaviors. Union involvement in HR is irrelevant, so choice B is incorrect. Unclear employee roles and subjective performance appraisal systems encourage political behavior among workers, so choices C and D, which are the opposite of these, are incorrect.

12. **The correct answer is B.** The negotiator role involves bargaining with others to obtain advantages, so choice B is correct. The liaison and figurehead are both interpersonal roles that involve developing and maintaining good relationships with people, so choices A and C are incorrect. The disseminator role relates to providing information to subordinates, so choice D is incorrect.

13. **The correct answer is C.** Members of a command group report to the same manager, so choice C is correct. Task group members are more likely to work in different departments, so choice A is incorrect. Command group members may or may not belong to a union, so choice B is incorrect. Friendship group members interact outside of work, so choice D is incorrect.

14. **The correct answer is D.** Both task demands and role demands are organizational factors, so choices A and C are incorrect. Family problems are categorized as personal factors, so choice B is also incorrect. Since changes in technology are considered to be external to the individual and the organization, but rather driven by innovations in society, choice D is the correct answer.

15. **The correct answer is D.** Leadership style is determined by subordinate preference and task structure, according to the path-goal theory. Leader characteristics, personal rewards, and group relationships are not relevant to path-goal theory, so choices A, B, and C are incorrect.

16. **The correct answer is A.** Leader-member exchange studies have shown that the relationship between leaders and followers is even stronger when employees have higher levels of autonomy and control over their job performance. Leaders who are open to experiences are typically strong, but this is not linked to LMX theory, which means choice B is incorrect. Choices C and D aren't necessarily associated with LMX theory.

17. **The correct answer is B.** Immediate feedback and speed are the main advantages of oral communication. Emotions are not necessarily expressed clearly through oral communication, so choice A is incorrect. Noise problems remain with oral communication, so choice C is incorrect. Written communication is typically more logical because people have time to consider what they want to communicate, so choice D is incorrect.

18. **The correct answer is C.** The storming stage is characterized by intragroup conflict regarding group leadership, and it ends with a clarified hierarchy. Hierarchy is typically not established during the norming, forming, or performing stages of group development, choices A, B, and D.

19. **The correct answer is B.** Group decision-making is advantageous because it incorporates more viewpoints, members typically have diversity in their knowledge, and there tends to be a higher degree of acceptance for group decisions. Therefore, choices A, C, and D are incorrect. Choice B is correct since individual decisions take less time than group decisions.

20. **The correct answer is B.** Critics of the Fiedler model find the questionnaire and variables confusing and participants' scores unreliable. Choices A, C, and D are criticisms, but not necessarily associated with Fiedler's contingency theory.

21. **The correct answer is C.** Anthropology, psychology, and sociology all contribute to organizational behavior. Therefore, Choices A, B, and D are incorrect and choice C is incorrect since geology is an earth science.

22. **The correct answer is C.** Bounded rationality assumes that individuals face limitations when making decisions: limited information, limited capacity, and limited time. Choices A and B are decision-making models that don't account for such limitations. Choice D is not related to the decision-making process.

23. **The correct answer is A.** The affective circumplex model is a way to delineate emotions according to how they fall on two dimensions: energy and pleasantness. Deep acting occurs when individuals change the emotions they feel so that it matches the emotions they are displaying. Emotional contagion refers to when an individual's emotion causes others to feel the same way. Therefore, choices B, C, and D are incorrect.

24. **The correct answer is C.** Performance norms indicate how hard group members should work, so choice C is correct. Communication, behavior, and roles are less likely to be indicated by performance norms, so choices A, B, and D are incorrect.

25. **The correct answer is B.** Departmentalization involves grouping jobs by product, function, or geography for the purpose of coordinating tasks. Formalization is the degree to which rules govern jobs, so choice A is incorrect. Work specialization divides labor into separate jobs to improve productivity, so choice C is incorrect. Centralized organizations rely on top managers to make decisions, so choice D is incorrect.

26. **The correct answer is A.** The MBTI is the most frequently used personality-assessment tool. Choices B, C, and D are less popular tools for assessing personality.

27. **The correct answer is C.** The division of labor, or work specialization, was established by Henry Ford. Ford is not credited for establishing departmentalization, span of control, or formalization, so choices A, B, and D are incorrect. Span of control, choice B, originated in the military.

answers post-test

28. **The correct answer is C.** Leadership, organizational policies and practices, and organizational myths are all important in translating culture to employees, so choices A, D, and B are incorrect. Since culture comes from within an organization, a competitors' products and services would not drive it, so choice C is the best answer.

29. **The correct answer is D.** Each management role is connected to another, so choice D is correct. Mintzberg's study doesn't suggest that some roles are more important or more related to success, so choices A and B are incorrect. Roles are equally distributed among interpersonal, information, and decisional, so choice C is incorrect.

30. **The correct answer is B.** Bureaucracies are characterized by standardization, depart-mentalization, and centralized authority, making choice B correct and choices C and D incorrect. Dual chains of command are an element of the matrix structure, so choice A is also incorrect.

31. **The correct answer is C.** Changing job specifications is least likely to occur during the process of organizational development, so it is the correct answer. A firm is more likely to collect survey feedback about perceptions, hire an outside consultant to assess processes, and implement team building activities. So, choices A, B, and D are things that an organization would do in implementing an organizational development strategy, and thus incorrect answers to the question.

32. **The correct answer is A.** Relationship conflicts stem from personality clashes between group members, and such conflicts are nearly always dysfunctional. Task conflicts and process conflicts are functional conflicts that can enhance group performance, so choices B, C, and D are incorrect.

33. **The correct answer is A.** Challenge stressors are linked to workload, deadlines, and pressure to complete tasks. Hindrance stressors prevent individuals from reaching their goals, such as bureaucracy and politics, so choice C is incorrect. Since stressors are categorized as either hindrance or challenge, choices B and D are also incorrect

34. **The correct answer is B.** The extent to which employees identify with and care about their jobs is termed job involvement. Job satisfaction refers to an employee's positive or negative feelings about a job, so choice A is incorrect. Employee engagement relates to enthusiasm, so choice C is incorrect. Choice D is not an organizational behavior term.

35. **The correct answer is B.** In the cognition and personalization stage, parties determine what a conflict is about, and emotions play a role in shaping conflict perceptions. Conditions create conflict opportunities earlier in the process, so choice A is incorrect. Choices C and D occur later in the process.

36. **The correct answer is D.** Organizational culture research comes from anthropology. In the 1970s, anthropology researchers introduced it to the field of organizational behavior in an effort to increase the use of anthropology concepts in OB research. Culture research was not traditionally studied in psychology, social psychology, or sociology. Therefore, choices A, B, and C are incorrect.

37. **The correct answer is A.** Evidence-based management calls for managers to base decisions on the best available scientific evidence rather than feelings and intuitions. Choice B, analytical management, uses mathematical models to develop solutions to business problems. Choice C, strategic management, is the process for designing and implementing competitive steps to enhance the performance of an organization. Choice

D, rational management, seems like a good answer, but is meant to distract from the correct answer.

38. **The correct answer is A.** Respecting individuals, openly confronting problems, and encouraging participation in decision-making are all central to organizational development. So, choices B, C, and D are incorrect and choice A is the best answer. Organizational development actually works to de-emphasize hierarchical control and authority

39. **The correct answer is C.** Contrast effect occurs when a person is evaluated based on comparisons to another person. Halo effect involves making a general impression based on one characteristic, so choice A is incorrect. Choice B is incorrect because John hasn't based his judgments on group associations. Selective perception is a problem associated with narrow interpretations, so choice D is incorrect.

40. **The correct answer is B.** Appreciative inquiry involves the identification of unique strengths in an organization and building on these qualities to improve performance. Process consultation and intergroup development are other organizational methods, so choices A and C are incorrect. A SWOT (strengths, weaknesses, opportunities, threats) analysis is used for marketing purposes, so choice D is incorrect.

41. **The correct answer is B.** There is no evidence to suggest that employee loyalty has an impact on stress, motivation, or decision-making outcomes. Therefore, choices A, C, and D are incorrect and B is the best choice.

42. **The correct answer is C.** Sensitivity training changes behavior using things such as diversity training and executive coaching. Process consultation involves hiring an outside consultant to help

managers identify processes that need to be improved. Team building entails interactive group activities to improve group trust and communication. Therefore, choices A, B, and D are incorrect and choice C is the best answer.

43. **The correct answer is A.** Conflict-stimulation methods include realigning work groups and changing rules. Conflict-resolution, not conflict-stimulation, methods include problem-solving sessions, compromising, and expanding resources, so choices B, C, and D are incorrect.

44. **The correct answer is B.** According to attribution theory, consensus, consistency, and distinctiveness are the primary factors that determine whether a person's behavior is internally or externally caused, so choices A, C, and D are incorrect. Personality is not a factor, which means choice B is correct.

45. **The correct answer is D.** Transformational leadership theory and charismatic leadership theory both suggest that leaders articulate a vision and are inspirational. Choices A, B, and C are less similar to transformational leadership theory. Choice A, LMX theory, is about the relationship between leaders and followers and indicates that the more autonomy employees have, the stronger the relationship. Choice B, contingency theory, posits that situational variables determine whether specific leadership traits and behaviors are effective. According to choice C, behavioral theory, effective leaders have different behaviors than ineffective leaders.

46. **The correct answer is A.** The interactionist school of thought views conflict as a positive activity in some cases and should be encouraged in those situations in order to improve group performance. However, interactionists believe that some conflict is harmful, so choice B is incorrect; be careful of universal qualifiers like "always"

and "everyone." Leadership and group size are not an issue, so choices C and D are incorrect.

47. **The correct answer is D.** Lewin's three-step model, Kotter's eight-step plan, and action research all have different approaches to changing the organization, but none of them focus specifically on using training to change attitudes, beliefs and values of employees. Therefore, choices A, B, and C are incorrect and D is the best response.

48. **The correct answer is B.** Communication apprehension occurs when a person feels tense about communicating orally, and it is a type of communication barrier that affects nearly 20 percent of all workers. Choices A, C, and D are not related to communication anxiety.

49. **The correct answer is D.** Failing to show appreciation for help or failing to compliment employees for working hard are examples of extinction. Negative reinforcement involves removing an undesirable consequence, so choice B is incorrect. Choices A and C are incorrect because Raj has not been rewarded or punished by his manager.

50. **The correct answer is A.** The four functions of communication in an organization are controlling behavior, choice B; expressing emotion, choice C; fostering motivation, choice D; and providing information. Increased performance may result from clear communication, but it isn't a primary function, which means choice A is the best answer.

51. **The correct answer is D.** Individuals who score high on openness to experience are more creative, but more susceptible to workplace accidents. Extraversion, agreeableness, and emotional stability are not necessarily associated with risky behavior at work, so choices A, B, and C are incorrect.

52. **The correct answer is B.** The model of bounded rationality assumes that there are three limitations when making decisions: only a limited information about possible alternatives is available, individuals have a limited capacity to evaluate available information, and only a limited amount of time is available for making decisions. Therefore, choices A, C, and D are incorrect. Choice B is the only option that is not part of Simon's theory of bounded rationality, and thus is the correct answer.

53. **The correct answer is B.** Research indicates that smaller groups complete tasks more quickly than larger groups and that employees work more effectively in smaller rather than larger groups. So, choice B is correct and choice D is incorrect. A manager benefits from encouraging competition and rewarding groups rather than individuals, so choices A and C are incorrect.

54. **The correct answer is D.** Leadership can influence organizational culture, but it is not the same as it, so A is incorrect. Organizational design and organizational structure refer to how the organization is configured in terms of things like power and employees and so choices B and C are also incorrect. Therefore, choice D is the best answer.

55. **The correct answer is B.** Variable interval schedules apply reinforcers after varying periods of time. Choices A and C are incorrect because Ludi didn't receive bonuses after every success. Variable ratio schedules apply reinforcers after a variable number of responses, which isn't suggested by the information, so choice D is incorrect.

56. **The correct answer is A.** The purpose of the third and final step of Lewin's model is to ensure that organizational changes are permanent. Employees are prepared and a plan is made in the first step, so choices B

and D are incorrect. Plans are implemented in the second, so choice C is incorrect.

57. **The correct answer is B.** Using effective training programs, regular exercise, and realistic goal setting are all methods to decrease work stress in employees. Therefore, choices A, C, and D are incorrect. Job reassignment is incorrect because research has not shown that it is effective at minimizing work stress. Therefore, choice B is the best answer.

58. **The correct answer is C.** Agreeableness is associated with high job performance, low levels of career success, and poor negotiation skills, so choice C is correct and choices A and B are incorrect. Conscientiousness implies better attention to detail, so choice D is incorrect.

59. **The correct answer is B.** Job rotation involves periodically shifting a worker from one task to another, a technique that reduces boredom in highly routine jobs. Choices A and C are not related to job rotation. Job enrichment expands an employee's responsibilities, so choice D is incorrect.

60. **The correct answer is C.** According to the Rokeach Value Survey, values can be divided into two types: (1) terminal values and (2) instrumental values. Equality is a terminal value, so choice C is correct. Honesty, sincerity, and dependability are instrumental values, so choices A, B, and D are incorrect.

answers post-test

Human Resource Management

OVERVIEW

The DSST® Human Resource Management exam is a multiple-choice exam designed to evaluate whether candidates possess the knowledge and understanding that would be gained by taking a lower level college course in human resource management which includes the following content: overview of the human resource management field; human resource planning, staffing, training and development; performance appraisals; compensation issues; safety and security issues; employment law; and labor relations.

Chapter 5

DIAGNOSTIC TEST ANSWER SHEET

1. Ⓐ Ⓑ Ⓒ Ⓓ   5. Ⓐ Ⓑ Ⓒ Ⓓ   9. Ⓐ Ⓑ Ⓒ Ⓓ   13. Ⓐ Ⓑ Ⓒ Ⓓ   17. Ⓐ Ⓑ Ⓒ Ⓓ
2. Ⓐ Ⓑ Ⓒ Ⓓ   6. Ⓐ Ⓑ Ⓒ Ⓓ   10. Ⓐ Ⓑ Ⓒ Ⓓ   14. Ⓐ Ⓑ Ⓒ Ⓓ   18. Ⓐ Ⓑ Ⓒ Ⓓ
3. Ⓐ Ⓑ Ⓒ Ⓓ   7. Ⓐ Ⓑ Ⓒ Ⓓ   11. Ⓐ Ⓑ Ⓒ Ⓓ   15. Ⓐ Ⓑ Ⓒ Ⓓ   19. Ⓐ Ⓑ Ⓒ Ⓓ
4. Ⓐ Ⓑ Ⓒ Ⓓ   8. Ⓐ Ⓑ Ⓒ Ⓓ   12. Ⓐ Ⓑ Ⓒ Ⓓ   16. Ⓐ Ⓑ Ⓒ Ⓓ   20. Ⓐ Ⓑ Ⓒ Ⓓ

POST-TEST ANSWER SHEET

1. Ⓐ Ⓑ Ⓒ Ⓓ   13. Ⓐ Ⓑ Ⓒ Ⓓ   25. Ⓐ Ⓑ Ⓒ Ⓓ   37. Ⓐ Ⓑ Ⓒ Ⓓ   49. Ⓐ Ⓑ Ⓒ Ⓓ
2. Ⓐ Ⓑ Ⓒ Ⓓ   14. Ⓐ Ⓑ Ⓒ Ⓓ   26. Ⓐ Ⓑ Ⓒ Ⓓ   38. Ⓐ Ⓑ Ⓒ Ⓓ   50. Ⓐ Ⓑ Ⓒ Ⓓ
3. Ⓐ Ⓑ Ⓒ Ⓓ   15. Ⓐ Ⓑ Ⓒ Ⓓ   27. Ⓐ Ⓑ Ⓒ Ⓓ   39. Ⓐ Ⓑ Ⓒ Ⓓ   51. Ⓐ Ⓑ Ⓒ Ⓓ
4. Ⓐ Ⓑ Ⓒ Ⓓ   16. Ⓐ Ⓑ Ⓒ Ⓓ   28. Ⓐ Ⓑ Ⓒ Ⓓ   40. Ⓐ Ⓑ Ⓒ Ⓓ   52. Ⓐ Ⓑ Ⓒ Ⓓ
5. Ⓐ Ⓑ Ⓒ Ⓓ   17. Ⓐ Ⓑ Ⓒ Ⓓ   29. Ⓐ Ⓑ Ⓒ Ⓓ   41. Ⓐ Ⓑ Ⓒ Ⓓ   53. Ⓐ Ⓑ Ⓒ Ⓓ
6. Ⓐ Ⓑ Ⓒ Ⓓ   18. Ⓐ Ⓑ Ⓒ Ⓓ   30. Ⓐ Ⓑ Ⓒ Ⓓ   42. Ⓐ Ⓑ Ⓒ Ⓓ   54. Ⓐ Ⓑ Ⓒ Ⓓ
7. Ⓐ Ⓑ Ⓒ Ⓓ   19. Ⓐ Ⓑ Ⓒ Ⓓ   31. Ⓐ Ⓑ Ⓒ Ⓓ   43. Ⓐ Ⓑ Ⓒ Ⓓ   55. Ⓐ Ⓑ Ⓒ Ⓓ
8. Ⓐ Ⓑ Ⓒ Ⓓ   20. Ⓐ Ⓑ Ⓒ Ⓓ   32. Ⓐ Ⓑ Ⓒ Ⓓ   44. Ⓐ Ⓑ Ⓒ Ⓓ   56. Ⓐ Ⓑ Ⓒ Ⓓ
9. Ⓐ Ⓑ Ⓒ Ⓓ   21. Ⓐ Ⓑ Ⓒ Ⓓ   33. Ⓐ Ⓑ Ⓒ Ⓓ   45. Ⓐ Ⓑ Ⓒ Ⓓ   57. Ⓐ Ⓑ Ⓒ Ⓓ
10. Ⓐ Ⓑ Ⓒ Ⓓ   22. Ⓐ Ⓑ Ⓒ Ⓓ   34. Ⓐ Ⓑ Ⓒ Ⓓ   46. Ⓐ Ⓑ Ⓒ Ⓓ   58. Ⓐ Ⓑ Ⓒ Ⓓ
11. Ⓐ Ⓑ Ⓒ Ⓓ   23. Ⓐ Ⓑ Ⓒ Ⓓ   35. Ⓐ Ⓑ Ⓒ Ⓓ   47. Ⓐ Ⓑ Ⓒ Ⓓ   59. Ⓐ Ⓑ Ⓒ Ⓓ
12. Ⓐ Ⓑ Ⓒ Ⓓ   24. Ⓐ Ⓑ Ⓒ Ⓓ   36. Ⓐ Ⓑ Ⓒ Ⓓ   48. Ⓐ Ⓑ Ⓒ Ⓓ   60. Ⓐ Ⓑ Ⓒ Ⓓ

answer sheet

HUMAN RESOURCE MANAGEMENT DIAGNOSTIC TEST

Directions: Carefully read each of the following 20 questions. Choose the best answer to each question and fill in the corresponding circle on the answer sheet. The Answer Key and Explanations can be found following this Diagnostic Test.

1. With what is the field of industrial psychology concerned?
   A. Training management personnel
   B. Hiring and firing employees
   C. Employee testing and assignment
   D. Trade unions and collective bargaining

2. Which of the following is NOT part of the strategic planning process for HRM?
   A. Identify employee skills that will enable the organization to attain its goals
   B. Determine the organization's goals
   C. Identify employees who exhibit desired skills
   D. Create policies that will produce the desired employee skills

3. Job evaluations are done by comparing
   A. salary incentives among employees in different departments.
   B. evaluations done by supervisory personnel.
   C. employee responses to exhaustive questionnaires.
   D. responsibilities and skills required for various jobs.

4. The human resource manager is expected to
   A. provide personalized and helpful service to customers.
   B. identify which workers deserve bonuses.
   C. plan the number of employees that an organization will need.
   D. give tours to visiting customers.

5. Which of the following is NOT included in employment law?
   A. Civil Rights Act Title VII
   B. Americans with Disabilities Act
   C. Family and Medical Leave Act
   D. Selective Service Act

6. Ergonomics covers such workplace issues as
   A. repetitive motion disorders.
   B. the prevention of food poisoning.
   C. traffic flow and overcrowding.
   D. the inhalation of hazardous gases.

7. In a structured job interview, the questioner will
   A. ask questions as he or she thinks of them.
   B. be joined by a panel of managers.
   C. expect certain acceptable responses.
   D. encourage the applicant to speak spontaneously.

8. Disciplinary action taken against a worker
   A. should not depend on the worker's seniority.
   B. may be more lenient with a first offender.
   C. usually begins with an oral warning.
   D. is usually administered by the worker's union.

9. Which of the following is true about the Social Security Act of 1935?
   A. It is a voluntary benefit.
   B. It is a form of discretionary benefits.
   C. It is a means of workers' compensation.
   D. It is a mandatory benefit.

10. Which of the following is an example of a soft skills training topic?
    A. Time management strategies
    B First aid techniques
    C Current tax laws
    D. Manufacturing quality control

11. A recruiter is permitted to take into account an applicant's
    A. family responsibilities.
    B. previous work history.
    C. country of origin.
    D. posture and dress.

12. What right of workers does the Wagner Act of 1935 protect?
    A. Working in a closed shop
    B. Enacting right-to-work laws
    C. Choosing shop stewards
    D. Bargaining collectively

13. Which of the following is NOT a requirement of the Worker Adjustment and Retraining Notification Act (WARN)?
    A. Give 60 days advance notice of the closing of a plant
    B. Notify the workforce of their right to organize in a union
    C. Provide workers with retirement benefits
    D. Close their business for all federal holidays

14. Which of the following describes an apprenticeship program?
    A. New employees learn how to use simulated versions of the real equipment they will be working on.
    B. Employers provide informal training through coaching and on-the-job experience.
    C. New employees learn their jobs through on-the-job training and mentoring.
    D. New employees learn their jobs through a structured combination of classroom instruction and on-the-job training.

15. Any worker who leaves his or her home country to work in a foreign branch is a/an
    A. third-country national.
    B. domestic worker.
    C. expatriate.
    D. agent.

16. Which of the following is the primary goal of OSHA?
    A. Providing employee training
    B. Preventing workplace accidents
    C. Requiring employee health coverage
    D. Monitoring corporate ethics

17. The passage of the Taft-Hartley Act marked a change from the way
    A. legislation had favored unions.
    B. states controlled the growth of unions.
    C. legislation always favored management.
    D. businesses bargained with unions.

18. A problem can arise with a performance evaluation if
    A. the employee being assessed is about to retire.
    B. the benefits administrator is not involved.
    C. the supervisor shows bias in favor of some employees.
    D. there have been multiple complaints about the supervisor.

19. Diversity in the workforce does NOT include being concerned with
    A. perceived differences.
    B. race, gender, or marital status.
    C. varied lifestyles.
    D. computer skills.

20. Which of the following describes a pay follower?
    A. A firm that pays less than other companies in the same field
    B. A firm that hires only the most experienced workers
    C. A firm that rarely promotes anyone from the outside into management because of the pay differential
    D. A firm that does not offer incentives to employees

diagnostic test

ANSWER KEY AND EXPLANATIONS

1. C	5. D	9. D	13. A	17. A
2. C	6. A	10. A	14. D	18. C
3. D	7. C	11. B	15. C	19. D
4. C	8. C	12. D	16. B	20. A

1. **The correct answer is C.** Choice A is incorrect because industrial psychology is not concerned with training. Choice B is incorrect because this field is not involved with hiring or firing workers. Choice D is incorrect because industrial psychology does not encompass trade unions and collective bargaining.

2. **The correct answer is C.** Identifying employees who already possess the skills and behaviors required to enable an organization to attain its goals is not part of HRM's strategic planning process, so it is the correct answer to the question. Choices A, B, and D are steps in the strategic planning process.

3. **The correct answer is D.** Choice A is incorrect because incentives are not considered in job evaluations. Choice B is incorrect because there is likely to be only one supervisor involved. Choice C is incorrect because questionnaires are used for job analysis, not for performance appraisals.

4. **The correct answer is C.** Choices A and D are incorrect because a human resource manager does not deal with customers. Choice D is also incorrect because that is likely to be done only in consultation with the direct supervisor. Choice B is incorrect because bonuses are determined by managers.

5. **The correct answer is D.** Choices A, B, and C are incorrect because employment law includes the Title VII of the Civil Rights Act, the Americans with Disabilities Act, and the Family and Medical Leave Act. The Selective Service Act deals with military service.

6. **The correct answer is A.** Ergonomics involves fitting workplace conditions and job demands to the capabilities of workers. Choice B is incorrect because food poisoning is not related to ergonomics. Choice C is incorrect because traffic flow and overcrowding are not ergonomic issues. Choice D is incorrect because ergonomics does not deal with the inhalation of gases. That would be an OSHA (Occupational Safety and Health Administration) issue.

7. **The correct answer is C.** Choice A is incorrect because asking random questions is not part of a structured interview. Choice B is incorrect because a panel of interviewers is not an aspect of a structured job interview. Choice D is incorrect because answering spontaneously would defeat the aim of a structured interview, which requires only certain acceptable answers.

8. **The correct answer is C.** Choice A is incorrect because seniority should not influence whether disciplinary action is taken or not, although a long-time employee with a spotless record may be treated more leniently than one with a series of infractions. Choice B is incorrect because although leniency for a first offense may be true in some cases, it is not a given. Choice D is incorrect because although the union may have set rules on discipline, the union is not involved in administering worker discipline.

9. **The correct answer is D.** Choice A is incorrect because Social Security is not a voluntary benefit, nor is it a discretionary benefit, choice B. Choice C is incorrect because workers' compensation is a separate issue.

10. **The correct answer is A.** Soft skills, such as time management, problem solving, and interpersonal communication, are important to job success, but are not related to a specific type of job. Choice B would likely be covered in a safety course, while choices C and D would be addressed in professional training sessions.

11. **The correct answer is B.** Choices A and C are incorrect because taking into account family responsibilities and an applicant's country of origin would be a form of bias. Choice D is incorrect because considering posture and dress might influence interviewers and would also be a form of bias.

12. **The correct answer is D.** The Wagner Act, also known as the National Labor Relations Board, protects the rights of workers to organize and bargain collectively. Choice A is incorrect because the Wagner Act does not deal with closed shops, which require union membership to work in a company. Choice B is incorrect because workers don't enact laws; legislatures do. Right-to-work laws are state laws that make it illegal to refuse to hire someone because he or she doesn't belong to a union. Choice C is incorrect because choosing a shop steward is a union membership decision that doesn't involve company management.

13. **The correct answer is A.** Choices B, C, and D are covered by WARN. The right to organize is protected under the National Labor Relations Board Act, commonly known as the Wagner Act.

14. **The correct answer is D.** Apprenticeship programs are formal structured programs that combine classroom learning with on-the-job training. Choice A describes vestibule training, not an apprenticeship program. Choices B and C say essentially the same thing and are both incorrect.

15. **The correct answer is C.** Choice A is incorrect because a third-party national comes neither from the home country of the global business, nor the host country of its branch. Choice B is incorrect because a domestic worker would be a citizen of the host country. Choice D is incorrect because while an agent may seem like a logical answer, it doesn't fit the description in the question.

16. **The correct answer is B.** The Occupational Safety and Health Administration (OSHA) oversees workplace health and safety. The agency sets safety standards and ensures compliance to reduce the frequency and severity of workplace accidents, so choices A, C, and D are incorrect.

17. **The correct answer is A.** Choice B is incorrect because states did not—and do not—control the growth of unions. Choice C is incorrect because the Taft-Hartley Act was a reaction to legislation that favored unions, not management. Choice D is incorrect because the Act did not directly affect collective bargaining.

18. **The correct answer is C.** Choice A is incorrect because retirement would not be an issue in an evaluation. Choice B is incorrect because the benefits administrator should not be involved in performance evaluations. Choice D is incorrect because although there may have been multiple complaints about the supervisor, they would be regarded as a separate issue.

19. **The correct answer is D.** This question is looking for the answer that doesn't fit. Since

choices A, B, and C are true examples of diversity in the workplace, they are incorrect. Perceived differences, choice A, is an issue in creating diversity in the workplace. Similarly, choice B, race, gender, and marital status, are issues in creating diversity in the workplace. Choice C is incorrect because varied lifestyles are also an issue in creating diversity in the workplace. Only choice D, computer skills, is not a diversity issue.

20. **The correct answer is A.** Choice B is incorrect because hiring the most experienced workers would more likely be true of a pay leader. Choices C and D are incorrect because although they may seem like possible answers, neither describes a pay follower.

answers diagnostic test

DIAGNOSTIC TEST ASSESSMENT GRID

Now that you've completed the diagnostic test and read through the answer explanations, you can use your results to target your studying. Find the question numbers from the diagnostic test that you answered incorrectly and highlight or circle them below. Then focus extra attention on the sections within the chapter dealing with those topics.

Human Resource Management		
Content Area	Topic	Question #
An Overview of the Human Resource Management Field 8%	• Historical development • HR functions • Role/qualification of the HR manager • Ethical aspects of HR decision making	1, 4
Human Resource Planning 9%	• Strategic HR issues • Workforce diversity/inclusion • Job analysis and job design	2, 19
Staffing / Talent Acquisition 11%	• Recruiting • Selection • Promotions and transfers • Reduction-in-force • Voluntary turnover, retirement, succession planning	7, 11
Training and Development 8%	• Onboarding • Career planning • Principles of learning • Training programs and method • Development programs s	10, 14
Performance Management (Appraisals) 12%	• Reasons for performance evaluation • Techniques • Challenges	8, 18

Human Resource Management (continued)		
Compensation and Benefits / Total Rewards 12%	• Job evaluation • Wage and salary administration • Compensation systems • Benefits—mandatory/voluntary	3, 20
Safety and Health 9%	• Occupational accidents and illness • Quality of work life and wellness • Workplace security	6, 16
Employment Law 16%	• Equal employment opportunity laws • Compensation and benefits related laws • Benefits—mandatory/voluntary • Health, safety, and employee rights laws	5, 9, 13
Labor Relations 10%	• Role of labor unions • Labor laws • Collective bargaining • Unionized vs. non-unionized work settings • Contract management	12, 17
Current Issues and Trends 5%	• HR information systems • Changing patterns of work relationships • Global HR environment • Social media • Corporate social responsibility and sustainability	15

....
GET THE FACTS
....

To see the DSST® Human Resource Management Fact Sheet, go to *http://getcollegecredit.com/ exam_fact_sheets* and click on the **Business** tab. Scroll down and click the **Human Resource Management** link. Here you will find suggestions for further study material and the ACE college credit recommendations for passing the test.

AN OVERVIEW OF THE HUMAN RESOURCE MANAGEMENT FIELD

Human Resource Management (HRM) is concerned with a company's employees, that is, its human resources. The primary goal of HRM is to suggest ways to manage the workplace so that all personnel contribute to the overall success of the company and are appropriately compensated for their contributions.

HISTORICAL DEVELOPMENT

One of the earliest forms of personnel management was known as industrial welfare. During the Industrial Revolution of the nineteenth century, legislation expanded the responsibilities of those concerned with supervising personnel. For example, new laws regulated the work hours of children and women, and supervisors were required to see that those laws were observed.

Other developments further influenced personnel management. Frederick Taylor, a U.S. mechanical engineer, is considered to be the founder of what became known as scientific management. Taylor promoted incentive systems that rewarded workers for meeting or exceeding objectives. He believed that pay should be linked to productivity, thus motivating workers to earn more by being more productive.

Others were also at work on ideas to improve management. During World War I, the new field of industrial psychology was beginning to be applied to the workplace. Industrial psychology is the branch of applied psychology concerned with the effective management of a labor force. For example, testing was introduced to evaluate military personnel so that they would be assigned to appropriate tasks. After the war, employee testing and assignment became a standard procedure in private industry.

In the early part of the twentieth century, many companies began to establish departments whose purpose it was to ensure workers' productivity by increasing job satisfaction, which, in turn, would increase productivity. These departments would eventually evolve into what became known as personnel departments. At first, these departments were concerned mainly with hiring suitable employees, but as their responsibilities became more complex, many personnel departments evolved into the HRM departments of today.

HUMAN RESOURCE FUNCTIONS

Management functions have gradually expanded beyond (1) staffing and (2) training and development. A modern human resources department may have to deal with many issues, including the following:

- Trade unions and collective bargaining
- Laws guaranteeing civil rights and equal opportunity employment
- Outsourcing
- Globalization
- Information technology
- Pensions and benefits
- The use of part-time and temporary employees
- Mergers and takeovers
- Federal, state, and local laws
- Flextime and job sharing
- Health-care costs

In many organizations, HRM is considered a strategic partner in developing the business.

THE ROLE AND QUALIFICATIONS OF THE HUMAN RESOURCE MANAGER

In the past, human resource (HR) managers primarily handled administrative tasks—hiring workers, processing payroll, and filling out forms. However, the role of HR managers has expanded over time to involve both administrative and strategic tasks. Staffing, developing workplace policies, administering compensation and benefits, facilitating employee growth and retention, upholding laws related to the workplace, and addressing worker safety issues are just some of the many issues handled by HR managers.

Effective HR managers work alongside other departments and managers to meet the needs of employees and the organization. In many organizations, HR managers work in consultation with line managers—those persons with the direct managerial responsibility for employees. HR managers and line managers jointly evaluate employee performance, determine training and development needs, and make decisions about promotions and transfers. In organizations in which HRM is used strategically, HR managers work with senior management to develop strategic goals for the organization and forecast future employment needs.

Successful HR managers possess a wide range of skills to juggle tasks, technology, and people on a daily basis. One of the most important skills needed is organization because HR managers handle personnel files, employee benefits, government paperwork, and many other types of information. Strong time management skills and personal efficiency support an HR manager's organizational capabilities. Negotiation skills are also essential since the HR department typically works with job candidates and current employees to reach salary terms that are acceptable to both parties. Problem-solving capabilities also facilitate success in the HR field because HR managers often work on the front lines handling conflicts between employees.

Strong communication skills are critical for most jobs and especially in the HR profession which involves interacting with both upper-level managers and employees on a regular basis. In addition to speaking in front of groups, HR managers must communicate verbally, in writing, and through social media platforms. Effective communication skills enable HR managers to motivate employees and help them set personal goals that align with company objectives. The ability to communicate clearly with employees and recognize their achievements demonstrates the kind of leadership skills expected of HR managers.

ETHICAL ASPECTS OF HUMAN RESOURCE DECISION MAKING

Ethics is a system of moral principles intended to govern a person's or group's behavior. In business, adhering to such a set of principles includes, but is not limited to, following laws and regulations. A major difficulty that the manager faces is the realization that while something may be legal, it is not necessarily moral. Because the goal of the company is to make a profit, the manager must decide whether an action that might be profitable is also morally justified, based on the company's ethical guidelines.

HR managers face ethical decisions every day, and sometimes it may not be easy to make those decisions. In interviewing a prospective employee, for example, the HR manager might have to decide whether to explain a potentially difficult situation the new employee would face, such as taking the place of a highly popular manager who was terminated. HR managers negotiate salaries, manage employee conflicts, evaluate employee performance, and handle other situations involving confidential information, so a strong ethical foundation is essential.

HUMAN RESOURCE PLANNING

The role of the HR department has changed greatly from the days of overseeing hiring and firing. Today's HR department is a strategic partner with upper management in setting goals and executing the company's strategic plan.

STRATEGIC HUMAN RESOURCE ISSUES

An HR manager is expected to identify the employee skills and behaviors required to meet the company's goals now and in the future. For example, a company may focus on providing customers with personalized and helpful service. To implement this strategy, therefore, the company will seek to hire employees they feel have empathy for others. Training and rewards will center on meeting that goal and should reach every level in the company.

Evaluation of the strategy should be ongoing so that management can make adjustments as needed over time. HRM works closely with company management to carry out and monitor how well employees are achieving the projected goals.

Familiarity with department managers and personnel enables HR managers to understand the strengths and weaknesses of the workforce and to anticipate future staffing needs. Tools such as trend analysis, ratio analysis, and scatter plots help HR managers to forecast staffing requirements, which enables them to support the strategic goals of the organization more effectively. Depending on the goals of the organization, HR managers will need to evaluate the current staff, determine how many people to hire, when to hire them, and what skills the new workers should possess.

Strategic HR also involves developing compensation plans and reward systems that will attract and retain the best talent. Developing training programs that equip employees for their jobs and support business goals are also important components of strategic HR plans. Strategic HRM optimizes an organization's human resources to ensure organizational success.

WORKFORCE DIVERSITY AND INCLUSION

The concept of diversity in the workforce has evolved over the years. Originally, its meaning was fairly narrow and mainly related to race and gender. Today diversity, which refers to the differences between people, also encompasses age, religion, disabilities, country of origin, marital status, socioeconomic status, family responsibilities, and sexual orientation. In terms of HRM, diversity management involves recognizing and proactively managing the unique needs of today's workforce and establishing an inclusive work environment often through policies and strategies. Being inclusive requires employers to be open-minded and supportive, so that all employees feel welcome and valued. A cohesive workforce is one in which employees work well together. Prospective employees are drawn to a company with that kind of reputation, and customers benefit from the harmonious environment. As an added bonus, studies indicate that corporate bottom lines benefit from workforce diversity as well.

JOB ANALYSIS AND JOB DESIGN

Job analysis and job design are part of the process of determining specific tasks to be performed, what methods are used in performing those tasks, and how the job relates to other work in the organization. Through this system, the HRM can identify the skills, duties, and knowledge necessary for performing certain jobs.

This process applies as new jobs are created or old ones are redesigned because of changing requirements or procedures. Job analysis and job design can provide information needed for staffing, training and development, compensation, and safety and health, all of which are crucial to the development of job descriptions. HRM might gather this information by means of (1) observation, (2) questionnaires, (3) interviews, (4) employee logs of their duties, or (5) a combination of methods.

STAFFING AND TALENT ACQUISITION

Staffing includes a variety of aspects, such as recruitment and selection in order to ensure that an organization has the right employees in the right jobs to execute the company's strategic plan and achieve its goals.

RECRUITING

Recruiting is a process. The first step is deciding, as part of planning and forecasting, what positions to fill. Next, recruiters have to build up a pool of candidates drawn from both (1) internal and (2) external sources. For internal recruiting, HRM consults personnel records to identify employees with the right skills set, and then interviews them for the position. The law requires jobs to also be posted, and workers may respond to job postings when they find a job description that seems to match their skills and experience.

Today's HR managers use a variety of methods to recruit externally. Job search websites like Indeed. com, Monster.com, and CareerBuilder.com are effective tools for posting available positions and identifying possible candidates. Social media also serves as a modern recruiting tool. LinkedIn, for example, the business-focused social networking site, enables HR managers to find and be introduced to potential job candidates. Some firms also use social media platforms like Facebook and Twitter to post jobs and engage with candidates. Other online recruiting options include the company website and professional association websites. More traditional methods such as job fairs, help-wanted ads, and college recruiting and internships allow recruiters to screen candidates for education, attitude, motivation, and communication skills.

Some firms also turn to outside sources for their recruitment needs. Executive search firms focus on filling upper-management and CEO positions and charge hefty fees for the task. If a business needs to fill a position temporarily, such as when a permanent employee takes medical leave, a staffing firm may be contacted.

SELECTION

How long the actual selection of staff takes can be affected by various factors, including (1) company rules and (2) legal considerations. Company rules on hiring and promotion may depend on the level of the position. For example, someone being considered for an executive position will probably be subject to more scrutiny than an applicant for a clerical position.

Legal considerations involve making sure that hiring is not discriminatory in any way and meets all the requirements of legislation governing hiring. Even when the parties involved in the selection process are confident in their final choice, the candidate may be required to undergo a physical exam before being officially hired. Following up on references and checking the accuracy of résumés may also extend the vetting process.

Interviewing—(1) structured or (2) unstructured—makes up a significant part of the selection process. In an unstructured interview, interviewers ask questions as they think of them. For a structured interview, though, the types of questions are predetermined. Even responses that are considered acceptable are delineated in advance.

Some interview questions are intended to explore the applicant's job skills. For example: What courses did you take in college that involved using your organizational skills? Other questions might be more situational, such as asking how the person would react to certain circumstances. Or a question might call on an applicant to describe particular situations in his or her work experience and explain how the candidate handled them.

Applicants may have to submit to several interviews, gradually moving up the levels of management. Some companies conduct panel interviews, with the candidate being interviewed simultaneously by a group of managers or peers who will be working with the candidate or a combination of both.

PROMOTIONS AND TRANSFERS

When promotions or transfers are considered for company personnel, HRM considers past experience and measurable competence. Still, there is no guarantee that even a high-performing employee will do as well in another position, which suggests that his or her future performance should be monitored in the first few months.

Transfers, which are usually lateral moves, generally mean being responsible for familiar tasks and decisions. Though such moves do not usually mean a higher paycheck, it may be desirable for the employee for other reasons. These might include better working hours, less commuting, or simply the need for a change of environment.

REDUCTION-IN-FORCE

A reduction-in-force, or RIF, may be the result of such external factors as an economic downturn or a merger or buyout by another company. An RIF that follows a merger or buyout occurs because when the two companies combine, there is a duplication of some staff positions. An internal cause of downsizing might be a company's own plans for reorganizing its work groups or its business.

An RIF is generally permanent. A layoff, on the other hand, is the discharge, often temporary, of workers. Those employees may be rehired once economic conditions improve. To minimize layoffs during a downturn, a company may try reducing everyone's hours and scheduling periodic plant closings or unpaid vacations.

The HR department may be called on to conduct termination interviews in which department personnel break the news to terminated workers and explain their severance packages. A company may also provide outside help in the form of the services of an outplacement firm, which counsels the affected employees by providing instruction on how to strengthen their job-search skills and rewrite their résumés. Outplacement firms may also provide office space and some secretarial help for a period of time for affected employees.

The HR department also needs to deal with the "survivors," the employees who have retained their positions in an RIF situation. An RIF is likely to affect, at least temporarily, the morale of those left behind, challenging their sense of security. The more sensitively the HR department handles the situation, the better the adjustment the remaining staff will make.

VOLUNTARY TURNOVER, RETIREMENT, AND SUCCESSION PLANNING

Because of the cost and time involved in recruiting and training new workers, companies remain alert to the rate of employee turnover. So, for example, when personnel from the HR department conduct exit interviews with workers who are resigning voluntarily, they will analyze the workers' responses to certain questions. The aim is to gain insight about why these people are leaving, including their perception of how the company has treated them. Information gathered this way may help the firm in the future to retain high-quality employees.

Retirement is another type of voluntary turnover, at least more so than it has been in the past. Though mandatory retirement age requirements still exist in some companies, there has been a trend in recent years toward phased retirement, which results in retirement being a process rather than an abrupt end to workers' jobs. Phased retirement allows workers to move gradually from full-time work to full retirement. They might begin by reducing the number of hours they work, gradually decreasing those hours over time. This may benefit the company, too, in that it allows management to reduce labor costs without the upheaval of an RIF. The benefit to older workers is that they can keep their benefits while working shorter hours.

Another way a firm may reduce its labor costs without laying off workers is by offering early retirement packages. These offer senior employees benefits that they would not receive if they retired later. However, workers do have the option of turning down such offers. There can also be a disadvantage to the company in making such offers. If it makes the offer to a whole class of workers (for example, senior employees), it risks losing some of its most experienced and able personnel.

With the growing number of retirements among the baby boomer generation, many firms are focusing their attention on succession planning. Succession planning prepares for the fact that turnover occurs by developing employees within the organization who can fill senior positions in the future. An effective succession plan identifies key positions and the potential personnel who could be groomed to fill those positions. By training, motivating, and developing such employees for senior positions, an organization ensures a smooth transition when current top executives retire or resign

TRAINING AND DEVELOPMENT

A large segment of an HR manager's responsibilities involves the training and development of an organization's employees, from top management to hourly workers.

ONBOARDING

First impressions in business are important because it is within the first six months of employment that many new hires decide whether to stay or leave. Many firms develop employee onboarding programs to improve the retention rates of new hires. Onboarding refers to the process of integrating new employees into a firm and its culture and providing them with the necessary tools and information to be successful, productive, and engaged. In the past, many organizations focused only on new employee orientation, which is a component of onboarding that takes place during the first few days on the job and primarily involves completing paperwork and covering company policies and procedures. However, onboarding is an ongoing process that can last for months with the objective of making new employees want to work at the firm.

The HR department is likely to be involved in onboarding, but other personnel may take part: (1) line managers wishing to establish a productive relationship with a new employee, and (2) peers who can anticipate a new employee's interests and concerns. Some employers may institute a buddy system, with a peer becoming a mentor to the new worker. Other employers may use a team approach, thus providing the newest member with ready access to different knowledge skills.

CAREER PLANNING

How an employee's career develops is important to both that worker and the company itself. Career planning is the ongoing process by which both the individual and the company are involved in that worker's development.

Self-assessment is a vital part of an employee's career planning. It involves recognizing one's interests, skills, and goals. Knowing one's strengths and weaknesses can help a person make the correct career choices and avoid mistakes that lead to job dissatisfaction. For example, if someone accepts a position that is not sufficiently challenging, it can lead to a bored employee making careless mistakes. On the other hand, the challenged worker who can apply his or her skills to a task and feel successful will not only find job satisfaction, but will also contribute to the company's success.

Some companies assist employees in planning their career paths by providing informative materials, personal guidance, and workshops. They might also compensate employees for approved outside courses, including those using e-learning and computer applications.

PRINCIPLES OF LEARNING

It probably is not logical to expect a single list of the principles of learning to apply to all learning situations. However, the following list recognizes the special requirements of the workplace:

- *Employee Motivation:* This can take many forms. The possibility of promotion, for example, can motivate employees to learn because employees will feel that their ability, training, and experience are likely to be recognized and rewarded.

- *Recognition of Individual Differences:* It is important that workers be rewarded for their particular capabilities by being assigned to learning tasks that recognize and challenge those abilities.

- *Transfer of Learning* (from one position to another): Workers can carry over certain skills from one assignment to another. A management that recognizes and acts on this fact prevents workers from being locked into one career path, especially if it is not a satisfying one.

- *Meaningful Materials:* Print, computer applications, DVDs, online programs, workshops—these are all available for educating workers. To be effective, materials should be up-to-date and directly related to the skills that learners need to master for their jobs. A review by supervisory personnel helps to ensure that the materials are current and appropriate to the company's and the workers' goals.

Management should also recognize that learning can take place both (1) formally and (2) informally. Formal learning may be company-sponsored or the result of individual initiative. It may take place in a classroom, workshop, or online. Informal learning is on-the-job learning, resulting from working and exchanging ideas with colleagues. It is an inexpensive form of learning, and companies are wise to encourage it.

An apprenticeship is another method for learning job-related knowledge and skills. It requires a combination of formal instruction and on-the-job training by a knowledgeable staff member with good communication skills.

TRAINING PROGRAMS AND METHODS

Training includes all those activities designed to provide learners with the knowledge and skills they need to do well in their present jobs. Companies with a reputation for encouraging learning are at an advantage in several ways. For one, training and development programs help in recruiting new workers concerned about how they will advance during their tenure at a company. It is likely, too, that a reputation for learning will attract more highly qualified applicants.

Any training must be done in context—the context being an analysis of the company's actual needs. HRM must ask itself the following types of questions:

- Which workers need to be trained?
- What do they need to learn?
- What do they need to do differently from what they are doing now?
- Will this training help advance the goals of the organization?

Training methods vary from company to company and include (1) instructor-led sessions, (2) online training, (3) virtual classrooms, and (4) case studies. Perhaps the most common one is a class led by an instructor. This method is especially effective with a small group and an instructor who encourages lively discussion. Online, or e-learning, delivered by computer or mobile device has become more and more popular. It not only allows more flexibility in terms of time and distance, but it is also cost-effective once the program is developed. A typical training session ends with a survey to elicit feedback on the effectiveness of the training.

One method often used for management training is the case study. A group leader presents a simulated situation in which a manager is required to analyze the case and then suggest solutions to the problem. The leader must be able to keep the discussion positive and productive. Role-playing and business games similarly involve participants' decision-making skills.

DEVELOPMENT PROGRAMS

Development programs are also concerned with learning, but center on the skills and knowledge that go beyond the trainee's present job. Development involves individual career planning within the context of organizational development. Human resource development is a major responsibility of the HR department.

Management development seminars and conferences may emphasize such skills as assertiveness training for women, cost accounting, and developing emotional intelligence. While these might not be the types of courses one would find in a college curriculum, they may enhance a management candidate's qualifications for a supervisory position.

As a further stimulus to improving management skills, a company might employ executive coaches from an outside firm. The coach identifies the candidate's strengths and weaknesses, and then helps that executive capitalize on his or her strengths. Coaching, while expensive, has proven to be effective, as shown by assessments from both subordinates and supervisors.

PERFORMANCE MANAGEMENT

Pay, promotion, and retention are based on performance appraisals. These evaluations are the way a firm's employees become aware of their standing in the company. Performance appraisals are formal evaluations as opposed to the ongoing assessment of employees' performance that managers should be conducting.

REASONS FOR PERFORMANCE EVALUATION

Long before the performance appraisals are actually carried out, the process should begin with the supervisor setting the performance standards, or criteria, which employees are expected to meet. These standards should be based on (1) appropriate traits, such as attitude and appearance; (2) appropriate behaviors, such as diligence and organizational skill; (3) competencies, such as business knowledge and interpersonal skills; (4) achievement of goals; and (5) potential for improvement.

Once the appraisals have been conducted, the supervisor works with employees to develop a plan to eliminate any deficiencies. If a worker performs well, he or she will benefit from immediate feedback. Similarly, if worker performance is less than ideal, the sooner the worker receives feedback, the sooner he or she can, in conjunction with the supervisor, take the necessary steps to improve performance.

TECHNIQUES

A variety of performance evaluation techniques are used by firms. Some companies use a packaged form, either paper or online, that lists the areas on which the employee is to be graded. The types of rankings may vary. For example, the supervisor may have to choose a number from 1 to 7 that he or she believes best represents the employee's progress, with the highest number representing the highest achievement. Another approach, the management by objectives (MBO) method, involves a supervisor judging an employee on the basis of whether previously defined objectives have been met. The 360-degree approach requires gathering performance feedback from co-workers, customers, direct reports, and managers. The Behaviorally Anchored Rating Scales (BARS) method compares employee performance against specific job-related behaviors. Assessment centers use multiple evaluation tools to evaluate employees, while the critical incident method requires managers to document specific examples of exceptional performance and examples of less-than-stellar performance.

CHALLENGES

Performance appraisals are supposed to be based on fair-minded criteria, but they are subjective, and biases and stereotyping can creep in. A manager may be too lenient with one worker and too strict with another. If an employee's view of his or her performance is more positive than the supervisor's evaluation, it can result in a perception of unfair treatment. Also, the evaluation process can be manipulated if the manager wishes to favor one employee or disparage another.

On the other hand, some of the unpleasantness of a poor performance appraisal can be avoided if managers handle problems, such as repeated lateness, as they occur rather than waiting several months to act on issues that need correction. Day-to-day communication and corrective measures can prevent crises from occurring during formal evaluations.

COMPENSATION, BENEFITS, AND TOTAL REWARDS

Compensation is the pay and rewards, such as money bonuses or stock awards, which employees get in exchange for their work. Compensation may be (1) direct or (2) indirect. The former includes salary, wages, commissions, and bonuses, whereas the latter are benefits such as paid vacations, holidays, and medical insurance. In order to attract, motivate, and retain effective employees, many firms offer total rewards packages that consist of compensation, health and dental insurance, performance bonuses, stock options, company-sponsored training, wellness programs, flexible schedules, employee discount programs, and many other perks and benefits.

Job Evaluation

Job evaluation is the formal and systematic comparison of a firm's positions. The comparison is designed to determine the value of one job in relation to others. Basically, it attempts to compare the effort, responsibility, and skills required to perform each job. Compensation for each position is then based on this evaluation.

The process begins with the creation of a job analysis for each position. This information is then used to prepare a job description. HRM might then assign rankers to rank the jobs. The rankers must be consistent in the factors they use to make their rankings. Once they have sorted the job descriptions, using the standard of ranking the most difficult job as the highest, the next step may be to assign each rank to a particular pay grade. A pay grade is made up of all jobs that fall within a certain range.

Rankers work independently of one another, but then meet to adjust and average the ratings. When the wages are plotted on a graph, they should reveal a wage curve that can show the relative value of and the average wage for each job.

Of course, most companies do not pay just one rate for all jobs in a particular pay grade. Instead, there may be a number of levels, or steps, within each pay grade. Finally, an employer must account for individual circumstances (such as years of service) before establishing a pay rate for each worker.

Wage and Salary Administration

Clearly, the task of administering wages is complex. The compensation manager in the Human Resources department is responsible for recommending financial compensation by establishing pay rates for various grades. In determining direct financial compensation, the manager must take into account the following factors:

- The company's policies on salaries
- The ability of the company to pay

- Employee job performance
- Employee skills and competencies
- Employee experience
- Employee potential
- Labor union contracts
- Legislation
- Economy
- Cost of living
- Job evaluations

In addition to evaluating these criteria in-house, an administrator has the option of accessing various Internet sites that report on what other firms are paying for comparable jobs. These sites also report on benefits. Besides private, commercial firms, businesses can consult the U.S. Department of Labor's Bureau of Labor Statistics online database of compensation for various industries.

Compensation Systems

The systems that govern decisions on compensation vary from company to company. These compensation policies provide managers with general guidelines for making decisions about compensation. Based on these decisions, a company might fall into one of three categories:

1. *Pay Leaders:* Those firms that pay higher compensation than their competitors. Higher-paying companies then logically expect to attract the most highly qualified workers.

2. *Market Rate:* Also called the going rate. This is the rate perceived to be the average for similar jobs in the industry.

3. *Pay Followers:* Companies that pay less than their competitors. The decision to pay less may be based on the firm's financial condition. It could also reflect the fact that the firm does not believe it requires highly qualified workers.

While these compensation policies indicate a desire to ensure consistency, other factors can alter a policy. For example, there may be pressure to retain high performers through the inducement of a higher salary and/or generous benefits. Other factors that affect such decisions include the following:

- The labor market of potential employees
- Labor unions and their contracts with employers
- The current economy
- Legislation regulating some salaries

The distinction between (1) exempt and (2) non-exempt workers is an example of legislation that affects compensation. By law, companies are expected to adhere to a government policy of classifying workers as either exempt or non-exempt. Exempt workers are those salaried employees categorized as executive, administrative, professional, or outside salespeople. Non-exempt employees, on the other hand, receive an hourly wage and are covered by laws regulating minimum wage, overtime, and other rights and protections.

Many companies offer incentive plans that, under certain circumstances, give employees additional compensation beyond their salaries or hourly pay. Salespeople, for example, may receive a fixed salary plus commissions for sales that meet or surpass a set quota. Such sales commissions are an example of performance related pay.

Other programs recognize worker achievements by awards that may or may not be monetary in nature. These can include employee stock ownership plans (ESOP), gift certificates, and merchandise, as well as profit-sharing plans and cash rewards. Some publicly traded firms offer executive compensation in the form of bonuses and stock options to CEOs, CFOs, managing directors, and other upper-level managers for their efforts on behalf of the organization.

Benefits: Mandatory and Voluntary

The compensation manager is also expected to administer indirect financial compensation, or benefits. Some benefits are mandatory while individual firms initiate others. Examples of mandatory, or legally required, benefits include the following:

- *Social Security:* The original Social Security Act of 1935 was created to provide benefits for retired workers. Amendments to the Act have since added other kinds of protection for workers.
  - *Disability insurance* provides for workers who are completely disabled.
  - *Survivors' benefits* help a worker's survivors—the widow or widower and unmarried children—if the employee dies. *Medicare* offers hospital and medical insurance for workers over 65.

Although the retirement age to be eligible for Social Security benefits has gradually risen over the years, eligibility for Medicare benefits remains age 65 for most people. Employees and employers contribute to the Social Security fund.

- *Unemployment Compensation:* If workers lose their jobs through no fault of their own, they become eligible for unemployment compensation, a joint federal-state program. This insurance program provides temporary benefits payments for a certain number of weeks, typically up to 26 weeks or until the worker finds another job, whichever comes first. It is funded by a payroll tax paid by employers. In times of severe economic downturn, Congress may extend the compensation period as it did during the recession that began in 2007. While the federal government provides guidelines for the program, it is administered by the states. This means that the benefits, including the time period, can vary from one state to another.
- *Workers' Compensation:* If a worker incurs expenses due to a job-related accident or illness, he or she can be reimbursed through this program. Workers' comp, as it is commonly called, also provides some income replacement. Employers purchase the insurance independently through private insurance companies, but the program is subject to federal regulation and is administered by the states.

Discretionary benefits are a form of indirect financial compensation, and individual employers can decide which to offer. The same factors that determine the level of direct compensation—salaries, wages, commissions, and bonuses—influence the types and amount of discretionary benefits employees receive. Some of the most common discretionary benefits include the following:

- Paid vacations
- Sick pay
- Medical benefits
- Life insurance
- Retirement plans
- Stock option plans
- Child care
- Scholarships for dependents

Retirement plans may be one of two types: defined benefits and defined contribution. A defined benefits plan gives retirees a specific amount of income upon retirement. It may be a lump sum or a monthly pension amount and is funded by employers. Under a defined contribution plan, employees don't receive a specific amount of money to fund their retirement. They contribute a portion of their salary toward retirement and employers may or may not also contribute. A 401(k) plan is an example of a defined contribution plan.

Another type of indirect compensation is the voluntary benefit. Voluntary benefits are those offered to employees by a company, but for which employees have to pay because the company feels it cannot afford to do so. However, the company usually pays the administrative costs, and employees benefit because they pay a group rate. These include the following:

- Term life insurance
- Vision insurance
- Long-term care insurance
- Dental insurance
- College savings plans

SAFETY AND HEALTH

Workers' safety and health are important to companies because lost time on the job cuts into productivity, raises health-care costs, and could lead to lawsuits, depending on the nature and cause of the injuries. Safety refers to protecting employees from physical injury on the job, and health is the physical and mental well-being of employees.

OCCUPATIONAL ACCIDENTS AND ILLNESS

The Occupational Safety and Health Act of 1970 was passed specifically to ensure worker safety and health in the United States. It established the Occupational Safety and Health Administration (OSHA) that works with employers to create good working environments. The agency's rules and regulations have helped eliminate many workplace-related fatalities, injuries, and illnesses and reduced the cost to companies of such injuries and illnesses.

If an employee feels endangered by conditions in the workplace, he or she may complain to OSHA, thus possibly initiating an OSHA inspection. The Act protects any employee who requests an inspection, refuses unsafe work, or complains about a dangerous workplace. If the OSHA inspector finds unsafe conditions, this can result in financial penalties for the company. Follow-up inspections check to make sure that the recommendations for improvement have been followed. If conditions have not improved, this results in further penalties.

While it is probably impossible to eliminate every cause of injury or illness on the job, companies can focus on the following areas to reduce hazards and the organization's liability:

- *Unsafe Worker Behavior:* Safety promotion campaigns can improve worker attitudes. It is a fact that workers suffer more injuries when they are new to a job, so placing an emphasis on safety during the first few months of employment can have a significant effect.

- *Unsafe Working Conditions:* A company may find that it must alter working conditions to meet OSHA standards. Though worker safety is the company's responsibility, employees should be encouraged to suggest their own solutions to unsafe conditions. Management must inform all workers of any hazards and take steps to correct them.

- *Job Hazard Analysis (JHA):* JHA requires the assessment of work activities and the workplace to establish whether adequate precautions have been taken to prevent injuries. It involves the systematic identification of potential hazards in the workplace as a step to controlling the possible risks involved. OSHA provides online forms and checklists that employers can download and use to evaluate workplace conditions. Some hazards are obvious, like slippery floors in an area that has a great amount of foot traffic. Others are less so, requiring the kind of expertise a safety engineer can offer. Categories that are analyzed for hazards on such forms are fire prevention, work environment, working/walking surfaces, ergonomics, emergency information (postings), emergency exits, electrical systems, and material storage. The following are examples of OSHA questions relating to fire prevention. Respondents are asked to choose from three possible answers: Yes, No, and N/A (not applicable).

    o Are employees trained on the use of portable fire extinguishers?

    o Is heat-producing equipment used in a well-ventilated area?

    o Are fire alarm pull stations clearly marked and unobstructed?

- *Ergonomics:* Studying people's efficiency in their working environment and then designing the workplace so that employees can function without pain is called ergonomics (from the Greek word *ergon*, "work"). It requires fitting the machine or movements to the worker rather than asking the worker to make the adjustment to such stressful motions as twisting one's whole body. In this way, employers have been able to reduce repetitive motion disorders like carpal tunnel syndrome, bursitis, and tendonitis.

- *Accident Investigation:* It is important that firms investigate any accident; determine the cause; and take steps to prevent other, similar accidents. At the same time, collecting accurate data about accidents over a set period can be valuable, especially if this shows either an increase or a decrease in the frequency and severity of accidents.

QUALITY OF WORK LIFE AND WELLNESS

Quality of work life can be defined as the extent to which employees can enhance their personal lives through their work environment and experiences. Healthy employees equate to less absenteeism, lower health-care costs, and increased productivity, so many organizations offer employee wellness programs that include vaccination clinics, nutrition education, exercise programs, health screenings, and substance abuse programs.

Additional policies and opportunities enhance the quality of work life:

- *Flextime:* Schedule flexibility
- *Compressed Work Week:* Allowing employees to work the same number of hours, but in fewer days
- *Telecommuting:* Working from home
- *Job Sharing:* Two part-time workers splitting one job
- *Part-Time Work:* Giving employees time to take care of personal needs
- A family-friendly workplace with child care
- A generous benefits program

WORKPLACE SECURITY

A feeling of safety in the workplace has come to mean more than just job security. Unfortunately, there have been many cases of workplace violence. Some of the incidents have been carried out by angry workers against fellow employees. The perpetrators are often people who believe that they have not been treated well by management or who have been victims of bullying by the coworkers they are targeting.

Sometimes, violence is carried out by an outsider. Often, the outsider is not targeting the company, but aims to harm someone with whom he has had a personal relationship, such as an estranged wife or girlfriend. Women are the usual victims in these types of attacks. Even dissatisfied customers have been known to react violently to circumstances and attack employees of a company they have a grudge against. Robbery is also a problem for some companies, especially retail establishments.

HRM does have some options for reducing workplace violence, which include the following:

- Keep a minimal amount of cash on hand in retail businesses
- Install a silent alarm system to alert security
- Install surveillance cameras
- Train workers in conflict resolution
- Screen employees for a history of violent behavior, including sexual harassment
- Question unexplained gaps in an applicant's employment
- Check for criminal records involving violence
- Prohibit firearms or other weapons in the facility

Training supervisors to recognize employees who display a tendency to react aggressively to situations, threaten others, or demonstrate antisocial behavior may also prevent a worker from acting violently.

EMPLOYEE RIGHTS AND DISCIPLINE

Most employees are hired and hold their jobs at their employer's discretion. This is known as employment at will, meaning that neither party acknowledges a time limit on that connection. Therefore, either party can terminate the relationship, with due notice. There are, however, some limits on terminating an employee, for example, where legislation or union rules govern such actions. A wrongful termination suit brought by a terminated employee would have to be based on promises or guarantees made by the company, but not adhered to. Then it is up to the claimant to prove that such assurances were made.

Disciplinary Procedures

Prior to termination, there are procedures for dealing with infractions, and it may fall to the HR manager to administer discipline to workers who do not come up to company standards or have failed to follow company rules. The disciplinary action usually occurs only after all other strategies to improve the workers' performance have failed.

Disciplinary actions may take different approaches. It is a given, though, that the action cannot be personal; that is, it should not show either bias or favoritism. Also, the disciplinary action should be taken immediately. It should not be delayed, for example, until the employee's next review, which might be weeks or months away.

Though company rules should be administered consistently, it is realistic to assume that the HR manager might act differently depending on circumstances. For example, if dealing with a first infraction by a new employee, the HR manager might be more lenient in his or her approach. Likewise, if a long-time employee's record has been exemplary until this infraction, the manager might correct the employee's behavior without administering a penalty. Flexibility then becomes a matter of judgment.

Ideally, the manager would apply the minimum penalty to any first offender. The manager would also have to balance the need to avoid damaging employee morale with making sure that all employees understand the need to follow company rules.

The sequence of disciplinary steps begins with an oral warning, followed, if necessary, by a written warning. Beyond that, the HR manager would have to consider whether the situation warrants suspension or termination. Another alternative is demotion, usually with a reduction in pay. In a union situation, this must be handled according to the firm's agreement with the union.

Whatever the resolution, the HR manager should handle any disciplinary action with consideration for the employee's likely emotional reaction as well as that of his or her colleagues. In all cases, the manager's interaction with the employee should be private and never carried out in front of others.

Termination

Termination requires sensitivity and honesty, with the manager explaining what actions warranted the termination. Where there is a union agreement, the manager must follow the rules governing termination with cause. Before it comes to this end, though, it is important that the manager keep in mind that it may be more expensive to hire a replacement than to retain an experienced worker who might only need a period of readjustment.

EMPLOYMENT LAW

Most employees are hired and hold their jobs at their employer's discretion, which is known as employment-at-will, meaning that neither party acknowledges a time limit on the employer–employee relationship. Therefore, either party can terminate the relationship, with due notice. There are, however, some limits on terminating an employee, for example, where legislation or union rules govern such actions. A wrongful termination suit brought by a terminated employee would have to be based on promises or guarantees made by the company, but not adhered to. Then it is up to the claimant to prove that such assurances were made. As the following table shows, there are a number of laws that govern employee management. There are four categories of employment laws: equal employment; compensation and benefits; health, safety, and employee rights; and union laws. An HR manager needs to be familiar with all of them in order to see that they are administered properly.

EMPLOYMENT LAWS

Equal Employment Laws	
Civil Rights Act Title VII	Makes it unlawful for an employer to discriminate against any individual because of race, color, religion, sex, or national origin
Americans with Disabilities Act (ADA)	Prohibits discrimination against workers with disabilities employed by certain federal contractors and subcontractors
Age Discrimination in Employment Act (ADEA)	Prohibits discrimination against workers within certain age ranges, the ranges changing as the law is amended
Compensation and Benefits	
Employment Retirement Income Security Act (ERISA)	Sets minimum standards for pension programs in private industry to protect employees' contributions
Family and Medical Leave Act (FMLA)	Provides certain employees with up to 12 weeks of unpaid leave under certain circumstances related to family needs
Fair Labor Standards Act (FLSA)	Sets provisions for minimum wage, maximum hours, conditions for overtime pay, equal pay, recordkeeping, and child labor; distinguishes between exempt and non-exempt employees

Health, Safety, and Employee Rights	
Occupational Safety and Health Act of 1970	Requires employers to provide a safe and healthy working environment
Worker Adjustment and Retraining Notification Act (WARN)	Requires 60 days advance notice of a plant closing or mass layoff
Union Laws	
National Labor Relations Act (NLRA)	Supports the right of labor to organize and engage in collective bargaining
Taft-Hartley Act	Prohibits unfair union labor practices, enumerates the rights of employees and employers, allows the U.S. president to bar national emergency strikes
Civil Service Reform Act	Regulates most labor management relations in the federal service

LABOR RELATIONS

A union is an organization of workers who find strength in coming together to deal with their employer. Generally, unions organize because of dissatisfaction with management policies. They strive to improve (1) wages, (2) hours, (3) working conditions, and (4) benefits for their members.

ROLE OF LABOR UNIONS

Although unions, or at least associations of workers, have been in the United States since the eighteenth century, it was not until the 1930s that unions in the United States began to grow in members and in significance. Until then, lawmakers and court decisions had favored management. But then, during the Great Depression, millions of workers were unemployed, and those who had jobs, especially factory jobs, worked long hours for little pay in unsafe and unhealthful working conditions.

The 1930s saw the passage of several laws that strengthened the rights of workers to organize and of unions to negotiate for their members. Probably the most important of these laws was the National Labor Relations Act of 1935 (also known as the Wagner Act, after Robert F. Wagner, then a U.S. Senator from New York, who sponsored the bill). The NLRA protected the rights of workers to organize and to bargain collectively.

After the passage of the Wagner Act, union membership showed a large increase. However, public attitudes shifted after a number of costly strikes following World War II. Although then-president Harry Truman vetoed the law, Congress overrode his veto to pass the Labor Management Relations Act, also known as the Taft-Hartley Act. The intention of the law was to allow for a more even-handed approach toward labor and management. It placed restrictions on both sides, but probably the most significant one was Section 14b, which allows states to pass right-to-work laws that restrict closed shops. In a closed shop, membership in a union is a condition for being hired and for continued employment.

COLLECTIVE BARGAINING

Beginning with the Wagner Act, both management and labor have been required, by law, to engage in collective bargaining. That is, they must sit down together to negotiate wages, hours, and terms and conditions of employment in good faith. While neither side is forced to accept any demands offered by the people on the other side of the table, it is expected that both sides will negotiate honorably, that is, with sincerity of intention; in other words, "in good faith." Representing the union is the shop steward, a person elected by workers to represent them in these and other dealings with management.

Once the two sides have reached an agreement, the union membership must ratify the agreement. Once management and the union have approved of the deal, it becomes part of the contract between them for the period called for in the contract, usually about three years. A contract generally covers such issues as (1) wages and (2) overtime and such special situations as (3) hazard pay, (4) layoff or severance pay, (5) holidays, (6) vacations, and (7) family care provisions. (8) Grievance procedures, (9) work breaks, (10) strikes, and (11) lockouts as well as (12) management rights are also covered. Items that may not be negotiated are discriminatory treatment of employees, separation of races in the workplace, and a closed shop. The latter requires that a worker join a union in order to be hired. All three are illegal.

UNIONIZED VERSUS NONUNIONIZED WORK SETTINGS

Management in nonunionized work situations probably look at their circumstances as easier than those in a company with a strong union. In a sense, that is the difference between an environment that allows collective bargaining and one that does not have that option. In the first case, bargaining is done by the shop steward on one side and management on the other. Because the shop steward is representing the interests of a whole class of people, the bargaining can be tough. On the other hand, where there is no union, the bargaining must be done on a person-by-person basis.

CONTRACT MANAGEMENT

Most collective bargaining agreements, or CBAs, include grievance procedures to clarify the process for handling contract violations. While contracts and procedures vary, HR departments are typically involved in addressing grievances because of their knowledge about the specific contract and relevant laws. The first step in the grievance process usually involves a discussion between the manager, employee, HR representative, and union representative and results in a written decision from management. In some cases, grievances are escalated to the national union, and arbitrators are brought in to facilitate a mutual agreement.

CURRENT ISSUES AND TRENDS

There are three major trends in HRM today that bear watching: (1) workforce diversity, (2) human resource information systems, and (3) changing patterns of work relationships.

WORKFORCE DIVERSITY

The meaning of the term *diversity in the workforce* has expanded over the years. Originally, its meaning was fairly narrow and mainly concerned with (1) race and (2) gender. Today, it encompasses many perceived differences, such as (3) age, (4) religion, (5) disabilities, (6) country of origin, (7) marital status, (8) family responsibilities, and (9) sexual orientation. The overriding aim is for a diversified workforce that reflects the general population.

Being inclusive requires that employers be open-minded and supportive, so that all employees feel welcome and valued. A cohesive workforce is one in which employees work well together. Prospective employees are drawn to a company with that kind of reputation, and customers benefit from the harmonious environment. As a result, the bottom line benefits.

HUMAN RESOURCE INFORMATION SYSTEMS

Increasingly sophisticated technology is allowing companies to implement highly useful human resource information systems (HRIS). An HRIS allows HR to collect and store, in one place, the vast amount of data it needs to research and track information about such things as recruitment and hiring, compliance with legislation and regulations, and the administration of the benefits program. It can identify the costs associated with various activities and present graphs to show inventory levels and disclose profit levels over a set period of time. It allows the production department to fill orders and accounting to bill the right customers in a timely manner. Employees may also have access to information about programs that they can enroll in, insurance coverage, benefits, and retirement plans.

CHANGING PATTERNS OF WORK RELATIONSHIPS

Changes in the workplace are a reflection of the varied lifestyles of the workforce. At one time, employers hired new workers, assigned them a workstation, and expected them to present themselves there at the usual starting time. Of course, such situations still occur, but many organizations are recognizing that younger workers desire a work–life balance and job flexibility. Technology has allowed for greater flexibility in work arrangements but also raises issues related to virtual offices, contingent workers, unconventional work arrangements, outsourcing, employee leasing, and training methods like e-learning and m-learning.

For example, with the virtual office, workers may not even have to appear in person, only electronically. A virtual office may be an actual place, but most importantly, it is equipped with telecommunication links that enable workers to connect. However, the office doesn't have to be a fixed place anymore. The computer itself can become the office, and its operator can function just about anywhere.

Contingent workers also have a nontraditional connection with a firm. The "contingency" is that they are subject to chance, that is, to the needs of the employer at a particular time. They may work as part-timers, temporary employees, or independent contractors. Their temporary availability allows the company flexibility and lower expenses than an on-site employee. There are none of the extra costs, such as vacation time or company contributions to medical insurance. The drawback for the employees, though, is that they are readily disposable. Still, companies that utilize contingent workers are going beyond the kind of workers needed only for unskilled jobs. The contingent workers can also be engineers, technicians, and specialists in various fields, including the law.

There are also other unconventional work arrangements. One is the autonomous work group. Under this arrangement, workers are part of a team that decides for itself how the work should be distributed among members of the team.

Outsourcing and employee leasing are other recent options in the business world. Outsourcing involves hiring workers outside the company to do work that was previously done in-house. Employee leasing is perhaps one of the more far-reaching alternatives to standard hiring practice. A company releases its employees, who are then hired by a professional employer organization (PEO). The PEO pays the workers and the expenses normally associated with permanent employees: workers compensation, payroll taxes, and employee benefits

Employees and employers also appreciate flexible training options, which can be cost effective for the organization and convenient for the employees. For example, training in the format of electronic learning (e-learning) allows employees to access online training and development programs. Mobile learning, known as m-learning, enables employees to access training programs via mobile devices like smartphones and laptops.

GLOBAL HR ENVIRONMENT

While conducting business in a global environment has become commonplace, it remains complex and challenging. An international HRM office becomes very important to an organization because it is vital that a company's staff be trained to handle the unique challenges of working globally. Among the factors that HRM on the global level must deal with are cultural, legal, and economic differences, as well as political risks.

Companies doing business in the global market may transfer personnel from their domestic offices to work in their satellite firms abroad. These workers are often called expatriates. In addition, U.S. companies often hire nationals from their host countries or even third-country nationals. For this mixed group of people to work well together, there must be a common language, such as English. For the U.S. workers, having a second language is a plus. In some cases, though, a translator may be necessary. Workers who remain in this country, but interact with global offices, may need training to work effectively in an international environment. Employees selected for overseas assignments receive orientation and training before departure and online training, development, and support while abroad. Coordination among offices in multiple countries frequently depends on e-mail, instant messaging, and virtual meetings and differences in time zones are a consideration as well.

Of primary importance is the fact that management cannot assume that U.S. ways of doing business are universal. Having different cultural and business backgrounds will affect the interactions between the U.S. corporation and personnel from the host country, further reflecting the importance of training in cultural sensitivity. Managers and expatriates also need to be aware that not only are there likely to be cultural differences, but also political, legal, and economic ones. Consideration must also be given to helping the families of expatriates adjust to their new environment such as by finding jobs for spouses and schools for children.

SOCIAL MEDIA

Another important trend that is crucial for HR managers to consider is the use of social media. Although many managers report anecdotally reviewing job applicants' social media sources prior to hiring, all aspects of the employee hiring process must be documented and validated. In other words, if a manager is reviewing a potential applicant's Facebook account, there must be documented evidence that the evaluation of the Facebook account is reliable (consistently measured) and valid (job related). This is an important ethical issue that HR managers must consider to avoid potential problems related to intentional (disparate treatment) or unintentional (disparate impact) discrimination.

CORPORATE SOCIAL RESPONSIBILITY AND SUSTAINABILITY

An increasing number of organizations are focusing on corporate social responsibility (CSR) and sustainability, and HR can play a key role in the implementation of such efforts, which need employee participation to be successful. Encouraging employees to participate in company-sponsored volunteer activities, creating recognition programs to celebrate employee efforts, encouraging green practices, and incorporating CSR into recruitment programs are just a few ways that HR managers can support CSR and sustainability.

SUMMING IT UP

- The field of **human resource management** (HRM) traces its roots back to the Industrial Revolution and a form of personnel management known as industrial welfare. Forerunners of contemporary HRM include the work of Frederick Taylor, industrial psychology, and personnel departments.

- Human resource functions include (1) **staffing** and (2) **training and development.** Newer responsibilities include (3) **performance appraisals**, (4) **compensation**, (5) **safety and health issues**, (6) **employee rights** and **discipline**, and (7) **forecasting staffing**.

- HRM works with line managers, employees, and senior management.

- Effective HR managers are **organized**, possess strong **negotiation skills**, and **communicate clearly**.

- HR departments may be used as a strategic partner with upper management to set goals and execute an organization's strategic plan. HRM assists by predicting future staffing needs through the use of (1) **trend analysis**, (2) **ratio analysis**, or (3) **scatter plots**, as well as (4) **forecasting** the training needs that will be required.

- **Diversity management** involves recognizing and proactively managing the unique needs of today's workforce and establishing an inclusive work environment often through HR policies and strategies.

- **Job analysis** and **job design** are part of the process of determining (1) specific tasks to be performed, (2) the methods to be used in performing those tasks, and (3) how the job relates to other work in the organization.

- **Staffing** involves (1) recruiting, (2) selection, (3) promotions and transfers, (4) reduction-in-force, (5) layoffs, and (6) voluntary turnover. **Candidates** may come from (1) internal or (2) external sources. Selection of staff can be **influenced** by (1) company rules and (2) legal considerations. Voluntary turnovers may occur because of (1) resignations and (2) retirements.

- **Onboarding** is the process of integrating new employees into an organization and its culture and giving them the tools and information to be successful, productive, and engaged.

- **Principles of learning** that need to be recognized in the workplace include (1) the need to motivate employees, (2) recognition of individual differences in learning, (3) the ability of employees to transfer learning, and (4) the need to provide meaningful materials.

- **Training methods** today can take a variety of forms, including (1) instructor-led sessions, (2) online training, (3) virtual classrooms, and (4) case studies. One-on-one coaching may also be appropriate.

- **Development programs** center on the skills and knowledge that go beyond the trainee's present job to deal with career planning.

- Pay, promotion, and retention are based on **performance appraisals**, which are formal evaluations of an employee as opposed to the ongoing assessment of performance that managers should be conducting.

- **Job evaluation** is the formal and systematic comparison of a firm's positions. It attempts to compare the effort, responsibility, and skills required to perform each job; compensation for each position is based on job evaluation.

- An organization's **compensation policies** classify it as a (1) pay leader, (2) market rate, or (3) pay follower.

- Employees are either (1) **exempt** or (2) **non-exempt**. The latter is governed by legislation regulating minimum wage, overtime, and other rights and worker protections.

- **Mandatory benefits** include (1) Social Security, (2) unemployment compensation, and (3) workers' compensation. Common discretionary benefits include (1) paid vacations, (2) sick pay, (3) medical benefits, (4) life insurance, (5) retirement plans, (6) stock option plans, (7) child care, and (8) scholarships for dependents. There are also voluntary benefits, such as vision and dental insurance.

- **The Occupational Safety and Health Administration** (OSHA) is charged with creating safe work environments in U.S. worksites. Areas that companies should focus on to create safe and healthy working conditions are (1) unsafe worker behavior, (2) unsafe working conditions, (3) Job Hazard Analysis to assess worksites, (4) ergonomics, and (5) accident investigation.

- **Quality of work life** is the extent to which employees can enhance their personal lives through their work environment and experiences.

- **Employment law** is divided into four categories: (1) equal employment, (2) compensation and benefits, (3) health, safety, and employee rights, and (4) unions.

- **Labor unions** strive to improve (1) wages, (2) hours, (3) working conditions, and (4) benefits for their members. A union contract generally covers such issues as (1) wages and (2) overtime and such special situations as (3) hazard pay, (4) layoff or severance pay, (5) holidays, (6) vacations, and (7) family care provisions.

- HRM assists **multinational organizations** to recruit, select, assist, and train employees for working abroad. Among the factors that HRM on the global level must deal with are (1) **culture**, (2) **different legal systems**, (3) **political risks**, and (4) **different economic systems**.

- Current HRM **issues** and **trends** to monitor include human resource information systems, changing patterns of work relationships, the global HR environment, social media, and corporate social responsibility and sustainability.

HUMAN RESOURCE MANAGEMENT POST-TEST

Directions: Carefully read each of the following 60 questions. Choose the best answer to each question and fill in the corresponding circle on the answer sheet. The Answer Key and Explanations can be found following this post-test.

1. Which of the following is part of the staffing function of HRM?
   A. Reporting workplace accidents
   B. Developing workplace security policies
   C. Motivating employees with career goals
   D. Negotiating compensation with job candidates

2. What must happen before workers have a performance evaluation?
   A. They must be told what their deficiencies are.
   B. They must be told what the performance criteria are.
   C. They must do a self-analysis and share it with the supervisor.
   D. They must be informed of any raise they will receive.

3. Which of the following describes m-learning?
   A. Using a personal computer to access online training portals
   B. Using a smartphone or tablet to access online training portals
   C. Using a company computer to access corporate training modules
   D. Using in-person orientation sessions to access training modules

4. Accidents due to unsafe worker behavior often occur
   A. after an OSHA inspection.
   B. right after a job hazard analysis.
   C. during a worker's first few months of employment.
   D. in a series of accidents.

5. Human resources are a company's
   A. customers.
   B. employees.
   C. supervisors.
   D. management.

6. A good performance review will depend mainly on whether the worker has
   A. met all the objectives expected of him or her.
   B. ever been promoted before.
   C. been with the firm for twenty or more years.
   D. a friendly relationship with his or her supervisor.

7. What is the function of a job analysis?
   A. To determine what skills are needed for certain jobs
   B. To make employees aware of why they are being terminated
   C. To develop pay ranges
   D. To create and maintain up-to-date files on each employee

8. What is the first step in a job evaluation?
   A. Job analysis
   B. Job ranking
   C. Pay grade
   D. Job description

9. Orientation generally includes
   A. a test about the company's expectations about new employees' performance.
   B. a chance for new employees to explain what they expect from their employment in the company.
   C. six months for new employees to prove their value to the firm.
   D. information about the firm's history.

10. What is Frederick Taylor known for?
    A. As an industrial psychologist
    B. As the founder of scientific management
    C. As head of the first craft union
    D. As the originator of personnel departments

11. Alternatives to having a supervisor evaluate an employee include all of the following EXCEPT
    A. peer reviews.
    B. written tests.
    C. evaluation by subordinates.
    D. appraisal by team members.

12. Which of the following would require that a job design be altered?
    A. Procedures and requirements for the job change.
    B. New employees replace more experienced ones.
    C. Hiring exceeds demand for products or services.
    D. Weaknesses in the workforce reveal themselves.

13. How can managers avoid accusations of bias in the evaluation process?
    A. By submitting their critiques in writing to their subordinates
    B. By ignoring minor deficiencies and concentrating on major problems
    C. By acting on problems in all workers' performance as they arise
    D. By having HR sit in all performance appraisals

14. Which of the following describes employment at will?
    A. An employee may not terminate employment unless the company agrees.
    B. An employee may or may not choose to sign a contract of employment.
    C. An employer may terminate an employee for any reason or for no reason.
    D. An employer may revoke an employee's contract.

15. Workplace diversity refers to which of the following?
    A. Employing workers from a range of ages and ethnicities
    B. Seeking highly skilled and knowledgeable employees
    C. Operating both domestically and internationally
    D. Providing multicultural training to employees

16. Which of the following describes the planning function of HRM?
    A. Researching wage trends
    B. Interviewing job candidates
    C. Providing e-learning opportunities
    D. Recruiting through social media

17. Which of the following statements is NOT true?
    A. A pay grade is made up of all jobs that fall within a certain range.
    B. The purpose of a pay curve is to help managers develop a progression between pay grades.
    C. Most companies pay one rate for all jobs in a pay grade.
    D. A wage curve shows the relative value of all jobs.

18. A reduction in workforce may occur because of
    A. a merger with or buyout by another company.
    B. attrition.
    C. errors in predicting job needs.
    D. inadequate training programs to match employees with required skills sets.

19. Generally, unions organize an industry because of dissatisfaction with
    A. the job market.
    B. the economy.
    C. management policies.
    D. globalization

20. Which of the following laws is applicable when an employer is planning a mass layoff?
    A. NLRA
    B. ADA
    C. FLSA
    D. WARN

21. The Americans with Disabilities Act applies to discrimination against
    A. workers employed by certain federal contractors.
    B. certain age ranges, the ranges changing over time.
    C. retired workers whose funds have been mismanaged.
    D. workers reporting hazards to OSHA.

22. Which of the following objectives would be most helpful in evaluating an employee's performance?
    A. Work efficiently.
    B. Produce the project on time and on budget.
    C. Create a new ad campaign by September 15, 2012.
    D. Develop ten informational fact sheets on Bike X by June 15, 2012.

23. The HR department is able to create a job description by means of
    A. questionnaires.
    B. observation.
    C. interviews of employees in the job.
    D. a combination of questionnaires, observation, and interviews of employees in the job.

24. What is the primary purpose of a job hazard analysis?
    A. To teach workers about ergonomics
    B. To identify work activities that are dangerous
    C. To encourage workers to apply for disability insurance
    D. To monitor workers in their first few months on the job

25. In establishing pay rates, the compensation manager must take into account all of the following factors EXCEPT
    A. the company's policies on salaries.
    B. the company's ability to pay.
    C. movement in the stock market in the short term.
    D. what the company president will receive at retirement.

post-test

26. Which of the following describes a defined benefit plan?
    A. The amount that the retiree receives is fixed at a certain amount for life.
    B. The amount that the retiree receives depends on how much the company invests for the employee and how well the investment does.
    C. A defined benefit plan is another name for a 401(k) plan.
    D. It is a trust that holds company stock and divides the stock among employees based on their earnings.

27. Which of the following statements is NOT true about phased retirement?
    A. Workers have to retire by age 70.
    B. Workers can adjust gradually to a new lifestyle while still working.
    C. Workers can reduce their hours, but keep their benefits while they continue working.
    D. Employers have a ready-made resource for mentoring younger workers by using phased retirement of experienced workers.

28. OSHA provides industry-specific health and safety standards for which type of business?
    A. Publishing
    B. Construction
    C Auto sales
    D. Agriculture

29. The right of labor to organize and engage in collective bargaining is covered by which of the following laws?
    A. Employee Retirement Income Security Act
    B. National Labor Relations Act
    C. Age Discrimination in Employment Act
    D. Taft-Hartley Act

30. Human Resource Information Systems allow for the
    A. control of Internet communications.
    B. setting up of virtual offices.
    C. collection and storage of vast amounts of data.
    D. monitoring of flexplace and flextime work arrangements.

31. Which of the following describes trend analysis for forecasting staffing needs?
    A. HRM develops a forecast based on the ratio between factors.
    B. HRM considers a variety of factors, both current and in the past.
    C. HRM creates a visual representation of variables, such as the number of departments in an organization and the number of employees in each department.
    D. HRM looks at staffing needs in an organization's departments over a period of time.

32. In collective bargaining, it is important that
    A. union members be allowed to sign authorization cards that the union may act for it.
    B. grievances be settled first.
    C. both sides be willing to make concessions.
    D. unions not "salt" the workplace.

33. According to the ADEA, an employer is prohibited from discriminating against which of the following?
    A. Employees who have a disability
    B. Employees who take maternity leave
    C. Employees who are aged 40 or older
    D. Employees who belong to a union

34. Which of the following describes an autonomous work group?
    A. Team of workers deciding for themselves how to handle work assignments
    B. Third-party contracted work team
    C. An outsourcing group
    D. A professional employer organization

35. Which law has been most effective in limiting discrimination in the workplace?
    A. Fair Labor Standards Act
    B. Civil Service Reform Act
    C. National Labor Relations Act
    D. Civil Rights Act Title VII

36. Outplacement is a company's way of trying to
    A. reduce the size of its staff through voluntary turnover.
    B. help terminated workers strengthen their job-search skills.
    C. learn how workers feel about how the firm treated them.
    D. gauge how much turnover there has been.

37. Which of the following is a provision of the Taft-Hartley Act?
    A. Employees could refuse to join a union.
    B. Unions no longer had to give employers notice of an impending strike.
    C. The U.S. president was no longer allowed to halt a strike on the basis of a national emergency.
    D. Employers may not publicize negative opinions about unions among their workers.

38. Which of the following could result in a wrongful termination suit?
    A. The company did not adhere to guarantees made to the employee when hiring.
    B. The company found unexplained gaps in an applicant's employment.
    C. The company does not train workers in conflict management.
    D. The company does not guarantee worker safety.

39. Surveys presented at the end of a training experience measure
    A. the need for additional training.
    B. immediate feedback on the program.
    C. changes in the participants' behaviors.
    D. changes in the results that the organization is experiencing because of the training.

40. What was the primary goal of Frederick Taylor's theory of management?
    A. Measuring product quality
    B. Improving labor productivity
    C. Reducing the workforce
    D. Evaluating employee performance

41. What does a right-to-work law do?
    A. Requires employers to hire only union members
    B. Removes the right to strike from unions
    C. Removes the requirement that workers in a union shop pay union dues whether they belong to the union or not
    D. Requires that the union steward negotiate wages for all workers

42. The four-fifths rule is used to determine which of the following?
    A. Wage rates
    B. Workplace diversity
    C. Adverse impact
    D. Performance rankings

43. Worker development is concerned mainly with
    A. fine-tuning employees' current skills sets.
    B. employee job satisfaction.
    C. employees' future career paths.
    D. improving employee weaknesses.

44. A company that is paying the market rate in salaries is
    A. paying no more than average.
    B. paying less than all its competitors.
    C. paying the highest compensation in the field.
    D. attracting the most highly qualified workers.

45. What is the purpose of exit interviews of workers who leave an organization voluntarily?
    A. To gain insight on why they are leaving
    B. To have them fill out termination paperwork
    C. To try to persuade them to stay by offering incentives
    D. To ask them to recommend replacements

46. Which of the following is NOT a category analyzed for hazards under OSHA regulations?
    A. Walking surfaces
    B. Emergency exits
    C. Coin-operated machines
    D. Electrical systems

47. Which of the following is a true statement about performance appraisals?
    A. The basis for evaluation at a PA is the set of goals the employee and supervisor set at the last PA.
    B. The supervisor prepares all paperwork for a PA.
    C. Supervisors are more likely to schedule PAs with employees who have problems in order to get them over with.
    D. Rating all employees in a department as average favors all the employees.

48. Which performance appraisal method focuses on the behaviors necessary for a specific position or job task at a firm?
    A. Assessment center method
    B. MBO
    C. Forced distribution method
    D. BARS

49. An organization would likely use a staffing firm for which of the following purposes?
    A. To fill high-level positions
    B. To hire temporary workers
    C. To manage payroll issues
    D. To recruit on college campuses

50. What development made the passage of ERISA necessary?
    A. Compensation and benefits programs became too expensive for most organizations.
    B. Health, safety, and employee rights were being abused by companies.
    C. Some retirement funds were mismanaged, and workers lost their retirement benefits.
    D. Union contracts did not cover members' retirement needs.

51. The principle of transfer of learning means that workers
    A. are motivated to continually learn new skills.
    B. learn by asking questions of mentors.
    C. can avoid being locked into one career path.
    D. must inform management of their online studies.

52. An agreement between a company and a labor union typically covers
    A. check card procedures.
    B. automatic payroll deduction of union dues.
    C. arbitration procedures.
    D. closed shop provisions.

53. Which of the following best describes disparate impact discrimination?
    A. A supervisor harasses a female employee because of her gender.
    B. African-American job applicants are tested for specific job skills at a higher rate than applicants of other racial groups.
    C. A supervisor harasses a Catholic employee because of his religion.
    D. Muslim job applicants are hired at a lower rate compared to other ethnic groups because of unintentional flaws in the selection process.

54. Which situation or condition would most likely attract an OSHA inspector's attention?
    A. No employees over the age of 40
    B. Lack of any retirement program
    C. Foreign-born workers who do not speak English
    D. The lack of well-marked emergency exits

55. The categories of exempt and non-exempt workers differ in that
    A. non-exempt employees are covered by laws regulating minimum wage.
    B. neither category is defined by legislation.
    C. exempt employees receive an hourly wage and non-exempt employees receive salaries.
    D. non-exempt employees include outside salespeople and this is not a category of exempt workers.

56. Which performance appraisal method relies on feedback from an employee's managers, co-workers, and direct reports?
    A. 360-degree appraisal
    B. Critical incidents method
    C. Grading method
    D. Paired comparison approach

57. Employee stock ownership plans are a form of
    A. monetary compensation.
    B. gift certificates.
    C. commissions.
    D. nonmonetary compensation.

58. Which statement about the FMLA is true?
    A. The FMLA applies to personal and family illnesses.
    B. The FMLA is limited to government employees.
    C. The FMLA provides six weeks of paid maternity leave.
    D. The FMLA applies to employers with at least 20 employees

59. E-learning for employees is popular because
    A. it is highly flexible.
    B. it is easy.
    C. it is not costly to prepare or purchase training materials.
    D. of its lack of assessments and tests.

60. Which of the following is true about worker's compensation?

  A. Worker's compensation pays benefits to workers who lose their jobs in a recession.

  B. It is similar to Social Security payments.

  C. It is a form of disability insurance.

  D. It reimburses a worker for expenses incurred in a job-related accident.

ANSWER KEY AND EXPLANATIONS

1. D	**13.** C	**25.** C	**37.** A	**49.** B
2. B	**14.** C	**26.** A	**38.** A	**50.** C
3. B	**15.** A	**27.** A	**39.** B	**51.** C
4. C	**16.** A	**28.** B	**40.** B	**52.** B
5. B	**17.** C	**29.** B	**41.** C	**53.** D
6. A	**18.** A	**30.** C	**42.** C	**54.** D
7. A	**19.** C	**31.** D	**43.** C	**55.** A
8. A	**20.** D	**32.** C	**44.** A	**56.** A
9. D	**21.** A	**33.** C	**45.** A	**57.** D
10. B	**22.** D	**34.** A	**46.** C	**58.** A
11. B	**23.** D	**35.** D	**47.** A	**59.** A
12. A	**24.** B	**36.** B	**48.** D	**60.** D

1. **The correct answer is D.** The staffing function relates to the hiring process and includes recruiting employees and negotiating compensation. Choices A and B relate to the function of protecting workers, not hiring them. While motivating employees is an important HRM task, doing so is not part of the staffing function, which makes choice C incorrect.

2. **The correct answer is B.** Choice A is incorrect because discussion of deficiencies happens during a performance appraisal, not before. Choice C is incorrect because self-analyses are not shared with supervisors. Choice D is incorrect because that happens during or after the evaluation, but not before.

3. **The correct answer is B.** Choices A and C are incorrect because m-learning occurs on mobile devices such as smartphones, tablets, or laptops. Choice D is incorrect because m-learning occurs remotely rather than in-person.

4. **The correct answer is C.** Choice A is incorrect because there is no evidence to support a causal relationship between OSHA inspections and accidents, nor between a job hazard analysis, choice B, and accidents. Choice D is incorrect because there is no evidence to support the idea that accidents happen in a series.

5. **The correct answer is B.** Choice A is incorrect because customers are not part of the organization. Choices C and D are incorrect because while supervisors and management are part of an organization's human resources, they are only parts.

6. **The correct answer is A.** Choice B is incorrect because meeting the current objectives is the most important criterion. Choice C is incorrect because length of employment is not important when it comes to assessing current performance. Choice D is incorrect because a friendly relationship with the supervisor could result in a subjective performance appraisal by the supervisor.

7. **The correct answer is A.** Choice B is incorrect because a performance evaluation, not a job analysis, would be useful in explaining why an employee is being terminated. Choice C is incorrect because

a salary survey and a job evaluation are used to help determine pay ranges, not a job analysis. Choice D is incorrect because the analysis is independent of any single employee's records.

8. **The correct answer is A.** Choice B is incorrect because job ranking is used in the job evaluation process. Choice C is incorrect because pay grades are based on information found through job evaluation. Choice D is incorrect because a job description is just that, a description of a job and not a step in the process of job evaluation.

9. **The correct answer is D.** The purpose of orientation is to provide new employees with information about their employer. Choice A is incorrect because orientation is not a testing situation. Choice B is incorrect because discussing a new employee's expectations for his or her employment is not part of orientation. Choice C is incorrect because proving an employee's value to a company is a matter of working for the company, not learning about it.

10. **The correct answer is B.** Frederick Taylor is known as the founder of scientific management. Choice A is incorrect because he was not an industrial psychologist. Choice C is incorrect because he was not involved in the union movement; the first craft unions were founded in Great Britain and the United States in the mid-1800s. The largest in the United States was the American Federation of Labor, which organized a federation of craft unions in 1886. Choice D is incorrect because Taylor was not involved in the development of personnel departments, which came much later than Taylor, who died in 1915.

11. **The correct answer is B.** You're looking for the wrong answer in *except* and *not* questions, and the answer that doesn't fit in this series is choice B. Written tests are not used as an alternative to having a supervisor evaluate an employee. Choices A, C, and D—peer review, subordinates' evaluating an employee who reports to a higher-level supervisor, and team member appraisals—are all alternative methods of employee evaluation and so incorrect answers to the question.

12. **The correct answer is A.** Choice B is incorrect because new employees would not affect job design. Choice C is incorrect because having too many employees for the amount of work required to meet demand would affect staffing, but not job design. Choice D is incorrect because weaknesses in the workforce should not be remedied by changing the job design.

13. **The correct answer is C.** Choice A is incorrect because that would not solve the problem. Choice B is incorrect because that would not be helpful to the employee, the supervisor, or the organization. Choice D is not a practical solution and doesn't help the manager learn good skills, so eliminate it.

14. **The correct answer is C.** Employment at will means that there is no written contract between employee and employer that specifies a set period of employment. Either party may terminate employment at any time; the employer may or may not give a reason for termination. Choice A is incorrect because employment at will doesn't require the agreement of the employer. Choices B and D are incorrect because there is no contract involved in employment at will.

15. **The correct answer is A.** A diverse organization has employees of different ages, genders, ethnicities, religious backgrounds, and physical abilities. Although most organizations seek highly skilled employees, doing so doesn't mean a company is diverse, which makes choice B incorrect. The location of a company's business does not relate to its

diversity, so choice C is incorrect. Multicultural training may or may not be offered by a diverse organization, so choice D is incorrect.

16. **The correct answer is A.** The planning function of HRM involves tasks such as researching wage trends and monitoring the labor market. Choices B and D are incorrect because they relate to the staffing function of HRM. The development function of HRM involves providing training opportunities, so choice C is incorrect.

17. **The correct answer is C.** You want the answer that is *not* true, so eliminate choices A, B, and D because they are all true statements related to pay grades and wage, or pay, curves. Choice C is not true about pay grades and wage curves, so it's the correct answer.

18. **The correct answer is A.** Choice B is incorrect, because attrition is not hiring employees to replace those who leave voluntarily or are terminated for cause. It is a method used as an alternative to an RIF. Choice C is incorrect because it is likely that an error in predicting job needs would be corrected by other means, such as choice B, before an RIF would be necessary. Choice D is incorrect because training programs would be revised before employees would be let go.

19. **The correct answer is C.** Choices A, B, and D are incorrect because none of these—the job market, the economy, or globalization—would have a direct influence on the decision to organize. They may all, however, have an influence on management policies.

20. **The correct answer is D.** The Worker Adjustment and Retraining Notification Act (WARN) requires employers to give employees 60 days' notice before a plant closing or mass layoff. The National Labor Relations Act (NLRA) supports the right to organize, so choice (A) is incorrect. The Americans with Disabilities Act (ADA) prohibits discrimination against applicants with disabilities, and the Fair Labor Standards Act (FLSA) relates to wages and working conditions, which means choices B and C are incorrect.

21. **The correct answer is A.** Choice B is incorrect because age discrimination is prohibited under the Age Discrimination in Employment Act (ADEA). Choice C is incorrect because pensions are guaranteed under the Employment Retirement Income Security Act (ERISA). Choice D is incorrect because the Occupational Safety and Health Administration (OSHA) deals with issues of worker safety and health.

22. **The correct answer is D.** Employee objectives need to be clearly stated and quantifiable. Only choice D meets both criteria. Choice A can be eliminated because it is vague, as is choice B. Choice C is better, but doesn't indicate what the ad campaign is for.

23. **The correct answer is D.** Choices A, B, and C alone are not the best answers. The best answer combines all three: questionnaires, observation, and interviews.

24. **The correct answer is B.** Choice A is incorrect because ergonomics refers to only one issue considered in identifying workplace hazards. Choice C is incorrect because disability coverage is provided through workers' comp, which almost all companies must carry by law; some companies also buy additional disability insurance for employees. Choice D is incorrect. Although many accidents may occur in a worker's first few months, the primary purpose of job hazard analysis is to protect all workers.

answers *post-test*

25. The correct answer is C. Movement in the stock market doesn't usually affect company policy on salaries in the short term. Choice A is incorrect because a company's policies on salaries are something the compensation manager must take into account. Choice B is incorrect because the company's ability to pay is something that does affect salaries. Choice D is incorrect because even if the company president's retirement benefits are expensive, they are not covered under salary policies.

26. The correct answer is A. At one time, the defined benefit plan, which means that the amount the retiree receives is fixed at a certain amount for life, was the typical pension plan for companies that offered pensions to their employees. Today, companies are moving to choice B, which defines a defined contribution plan. Choice C is incorrect because a 401(k) is a form of defined contribution plan, so eliminate it. Choice D is incorrect because it describes an employee stock option plan (ESOP).

27. The correct answer is A. Choices B, C, and D are all true about phased retirement, so they are incorrect answers to the question, whereas choice A is not true and the correct answer. There is no set age for retirement; however, age 70 is the age at which people must begin taking their Social Security benefits. Note that although working fewer hours means a reduction in pay, employees keep their benefits.

28. The correct answer is B. The dangerous nature of the construction industry has resulted in specific health and safety guidelines from OSHA. Businesses in the publishing, sales, and farming industries must comply with general OSHA guidelines but lack specific standards, so Choices A, C, and D are incorrect.

29. The correct answer is B. Choice A is incorrect because ERISA deals with retirement programs. Choice C is incorrect because ADEA deals with discrimination against workers within certain age ranges. Choice D is incorrect because the Taft-Hartley Act deals mainly with unfair union labor practices and also enumerates the rights of employees and employers.

30. The correct answer is C. Choice A is incorrect because HRIS does not control Internet communications. Choice B is incorrect because setting up virtual offices isn't the purpose of HRIS. Choice D is incorrect because HRIS does not monitor flexplace and flextime work arrangements, though HRIS may collect data about them.

31. The correct answer is D. Choice A is incorrect because it describes a form of forecasting called ratio analysis. Choice B is incorrect because HRM would consider only past staffing needs, not a variety of factors. Choice C is incorrect because it describes scatter plot analysis.

32. The correct answer is C. Choice A is incorrect because authorization cards are used to prove that a large number of a site's workers are interested in joining the union. It is the second step in a unionization effort. Choice B is incorrect because dealing with grievances is separate from contract negotiations. Choice D is incorrect because "salting" a workplace involves having union members go to work for nonunion companies in an effort to organize the companies.

33. The correct answer is C. The Age Discrimination in Employment Act (ADEA) prohibits discrimination based on age. The Americans with Disabilities Act (ADA) prohibits discrimination against applicants with disabilities, so choice A is incorrect. Maternity leave is addressed by the Family and Medical Leave Act (FMLA), so choice

B is incorrect. Labor laws such as the NLRA protect union members, so choice D is incorrect.

34. **The correct answer is A.** Choices B and C are both incorrect because they describe outsourcing. Choice D is incorrect because a PEO hires employees laid off by a company, pays them and their benefits, and leases their services to companies.

35. **The correct answer is D.** Choice A is incorrect because the FLSA deals mainly with minimum wage, maximum hours, overtime pay, equal pay, recordkeeping, and child labor provisions, as well as distinguishing between exempt and non-exempt employees. Choice B is incorrect because the CSRA is concerned with labor management relations in the federal service. Choice C is incorrect because the NLRA supports the right of labor to organize and engage in collective bargaining.

36. **The correct answer is B.** Choice A is incorrect because outplacement is not related to voluntary turnover. Choice C is incorrect because learning how terminated employees feel about the company is the purpose of the exit interview. Choice D is incorrect because turnover generally relates to voluntary termination, whereas outsourcing is for workers terminated involuntarily. Also, outplacement has nothing to do with monitoring.

37. **The correct answer is A.** By giving workers the right to not join a union, the Taft-Hartley Act banned the closed shop. Choice B is incorrect because unions are required under the law to notify a company 60 days in advance of an impending strike. Choice C is incorrect because it is the opposite of what the law says; the U.S. president may intervene and apply for an injunction to halt the strike. Choice D is incorrect because the Taft-Hartley Act allows employers to give

their side of what unionization may do to the company and to their jobs in the future.

38. **The correct answer is A.** A wrongful termination suit is brought by a former employee. Choice B is incorrect because unexplained gaps should be apparent on a person's resumé and be dealt with during an interview. Also, it is illogical to consider that a former employee would begin a lawsuit because of an omission on his or her part. Choice C is incorrect because conflict management training is not a requirement. Choice D is incorrect because not guaranteeing worker safety is illegal.

39. **The correct answer is B.** Choice A is incorrect because the need for additional training will be measured on how well participants learned the information and put it into practice. Choice C is incorrect because any possible changes in behavior related to the training have not yet taken place. Choice D is incorrect because the employees have not yet had an opportunity to put into practice—or not—what they've learned during the training.

40. **The correct answer is B.** In his scientific management theory, Taylor proposed that labor productivity would improve if work processes were simplified. Taylor did not try to quantify product quality, so choice A is incorrect. Improving efficiency rather than reducing the workforce was the focus of Taylor's theory, so choice C is incorrect. Choice D is incorrect because Taylor focused on work processes rather than individual employees.

41. **The correct answer is C.** Choice A is incorrect because employers can hire both union and nonunion workers regardless of whether a state has a right-to-work law. Choice B is incorrect because right-to-work laws are state laws, and federal law guarantees the right to strike; federal law

takes precedence over state law. Choice D is incorrect because the union has a panel of union members that negotiate contract terms, including wages.

42. **The correct answer is C.** Adverse impact, which refers to hiring practices that seem neutral but actually discriminate against a protected group, is estimated with the four-fifths, or 80%, rule set by the EEOC's Uniform Guidelines on Employee Selection Procedures. For example, assume that a company has 100 total job applicants consisting of 80 males and 20 females, and the company selects 60 males and five females. Adverse impact is demonstrated because 75% of males were selected in comparison to 25% of women, and 25/75 equals 33%, which is less than the 80% requirement. The four-fifths rule is the primary method of determining adverse impact, so choices A, B, and D are incorrect.

43. **The correct answer is C.** Choice A is incorrect because development is mainly concerned with future skills, not present skills; improving skills is the work of training programs. Choice B is incorrect because worker development is concerned with future positions, not current job satisfaction. Choice D is incorrect because although an employee's weaknesses are of concern, strengthening skills and knowledge would be only one part of the plan for his or her future and would involve training.

44. **The correct answer is A.** Choice B is incorrect because a pay follower pays less than its competitors. Choice C is incorrect because paying the highest rate describes a pay leader. Choice D is incorrect because it is unlikely that a company paying average compensation would attract the most highly qualified workers.

45. **The correct answer is A.** Choice B is incorrect because while employees may need to fill out paperwork, this is not the purpose of an exit interview. Choice C is incorrect because it is not the place of HRM to offer incentives; that would be done by the supervisor, if interested, at the time the employee resigns. Choice D is incorrect because while that may occur, it is not the purpose of an exit interview.

46. **The correct answer is C.** While it is possible that an employee might get his or her hand caught in a vending machine, vending machines are not a category of hazards under OSHA regulations, so choice C is the correct answer. Choices A, B, and D are incorrect answers because they are categories analyzed for hazards.

47. **The correct answer is A.** Choice B is incorrect because the employee completes his or her own evaluation form, which will be used with the supervisor's during the PA interview. Choice C is incorrect because human nature being what it is, supervisors who have to deliver unpleasant information tend to put off those PAs. Choice D is known as the central tendency error and is incorrect because it favors the underachiever, but not the overachiever.

48. **The correct answer is D.** The Behaviorally Anchored Rating Scales (BARS) method compares employee performance against specific job-related behaviors. Assessment centers use multiple evaluation methods and do not focus only on job task behaviors, so choice A is incorrect. Choice B is incorrect because the management-by-objectives method focuses on goal setting rather than behaviors. Forced distribution is a method of ranking employees after they have been evaluated, so choice C is incorrect.

49. **The correct answer is B.** Staffing firms are often used to fill short-term or temporary positions at a company. Executive search firms specialize in filling executive positions,

so choice A is incorrect. Staffing firms fill open positions and do not handle payroll problems, so choice C is incorrect. A firm's HR personnel typically recruits on college campuses, so choice D is incorrect.

50. **The correct answer is C.** ERISA is the Employment Retirement Income Security Act, which protects retirement funds. Choice A is incorrect because the passage of ERISA was separate from the cost of compensation and benefits packages. Choice B is incorrect because ERISA deals only with retirement benefits. Choice D is incorrect because union contracts usually do cover retirement benefits.

51. **The correct answer is C.** Choice A is incorrect because transfer of skills involves taking what one has learned in one job to a new job. Choice B is incorrect because transfer of skills does not refer to passing on information, but to applying it to a new position. Choice D is incorrect because transfer of learning has nothing to do with a requirement for employees to inform management when they take courses.

52. **The correct answer is B.** Choice A is incorrect because the check card, or authorization card, is part of the process of organizing a workplace by a union. It is used in place of an election to determine if the workers wish to unionize. Choice C is incorrect because any arbitration procedure is set at the time of contract negotiation. Choice D is incorrect because a closed shop is illegal and, therefore, could not be part of bargaining agreement.

53. **The correct answer is D.** Choices A, B, and C are incorrect because they describe situations of disparate treatment discrimination. Unlike disparate impact discrimination, disparate treatment discrimination involves intentionally discriminating against

employees or job applicants because of their race, religion, or gender.

54. **The correct answer is D.** Choice A is incorrect because OSHA is concerned with worker safety, not age discrimination, which is the responsibility of the ADEA. Choice B is incorrect because OSHA is concerned with hazardous working conditions, not retirement funds. Choice C is incorrect because OSHA is concerned with workplace injuries and illnesses, not foreign-born workers who may or may not be illegal, unless they are affected by those injuries or illnesses.

55. **The correct answer is A.** Choice B is incorrect because the categories are defined by legislation. This answer choice is also wrong because the question asks about the difference between the two categories and this answer choice gives a similarity. Choice C is incorrect because the opposite is true; non-exempt employees receive an hourly wage and exempt employees receive salaries. Choice D is incorrect because non-exempt employees don't include outside salespeople; they belong in the category of exempt workers.

56. **The correct answer is A.** In the critical incidents method B, one rater evaluates an employee's key job behaviors. The grading method C involves a manager assigning grades to an employee for specific performance categories. Choice D is incorrect because the paired comparison method involves comparing the performance of two employees, but only one rater is involved.

57. **The correct answer is D.** Choice A is incorrect because stock options are not considered monetary compensation. Choice B is incorrect because stock options are not in the form of gift certificates. Choice C is incorrect because commissions are not the same as stock options.

58. **The correct answer is A.** The Family and Medical Leave Act (FMLA) provides leave for childbirth, adoption, and illness. FMLA applies to public and private employers with at least 50 employees, so choices (B) and (D) are incorrect. The FMLA allows 12 weeks of unpaid leave, so choice (C) is incorrect.

59. **The correct answer is A.** Choice B is incorrect because e-learning can be on the level of college courses. Choice C is incorrect because preparing or purchasing training materials can be expensive, though over time, e-learning can be cost-effective, if enough employees use the programs. Choice D is incorrect because e-learning may have assessments and tests, depending on the type of training involved.

60. **The correct answer is D.** Worker's compensation is an insurance program in that companies with a certain number of minimum employees must carry to pay medical, death, and income benefits to workers who are injured on the job or contract work-related illnesses. But it is not the same as disability insurance, so choice C is incorrect. Choice A is incorrect because worker's comp isn't related to job loss from a recession, nor is it related to Social Security payments, so choice B is also incorrect.

Technical Writing

OVERVIEW

- **Test Answer Sheets**
- **Technical Writing Diagnostic Test**
- **Answer Key and Explanations**
- **Diagnostic Test Assessment Grid**
- **Theory and Practice of Technical Writing**
- **The Purpose of Technical Documents**
- **The Technical Writing Process**
- **Document Design**
- **Revising, Editing, and Final Sections**
- **Summing It Up**
- **Technical Writing Post-test**
- **Answer Key and Explanations**

The DSST Technical Writing exam covers multiple topics related to technical writing including the theory and practice of technical writing; the purpose, content, and organizational patterns of common types of technical documents; information design; and technical editing.

DIAGNOSTIC TEST ANSWER SHEET

1. Ⓐ Ⓑ Ⓒ Ⓓ   5. Ⓐ Ⓑ Ⓒ Ⓓ   9. Ⓐ Ⓑ Ⓒ Ⓓ   13. Ⓐ Ⓑ Ⓒ Ⓓ   17. Ⓐ Ⓑ Ⓒ Ⓓ
2. Ⓐ Ⓑ Ⓒ Ⓓ   6. Ⓐ Ⓑ Ⓒ Ⓓ   10. Ⓐ Ⓑ Ⓒ Ⓓ   14. Ⓐ Ⓑ Ⓒ Ⓓ   18. Ⓐ Ⓑ Ⓒ Ⓓ
3. Ⓐ Ⓑ Ⓒ Ⓓ   7. Ⓐ Ⓑ Ⓒ Ⓓ   11. Ⓐ Ⓑ Ⓒ Ⓓ   15. Ⓐ Ⓑ Ⓒ Ⓓ   19. Ⓐ Ⓑ Ⓒ Ⓓ
4. Ⓐ Ⓑ Ⓒ Ⓓ   8. Ⓐ Ⓑ Ⓒ Ⓓ   12. Ⓐ Ⓑ Ⓒ Ⓓ   16. Ⓐ Ⓑ Ⓒ Ⓓ   20. Ⓐ Ⓑ Ⓒ Ⓓ

POST-TEST ANSWER SHEET

1. Ⓐ Ⓑ Ⓒ Ⓓ   13. Ⓐ Ⓑ Ⓒ Ⓓ   25. Ⓐ Ⓑ Ⓒ Ⓓ   37. Ⓐ Ⓑ Ⓒ Ⓓ   49. Ⓐ Ⓑ Ⓒ Ⓓ
2. Ⓐ Ⓑ Ⓒ Ⓓ   14. Ⓐ Ⓑ Ⓒ Ⓓ   26. Ⓐ Ⓑ Ⓒ Ⓓ   38. Ⓐ Ⓑ Ⓒ Ⓓ   50. Ⓐ Ⓑ Ⓒ Ⓓ
3. Ⓐ Ⓑ Ⓒ Ⓓ   15. Ⓐ Ⓑ Ⓒ Ⓓ   27. Ⓐ Ⓑ Ⓒ Ⓓ   39. Ⓐ Ⓑ Ⓒ Ⓓ   51. Ⓐ Ⓑ Ⓒ Ⓓ
4. Ⓐ Ⓑ Ⓒ Ⓓ   16. Ⓐ Ⓑ Ⓒ Ⓓ   28. Ⓐ Ⓑ Ⓒ Ⓓ   40. Ⓐ Ⓑ Ⓒ Ⓓ   52. Ⓐ Ⓑ Ⓒ Ⓓ
5. Ⓐ Ⓑ Ⓒ Ⓓ   17. Ⓐ Ⓑ Ⓒ Ⓓ   29. Ⓐ Ⓑ Ⓒ Ⓓ   41. Ⓐ Ⓑ Ⓒ Ⓓ   53. Ⓐ Ⓑ Ⓒ Ⓓ
6. Ⓐ Ⓑ Ⓒ Ⓓ   18. Ⓐ Ⓑ Ⓒ Ⓓ   30. Ⓐ Ⓑ Ⓒ Ⓓ   42. Ⓐ Ⓑ Ⓒ Ⓓ   54. Ⓐ Ⓑ Ⓒ Ⓓ
7. Ⓐ Ⓑ Ⓒ Ⓓ   19. Ⓐ Ⓑ Ⓒ Ⓓ   31. Ⓐ Ⓑ Ⓒ Ⓓ   43. Ⓐ Ⓑ Ⓒ Ⓓ   55. Ⓐ Ⓑ Ⓒ Ⓓ
8. Ⓐ Ⓑ Ⓒ Ⓓ   20. Ⓐ Ⓑ Ⓒ Ⓓ   32. Ⓐ Ⓑ Ⓒ Ⓓ   44. Ⓐ Ⓑ Ⓒ Ⓓ   56. Ⓐ Ⓑ Ⓒ Ⓓ
9. Ⓐ Ⓑ Ⓒ Ⓓ   21. Ⓐ Ⓑ Ⓒ Ⓓ   33. Ⓐ Ⓑ Ⓒ Ⓓ   45. Ⓐ Ⓑ Ⓒ Ⓓ   57. Ⓐ Ⓑ Ⓒ Ⓓ
10. Ⓐ Ⓑ Ⓒ Ⓓ   22. Ⓐ Ⓑ Ⓒ Ⓓ   34. Ⓐ Ⓑ Ⓒ Ⓓ   46. Ⓐ Ⓑ Ⓒ Ⓓ   58. Ⓐ Ⓑ Ⓒ Ⓓ
11. Ⓐ Ⓑ Ⓒ Ⓓ   23. Ⓐ Ⓑ Ⓒ Ⓓ   35. Ⓐ Ⓑ Ⓒ Ⓓ   47. Ⓐ Ⓑ Ⓒ Ⓓ   59. Ⓐ Ⓑ Ⓒ Ⓓ
12. Ⓐ Ⓑ Ⓒ Ⓓ   24. Ⓐ Ⓑ Ⓒ Ⓓ   36. Ⓐ Ⓑ Ⓒ Ⓓ   48. Ⓐ Ⓑ Ⓒ Ⓓ   60. Ⓐ Ⓑ Ⓒ Ⓓ

answer sheet

TECHNICAL WRITING DIAGNOSTIC TEST

> **Directions:** Carefully read each of the following 20 questions. Choose the best answer to each question and fill in the corresponding circle on the answer sheet. The Answer Key and Explanations can be found following this Diagnostic Test.

1. Which of the following summarizes only the scope and purpose of a document?
   - A. Informative abstract
   - B. Executive summary
   - C. Descriptive abstract
   - D. Closing summary

2. Which sequencing method would be most appropriate for the description of a new car model?
   - A. Spatial
   - B. Sequential
   - C. Chronological
   - D. Cause and effect

3. Which type of proposal would most likely be written by a university professor to request funding from a government agency for a scientific study?
   - A. Internal proposal
   - B. Sales proposal
   - C. Routine proposal
   - D. Grant proposal

4. The primary focus of most technical writing is
   - A. undocumented opinion.
   - B. global integration.
   - C. factual information.
   - D. supplemental data.

5. Which of the following is written specifically for repair technicians?
   - A. User manuals
   - B. Training manuals
   - C. Service manuals
   - D. Operator manuals

6. An informal tone in a document is most appropriate when writing to
   - A. colleagues.
   - B. customers.
   - C. superiors.
   - D. academics.

7. It is most appropriate for a technical document conclusion to
   - A. interpret findings.
   - B. present a new idea.
   - C. cite useful references.
   - D. define technical terms.

8. Which of the following is true of white papers?
   - A. Their purpose is to inform an internal audience about a new project offering.
   - B. They do not play a role in a company's branding efforts.
   - C. They exhibit an objective tone.
   - D. They do not include visual aids.

9. The literal meaning of a word is its
   - A. connotation.
   - B. subordination.
   - C. denotation.
   - D. abstraction.

diagnostic test

10. All of the following are strategies to promote concise writing EXCEPT
    A. eliminating unnecessary words.
    B. repeating major points and key words.
    C. eliminating redundancy.
    D. eliminating superfluous detail.

11. A brief definition of a technical term should be explained in a document's
    A. appendix.
    B. glossary.
    C. bibliography.
    D. table of contents.

12. Which of the following would most likely be written when a business is considering the development of a new service?
    A. Feasibility report
    B. Internal memo
    C. Progress report
    D. Solicited proposal

13. Which of the following involves the use of a synonym to explain the meaning of an unfamiliar word?
    A. Sentence definition
    B. Expanded definition
    C. Parenthetical definition
    D. Definition by components

14. The major difference between instructions and procedures is that procedures are intended for
    A. unskilled users.
    B. groups of people.
    C. sales personnel.
    D. new employees.

15. Learning as much as possible about the readers of a technical document is known as audience
    A. purpose.
    B. analysis.
    C. planning.
    D. adaptation.

16. Below, some part of the sentence or the entire sentence is underlined. Beneath this sentence, you will find four ways of phrasing the underlined part. Choice A repeats the original; the other three are different. If you think the original is better than any of the alternatives, choose choice A. Otherwise, choose one of the others. In choosing answers, pay attention to grammatical correctness, appropriate word choice, and smoothness and effectiveness of sentence construction.

    Prior to welding, a visual inspection at 1X magnification will be performed and the surface is smooth and clean.
    A. Prior to welding, a visual inspection at 1X magnification will be performed and the surface is smooth and clean.
    B. Prior to welding, a visual inspection at 1X magnification will be performed to ensure the surface is smooth and clean.
    C. Prior to welding, a visual inspection at 1X magnification will be performed so the surface is smooth and clean.
    D. Prior to welding, a visual inspection at 1X magnification will be performed, yet the surface is smooth and clean.

17. Which of the following graphics is best for tracing steps in a process?
    A. Table
    B. Flowchart
    C. Pie chart
    D. Line graph

18. All of the following are elements of most laboratory reports EXCEPT

   A. costs.

   B. results.

   C. equipment.

   D. procedures.

19. Which of the following demonstrates proper parallel structure?

   A. The goal of this progress report is to update management about current system upgrades, problems that have pushed back the timeline for the upgrade, and to present a revised timeline for project completion.

   B. The goal of this progress report is to update management about current system upgrades and problems that have pushed back the timeline for the upgrade. It also presents a revised timeline for project completion.

   C. Both A and B

   D. Neither A nor B

20. All of the following are true of executive summaries EXCEPT

   A. their length will vary, depending on the length of the document they summarize.

   B. they highlight important points from all major document sections.

   C. they are often persuasive.

   D. they are part of a document's back matter.

diagnostic test

ANSWER KEY AND EXPLANATIONS

1. C	5. C	9. C	13. C	17. B
2. A	6. A	10. B	14. B	18. A
3. D	7. A	11. B	15. B	19. B
4. C	8. C	12. A	16. B	20. D

1. **The correct answer is C.** A descriptive abstract summarizes in a few sentences the scope and purpose of a document. Choices B and D review the main points of a document. Choice A summarizes a report rather than just the scope and purpose.

2. **The correct answer is A.** The spatial method of development is used to describe the physical appearance of something, such as a new car. The sequential method, choice B, is for explaining systematic instructions. Chronological order, choice C, explains a sequence of events, such as a car accident. The description of a car involves no cause-and-effect relationship, so choice D is incorrect.

3. **The correct answer is D.** A professor requesting funding from the government for a study would submit a grant proposal. Internal and routine proposals are submitted within organizations, so choices A and C are incorrect. A sales proposal is used to gain business, so choice B is incorrect.

4. **The correct answer is C.** Presenting facts is the main focus of technical documents. Technical documents may include expert opinions and supplemental data, such as statistics, but essential facts are the focal point. Technical writers need to consider whether a document will be read on a global level, but global integration is not a key consideration.

5. **The correct answer is C.** Service manuals are written for repair technicians, and they contain troubleshooting charts to help diagnose equipment problems. User manuals, choice A, are written for the people who use a product, not repair it. Training manuals, choice B, are used as teaching tools with certain vocations, and operator manuals, choice D, are for trained equipment operators.

6. **The correct answer is A.** An informal tone in technical writing is appropriate for colleagues and subordinates in most cases. Superiors and academics, such as professors, require a formal or semiformal tone. A semiformal or formal tone is also appropriate when communicating with customers.

7. **The correct answer is A.** The conclusion of a technical document should interpret findings presented in the report. New ideas should not be introduced in a conclusion, so choice B is incorrect. References are cited in a bibliography, so choice C is incorrect. Technical terms, choice D, should have been defined in the body of a document, so it would be too late to explain them in the conclusion (choice D).

8. **The correct answer is C.** Even though white papers do not contain the same kind of language as a brochure or proposal, the purpose of a white paper is, ultimately, to support a company's sales and marketing efforts (making choice B incorrect). Choice A is incorrect because the audience for a white paper is external and while white papers may contain content that informs the readers about a particular perspective or

product, ultimately the goal is to persuade the audience to adopt a similar perspective. Choice D is incorrect because it is not always clear whether the audience for a white paper will be highly or even semi-technical. Visual aids help to make technical content accessible to laypersons.

9. **The correct answer is C.** The denotation of a word is its literal meaning or dictionary definition. A word's connotation, choice A, is the associations it brings to mind for different people, which may be positive or negative. Choices B and D are incorrect and have no relation to the meaning of words.

10. **The correct answer is B.** Concise writing eliminates unnecessary words and details. These elements are considered unnecessary if they do not clarify the main point of a document. Choices A, C, and D are all strategies designed to trim sentence content that does not clarify a main point. Choice B, on the other hand, offers a strategy to promote unity within a document.

11. **The correct answer is B.** The glossary is where a writer defines technical and unfamiliar terms from a document. Expanded definitions may require an appendix (choice A), but terms defined briefly should be included in a glossary. Bibliographies (choice C) cite references used for a document, and a table of contents (choice D) lists where information can be located in a report or proposal.

12. **The correct answer is A.** Feasibility reports are written when a business is considering a major change, such as developing a new service or moving a manufacturing facility. Memos are written to request information or announce policies within an organization, so choice B is incorrect. Progress reports, choice C, describe the status of a large project, and solicited proposals, choice D, are persuasive documents written to earn business.

13. **The correct answer is C.** Parenthetical definition involves using a synonym or phrase to explain the meaning of an unfamiliar term in a document. Expanded definitions, choice B, and sentence definitions, choice A, are lengthier than a word or phrase. Choice D is a type of expanded definition.

14. **The correct answer is B.** Procedures are used to clarify the rules and expectations that group members should follow in different situations. Instructions are the steps taken to complete a task. Procedures are for skilled individuals, so choice A is incorrect. Choices C and D are not the primary focus of procedures.

15. **The correct answer is B.** Audience analysis refers to gathering information about the readers of a technical document in preparation for writing. Technical writers often adapt their messages (choice D) *after* learning about the needs and knowledge of readers. The purpose of a technical document is an important aspect of writing preparation, but the terms used in choices A and C do not describe audience analysis.

16. **The correct answer is B.** The original sentence exhibits faulty coordination, meaning that both coordinate clauses are positioned as equal when in reality they contain unequal ideas. Choice B converts "the surface is smooth and clean" into a subordinate clause. Although choice C likewise converts the second clause into a subordinate one, the use of "so" incorrectly implies that the clean surface is the result of the inspection. The use of "yet" in choice D inappropriately introduces a change in the direction of the logic.

17. **The correct answer is B.** Flowcharts are appropriate for tracing the steps or decisions in any type of procedure or process. A table, choice A, helps organize explanations and numbers. Pie charts, choice C, relate parts

to the whole. Line graphs, choice D, show changes over time.

18. **The correct answer is A.** Results, equipment, and procedures are key elements usually included in laboratory reports. In order for a test to be repeatable, an author must identify all equipment and procedures used. The costs associated with laboratory testing are not included in a laboratory report in most instances.

19. **The correct answer is B.** The third item in the list presented in choice A exhibits a different grammatical structure from the first two list items. Choice B corrects the problem by splitting the long sentence into two.

20. **The correct answer is D.** An executive summary precedes a technical document so it is part of its front matter. Unlike an abstract which remains consistent in length, regardless of the length of the document it summarizes, an executive summary should be approximately 10 percent of the length of the original document, so a longer document requires a longer executive summary. Its structure mirrors the document's structure and each section of an executive summary presents summary content from each section. Their purpose is often persuasive as an executive summary is often the only portion of a document that a decision maker will read.

DIAGNOSTIC TEST ASSESSMENT GRID

Now that you've completed the diagnostic test and read through the answer explanations, you can use your results to target your studying. Find the question numbers from the diagnostic test that you answered incorrectly and highlight or circle them below. Then focus extra attention on the sections within the chapter dealing with those topics.

Technical Writing		
Content Area	**Topic**	**Question #**
Theory and Practice of Technical Writing	• Understanding contexts, purpose, and importance	4, 6, 15
Purpose of Technical Documents	• Informing • Persuading and making recommendations	3, 5, 8, 14, 18
Technical Writing Process	• Individual and/or collaborative writing • Choice of medium • Drafting and organizing content • Research (primary and secondary)	2, 7, 9
Document Design	• Elements of document design • Strategies of document design	11, 12, 13, 17
Revising, Editing, and Final Sections	• Revising • Editing • Miscellaneous writing pieces	1, 10, 16, 19, 20

GET THE FACTS

To see the DSST® Technical Writing Fact Sheet, go to *http://getcollegecredit.com/exam_fact_sheets* and click on the **Technology** tab. Scroll down and click the **Technical Writing** link. Here you will find suggestions for further study material and the ACE college credit recommendations for passing the test.

THEORY AND PRACTICE OF TECHNICAL WRITING

Technical writing refers to any written communication pertaining to a job, such as manuals, instructions, reports, and proposals. Although the subject is usually technical, any document that contains industry-specific language is a type of technical writing. Almost every career involves an element of technical writing—science, engineering, business, health sciences, and technology. Doctors maintain patient records, scientists write lab reports, software engineers write manuals, and managers write personnel evaluations. Understanding the specific elements of technical communication is essential in the information-driven twenty-first century. On your DSST Technical Writing exam, about 14 percent of the questions you see will cover the theory and practice of technical writing.

UNDERSTANDING CONTEXT, PURPOSE, AND IMPORTANCE

Technical documents are generally targeted for a specific audience—a technician who is hired to repair malfunctioning computer equipment might be the audience for a procedural manual. A busy executive who must make a decision to invest in new computers might be the audience for a technical proposal.

Just as different technical documents are written for different audiences, they are also written for different purposes. A process description might help the technician understand the steps involved in repairing broken computers while a formal proposal might convince the CEO to purchase new computers instead of repairing the broken ones.

To make sure that they reach their intended audience and achieve their purpose, technical documents are well organized and highly structured. Often, they contain visual aids to reinforce their message. The writing style is concise and the tone is objective. This means that unlike essays written for class or poetry written for pleasure, technical writing focuses on facts rather than personal thoughts, feelings, and attitudes.

Purpose

Purpose refers to what a technical writer wants the reader to know, believe, or do after reading a piece of technical writing. The two most common purposes for technical documents are as follows:

Technical Purpose		
Purpose	**Definition**	**Example Document Types**
Inform	Teaches a reader about a particular topic	• Manuals • Process or mechanism descriptions • Instruction sheets • Fact sheets • Progress reports • Research/lab reports • Incident reports • Feasibility reports
Persuade	Convinces a reader to take action or adopt a specific perspective	• Proposals • White papers • Grants

As the table implies, an informative document helps readers learn information. Persuasive documents make recommendations and encourage readers to take action or adopt a specific point of view. Many types of technical documents might achieve either (or both) purposes, depending on the situation.

To determine the purpose of a technical document, writers should ask the following questions:

- What action do I want people to take after reading the document?
- What do I want to convince readers of?
- What do I want people to know after reading the document?
- Do I want my readers to learn something, buy something, or change their minds about something?

The answers to these questions should be as specific as possible to simplify the writing task and to guarantee that the document achieves the writer's goal.

AUDIENCE AND AUDIENCE ANALYSIS

The audience refers to the intended reader (or readers) of a technical document. In order for technical writing to achieve its purpose the author must consider the audience's point of view. In fact, the audience should be the chief consideration when planning and writing a technical document.

To make sure they are properly considering their audience, technical writers conduct an audience analysis. Audience analysis refers to learning as much as possible about the individuals who will use a specific document. Understanding the knowledge, interests, and needs of readers enables a writer to adapt a message and tailor it to the specific audience.

One important factor is the technical experience of the reader. Readers with different levels of technical experience require different amounts of explanation and technical detail. The technical background of the audience determines whether terms need to be explained. As shown in the table, below, readers who have a technical background and who are familiar with the subject of a technical document need only straightforward data, but those unfamiliar with terminology expect interpretations and recommendations.

Audience Technicality Level		
Document User	**Necessary Information**	**Example**
Highly technical	Audience consists of experts in the subject matter; data does not require lengthy explanation	A physician giving a report to a surgeon about a patient's lab results and symptoms
Semi-technical	Audience consists of people with some technical knowledge but less than experts; data needs some explanation	A physician giving a report to first-year medical students regarding a patient's lab results and symptoms
Nontechnical	Audience consists of laypersons with no training in the subject matter; data needs to be translated into simple language that can be easily understood	A physician giving a report to a patient's spouse regarding lab results, symptoms, and treatment options

Here are the other important considerations when conducting an audience analysis:

Audience Analysis	
Is the reader a technical expert, proficient in technical material, or a layperson?	• Determine appropriate level of technical detail and amount of explanation needed • Determine whether it is appropriate to use technical language (jargon) • Determine whether to use visual aids
How much does the reader know about the topic?	• Provide a brief summary of content that is well-known to readers • Add detail or explanation about topics that readers are unfamiliar with
How interested is the reader in the topic?	• Use knowledge of interests to determine what content to include in technical document

Audience Analysis (continued)	
Does the reader share the author's point of view or priorities?	• Determine what evidence is needed to convince the reader to agree • Determine what information is needed to appeal to the reader's priorities or perspective
What role does the reader play and what will he or she need to do after reading the document?	• Write different content for people who play different roles—for example, provide technical details for technicians; include information on the bottom line and associated risks and benefits for decision makers • Determine what tone is appropriate for the audience—adopt a formal tone with executives or supervisors; use a semi-formal or informal tone with peers or subordinates
What is the reader's background/cultural/belief system	• Consider whether and how these factors are likely to impact your reader's perception of your writing style or content
What is the reader's personality or learning preference?	• Determine appropriate tone • Determine appropriate medium (formal or informal proposal) • Include many facts and present them in a logical order for analytical readers • Focus on the big picture for creative readers
Will the audience consist of more than one type of reader?	• Consider whether to include supplemental sections, such as glossaries or appendixes

EVALUATING DATA VALIDITY AND RELIABILITY

Technical writers often conduct research so they can include data or evidence in their documents. Evidence refers to any information used to support or refute a claim. Ethical technical writers strive for balanced evidence, which means they avoid exaggeration and include all pertinent facts. Factual statements, statistics, and expert opinions are examples of hard, verifiable evidence. Soft evidence refers to uninformed opinions and unverified data.

Before writing any technical document, a technical writer must evaluate the information and evidence that will be included to ensure it is valid and reliable. Thus, he or she must carefully choose which sources of information to include. A printed source or electronic content published by a university or other respected organization is most likely reliable. A source found on the Internet may or may not be.

To determine whether a source is reliable, consider the following guidelines:

Evaluating Sources of Evidence		
Author	• Who wrote the source? • What is the author's perspective? • What are the author's credentials and expertise?	• Is the author an expert in the field? • Is the source objective? • Is the information reliable?
Document Purpose	• What does the author want a reader to do after reviewing the content? • Why was the content created? • What is the website's sponsor and domain type (i.e., .edu, .com, .gov, .net)?	• Is the information biased? • Is the information being used to facilitate profit or information sharing?
Publication	• Who published the source? • Is the document peer-reviewed? • Was the content self-published?	• Is the information reliable? • Is the information accurate?
Format	• What medium does the author use?	• Is the format appropriate for the audience?
Relevance	• Is the information related to the document? • Do facts and figures support the document's point of view?	• Is the content appropriate for the audience? • Is the evidence presented likely to convince an audience? • Is the author presenting himself as a credible researcher?

Evaluating Sources of Evidence (continued)		
Publication Date	• When was the source written? • Has information been updated?	• Is the information current? The source of the information should be as current as possible, although some information changes very quickly. Information regarding technology is often outdated in a few months, so a document about diabetes treatments or data mining requires the most current research. (NOTE: Some topics, such as workplace ethics and flexible scheduling, benefit from including both recent and historical research.)
Credibility	• Does the author cite sources? • What sources did the author cite? • What kind of links does the author include on the web page?	• Is the author ethical? • Is the information reliable? • Is the information biased?

For the most valid data, technical writers should avoid relying on a single source to provide information and should instead acquire a consensus from many different sources.

ESTABLISHING THE APPROPRIATE STYLE

Although different types of writing may address the same or similar subjects, the approach differs depending on the type of writing. A personal essay, for example, is expressive writing that shares the author's experience, observations, or feelings. A research paper, on the other hand, does not convey information gathered from personal experience; rather, it discusses information discovered through study. A personal essay on the topic of animal rights might focus on the fact that the author felt upset and angry after witnessing animal abuse. Meanwhile, an informative, research-based essay on the same subject might discuss what animal rights activists have published on the subject of the ethical treatment of animals.

Technical writing often shares information that a reader needs to understand a specific topic or perform an action. It might require library or field research (information gathered from surveys or questionnaires) or scientific study. Regardless of the purpose, technical writing requires a writer to present information precisely, accurately, and objectively.

Tone

The attitude expressed by a writer toward a subject is the tone of a document. For technical writing, tone depends on the purpose, audience, and method of communication. Tone indicates the distance between a writer and a reader; it also indicates the attitude of the author toward the topic and the audience. Although no rules exist for determining the most appropriate tone for a technical document, the following guidelines may be useful to writers:

- Use a formal or semiformal tone when the writing is intended for superiors or professionals.
- Use a semiformal or informal tone when the writing is intended for colleagues and subordinates.
- Use an informal tone when a conversational style is desired, but avoid being too informal with profanity, slang, or poor grammar.

THE PURPOSE OF TECHNICAL DOCUMENTS

The purpose of a technical document refers to the goal that the author wants to accomplish. Different types of technical documents have different purposes. This section discusses some of the most common document types and their purposes—on your exam, around 23 percent of the questions you face will ask you about the purpose of technical documents.

DOCUMENTS THAT INFORM

Reports

Reports often provide the basis for decision making in the workplace, and they may be formal, informal, informational, or analytical:

- Informational reports focus on providing straightforward information—results of a customer survey, minutes of a department meeting, or profits and losses for the month.
- Analytical reports evaluate information, draw conclusions, and make recommendations.
- Formal reports are typically lengthy, require extensive research, and involve multiple writers.
- Informal reports lack extensive planning or research, and they often take the form of a memorandum.

Executives and employees write numerous types of reports in the workplace, but progress reports, feasibility reports, and laboratory reports are the focus of this review.

Progress reports, also known as status reports, keep the reader informed about activities, problems, and progress related to a large project. A project involving numerous steps may require the submission of regular progress reports—daily, weekly, or monthly. Progress reports are extremely useful with managerial decisions regarding work schedules, task assignments, funding, and supplies.

When writing a progress report, it is important for technical writers to think about the reader's questions and consider which ones are most important. The table below lists some of questions that clients and managers often expect progress reports to answer. It also contains advice for how to organize a progress report and cultivate an informative tone.

Progress Report Overview		
Questions	**Organization**	**Tone/Content**
Which tasks have been completed?	• Use lists, headings, and subheadings when discussing multiple tasks	• Use past tense • Be detailed, clear, and accurate
Which tasks must be completed in the future?	• Use lists, headings, and subheadings when discussing multiple tasks	• Use future tense
What problems have impacted the work?	• Use lists or describe any problems in paragraph format	• Describe items impacting work quality • Describe project obstacles • Be honest • Report facts, avoid placing blame
When will all tasks be complete?	• Consider using a chart or table to outline the timeline	• If problems have stalled progress, provide a new anticipated completion date.

The structure of a progress report often depends on the business, and many companies have specific forms they require for progress reports. However, every progress report pertaining to the same project should be organized in the same manner for the sake of consistency. In general, the first progress report submitted for a project includes an introduction or overview that states the project, necessary materials, and anticipated completion date. Follow-up reports explain what work has been completed, what work remains to be done, scheduling information, budget updates, and recommendations.

When a business considers the purchase of new equipment, development of a new product, or relocation of manufacturing facilities, executives initially attempt to assess the likelihood that the project or change will succeed. **Feasibility reports** help executives determine if an idea or a plan is both possible and practical. In some cases, a course of action may be possible but impractical because it would lower productivity or raise costs. Feasibility reports should address a variety of questions:

- Is this plan likely to succeed?
- What are the benefits and risks of the plan?
- What are other options?

- Is funding available?
- How would employees be affected?

Feasibility reports often begin with a purpose statement, such as, "The purpose of this report is to determine the feasibility of moving our manufacturing facilities overseas." The length of a feasibility report depends on the size of the project, but most follow a similar structure:

- Introduction: contains background information and purpose statement
- Body: presents a review of options being considered based on carefully selected evaluation criteria such as costs and resources needed
- Conclusion: presents an interpretation of the findings
- Recommendation: provides the author's opinion regarding the most feasible option based on the criteria discussed in the body of the report

Although the structure and length of feasibility reports varies, they should always review possible alternatives, provide specific recommendations, and include enough details to support the author's recommendations.

Laboratory reports relay information gathered from an investigation or from laboratory testing. The format of a laboratory report varies by profession and organization, but basic elements exist in almost all laboratory reports:

- The reason for conducting the test or investigation
- Equipment and procedures used during the investigation
- Problems, results, and conclusions

The most critical aspect of laboratory reports is the equipment and procedures used during testing. Duplicating the test and assessing the accuracy of the investigation depend upon the equipment used and the procedures followed.

MANUALS

Manuals are documents that help people understand how to assemble, use, and repair products. Nearly every product sold to consumers—from waffle irons to automobiles—includes a manual. Different types of manuals serve a variety of purposes and audiences.

Types of Manuals	
User Manuals	Written for both skilled and unskilled users of a product; include instructions regarding setup, operation, and maintenance as well as safety warnings and troubleshooting tips
Tutorials	Written as a self-study guide for the users of a product; intended to guide first-time users through the steps involved in operating a product
Training Manuals	Major teaching tool in vocational jobs; used to train people in a procedure or skill and often paired with audiovisual information

Types of Manuals (continued)	
Operator's Manuals	Written for trained operators of construction, computer, or manufacturing equipment for use on the job; includes instructions and safety information
Service Manuals	Written for repair technicians; contain troubleshooting charts for diagnosing problems

Before writing a manual, an author must consider whether the typical reader is a novice user, intermediate user, or expert user of the product or service. Audience determines the details to include and the terminology to use.

INSTRUCTIONS AND PROCEDURES

Instructions and procedures are two aspects of technical documentation that require clarification because they are frequently confused. Instructions are the steps required to complete a specific task safely and efficiently, such as installing a memory card into a laptop. People who have never performed a certain task are the typical audience for instructions. Printed manuals, online documentation, and brief reference cards are examples of common instructional documents. Instructional documents must be accurately written because consumers who are injured by a product due to faulty instructions may sue the technical writer. The misuse of power tools, medications, and cleaning products can lead to serious injuries, so all safety information and potential risks must be clearly explained to users in instructional documents.

Instructions that act as guidelines for people familiar with a task are called procedures. Procedures ensure safety within a group. For example, most businesses have written safety procedures that explain how to evacuate a building during a fire. Safety procedures include how to assist personnel with special needs, where to meet after evacuation, and who to contact for assistance. Written procedures also help maintain consistency. For example, police departments have specific procedures to follow when investigating a crime scene to ensure that officers gather, label, and store evidence correctly. Procedures help members of a group learn the expectations and rules related to a specific task.

PROCESS DESCRIPTIONS

A process description or a process explanation describes how something works and breaks down a process into steps or parts. The steps required to manufacture a DVD or the way a bank reviews loan applications are both typical subjects of process explanations. Well-written process descriptions include enough details so another person is able to follow the process through each step.

A process description begins with an introduction that provides an overview of the process or explains the importance of learning the process. Defining terminology and including visual aids helps make the process clear for readers. A technical writer clarifies each step of a process with transitional phrases and topic headings that indicate to readers that one stage is complete and another is beginning.

A conclusion wraps up the process description by summarizing the major stages and describing a complete cycle of the process.

An item or process is best described in a specific order to enable the audience to understand. Technical writers use spatial sequence to describe a mechanism at rest and to explain what an object is, what it does, and what it looks like. Technical writers use functional sequence when describing a mechanism that is in action and discussing how a mechanism works. When describing the order of assembly and explaining how a mechanism is put together, technical writers use chronological sequence.

DOCUMENTS THAT PERSUADE/MAKE RECOMMENDATIONS

Proposals

Proposals are documents written to persuade readers to take some type of action. The intention of a proposal may be to offer a solution to an identified need or organizational problem, persuade an audience to support a plan, authorize a project, or purchase a product. Reports and proposals have similar elements, but they differ in purpose. Although the recommendations section of a report may be somewhat persuasive, the majority of a report is informative. In contrast, a proposal is entirely persuasive in nature.

Numerous types of proposals are used in the workplace, and the organizational pattern, formality, and length of each kind varies. An internal proposal is submitted to personnel within an organization; an external or sales proposal is submitted to clients or potential customers. Short proposals include an introduction, body, and conclusion. In contrast, long proposals are divided into front matter, body, and back matter. Front matter refers to the content that precedes the main proposal and includes the cover letter, title page, table of contents, and list of figures. The body includes the executive summary, introduction, problem description, rationale, cost analysis, personnel expertise, statement of responsibilities, organizational sales pitch, request for approval, and the conclusion. Back matter refers to the content that follows the main proposal content; it includes appendixes, a bibliography, and a glossary of terms.

Types of Proposals	
Routine internal proposal	Written in short proposal format; used frequently in organizations for minor spending requests
Formal internal proposal	Used when requesting large amounts of money
Solicited proposal	External proposal written in response to a request for proposals (RFP) or an invitation for bids (IFB)
Unsolicited proposal	External proposal written and submitted without request
Sales proposal	External proposal that may be short or long depending on size of potential sale
Grant or research proposal	External proposal written to request funding for a project or study

White Papers

A white paper is a document that an organization uses to present its position on an issue to an audience outside the organization or to propose a solution for a pressing problem to potential clients. They are considered persuasive because they are often used for marketing purposes or to sell information or products. Often, potential clients consider white papers when making decisions about which solution represents their best option.

White papers can be difficult to write because they are written for diverse, often unknown audiences. For example, they may be written for the general public or for companies that might be searching for a solution to a particular problem. Even though writers of white papers may not know their audience well, they must focus on reader needs if they hope to convince people that their proposed solution or perspective is valid.

Even though white papers play a role in the sales and marketing process, they rely on objective analysis, research, and a thorough, informative treatment of paper content. Writers of white papers must be mindful to balance informative and persuasive content and avoid producing a document that reads like a technical report or sales brochure.

While the structure of a white paper may vary depending on the organization and context, there are certain techniques that you as a writer may use to achieve both an objective tone and a persuasive purpose:

- Focus on benefits.
- Use informative illustrations and other visuals to emphasize written content.
- Discuss topics from the reader's perspective.
- Focus on problem solving or the ways in which a particular product might address a need.
- Include evidence from subject matter experts and scientific or research studies.
- Use headings to help readers follow the discussion.
- Consider alternative solutions or perspectives.
- Document research properly.

Grant Proposals

Grant proposals are written to request funding for a specific project or study. Often, they require technical writers to address very specific content and follow explicit instructions so that grantmakers (organizations that provide funds to grant winners) can expedite the proposal review process. Reviewers are not likely to read past the point where proposals demonstrate a lack of compliance with instructions, so attention to detail is critical.

Although the structure and content of grant proposals vary depending on the grantmaker's instructions, grant writers can expect to provide a cover letter and an executive summary and include the following content:

- Problem statement
- Work schedule
- Budget

- Qualifications
- Conclusions
- Appendices

Further, grant writers must strive to be as clear and specific as possible while adhering to limits set by grantmakers.

THE TECHNICAL WRITING PROCESS

Like all writing, technical writing is a process. This means that there are steps that technical writers must take to express and refine their ideas. On the DSST Technical Writing exam, around 14 percent of exam questions will ask you about the technical writing process.

Generally, the steps of the technical writing process are as follows:

- Planning—analyzing audience; determining structure, purpose, scope, and content
- Researching—gathering the information to be discussed in a technical document
- Drafting—producing a technical document that will later be refined after team or individual review
- Revising—determining whether additions or changes are needed to the content or structure of a technical document
- Editing—determining whether a technical document is grammatically and technically correct
- Publishing—delivering the technical content to the audience

The process is by no means linear; writers often perform many of these steps out of order or repeat steps as needed. For example, a writer who is in the drafting phase may discover that more research is needed to inform or persuade an audience.

INDIVIDUAL AND COLLABORATIVE WRITING

Technical documents may be written by individuals or project teams. When technical documents are often long and complex, they are frequently written by project teams as opposed to individual authors. When more than one person authors a technical document they are engaged in **collaborative writing**. Collaborative writing requires technical authors to navigate the challenges presented by the complex writing process and the challenges of collaboration. It, therefore, requires strong communication and interpersonal skills.

Collaborative writing requires that project teams complete a number of tasks to help them stay organized and avoid obstacles. They include:

- Establishing an agenda and common goal
- Identifying writing tasks and dividing those tasks among members of the project team
- Identifying roles for group members
- Tracking ideas

- Developing a system for document management and version control
- Managing conflict

Planning and preparing a technical document can be challenging in a collaborative environment. Team members should consult with one another and meet regularly to discuss ideas and ensure that the document reflects the entire team's decisions.

Further, different writers have different styles, so creating a consistent voice and strong links between independently developed pieces of content can be difficult. A collaborative document requires heavy editing to standardize the writing style and tone, and weave the content together in a visually and linguistically cohesive document. Generally, this work is completed by a single person, referred to as an editor or a revision manager.

CHOICE OF MEDIUM

Medium refers to the way in which technical writers communicate information in a technical document. More specifically, it refers to the way in which the writing will be delivered. For example, an informal report that is composed using the memo form might be delivered by e-mail. Writers should consider the context and the audience's expectations when choosing a medium. Official correspondences and formal communications should be included as attachments to e-mails or distributed in paper format while informal communications might be included in the body of an e-mail message.

DRAFTING AND ORGANIZING TECHNICAL CONTENT

Technical documents are often lengthy, so it is common for writers to include a summary of information, introduction, conclusion, definitions, and report supplements to aid readers.

Introductions

The purpose of an introduction is to help the reader understand the scope, purpose, and structure of a technical document. An effective introduction captures the reader's attention and provides enough context to help the reader understand what he or she will read in the body and supporting sections of the document.

Conclusions

The purpose of a conclusion in a technical document is to summarize information, interpret findings, and offer recommendations. Conclusions offer an author a final opportunity to emphasize a significant point that will remain with the reader. Throughout a document, writers explain evidence, but the conclusion sums up the analysis and leads to a recommendation—if the document requires the author's opinion.

Depending on the type of document, a conclusion should have certain characteristics:

- Summary: represents the main points of the document
- Interpretation: coincides with findings presented in the document
- Recommendations: agree with purpose, evidence, and interpretations of the document

The purpose of the document and the reader's needs dictate the content of a conclusion. For example, a report may end with a recommendation, yet it may be more advantageous to conclude a sales proposal with a persuasive statement regarding the benefits of purchasing a product. Other methods of effectively concluding a document involve ending with a thought-provoking statement or quotation, asking readers to take action, making predictions, and presenting ideas to consider. Regardless of the approach used to conclude a document, writers should never introduce a new topic. Conclusions should always refer to the information and ideas presented in the document.

Definitions

Defining unfamiliar terms and concepts is critical for the clarity of a technical document. Definitions help readers understand the precise meaning of a word, concept, or process. Within various types of technical documents, definitions may have legal implications. For example, contracts and employee handbooks require clear definitions to ensure that all parties understand the legal terms and responsibilities. Technical writers employ a variety of methods when defining terms in documents.

Methods for Defining Terms	
Parenthetical definition	Use a synonym or a clarifying phrase to explain the meaning of an unfamiliar word; easy to set up links in electronic documents
Sentence definition	Used for complex terms or when term has multiple meanings. Follows a fixed pattern: indicate the item to be defined, the class in which the item belongs, and the features that make the item unique from others in same class
Expanded definition	Used when extensive details are required about an item; may be a paragraph or numerous pages depending on the audience and purpose

Parenthetical and sentence definitions are appropriate when a reader only requires a general understanding of a term or a concept. However, expanded definitions may be necessary when a reader needs to know how something works or when a reader is semi-technical or nontechnical. Definitions can be expanded in a variety of ways:

- Etymology: describe the term's origin, such as Greek or Latin words
- Background: discuss history, development, and applications for the term unless readers are only attempting to perform a task related to the term
- Negation: explain what the term does not mean
- Operation: explain how an item or process works
- Analysis of parts: explain how each element of a complex item works, which is especially beneficial to laypersons attempting to understand a technical subject

- Visuals: show the meaning of a process or concept
- Comparison and contrast: compare or contrast unfamiliar information with information the reader understands
- Examples: use those that match a reader's level of comprehension to describe how an item is used or how it works

Including definitions in a document promotes reader understanding, but determining where to place definitions can be tricky. If four or fewer terms need to be explained, then parenthetical definitions or hypertext links are appropriate because the flow of the text will not be disrupted.

However, more than four terms requiring clarification calls for sentence definitions placed in the glossary of the document. Expanded definitions belong in the introduction if the term is essential to understanding the entire document. An expanded definition that explains a major point belongs in that specific section. An appendix is appropriate for an expanded definition that is merely a reference in a document and not essential to understanding a key point.

Report Supplements

Long documents need to be accessible to readers who may not have the time or interest to read the full text, and, as such, report supplements are beneficial tools. Like formal proposals, long documents have both front matter and back matter. The table of contents is part of the front matter, and the glossary and appendixes are part of the back matter.

Table of Contents

A formal document longer than ten pages usually includes a table of contents to simplify the process of locating information. Most writers place the table of contents after the title page and abstract but before the list of tables, the foreword, and the preface. A table of contents shows what is contained in a document and on what pages information can be located. In the table of contents, list the major headings of a document in the order in which they appear and include subheadings as well. Front matter is listed in Roman numerals, and page numbers begin with the first page of the report, most likely the introduction.

Glossary

The glossary of a document is an alphabetical listing of definitions. Technical terms, or those that have a unique meaning in the document, require definitions for reader comprehension. A glossary defines technical terms without breaking the flow of a document. Technical documents intended for laypersons may require a glossary, yet an audience of skilled readers may not need technical terms defined at all. In general, a document containing more than five technical terms calls for a glossary. Explain the meaning of five or fewer technical terms either within the text or in a footnote. Definitions should be concise and clear to enhance reader understanding. Insert a glossary after the appendixes and the bibliography in the back matter of a long document.

Appendix

An appendix is part of the back matter of a document, and it serves the purpose of clarifying or supplementing information presented in the text's body. Documents may contain more than one appendix, but each appendix should address only one piece of information. Arrange multiple appendixes in a document in the order in which the information appears in the body. Each appendix begins on a new page and is identified with a letter (beginning with A) and an appropriate title. A document containing only one appendix does not require letters, only Appendix as the title. The following is a list of typical information that would be appropriate for an appendix:

- Experiment details
- Complicated formulas
- Interview questions and answers
- Quotations longer than one page
- Maps and photographs
- Sample questionnaires, tests, and surveys
- Large visual aids

Keep in mind that information is generally included in an appendix if it would interfere with the main body text or is too detailed or lengthy for the primary reader. However, writers should not include irrelevant information in appendixes or use too many of them.

RESEARCH

Technical writers often conduct research so that they have enough valid data to support their conclusions and recommendations. There are two types of research that may assist technical writers in gathering appropriate data.

Primary Research

Primary research refers to any data that writers collect themselves. Examples of primary research include surveys, questionnaires, interviews, or recorded observations about people, events, or products. The following questions can help guide technical writers in conducting primary research:

- What do I want or expect to find out?
- How will I go about finding out what I want to know? What methods will I use? (This is referred to as a research methodology.)
- What do I know or believe about this topic? (The goal is to identify biases and think about ways to keep them from influencing your research methods.)
- Who am I going to speak with or study? (The people you will observe or question are referred to as research subjects or participants.)
- How will I find people to participate in my study?

Once information is gathered, technical writers analyze and organize the information based on criteria that they develop so that they can look for patterns or gain a deeper understanding of how a product or process works.

Secondary Research

Secondary research refers to a review of the studies that other people conducted and the data they gathered and analyzed as a result of those studies. It is useful when technical writers need to understand what is already known about a topic or what possible solutions exist to solve a complicated problem. Secondary research is sometimes used to help prepare a technical writer for primary research. Conducting secondary research can help a technical writer identify what data is needed or what research methods would be the most effective. Often, it is the only kind of research that a technical writer will perform.

DOCUMENT DESIGN

It's often said that appearance is everything, and for technical documents—whether a report, memo, manual, proposal, or e-mail—this is definitely true. The proper use of titles and headings, page design, and visuals is extremely important when writing and composing technical documents. Document design questions will comprise about 18 percent of your DSST Technical Writing exam.

ELEMENTS OF, AND STRATEGIES FOR, DESIGN

Page design can emphasize certain aspects of a document and visually indicate the organization of information. Authors should keep readers in mind when designing pages and focus on using page design elements consistently throughout a document. The following elements of page design are effective tools for enhancing the appearance of a technical document.

Page Design Elements	
Justification	Margins justified on the left are easier to read; fully justified appropriate for multiple columns.
Headings	Indicate organizational structure and help readers find information; type size or font should differ from main text.
Lists	Useful in presenting steps, materials, and recommendations.
Headers and footers	Often include section topic, date, page number, and title of document.
Columns	Single-column for larger typeface; double for smaller typeface. Avoid orphans and widows. Orphan is a word on a line by itself at the end of a column. Widow is a single line carried over to the top of a column.
Color	Useful in highlighting sections of a document to draw reader attention.
White space	Blank space between paragraphs and between sections visually helps readers know when one idea or section is beginning or ending.

Readers often base their decision to read a technical document upon the **title**. Well-written titles indicate a variety of information about a document—topic (the subject of the technical document), tone, scope (what topics are included and what level of detail is provided in a technical document), purpose, and more. The most useful titles are concise yet specific. Avoid sentence form and redundancies in titles. The subject line acts as the title for memos and e-mails.

Within the body of a technical document, **headings** serve as titles of sections and subtopics. Headings have a number of purposes, especially in lengthy reports:

- Help readers find a particular section
- Divide information into logical pieces
- Highlight main points and topics
- Signal topic changes

Headings can be real time-savers for readers and make a technical document more accessible. The way in which a heading is phrased depends on its function in the document. A topic heading is a brief phrase or word that is most appropriate when there are many subtopics in a document; however, they can be too vague for readers. Statement headings require a sentence or a detailed phrase and are useful when a specific detail about a topic needs to be addressed. Question headings draw readers into the topic, but they may be too informal for some documents.

Visuals also improve a document's readability and appearance. A technical writer who needs to explain an idea more clearly than is possible with words will often turn to visuals. Drawings, photographs, and maps show readers what something looks like. Graphs and tables illustrate numbers and quantities. Flowcharts, diagrams, and organizational charts clarify relationships.

As with most elements of technical writing, audience and purpose determine what visuals should be utilized in a document. For example, numerical tables and schematics are most appropriate for expert readers who are able to interpret information sufficiently. Basic graphs and diagrams are suitable for audiences with limited technical knowledge.

In general, technical writers use visuals when readers need to focus on a particular idea. Visuals serve to instruct or persuade the reader, and they draw the reader's attention to an important concept. Including visuals is also beneficial when an author anticipates that a document will be consulted by readers unfamiliar with the topic or by readers who only need to read specific sections of a document.

Types of Visuals	
Tables	Data organized for easy comparison
Bar graphs	Translate numbers into shapes or colors; show comparisons
Line graphs	Show trends and changes over time, cost, size, rates, and other variables
Pie charts	Show parts of a whole
Gantt charts	Show how the phases of a project relate to each other
Pictograms	Use images or icons to represent quantities; useful for non-experts to grasp ideas
Flowcharts	Show steps in a process

Types of Manuals (continued)	
Schematic diagrams	Show how components of a principle, process, or system function together
Drawings	Show real or imaginary objects; highlight specific parts; use exploded view to show how parts fit together

Visuals are especially effective when placed near the text they are clarifying. Especially large or lengthy visuals should be included in an appendix.

REVISING, EDITING, AND FINAL SECTIONS

If the appearance and content of a technical document are sound, but the writing is not readable, then the writer has not met the audience's needs. Thus, revising and editing are important steps in writing technical documents. Revision considers whether a document is complete, properly scoped, appropriate for the audience, and well-structured. Editing considers whether a document is grammatically correct, properly formatted, and free of typos, broken hyperlinks, spelling mistakes, and sentence-level errors. Some tasks, such as considering whether a document is concisely written, occur during both levels of review. Questions that cover reading, editing, and final sections will make up about 31 percent of your DSST Technical Writing exam.

REVISING FOR COMPLETENESS

When technical writers consider whether their documents are complete, they evaluate whether they have treated their topic thoroughly enough. Specifically, they consider whether they have provided all necessary information to the reader, whether they have addressed all the questions they posed in the planning stages or anticipated questions a reader might have, and whether additional content is needed to ensure a document meets its purpose. Some questions writers can use to assess completeness are as follows:

- Has the document's purpose been fulfilled? Why or why not?
- Does the body of the document provide all the information required to understand the conclusion, recommendation, or results? If not, does the document provide guidance as to where readers can find the necessary information (e.g., is the information located in an appendix)?
- Does the document provide enough evidence to support important findings, recommendations, or results?
- What questions will the audience have after reading the document?

REVISING FOR CONCISENESS

Writing with conciseness involves removing unnecessary words, phrases, and sentences from a document without impeding clarity. Concise does not necessarily mean brief, because lengthy reports may be concise. Two kinds of wordiness plague documents. One type of wordiness involves giving readers unnecessary information. Another kind involves using too many words to convey relevant information. Use the fewest words possible to express a concept, but do not omit information that is required for clarity.

Wordiness is a normal occurrence during draft writing, but editing should repair the problem. For example, eliminate phrases like "basic and fundamental" or "each and every" because they bog down a document with redundancies. Excess qualification, such as "completely accurate," adds to the wordiness of a document as well. Introductory phrases like "in order to," "due to the fact that," and "through the use of" can be easily replaced with single words—"to," "because," and "by."

Another way to achieve conciseness is by using parallel sentence structure. Such a structure requires elements of a sentence to be similar in function and grammatical form. Parallelism enhances meaning, achieves emphasis, and eliminates wordiness as indicated in the following examples:

- **Not parallel:** Our new SUV has other features such as a moon roof, a DVD player, and switching to four-wheel drive.
- **Parallel:** Our new SUV has other features such as a moon roof, a DVD player, and a four-wheel drive option.

Parallel sentence structure is especially important when developing outlines, and creating tables of contents because it helps readers understand how the different parts of a document are related.

REVISING FOR ACCESSIBILITY AND ORGANIZATION

Accessibility refers to how easy it is for a writer to read a technical document, follow its logic, and comprehend its content. An accessible document is one that is well organized and clear. Effective formatting and heading use can also contribute to document accessibility.

Unity and Sequence

The unity of a document refers to its single purpose and its presentation of information. A paragraph that exhibits unity pertains to one idea and does not deviate from it. When editing a technical document, an author needs to question whether each paragraph concentrates on a single topic, whether the entire document focuses on achieving one purpose, and whether all ideas flow logically together.

Information presented in a logical sequence creates a readable document. Certain sequence patterns, or methods of development, are useful when creating technical documents.

Sequence Patterns	
Spatial	Describes the physical appearance of an object or area beginning at one point and ending at another; useful for product or mechanism descriptions
Chronological	Follows sequence of events; useful for explanations of how something is done or how an accident occurred
Sequential	Used for writing step-by-step instructions
Cause and Effect	Begins with either the cause or the effect; useful in reports discussing problems and solutions
Emphatic	Emphasizes important information; reasons or examples are arranged in decreasing or increasing order of importance; used when making recommendations or proposals
Comparison	Used when writing about one subject that is similar to another

Most writers blend various methods of development or use more than one in a single document. During the editing process, writers need to consider the unity of each paragraph and the way in which the paragraphs and sections link together.

Transitional Phrases

Transitional phrases are like road signs that help the reader understand the logic of a technical document. They build unity and clarify the connection between different sections of a document. The smooth flow of ideas within a paragraph or between paragraphs is accomplished with the use of appropriate transitions. Readers are more easily able to make connections and understand the relationships between concepts when an author uses transitions in a document. Creating unity with transitions can be achieved in a number of ways:

- Using transitional words and phrases
- Repeating major points or key words
- Summarizing information presented in a previous paragraph
- Using numbers to indicate steps in a process (first, second, third)

The table below presents some common transition words and phrases.

Transition Type	Purpose	Examples
Additions	Provide evidence and further explanation	Moreover; furthermore; besides; again; and; in addition; equally importantly; another example
Contrast	Shows a change in the direction of the logic	But; yet; however; still; nevertheless; on the other hand; on the contrary; in contrast; at the same time; although
Comparison	Shows similarities between points or examples	Similarly; likewise; in the same way
Clarification	Explain a point	In other words; to restate; put another way; indeed; in short; for example; for instance, to illustrate; such as
Results	Signals discussion of findings	Thus; as a result; therefore; hence; consequently; subsequently
Time	Indicates a time relationship, sequence or chronology	Meanwhile; immediately; shortly; afterward; later; after a few minutes (hours, weeks, months, years, etc.); first (second, third, etc.); finally
Summary	Conclude, summarize, restate ideas	In summary; on the whole; in short; as stated; in conclusion

Clarity

A logical presentation of information and clearly written sentences improve the overall clarity of a technical document. Editing for clarity requires focusing on sentence construction and word choice. Avoid ambiguity with clear phrasing, appropriate punctuation, and agreement between pronouns and antecedents.

Proper word choice also promotes clarity because choosing a precise word helps technical writers avoid vagueness. To be precise, technical writers must be aware of the denotation and connotation of words. The **denotation** of a word is its literal meaning, or the definition found in a dictionary. The **connotation** of a word refers to the associations that a word has—both positive and negative. For example, the denotative meaning of school is a building where people receive an education, but the connotative meaning of school varies. For some people, school may generate negative memories of difficult classes, but other people may think about fun experiences with friends. Words used in technical documents should have precise denotations and appropriate connotations for both the audience and purpose.

Emphasis and subordination are likewise necessary for clarity in writing. Stressing important ideas by positioning key words or ideas first or last in a sentence is known as **emphasis**. By organizing information in a paragraph from familiar to unfamiliar, a writer is also able to place emphasis on a key concept. **Subordination** in a sentence shows that a less important concept is dependent upon a more important concept. Subordinating conjunctions, such as because, if, while, which, and since indicate relationships in a sentence:

- A sedentary lifestyle is linked to obesity. A lack of exercise also puts people at risk for high blood pressure. (The two ideas are equally important.)
- A sedentary lifestyle, which is a risk factor for high blood pressure, is linked to obesity. (The risk factor for high blood pressure is subordinated, and the link to obesity is emphasized.)
- A sedentary lifestyle, which is linked to obesity, is a risk factor for high blood pressure. (The risk factor for obesity is subordinated, and the link to high blood pressure is emphasized.)

Failure to use emphasis and subordination will result in clauses and sentences that have equal importance in a document. Readers will be required to determine which concepts are most important, and their assumptions may not be what the author intended.

Reviewing for Accuracy

If an organization presents flawed or erroneous information in a technical document, its credibility suffers and the organization may be subjected to unwanted consequences. As mentioned earlier, readers might sue if they suffer injury as a result of reviewing inaccurate information; it is important that a subject matter expert reviews a document for technical accuracy. Some areas of focus are as follows:

- Facts are correct and derived from credible sources.
- Evidence supports the claims made.
- Third-party review occurs when information is in dispute.
- Limitations are noted—for example, the reviewer of a proposal for IT support considers whether a proposed solution only pertains to specific hardware or software.
- Written procedures are tested for completeness, ease of use, and accuracy.

During the editing process, a technical writer or editor also reviews a document for errors such as wrong words, word omissions, spelling errors, punctuation issues, subject-verb agreement, and other problems related to writing mechanics. Grammatical review occurs as follows:

- Personal review: technical writers review their own work
- Peer review: a colleague or technical editor is called upon to review the work
- Technological review: spelling and grammar checkers, such as the review features in Microsoft Office™ software or programs like Grammarly™ are used to review work

Grammatical review is important as readers often make judgements about an author's attention to detail or writing ability when they encounter writing-related errors.

FINAL SECTIONS

Cover Letters

Just like a job seeker uses a cover letter to introduce her or his resume or qualifications to potential employers, a technical writer uses a cover letter to introduce the audience to a document and its ideas or recommendations. The cover letter is often the first piece of writing that a decision maker or potential client sees, so it is important to make a strong first impression. This is particularly true of proposals.

The purpose of a proposal is to facilitate a sale or propose a solution to a problem. A cover letter assists in the fulfilment of that purpose by enticing the reader to review the executive summary and enough of the body of the proposal that they are convinced the ideas it proposes represent the best possible solutions for his or her organization.

A technical writer cannot be sure if an audience will read further than the cover letter so it is important that the cover letter provide a concise, clear summary of a document's content. As the cover letter should be no longer than a page, a technical writer should prioritize and include only the one or two most important points. To assist in identifying those points, a technical writer might ask the following question:

- What would I tell the readers if I only had one minute to educate them about my solution, findings, or recommendation?

For a proposal cover letter, the answer to this question should focus heavily on the following:

- Solutions for the potential client's problem or needs
- The benefits that the solution would offer to the potential client

A cover letter is a formal document and so it should be presented on business letterhead, properly formatted with a header, a date of submission, and a greeting. If the technical writer does not know the recipient of the document well, a formal greeting (such as "Dear Mr./Ms.") should be used. The reader's first name can be used if the writer knows the recipient well and regularly uses that form of address.

The content of a cover letter varies depending on the organization and context. However, it generally contains the following content:

- Overview of the problem
- Overview of the proposed solution, recommendation, or findings
- Contact information

For documents with a persuasive purpose, the cover letter should also provide insight into proposal benefits and a call to action—or a statement of what the writer hopes the reader will do after reviewing the document.

Summaries and Abstracts

Closing summaries, executive summaries, informative abstracts, and descriptive abstracts are four types of summarized information often included in technical documents.

Summaries and Abstracts	
Closing summary	Included either at the beginning of the conclusion or at the end of the body; reviews main points and findings
Executive summary	Included before full report; combines main points of a report or proposal; often persuasive
Informative abstract	Included before full report; summarized version of report
Descriptive abstract	Included on the title page; summarizes in a few sentences the scope and purpose of the document

Informative abstracts and executive summaries are often confused because they are similar. An **abstract** is a summary of a written document that enables readers to determine whether to read an entire article. An **executive summary** combines the main points of a report or proposal, and it is often the only section of a longer document that is read. Executive summaries follow the same sequence as the full document with subheadings to assist the reader. Most executive summaries are 10 percent of the length of the original document, while most abstracts are approximately 200 words long, regardless of the length of the original article.

SUMMING IT UP

- **Technical writing** is any written communication pertaining to a job—manuals, instructions, reports, and proposals. Most technical communication helps readers understand a process, concept, or technology.

- **Audience analysis** means learning about the individuals who will use a specific document—their technical and cultural backgrounds, experience and training, attitudes about subject matter, and needs and interests.

- The **sources** and **evidence** used in a technical document should be both valid and reliable. For the most valid data, avoid relying on a single source for information and instead acquire a consensus from many different sources. A printed source published by a university or other respected organization is most likely reliable.

- **Progress** or **status reports** keep readers informed about activities, problems, and steps forward related to a large project, whether on a daily, weekly, or monthly basis.

- **Feasibility reports** help executives determine if an idea or a plan is possible and practical. They should review possible alternatives, provide specific recommendations, and include details to support the author's recommendations.

- **Laboratory reports**, which relay information gathered from an investigation or laboratory testing, include the reason for conducting the investigation, equipment and procedures used, and problems, results, and conclusions.

- **Manuals** (user, tutorial, training, operator, and service) help people understand how to assemble, use, and repair products. An author must consider whether the reader is a novice, intermediate, or expert user of the product or service.

- **Instructions** are the steps required to complete a specific task safely and efficiently. People who have never performed a certain task are the typical audience for instructions, which must be accurately written to avoid causing injuries to consumers.

- **Procedures** are instructions that act as guidelines for people familiar with a task. Safety procedures include how to assist personnel with special needs, where to meet after evacuation, and who to contact for assistance.

- A **process description** or **explanation** describes how something works. Spatial sequence is used to describe a mechanism at rest. Functional sequence is used to describe a mechanism in action. Chronological sequence is used to describe the order of assembly.

- **Proposals** persuade readers to take some type of action. Long proposals are divided into front matter (cover letter, title page, table of contents, and list of figures), body (executive summary, introduction, problem description, rationale, cost analysis, personnel expertise, statement of responsibilities, organizational sales pitch, request for approval, and conclusion), and back matter (appendixes, bibliography, and glossary of terms).

- A **white paper** is a document that an organization uses to present its position on an issue to an audience outside the organization or to propose a solution for a pressing problem to potential clients. They are considered persuasive because they are often used for marketing purposes or to sell information or products.

- **Grant proposals** are written to request funding for a specific project or study. Often, they require technical writers to address very specific content and follow explicit instructions so that grantmakers (organizations that provide funds to grant winners) can expedite the proposal review process.

- **Technical documents** may be written by individuals or project teams. When technical documents are often long and complex, they are frequently written by project teams as opposed to individual authors. When more than one person authors a technical document they are engaged in collaborative writing. **Collaborative writing** requires technical authors to navigate the challenges presented by the complex writing process and the challenges of collaboration. It, therefore, requires strong communication and interpersonal skills.

- **Medium** refers to the way in which technical writers communicate information in a technical document. More specifically, it refers to the way in which the writing will be delivered.

- **Technical writers** often conduct research so that they have enough valid data to support their conclusions and recommendations. There are two types of research that may assist technical writers in gathering appropriate data—**primary** and **secondary research**.

- The purpose of a **conclusion** in a technical document is to summarize information, interpret findings, and offer recommendations.

- **Definitions** help readers understand the meaning of a word, concept, or process. Use parenthetical definitions for four or fewer terms. Place expanded definitions in the introduction if the term is essential to understanding the entire document or in an appendix if not essential to understanding a key point. Use sentence definitions if more than four terms require clarification and place them in the glossary.

- **Headings** serve as titles of sections and subtopics within the body of a technical document.

- **Page design elements** include justification, headings, lists, headers and footers, columns, color, and white space.

- **Audience** and **purpose** determine which visuals should be used in a document. Numerical tables and schematics are best for expert readers; basic graphs and diagrams are best for those with limited technical knowledge.

- For technical writing, **tone** (a writer's attitude toward a subject) depends on the purpose, audience, and method of communication. Use a formal or semiformal tone for superiors or professionals, a semiformal or informal tone for colleagues and subordinates, and an informal tone when a conversational style is desired.

- **Information sequence methods** include spatial, chronological, sequential, cause and effect, emphatic, and comparison.

- A word's **denotation** is its literal meaning; **connotation** refers to the word's positive and negative associations.

- When technical writers consider whether their documents are **complete**, they evaluate whether they have treated their topic thoroughly enough. Specifically, they consider whether they have provided all necessary information to the reader, whether they have addressed all the questions they posed in the planning stages or anticipated questions a reader might have, and whether additional content is needed to ensure a document meets its purpose.

- **Concise** writing involves removing unnecessary words, phrases, and sentences without impeding clarity. Check for parallel sentence structure so that elements of a sentence are similar in function and grammatical form.

- **Accessibility** refers to how easy it is for a writer to read a technical document, follow its logic, and comprehend its content. An accessible document is one that is well organized and clear. Unity, sequencing, transitions, and clarity all contribute to a document's accessibility.

- The **unity** of a document refers to its single purpose and its presentation of information. A paragraph that exhibits unity pertains to one idea and does not deviate from it.

- **Transitional phrases** are like road signs that help the reader understand the logic of a technical document. They build unity and clarify the connection between different sections of a document.

- If an organization presents **flawed or erroneous** information in a technical document, its credibility suffers and the organization may be subjected to unwanted consequences. As mentioned earlier, readers might sue if they suffer injury as a result of reviewing inaccurate information so it is important that documents be reviewed for technical accuracy by a subject matter expert.

- **Grammatical review** is important as readers often make judgements about an author's attention to detail or writing ability when they encounter writing-related errors.

- Just like a job seeker uses a cover letter to introduce his resume or qualifications to potential employers, a technical writer uses a **cover letter** to introduce the audience to a document and its ideas or recommendations. The cover letter is often the first piece of writing that a decision maker or potential client sees, so it is important to make a strong first impression.

- **Closing summaries, executive summaries, informative abstracts,** and **descriptive abstracts** are four types of summarized information often included in technical documents. An executive summary combines the main points of a report or proposal and is often the only section of a longer document that is read.

TECHNICAL WRITING POST-TEST

Directions: Carefully read each of the following 60 questions. Choose the best answer to each question and fill in the corresponding circle on the answer sheet. The Answer Key and Explanations can be found following this post-test.

---

1. Which of the following transitions is most appropriate for indicating a logical relationship between two ideas?
   A. Meanwhile
   B. Therefore
   C. Furthermore
   D. Specifically

2. The type of report that provides information regarding which tasks of a large project need to be completed is a(n)
   A. investigative report.
   B. feasibility report.
   C. progress report.
   D. test report.

3. All of the following are examples of white space EXCEPT:
   A. margins.
   B. space between paragraphs.
   C. headers.
   D. gutters.

4. All of the following are true of secondary research EXCEPT:
   A. It focuses solely on first-hand study.
   B. It can help researchers conduct more thorough primary research.
   C. It requires the use of reliable and credible sources.
   D. It is sometimes the only kind of research a technical writer performs.

5. All of the following are questions that a technical writer could use to evaluate a laboratory report for completeness EXCEPT:
   A. Are the recommendations justified?
   B. Is the purpose of the report clear?
   C. Is there enough evidence to support the findings in the analysis section?
   D. Will the audience have questions about the research methods section?

6. Which of the following may be too informal for a proposal?
   A. Question headings
   B. Statement headings
   C. Minor topic headings
   D. Major topic headings

7. Modifying the language used in a document to make it suitable for specific readers is an example of
   A. abstracted information.
   B. audience adaptation.
   C. documented research.
   D. audience analysis.

8. The primary purpose of a progress report is to
   A. report on a change in a project timeline.
   B. recommend a change in procedure.
   C. report on project completion.
   D. persuade a supervisor to approve additional resources for a project.

9. Which of the following does NOT need revision to correct an error in parallel structure?

A. Although the exact cause of diabetes is uncertain, medical experts believe that both heredity and environment are significant factors.

B. Achilles tendinitis is common among individuals who either play sports, such as basketball, or that suddenly increase the frequency of exercise.

C. People diagnosed with epilepsy usually take medication to reduce the frequency, intensity, and a dangerous accident related to a seizure.

D. Food and airborne allergies can cause symptoms that affect the skin, sinuses, digestive system, and breathing ability.

10. Which of the following does NOT require revision to correct an error in parallel structure?

A. Mass defect—or loss—occurs when protons and neutrons combine to form a nucleus.

B. The software was neither Windows compatible nor was it UNIX compatible.

C. The Hepatitis B virus is transmitted through blood, causes inflammation of the liver, and associated symptoms are flu-like in nature.

D. The Antikythera mechanism was used to predict eclipses, track the lunar calendar, and many people consider it the first analog computer.

11. Feasibility reports are most often written to help determine whether an idea is

A. successful and profitable.

B. necessary and reliable.

C. possible and practical.

D. new and promising.

In items 12–13, some part of the sentence or the entire sentence is underlined. Beneath each sentence, you will find four ways of phrasing the underlined part. Choice A repeats the original; the other three are different. If you think the original is better than any of the alternatives, choose answer A. Otherwise, choose one of the others. In selecting answers, pay attention to grammatical correctness, appropriate word choice, and smoothness and effectiveness of sentence construction.

12. Symptoms of lupus include a low red blood cell count and swollen feet and hands.

A. Symptoms of lupus include a low red blood cell count and swollen feet and hands.

B. People who suffer from lupus often have a low red blood cell count and show signs of swelling in the feet and hands.

C. Symptoms of lupus include anemia and edema.

D. Symptoms of lupus include a low red blood cell count as well as swollen feet and hands.

13. Following the experiment, the laboratory assistant reported that the sample showed no signs of contamination.

A. Following the experiment, the laboratory assistant reported that the sample showed no signs of contamination.

B. The laboratory assistant following the experiment reported that the sample showed no signs of contamination.

C. The laboratory assistant reported following the experiment that the sample showed no signs of contamination.

D. The laboratory assistant reported that the sample showed no signs of contamination following the experiment.

14. Equipment and procedures must be included in a laboratory report for the purpose of
    A. understanding results.
    B. duplicating the test.
    C. explaining the data.
    D. recalling information.

15. Which of the following should be addressed when editing an informal sales proposal for computer software solutions?
    A. The proposal does not note that its solution is not compatible with LINUX operating systems.
    B. The following sentence appears in the executive summary: "With a virtual desktop application, Company X can improve it's mobile computing capabilities by 59 percent."
    C. Both A and B
    D. Neither A nor B

In items 16–18, some part of the sentence or the entire sentence is underlined. Beneath each sentence, you will find four ways of phrasing the underlined part. Choice A repeats the original; the other three are different. If you think the original is better than any of the alternatives, choose answer A. Otherwise, choose one of the others. In selecting answers, pay attention to grammatical correctness, appropriate word choice, and smoothness and effectiveness of sentence construction.

16. Natural gas is often found in coal beds where it was created by microorganisms, and it consists mostly of methane.
    A. Natural gas is often found in coal beds where it was created by microorganisms, and it consists mostly of methane.
    B. Natural gas, which consists mostly of methane, is often found in coal beds where it was created by microorganisms.
    C. Natural gas is often found in coal beds, was created by microorganisms, and consists mostly of methane.
    D. Natural gas is often found in coal beds and consists mostly of methane where it was created by microorganisms.

17. The new arena next to the highway is touted for its state-of-the-art design.
    A. The new arena next to the highway is touted for its state of-the-art design.
    B. The new arena is next to the highway, and it is touted for its state-of-the-art design.
    C. The new arena is touted for a state-of-the-art design, and it is located next to the highway.
    D. The new arena, touted for its state-of-the-art design, is next to the highway.

18. The vice president was wrongly accused of mishandling the firm's largest marketing project by the stockholders.
    A. of mishandling the firm's largest marketing project by the stockholders.
    B. by the firm's largest marketing project of mishandling the stockholders.
    C. of mishandling by the stockholders in the firm's largest marketing project.
    D. by the stockholders of mishandling the firm's largest marketing project.

post-test

19. The main difference between laboratory reports and feasibility reports is that feasibility reports include
    A. informal language.
    B. instructions.
    C. test results.
    D. recommendations.

20. A document intended for an audience of subject matter experts would most likely be written in language that is
    A. highly technical.
    B. semi-technical.
    C. indefinite.
    D. subjective.

21. Clarity in a technical document can best be achieved by
    A. using abstract terms.
    B. eliminating transitions.
    C. including many appendixes.
    D. writing in parallel structure.

22. A word on a line by itself at the end of a column is known as a(n)
    A. orphan.
    B. header.
    C. outlier.
    D. widow.

23. A memo regarding salary cuts would most likely be organized
    A. functionally.
    B. indirectly.
    C. spatially.
    D. directly.

24. Which of the following visuals would be appropriate to use when showing steps in a process?
    I. Flowchart
    II. Schematic diagram
    III. Representational diagram
    A. I only
    B. III only
    C. I and II only
    D. I, II, and III

25. The glossary of a technical document is typically placed
    A. in an appendix.
    B. before the introduction.
    C. in the front matter.
    D. after the bibliography.

26. A visual that shows how the phases of a project relate to one another is known as a
    A. prose table.
    B. pictogram.
    C. bar graph.
    D. Gantt chart.

27. What is the purpose of the conclusion in a feasibility report?
    A. Express an opinion
    B. Interpret the findings
    C. Introduce alternatives
    D. Review the costs

28. All of the following are methods for improving the unity of a document EXCEPT
    A. using transitions.
    B. repeating key points.
    C. using enumeration.
    D. explaining word origins.

29. A technical writer who wants to show what percentage of total monthly sales was generated by each department would most likely use a(n)
   A. tree chart.
   B. pie graph.
   C. line graph.
   D. organizational chart.

30. Which of the following visuals is most appropriate for nontechnical readers?
   A. Multiline graph
   B. Schematic diagram
   C. Pictogram
   D. PERT chart

31. All of the following are elements of the audience to consider when writing technical documents EXCEPT
   A. methods.
   B. attitude.
   C. needs.
   D. culture.

32. What is the customary place in a document to include a descriptive abstract?
   A. At the end of the body
   B. In the conclusion
   C. On the title page
   D. In the appendix

33. Which of the following is included in the back matter of a long proposal?
   A. Bibliography
   B. Cost analysis
   C. Conclusion
   D. Rationale

34. A line graph is most appropriate for showing
   A. parts of a whole.
   B. changes over time.
   C. phases of a project.
   D. sequence of events.

35. Unlike other types of technical documents, proposals are primarily written to
   A. persuade readers.
   B. describe products.
   C. analyze audiences.
   D. compare options.

36. Which of the following guidelines applies to preparing appendixes for a technical document?
   A. Use numbers to identify appendixes.
   B. Use a separate appendix for each major item.
   C. Limit each appendix to one page in length.
   D. Arrange appendixes in order of importance.

37. The conclusion of a sales proposal would most likely include
   A. a discussion of a competitor's weaknesses.
   B. persuasive statistics not presented in the body.
   C. background information about procedures used.
   D. a persuasive statement about a company's strengths.

38. Which of the following is written to request approval for hiring an additional part-time employee?
   A. Formal internal proposal
   B. Progress report
   C. Routine internal proposal
   D. Feasibility report

post-test

Questions 39 and 40 refer to the following group of numbered sentences:

1. Every spot holds many identical DNA strands.
2. The spots reflect a unique DNA sequence and represents one gene.
3. A Microarray is a technique that scientists use to evaluate whether genes are turned on and off.
4. Computer databases are used to keep track of the DNA sequence and position of each spot.
5. Rows and columns comprising thousands of spots are arranged on a glass surface.

39. If the sentences are reorganized into a cohesive paragraph, which represents the fourth sentence?
    A. 1
    B. 3
    C. 4
    D. 2

40. Which transition word or phrase should be used to join sentences 1 and 2?
    A. However
    B. And
    C. In sum
    D. For example

41. Information in a technical document is best divided into logical pieces by
    A. titles.
    B. headings.
    C. footers.
    D. headers.

42. A status report provides information about accomplishments related to
    A. multiple departments in an organization.
    B. multiple projects in a given period.
    C. one employee in an organization.
    D. one project during a given period.

43. Which section of a long proposal is most often the only one read by an audience?
    A. Costs
    B. Methods
    C. Executive Summary
    D. Statement of Problem

44. Which of the following is the best way to determine the reliability of a printed source?
    A. Publisher
    B. Readability
    C. Soft evidence
    D. Publication date

45. Which of the following is the primary benefit of headings in a technical document?
    A. Improve readability
    B. Clarify style and tone
    C. Enhance visual design
    D. Summarize main points

46. Feasibility reports should include all of the following EXCEPT
    A. a review of all alternatives.
    B. specific recommendations.
    C. procedures and instructions.
    D. an interpretation of various options.

47. Which of the following is content appropriate for a grant proposal?
    A. Problem statement
    B. Budget and schedule
    C. Qualifications
    D. All of the above

48. In which of the following situations would a drawing be most appropriate to include in a report?
- **A.** To record the development of an event over time
- **B.** To save space and add visual appeal for laypersons
- **C.** To show cutaway views of internal mechanisms
- **D.** To show distances and locations of specific sites

49. A cover letter for a formal proposal composed in response to an RFP should contain all of the following EXCEPT a
- **A.** concise overview of the solution.
- **B.** formal salutation and professional closing.
- **C.** summary of benefits for the client.
- **D.** paragraph describing the features of the solution.

50. Which of the following sentences does NOT need to be revised for clarity?
- **A.** The CEO told human resources many times that the firm needed another sales agent.
- **B.** Being so familiar with medical equipment, I would appreciate your assistance with the sales presentation for the pediatric clinic.
- **C.** The office manager resents the vice president because he performed poorly during the first quarter of the year.
- **D.** All active-duty police officers are not required to submit daily trip reports.

51. Terms included in a document's glossary are
- **A.** limited to technological concepts.
- **B.** listed in the order they appear.
- **C.** arranged alphabetically.
- **D.** explained in full detail.

52. Which of the following would a trained bulldozer driver use to review safety procedures?
- **A.** Tutorials
- **B.** Service manual
- **C.** Training manual
- **D.** Operator manual

53. Which of the following communication situations would require writers to establish a common goal, manage conflict, and develop a system for version control?
- **A.** A progress report written by a project manager to update management on a change to the project schedule
- **B.** A sales proposal written by a team of subject matter experts in response to a government request for proposal (RFP)
- **C.** A description of a new performance review process written by the HR manager
- **D.** An informal sales proposal written by a sales associate for a well-known client

54. Which of the following elements of a long proposal would include the problem statement?
- **A.** Product description
- **B.** Cost analysis
- **C.** Background
- **D.** Site preparation

55. Which of the following best indicates what an author wants a reader to know, believe, or do after reading a technical document?
- **A.** Executive summary
- **B.** Topic
- **C.** Purpose statement
- **D.** Outline

post-test

56. The main difference between an informative abstract and an executive summary is that executive summaries are
    A. presented orally.
    B. slightly persuasive.
    C. placed in the conclusion.
    D. always 200–250 words.

57. Which of the following most improves the validity of information used in a technical document?
    A. Statistical data
    B. Website graphics
    C. Multiple sources
    D. Website sponsorship

58. The front matter of a long proposal includes all of the following EXCEPT a(n)
    A. title page.
    B. introduction.
    C. cover letter.
    D. list of figures.

59. The major difference between procedures and manuals is that manuals
    A. assert opinions.
    B. specify actions.
    C. discuss results.
    D. provide guidelines.

60. When writing an informative abstract, assume that the audience consists of
    A. readers with different levels of knowledge.
    B. academics from different subject areas.
    C. highly technical subject-matter experts.
    D. readers with no technical interests.

ANSWER KEY AND EXPLANATIONS

1. B	**13.** D	**25.** D	**37.** D	**49.** D
2. C	**14.** B	**26.** D	**38.** C	**50.** A
3. C	**15.** C	**27.** B	**39.** D	**51.** C
4. A	**16.** B	**28.** D	**40.** B	**52.** D
5. B	**17.** D	**29.** B	**41.** B	**53.** B
6. A	**18.** D	**30.** C	**42.** D	**54.** C
7. B	**19.** D	**31.** A	**43.** C	**55.** C
8. C	**20.** A	**32.** C	**44.** A	**56.** B
9. A	**21.** D	**33.** A	**45.** A	**57.** C
10. A	**22.** A	**34.** B	**46.** C	**58.** B
11. C	**23.** B	**35.** A	**47.** D	**59.** D
12. A	**24.** C	**36.** B	**48.** C	**60.** A

1. **The correct answer is B.** Transitions such as *therefore*, *consequently*, and *as a result* indicate logical relationships. Choice A is a transition used to show time. Choice C is used when an additional point is being made. Choice D is appropriate for introducing examples.

2. **The correct answer is C.** Progress reports keep supervisors up to date on the status of a project. Choice A is a report written when information is requested about a particular subject. Choice B is a report that enables executives to determine whether an idea is possible and practical. A test report (choice D) is similar to a laboratory report but smaller and less formal.

3. **The correct answer is C.** White space is sometimes referred to as negative space because it is devoid of text or content. Choices A, B, and D all contain examples of space in a document that do not contain content. Although white space might be present above or below a header, a header contains content, and thus, is not, itself, an example of white space.

4. **The correct answer is A.** Firsthand study (sometimes called field research) is within the scope of primary research, not secondary. When technical writers conduct secondary research (sometimes called library research), they review studies conducted and data gathered by other researchers. They may also review articles, books and other sources of information. Secondary research can be very useful in guiding technical writers who are conducting primary research because secondary research gives technical writers a sense of what information is available, what methods have been used, and what other people have discovered. Since the information gathered will be used to support or refute findings or inform a research study, it must be extracted from credible sources. Choice D is incorrect because technical writers often rely solely on secondary research to draw conclusions.

5. **The correct answer is B.** Choice B asks the technical writer to consider whether the language is appropriate for the established purpose. It does not consider whether the

writer has provided enough information for the document to achieve its purpose. choices A and C focus on whether the report has provided sufficient and appropriate evidence. choice D presents a question that a technical writer could use to consider whether additional steps are necessary.

6. **The correct answer is A.** Question headings are useful in drawing readers into reading about a specific topic, but they are too informal for some documents, such as proposals. Statement headings are more detailed than minor and major topic headings. However, choices B, C, and D are all appropriate for proposals.

7. **The correct answer is B.** Audience adaptation refers to modifying the information in a technical document to make it appropriate for a specific audience. Audience adaptation often occurs after a writer has analyzed the audience, so choice D is incorrect. Abstracts, choice A, and documented research, choice C, are elements of many technical documents, but neither refers to changing the language to suit the needs of readers.

8. **The correct answer is C.** Progress reports do note changes to the project timeline when a project team encounters setbacks, but that is not the primary purpose of a progress report. A progress report provides an update on the status of a project under completion. Choice B is more appropriate for a recommendation report while choice D is more appropriate for a short, informal proposal.

9. **The correct answer is A.** Choice A is written in parallel structure, which means that all elements in the sentence are alike in both form and function. Choice B is incorrect because "that suddenly" should be "who suddenly" to match "who either play." Choice C is incorrect because "a dangerous accident" should be changed to "danger." Choice D is

incorrect because "breathing ability" should be changed to "airways."

10. **The correct answer is A.** Parallel structure requires words or phrases in sequence to exhibit the same form. In choice B, "nor was it" should be replaced by "nor." In choices C and D, the last phrase in the sequence does not begin with a verb even though the first and second phrases do.

11. **The correct answer is C.** Possible *and* practical are the key ideas behind feasibility reports. An idea may be possible or promising, but whether it is practical determines if a company will go through with it. Choices A, B, and D are incorrect.

12. **The correct answer is A.** Choice A is written concisely, is grammatically correct, and contains simple language that is not likely to confuse an audience who is unfamiliar with medical terminology. Choice B adds unnecessary words that do not help the reader understand the meaning of the sentence. Similarly, the transitional phrase "as well as" in choice D is wordy. Choice C uses medical jargon that might confuse general audiences.

13. **The correct answer is D.** In the original, the underlined content represents a misplaced modifier. A modifier is a phrase that provides more information about other words or phrases in a sentence. Modifiers must be placed as close as possible to the words or phrases that they modify. In this example, the modifier "following the experiment," modifies the uncontaminated sample and so it must be placed as close as possible to the phrase. In choices A, B, and C, the modifier is not placed in close proximi"ty to the content it modifies.

14. **The correct answer is B.** Duplicating the test requires clearly written information about the equipment used and the procedures

followed. Results and Conclusions are two other sections of a lab report that apply to choices A and C.

15. **The correct answer is C.** Choice A requires attention because it identifies a limit of the potential solution. The technical writer should add a note indicating that the solution is not compatible with the LINUX operating system. Choice B contains a common grammatical mistake—a misplaced apostrophe. To indicate possession, the writer should use "its" instead of "it's."

16. **The correct answer is B.** Choice B moves the information about methane closer to natural gas and places emphasis on the detail about coal beds. In choice C, the verb tense changes from present to past. The pronoun "it" in choice D is too far from natural gas, so the sentence is confusing.

17. **The correct answer is D.** The pronoun "its" needs to be close to "aren" a for the sake of clarity. Choices A and B have the pronoun too far from "arena." Choice C is unnecessarily wordy.

18. **The correct answer is D.** The stockholders did the accusing, so "by the stockholders" should be near "accused." Choices A and C fail to do this. Choice B falsely changes the entire meaning of the sentence.

19. **The correct answer is D.** Feasibility reports include a recommendations section, but laboratory reports do not. Feasibility reports most likely include formal, rather than informal, language. Lab reports include procedures and test results, so choices B and C are incorrect.

20. **The correct answer is A.** A document containing highly technical language is most appropriate for an audience that consists of subject matter experts, who would not require extensive explanations of data or terms. Semi-technical language is appropriate for an audience that consists of people with some technical knowledge but who are not quite as knowledgeable as experts. Technical writing language is precise and objective, so choices C and D are incorrect.

21. **The correct answer is D.** Writing in parallel structure, eliminating excess words, and sequencing information can enhance clarity in a document. Concrete terms are clearer than abstract ones, so choice A is incorrect. Transitions improve clarity, so choice B is incorrect. Appendixes do not necessarily improve clarity, choice C, and too many appendixes clutter a document with irrelevant information.

22. **The correct answer is A.** When using columns in a document, orphans and widows should be avoided. An orphan is a word on a line by itself at the end of a column. A widow is a single line carried over to the top of a column. A header is information placed at the top of every page, such as the date and page number. An outlier is a statistical term.

23. **The correct answer is B.** Indirect patterns are used in memos when presenting bad news to employees, such as layoffs and salary cuts. Direct patterns present the main point first, and indirect patterns present the main point last. Choices A and C are not terms used for the structure of memos.

24. **The correct answer is C.** Flowcharts and schematic diagrams are appropriate for showing steps in a process or the relationships in a system. A representational diagram presents a realistic but simplified illustration of an item. Choices A, B, and D are incorrect.

25. **The correct answer is D.** A document's glossary is usually placed after the bibliography and appendixes. Choice A is incorrect because a glossary is separate from the appendixes. Choices B and C are incorrect

because the glossary is part of a document's back matter.

26. **The correct answer is D.** Gantt charts show how the phases of a project interrelate. Prose tables, choice A, organize verbal descriptions or instructions. Pictograms, choice B, are tables with representative symbols. Bar graphs show comparisons, so choice C is incorrect.

27. **The correct answer is B.** The conclusion of a feasibility report interprets the findings of the study. The recommendation section is used to express the author's opinion, so choice A is incorrect. Options and costs are reviewed in the body of the report, so choices C and D are incorrect.

28. **The correct answer is D.** Numbering steps in a process and using transitions are both effective ways to enhance unity, so choices A and C are incorrect. Repeating key terms and major points, choice B, helps the reader keep the purpose of a document in mind. Explaining word origins, choice D, is appropriate for some documents, but it does not necessarily improve unity.

29. **The correct answer is B.** A pie graph is used to relate parts to a whole, so it is the best visual for showing what percentage of total sales each department generated. Tree charts, choice A, show how different aspects of an idea relate to one another. Line graphs, choice C, show how things change. An organizational chart, choice D, would show how each department in a group is connected.

30. **The correct answer is C.** A pictogram uses symbols instead of lines and bars to represent numerical amounts, so it is appropriate for nontechnical readers. A PERT chart, choice D, is similar to a Gantt chart and is used to schedule activities on a project. Choices A and B are less appropriate for nontechnical readers.

31. **The correct answer is A.** When performing an audience analysis, a technical writer should consider the attitude readers have toward the subject matter as well as the needs of the audience. Culture is a consideration when an international audience will read a document. Method is not an aspect of audience analysis, so choice A is the correct answer.

32. **The correct answer is C.** Descriptive abstracts are included on the title page of documents. Choices A and B are where closing summaries are inserted. The appendix is not a typical location for summaries or abstracts, so choice D is incorrect.

33. **The correct answer is A.** The back matter of a long proposal includes the appendixes, bibliography, and glossary. Among other information, the body of a long proposal includes the cost analysis, rationale, and conclusion. Choices B, C, and D are incorrect.

34. **The correct answer is B.** Changes over time are best illustrated with a line graph. Choice A is shown in a pie graph, and choice C involves a Gantt chart. A sequence of events, choice D, is indicated in a flowchart.

35. **The correct answer is A.** Proposals differ from other technical writing because their purpose is to persuade readers. Product description is an aspect of many different kinds of technical documents, so choice B is incorrect. Audience analysis occurs with most technical documents, so choice C is incorrect. Feasibility reports often compare options, so choice D is incorrect.

36. **The correct answer is B.** Each appendix should relate to one major item. Letters are used to identify each appendix, so choice A is incorrect. Appendixes may be longer than one page, and they should be arranged in the order in which they are mentioned in the text, so choices C and D are incorrect.

37. **The correct answer is D.** It is appropriate to include a persuasive pitch for a company, product, or service in the conclusion of a sales proposal. The conclusion should not be used to introduce new statistics or other information not presented in the body, so choice B is incorrect. A competitor's weaknesses and background information is not appropriate in a sales proposal conclusion.

38. **The correct answer is C.** Routine internal proposals are written for minor spending requests and permission to hire new employees. Choice A is used when requesting large amounts of capital. Progress reports describe how a project is going, and feasibility reports discuss the practicality of an idea.

39. **The correct answer is D.** If chronological sequencing is employed, the correct order of sentences should be 3, 5, 1, 2, 4.

40. **The correct answer is B.** Both sentences provide descriptive content about what a spot contains, thus, they can be joined using a transition that indicates addition. Choice A contains a transition word that indicates contrast, which does not accurately describe the relationship between sentences 1 and 2 as they both describe the spot. Choice C is used to summarize and D is used to clarify a point through the use of example.

41. **The correct answer is B.** Headings serve to divide information in a document into logical pieces easily recognized by readers. Headers, choice D, and footers, choice C, are at the top and bottom of pages and usually indicate the page number and date of a document. Titles, choice A, provide readers with an indication of the subject of a document.

42. **The correct answer is D.** A status report, which is also called a progress report, summarizes the accomplishments related to one project during a given period. A periodic activity report summarizes general activities in a given period, which may relate to one employee or multiple departments in an organization.

43. **The correct answer is C.** The executive summary combines the main points of a proposal, and it is often the only section of a longer document ever read by an audience. Executive summaries follow the same sequence as the full document, but they are 10 percent of the length. Choices A, B, and D are proposal sections, but a concise version of each are included in the executive summary.

44. **The correct answer is A.** A printed source published by a university, professional organization, or museum is most likely reliable. Readability, choice B, helps the audience understand information but does not increase reliability. Soft evidence is less reliable than hard evidence, so choice C is incorrect. The publication date, choice D, is important in determining whether a source is current, but it is less important when determining reliability.

45. **The correct answer is A.** Headings improve the readability of technical documents by helping readers easily locate information and recognize when topics have changed. Style and tone may be illustrated by document titles but less so with headings. Although headings break up the monotony of paragraphs, they do not necessarily enhance the visual appeal of a document like graphs and charts do. Headings are not so specific that they summarize main points, but they do indicate the subject addressed in a section.

46. **The correct answer is C.** A feasibility report should include a review of possible alternatives, specific recommendations, and an interpretation of options. Procedures and instructions are not elements of feasibility reports, so choices A, B, and D are incorrect.

47. **The correct answer is D.** Even though grantmakers often have very specific and unique requirements, technical writers can expect to be asked to provide insight into project logistics. Like other types of proposals, grant proposals have a persuasive purpose; the technical writer must convince the grantmaker that the proposed project has value.

48. **The correct answer is C.** A drawing is effective in a report when a cutaway view of an internal mechanism is needed. Choice A calls for a photograph rather than a drawing. Choice B describes why symbols and icons are included in some reports. Maps are useful to illustrate locations and distances (choice D).

49. **The correct answer is D.** A paragraph describing the details of a solution is inappropriate for two reasons. Firstly, a proposal presents persuasive content and its cover letter should be similarly persuasive; thus it should focus on benefits for the client, rather than technical specifications. The technical specifications appear in the body of the proposal. Secondly, a cover letter is intended to provide a concise statement of value for the client. A paragraph is too lengthy. Choice A represents a stronger design choice. Choice B is a cover letter element that contributes to a professional, courteous tone.

50. **The correct answer is A.** Choice A is written clearly, while choices B, C, and D are not. Choice B should be reworded to say "since you are so familiar." It is unclear in choice C whether he refers to the manager or the vice president. "All" and "not" in choice D create a confusing sentence.

51. **The correct answer is C.** Glossary terms are arranged alphabetically just like a dictionary. Terms are typically technical ones used in the field, (technology, medicine, business, or science), so choice A is incorrect. Appendixes

are listed in the order they appear, but not glossary terms, so choice B is incorrect. Items in a glossary should have clear and concise explanations, so choice D is incorrect.

52. **The correct answer is D.** Trained operators of construction and manufacturing equipment turn to operator manuals for reviewing safety information. Tutorials, choice A, and training manuals, choice C, are for unskilled users of a product or piece of equipment. Service manuals, choice B, are used by repair technicians.

53. **The correct answer is B.** Common goals, conflict management, and version control are all requirements of collaborative writing. A collaborative document is one that is produced by more than one person. Choice B is the only choice that indicates that the written document will be produced by more than one author.

54. **The correct answer is C.** The background section of a long proposal describes the problem that a proposal attempts to address. A general description of the product or service offered by a company is included in choice A. An itemization of cost estimates is provided in choice B. Site preparation refers to any modifications that are necessary to a customer's facilities.

55. **The correct answer is C.** The purpose of any kind of technical communication is what readers should know, believe, or do after reading a document. Although an executive summary, choice A, may include the purpose of a document, it serves to present a concise version of the full document. The topic is the subject matter of the document and does not necessarily indicate the author's purpose, so choice B is incorrect. Choice D is incorrect because the outline helps organize information and does not specify an author's objective.

56. **The correct answer is B.** Executive summaries are slightly persuasive because the writer is trying to convince readers of what to think or do. Abstracts and summaries are both typically read, so choice A is incorrect. Only a closing summary is placed in the conclusion, so choice C is incorrect. Informative abstracts are always 200–250 words, while executive summaries are 10 percent of the document's length.

57. **The correct answer is C.** Multiple sources improve the validity of information presented in a technical document. Statistical data may be necessary in many documents, but if the data comes from only one source, it may not be reliable. The graphics and sponsorship of a website do not improve the validity of information on the site.

58. **The correct answer is B.** The front matter of a long proposal includes the cover letter, title page, table of contents, and list of figures.

The introduction is part of the body of a long proposal. However, short proposals are divided into introduction, body, and conclusion.

59. **The correct answer is D.** Manuals provide guidelines and serve as a reference tool for users. Procedures specify what actions group members must take during certain situations, so choice B is incorrect. Manuals are not persuasive, so choice A is incorrect. Results are not discussed in manuals, so choice C is incorrect.

60. **The correct answer is A.** Informative abstracts are written for general audiences that consist of readers with different levels of knowledge. Informative abstracts should not be written only for experts and academics, so choices B and C are incorrect. Many readers of abstracts do not have the time to read an entire report, but that does not mean they have no interest at all.

answers post-test

Principles of Statistics

OVERVIEW

Statistics is the branch of math that deals with collecting, analyzing, and interpreting data. Data refers to a set of values that represent information of interest. The DSST® Principles of Statistics exam covers topics such as probability, correlation, regression, sampling distribution, and inferential statistics. This chapter will review everything you need to know to approach your DSST Principles of Statistics exam with confidence.

Chapter 7

DIAGNOSTIC TEST ANSWER SHEET

1. Ⓐ Ⓑ Ⓒ Ⓓ   5. Ⓐ Ⓑ Ⓒ Ⓓ   9. Ⓐ Ⓑ Ⓒ Ⓓ   13. Ⓐ Ⓑ Ⓒ Ⓓ   17. Ⓐ Ⓑ Ⓒ Ⓓ
2. Ⓐ Ⓑ Ⓒ Ⓓ   6. Ⓐ Ⓑ Ⓒ Ⓓ   10. Ⓐ Ⓑ Ⓒ Ⓓ   14. Ⓐ Ⓑ Ⓒ Ⓓ   18. Ⓐ Ⓑ Ⓒ Ⓓ
3. Ⓐ Ⓑ Ⓒ Ⓓ   7. Ⓐ Ⓑ Ⓒ Ⓓ   11. Ⓐ Ⓑ Ⓒ Ⓓ   15. Ⓐ Ⓑ Ⓒ Ⓓ   19. Ⓐ Ⓑ Ⓒ Ⓓ
4. Ⓐ Ⓑ Ⓒ Ⓓ   8. Ⓐ Ⓑ Ⓒ Ⓓ   12. Ⓐ Ⓑ Ⓒ Ⓓ   16. Ⓐ Ⓑ Ⓒ Ⓓ   20. Ⓐ Ⓑ Ⓒ Ⓓ

POST-TEST ANSWER SHEET

1. Ⓐ Ⓑ Ⓒ Ⓓ   13. Ⓐ Ⓑ Ⓒ Ⓓ   25. Ⓐ Ⓑ Ⓒ Ⓓ   37. Ⓐ Ⓑ Ⓒ Ⓓ   49. Ⓐ Ⓑ Ⓒ Ⓓ
2. Ⓐ Ⓑ Ⓒ Ⓓ   14. Ⓐ Ⓑ Ⓒ Ⓓ   26. Ⓐ Ⓑ Ⓒ Ⓓ   38. Ⓐ Ⓑ Ⓒ Ⓓ   50. Ⓐ Ⓑ Ⓒ Ⓓ
3. Ⓐ Ⓑ Ⓒ Ⓓ   15. Ⓐ Ⓑ Ⓒ Ⓓ   27. Ⓐ Ⓑ Ⓒ Ⓓ   39. Ⓐ Ⓑ Ⓒ Ⓓ   51. Ⓐ Ⓑ Ⓒ Ⓓ
4. Ⓐ Ⓑ Ⓒ Ⓓ   16. Ⓐ Ⓑ Ⓒ Ⓓ   28. Ⓐ Ⓑ Ⓒ Ⓓ   40. Ⓐ Ⓑ Ⓒ Ⓓ   52. Ⓐ Ⓑ Ⓒ Ⓓ
5. Ⓐ Ⓑ Ⓒ Ⓓ   17. Ⓐ Ⓑ Ⓒ Ⓓ   29. Ⓐ Ⓑ Ⓒ Ⓓ   41. Ⓐ Ⓑ Ⓒ Ⓓ   53. Ⓐ Ⓑ Ⓒ Ⓓ
6. Ⓐ Ⓑ Ⓒ Ⓓ   18. Ⓐ Ⓑ Ⓒ Ⓓ   30. Ⓐ Ⓑ Ⓒ Ⓓ   42. Ⓐ Ⓑ Ⓒ Ⓓ   54. Ⓐ Ⓑ Ⓒ Ⓓ
7. Ⓐ Ⓑ Ⓒ Ⓓ   19. Ⓐ Ⓑ Ⓒ Ⓓ   31. Ⓐ Ⓑ Ⓒ Ⓓ   43. Ⓐ Ⓑ Ⓒ Ⓓ   55. Ⓐ Ⓑ Ⓒ Ⓓ
8. Ⓐ Ⓑ Ⓒ Ⓓ   20. Ⓐ Ⓑ Ⓒ Ⓓ   32. Ⓐ Ⓑ Ⓒ Ⓓ   44. Ⓐ Ⓑ Ⓒ Ⓓ   56. Ⓐ Ⓑ Ⓒ Ⓓ
9. Ⓐ Ⓑ Ⓒ Ⓓ   21. Ⓐ Ⓑ Ⓒ Ⓓ   33. Ⓐ Ⓑ Ⓒ Ⓓ   45. Ⓐ Ⓑ Ⓒ Ⓓ   57. Ⓐ Ⓑ Ⓒ Ⓓ
10. Ⓐ Ⓑ Ⓒ Ⓓ   22. Ⓐ Ⓑ Ⓒ Ⓓ   34. Ⓐ Ⓑ Ⓒ Ⓓ   46. Ⓐ Ⓑ Ⓒ Ⓓ   58. Ⓐ Ⓑ Ⓒ Ⓓ
11. Ⓐ Ⓑ Ⓒ Ⓓ   23. Ⓐ Ⓑ Ⓒ Ⓓ   35. Ⓐ Ⓑ Ⓒ Ⓓ   47. Ⓐ Ⓑ Ⓒ Ⓓ   59. Ⓐ Ⓑ Ⓒ Ⓓ
12. Ⓐ Ⓑ Ⓒ Ⓓ   24. Ⓐ Ⓑ Ⓒ Ⓓ   36. Ⓐ Ⓑ Ⓒ Ⓓ   48. Ⓐ Ⓑ Ⓒ Ⓓ   60. Ⓐ Ⓑ Ⓒ Ⓓ

answer sheet

PRINCIPLES OF STATISTICS DIAGNOSTIC TEST

> **Directions:** Carefully read each of the following 20 questions. Choose the best answer to each question and fill in the corresponding circle on the answer sheet. The Answer Key and Explanations can be found following this Diagnostic Test.

1. The heights of seven people, in inches, were measured to be 51", 59", 59", 59", 59", 59", and 60". Which of the following describes the value of 51" in this data set?
   A. Mean
   B. Median
   C. Mode
   D. Outlier

2. A committee consists of 10 people. From among these, a subcommittee of 3 people is to be formed. How many different subcommittees are possible?
   A. 30
   B. 120
   C. 720
   D. 1000

3. A student receives a score of 86 on an exam for which the class distribution is approximated by the normal curve $N(80,5)$. What is this student's z-score?
   A. -1.2
   B. 1.0125
   C. 1.2
   D. 6

4. There are two new antibiotics, Drug A and Drug B, available to treat bacterial bronchitis. Researchers want to know whether either one of these is more effective than the other. If the proportion of bacterial bronchitis patients who are cured by these drugs are ρ_a and ρ_b, respectively, which pair of null and alternative hypotheses best represent this scenario?

   A. $H_0 : \rho_a < \rho_b$ and $H_a : \rho_a \neq \rho_b$
   B. $H_0 : \rho_a = \rho_b$ and $H_a : \rho_a > \rho_b$
   C. $H_0 : \rho_a = \rho_b$ and $H_a : \rho_a < \rho_b$
   D. $H_0 : \rho_a = \rho_b$ and $H_a : \rho \neq \rho_b$

5. A standard 6-sided die is rolled. What is the probability that it shows either an even number or a 3?
   A. $\dfrac{1}{6}$
   B. $\dfrac{4}{5}$
   C. $\dfrac{1}{2}$
   D. $\dfrac{2}{3}$

6. Which of the following is NOT a possible value of the correlation coefficient r?
   A. -1.21
   B. -0.85
   C. 0
   D. 0.91

7. In a population of 10 million bacteria, the average amount of time it takes for a single bacterium to divide itself is 37 minutes, and the standard deviation of the times is 2 minutes. If the times are normally distributed, in what range of times would you expect to find approximately 95% of the values?
   A. 33–37 minutes
   B. 35–39 minutes
   C. 33–41 minutes
   D. 31–43 minutes

8. The mean of a population is 2, and the standard deviation is 0.5. If the sample size is 100, which of the following best represents the sampling distribution of the mean for this population?

    A. $N(2,0.05)$

    B. $B(2,0.05)$

    C. $N(2,0.5)$

    D. $B(2,0.5)$

9. In a one-sample t-test, a researcher chooses a significance level of $a = 0.01$. The calculated t-statistic is 2.91, which corresponds to a p-value of 0.00675. Since $p < a$, the null hypothesis is rejected. What is the probability that this rejection was erroneous, i.e., that the null hypothesis is, in fact, true?

    A. 0.675%

    B. 1%

    C. 2.91%

    D. 5%

10. Based on a set of data points with x-values ranging from 1 to 15, a least-squares regression calculation produces the line $y = \frac{4}{5}x + 3$. Using this model, one can predict the value of y when $x = 20$. What is the predicted value? Is this an example of interpolation or extrapolation?

    A. 19; interpolation

    B. 19; extrapolation

    C. 21.25; interpolation

    D. 21.25; extrapolation

11. A pre-election survey asks for the age and state of residence of likely voters. What data types are being collected in this survey?

    A. Categorical only

    B. Categorical and ordinal only

    C. Categorical and numerical only

    D. Categorical, numerical, and ordinal

12. A farmer wants to test 4 different fertilizers to see which one produces the tallest tomato plants. He divides his field into 4 sections, and uses a different fertilizer in each. At the end of the growing season, he measures the heights of a sample of tomato plants from each section, and finds the means of each sample. What type of hypothesis test would be most appropriate for him to conduct?

    A. ANOVA

    B. t-test for a mean

    C. t-test for the difference of two means

    D. z-test for a proportion

13. Which of the following is a valid discrete probability distribution?

    A.

X	1	2	3
$P(X)$	0.5	−0.3	0.8

    B.

X	1	2	3
$P(X)$	0.4	0.4	0.1

    C.

X	1	2	3
$P(X)$	0.7	0.1	0.3

    D.

X	1	2	3
$P(X)$	0.5	0.3	0.2

14. Which of the following scatter plots shows the strongest positive correlation?

A.

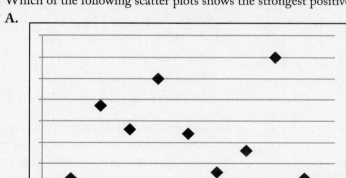

B.

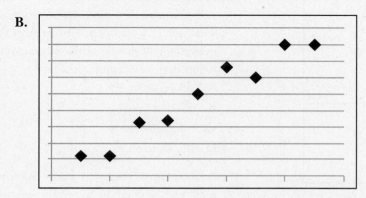

C.

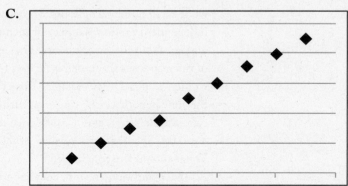

D.

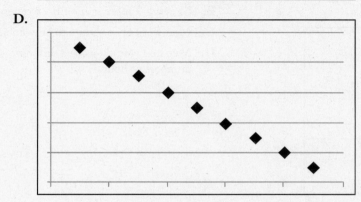

diagnostic test

15. Consider the following boxplots, which represent data sets A and B, respectively:

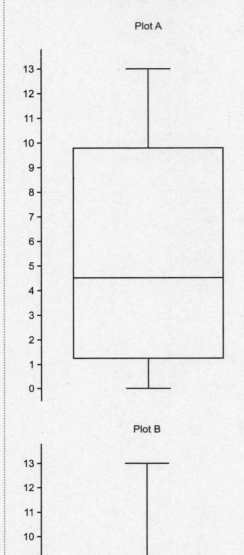

Plot A

Plot B

Which of the following statements about these data sets is false?

A. A has a larger median than B.

B. A has a larger range than B.

C. A has a larger IQR than B.

D. A has a larger 3rd quartile than B.

16. In a sample of 100 people from a population of 1,000, it is found that 58 of them would prefer to drive an SUV rather than a sedan. Given that the 95% of normally distributed data lies between −1.96 and 1.96 standard deviations from the mean, what is a 95% confidence interval for the percentage of people in the larger population that would prefer a sedan?

A. 38.9% to 45.1%

B. 37.1% to 46.9%

C. 32.3% to 51.7%

D 48.3% to 67.7%

17. A sociologist wants to know whether men and women in a certain country work equal numbers of hours. She surveys independent random samples of men and women about their work hours. The mean of the responses from men is μ_M and from women is μ_W. The sociologist then tests the null hypothesis $H_0 : \mu_M = \mu_W$ using a two-sample t-test, and a confidence level $a = 0.05$. She obtains a p-value of 0.028. What should she conclude?

A. Men and women work equal hours.

B. Men work more hours than women.

C. Men work fewer hours than women.

D. Men and women work a different numbers of hours.

18. A biased coin has a $\frac{3}{5}$ probability of landing on heads when flipped. If the coin is flipped 250 times, which expression represents the expected value of the number of heads obtained in these flips?

    A. $250 \cdot \frac{2}{5}$

    B. $\left(\frac{3}{5}\right)^{250}$

    C. $250 \cdot \frac{3}{5}$

    D. $\frac{3}{5}$

19. Linear regression is performed on a data set consisting of ordered pairs (x,y). The r^2 value is calculated to be 0.89. Which of the following conclusions is implied by this result?

    A. x and y are strongly correlated

    B. x and y are positively correlated

    C. x and y are negatively correlated

    D. x and y are not correlated

20. A school principal wants to find out how many students are in favor of a new "healthy food in school" initiative. Which of the following is the best way to choose a sample of students from among the entire population of the school?

    A. On a typical school day, have every freshman language arts class complete a survey that asks for their opinions.

    B. On a typical school day, ask every student waiting in line to buy lunch at the cafeteria for their opinion.

    C. On a typical school day, stop every fifth student who walks into the building and ask his or her opinion on the topic.

    D. On a day when all seniors are absent, stop every fifth student who walks into the building and ask his or her opinion on the topic.

ANSWER KEY AND EXPLANATIONS

1. D	5. D	9. B	13. D	17. D
2. B	6. A	10. B	14. C	18. C
3. C	7. C	11. C	15. B	19. A
4. D	8. A	12. A	16. C	20. C

1. **The correct answer is D.** An outlier is a value in a data set that is significantly far away from where the rest of the data lies. Since all of the other values are either 59 or 60, 51 is considered an outlier. Choice A is incorrect since the mean is 58. Choice B is incorrect since the median is 59. Choice C is incorrect since the mode is 59.

2. **The correct answer is B.** Since the order in which the 3 people are chosen does not matter, and each person cannot be chosen more than once, this problem is represented by the combination $C(10,3)$. We can then calculate $C(10,3) = \dfrac{10!}{7!3!} = \dfrac{10 \cdot 9 \cdot 8}{3 \cdot 2 \cdot 1} = 120$. If the order did matter, the answer would be $P(10,3) = 720$ (choice C), whereas $3 \cdot 10 = 30$ (choice A) and $10^3 = 1,000$ (choice D) are not relevant to situations in which we are selecting items without repetition.

3. **The correct answer is C.** The standardized score, or z-score, is $z = \dfrac{x - \mu}{\sigma}$, where x is the data point, μ is the population mean, and σ is the standard deviation. Here, we are given $x = 86$, $\mu = 80$, and $\sigma = 5$, so $z = \dfrac{86 - 80}{5} = 1.2$. The given score is higher than the mean, so the z-score must be positive, and therefore choice A cannot be correct. Choice B is incorrect since it reverses the role of μ and σ in the calculation. Choice D represents the difference between 86 and 80, but it is not standardized (i.e., divided by σ).

4. **The correct answer is D.** The null hypothesis always represents the default position in the absence of evidence. In this case, it means that there is no difference in efficacy between the antibiotics, so $\rho_a = \rho_b$. In addition, the researchers want to know whether either drug is more effective than the other, and are not specifically proposing which one might be better. Therefore, the alternative hypothesis is two-sided, or $\rho_a \neq \rho_b$. Choices B and C are incorrect as they have one-sided alternative hypotheses, while choice A has an incorrect null hypothesis.

5. **The correct answer is D.** The first event under consideration consists of 2, 4, and 6, and the second event contains only the 3. Since these events are mutually exclusive, we can simply add their respective probabilities. The first has a probability of $\dfrac{3}{6}$, and the second has a probability of $\dfrac{1}{6}$, so combined their probability is $\dfrac{3}{6} + \dfrac{1}{6} = \dfrac{4}{6}$, or $\dfrac{2}{3}$. Choices A and C each neglect to include one of the two events, and choice B incorrectly counts the number of possibilities in the problem.

6. **The correct answer is A.** The correlation coefficient, r, is a value that indicates the strength of the association between two variables. It always has a value in the interval $-1 \leq r \leq 1$, and choice A is the only one that does not satisfy this condition. A negative value (choice B) indicates a negative correlation,

0 (choice C) indicates no correlation at all, and a positive value (choice D) indicates a positive correlation.

7. **The correct answer is C.** A normal distribution contains approximately 95% of its data within 2 standard deviations of the mean. Since the mean is 37 and the standard deviation is 2, this interval starts at $37 - 2 \cdot 2 = 33$ and ends at $37 + 2 \cdot 2 = 41$. An interval that contains a single standard deviation on either side (choice B) contains 68% of the data, while an interval using 3 standard deviations (choice D) contains 99.7%. Choice A is incorrect since it represents an interval entirely below the mean.

8. **The correct answer is A.** By the central limit theorem, the mean of the sampling distribution for a mean can be approximated by $N\left(\mu, \sigma / \sqrt{n}\right)$, where μ is the population mean, and σ is the standard deviation. Since $n = 100$, we have $\sigma / \sqrt{n} = 0.5 / 10 = 0.05$. The sampling distribution does not follow a binomial distribution (choices B and D), and choice C neglects the denominator of $\sqrt{n}$ in the standard deviation.

9. **The correct answer is B.** An erroneous rejection is a type I error. The probability of this occurring is always equal to the significance level, α, which in this case is 0.01, or 1%. Choice A is wrong because although the p-value does represent a probability, it is associated with the particular sample chosen, not all possible samples. Choice C is wrong because the t-statistic does not represent any probability at all. Although 5% (choice D) is a value commonly used for α, a different one was specified in this scenario.

10. **The correct answer is B.** When 20 is substituted for x in the equation, it becomes $y = \frac{4}{5} \cdot 20 + 3 = 19$, so the predicted value is $y = 19$. Since 20 lies outside of the range of the original data points, this is an example of extrapolation. It would be interpolation if one was predicting a y for an x within the original range (choices A and C). Choices C and D incorrectly substitute the 20 for y, and solve for x.

11. **The correct answer is C.** Age is an example of numerical data. It is represented as a number, and it makes sense to compare and perform arithmetic on these numbers. State of residence is a categorical variable. Responses are divided into categories, but cannot be ranked or operated upon arithmetically. Choices A and B are wrong because they do not include numerical. Choices B and D are wrong because they include ordinal, which is not one of the data types represented in this survey.

12. **The correct answer is A.** ANOVA, or analysis of variance, is the procedure used to compare means from more than two samples. A t-test is used to either check the value of a single mean (choice B) or compare means for two samples (choice C). A z-test (choice D) is generally used with proportions, not means.

13. **The correct answer is D.** A discrete probability distribution must satisfy two conditions: each probability must be between 0 and 1, and the sum of the probabilities must be 1. Choice D is the only one that satisfies all of these conditions. Choice A includes a negative probability, while choices B and C do not have probabilities that sum to 1.

14. **The correct answer is C.** The points in choice C lie almost perfectly in a straight line that rises to the right, which indicates a very strong positive correlation. Choice B also shows a positive correlation, but the points are not as tightly clustered around the same line. Choice D shows a strong negative correlation, while choice A shows little to no correlation of any kind.

15. **The correct answer is B.** The range is represented by the distance between the top and bottom of the plot, and these are equal in the two plots shown. The median is the center line, and this is higher in A than in B, so choice A is wrong. The IQR is represented by the height of the box, and this is larger in A than in B, so choice C is wrong. The 3rd quartile is the top of the box, and this is also higher in A than in B, so choice D is wrong.

16. **The correct answer is C.** The margin of error for a proportion confidence interval is $m = z^* \cdot \sqrt{\dfrac{\hat{p}(1 - \hat{p})}{n}}$. Here we are given

    $z^* = 1.96$, $n = 100$, and $\hat{p} = 1 - 0.58$

    $= 0.42$, so we get

    $m = 1.96 \cdot \sqrt{\dfrac{0.42 \cdot 0.58}{100}} \approx 0.097$.

    The confidence interval is of the form $\hat{p} \pm m = 0.42 \pm 0.097$; that is, from 32.3% to 51.7%. Choice A is wrong because it uses the population size, 1000, as n, in place of the sample size, 100. Choice B neglects the factor of 1.96 in the margin of error, while Choice D incorrectly uses $\hat{p} = 0.58$ instead of 0.42.

17. **The correct answer is D.** Since the test is to determine whether the number of hours are the same or different, the alternate hypothesis is $H_a : \mu_M \neq \mu_W$. The p-value of 0.028 is less than α, so the null hypothesis should be rejected in favor of the alternate hypothesis. Therefore, the sociologist should conclude that men and women work different numbers of hours. Choice A is wrong because the p-value is sufficiently low to reject the null hypothesis. The other choices incorrectly assume that the alternate hypothesis is one-sided; $H_a : \mu_M > \mu_W$ (choice B) or $H_a : \mu_M < \mu_W$ (choice C).

18. **The correct answer is C.** This situation is modeled by a binomial distribution, where $n = 250$ and $p = \dfrac{3}{5}$. The expected value of a binomial distribution is simply $np = 250 \cdot \dfrac{3}{5}$. Choice A incorrectly uses the probability of tails in place of the probability of heads. Choice B represents the probability of the coin landing on heads in all of the 250 flips, while choice D neglects to account for the 250 repetitions of the experiment.

19. **The correct answer is A.** An r^2 value near 1 indicates a strong correlation, while values near 0 indicate little to no correlation. 0.89 is close to 1, so the correlation is strong. Since r^2 is a squared value, it cannot be negative, and therefore there is no way to know if the correlation is positive or negative (choices B and C). Choice D comes to the wrong conclusion based on the value of r^2.

20. **The correct answer is C.** Stopping every fifth student, without taking any other criteria into account, ensures that the sample is as random as possible, and does not systematically exclude students with certain characteristics. Choice A is wrong because only freshmen are surveyed, so the sample is not representative of the population. Choice B is wrong because it excludes students who bring lunch from home rather than buying it in school; since the question is about food in school, there is reason to think that opinions might differ between these groups. Choice D is wrong because seniors are excluded, so the sample is not representative of the population.

DIAGNOSTIC TEST ASSESSMENT GRID

Now that you've completed the diagnostic test and read through the answer explanations, you can use your results to target your studying. Find the question numbers from the diagnostic test that you answered incorrectly and highlight or circle them below. Then focus extra attention on the sections within the chapter dealing with those topics.

Principles of Statistics		
Content Area	**Topic**	**Question #**
Foundations of Statistics	• Data types and levels of measurement, sample vs. population, and distribution • Sampling methods • Descriptive statistics • Visual representation of data	1, 11, 15, 20
Probability	• Basic concepts • Probability rules for dependent and independent events • Combinations and permutations • Discrete distributions • Continuous distributions	2, 5, 13
Correlation and Regression	• Scatter plots • Linear correlation • Linear regression • Prediction using the linear mode	6, 10, 14, 19
Sampling Distributions	• Basic understanding of standard scores such as Z and T scores • The law of averages, expected values, standard error, normal approximation, sample size, sample average and estimating accuracy of a sample • Central limit theorem	3, 7, 8, 18

Principles of Statistics (continued)		
Inferential Statistics	• Confidence intervals • Null and alternate hypothesis, confidence level and power • Type i and type ii errors and levels of significance • Inference for the mean or the proportion of a population • Comparing two sample means and proportions • Comparing the means of more than two samples • Non-parametric	4, 9, 12, 16, 17

GET THE FACTS

To see the DSST® Principles of Statistics Fact Sheet, go to ***http://getcollegecredit.com/exam_fact_sheets*** and click on the **Math** tab. Scroll down and click the **Principles of Statistics** link. Here you will find suggestions for further study material and the ACE college credit recommendations for passing the test.

FOUNDATIONS OF STATISTICS

DATA TYPES

Numerical data can be counted or measured. For example, it answers questions like: How many fish are there in a net? How many feet across is the room you are sitting in? What is the speed of sound? How tall are you?

Numerical data is further categorized as either discrete or continuous. **Discrete** data represents units that can be counted. The range can be potentially infinite—for example, how many times is a particular coin flipped before it shows heads? Discrete data can also be limited—for example, how many steps does it take a particular person to walk one mile? In each case, there are countable units. It may take 1 flip, 2 flips, 10 flips, or 20 flips of the coin to show heads, but it will never take 3.5 flips. Similarly, a person walking does not take fractions of a step.

Continuous data can be absolutely any value in a range, and can't be directly counted. For example, if a wedge of cheese is cut from a 10-pound wheel, how much might the wedge weigh? The wedge can have any weight between 0 and 10 pounds—for example, 0.0001 pounds or 3.278944 pounds—and it is impossible to list all the values, even with an infinite amount of time.

Categorical data is not counted or measured as a number. Rather, it represents information that can be divided into categories. Marital status is a good example. A person can be married, unmarried, divorced, separated, or widowed. Other examples are zip codes, favorite foods, or voting preferences. Note that a zip code looks like a number, but it does not act as a number in analysis—one would never find the average of zip codes, or say that one is greater than another—so it is not numerical data.

The last category is ordinal data. **Ordinal** data is categorical data that has been organized into meaningful numbers. For an example of ordinal data, consider a voting survey in which people are asked how likely they are to vote in an election on a scale of 0 to 5, where 0 means they will not vote and 5 means they will certainly vote. The answer given is categorical, but if there are 100 ratings on this scale, the numbers can be compared with one another and analyzed numerically. If the average is 2.7, a lower turnout is predicted than if the average is 4.8.

Levels of Measurement

Related to types of data is the notion of **levels of measurement**. These levels describe exactly how variables in a study are measured. There are four levels: nominal, ordinal, interval, and ratio.

The **nominal** level of measurement describes categories that are not ranked or related. For example, consider different types of cars: sports cars, minivans, sedans, etc. Each car fits in a category, but they are not ranked, and there are no relationships among the categories. Minivans are not greater than sedans or vice versa.

Ordinal measurement still places data into categories, but the categories are ranked; that is, they are placed in relative order to one another. The terms first, second, third, etc., are clues that the ordinal level of measurement is being used. An example is the finishing place of each runner in a race. There is a runner who comes in first, one who comes in second, and so on. For any pair of runners, they can be directly compared in the sense that one comes before the other.

The **interval** level of measurement places a set distance between categories of data. For example, consider the sizes of shirts. There is the same distance between a size 2 and a size 3 as between size 15 and size 16. Note that in interval data, 0 is simply the name of a category, and does not necessarily refer to a quantity (A shirt of size 0 is just a very small shirt, not a shirt with no size!).

Finally, at the **ratio** level, 0 actually means 0, as in nothing. For example, consider counting the number of trees in a forest. A value of 0 trees means that there is not a single tree.

SAMPLING METHODS

Before data can be analyzed, it needs to be collected. That sounds simple, but it is not always so easy in practice.

The **population** of a study refers to all members of the group under consideration. This might refer to a literal population (for example, in a nationwide poll), or it might mean a limited study group, like the bacteria colonies in a biologist's lab. Often it is impractical, expensive, or unnecessary to study the entire population, so a statistician only analyzes a portion of that population, called a **sample**.

ALERT

If it doesn't make sense to perform arithmetic on the values in a set, the data is categorical.

Deciding how to pick a sample from a population is a crucial step in statistical analysis. The method used to choose a sample is called the **sample design**. The key to choosing a sampling method is making sure that the sample is truly representative of the entire population. For example, if examining samples of milk from a dairy, the samples must be chosen from among all the different sources of milk. If only the freshest samples are chosen, the milk will be deemed better than it really is—this is poor design.

Another example of a poor design is called a **voluntary response sample**. In this type of sample, the entire population is surveyed, but data is only collected from those who choose to complete the survey. This means the sample consists entirely of people that make the effort to respond, typically those with strong opinions. Many others might have feelings on the subject but fail to answer the survey. Finally, a sample that is not reflective of the population is said to be **biased**. The best way to avoid bias is to make sure that the sample is chosen by some impersonal, impartial means.

There are a variety of sampling methods, but the best samples are probability samples. In a **probability sample**, each member of a population has a known, positive chance of being chosen. Note that the probabilities are not necessarily the same for each member. There are several types of probability samples.

A **simple random sample**, or **SRS**, has the property that in the study population, every subset of *n* individuals has the same probability of being chosen. This does not mean that every individual has an equal chance of being chosen (although that is often the case). Rather, any group of 10 individuals have the same chance of being chosen as any other group of 10 individuals. In an SRS, the sample must be chosen truly randomly—for example, by assigning every individual a number and then using a random number generator to choose from among them.

Stratified random samples are more complicated, but more powerful. In a stratified sample, the population is first categorized into groups of similar individuals called **strata**. For example, people in a study might first be split into strata based on whether they live in an urban, suburban, or rural setting. Once this stratification is done, a random sample is chosen from within each stratum. A stratified design can often be smaller and easier to carry out since individuals in each stratum are similar. A relatively small sample from each stratum can yield results that are as good as, or even better than, a larger SRS.

Multistage sampling is another technique. It is especially useful in narrowing down a sample from a large, diverse population. The U.S. Census Bureau and most major pollsters use multistage sampling. In this method, increasingly smaller samples are chosen. For example, say one wants to conduct a study regarding the restaurants of the Greek islands. There are hundreds of inhabited islands, and thousands of restaurants, so it is not possible to visit them all. First, a random sample of islands are chosen—that's stage one. Next, within each of these islands, a random sample of towns are chosen—that's stage two. Finally, within each town, a random sample of restaurants are chosen—that's stage three. The sample at each stage may be an SRS, or even stratified.

Even with an unbiased sample, there are still potential pitfalls in the data collection stage. **Undercoverage** results when some groups are left out of or are underrepresented in the sample. For example, if an ornithologist is counting bird species in the rainforest, shy or nocturnal birds are less likely to be noticed and thus less likely to be counted. **Nonresponse** is a similar problem that occurs when an individual chosen as part of a sample does not participate, whether by accident or because of a lack of cooperation.

A problem that can plague surveys is **response bias**. Respondents sometimes lie, especially about embarrassing or illegal activities. The way a question is worded is also vitally important, and can bias the response. For example, imagine a study that aims to see if people will agree to have a particular blood test done. Consider two different ways of phrasing a question: "Will you get the test if 60 percent of doctors recommend it?" and "Will you get the test if 40 percent of doctors do not recommend it?" Although the questions are essentially the same, they have completely different tones, and will likely elicit different answers.

DESCRIPTIVE STATISTICS

Descriptive statistics provide basic summary information of a data set, particularly its distribution. The **distribution** of a data set is the pattern of variation within it, and it is often summarized with a few key values. The complete spread of values in a distribution is called the **range**. The **center** of a distribution refers to the values near the middle of the range, and the **spread** of a distribution describes how far the values in the distribution spread out from the center.

Center of a Distribution

The most common measure of center is the **mean** (sometimes called the average), symbolized by either $\bar{x}$ (when the data under consideration is a sample), or μ (when a full population is being considered). To find the mean for a set of n observations, add the values of every observation and then divide by n.

$$\bar{x} = \frac{x_1 + x_2 + \ldots + x_n}{n} = \frac{1}{n}\sum x_i$$

The symbol Σ means "sum of," and x_i refers to the different values of each observation.

For example, say a forester is measuring the heights of a sample of shrubs edging a field. She measures 5 shrubs. The shrubs are 3, 4, 6, 9, and 11 feet tall. What is the mean height of her sample? To find the mean for the shrub heights, we add them all and divide by 5:

$$\frac{3 + 4 + 6 + 9 + 11}{5} = \frac{33}{5} = 6.6 \text{ feet}$$

Though the mean is commonly used and easy to calculate, one of the problems with it as a descriptive statistic is that it is susceptible to outliers. An **outlier** is a value in a data set that falls well outside most of a distribution. In the previous example, suppose the last shrub was 25 feet tall, rather than 11. Recalculating the mean with this value gives a result of 9.4 feet. Just one large value, 25, raised the mean from 6.6 to 9.4, a jump of more than 40 percent.

Since it is susceptible to extreme values, we say that the mean is not a **resistant** measure of the center.

A descriptive statistic that is resistant to extreme values is the median. The **median**, M, is the number in a data set such that half the observations fall below it and half fall above it. The median is not calculated by means of a formula; rather, it is the midpoint of the data set.

Let's look at the shrub heights again: 3, 4, 6, 9, and 11. For this data, $M = 6$; two values (3 and 4) are below 6, and two values (9 and 11) are above it. Note that unlike with the mean, changing the 11 to 25 does not affect the median at all. If the shrubs are 3, 4, 6, 9, and 25 feet tall, the median is still 6.

The easiest way to find a median is to arrange the observations in order of increasing value. The forester will probably measure the shrubs in the order she first sees them, so her data might initially look like this: 4, 9, 3, 6, 11. It is much easier to see the median when they are in order: 3, 4, 6, 9, 11.

When there are an odd number of observations, as in the shrub example, the median is simply the center value in the list once it has been put in order. When there are an even number of observations, the median is the mean of the two center observations in the ordered list.

For example, if the forester measures six shrubs of 3, 4, 6, 9, 11, and 15 feet, then the median is the mean of 6 and 9, or 7.5.

The **mode** is the value in a data set that occurs most often. It is often near the center, but not always. For example, suppose a teacher is looking at the distribution of grades on a test, and she sees the following scores:

$$50, 65, 78, 78, 78, 80, 83, 83, 86, 86, 88, 91, 95$$

The mode is 78, since it was the most common grade.

If multiple values are tied for most appearances in the data set, the distribution is said to be **multi-modal** (or bimodal if there are exactly two such values).

Spread of a Distribution

To accurately describe a distribution, we need descriptors for both the center and the spread. The quickest way to analyze a distribution's spread is using percentiles. The nth **percentile** is the value such that n% of the observations fall at or below that value. For example, the 34th percentile is greater than or equal to 34% of observations and less than or equal to 66%.

The percentiles used most often are called **quartiles**. The **first quartile**, or Q_1, is the 25th percentile. The **second quartile**, or Q_2, is the 50th percentile, and the **third quartile**, or Q_3, is the 75th percentile. Note that the second quartile is simply the median.

The distance between the first and third quartiles is called the **interquartile range**, or IQR. The IQR is calculated as $IQR = Q_3 - Q_1$. It is a useful descriptive statistic since it covers both the center and half of the spread.

IQR can also provide a quick test for outliers. An observation more than $1.5 \cdot IQR$ above the third quartile or below the first quartile might well be an outlier.

Together with the minimum and maximum values in the set, we use the quartiles to get the **five-number summary**—five numbers that map out the entire range and basic shape of a distribution:

$$\min, Q_1, Q_2, Q_3, \max$$

ALERT

Don't immediately look to the center of a list for the median; you must first make sure it is in order.

When the mean is used as the measure of center, use the standard deviation for spread. If the median is used for center, use quartiles for spread.

A more precise way to measure spread is the **standard deviation**, a calculation of how far the actual observations fall from the mean. The **sample standard deviation** s is calculated based on the average square deviation from the mean:

$$s = \sqrt{\frac{1}{n-1} \sum (x_i - \overline{x})^2}$$

Though it can seem daunting, calculating a standard deviation consists primarily of plugging in the value of each observation for x: the first value is x_1, the second is x_2, all the way to the last observation, x_n. For example, consider a data set with four values: 1, 2, 5, and 7. The mean is $\overline{x} = 3.75$. The standard deviation is then calculated as follows:

$$s = \sqrt{\frac{1}{4-1}((1-3.75)^2 + (2-3.75)^2 + (5-3.75)^2 + (7-3.75)^2)} \approx 2.754$$

In the case of a **population standard deviation**, the value is denoted by σ instead of s, and the formula is slightly different:

$$\sigma = \sqrt{\frac{1}{n} \sum (x_i - \mu)^2}$$

The key feature of the standard deviation is that the smaller it is, the more tightly the observations are centered around the mean; the larger it is, the more spread out they are. The standard deviation is never negative, and it is only 0 when there is no spread at all—that is, when all observations are equal. The standard deviation should only be used together with the mean, not the median. Just like the mean, the standard deviation is easily influenced by outliers.

Measures of spread do not change under translations, while measures of center do. Everything changes when the data is scaled.

Transformations

A **transformation** is an operation that is performed on each value in a data set. If each value has a fixed number added to it, we say that the data has been **translated**, or **shifted**. If each value is multiplied by a fixed value, we say that it has been **scaled**. For example, translating the data by 2 means replacing each value x with $x + 2$. Similarly, scaling the data by 3 means replacing each value x by $3x$. When data has been transformed in either or both of these ways, the statistics behave in predictable ways. These behaviors are summarized below.

	Translate: $x \rightarrow x + c$	**Scale:** $x \rightarrow cx$
Mean	$\overline{x} \rightarrow \overline{x} + c$	$\overline{x} \rightarrow c\overline{x}$
Median	$m \rightarrow m + c$	$m \rightarrow cm$
IQR	No change	$IQR \rightarrow c \cdot IQR$
Standard Deviation	No change	$s \rightarrow cs$

DATA VISUALIZATION

Data is usually easier to understand and analyze when the distribution can be visualized—that is, when it is represented graphically. There are three common types of graphics: stemplots, histograms, and boxplots.

Stemplots

A **stemplot** is a quick visual summary of a data set that includes every value. It is made by splitting each observation into a **stem** and a **leaf**. The stem is the value with its final digit discarded, and the leaf is the final digit.

For example, suppose 6 runners can complete one lap of a track in 42, 45, 51, 53, 55, and 62 seconds. The stem of the 42 is 4; its leaf is 2. To create a stemplot, line up the stems vertically and then add the leaves to the right of each stem.

```
4 | 2  5

5 | 1  3  5

6 | 2
```

Histograms

A **histogram** is a graph of the frequency of each observation in your data set. The horizontal axis shows each observation or category of observation, and the vertical axis shows how often each of these values occurs. There is no gap between the columns.

For example, this histogram shows the times that the students in Mr. Gordon's 8th grade gym class took to complete a 1-mile course, rounded to the nearest half-minute.

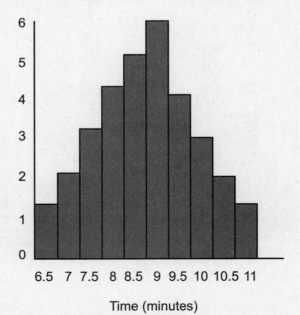

A quick look gives much information. The mode, for example, is 9 minutes. The center is also somewhere near 9. The distribution is roughly symmetric.

Or consider the same class with a different histogram.

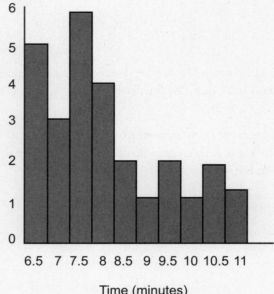

Now there are many more fast runners in the class. More of the data is on the lower end of the range rather than near the middle, leaving a long tail on the right side. This distribution is said to be **skewed** to the right; slower runners would skew the distribution to the left.

A gap in a histogram, such as at 15 minutes below, indicates that there is no observation at that value. No runner completed the course in 15 minutes.

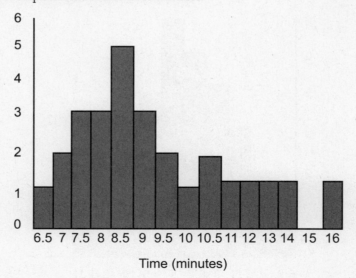

Boxplots

Another good visual representation of data is a **boxplot**, a graphical representation of the 5-number summary.

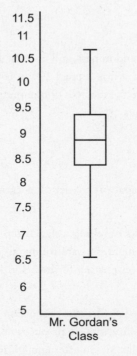

The bottom and top edges of the box represent the first and third quartiles, respectively; a line through the box gives the location of the second quartile, or median. The "whiskers" at each end encompass the total range of the distribution, excluding outliers, which are shown as individual dots beyond the range of the whiskers.

Boxplots are useful for comparing two related distributions.

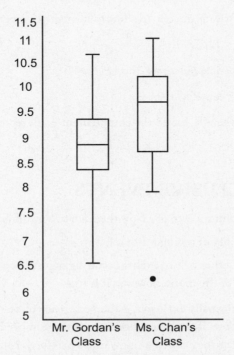

These boxplots compare Mr. Gordon's students' times to Ms. Chan's students; clearly Ms. Chan's students tend to be slower, and there is less variation among them.

Around 15 percent of the questions on the DSST Principles of Statistics exam will cover probability concepts.

PROBABILITY

Probability is the mathematics of randomness and chance. Imagine flipping a coin: what is the chance it will come up heads? What if it is flipped 100 times? What are the chances of getting a head on any particular flip? What are the chances of obtaining exactly 43 heads in these 100 flips? Probability will answer these questions.

BASIC CONCEPTS

For a given experiment, the **sample space** is the set of all possible outcomes. An **event** consists of a subset of the sample space.

For example, if an experiment consists of rolling a standard 6-sided die, the sample space contains the outcomes 1, 2, 3, 4, 5, and 6. Some events are rolling an even number (consisting of the 2, 4, and 6), rolling a number less than 3 (consisting of the 1 and 2), and rolling a 1 or 6 (consisting of the 1 and 6).

The **probability** of an event E, denoted $P(E)$, is the proportion of times that event occurs in repeated trials. Repetition is crucial to probability; any single outcome does not have much significance. A random phenomenon cannot be predicted, but after enough repetitions a pattern may emerge.

The coin flip is a great example. Nobody knows, or can predict, what will happen on any given flip. However, over the course of 100 flips you should expect to see approximately 50 heads and 50 tails, so the probability of each is $\frac{1}{2}$. Similarly, the probability of getting any particular number on a single roll of a die is $\frac{1}{6}$.

The definition of probability leads directly to a few fundamental properties:

For any event E, $0 \leq P(E) \leq 1$.

If E contains all possible outcomes, then $P(E) = 1$.

If E is impossible, then $P(E) = 0$.

$P(\overline{E}) = 1 - P(E)$ where $\overline{E}$, called the **complement** of E, represents all outcomes that are not in E.

MUTUALLY EXCLUSIVE EVENTS

What is the probability of rolling a 2 or a 5? Now there are two possibilities, each with a probability of $\frac{1}{6}$. Therefore, the probability of rolling a 2 or a 5 is $\frac{1}{6} + \frac{1}{6} = \frac{2}{6}$, or $\frac{1}{3}$. Note that it is not always true that the probability of either of two events occurring is just the sum of the individual probabilities. In a large category of situations, however, it is true.

Two events are said to be **mutually exclusive** if the occurrence of one implies that the other did not occur. In the example above, if the event A consists of the number 2, and event B consists of 5, it is impossible for both events to occur on a single roll. Therefore, A and B are mutually exclusive.

For mutually exclusive events, a simple rule holds. Sometimes called the **addition rule**, it says that if A and B are mutually exclusive events, then $P(A \text{ or } B) = P(A) + P(B)$.

If A and B are not mutually exclusive, the situation is a little more complicated. The formula is $P(A \text{ or } B) = P(A) + P(B) - P(A \text{ and } B)$. This last term adjusts the answer to account for double counting of outcomes that are represented in both A and B.

For example, suppose we are interested in the probability of rolling either an even number or a prime number. The even numbers are represented by 2, 4, and 6, while the prime numbers are 2, 3, and 5. The number 2 is in both, so if we simply add together their respective probabilities, we get $\frac{3}{6} + \frac{3}{6} = 1$, which is clearly incorrect. Applying the full formula just given, we instead get the correct answer of $\frac{3}{6} + \frac{3}{6} - \frac{1}{6} = \frac{5}{6}$, where the $\frac{1}{6}$ represents the probability of the 2, which is counted as part of both $\frac{3}{6}$ terms.

INDEPENDENT AND DEPENDENT EVENTS

The addition rule applies when looking at the probability of either of two events occurring. Another common situation is trying to find the probability of two events *both* occurring. For example, suppose a die is rolled twice. What is the probability of rolling a 1 and then a 6? The rule that applies in this situation, the **multiplication rule**, says that $P(A \text{ and } B) = P(A) \cdot P(B)$.

Applying this rule, $P(1 \text{ and then } 6) = P(1) \cdot P(6) = \frac{1}{6} \cdot \frac{1}{6} = \frac{1}{36}$. In this example, there is a subtle but important property involved. The probability of the second event, getting a $\frac{1}{6}$ on the second roll, is not affected by what happens on the first roll. It is always $\frac{1}{6}$. Events of this sort, in which one occurring does not affect the probability of the other, are called **independent events**. When dealing with independent events, applying the multiplication rule is particularly simple.

Sometimes, however, one may come across **dependent events**, in which the first event occurring affects the probability of the second event. For example, suppose one has a bag that contains 3 blue marbles and 7 red marbles. An experiment involves reaching into the bag and drawing a marble, and then drawing a second marble. Suppose we are interested in finding the probability of getting a red marble and then a blue marble. Although the multiplication rule still applies, one has to be careful about the probability of the second event.

The probability of pulling a red marble on the first draw is $\frac{7}{10}$, as expected. However, the probability of getting a blue marble on the second draw is $\frac{3}{9}$, since there are only 9 marbles remaining after the first draw. Therefore, the multiplication rule tells us that the combined probability of the two events is $\frac{7}{10} \cdot \frac{3}{9} = \frac{21}{90} = \frac{7}{30}$.

Note that if the first marble were put back in the bag before drawing again, the events would be independent. In that case, the answer would be $\frac{7}{10} \cdot \frac{3}{10} = \frac{21}{100}$.

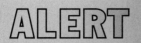

When calculating a probability of the form *P*(*A* and *B*), you should first make sure to check whether *A* and *B* are independent.

PERMUTATIONS AND COMBINATIONS

Since calculating probabilities often involves counting numbers of possibilities, it is important to develop techniques for doing so in a variety of situations.

Counting Principle

The **counting principle** says that if task *A* can be accomplished in *m* ways, and task *B* can be accomplished in *n* ways, then the combination of tasks *A* and *B* can be accomplished in $m \cdot n$ ways.

For example, if a deli offers sandwiches with 3 choices of bread, 4 choices of meat, and 2 choices of condiment, the total number of different sandwiches one can order is (3)(4)(2) = 24.

As another example, consider four people who are choosing between water, coffee, and tea to have with their breakfast. Since each person has three choices, there are (3)(3)(3)(3) = 81 different possible outcomes.

Permutations

Ten runners are participating in a 5-kilometer race. Gold, silver, and bronze medals are to be awarded to first, second, and third place finishers, respectively. How many different ways of assigning the medals to the runners are possible? The counting principle lets us answer this question, but as with calculating probabilities of dependent events, care must be taken.

The gold medal can end up being awarded to any of the 10 runners. However, after that is done, there are only 9 contestants remaining who might take the silver medal, and then only 8 who can win the bronze. Thus, the total number of possible assignments is (10)(9)(8) = 720.

There are certain properties of this example that are characteristic of a wide variety of situations. These are the following:

> There are *n* objects that can potentially be chosen.
>
> *r* of the objects are to actually be chosen (without repetition).
>
> The order in which the objects are chosen is important.

The different possible choices in a situation that satisfies these conditions are called **permutations**, and the total number of choices is denoted as $P(n,r)$.

In this example, $n = 10$ and $r = 3$. There is no repetition since a runner cannot win more than one medal, and the order is important because the different medals are not interchangeable; we need to know not only which three runners get them, but also which runner gets each particular medal. Linda getting the gold, John the silver, and Sue the bronze is a different outcome than John getting the gold, Sue the silver, and Linda the bronze! The answer we are looking for is $P(10,3)$, and we have calculated that it is 720.

Although the counting principle can always be used in these situations as shown, there is also an explicit formula that gives the correct answer:

$$P(n,r) = \frac{n!}{(n-r)!}$$

Here, $n!$ represents a factorial, which is defined by the product of all the numbers from n down to 1. That is:

$$n! = n \cdot (n-1) \cdot (n-2) \ldots 2 \cdot 1$$

Going back to the previous example, we can calculate as follows:

$$P(10, 7) = \frac{10!}{(10-3)!} = \frac{10!}{7!} = \frac{10 \cdot 9 \cdot 8 \cdot 7 \cdot 6 \cdot 5 \cdot 4 \cdot 3 \cdot 2 \cdot 1}{7 \cdot 6 \cdot 5 \cdot 4 \cdot 3 \cdot 2 \cdot 1} = 10 \cdot 9 \cdot 8 = 720$$

This matches the answer we got using the counting principle. Note that in the second-to-last step, all of the factors from 7 to 1 cancel from the numerator and denominator. A similar situation arises when calculating any permutation.

Combinations

A variation on a permutation is when the first two conditions given are met, but the last one is not; that is, the order of the choices does not matter. The different possibilities in a situation like this are referred to as **combinations**, and the answer is denoted by $C(n,r)$. The formula for counting them is:

$$C(n,r) = \frac{n!}{r!(n-r)!}$$

Note the extra factor of $r!$ in the denominator when compared with the permutation formula.

For example, suppose a club has 23 members, and they need to choose a 3-person committee. There is no distinction between the committee members. The order does not matter, so this is a combination problem with $n = 23$ and $r = 3$. Thus, the total number of committees is calculated as follows:

$$C(23,3) = \frac{23!}{3!(23-3)!} = \frac{23!}{3!\,20!} = \frac{23 \cdot 22 \cdot 21}{3 \cdot 2 \cdot 1} = 1,771$$

PROBABILITY DISTRIBUTIONS

In the context of probability, a **distribution** contains information about the different possible outcomes of an experiment and the probability of each one of them.

Discrete Distribution

A **discrete distribution** describes a situation in which the possible outcomes are discrete; that is, they can be listed, even if the list is potentially infinite. If X is a variable that holds the value of the experimental outcome, we call it a **random variable**.

For example, if we let X represent the number shown on a die when it is rolled, then X is a **discrete random variable**, and its distribution is represented by the following table.

To determine if a problem involves permutations or combinations, look for a few key words: *order, arrange, line-up, in a row*. If any of these are involved, the problem likely involves permutations. Another indication that permutations are involved is when there is a distinction in the items being chosen, such as 1st, 2nd, and 3rd places in a race.

X	1	2	3	4	5	6
$P(X)$	$\frac{1}{6}$	$\frac{1}{6}$	$\frac{1}{6}$	$\frac{1}{6}$	$\frac{1}{6}$	$\frac{1}{6}$

Now suppose we start flipping a coin repeatedly, and let X be the random variable that represents how many flips it takes for it to first land on heads. If the first flip is heads, $X = 1$. If the first is tails but the second heads, $X = 2$, and so on. Clearly, X can take on any positive value without bound, so the list of possible values is infinite; despite this, X is discrete, since we can systematically list its possible values. The beginning of the distribution would look like this:

X	1	2	3	4	5	
$P(X)$	$\frac{1}{2}$	$\frac{1}{4}$	$\frac{1}{8}$	$\frac{1}{16}$	$\frac{1}{32}$	...

Any discrete distribution has to satisfy the following conditions:

Each probability is between 0 and 1.

The sum of the probabilities is 1.

Note that it is possible for an infinite number of probabilities to sum to 1, as in the most recent example.

Binomial Distribution

A commonly encountered discrete distribution is the result of a binomial experiment. A binomial experiment consists of repeating a smaller experiment, called a trial, repeatedly. One then counts the number of times that different results are obtained. Specifically, the following conditions need to be satisfied:

Each trial has only two possible results, referred to as success and failure.

The experiment consists of repeating the trial some number of times.

The probability of success in any single trial must stay fixed for all trials.

The probability of success is called p, and the number of trials is called n. The random variable of interest, X, is the number of successes obtained in these n trials; the possible values for X are all positive integers from 0 to n. The distribution of this variable is called a **binomial distribution**, and is denoted by $B(n,p)$.

Probabilities in a binomial distribution are calculated by means of a formula that includes the combination formula discussed previously. Specifically, the probability of exactly k successes in the n trials is given by:

$$P(X = k) = C(n,k) \times p^k(1 - p)^{n - k}$$

The classic example of a binomial experiment is repeated coin flips. If we flip a coin 50 times, we can count the number of heads that result. Here, $p = \frac{1}{2}$, $n = 50$, and the number of heads in these 50 flips follows the distribution $B(50, \frac{1}{2})$. Intuitively, one would expect that the most likely number of successes in these 50 trials is 25, since $\frac{1}{2} \cdot 50 = 25$. The exact value of this probability is calculated as follows:

$$P(X = 25) = C(50, 25) \cdot \left(\frac{1}{2}\right)^{25} \left(1 - \frac{1}{2}\right)^{25} \approx 0.112$$

Since they involve both combinations and exponents, these probabilities are generally found using calculators that have special functions for these operations.

Expected Value

The **expected value**, E, of a random variable X that takes on possible values $x_1, x_2, \ldots$ is

$$E = \sum x_i P(x_i)$$

That is, each possible value is multiplied by its probability, and these products are summed.

For a binomial distribution, the formula can be greatly simplified, and it is consistent with the intuition that 25 should be the most likely number of heads to obtain in 50 flips of a coin. Specifically, if X is a binomial random variable, the expected value of X is $E = np$, where n and p are as described in the previous section.

For example, suppose a bag contains one yellow marble and three black marbles. A marble is selected from the bag, and then replaced. This is repeated ten times. What is the expected value of how many times the chosen marble will be black? This is a binomial experiment with $n = 10$ and $p = \frac{3}{4}$. Therefore, the expected value is $10 \cdot \frac{3}{4} = 7.5$.

Note that the expected value is not necessarily even a possible outcome, as seen in the previous example.

The expected value of random variable X is also called its mean, and denoted by μ_x; for a binomial random variable, we have seen that $\mu_x = np$. Similarly, one can calculate a standard deviation for a random variable X, denoted by μ_x. For a binomial random variable, the standard deviation is given by $\mu_x = \sqrt{np(1 - p)}$.

Continuous Distribution

If the outcome of an experiment cannot be described by a discrete variable, it is said to be **continuous**. A continuous random variable can take on any of infinitely many values, and they cannot be systematically listed. For example, consider randomly choosing a real number between 0 and 1. The random variable describing the outcome of this experiment is continuous.

With a continuous distribution, there is no way to easily represent the probabilities involved as you do with discrete distributions. Rather, the only way to describe the probabilities is by providing a curve called the **density curve** for the distribution. The probabilities are then calculated as the areas under certain sections of the density curve.

A density curve must satisfy the following conditions:

The curve has no negative values.

The total area under the curve is 1.

Normal Distribution

The most commonly encountered type of continuous distribution is called a **normal distribution**. In a data set that conforms to a normal distribution, the median, mode, and mean are all the same. Additionally, the density curve is always symmetric around the mean. A smaller standard deviation will result in a taller, tighter curve, and a larger standard deviation will result in a shorter, broader curve. Regardless, most of the data lies within a single standard deviation of the mean, and virtually all of the data is within three standard deviations of the mean.

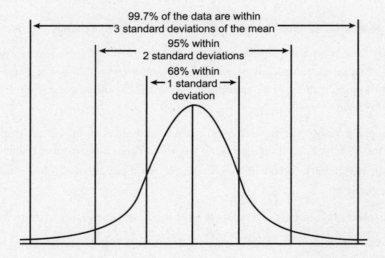

A normal distribution with mean μ (*mu*) and standard deviation σ (*sigma*) is denoted by $N(\mu,\sigma)$. The distribution $N(0,1)$, with mean 0 and standard deviation 1, is called the **standard normal distribution**. Although data that is perfectly described by a normal distribution is uncommon, it is a useful approximation for a large class of examples, especially when working with large data sets.

CORRELATION AND REGRESSION

In the previous sections, we examined one variable at a time. In the real world, however, it is more common to consider whether or not there is a connection between two different variables. When discussing multiple variables, we need to split them into two categories: **explanatory** (or independent) variables and **response** (or dependent) variables. Explanatory variables explain (or cause) changes in response variables. For example, consider a study that examines how heart rate responds to different intensities of exercise. The harder a person exercises, the more their heart rate increases.

Exercise is influencing the heart rate, so exercise intensity is the explanatory variable. Heart rate is being affected, so heart rate is the response variable.

SCATTERPLOTS

A **scatterplot** is a graph that shows the relationship between a response variable and an explanatory variable. The explanatory variable is plotted on the horizontal axis, and the response variable on the vertical axis.

Here is a scatterplot showing the measured heart rate of 10 people exercising at various intensities, where intensity is measured on a scale of 0–5, and heart rate is measured in beats per minute (BPM).

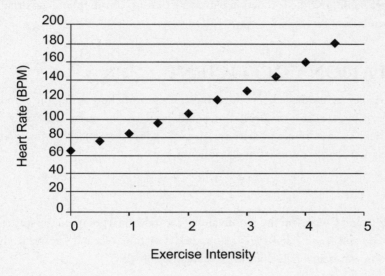

> **TIP**
>
> If a line drawn through most of the points rises to the right, the variables are positively correlated. If it falls to the right, they are negatively correlated.

The graph shows that heart rate increases as exercise intensity increases. This kind of relationship is called a **positive correlation**. If heart rate decreased as exercise intensity increased, the line would be sloping down to the right, and the relationship would be called a **negative correlation**.

Let's look at another scatterplot:

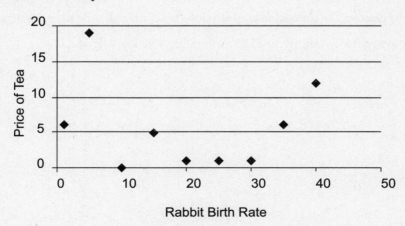

Here it appears that there is no correlation at all between the variables.

It is important to realize that a correlation (whether positive or negative) between two variables does not necessarily imply that there is a causative relationship between the variables. In the exercise example above, one may hypothesize that an increase in exercise intensity causes an increase in heart rate. The scatterplot makes this seem plausible, but knowledge of anatomy and cardiology is necessary to really be confident in this hypothesis.

Consider two variables that have no obvious connection: rate of ice cream consumption, and number of deaths by drowning. A scatterplot of data may well show a positive correlation between these variables. Does this mean that eating ice cream causes drownings? Of course not. It may simply mean that during the summer, when people are more likely to eat ice cream, they are also more likely to swim, and therefore more drownings occur. This hidden factor—the season—is called a **confounding variable**, and the correlation between ice cream consumption and drowning is called a **spurious correlation**.

CORRELATION COEFFICIENT

When two variables are correlated, one often wants to quantify how strong the correlation is. One way of doing so is by calculating a **correlation coefficient**, usually referred to simply as r. If x and y are the two variables in question, and there are n points on the scatterplot showing their relationship, then the correlation coefficient is defined as follows:

$$r = \frac{1}{n-1} \Sigma \left(\frac{x_i - \bar{x}}{s_x} \right) \left(\frac{y_i - \bar{y}}{s_y} \right)$$

In this formula, x_i and y_i represent the coordinates of the individual points on the scatterplot, $\bar{x}$ and $\bar{y}$ are the means of x and y, and s_x and s_y are the standard deviations of x and y, respectively. Calculating r is fairly tedious, and is generally done using statistical software.

Remember the following important properties of the correlation coefficient:

r is always between −1 and 1.

r close to 0 means there is a weak correlation between the variables, while r close to −1 or 1 indicates a strong correlation.

If r is positive, the correlation is positive; if r is negative, the correlation is negative.

r is susceptible to outliers, just like the mean and standard deviation.

LINEAR REGRESSION

In addition to calculating the strength of a correlation, you can examine the nature of the relationship between the variables more closely. One way to do that is to find the equation of a line that passes through or near to most of the points on a scatterplot.

In the exercise example from above, the points seem to lie approximately on a straight line.

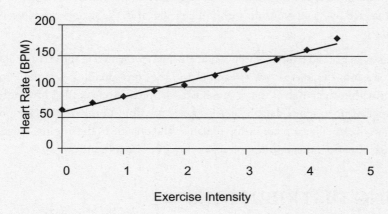

A line that is fit to the points on a scatterplot is called a **regression line**. The most common method of finding such a line is called **least squares regression**. The name comes from the following example:

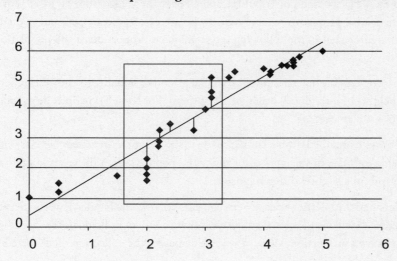

Although the line goes through some of the points, it does not go directly through most of them. The distance between the points and the line, shown as the short vertical segments, represents the lack of a perfect fit. The least squares regression line represents the line that best fits the data, in the sense that the sum of the squares of these errors is as small as possible.

Recall that a line in the xy-plane can be represented by the equation $y = mx + b$, where m is the slope and b is the y-intercept. These values for a least squares regression line are given by the following:

$$m = r \cdot \frac{s_y}{s_x} \text{ and } b = \overline{y} - m\overline{x}$$

As before, s_x and s_y are the standard deviations, and $\overline{x}$ and $\overline{y}$ are the means of x and y, respectively. Again, these values are generally calculated with the help of statistical software.

To assess how well a regression line fits the data, the statistic r^2 is used—this is simply the square of the correlation coefficient r. The value r^2 can be interpreted as the fraction of the variation in y that can be explained by its relationship with x. The larger it is, the stronger the linear relationship between x and y.

A regression line can be used to predict values that are not represented in the existing data set; simply plug a value for x into the line $y = mx + b$ and obtain the corresponding y. If the x for which you are finding y is within the range of the original data, the prediction is called **interpolation**. If it is outside the range of the original data, it is called **extrapolation**. In the case of extrapolation, there is an assumption that the linear relationship remains valid outside of the original range. Depending on the particular situation, this assumption may or may not be warranted.

SAMPLING DISTRIBUTIONS

Suppose a researcher is interested in analyzing the distribution of heights in a population of 10,000 adults whose heights are from 50" to 75". If X is the height of a randomly chosen person within this population, then X has a certain distribution, spread over the values from 50 to 75. For example, it may be that there are 4 people who are 50" tall, 3 who are 51", 5 who are 53", and so on. Specifically, the researcher is interested in the following question: what proportion of the population is at least 60" tall?

However, it is not feasible to measure all their heights individually, so the researcher decides to measure the heights of a random sample of 50 of them. For these 50 people, he calculates that 48 of them, or 96%, are at least 60".

How does this result, obtained from a sample, relate to the question the researcher is trying to answer? Is it a reasonable estimate of the answer for the entire population? A different sample of 50 people would likely result in a slightly different answer.

To better understand the questions raised here, consider what would happen if we looked at all possible samples of size 50. Each one of them would have its own count of individuals that are at least 60" tall, and therefore its own proportion. What if we could analyze the collection of all these proportions?

Sampling Distribution of a Proportion

The discussion above can be generalized. Consider a population of interest, and a characteristic that each individual in the population may or may not have. The proportion of those with the characteristic is called the **population proportion**, and is denoted by p.

Now consider taking a sample of n individuals from this population. n is called the **sample size**. For this sample, we can count the number of individuals that do have this characteristic; let's call this number the **sample count**, c. Similarly, we can calculate the **sample proportion**, denoted by $\hat{p}$, by dividing $\frac{c}{n}$.

NOTE

Around 20 percent of the questions on the DSST Principles of Statistics exam will test you on sampling distributions.

Now consider *all possible samples* of size n. Each sample comes with a sample proportion, so we now find ourselves with a large set of sample proportions. This set forms a distribution, called a **sampling distribution**. As with any distribution, it has a mean and a standard deviation.

If n is sufficiently large, the distribution of the sample proportions is approximately normal. That is, it closely resembles a normal distribution. Specifically, the distribution is as follows:

	Mean (μ)	Standard Deviation (σ)	Normal Approx.
Sample proportions	p	$\sqrt{\dfrac{p(1-p)}{n}}$	$N\left(P, \sqrt{\dfrac{p(1-p)}{n}}\right)$

For example, distribution of sample proportions might be represented by the following histogram, in which the overlaid curve shows the normal approximation. The sections of the bars that extend above the curve, and the sections of empty space below the curve, represent the differences between the actual distribution and the normal approximation. As the sample size n increases, these differences continually grow smaller.

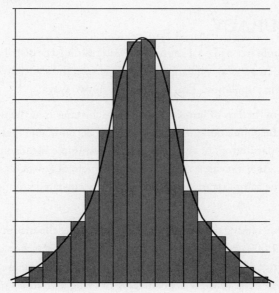

SAMPLING DISTRIBUTION OF A MEAN

Returning to the example that started this discussion, suppose the researcher was instead interested in the mean height of the population. A similar construction follows.

The **population mean** is written as μ, and the **population standard deviation** as σ. The corresponding means of each sample are called **sample means** and **sample standard deviations,** and are written as $\bar{x}$ and s, respectively.

The means all possible samples of size n form a distribution. The connections between this sampling distribution and the population parameters μ and σ are given by the following:

The mean of the sampling distribution is μ.

The standard deviation of the sampling distribution is $\frac{\sigma}{\sqrt{n}}$.

In addition, if the sample size is sufficiently large, then the sampling distribution is normal. Symbolically, if the population has distribution $N(\mu,\sigma)$, then the sample means have distribution $N(\mu, \frac{\sigma}{\sqrt{n}})$. This fact, among the most powerful and important ideas in statistics, is called the **central limit theorem**.

STANDARD ERROR

The population standard deviation, σ, appears in the formula for the standard deviation of a sampling distribution of a mean. In the most commonly encountered scenarios, however, this value is unknown; indeed, calculating it would require having the data for the entire population!

When σ is unknown, you can estimate it using s, the sample standard deviation. In doing so, however, further uncertainty is introduced. This uncertainty will be important later in our discussion of confidence intervals and hypothesis testing. When the standard deviation is computed in this way, using s instead of σ, it is often referred to as the **standard error** of the sampling distribution.

SAMPLE ACCURACY

As we have seen, the sample size n plays a large role in determining the distribution of sample counts, means, and proportions. In general, the larger the sample size, the more we can expect the samples to be representative of the population. This can be seen in two ways.

First, this is formalized in the **law of large numbers**, which states that the mean of a sampling distribution will approach the population mean as n increases. Second, note that in each of the formulas given above for the standard errors of the distributions of sample means and sample proportions, the denominator is $\sqrt{n}$. As n increases, this denominator increases, which causes the standard error to *decrease*. As a result, the sample statistics are more tightly clustered around the true value for the population as a whole.

At some point, however, increasing the sample size too much makes the entire process meaningless—if a population consists of 1,000 people, and you decide to measure some characteristic of 900 of them, you might as well go the rest of the way and just measure all 1,000 of them! Statistical studies are often expensive and time-consuming, so there is great value in being able to decrease the needed sample size. The key, therefore, is trying to perform a balancing act; a sample needs to be small enough to be feasible, but large enough to give meaningful and accurate statistical results.

Another factor to consider is the variability of the population as a whole. The lower this is, the smaller the standard error for the sampling distribution will be. For example, recall that the standard error for the sampling distribution of means is $\frac{\sigma}{\sqrt{n}}$. If σ (the population standard deviation) is small, this fraction will be small; in fact, it has exactly the same effect as increasing the sample size! Unfortunately, however, a statistician does not have the ability to choose σ the same way that he or she can decide on the sample size.

NOTE

The *gambler's fallacy* states that if a single outcome has occurred many times consecutively, then it is unlikely to occur again on the next iteration of the experiment. This is incorrect, though, and sometimes confused with the law of large numbers.

STANDARD SCORES

When working with distributions that are normal, or approximately normal, it is often most convenient to perform calculations with the standard normal distribution. Fortunately, any normally distributed data can be scaled in such a way as to make it follow a standard normal distribution. Data that has been scaled in this way is called **standardized**.

Standardizing data consists of calculating a standard score, or z-**score**, for each value in the set. The z-score for a value x is defined by

$$z = \frac{x - \bar{x}}{s}$$

where, as usual, $\bar{x}$ is the mean and s is the standard deviation. Essentially, the z-score represents how many standard deviations above or below the mean an observed value lies.

For example, a z-score of 1.38 means that the observation is 1.38 standard deviations greater than the mean, while a z-score of -0.66 means that the observation is 0.66 standard deviations below the mean. Even if two observations come from different distributions, they can now be meaningfully compared.

In a sampling distribution of a mean, a z-score is given by

$$z = \frac{\bar{x} - \mu}{\frac{\sigma}{\sqrt{n}}}$$

When the standard error $\frac{s}{\sqrt{n}}$ has to be used in place of $\frac{\sigma}{\sqrt{n}}$, the distribution is no longer best approximated by a normal distribution, but rather by a modified version of one called a **Student's t-distribution**. In this context, instead of z-scores, we consider standardized t-scores:

$$t = \frac{\bar{x} - \mu}{\frac{s}{\sqrt{n}}}$$

INFERENTIAL STATISTICS

The true power of statistics lies in its ability to show how a relatively small sample can provide information about the larger population. Can we estimate the mean of a population based on the mean of a sample? If we can, how confident should we be in this estimate? Can samples from two populations tell us whether the populations have significantly different distributions? These are exactly the kinds of questions that are answered by **inferential statistics**.

NOTE

Around 25 percent of the questions on the DSST Principles of Statistics exam will cover concepts about inferential statistics.

CONFIDENCE INTERVALS

A **confidence interval** is a range of values for which there is a known probability that a population parameter is contained within it.

For example, recall that the distribution of sample means for a large population can be approximated by a normal distribution with mean μ, the population mean. Also, as seen earlier, 95% of normally distributed data lies within (approximately) 2 standard deviations of the mean. Combining these facts, we find a 95% probability that any given sample has a mean within 2 standard deviations of the population mean.

In other words, for 95 out of every 100 possible samples, an interval that extends 2 standard deviations in either direction from the sample mean will contain the population mean. Of course, this means that 5 of the 100 samples will *not* have this property, hence the importance of presenting the interval along with a confidence level.

The general form of a confidence interval of confidence level C is $x \pm m$, where x is an estimate of the parameter being considered, and m is the margin of error. The confidence level C is usually expressed as a percentage (e.g., 90%, 95%). The margin of error is a measure of the accuracy of the estimate, and it takes into account both information about the sample and the confidence level.

The methods for computing m will vary based on sample design and how much information is known about the population. However, regardless of the situation, C and m have the same relationship: as C increases, m also increases. Simply, if we want to be more confident that we have found the population parameter, we are going to necessarily obtain a wider interval.

Of particular importance in computing m is the role of **critical values**; these can come from either a normal distribution, in which case they are denoted z^*, or from a Student's t-distribution, in which case they are denoted by t^*. Critical values are dependent on the confidence level. For example, the value of z^* at a 95% confidence level is 1.96, because approximately 95% of the data in a standard normal distribution lies between −1.96 and 1.96. In the case of critical t-values, another parameter needed is called degrees of freedom, often abbreviated df. In either case, the critical value can be looked up in a table or computed using software.

Confidence Interval for a Mean

A confidence interval for a population mean is given by the following:

$$\bar{x} \pm z^* \cdot \frac{\sigma}{\sqrt{n}}$$

If the value of σ is unknown, it is approximated by s, and the confidence interval becomes:

$$\bar{x} \pm t^* \cdot \frac{s}{\sqrt{n}}$$

where t^* is calculated using $df = n - 1$.

Consider an example in which one is interested in the mean μ of a population of 10,000 individuals, for which the standard deviation is known to be σ = 5. Taking a sample of size $n = 100$, the sample mean $\bar{x}$ is found to be 30.

Following the above formula, the confidence interval is:

$$30 \pm 1.96 \cdot \frac{5}{\sqrt{100}} = 30 \pm 0.98$$

Confidence Interval for a Proportion

In a similar manner, we can form confidence intervals for population proportions:

$$\hat{p} \pm z^* \cdot \sqrt{\frac{\hat{p}(1 - \hat{p})}{n}}$$

For example, suppose that from a town with a population of 22,000 people, we choose a sample of 100 and find that 75 of them are in favor of putting a new traffic light at a busy intersection.

The sample proportion is $\frac{75}{100} = 0.75$, so a 95% confidence interval for p is

$0.75 \pm 1.96\sqrt{\frac{0.75(0.25)}{100}} = 0.75 \pm 0.085$. In other words, we can say with 95% confidence that the

proportion of the population that stands in favor of the new traffic light is between 66.5% and 83.5%.

Note that unlike with the mean, not knowing the population standard deviation here does not change anything; we can calculate it using $\hat{p}$ and still use z^* values.

Confidence Interval for the Difference of Two Means

Although single populations can be of great interest to researchers, it is more often the case that one wants to compare the means of different populations. In this case, a confidence interval can be formed for the difference between the means. The notation used here is given in the following table.

	Population Mean	Population Standard Deviation	Sample Size	Sample Mean	Sample Standard Deviation
Population 1	μ_1	σ_1	n_1	$\overline{x}_1$	s_1
Population 2	μ_2	σ_2	n_2	$\overline{x}_2$	s_2

If the population standard deviations σ_1 and σ_2 are known, the confidence interval is given by:

$$(\overline{x}_1 - \overline{x}_2) \pm z^* \cdot \sqrt{\frac{\sigma_1^2}{n_1} + \frac{\sigma_2^2}{n_2}}$$

Usually, they will not be known. As before, they are estimated using s_1 and s_2, respectively, and a t-distribution is used:

$$(\overline{x}_1 - \overline{x}_2) \pm t^* \cdot \sqrt{\frac{s_1^2}{n_1} + \frac{s_2^2}{n_2}}$$

The number of degrees of freedom is the smaller of $n_1 - 1$ and $n_2 - 1$.

Confidence Interval for the Difference of Two Proportions

Similarly, a confidence interval can be formed for the difference in the proportions of two populations. The notation is similar.

	Population Proportion	Sample Proportion	Sample Size
Population 1	p_1	$\hat{p}_1$	n_1
Population 2	p_2	$\hat{p}_2$	n_2

The confidence interval is given by:

$$(\hat{p}_1 - \hat{p}_2) \pm z^* \cdot \sqrt{\frac{\hat{p}_1(1 - \hat{p}_1)}{n_1} + \frac{\hat{p}_2(1 - \hat{p}_2)}{n_2}}$$

HYPOTHESIS TESTING

Much of statistical testing concerns comparing observed data with a **hypothesis** in order to see if that hypothesis is accurate. For example, suppose one believes that males in the United States are taller than females. That's a hypothesis. One can then compare the means of samples of males and females and see if males are indeed taller. Statistical tests will then determine if the sample data is convincing.

It is standard in hypothesis testing to test the evidence for a hypothesis against a null hypothesis. The **null hypothesis** is that the hypothesis being proposed is untrue. In the example with heights, the null hypothesis would be that males and females have similar heights. The null hypothesis is abbreviated H_0. The hypothesis you propose—the hypothesis for which you have collected evidence to see if it is true—is called the **alternate hypothesis**. In our example, the alternative hypothesis is that males in the United States are taller than females. We write the alternative hypothesis as H_a.

The alternate hypothesis can be **one-sided** or **two-sided**, depending on the available outcomes. For example, if you hypothesize that people will lose weight on a specific exercise regime, that is one-sided; weight can go in only one direction, down. However, if you are testing to see just whether weight *changes* over the course of the exercise program, that would be two-sided; the null hypothesis would be that weight remains unchanged and is rejected if weight goes up or down. Two-sided hypotheses are more common and often more useful.

The problem with the hypothesis-testing construct is that it is binary—the hypothesis is either accepted or not. But what if it's probably true, but you aren't completely sure? This is where **significance level** comes in. It is far more precise to express the evidence in favor of the alternate hypothesis in terms of probability that it is correct. Expressing the likelihood of the alternate hypothesis being correct in this way is called the **p-value**. The lower the p-value, the higher the probability that H_a is actually correct.

To calculate a p-value, a **test statistic** is used. A test statistic is a value calculated from a sample. The p-value is then the probability of obtaining this test statistic under the assumption that H_0 is correct. A low p-value means that the probability of obtaining the test statistic is low; this will generally lead

TIP

When looking up or calculating a *p*-value, it is important to note whether the test is *one-tailed* or *two-tailed*. This corresponds to having a one-sided or two-sided alternate hypothesis.

one to conclude that H_0 is incorrect. This is referred to as **rejecting** H_0. Although p-values can be calculated for different statistics using tables, it is much easier to use statistical software.

In advance of conducting the sample statistic, it is important to decide how low the p-value would have to be to indicate rejection of H_0. This threshold is called the significance level, and is denoted by α. If a p-value is less than or equal to α, than the data (supporting H_a) are said to be statistically significant at level α.

Errors and Power

There are two ways in which a hypothesis test can go awry. The first is if the null hypothesis is rejected when it is actually true. This is called a **type I error**. Alternatively, the opposite can happen: the alternate hypothesis is rejected in favor of the null hypothesis when actually the alternate hypothesis is true. That is called a **type II error**. In these terms, the significance level α is equivalent to the probability of a type I error occurring. The probability of a type II error is called β.

The **power** of a hypothesis test is defined to be $1 - \beta$. To understand the notion of power in this context, recall the relationship between C and m in the context of confidence intervals: as C increases, so does m. In other words, one might have high confidence that the desired value is in a given interval, but if the interval is so broad that it covers most of the population then it isn't useful. For a sample to be truly useful, it needs to produce not only a high level of confidence, but also a relatively small margin of error. This is equivalent to saying that the corresponding hypothesis test has high power.

By the definition of power, it is clear that as power increases, the probability of a type II error decreases. Hence, power can be thought of as the ability of a test to properly detect an alternative hypothesis. Power can be increased by:

> an increase in the sample size n
>
> a decreasing α
>
> a decrease in the standard deviation
>
> changing the alternate hypothesis to be farther away from the null hypothesis

For example, if hypothesizing that a certain plant food increases growth rate, the null hypothesis would be no growth with the food. An alternate hypothesis proposing 50 percent faster growth would lead to a test with more power than if it proposed only 10 percent faster growth. If such a large effect exists it will be detected with high power.

t-Test for a Mean

When testing a hypothesis concerning the value of a population mean, the null hypothesis will be of the form $H_0 : \mu = \mu_0$. A **one-sample t-test** is used, and the test statistic is:

$$t = \frac{\overline{x} - \mu_0}{\frac{s}{\sqrt{n}}} \ , df = n - 1$$

TIP

In most research areas, significance levels of 0.05 (5%) or 0.01 (1%) are standard.

As an example, consider a researcher studying a new medication for tension headaches, and suppose it is known that without treatment, tension headaches subside on their own in a mean time of 5 hours. For the medication to be effective, it must reduce this time. If μ is the mean time it takes these headaches to subside when patients are treated with this new medication, then the null and alternative hypotheses for this test are $H_0: \mu = 5$ and $H\alpha : \mu < 5$, respectively. Let us choose $\alpha = 0.05$ as our significance level.

To perform the test, we take a sample of 30 patients and collect data on how quickly this medication relieves their headaches. The results have a mean of 4.5 hours, and a standard deviation of 1.3 hours. Given these numbers, we can calculate the test statistic:

$$t = \frac{4.5 - 5}{1.3 / \sqrt{30}} \approx -2.11$$

Using software or a table of values, we can look up this t-statistic, and find that the associated p-value is $p = 0.0218$. Since this is less than our chosen α, the effect is statistically significant and we reject H_0. Note that if we had instead chosen $\alpha = 0.01$, for example, the p-value would not have been significant enough to reject H_0.

t-Test for the Difference of Two Means

A similar procedure can be used to compare the means of two different populations, as long as the populations are completely distinct and the samples are independent of each other. The same variable has to be measured in both groups. We have seen before that we can do a rough comparison of two populations by making a stemplot or boxplot of each and comparing them side by side, but to make sure that any differences are statistically significant, we need to perform a hypothesis test.

Here, the null hypothesis has the form $\mu_1 - \mu_2 = \Delta$, and the test statistic is

$$t = \frac{(\bar{x}_1 - \bar{x}_2) - \Delta}{\sqrt{\frac{s_1^2}{n_1} + \frac{s_2^2}{n_2}}}$$

and the number of degrees of freedom is the smaller of $n_1 - 1$ and $n_2 - 1$.

z-Test for a Proportion

We can also perform hypothesis tests for one-sample and two-sample proportions. The notation is the same as with confidence intervals.

The test statistic for a one-sample proportion test with $H_0: p = p_0$ is

$$z = \frac{\hat{p} - p_0}{\sqrt{\frac{\hat{p}(1 - \hat{p})}{n}}}$$

z-Test for the Difference of Two Proportions

The test statistic for a two-sample proportion test with $H_0 : p_1 - p_2 = \Delta$ is

$$z = \frac{(p_1 - p_2)}{\sqrt{p(1 - p)\left(\dfrac{1}{n_1^2} + \dfrac{1}{n_2^2}\right)}}$$

where $\hat{p}$, called the **pooled proportion**, is defined by $\hat{p} = \dfrac{\hat{p}_1 n_1 + \hat{p}_2 n_2}{n_1 + n_2}$.

ANOVA

We have previously seen how to compare the means or proportions of two populations. What about when there are more than two populations to compare? For example, a corporate sales analyst might want to compare mean sales across four different geographic regions.

Analysis of variance, or **ANOVA**, is a method of comparing means using samples drawn from at least three different populations. ANOVA determines whether or not the differences in sample means are statistically significant. Are the observed differences due to chance, or due to genuine differences in the populations?

As with the two-sample t-test, it is always a good idea to examine side-by-side boxplots when comparing multiple means. If the groups have very different medians and low in-group variation, it is likely that the means are truly different. However, if the medians are different but variation is high, maybe the populations aren't really that different after all; this is what ANOVA works to determine.

Hypothesis testing with ANOVA is more complex than with one or two samples. The null hypothesis, H_0, is that the means of all groups are equal. The alternate hypothesis, that not all of the means are equal, can be true in a variety of different ways. It may be that all of the means are different, or it may be that some are the same but one or more are different from the rest.

The details of ANOVA calculations are beyond the scope of this chapter, but in general, it works by comparing variance between groups with the n-group variance of each group. The populations being compared must all have normal distributions, and the samples should ideally all be of the same size. ANOVA assumes that the in-group variances are close to each other; if this is not the case, ANOVA should not be used. The rule of thumb is that the largest standard deviation must be less than twice as large as the smallest standard deviation in the populations being compared. The power of an ANOVA test will be highest with large sample sizes, high variation among the different sample means, and low standard deviations within each group.

When using computer software to calculate ANOVA statistics, the results are generally presented as a table, containing many pieces of information. The most important of these are the F-value and the p-value. The F-value is the test statistic, analogous to the t-statistic in other hypothesis tests. The p-value, as usual, is the probability of obtaining these results under the assumption of the null hypothesis; if this is less than the predetermined α, then H_0 should be rejected.

Non-Parametric Procedures

All the procedures discussed so far apply to populations that are normally distributed, or whose sampling distributions can be approximated with normal distributions. However, this certainly does not apply to all data! There are some models available for non-normal data, but they don't always apply.

One strategy in a situation like this is to apply a transformation to the data; sometimes, an appropriate transformation will make the data normal. Some common transformations to consider attempting:

Take the square root of every observation.

Divide by a constant.

Take the logarithm.

If transforming the data does not help, the most common approach is to apply procedures that make inferences without relying on distributions at all. These are called **non-parametric** procedures. Since these generally less powerful tests don't rely on distributions, they don't compare means. Rather, medians are usually the focus.

The simplest non-parametric test is the **sign test**. It's a test based on counts; pairs of data points are compared and the test statistic is simply the count of pairs that have positive differences. The sample size, n, does not include pairs that have no difference, and p-values are calculated based on the binomial distribution. As usual, this is most easily done with software.

Another common non-parametric test is the **Mann-Whitney U test**, which tests hypotheses about differences between randomly selected values from different samples. It is almost as powerful as a t-test.

SUMMING IT UP

- Data can come in three different forms. **Numerical** data is represented by numbers that can be manipulated arithmetically. **Categorical** data simply divides values into categories that have no numerical meaning. **Ordinal** data is divided into categories, but these are placed in a particular order in a meaningful way. Numerical data is **discrete** if the possible values can be listed (even if the list is potentially infinite), and **continuous** otherwise.

- **Nominal** data points are purely categorical, with no relation to one another. **Ordinal** measurement places data into ordered categories. The **interval** level goes one step further by placing its categories at a fixed distance from each other; at this level, addition and subtraction are meaningful. Finally, at the **ratio** level, data is fully numeric; multiplication and division give meaningful results as well.

- Since **populations** are generally too large to study directly, **samples** are chosen from among them. Some of the most common sampling techniques are **simple random samples**, **stratified samples**, and **multistage samples**. These all use randomization to some extent. Poor sampling techniques, including voluntary surveys, lead to problems such **response bias** and **undercoverage**.

- **Descriptive statistics** provide a summary of a data set. The focus is usually on **center**—a measurement of where the middle of the data lies—and **spread**—a way of describing how the data is spread out.

- The **mean**, sometimes called the **average**, is represented by $\bar{x}$ (for a sample mean) or μ (for a population mean). In either case, it is the sum of the data points divided by the size of the set. The **median** is found by putting the data points in order and finding the point in the middle.

- The mean is susceptible to **outliers**; that is, a single point far away from the rest of the data will have a large influence on the mean. The **median** is resistant to outliers.

- One way of measuring the spread of a data set is in terms of percentiles. The **nth percentile** is a value in a data set such that $n\%$ of the values fall below it. The most commonly used percentiles are the 25th, called the **first quartile**, the 50th, which is the median, and the 75th, called the **third quartile**. The **five-number summary** is made up of these three percentiles along with the smallest and largest values in the set. The distance between the first and third quartiles is called the **interquartile range**, or **IQR**.

- When using the mean as a measure of center, the **standard deviation** is used as the measure of spread. The standard deviation is represented by s or σ for samples and populations, respectively, and is calculated by the formulas $s = \sqrt{\dfrac{1}{n-1}\sum(x_i - \bar{x})^2}$ and $\sigma = \sqrt{\dfrac{1}{n}\sum(x_i - \mu)^2}$.

  The smaller the standard deviation, the closer together the values in the data set are.

- A constant value can be added to every number; this is called a **translation**, or a **shift**. Each data point can be multiplied by a constant value; here, the data is said to be **scaled**. Translations cause measures of center to change, but measures of spread remain the same. When data is scaled, all measures of both center and spread are changed along with the data.

- A **visualization** is a graphical representation of a data set. The goal with visualizations is to create a picture that shows features of interest in the set—primarily the center and/or spread.

- A **stemplot** is a visual summary of data that shows every value in the set. Each data point is split into a **stem**—the value with the last digit discarded—and the **leaf**—the last digit. The values are then grouped together by stem, with the leaves listed alongside in order.

- A **histogram** does not show individual values, but rather uses bars to show how many of the values fall into each of several ranges. The shape of a histogram is a visual guide to the center and spread of a data set. A peak is often (but not always) near the center of the data, and the relative sizes of the bars are determined by the spread of the data. Histograms can be **symmetric** or **skewed**.

- A **boxplot** is a visual representation of the five-number summary. The 25th, 50th, and 75th percentiles form a **box**, showing the IQR. The **whiskers** on either end of the box extend to the smallest and largest values in the set, displaying the range of the entire set. If there are outliers, these are usually discarded when creating the whiskers, and shown separately as stars.

- **Probability** is the mathematics of randomness and chance. A **sample space** is the set of all possible outcomes of an experiment, and an **event** is of a subset of the sample space. The **probability** of an event is the proportion of times that event occurs, and is always a value between 0 and 1.

- Two events are **mutually exclusive** if they cannot occur at the same time. For such events A and B, the probability of one or the other follows the **addition rule**: $P(A \text{ or } B) = P(A) + P(B)$. If events are not mutually exclusive, then $P(A \text{ or } B) = P(A) + P(B) - P(A \text{ and } B)$.

- Events that do not influence each other are called **independent**; if they do influence each other, they are **dependent**. In either case, the **multiplication rule** says that $P(A \text{ and } B) = P(A) \cdot P(B)$, but care must be taken in the dependent case to adjust probabilities based on the prior outcome, A.

- If two tasks are completed in succession, and there are m and n ways of completing them, respectively, then the combined number of ways to complete the pair is $m \cdot n$. This is the **counting principle**.

- If r items are to be chosen from among n, and the order matters, the different ways of accomplishing this are called **permutations**. The number of possible ways is given by $P(n,r) = \dfrac{n!}{(n-r)!}$

- If r items are to be chosen from among n, and the order does not matter, the different ways of accomplishing this are called **combinations**. The number of possible ways is given by $C(n,r) = \dfrac{n!}{r!(n-r)!}$

- A **discrete probability distribution** is an assignment of a probability to each of the possible discrete outcomes of an experiment. The probabilities must sum to 1.

- A **binomial experiment** consists of a series of n independent trials with a fixed probability of success, p. The number of successes in these trials has a **binomial distribution**, written $B(n,p)$. In particular, the probability of exactly k successes is $C(n,k) \times p^k(1-p)^{n-k}$.

- The **expected value** of a probability distribution is $E = \sum x_i P(x_i)$. For a binomial distribution, this is equivalent to $E = np$.

- A **continuous probability distribution** applies when the possible outcomes of an experiment form a continuous set. It is described by means of a **density curve**, and probabilities are calculated based on specific areas under this curve.

- The most commonly encountered family of continuous distributions are normal distributions. A **normal distribution** $N(\mu,\sigma)$ is described by its mean (μ) and its standard deviation (σ). Approximately 68% of the data lies within 1 standard deviation of the mean; 95% within 2; and 99.7% within 3. $N(0,1)$ is called the **standard normal distribution**.

- A **scatterplot** is a two-dimensional graph that shows a relationship between two variables, called the **explanatory** and **response** variables. The explanatory variable is shown along the x-axis, and the response variable is shown along the y-axis. When one variable shows a tendency to rise as the other one rises, they are said to be **positively correlated**. If one falls as the other rises, they are **negatively correlated**.

- The **correlation coefficient**, r, is a measurement of how well correlated two variables are. It is always between −1 and 1. A value close to 0 indicates weak correlation, while values close to −1 and 1 represent strong positive and negative correlation, respectively. This value is susceptible to outliers.

- The process of finding a line that best fits a collection of points on a scatterplot is called **linear regression**, and it results in a line of the form $y = mx + b$. The most common method of doing this is called **least squares regression**. The line produced can be used to **interpolate**—predict values of y for values of x that are inside the range of the data, but not represented by the given points—or **extrapolate**—predict values of y for values of x that are outside the range of the data set. How well the line fits the data is measured by the square of the correlation coefficient r^2. This is always between 0 and 1; larger values indicate a better fit.

- When repeated samples of a particular **sample size** n are taken from a population, any statistics calculated from the samples form a **sampling distribution**.

- A **population proportion** is denoted p, and a **sample proportion** is denoted $\hat{p}$. The sampling distribution for $\hat{p}$ has mean p and standard deviation $\sqrt{\dfrac{p(1-p)}{n}}$. If n is large, it is approximately normal.

- The **distribution of sample means** from a population with mean μ and standard deviation σ has mean μ and standard deviation $\dfrac{\sigma}{\sqrt{n}}$. The **central limit theorem** says that as the sample size increases, this distribution can be approximated to an increasingly accurate degree by a normal distribution.

- If the standard deviation σ of a population is unknown, it is often approximated by the sample standard deviation, s. With this approximation, the standard deviation of the sampling distribution is called the **standard error**.

- The **law of large numbers** states that the mean of a sampling distribution will approach the population mean as the sample size increases. In addition, an increase in sample size causes a decrease in the standard deviation (or standard error) of the sampling distribution. For this reason, larger sample sizes tend to lead to more powerful statistical results.

- Any normal distribution can be **standardized** by replacing each data point by a **z-score**, calculated as $z = \frac{x - \bar{x}}{s}$. In the context of a sampling distribution of a mean, where the data points themselves are sample means, this turns into $z = \frac{\bar{x} - \mu}{\frac{\sigma}{\sqrt{n}}}$. If the standard error is being used, a t-score is usually more appropriate, and is $t = \frac{\bar{x} - \mu}{\frac{s}{\sqrt{n}}}$.

- A **confidence interval** is a range of values for which there is a known probability that a population parameter is contained within it. It is always of the form $x \pm m$, where x is an estimate, and m is the **margin of error** and is calculated based on sample data and a **confidence level**, C, that is associated with the interval. It usually involves a **critical** z (or t) value, written z^* (or t^*).

- A **hypothesis** is a proposition about a population that may or may not be true. When considering a hypothesis, it is usually tested against a **null hypothesis**, H_0, which states that the proposal is untrue. The **alternate hypothesis**, H_a, is the hypothesis being proposed. It can be either **one-sided** or **two-sided**. A **hypothesis test** is performed at a particular significance level, α, which should be decided upon before doing the experiment. The test is conducted by calculating the **test statistic**, which leads to a **p-value**. If $p < \alpha$, there is sufficient evidence to reject H_0. Otherwise, H_0 cannot be rejected, and H_a, therefore, remains unproven.

- A **type I error** occurs when the null hypothesis is incorrectly rejected; the probability of this happening is α, the significance level. A **type II error** occurs when the null hypothesis is erroneously not rejected; the probability of this happening is called β. The **power** of a hypothesis test is $1 - \beta$. Power can be increased by increasing the sample size, decreasing α, decreasing the standard deviation, or making the alternate hypothesis more extreme.

- **Analysis of variance**, or **ANOVA**, is a method of comparing the means of more than 2 populations at a time. The null hypothesis is that all means are equal; the alternate hypothesis is that at least one of the means is different. ANOVA is done using statistical software, which will produce an F-statistic and a p-value. Rejection of H_0 follows the same rules as with other hypothesis tests.

- When populations, or their sampling distributions, are not normal, there are two options to consider. First, a transformation can be attempted. Common ones include square roots, scaling, and logarithms. Otherwise, **non-parametric** procedures can be applied. These usually focus on medians rather than means. The **sign test** is a simple example of a non-parametric test.

PRINCIPLES OF STATISTICS POST-TEST

> **Directions**: Carefully read each of the following 60 questions. Choose the best answer to each question and fill in the corresponding circle on the answer sheet. The Answer Key and Explanations can be found following this post-test.

1. A zoologist measures the lengths, in feet, of 23 crocodiles. He finds that the mean length is 8 feet, and the standard deviation is 1.5 feet. Later, he realizes that his measuring instruments were incorrectly calibrated, and that each measurement should have 2 feet added to it. What are the correct values of the mean and the standard deviation, respectively?
   - **A.** 8 and 1.5
   - **B.** 10 and 1.5
   - **C.** 8 and 3.5
   - **D.** 10 and 3.5

2. In succession, a fair coin is flipped and a standard 6-sided die is rolled. What is the probability that the coin shows heads and the die shows 3?
   - **A.** $\frac{2}{3}$
   - **B.** $\frac{1}{12}$
   - **C.** $\frac{1}{3}$
   - **D.** 0

3. In a game at the county fair, a person has a 50% chance of winning \$1, a 50% chance of winning \$2, and a 25% chance of losing \$4. What is the expected value of the game?
   - **A.** \$0.25
   - **B.** −\$1
   - **C.** \$1.50
   - **D.** \$2.50

4. An environmental engineer wants to compare the median carbon output of two different models of cars. Which of the following would be the most appropriate statistical procedure for her to employ?
   - **A.** z-test
   - **B.** t-test
   - **C.** ANOVA
   - **D.** Sign test

5. An experiment produces an outcome x in the range $1 \leq x \leq 5$, where x is not restricted to being an integer. The probabilities in this continuous distribution are described by a density curve, C. Which of the following facts about C must be true?
   - **A.** C is highest at $x = 3$.
   - **B.** C has the same height at $x = 1$ and at $x = 5$.
   - **C.** The total area under the curve C between $x = 1$ and $x = 5$ is 1.
   - **D.** At some point between 1 and 5, C has a negative value.

6. Over the past decade, 44% of the applicants to a certain university have been female. In an effort to boost this number, the admissions office actively tries to recruit more girls. After two years of doing this, and collecting data about the applicants during these two years, what null hypothesis should they test to know if they have succeeded?
   - **A.** $\rho = 0.44$
   - **B.** $\rho > 0.44$
   - **C.** $\mu = 0.44$
   - **D.** $\mu > 0.44$

7. All of the following will increase the power of a hypothesis test EXCEPT
   A. increasing the sample size.
   B. decreasing the standard deviation.
   C. decreasing the confidence level.
   D. moving the alternate hypothesis closer to the null hypothesis.

8. The regression line $H = 0.8m + 20$ is used to predict the height, in inches, of a baby boy that is m months old, where $0 \leq m \leq 12$. Using this model, what is the predicted height of a 6-month old baby boy?
   A. 4.8 inches
   B. 20.8 inches
   C. 24.8 inches
   D. 68 inches

9. When normally distributed data are standardized, so that z-scores are applicable, what are the mean and standard deviation of the distribution to which they are fit?
   A. mean = 0, standard deviation = 0
   B. mean = 0, standard deviation = 1
   C. mean = 1, standard deviation = 0
   D. mean = 1, standard deviation = 1

10. Which of the following graphs would be most appropriate for examining the quartiles of a data set?
    A. Scatterplot
    B. Stemplot
    C. Histogram
    D. Boxplot

11. Which of the following best describes the correlation between the variables shown in the following scatterplot?

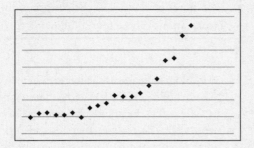

   A. Positive correlation
   B. Negative correlation
   C. Linear correlation
   D. No correlation

12. The organizer of an academic conference received 17 applications from graduate students who want to speak at the conference. He has to choose 5 of them, and decide on the order in which they will speak. Which expression represents the number of different lineups of speakers that are possible?
   A. $17 + 16 + 15 + 14 + 13$
   B. $C(17,5)$
   C. $P(17,5)$
   D. 17^5

13. What characteristics of a data set are described by its distribution?
   A. The method by which the data was collected, and highest value in the set
   B. The number of points in the data set, and the units that the numbers describe
   C. The range of the data set, its center, and how spread apart the values are
   D. The possible hypothesis tests that can be performed using it

14. If 30 ± 4 represents a 95% confidence interval for the mean of a population, which of the following values would have to be contained in a 90% confidence interval for the mean of the same population?
    A. 28
    B. 30
    C. 32
    D. 34

15. If a line passes exactly through every point in a data set, what can be said about the value of the correlation coefficient r for that data set?
    A. r is less than $\frac{1}{2}$
    B. r is greater than $\frac{1}{2}$
    C. r is either -1 or 1
    D. r is 0

16. A standard 6-sided die is rolled. What is the probability that it lands on either an even number or a 5?
    A. $\frac{1}{12}$
    B. $\frac{1}{6}$
    C. $\frac{1}{2}$
    D. $\frac{2}{3}$

17. In a town with 23,000 households, the mean annual household income is $48,000.
    A sample of 100 households has a mean income of $31,000. What is the most likely explanation for the large difference between the sample mean and the population mean?
    A. A type I error occurred.
    B. A type II error occurred.
    C. The sample was biased due to insufficient randomization.
    D. People lied about their income when asked.

18. The means of five populations are compared using ANOVA. The p-value is 0.031, which is less than the chosen α of 0.05. Which conclusion is best supported by this information?
    A. All five populations have the same mean.
    B. At least one of the five populations has a mean that is different than all the other means.
    C. There are at least two different means among the five populations.
    D. Each population has a different mean.

19. If samples of a sufficiently large size are repeatedly taken from a large population, which of the following is NOT necessarily true about the distribution of sample means?
    A. It is symmetric.
    B. It can be well approximated by a normal distribution.
    C. The mean is the same as the population mean.
    D. The standard deviation is the same as the population standard deviation.

20. When performing a hypothesis test, which of the following is a consequence of decreasing the significance level α?
    A. There is a higher risk of a type I error.
    B. There is a lower risk of a type I error.
    C. The sample size increases.
    D. The sample size decreases.

21. In a sample of one-hundred 2-ounce bags of M&Ms, the proportion of red candies is 13% red. In a different sample of one-hundred 16-ounce bags, the proportion of red candies is 15%. What hypothesis test would be most appropriate for testing whether or not this difference in proportions is statistically significant?
    A. One-sample t-test
    B. Two-sample t-test
    C. Two-sample z-test
    D. ANOVA

22. Which of the following variables does NOT form a discrete distribution?
    A. The number of days in a week that it rains
    B. The number of students enrolled in a university
    C. The position in line of a person waiting at a grocery store
    D. The position on a number line of a randomly chosen real number

23. Events E and F are independent. If the probability of event E is 10%, the probability of event F is 40%, and p represents the probability of these events occurring together, what can be concluded about p?
    A. It is equal to 0%.
    B. It is greater than 4%.
    C. It is less than 4%.
    D. It is equal to 4%.

24. A 90% confidence interval for the mean height of redwood trees in California is 27 ± 3. What does this tell you?
    A. With 90% confidence, the mean height of all redwood trees in California is between 24 and 30 feet.
    B. Ninety percent of redwood trees in California have a height between 24 and 30 feet.
    C. The mean height of redwood trees in California is 27 feet, and the standard deviation is 3 feet.
    D. If any 90 redwood trees in California are measured, their mean height will be between 24 and 30 feet.

25. A scatterplot is shown below, along with the regression line calculated using the least squares method.

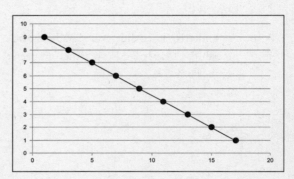

Which of the following is closest to the value of r^2 for this line?
    A. −0.5
    B. 0.0
    C. 0.5
    D. 1.0

26. If the probability that it will rain tomorrow is $\frac{4}{19}$, what is the probability that it will NOT rain tomorrow?
    A. 1
    B. $\frac{15}{19}$
    C. $\frac{4}{19}$
    D. 0

27. Find the mean, median, and mode of the following list: 7, 7, 9, 2, 6, 10, 1.
    A. mean = 6, median = 7, mode = 7
    B. mean = 7, median = 7, mode = 7
    C. mean = 6, median = 2, mode = 2
    D. mean = 6, median = 2, mode = 7

28. A certain population has a standard deviation of 20. Samples of size 16 are taken from the population. What is the standard error of the sample means?
    A. 1.25
    B. 5
    C. 16
    D. 20

29. A data set consists of ordered pairs (x, y) where the x coordinates range from −3 to 17. The data is fit by a linear model $y = −2x + 1$. Which of the following equations represent the process of extrapolating from this data?
    A. $y = −2(−3) + 1$
    B. $y = −2(0) + 1$
    C. $y = −2(16) + 1$
    D. $y = −2(18) + 1$

30. Which of the following characteristics apply to a normal distribution?
    A. Discrete and symmetric
    B. Continuous and symmetric
    C. Discrete and skewed
    D. Continuous and skewed

31. Using the same sample data, 90% and 95% confidence intervals are constructed. Which of these intervals will contain a larger range of values?
    A. The 90% interval will be larger.
    B. The 95% interval will be larger.
    C. The intervals will be the same size.
    D. Either interval could be larger, depending on the population.

32. A factory that produces gizmos has a failure rate of 2%. That is, every gizmo they produce has a 2% chance of being defective. In a shipment of 500 gizmos, what is the expected value of the number of defective gizmos?
    A. 250
    B. 100
    C. 10
    D. 2

33. The histogram below can represent which of the following data sets?

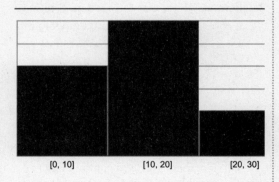

[0, 10]   [10, 20]   [20, 30]

    A. [0, 15, 16, 29, 19, 7]
    B. [11, 28, 13, 17, 14, 1]
    C. [2, 21, 28, 13, 14, 15]
    D. [10, 20, 30]

34. Of the following sampling techniques, which is least likely to lead to statistically valid conclusions?

    A. Simple random sample

    B. Stratified random sample

    C. Voluntary survey

    D. Multistage sample

35. A brand of potato chips is sold in 5-ounce bags. A skeptical consumer suspects that the bags are chronically underfilled, and do not, on average, actually contain 5 ounces To test this hypothesis, he purchases 30 bags of chips and measures the weight of the chips in each. If σ is the population mean, and *s* is the sample mean, which of the following sets of hypotheses does he want to test?

    A. $H_0 : \mu = 5, H_a : \mu \neq 5$

    B. $H_0 : \mu = 5, H_a : s < 5$

    C. $H_0 : \mu = 5, H_a : \mu < 5$

    D. $H_0 : s = 5, H_a : s < 5$

36. Two variables, *x* and *y*, are found to have a correlation coefficient of 0.92. Does this mean necessarily imply that *x* causes *y* or that *y* causes *x*? Why?

    A. Yes; 0.91 implies strong correlation, so one of the variables must cause the other.

    B. No; 0.91 is too small to imply strong correlation.

    C. No; there may be a confounding variable.

    D. No; only a negative correlation implies a causative relationship.

37. Which of the following does NOT generally affect the accuracy to which a sample represents the population from which it is drawn?

    A. Sample size

    B. Confidence level

    C. Population standard deviation

    D. Randomization in sampling

38. Each answer below shows a scatterplot along with a least-squares regression line. For which line do you expect the r^2 value to be closest to 0?

A.

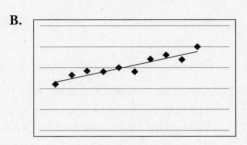

B.

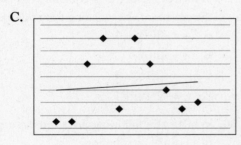

C.

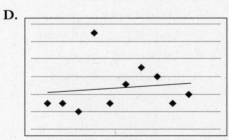

D.

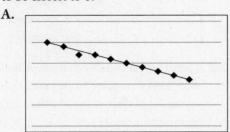

39. What kind of hypothesis test should be used to test a hypothesis of the form $\mu_1 = \mu_2 = \mu_3 = \mu_4$, where μ_i is the mean of sample i?
    A. Sign test
    B. ANOVA
    C. z-test
    D. t-test

40. When creating a confidence interval for a population mean, which of the following conditions is an indication that a z-value, rather than a t-value, can be used?
    A. The population standard deviation is known.
    B. The sample size is less than 100.
    C. The confidence level is more than 90%.
    D. The population mean is unknown.

41. A paleontologist searches for fossils in five neighboring sites. The number of fossils he finds at each site are 3, 5, 0, 10, and 1, respectively. These numbers are an example of what level of measurement?
    A. Nominal
    B. Ordinal
    C. Interval
    D. Ratio

42. Which of the following are NOT affected by sample size?
    A. Population mean
    B. Standard error
    C. Confidence interval
    D. Power

43. A teacher finds that her students tend to perform better on tests when they get more sleep. Which of the following scatterplots best represents this relationship between hours of sleep (on the *x*-axis) and test scores (on the *y*-axis)?

A.

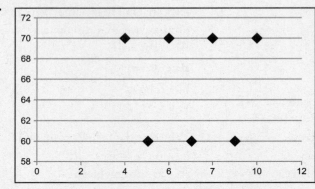

B.

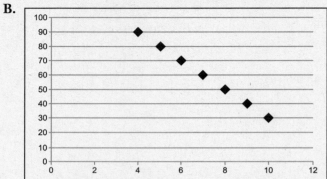

C.

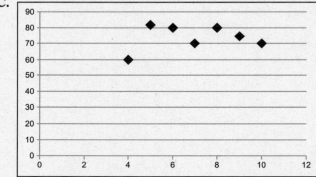

D.

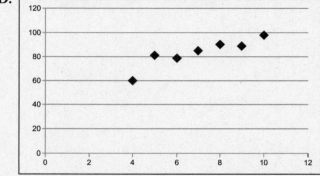

44. The null hypothesis $H_0: \mu = 7$ is tested against $H_a: \mu > 7$ with a significance level of $\alpha = 0.05$. The true value of μ is 7.3. However, due to a small sample size, the p-value for the test is 0.0512, so H_0 cannot be rejected. Which of the following describes this situation?
   A. Type I error
   B. Type II error
   C. Sample bias
   D. Confounding variable

45. Which of the following descriptive statistics are influenced by outliers?
   A. Mean and median
   B. Mean and standard deviation
   C. Median and IQR
   D. Standard deviation and IQR

46. Least squares regression is performed on a set of ordered pairs (x, y), where $\bar{x} = 5$ and $\bar{y} = 10$. If the slope is calculated to be $m = 6$, what is the value of the y-intercept b in the equation $y = mx + b$?
   A. −20
   B. 0
   C. 2
   D. 5

47. If the standard deviation of a population is 10, what sample size is necessary to ensure that the standard deviation of the sampling distribution for the mean will be less than or equal to 1?
   A. 4
   B. 10
   C. 16
   D. 100

48. Which of the following is NOT a reason to survey a sample chosen from a population, as opposed to the full population?
   A. The full population may not be known.
   B. It may be too expensive to survey the full population.
   C. Using a sample may result in more accurate statistical data.
   D. It may be too time-consuming to survey the full population.

49. A sample is selected from the students at a university in the following manner: 50 freshmen are randomly chosen, then 50 sophomores are randomly chosen, then 50 juniors, and finally 50 seniors. What kind of sample is being used in this scenario?
   A. Simple random sample
   B. Stratified random sample
   C. Multistage sample
   D. Voluntary response sample

50. If the sampling distribution of the sample means of a population, with sample size 100, is approximated by $N(450,4)$, what are the values of μ and σ for the population?
   A. $\mu = 450, \sigma = 4$
   B. $\mu = 45{,}000, \sigma = 400$
   C. $\mu = 450, \sigma = 400$
   D. $\mu = 450, \sigma = 40$

51. The hypothesis $H_0: \mu = 80$ is tested against $H_a: \mu > 80$ at a significance level of $\alpha = 0.01$. The p-value corresponding to the computed test statistic is $p = 0.004$. What conclusion is appropriate?
   A. $\mu = 81$
   B. $\mu > 80$
   C. $\mu = 80$
   D. $\mu < 81$

52. Consider the side-by-side boxplots below, representing populations A and B, respectively.

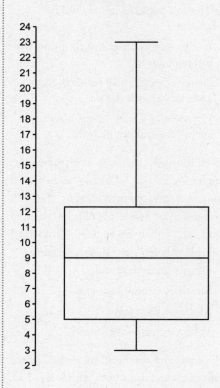

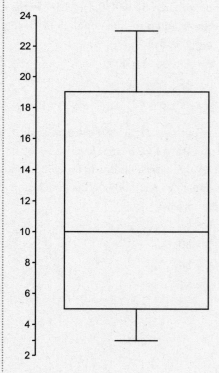

Which of the following statements is true?

A. Populations A and B have the same range.

B. Population A has a higher maximum than population B.

C. Population A has a higher median than population B.

D. Populations A and B have the same IQR.

53. Two population proportions are compared by testing the hypothesis $H_0 : p_1 = p_2$ against an alternative with $\alpha = 0.05$. The p-value is calculated to be $p = 0.052$. Which of the following conclusions is warranted?

A. The two proportions are definitely equal.

B. There is insufficient evidence to conclude that the proportions are not equal.

C. The two proportions are definitely not equal.

D. The first proportion is greater than the second.

54. If a population proportion is $p = 0.25$, which expression represents the standard deviation of the sampling distribution for this proportion with sample size 25?

A. 0.25

B. $\dfrac{0.25}{25}$

C. $\dfrac{\sqrt{0.25 \cdot 0.75}}{25}$

D. $\dfrac{\sqrt{0.25 \cdot 0.75}}{5}$

55. An organization consists of 32 women and 27 men. A committee consisting of 3 men and 3 women is to be chosen from among the members. Which of the following represents the number of different possible committees that can be chosen?

A. $C(59,6)$

B. $P(59,6)$

C. $C(32,3) \cdot C(27,3)$

D. $P(32,3) \cdot P(27,3)$

56. If two variables have a strong negative correlation, what can be said about the value of r^2 that results from performing least squares regression on these variables?

A. It will be close to -1.

B. It will be close to 0.

C. It will be close to 1.

D. It will be more than 1.

57. Ten software engineers were surveyed. The data collected includes how many years of experience they have and their current annual salary. The results are plotted below, where years of experience is on the x-axis and salary is on the y-axis. A best fit line, obtained using least squares regression, is shown as well.

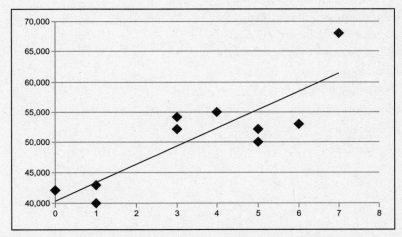

What best describes the correlation between years of experience and salary?

A. Positive correlation

B. Negative correlation

C. Quadratic correlation

D. No correlation

58. In a certain hypothesis test, the probability of a type II error is 20%. What does this mean?

   A. There is a 20% chance that the null hypothesis will be rejected.

   B. If the null hypothesis is true, there is a 20% chance that the test will erroneously conclude that it should be rejected.

   C. If the null hypothesis is false, there is a 20% chance that the test will fail to produce enough evidence to reject it.

   D. There is a 20% chance that the alternative hypothesis is false.

59. Based on a set of data points with x-values ranging from 40 to 90, a least-squares regression calculation produces the line $y = 3x - 10$. Using this model, one can predict the value of y when $x = 50$. What is the predicted value? Is this an example of interpolation or extrapolation?

   A. 20; interpolation

   B. 140; interpolation

   C. 20; extrapolation

   D. 140; extrapolation

60. If a sample of size 50 is taken from a population of size 1,000, and the sample is subsequently analyzed using a t-distribution (due to an unknown population standard deviation), how many degrees of freedom should be used?

   A. 49

   B. 50

   C. 999

   D. 1000

ANSWER KEY AND EXPLANATIONS

1. B	**13.** C	**25.** D	**37.** B	**49.** B
2. B	**14.** B	**26.** B	**38.** C	**50.** D
3. A	**15.** C	**27.** A	**39.** B	**51.** B
4. D	**16.** D	**28.** B	**40.** A	**52.** A
5. C	**17.** C	**29.** D	**41.** D	**53.** B
6. A	**18.** C	**30.** B	**42.** A	**54.** D
7. D	**19.** D	**31.** B	**43.** D	**55.** C
8. C	**20.** B	**32.** C	**44.** B	**56.** C
9. B	**21.** C	**33.** A	**45.** B	**57.** A
10. D	**22.** D	**34.** C	**46.** A	**58.** C
11. A	**23.** D	**35.** C	**47.** D	**59.** B
12. C	**24.** A	**36.** C	**48.** C	**60.** A

1. **The correct answer is B.** When data is translated by a fixed value (2, in this case), the mean is translated as well, but the standard deviation does not change. Therefore, the correct mean is 8 + 2 = 10, but the standard deviation remains 1.5. Choices A and C neglect to adjust the mean; choices C and D incorrectly adjust the standard deviation.

2. **The correct answer is B.** The probability of obtaining heads on a flip of a fair coin is $\frac{1}{2}$, and the probability of getting a 3 on a die is $\frac{1}{6}$. These events are independent, so we can simply multiply the probabilities to obtain $\frac{1}{2} \cdot \frac{1}{6} = \frac{1}{12}$. Choices A and C result from using the wrong operation—addition (choice A) or subtraction (choice C)—instead of multiplication. A probability is only 0 (choice D) when the event cannot occur, which is not the case here.

3. **The correct answer is A.** The expected value is obtained by multiplying each outcome by its probability, and then summing these products. Here we have

$0.25 \cdot 1 + 0.5 \cdot 2 + 0.25 \cdot -4 = 0.25$. Choice B simply adds the dollar amounts 1 + 2 + (−4) without taking the probabilities into account. Choice C neglects the possibility of losing money. Choice D includes all dollar amounts and probabilities, but mistakenly counts the $4 as positive instead of negative.

4. **The correct answer is D.** The sign test is the only choice that does not rely on a particular sampling distribution; it is a non-parametric test, and is used to test null hypotheses involving medians. A z-test (choice A) is generally used for testing one or two proportions, a t-test (choice B) is used for testing one or two means, and ANOVA (choice C) compares more than two means with one another.

5. **The correct answer is C.** For a curve to describe a continuous probability distribution, the total area underneath the curve must be 1. C is not necessarily highest in the middle, at $x = 3$ (choice A), and it does not necessarily have equal heights at the endpoints $x = 1$ and $x = 5$ (choice B), although both of these will be true if the

data is unimodal and symmetric. Choice D is wrong because the opposite is actually true; a density curve cannot have any negative values.

6. **The correct answer is A.** The null hypothesis always assumes that the default state of affairs remains; since the proportion, ρ, has been 0.44, the null hypothesis assumes that this number has not changed. Choice B is a likely candidate for the alternate hypothesis, but is certainly an incorrect null hypothesis. Choices C and D are wrong because they involve a mean, μ, rather than a proportion, ρ.

7. **The correct answer is D.** The power of a hypothesis test is increased when the alternate hypothesis is moved farther away from the null hypothesis, not closer. Increasing the sample size (choice A), decreasing the standard deviation (choice B) and decreasing the confidence level (choice C) all increase the power of a hypothesis test.

8. **The correct answer is C.** A regression line can be used to predict the response variable from a given value of the explanatory variable. In this case, substituting 6 for m gives $H = 0.8(6) + 20 = 24.8$. The other answer choices result from arithmetic errors: neglecting to add the 20 (choice A), performing operations in the incorrect order (choice B), or ignoring a decimal point (choice D).

9. **The correct answer is B.** The standard normal distribution, to which z-scores are applicable, is $N(0,1)$; that is, the mean is 0, and the standard deviation is 1. While the data could, in principle, be adjusted to have a mean of 1 (choices C and D), 0 is preferable as this makes the curve symmetric around the line $y = 0$. The standard deviation cannot be made to be 0 (choices A and C), as this could only occur if there were no variability in the data at all.

10. **The correct answer is D.** The box that features prominently in a boxplot, and the line through its center, are formed using the values of the 1st, 2nd, and 3rd quartiles. Stemplots (choice B) and histograms (choice C) allow one to visually estimate the locations of the quartiles, but do not explicitly show them in any way. A scatterplot (choice A) is only appropriate for showing two-variable data, and does not in any way refer to the quartiles of either variable.

11. **The correct answer is A.** As the values rise along the x-axis, they also rise along the y-axis, which means the variables are positively correlated. For the data to show negative correlation (choice B), the y-values would have to fall as the x-values rose. The points do not seem to lie along a straight line, so the correlation is not linear (choice C). There is clearly a relationship between the x and y coordinates, so choice D is incorrect.

12. **The correct answer is C.** The organizer needs to choose 5 of 17 people, without repetition, and the order matters. This is represented by a permutation, so the answer is $P(17,5)$. Choice A is wrong because the different numbers of choices have to be multiplied by each other, not added. Choice B is a combination, in which order does not matter—not the case in this problem. Choice D allows repetition, since the factors are each 17, and not decreasing as each choice is made.

13. **The correct answer is C.** Although there are various ways of describing the distribution of a data set, the characteristics that will generally be covered include the range, the center (usually the mean or median), and the spread (usually the IQR or standard deviation). The method of data collection (choice A), the units (choice B), and hypothesis tests (choice D) are all

characteristics that are interesting, but they are not relevant to the distribution.

14. **The correct answer is B.** The margin of error and confidence level have a direct relationship; if the confidence level is decreased, the margin of error decreases as well. Since the margin of error in the 95% interval is 4, the margin of error in the 90% interval must be less than 4. Although there is no way to know how much less it will be, the center of the interval, 30, is the only value guaranteed to remain. Even a very small margin of error, say 0.1, will still produce a confidence interval of the form 30 ± 0.1, which contains 30. 28 (choice A) and 32 (choice C) may or may not still be included. 34 (choice D), would certainly not be included.

15. **The correct answer is C.** If the line passes exactly through every point, the correlation is perfect; there are no errors. Therefore, the value of r will be either 1 or –1, depending on whether the correlation is positive or negative. Choices A and B are wrong because we cannot know if r is positive or negative. Choice D is wrong because r is certainly not 0; that would represent no correlation at all.

16. **The correct answer is D.** The even numbers are 2, 4, and 6, so the probability of rolling an even number is $\frac{3}{6}$. The probability of rolling a 5 is $\frac{1}{6}$. Since these are mutually exclusive events—that is, they cannot both occur together—we can simply add them. So the probability of rolling either an even number or a 5 is $\frac{3}{6} + \frac{1}{6} = \frac{4}{6} = \frac{2}{3}$. Choice A is incorrect since the $\frac{3}{6}$ and $\frac{1}{6}$ are multiplied rather than added as they should be. The other choices only take one of the two mentioned events into account—only the 5 (choice B), or only the even numbers (choice C).

17. **The correct answer is C.** If a sampling method was not random, the results are often not representative of the population. In this situation, there was likely a bias toward including lower-income households in the sample. Choices A and B are incorrect because type I and type II errors are related to hypothesis testing, which is not part of this scenario. While choice D is plausible, it is not likely to explain the clear bias towards lower incomes in the sample; there is no given reason to think that people would consistently underreport income.

18. **The correct answer is C.** ANOVA is used to test the null hypothesis that the means of all populations are equal to one another. If this hypothesis is rejected, it means that they are not all the same; in other words, that there are at least two different means among the populations. Choice A is clearly incorrect, since the null hypothesis is rejected when $p < \alpha$. Choice B is wrong since it may be that the five populations are split into just two means, where, for example, the first two are equal and the next three are equal. Similarly, choice D is incorrect.

19. **The correct answer is D.** The standard deviation of the sample means is related to the population mean, but is not the same as it. In particular, if the population standard deviation is σ, and the sample size is n, the standard deviation of the sample means will be $\sigma / \sqrt{(n)}$. The central limit theorem states that sample means are approximately normally distributed (choice B), which implies that the distribution is symmetric (choice A), and that their mean is the same as the population mean (choice C).

20. **The correct answer is B.** A type I error occurs when H_0 is rejected even though it is true. The probability of this occurring is α, the significance level of the test. Thus, a decrease in α is a decrease in the risk of

a type I error. The opposite occurs (choice A) when α is increased. Although sample size and significance level are both chosen before conducting the experiment, there is no direct relationship between them; changing α does not raise (choice C) or lower (choice D) the sample size.

21. **The correct answer is C.** When comparing proportions, a z-statistic can always be used, even though the population proportion (p) is unknown, and has to be approximated by the sample proportion $\hat{p}$. A t-test (choices A and B) is not necessary when dealing with proportions. ANOVA (choice D) is only used for comparing more than two samples.

22. **The correct answer is D.** The real numbers have no discrete structure—there is no unit size that separates values, and there is no notion of the next value in a list. This means that a discrete distribution cannot be formed by this variable. In all of the other answer choices, there is a discrete unit size: a number of days (choice A) or a number of students (choice B) are always counted in whole numbers. Choice C is different, as it involves ordinal data (first, second, third, etc.) but it is similar in the sense that there is discrete space between one possible value and the next.

23. **The correct answer is D.** When events are independent, their probabilities simply multiply to produce the joint ("and") probability. In this case, $0.1 \cdot 0.4 = 0.04 = 4\%$. If the events were not independent, the answer would certainly not be 4%; although without more information there is no way of knowing if it would be greater than 4% (choice B), less than 4% (choice C), or even 0% (choice A).

24. **The correct answer is A.** A confidence interval represents a range such that when constructed for all possible sample means, a known percentage of these intervals will contain the true population mean. Since

90% of similarly constructed intervals will contain the population mean, we can be 90% confident that this particular one, 27 ± 3 (which ranges from 24 to 30), will contain it. The 90% here represents a confidence level, not a percentage of the population (choice B). Choice C misinterprets the 27 and 3, and does not take the 90% into account at all, while choice D does not interpret the 90 correctly as a percentage.

25. **The correct answer is D.** The line fits the data perfectly, going directly through each point. This corresponds to an r^2 value of 1.0. A smaller value, such as 0.5 (choice C), would indicate some fit but also much error with the fit. A value of 0.0 (choice B), would indicate a line that doesn't fit the data at all. As a squared value, r^2 can never be negative (choice A).

26. **The correct answer is B.** If the probability of event A is x, then the probability of the complement of A is $P(\overline{A}) = 1 - x$. If the probability that it will rain is $\frac{4}{19}$, the probability that it will not rain is $1 - \frac{4}{19} = \frac{15}{19}$. It is neither certain (choice A) nor impossible (choice D) that it will rain. The only time the probabilities of an event and its complement will be equal (as in choice C) is when they are both equal to $\frac{1}{2}$.

27. **The correct answer is A.** The mean is $\frac{7 + 7 + 9 + 2 + 6 + 10 + 1}{7} = \frac{42}{7} = 6$. To find the median, we put the list in order: 1, 2, 6, 7, 7, 9, 10, and see that the middle number is 7. The mode is the number that appears most often, and this is 7 as well. Choice B incorrectly calculates the mean. Choices C and D both have the median as 2, which results if you forget to first put the numbers in order and simply take the middle value as it is written.

28. The correct answer is B. The standard error for the sample mean is $\sigma / \sqrt{n}$. Here, $\sigma = 20$ and $n = 16$, so the standard error is $\frac{20}{4} = 5$. Choice A incorrectly uses σ / n as the formula. Choices C and D neglect to take into account either the population standard deviation (choice C) or the sample size (choice D).

29. The correct answer is D. The equations all show the application of the equation to a particular value of x to predict a value of y. Extrapolation refers to doing this for a value of x outside of the original range of the data. Since the original data ranges from -3 to 17, 18 is the value that is outside. Choice A uses a value that is actually in the original data set. Choices B and C use values that may be in the original data set, or may lie between values in the original set—in this case, the process would be called interpolation.

30. The correct answer is B. A normal distribution is a continuous distribution that is symmetric and unimodal—the mean, median, and mode are all equal. Choices A and C misidentify it as discrete instead of continuous; choices C and D misidentify it as skewed, as opposed to symmetric.

31. The correct answer is B. When constructing a confidence interval, the margin of error increases as the confidence level increases. Since 95% is a higher confidence level than 90%, the margin of error will be larger, and therefore the interval will represent a larger range of values. Choice A has the relationship reversed. Choice C incorrectly assumes that the size of the confidence interval is independent of the confidence level. Choice D is wrong because the other parameters are all staying fixed; the population and sample are the same for both intervals, so the only factor that matters is the confidence level.

32. The correct answer is C. This situation can be modeled by the binomial distribution $B(500, 0.02)$ The expected value of a binomial distribution $B(n, p)$ is np, so here it is $500 \cdot 0.02 = 10$. The other choices either use incorrect values of p (20% in choice B) or simply perform the calculation incorrectly (choices A and D).

33. The correct answer is A. There are two values in the $[0, 10]$ range, three values in $[10, 20]$, and one in $[20, 30]$. Choices B and C are each missing a value in the smallest category. Choice D only has three values altogether, while the histogram clearly shows a total of six values.

34. The correct answer is C. A voluntary survey is generally a poor sampling technique. Because it is voluntary, the people who choose to respond may not be representative of the population as a whole; and because it is a survey, it is susceptible to response bias. Simple random samples (choice A), stratified random samples (choice B), and multistage samples (choice D) are all valid and powerful sampling techniques.

35. The correct answer is C. The null hypothesis is the default that he is trying to disprove—that the bags contain 5 ounces, on average. The alternate hypothesis is what he wants to discard the null hypothesis in favor of—that the average is less than 5. The null and alternate hypotheses always involve the population parameter (μ), and not the sample statistic (s), as choices B and D do. Choice A is incorrect because the alternate hypothesis is one-sided—his suspicion is that the bags contain less than 5 ounces, not simply something other than 5 ounces.

36. The correct answer is C. Correlation alone, no matter how strong, can never on its own imply that there is a causative relationship between two variables. It is always possible that a confounding variable is responsible for the correlation. Even though the correlation is strong (choice A), one variable does not necessarily cause the other. Choice B is wrong because 0.91 actually does represent a strong relationship. Choice D is wrong because whether the correlation is positive or negative is immaterial to the question of causation.

37. **The correct answer is B.** Although the confidence level plays alongside the accuracy of the sample in constructing a confidence interval, it does not in any way actually have an effect on the accuracy of the sample. Criteria that do have a significant effect on the expected accuracy of a sample include the sample size (choice A), the variation within the population (choice C), and a properly randomized sampling technique (choice D).

38. **The correct answer is C.** The line in choice C does not pass through or near most of the points, so the value of r^2 will be low, near 0. Choices A and B have lines that go through or close to all of the points, so r^2 will be close to 1. While choice D has some significant errors, the points are generally clustered closer to the line than they are in choice C.

39. **The correct answer is B.** The hypothesis compares 4 different sample means to one another. ANOVA is the test that is used to compare more than two sample means. The sign test (choice A) is a non-parametric test that is generally used to compare medians. The z-test (choice C) and the t-test (choice D) are used in various scenarios involving only 1 or 2 samples.

40. **The correct answer is A.** When the population standard deviation is known, z-values can be used in place of t-values. t-tests are generally less powerful than z-tests, because they include more uncertainty related to having an unknown population standard deviation. The size of the sample (choice B) and the confidence level (choice C), although important in constructing a confidence interval, are not deciding factors in choosing between the z- and t-distributions. Choice D is incorrect because the mean is certainly not known in this scenario—if it were known, there would be no reason to construct a confidence interval for it!

41. **The correct answer is D.** The values are represented by numbers that are meaningful arithmetically. The ratio of 10 to 5 being 2 means that he found twice as many fossils at the fourth site as at the first. It would make sense to talk about the mean number of fossils found, and the 0 truly represents a value of 0—there were no fossils found at the third site. These facts all point to the ratio level of measurement. At the interval level (choice C), the notion of division—ratios—would not make sense, and 0 would not represent a true absence of anything. At the ordinal level (choice B), it would only make sense to put the sites in order of least to greatest, but not to perform arithmetic on the data. Finally, at the nominal level (choice A), the values wouldn't even really represent numbers at all, but would simply be the names of categories.

42. **The correct answer is A.** By definition, the population mean includes every data point in the population, so it cannot be affected by anything related to choice of sample. Standard error (choice B) is calculated in different ways depending on parameter being estimated, but the one factor that is always included in the formula is the sample size. Similarly, the margin of error in a confidence interval (choice C) always includes the sample size. Though we have not seen an explicit formula for power (choice D) that includes the sample size, it is true that a larger sample size contributes to increasing the power of a test.

43. **The correct answer is D.** The points show a clear trend. The y-coordinates (test scores) tend to be higher when the x-coordinates (hours of sleep) are higher. It is not a perfect trend, but the correlation is clear. Choice A shows no relationship at all between hours of sleep and test scores. Choice B shows a very strong relationship between the variables, but it is opposite to the one described—it shows scores falling as hours of sleep increases. Choice C shows a very weak relationship between the variables; at a glance, it is not even clear whether the correlation is positive or negative.

44. **The correct answer is B.** A type II error occurs when H_0 is false but a hypothesis test fails to reject it. A type I error (choice A) describes the opposite situation: H_0 is true but is incorrectly rejected. Sample bias (choice C) is not relevant here—it may or may not have occurred, but it does not describe the error that happened. Choice D is incorrect because a confounding variable is of interest when trying to derive a causal relationship from a correlation between two variables, which is completely unrelated to the situation described here.

45. **The correct answer is B.** Since they include every data point in their calculations, mean and median are easily influenced by outliers; that is, a single value far away from the rest of the data has a significant effect on their values. Median (choice A) and IQR (choices C and D) are all calculated based only on one or two values closer to the center of the data set, so they are not influenced by extreme values.

46. **The correct answer is A.** The value for b is given by $b = \bar{y} - m\bar{x} = 10 - 6 \cdot 5 = -20$. All of the other answer choices either use the wrong formula or contain a computational error.

47. **The correct answer is D.** The standard deviation of the sampling distribution is $\sigma / \sqrt{n}$, where σ is the population standard deviation, and n is the sample size. The problem is asking for the value of n that will make this less than or equal to 1. In other words, we have to solve the inequality $10 / \sqrt{n} \leq 1$ for n. The solution is $n \geq 100$. A sample size of 4 (choice A) will result in a standard deviation of $10 / \sqrt{4} = 5$. Similarly, $n = 10$ (choice B) and $n = 16$ (choice C) will result in standard deviations of 3.16 and 2.5, respectively.

48. **The correct answer is C.** Conclusions based on data gathered from a full population are always more accurate than conclusions based on data that has been gathered from a sample. Samples are generally used, however, since the entire population may not be known or accessible (choice A), or it may be too expensive (choice B) or time-consuming (choice D) to survey the full population.

49. **The correct answer is B.** The population is first divided into four categories, or strata: freshmen, sophomores, juniors, and seniors. Then a random sample is selected from each stratum. This technique is known as stratified random sampling. The sample was not chosen randomly from the population as a whole, so this is not a simple random sample (choice A). Randomized choices were only made at a single level (when choosing students within each stratum), so this is not a multistage sample (choice C). Since the sample was not selected on the basis of students volunteering, this is not a voluntary response sample (choice D).

50. **The correct answer is D.** The central limit theorem says that the sampling distribution of a mean will be normal with sufficiently large samples. The mean of the sampling distribution is equal to the mean of the

population, so $\mu = 450$. The standard deviation of the sampling distribution, in this case 4, is given by the formula $\sigma / \sqrt{n}$. Solving $\sigma / \sqrt{100} = 4$ yields $\sigma = 40$. Choice B has incorrect values for both , while choices A and C have the wrong value for σ.

51. **The correct answer is B.** The p-value is less than α, so H_0 should be rejected in favor of $H\alpha$, which states that $\mu > 80$. Since H_0 is rejected, choice C is not correct. Choices A and D are incorrect because there is no justification for choosing any particular value for μ.

52. **The correct answer is A.** The range is the distance between the smallest and largest values in a data set. Since the boxplots show the same maximum and minimum values for A and B, they have the same range. Since the maximums are equal, choice B is wrong. Choice C is wrong because the median is represented by the center line in a boxplot, and it is higher for population B than for population A. The size of the box represents the IQR, and they are clearly not the same, so choice D is wrong.

53. **The correct answer is B.** Since $p > \alpha$, H_0 cannot be rejected, there is insufficient evidence to say that the proportions are not equal. Though choice A is similar, it is too strong a conclusion. The lack of rejecting H_0 is not the same as concluding that it is true. It may still be false, but at this time we have insufficient evidence to conclude that. Since $p > \alpha$, we certainly cannot accept any alternative hypothesis, whether that is that the proportions are not equal (choice C), or that the first is greater than the second (choice D).

54. **The correct answer is D.** The standard deviation of the sampling distribution f or a proportion is $\sqrt{\frac{p(1-p)}{n}}$. With

$p = 0.25$ and $n = 25$, this becomes

$$\sqrt{\frac{0.25 \cdot 0.75}{25}} = \frac{\sqrt{0.25 \cdot 0.75}}{5}.$$

The standard deviation is not the same as the population proportion (choice A), nor is it simply divided by the sample size (choice B). In choice C, the square root of 25 has not been taken.

55. **The correct answer is C.** The number of ways of choosing 3 of the 32 women is $C(32,3)$, and the number of ways of choosing 3 of the 27 men is $C(27,3)$. Since both of these sets of choices need to be made, the total number of committees is the product of these two values. Note that since there is no indication of the committee members playing different roles, this situation refers to combinations, not permutations (choices B and D). Also, since there are particular requirements for the number of women and men that must be chosen, the choices cannot be grouped together (choices A and B).

56. **The correct answer is C.** Since the value of r for these variables will be closed to -1, r^2 will be close to 1. As the square of r, r^2 will never be negative (choice A). Since the correlation is strong, it will be closer to 1 than to 0 (choice B). Since r is always between -1 and 1, its square can never exceed 1 (choice D).

57. **The correct answer is A.** Although the points do not all lie exactly on a line, there is a clear upward trend in salary as years of experience increases. This represents a positive correlation. If salary decreased as years of experience increased, that would be a negative correlation (choice B), and if there was no clear trend in either direction, that would be no correlation (choice D). Quadratic correlation (choice C) would produce a scatterplot in which the points formed a parabola.

58. **The correct answer is C.** A type II error is commonly known as a false negative; that is, failing to reject the null hypothesis when it is, in fact, false. Choice B describes a type I error. Type I and type II errors are both related to the probability of coming to erroneous conclusions, not to the probability of reaching these conclusions overall, so choices A and D are incorrect.

59. **The correct answer is B.** When 50 is substituted for x in the equation, it becomes $y = 3 \cdot 50 - 10 = 140$, so the predicted value is $y = 140$. Since 50 lies within the range of the original data points, this is an example of interpolation. It would be extrapolation if one was predicting a y for an x outside of the original range (choices C and D). Choices A and C incorrectly substitute the 50 for y and solve for x.

60. **The correct answer is A.** The number of degrees of freedom for the sampling distribution of a mean is $n - 1 = 50 - 1 = 49$. Choice B neglects to subtract 1 from the sample size. Choices C and D are incorrect because they are based on the population size, whereas the number of degrees of freedom is only related to the sample size.

Criminal Justice

OVERVIEW

- Test Answer Sheets
- Criminal Justice Diagnostic Test
- Answer Key and Explanations
- Diagnostic Test Assessment Grid
- Criminal Behavior
- The Criminal Justice System
- Law Enforcement
- The Court System
- Corrections
- Criminal Justice Post-test
- Answer Key and Explanations
- Summing It Up

The DSST® Criminal Justice exam consists of 100 multiple-choice questions that should be answered in 2 hours. The exam covers topics like criminal behavior; the roles of police and law enforcement at the federal, state and local levels; the U.S. court system and its structures; sentencing issues; and the criminal justice system including adult prison systems and juvenile correction alternatives.

Chapter 8

DIAGNOSTIC TEST ANSWER SHEET

1. Ⓐ Ⓑ Ⓒ Ⓓ   5. Ⓐ Ⓑ Ⓒ Ⓓ   9. Ⓐ Ⓑ Ⓒ Ⓓ   13. Ⓐ Ⓑ Ⓒ Ⓓ   17. Ⓐ Ⓑ Ⓒ Ⓓ

2. Ⓐ Ⓑ Ⓒ Ⓓ   6. Ⓐ Ⓑ Ⓒ Ⓓ   10. Ⓐ Ⓑ Ⓒ Ⓓ   14. Ⓐ Ⓑ Ⓒ Ⓓ   18. Ⓐ Ⓑ Ⓒ Ⓓ

3. Ⓐ Ⓑ Ⓒ Ⓓ   7. Ⓐ Ⓑ Ⓒ Ⓓ   11. Ⓐ Ⓑ Ⓒ Ⓓ   15. Ⓐ Ⓑ Ⓒ Ⓓ   19. Ⓐ Ⓑ Ⓒ Ⓓ

4. Ⓐ Ⓑ Ⓒ Ⓓ   8. Ⓐ Ⓑ Ⓒ Ⓓ   12. Ⓐ Ⓑ Ⓒ Ⓓ   16. Ⓐ Ⓑ Ⓒ Ⓓ   20. Ⓐ Ⓑ Ⓒ Ⓓ

POST-TEST ANSWER SHEET

1. Ⓐ Ⓑ Ⓒ Ⓓ   13. Ⓐ Ⓑ Ⓒ Ⓓ   25. Ⓐ Ⓑ Ⓒ Ⓓ   37. Ⓐ Ⓑ Ⓒ Ⓓ   49. Ⓐ Ⓑ Ⓒ Ⓓ

2. Ⓐ Ⓑ Ⓒ Ⓓ   14. Ⓐ Ⓑ Ⓒ Ⓓ   26. Ⓐ Ⓑ Ⓒ Ⓓ   38. Ⓐ Ⓑ Ⓒ Ⓓ   50. Ⓐ Ⓑ Ⓒ Ⓓ

3. Ⓐ Ⓑ Ⓒ Ⓓ   15. Ⓐ Ⓑ Ⓒ Ⓓ   27. Ⓐ Ⓑ Ⓒ Ⓓ   39. Ⓐ Ⓑ Ⓒ Ⓓ   51. Ⓐ Ⓑ Ⓒ Ⓓ

4. Ⓐ Ⓑ Ⓒ Ⓓ   16. Ⓐ Ⓑ Ⓒ Ⓓ   28. Ⓐ Ⓑ Ⓒ Ⓓ   40. Ⓐ Ⓑ Ⓒ Ⓓ   52. Ⓐ Ⓑ Ⓒ Ⓓ

5. Ⓐ Ⓑ Ⓒ Ⓓ   17. Ⓐ Ⓑ Ⓒ Ⓓ   29. Ⓐ Ⓑ Ⓒ Ⓓ   41. Ⓐ Ⓑ Ⓒ Ⓓ   53. Ⓐ Ⓑ Ⓒ Ⓓ

6. Ⓐ Ⓑ Ⓒ Ⓓ   18. Ⓐ Ⓑ Ⓒ Ⓓ   30. Ⓐ Ⓑ Ⓒ Ⓓ   42. Ⓐ Ⓑ Ⓒ Ⓓ   54. Ⓐ Ⓑ Ⓒ Ⓓ

7. Ⓐ Ⓑ Ⓒ Ⓓ   19. Ⓐ Ⓑ Ⓒ Ⓓ   31. Ⓐ Ⓑ Ⓒ Ⓓ   43. Ⓐ Ⓑ Ⓒ Ⓓ   55. Ⓐ Ⓑ Ⓒ Ⓓ

8. Ⓐ Ⓑ Ⓒ Ⓓ   20. Ⓐ Ⓑ Ⓒ Ⓓ   32. Ⓐ Ⓑ Ⓒ Ⓓ   44. Ⓐ Ⓑ Ⓒ Ⓓ   56. Ⓐ Ⓑ Ⓒ Ⓓ

9. Ⓐ Ⓑ Ⓒ Ⓓ   21. Ⓐ Ⓑ Ⓒ Ⓓ   33. Ⓐ Ⓑ Ⓒ Ⓓ   45. Ⓐ Ⓑ Ⓒ Ⓓ   57. Ⓐ Ⓑ Ⓒ Ⓓ

10. Ⓐ Ⓑ Ⓒ Ⓓ   22. Ⓐ Ⓑ Ⓒ Ⓓ   34. Ⓐ Ⓑ Ⓒ Ⓓ   46. Ⓐ Ⓑ Ⓒ Ⓓ   58. Ⓐ Ⓑ Ⓒ Ⓓ

11. Ⓐ Ⓑ Ⓒ Ⓓ   23. Ⓐ Ⓑ Ⓒ Ⓓ   35. Ⓐ Ⓑ Ⓒ Ⓓ   47. Ⓐ Ⓑ Ⓒ Ⓓ   59. Ⓐ Ⓑ Ⓒ Ⓓ

12. Ⓐ Ⓑ Ⓒ Ⓓ   24. Ⓐ Ⓑ Ⓒ Ⓓ   36. Ⓐ Ⓑ Ⓒ Ⓓ   48. Ⓐ Ⓑ Ⓒ Ⓓ   60. Ⓐ Ⓑ Ⓒ Ⓓ

answer sheet

CRIMINAL JUSTICE DIAGNOSTIC TEST

Directions: Carefully read each of the following 20 questions. Choose the best answer to each question and fill in the corresponding circle on the answer sheet. The Answer Key and Explanations can be found following this Diagnostic Test.

1. Crimes that are considered to be wrong by their very nature, such as assaults, theft, and murder are called
   - A. mala prohibita.
   - B. felonies.
   - C. mala in se.
   - D. organized crime.

2. Which theory states that being around criminal behavior influences an individual towards criminality?
   - A. Biological theory
   - B. Learning theory
   - C. Labeling theory
   - D. Psychological theory

3. A crime report that is generated on a yearly basis by the FBI for a statistical analysis and summary is called the
   - A. dark figure of crime.
   - B. UCR.
   - C. NIBRS.
   - D. NCVS.

4. The notion of a guilty state of mind is defined by which term?
   - A. Mala in se
   - B. Mens rea
   - C. Retribution
   - D. Probable cause

5. The notion that a person has the right to protect themselves from self-incrimination is found in the
   - A. Fifth Amendment.
   - B. Fourth Amendment.
   - C. First Amendment.
   - D. Eighth Amendment.

6. The right to counsel and to a speedy and public trial falls under the
   - A. Sixth Amendment.
   - B. Eighth Amendment.
   - C. Fifth Amendment.
   - D. Fourth Amendment.

7. The standard to convict an individual in criminal court is
   - A. reasonable suspicion.
   - B. probable cause.
   - C. beyond a reasonable doubt.
   - D. preponderance of the evidence.

8. The agency within the criminal justice system that is responsible for due process and sentencing offenders under the sentencing laws and guidelines is
   - A. corrections.
   - B. the judicial branch.
   - C. law enforcement.
   - D. the parole board.

diagnostic test

9. When Sir Robert Peel created the first London police force in 1829, the officers were called
   A. coppers.
   B. Londoners.
   C. bobbies.
   D. peelers.

10. Which years encompass the Community Policing Era, which has a focus on police community relations, where police assist with social service calls?
   A. 1840-1920
   B. 1920-1970
   C. 1970–present
   D. 2001–present

11. Law enforcement changes and evolves as it reflects societal needs. One of the major issues that law enforcement is facing present day is
   A. traffic control.
   B. sentencing of violent offenders.
   C. antiterrorism.
   D. auto larceny.

12. Law enforcement contains a high level of stress due to the nature of its work. A common result of stress that police officers face is
   A. high suicide rates among officers.
   B. divorce.
   C. alcohol abuse.
   D. All of the above

13. The Judiciary Act, passed in 1789, created which court?
   A. Criminal court
   B. Civil court
   C. Family court
   D. The Supreme Court

14. On a state level, the courts that handle misdemeanor cases and civil lawsuits up to a certain amount of money are known as
   A. courts of general jurisdiction.
   B. civil courts.
   C. Supreme Courts.
   D. courts of limited jurisdiction.

15. The judicial system is divided into an adult and juvenile court system. In the adult court system, the accused is known as the
   A. offender.
   B. perpetrator.
   C. complainant.
   D. defendant.

16. A grand jury can be convened to hear and review serious criminal offenses. If the grand jury determines probable cause, the next step for the defendant is
   A. initial appearance.
   B. sentencing.
   C. bail.
   D. arraignment.

17. One of the main principles of corrections in the United States is deterrence to control people's behavior. What are the two types of deterrence?
   A. General and specific
   B. Individual and community
   C. Incorporation and rehabilitation
   D. General and rehabilitation

18. The adult prison system is intended for individuals 18 years and older. Its main purpose is
   A. restitution.
   B. rehabilitation.
   C. punishment.
   D. retribution.

19. Which of the following are residential treatment programs within the juvenile system?
   A. Group homes
   B. Foster care
   C. Family group homes
   D. All of the above

20. Which amendment challenges the constitutionality of the death penalty as well as the methods of execution?
   A. Fourth Amendment
   B. Second Amendment
   C. Fifth Amendment
   D. Eighth Amendment

diagnostic test

ANSWER KEY AND EXPLANATIONS

1. C	5. A	9. C	13. D	17. A
2. B	6. A	10. C	14. D	18. C
3. B	7. C	11. C	15. D	19. D
4. B	8. B	12. D	16. D	20. D

1. **The correct answer is C.** *Mala in se* offenses are offenses that are wrong by their very own nature. Choice A is incorrect because *mala prohibita* crimes are prohibited by law, but may not be wrong in and of themselves. Choice B is incorrect because a felony is a classification of crime used to determine punishment. Choice D is incorrect because organized crime is a category of crime signifying organizations of smaller criminal networks.

2. **The correct answer is B.** Learning theory, suggested by Edwin Sutherland, states that values associated with deviant behavior are learned through interaction with family and friends. Choice A is incorrect because the biological theory refers to the idea that people have a genetic makeup for deviant behavior. Choice C is incorrect because the labeling theory believes that society creates deviance by creating rules. Choice D is incorrect because psychological theory states that deviant behavior can be found in those with personality conditions.

3. **The correct answer is B.** The Uniform Crime Report (UCR) is generated yearly after compiling statistics from local, state, and federal law enforcement agencies. Choice A is incorrect because the dark figure of crime is not a statistical analysis, but rather a component of crime that is not reported. Choice C is incorrect because the NIBRS is the National Incident-Based Reporting System, which is used by police officers when reporting more than one offense in a criminal incident. Choice D is incorrect because the NCVS is the National Crime Victimization Survey, which is used as a self-reporting survey for individuals who were victims of a crime.

4. **The correct answer is B.** Mens rea refers to the guilty state of mind. The term is derived from common law during colonial times. Choice A is incorrect because mala in se are offenses that are wrong in and of themselves. Choice C is incorrect because retribution is based on revenge and punishment. Choice D is incorrect because probable cause is a standard for an arrest.

5. **The correct answer is A.** The Fifth Amendment protects individuals from being forced by the State to answer questions that may incriminate themselves. Choice B is incorrect because the Fourth Amendment prohibits unreasonable searches and seizures. Choice C is incorrect because the First Amendment guarantees freedom of speech. Choice D is incorrect because the Eighth Amendment prohibits cruel and unusual punishment.

6. **The correct answer is A.** The Sixth Amendment covers a person's right to counsel as well as a speedy and public trial. Choice B is incorrect because the Eighth Amendment deals with cruel and unusual punishment. Choice C is incorrect because the Fifth Amendment is about double jeopardy and self-incrimination. Choice D

is incorrect because the Fourth Amendment deals with unreasonable searches and seizure.

7. **The correct answer is C.** Beyond a reasonable doubt is the legal standard for conviction in criminal court. Choice A is incorrect because reasonable suspicion is a standard for police to conduct stops and question people. Choice B is incorrect because probable cause is the standard for an arrest. Choice D is incorrect because the preponderance of evidence is used in a civil court proceeding.

8. **The correct answer is B.** The judicial branch has the responsibility through the courts to establish guilt or innocence through due process and hand down sentencing for guilty offenders. Choice A is incorrect because corrections departments enforce the sentencing by the courts. Choice C is incorrect because law enforcement is an overarching term for all that goes into enforcing the laws of the land and maintaining order. Choice D is incorrect because a parole board decides whether or not an offender should be released from prison.

9. **The correct answer is C.** The origin of the name "bobbies" for London police officers is derived from Sir Robert Peel's name. Therefore, choices A, B, and D are all incorrect.

10. **The correct answer is C.** The Community Policing Era picked up where the Professional Era ended in 1970, and continues to present day. Choice A is incorrect because 1840-1920 was the Political Era. Choice B is incorrect because 1920-1970 was the Professional Era. Choice D is incorrect because there is no defined era within that time span.

11. **The correct answer is C.** Since 9/11, policing in America has changed and departments and officers must be extremely vigilant in the fight against terrorism. Choice A is incorrect because traffic control has always been a police-related issue. Choice B is incorrect because this is not a police function at all, but a judicial issue within the court system. Choice D is incorrect because auto larceny is a crime that occurs on a regular basis, and the police have always combatted auto larceny as part of routine police work.

12. **The correct answer is D.** Because of the high level of stress that police officers face, they commonly fall prey to all of the listed choices.

13. **The correct answer is D.** The Judiciary Act created the Supreme Court, which then consisted of a Chief Justice and five Associate Justices.

14. **The correct answer is D.** Courts of limited jurisdiction only hear misdemeanor cases and, depending on the state, civil cases for small amounts of money. Choice A is incorrect because courts of general jurisdiction hear felony cases and civil cases for larger sums of money. Choice B is incorrect because civil courts do not hear any criminal cases. Choice C is incorrect because the Supreme Court hears cases involving Constitutional issues.

15. **The correct answer is D.** In adult court, the individual accused of a crime is known as the defendant.

16. **The correct answer is D.** Arraignment takes place after a grand jury has established probable cause; there, the defendant is brought before the judge to hear the charges that were found against him. Therefore, choices A, B and C are all incorrect because they are other steps within the judicial process.

17. **The correct answer is A.** General and specific are the two types of deterrence. General deterrence prevents criminal behavior within

a society. Specific deterrence targets the behavior of the individual offender.

18. **The correct answer is C.** The adult prison system is intended for punishment. Choice A is incorrect; restitution is part of corrections, but it is not part of the prison system. Choice B is incorrect because adult prison systems have fewer vocational and educational services than juvenile facilities. Choice D is incorrect because although retribution is a goal of corrections, it is not specific to adults and can be applied to any age group in which the punishment fits the crime.

19. **The correct answer is D.** Group homes, foster homes, and family homes are all part of juvenile treatment programs.

20. **The correct answer is D.** The Eighth Amendment challenges not only the death penalty but also the methods that are used for execution under the cruel and unusual punishment clause. Therefore, choices A, B and C are all incorrect as they do not relate to cruel and unusual punishment.

DIAGNOSTIC TEST ASSESSMENT GRID

Now that you've completed the diagnostic test and read through the answer explanations, you can use your results to target your studying. Find the question numbers from the diagnostic test that you answered incorrectly and highlight or circle them below. Then focus extra attention on the sections within the chapter dealing with those topics.

Criminal Justice		
Content Area	**Topic**	**Question #**
Criminal Behavior	• Defining Crime • Types of Crime • Theories of Crime • Measurement of Crime • Juvenile Delinquency	1, 2, 3
Criminal Justice System	• Historical Origins • Legal Foundations • Due Process • Criminal Justice Agencies	4, 5, 6, 7, 8
Law Enforcement	• History of Policing • Law Enforcement Roles & Responsibilities • Issues and Trends in Policing • The Nature of Law Enforcement	9, 10, 11, 12
Courts	• History of the Court System • Organization and Structure • Adult Court System • Juvenile Court	13, 14, 15
Court System	• Pretrial, Trial, and Post-Trial Process	16
Corrections	• Purpose • Intermediate Sanctions • Juvenile Correction Alternatives • Capital Punishment • Prison Organization • Prison Subculture	17, 18, 19, 20

GET THE FACTS

To see the DSST® Criminal Justice Fact Sheet, go to *http://getcollegecredit.com/exam_fact_sheets* and click on the **Social Sciences** tab. Scroll down and click the **Criminal Justice** link. Here you will find suggestions for further study material and the ACE college credit recommendations for passing the test.

This chapter reviews all the topics you'll see on your DSST Criminal Justice exam. The American criminal justice system is a large, complex, and vital institution that includes a variety of interconnected subsystems. It is one of the oldest institutions in America's history and is the cornerstone of its democracy. The criminal justice system, as with many other intuitions, has grown and evolved over time.

Because the criminal justice system is so complex, many people don't realize how interwoven it is within American society, and how it affects everyday lives. People outside of the criminal justice system think they have an idea about how the system works based on the news, television, movies, and social media. All of these variables may help shape people's beliefs and opinions about the criminal justice system, both in negative and positive ways—in reality, most of these depictions don't accurately portray the criminal justice system or its various agencies and personnel.

Why is this so important? People's beliefs and opinions about the effectiveness of the criminal justice process can affect its practices, policies, and conduct at all levels.

This chapter will help you understand the various levels and agencies that comprise the criminal justice system and prepare you for exam day.

You'll get an overview of how the criminal justice system operates, along with the various roles and parts of the system, with the understanding that each component is more complex than the general review provided here. The topics covered include criminal behavior, what defines it, how it's measured, the different types of crimes, and the different theories behind criminality and deviant behavior. We'll also examine the historical perspective of the criminal justice system within a legal framework, including due process.

Different agencies are also examined, including the police and how they're organized, as well as some of the issues and trends that today's police officers face. Additionally, we look at the occupational characteristics of police officers in today's society.

The court system is the next tier that will be covered, including its history and origin, and how it's structured—from the adult system to the juvenile system. The trial process will also be examined, along with the various sentencing issues and trends that the American court system faces.

The last part of the criminal justice system we'll cover is sometimes the least recognizable—corrections. How does corrections fit into American society and what is its role and purpose within the criminal justice system? Finally, we'll look into how prisons operate and what takes place behind their walls and bars.

CRIMINAL BEHAVIOR

DEFINING CRIME

Let's start with a basic definition. When asked to define *crime*, most people would simply say that it means breaking laws that have been written and established by elected officials. While this is partially correct, defining crime is a little more involved and complex. The formal definition of crime according to the manual *The American System of Criminal Justice* is as follows:

A specific act of commission or omission in violation of the law, where a punishment is prescribed

Let's examine the part of the definition that states "… act of commission …" Commission entails *doing* something. If I took a baseball bat and hit you with it, it would be an act of assault; if I stole your car, it would be an act of larceny. That's the easy part to understand—performing an act in violation of the law. The other part of the definition states "… act of commission *or omission*…" If commission means doing, then omission means *not* doing something. How does not doing something violate the law? Here's an example: the police, hospitals, and schools all have a mandatory reporting requirement for suspected child abuse. If someone from one of these agencies *fails* to report it, then that is a crime. Other examples include the failure to file your taxes—a crime of *not* doing something that's required by law. If you had a court date and *failed* to show up for your required appearance that would also be an omission—and would result in a court ordered bench warrant.

Finally, the definition and concept of crime must include some sort of prescribed punishment. In order for the law to work, punishment must be attached—it does not matter what the punishment is, just that there is a prescribed punishment. That being said, crimes need to be written down and codified, most likely in the penal law, in order to define which acts are illegal.

Crimes can be defined in two ways:

1. The first is **mala in se**. This means offenses that are wrong by their very nature—for example, murder, rape, robbery, and assault. We know just by the acts that they are immoral and wrong.

2. Next is **mala prohibita**. Here, the law prohibits certain offenses, but they are *not* wrong in and of themselves. This refers to crimes like gambling, drug use, and prostitution in some circumstances, or even minor infractions like speeding.

CRIME IN THE UNITED STATES

Crime in the United States follows particular trends and patterns, which are statistically compiled and classified across the country. Interestingly, the perception of crime may be different from what the actual statistics show. Let's examine some studies about crime trends from the past few years.

The Uniform Crime Reporting (UCR) Program shows that during the first 6 months of 2015, compared to 2014, violent crime was up by 1.7 percent, while property crime went down by 4.2 percent. In 2016, violent crimes increased by 4.1 percent and property crimes decreased by 1.3 percent from the previous year.

Some reports released for 2015 stated that crime levels remained the same from the prior year. That being said, even as crime levels off and sometimes declines, there are still increases in certain cities, and in specific crimes. As reported by *U.S. News & World Report*, the United States has seen historic decreases in overall crime. However, in 2015, even as crime remained at an all-time low, there was a slight increase in violent crimes compared to 2014. As per *U.S. News & World Report*, violent crime rose 3.9 percent across the entire year compared to 2014. This was largely attributed to gang violence and shootings. The murder rate also showed an increase nationwide—however, only three cities were largely responsible for this increase: Baltimore, Chicago, and Washington, D.C.

Still, overall crime appears to be on the decrease and at an all-time low, even as crime levels increase in Chicago, Charlotte, and Los Angeles and skew the national average. Statistics also indicate that males in the age range of 15 to 24 commit the majority of crimes nationwide.

Geography and race are key factors in tracking trends and patterns of crime, with violent crimes occurring more frequently in urban areas. The Uniform Crime Report also breaks down violent crime categories in cities with populations of 100,000 or more—the report shows a statistical significance between large cities with lower socioeconomic populations and violent crimes, including murder. Available statistics also demonstrate that most violent crimes are **intraracial**, meaning that both victims and offenders are from the same race.

THEORIES OF CRIME

For years, criminologists have pondered what causes crime. There are many theories—let's examine a few of the most popular ones, including the two primary schools of thought in the field of criminology.

Classical Criminology

Classical criminology views behavior as stemming from free will, and demands responsibility and accountability for all offenders. Punishment is a key factor in this theory; it demands punishment to deter individuals from committing further deviant acts. In order for this theory to function properly, the punishment needs to be predictable. This theory is applied in modern court procedures and philosophy. The American court system, for the most part, holds offenders accountable for their actions.

During the Age of Enlightenment, also known as the Age of Reason, social reformers enacted changes throughout society regarding crime and punishment. The prior Draconian methods of torture used to influence behavior began to shift towards more humane methods of punishment. The two most influential theorists in this field during the Age of Enlightenment were Cesare Beccaria and Jeremy Bentham.

Cesare Beccaria was an 18th century criminologist who believed in classical criminology. Beccaria wrote a famous book, *An Essay on Crimes and Punishment*, which essentially states that behavior stems from free will and people are accountable for their behavior. The book supports the notion that societies should protect themselves by preventing crime. Beccaria also believed the following ideas:

- Criminal behavior is rational; people choose to commit crimes after weighing out the pros and cons, and fear of punishment keeps people in check.

- Crime is an injury to society and people need to be punished accordingly.

- The accused has the right to a speedy trial and to bring forth evidence on his or her behalf.
- The purpose of punishment is deterrence.
- Swiftness of punishment is more important than its severity.
- Prisons should be more humane, with clear prisoner classifications based on age, sex, and the degree of the offense.

Jeremey Bentham was one of the great English thinkers regarding criminal law, and was known for his utilitarian philosophy. **Utilitarianism** is defined as the greatest possible balance of pleasure over pain, and that determining whether actions are morally right or wrong depends on the effects and results that they produce.

Utilitarianism believes that people behave in ways that bring about the greatest pleasure and avoid pain. Bentham, a reformer, emphasized deterrence and prevention (people seek to avoid pain and unpleasantness) in his views of crime and punishment.

Positivist Criminology

On the other side of the spectrum is the **positivist theory of criminology**, which views behavior as stemming from sociological, biological, and psychological factors. Proponents of this theory believe that punishment should be tailored to fit the individual and not the crime, that human behavior is controlled, and that there is no free will and no personal responsibility. Positivist criminologists use science to study crime and treat deviants, and believe that criminals have a different makeup than noncriminals.

One of the most famous biological criminologists was **Cesare Lombroso**, who felt there was a biological explanation for committing crimes. Lombroso believed that looking at people's physical traits could allow you to distinguish criminals from noncriminals—in other words, people are born criminals based on their physical genetic makeup. Lombroso, who visited insane asylums and other institutions for subjects, would measure and record people's physical traits. Some of the traits that he linked to criminal behavior included the size of a person's skull and forehead, deep-set eyes, an oversized nose, and large hands and fingers, among others.

The notion of criminality being linked to biological factors did not stop at Lombroso. Other psychologists also attempted to link deviant behavior to physical characteristics, including William Sheldon. Under the positivist explanation of deviant behavior, Sheldon created different categories that united or linked the biological and psychological makeups of individuals and behavior. These classifications included three different and distinct body types:

> **Endomorphs:** People who are round and soft had a tendency towards a "viscerotonic" type of personality, which means someone who is relaxed, comfortable, and considered an extrovert.

> **Mesomorphs:** People who are square and muscular and who have tendencies towards a "somotonic" personality, which means someone who is active, assertive, and aggressive.

> **Ectomorphs:** These are people who are thin and believed to have a tendency towards a "cerebrotonic" personality, which is someone who is introverted, thoughtful, and sensitive.

Sheldon used these classification systems to explain deviant behavior. He claimed that criminality and delinquency are derived from the mesomorphic category. His theory was that individuals who are firmly in the mesomorphic category are aggressive and lack sensitivity, and tend to exhibit criminal behavior.

Over time, as modern science and medicine became more advanced, the notion of linking physical traits and criminality did not withstand the test of time. Sheldon's theory, which at the time was considered innovative, later on became unsubstantiated as well.

The more modern biological explanation for deviant behavior looks at biological factors that predispose some people to exhibit criminal behavior. This theory relies on genetic makeup, which proponents say outweighs other social factors. One theory, called the **XYY chromosome theory**, is based on the premise that males who are born with an extra Y chromosome are more likely predisposed to deviant behavior and criminality.

Today's research investigates the notion of a link between genetic makeup and deviant behavior, and the connection with biological and environmental factors. Also under investigation is the notion of how injuries, such as head trauma, may affect behavior.

Psychological Theories

Let's discuss some of the primary psychological theories regarding why individuals commit crimes.

One of the most prominent theorists and psychologists in the world was **Sigmund Freud**. Freud was, and still is, one of the most famous, respected, and controversial figures in psychology. Among his many theories explaining human behavior is the **psychodynamic theory**. This theory suggests that unconscious forces and drives formed from early childhood control a person's personality and behavior. Freud believed that certain elements make up human personality and behavior. These elements are called the id, ego, and superego.

- The **id** is found in a person's unconscious self at birth. According to Freud, it drives the urges for food, sex, and other life necessities. The id's main concern is instant gratification. For example, a baby cries when he is hungry, thirsty, or needs to be changed. Freud does not say that a baby has immediate sexual desires to be fulfilled; rather, he is stating that those drives and urges are there and are buried, and have to be nurtured and developed.

- The **ego** balances out the id, trying to realistically satisfy its needs in a manner that is appropriate for society. When people develop an ego, they learn that the id cannot always be instantly gratified and compensated. This begins in early childhood.

- The **superego** provides people with a set of moral standards—in other words, your conscience, which is formed by your home environment during your formative years and society. The superego helps with judgment in determining right from wrong.

So, how does this relate to criminality? Freud's theory states that if the ego and/or the superego are not developed properly (for example, due to poor or absent parenting) then deviant behavior can arise. If the ego is damaged, the id takes over with impulsive behavior. If the superego is damaged, then there is no sense of morality and right from wrong.

Sociological Theories

Sociological explanations for criminality suggest that social conditions can affect individuals enough to cause criminal behavior. In other words, criminals are made by external factors.

Social Process Theories

Social process theories suggest that everyone has the potential to become a criminal depending on the following:

- The influences that drive a person towards or away from crime
- How one is regarded by others in his or her life

Edwin Sutherland was a criminologist who suggested that criminal behavior, like other behavioral traits, is learned through interaction with family and friends. Sutherland believed that people learn values and behaviors that are associated with crime. This is also known as the **differential association theory**, or the **learning theory**.

Sutherland believed that people learn values, attitudes, and motives by interacting with others. When it comes to criminality, a person "learns" how to become a criminal. In addition, there are many factors behind Sutherland's differential association theory that are taken into consideration, such as a person's socioeconomic background.

His theory can be explained through certain key points and assumptions:

- Criminal behavior is a learned behavior.
- The learning process for criminal behavior occurs through intimate personal relationships with others.
- The learning process for criminal behavior can be taught through techniques regarding how to commit crimes.
- People choose to become criminals because the favorable conclusions for committing a crime are more valued than the potential unfavorable conclusions.

Criminologists who subscribe to the **control theory** propose that criminal behavior occurs when the bonds that tie an individual to society are weakened or broken. These ties are often formed in family, church, and school. When these ties are broken, a person is more inclined to commit deviant behavior.

Labeling theory states that criminal behavior is not found in the individual; instead, crime is socially constructed. Society creates deviance by making rules and applying them to itself. When an individual acts a certain way, they are then perceived to be deviant and labeled as such, and this has the effect of a self-fulfilling prophecy on current and future behavior.

Emile Durkheim and **Robert Merton** believed in a theory called anomie. **Anomie** is defined as a breakdown in, and the disappearance of, the rules of social behavior. When the rules and norms that guide behavior are weakened or disappear, the result is deviant behavior.

TYPES OF CRIME

Different categories of crime have been established over the course of time. To help us understand these categories, let's start with some common definitions.

A **felony** is a crime carrying a penalty that ranges from incarceration for a minimum of one year to the death penalty.

A **misdemeanor** is a crime carrying a penalty of incarceration for no more than a year.

We know that there are hundreds of types of crimes under state or federal law; these include murder, manslaughter, larceny, assault, sexual assault, drug offenses, trespassing, and many more.

Let's examine some additional categories of crime:

Visible crime is defined as street crime or ordinary crime that can be observed and is usually most upsetting to the public. This does not literally mean you have to actually see the crime occur. It refers to such crimes as shoplifting, vandalism, and homicide.

Occupational crime is created through opportunities in an otherwise legal or legitimate business or occupation. For example, if you are a cashier at a supermarket, that is a legitimate job. But if you steal money out of the register while working, that is occupational crime, or white-collar crime. Edwin Sutherland developed this concept. Bribes, thefts by employees, and insider trading are all occupational crime.

Organized crime includes criminal acts in the fields of gambling, drugs, and prostitution that can be found through entities like the Mafia. There are many types of crime organizations, such as drug cartels. These entities have a structure and run like a business. One of the mechanisms that these organizations use is money laundering, which entails taking the profits from crime and filtering it through a legal business to make it clean so authorities cannot trace it.

Crimes without victims involve exchanges of illegal goods or services that are in strong demand in society. As a result, society as a whole is being injured, not one particular person. These crimes can overlap with organized crime, as well. Some of these crimes carry a moral weight. Is prostitution a victimless crime? Who is being harmed? And what about drug use? These are all debatable issues.

Political crime involves ideological issues or, in other words, crimes against the state. Terrorist acts fall under this label. These are not bribes to politicians—those are occupational crimes since being a politician is a legitimate occupation. Rather, these are crimes against a state or government.

Cybercrime includes offenses involving the use of computers, such as hacking into computer data-banks or setting up viruses to damage computers or computer systems.

Measuring crime levels and analyzing crime statistics is an extremely valuable tool in the criminal justice system. This information can show us key national trends in crime; at the same time, we can follow local crime statistics to examine if crime in a city or neighborhood is on the rise or decline, and what categories are increasing or decreasing. Crime reporting is also a very useful tool for crime detection and follow-up investigations. The criminal justice system relies on crime reports and statistics.

The Dark Figure of Crime

Before we get into reporting techniques, let's expand upon a key concept: **the dark figure of crime**. The dark figure of crime is a dimension of crime that is never reported to the police. This is not to say that the crime never took place, it was just never reported or recorded. It does not matter what the crime is, or how big or small—people will have many different reasons for not reporting it to the police.

If someone breaks into a car and steals a smartphone, it may not be worth the person's time and may be more of an inconvenience to them to file a report. Unfortunately, for a more serious crime like rape, the victim may feel ashamed or responsible, and does not want to face what might arise when reporting this crime.

Other issues arise when determining whether or not to report a crime. First, someone might fail to recognize that a crime has been committed. For instance, for crimes that involve fraud, the victim may not even realize that he or she was a victim of a fraudulent scheme.

Another factor of the dark figure of crime is when an incident is reported to the police but isn't processed. If a complainant calls the police and says that her car window was broken, the police may try to avoid the report by telling the car owner that her premiums might go up if the report goes to the insurance company. The complainant may then opt out of reporting the incident and decide to get the damages fixed out of pocket.

Another factor in the dark figure of crime is how the police classifies an incident. This type of scenario can go a couple of different ways. Depending on the incident, the police may take the report and reclassify the crime, perhaps even downgrading it, which affects crime statistics. Even though a crime is being reported the police might reclassify the incident, which may not lead to an accurate report. This type of practice has been monitored and addressed by police departments, and the process of correctly classifying crimes continues to evolve.

MEASUREMENT OF CRIME

When a crime report is completed and inputted, it becomes part of the **National Incident-Based Reporting System**, or **NIBRS**. In this report, the police officer details each offense that was committed during the crime. For example, if someone is robbed at gunpoint and also assaulted, although the robbery is the most severe charge, the assault and weapons charges are key and must be noted as well.

The NIBRS is a nationally recognized and utilized reporting system for police departments throughout the country. Any law enforcement agency that wants to use the NIBRS has to submit its request to the FBI. The law enforcement agency has to submit the structure of the report, crime categories, number of offenses collected per incident, and data values for incidents, which will then be reviewed for approval by the FBI.

National crime reports, called the **Uniform Crime Reports** or **UCR**, are updated and published every year by the FBI. All local police departments, including local, state, federal, and tribal departments, have to report their yearly statistics to the FBI. The FBI studies and analyzes these statistics and publishes these reports to the public. These reports are broken down into statistical categories, which allow us to analyze trends and patterns in crime.

Crimes reported to the FBI are put into categories, called Index Crimes. They include the following:

- Murder
- Burglary
- Rape
- Grand larceny
- Robbery
- Grand larceny, auto
- Felony assaults
- Arson

The UCR is extremely helpful and accurate, but because of the dark figure of crime, it may provide an incomplete picture of crime trends. In order to close the gap between the UCR and the dark figure of crime, the United States Department of Justice created the **National Crime Victimization Survey (NCVS)** in 1972.

The Department of Justice uses the Bureau of Justice Statistics to send out surveys two times a year to determine the number and types of crimes and victims that went unreported, in addition to reported incidents. Over the years, the surveys have been reorganized and are still used today by the Department of Justice to build a crime index.

The NCVS samples approximately 90,000 households and 160,000 people. It collects information on crimes that fall into the UCR's list of Index Crimes, with the exception of murder. The survey includes victims who experienced crime but did not report these crimes to the police.

The NCVS asks recipients to provide information about themselves, including age, sex, race, marital status, education, and income level. It also asks for any information about the offender as well, when available. The victim also answers questions as to why they reported, or did not report, the incident to the police.

JUVENILE DELINQUENCY

Juvenile delinquency is criminal behavior committed by a minor who falls under a particular age. What is most interesting and concerning about juvenile delinquency is how the criminal justice system finds ways to manage these young members of society, and the ever-changing philosophies about the causes of delinquency and the punishments that should be administered.

Let's examine some of the modern ideas about trends that can lead a young person to delinquency. The state of the economy and job market has always exhibited a correlation between juvenile delinquency and criminality in general. Let's assume that a poor economy or job rate leads to criminality in general. How does this relate to delinquency? The lack of availability of after-school jobs, and the structure and responsibility they provide, may drive kids to deviant behavior.

Other correlates for juvenile delinquency may exist in the social arena. As societies become more complex, something close to what we see in anomie tends to occur—more social issues develop and people, particularly kids, must encounter these issues on a daily basis without the maturity to know how to deal with them properly. These may include racial conflicts, physical or cyber-bullying, and the lure and power of social media.

Drug use has always been a common cause of juvenile delinquency. The rise of drug epidemics over the years, in connection with a poor economy, leaves time and opportunity for juveniles to become involved in delinquent behavior, including drug trafficking, turf wars among rival gangs that sell drugs, and increased street violence. Also, the social trend of designer drugs can lead to higher consumption by minors, leading to delinquency and deviant behavior.

Gangs and gang activity have a direct correlation with the rise of juvenile delinquency. It's estimated that there are approximately 800,000 gang members nationwide. Violence and weapons are typical in the lives of gang members, which of course lead to acts of criminal behavior. Research indicates that gangs fall into four categories.

- **Social gangs:** Members are involved in few delinquent acts including some drug use (with the exception of some marijuana and alcohol). Social gang members are more interested in social activities.

- **Party gangs:** Members concentrate on drug use and sales to support themselves and their personal use; there is little delinquent behavior in this group.

- **Serious delinquent gangs:** Members engage in serious delinquent acts and criminal behavior; drug dealing is not their main objective and drug use is typically for personal use.

- **Organized gangs:** Members are extremely involved in criminal behavior; drug use and sales are connected with other criminal acts; and violence is used to establish control over territory for drug sales and distribution. These gangs are very organized and can become formal criminal enterprises.

The average age of gang members has been changing in recent times; today, gang members may be as old as 55 or older. This indicates that gang members are staying with their gangs longer.

Gang research shows that young people can be involved with gangs as early as age 9, and by the time they're 12 can be full gang members. At the ages of 10 and 11, they have often committed some violent acts for initiation. By the age of 13, they may have fired their first gun, seen someone get killed, gotten their first tattoo, or been arrested.

Gangs have also seen an increase in female members. Some of the reasons may include financial opportunities through drug sales and theft, enhanced perception of identity and status, peer pressure, and broken families. Another possible reason could be for the excitement they get from belonging to a gang.

According to the National Youth Gang Survey, most gangs are made up of members with predominately black and Hispanic backgrounds. The average ethnic breakdown is as follows:

- Hispanic: 49 percent
- Black: 35 percent
- White: 9 percent
- Asian/Other: 7 percent

Gangs can also be broken down geographically. For instance, in Philadelphia and Detroit the majority of gang members are black. In New York and Los Angeles, gang members are mostly Hispanic.

Let's now look at what happens when accused criminals enter the criminal justice system. What are their rights? How does the system ensure a fair and just process?

THE CRIMINAL JUSTICE SYSTEM

The ideas that comprise the criminal justice system date back to Biblical times and the B.C. era, and come from all parts of the world. It has evolved over time and continues to evolve and grow, but there are still some core underlying principles regarding crime and punishment.

HISTORICAL ORIGINS AND LEGAL FOUNDATIONS

One of the earliest and most famous laws is the **Hammurabi code** (1750 B.C.E.). These were Babylonian laws written and codified to help keep the gods happy, and were based on the principle of retribution. **Retribution** is essentially payback—the idea that offenders need to be punished. Hammurabi had the notion to inflict pain unto offenders as they had to their victims. This pain is not necessarily physical; it also includes financial punishment. These laws dealt with all forms of societal behavior. The standard for these laws was based on "**lex talionis**," the notion of "an eye for an eye." For instance, if you broke somebody's bone, he would break your bone. If you were caught committing a robbery, the punishment was death.

As time passed, the criminal justice system evolved all over the world, and the United States was no exception. The origins of the criminal justice system in America derived from English tradition. During colonial times, the criminal justice system was based on common law and the notion of **mens rea**, which refers to a guilty mind, or knowledge of wrongdoing. The Catholic church also helped to guide and shape human behavior, values, and morals. The colonies used common law, based on judges' previous rulings and decisions, to assist or guide them, as there were no codified or written laws on the books.

These colonial laws were later reshaped and modified by William Penn. Prior to the Revolutionary War, Penn realized that there had to be a humane and compassionate component to the system. He believed in housing and rehabilitation for offenders and set up the first bail system.

Following the Revolutionary War, the creation of the U.S. Constitution led to equal rights and protections for citizens, and punishment for criminal offenders. In the early 1900s, Theodore Roosevelt helped usher in Progressive Era reform to the criminal justice system, and helped create national law enforcement agencies such as the FBI. Sentencing laws were also created during this time, along with the juvenile justice system.

DUE PROCESS

The American criminal justice system is built upon the notion of **due process**. Due process is fair treatment in all legal matters, whether civil or criminal. The concept of due process can be found in the Fifth Amendment of the Constitution, which states that no person shall be deprived of life, liberty, or property without having notice and a chance to present his or her side. The due process clause is also attached to the Fourteenth Amendment, which later applied these legal rights to all states as well.

Due process actually limits the powers of the state and federal governments, and requires them to follow certain procedural rules and laws. In addition, the responsibility to convict an individual of a crime in a criminal proceeding is placed upon the government or state, which must reach the standard that a person is guilty beyond a reasonable doubt.

In essence, due process grants the populace the protections of life, liberty, and property. But where do these protections come from and how are they applied? They are actually found in particular amendments to the **Bill of Rights**, the first 10 amendments of the U.S. Constitution. Let's take a closer look at some of the amendments that apply directly to criminal justice.

The **Fourth Amendment** includes the rights of people to be secure in their persons, houses, papers, and effects against unreasonable searches and seizures, and that no warrants shall be issued without probable cause.

The Fourth Amendment does give way to certain exceptions regarding police search and seizure, in specific cases. However, if the courts determine that the police acted unfairly or violated the Fourth Amendment clause and evidence was illegally seized, it would fall under the exclusionary rule.

The **exclusionary rule** states that when evidence is illegally obtained in searches and seizures it must be excluded from trial. In other words, the evidence would not be admissible at trial. This is also called "The Fruit of the Poisonous Tree" doctrine.

The **Fifth Amendment** protects the public from what is called double jeopardy—it stops prosecutors from subjecting a person to prosecution more than once in the same jurisdiction for the same offense. The Fifth Amendment also addresses self-incrimination, which simply means that the state cannot force someone to answer questions about himself or herself that may reveal a criminal act.

The **Sixth Amendment** includes the right to counsel and to a speedy and public trial, the right to confront witnesses, and the right to an impartial jury. This amendment ensures that there are no closed proceedings—all criminal trials must be fair and open. It protects the accused, or defendant, from government powers during a criminal proceeding. You also have the right to have legal representation protecting your rights and to cross-examine your accusers and witnesses against you.

The **Eighth Amendment** states that excessive bail shall not be required, nor excessive fines imposed, nor cruel and unusual punishment inflicted. Although this amendment prohibits excessive bail, this language is often open to interpretation, and often differs depending on the accused crime. Certain crimes like murder or rape may require that no bail is set, and the accused is remanded back to jail. Such a ruling must be reasonable, depending upon the circumstances set before the court and judge.

Cruel and unusual punishment is oftentimes open for debate, as the death penalty can be applied to capital cases. The death penalty has been an issue that has been debated, and contested from state to state, right up to the Supreme Court.

The criminal justice system is comprised of numerous agencies that work on both the state and federal levels. These different agencies are separate and unique, but are part of a complex and interconnected system. Each agency has its own set of goals, but all work towards the common goal of justice.

CRIMINAL JUSTICE AGENCIES

It would be impossible to list every individual agency within the criminal justice system; however, let's examine the various categories of these agencies and their roles.

The first group includes law enforcement and police. Again, we see law enforcement on both a state and federal level, including local or state police and federal agencies such as the FBI and DEA. The FBI and DEA belong to the Department of Justice, while FEMA and the U.S. Secret Service fall under the jurisdiction of the Department of Homeland Security. On the state level, it is not just the state police; it also includes conservation officers, environmental protection officers, and even parole officers. Local levels include law enforcement for towns and other municipalities.

Their roles are numerous, but mostly include keeping the peace by maintaining public order, apprehending offenders and violators who break laws, preventing crime through public awareness and educational programs, and providing social services that encompass other noncrime related matters.

The next agency level that takes part in the criminal justice system is the judicial branch, also known as the courts. There are many types of courts, including small claims court, civil court, bankruptcy court, and family court. The most common and recognizable is criminal court.

Courts are responsible for adjudicating each case, and as we've learned, due process plays a major role in American court proceedings. **Adjudication** is the process in which the courts determine if a defendant is guilty or not guilty. They must follow the rule of law and invoke fair procedures during this process. In addition, the courts impose sentencing, under the sentencing laws and guidelines, for offenders who are found guilty.

Our judicial system works as a **dual court system**, which means it separates state courts completely from national or federal courts. Each case is tried in its respective jurisdiction where laws were violated.

The last segment of the system falls under **corrections**. The correctional system is by far one of the oldest, and is also one of the most controversial and scrutinized. Corrections are used to punish offenders who break and violate the law. The correctional system takes on many forms, but we typically associate corrections with jails and prisons, which we'll explore in more detail later on in this chapter. The corrections system also consists of probation and parole. The purpose of corrections is a question that remains a topic of debate to this day—is it for punishment or rehabilitation? We'll look closer at different methods of correction, and their benefits and drawbacks, later on in this chapter.

LAW ENFORCEMENT

Let's now turn our focus to those who enforce the law on a daily basis—the police, which is the body that enforces societal law.

HISTORY AND ORGANIZATION

Law enforcement, as with most aspects of our laws, courts, and political structures, can be traced back to English tradition. One of the oldest systems, dating back to before the thirteenth century, was called frankpledge. **Frankpledge** is a system of ten household units (known as tithings) that work together to uphold the law and ensure each other's safety—and bring violators to court. The system also made all males above the age of 12 part of the tithings. When a crime was committed and a male became aware of it, he had a responsibility to inform the others (also known as a hue and cry) and to apprehend the offender. If the members failed to perform their duties, the tithing was fined.

The American system is largely based on the ideas of the founding father of policing, **Sir Robert Peel**, who in 1829 created the first London police force. In tribute, officers were called "bobbies" after him. Peel's philosophies now comprise much of modern policing today.

Peel had a four-part mandate. His goals were to do the following:

- Prevent crime without repressive force or use of the military
- Maintain public order by nonviolent means
- Reduce conflict between the police and public
- Show efficiency through the absence of crime

These mandates are still prevalent in today's policing.

American Policing—Historical Periods

American policing can be broken down into three historical periods.

The Political Era

The first period is the **Political Era**, which took place from 1840 to 1920. In this era, there were close ties between the police and political leaders. The police were loyal to the mayors and their parties—in other words, the police helped keep local politicians in power and the police were paid and received favors for their work and loyalty.

Corrupt politicians and their regimes used local police forces to harass and intimidate their political rivals. During this era, there was poor oversight and few regulations. This led to all sorts of corruption, which included discriminating against new immigrants and suppression of competing political parties.

Additionally, there were no standards or procedures to become a police officer, except for political connections, and for new officers training was limited. This bred more corruption. Newly appointed officers were often trained by veteran officers, who taught them all about the corrupt practices between the police, the community, and the politicians.

However, not everything in this era was bad or corrupt. As cities grew and with the influx of immigrants, police officers became extremely integrated within their communities. Officers were often seen as the only public servants on the street, and they took on a wide range of tasks that included community service—for instance, they served in soup kitchens, helped the homeless find shelter, and assisted immigrants in finding jobs.

In 1845, New York City created the first full-time paid police force. Because this era was filled with corruption, positions and ranks were paid off. For example, becoming a New York City police captain cost $10,000. Besides power, a lot of extra benefits and payoffs likely came along with that rank. However, this corrupt system couldn't last forever, and with the rise of reformers who wanted to change the relationship between the police and politicians, the second era of policing arose.

The Professional Model

The **Professional Model**, from 1920 through 1970, moved away from the corruption as the progressive movement began to influence policing. The progressives were largely made up of upper middle class and educated individuals. Some of their goals were to create a more efficient government and to have more services for the less fortunate in society. These reformers wanted the police and the police departments to become more professional.

August Vollmer, who was chief of police in Berkeley, California from 1909–1932, was one of the leading proponents of professional policing. He upgraded the police through technology, training, and even started a motorcycle unit.

In order for lasting change to happen, there were certain elements the reformers felt needed to be put in place:

- First, they wanted police to stay out of politics; they felt the police should be neutral when it came to political leaders. This is true today, as police departments do not endorse candidates for office.
- They wanted the police to be well trained. Training is a major component of professional policing. Training never ends for law enforcement—it is a constant reminder that as society

becomes more complex, policing has to continually evolve to reflect the changing needs of society.

- They wanted assurance that all laws would be enforced equally.

- There was a great call for police departments to use new technology, including day-to-day and in training, as well. This continues today—as technology advances, law enforcement must constantly stay trained in the latest weapons, non-lethal weapons, and computers, among other new developments.

- Finally, the reformers requested that the main task of the police be to fight crime.

Community Policing

This progressive era then moved into the next one, known as **Community Policing**. In the early 1970s, policing moved away from traditional crime fighting and moved toward services to benefit the community. Police departments did not want to isolate the community and hoped for a better relationship between the community and the police. This is not to say that the police stopped enforcing the law—rather, they expanded their roles to include more social service calls.

Community policing calls for the police to build partnerships with the communities that they serve. This movement broadened the responsibilities of the police. As this era of community policing continues, some criminologists suggest that a new model of policing should be established. As a result of 9/11 and other terrorist attacks, the next suggested era might be labeled **Homeland Security**. Time will tell what the next official era and its components will be in this ever-changing world.

STRUCTURING OF POLICE DEPARTMENTS

The structure of modern day police departments can be traced back to Sir Robert Peel. During his construction of the London police force, he realized that the military could not police the streets and communities for numerous reasons. However, during the transition from a military force to a police force, Peele realized that even though the military could not effectively patrol the streets, the police department should model itself structurally like the military to be most effective. As a result of this, we often refer to the police as a paramilitary organization.

As in the military, police departments have hierarchies that resemble military ranks. There may be differences between the two institutions, but there is no doubt that there is rank structure within police departments. This hierarchy is also called a **chain of command**. The chain of command provides structure that defines ranks and authority over subordinates. This structure creates accountability, discipline, and control. Another term that may be used to describe police structure is **command and control**.

A common rank structure in policing (in order from lowest to highest ranked) is as follows:

Commander

Captain

Lieutenant

Sergeant

↑

Detective

↑

Police Officer

After the rank of captain, titles and structure may vary depending on the particular police department.

Some roles and functions of police in our society seem obvious—for instance, the protection of life and property. This is actually a simplistic view of the responsibilities that police take on. Police forces can and do have more of a personal role in modern society, and the community involvement portion of their jobs is often overlooked. Their service includes community outreach, such as speaking at schools and businesses and promoting educational programs such as D.A.R.E., a drug prevention and awareness program.

Other police-sponsored programs may include running a police athletic league; offering the chance to ride along with a local patrol officer; and hosting local parades, picnics, and holiday parties. Social media is a key tool for the police to get out their message and promote community relations.

Other responsibilities that fall under the purview of the police are investigating crimes, gathering information, interviewing victims and witnesses, testifying in court, and establishing crime scenes when necessary. Most of these functions, including traffic enforcement, fall under the routines of patrol. While performing patrol duties, police may also respond to emergencies such as car accidents and medical calls.

Along with patrol duties, an officer's duties include service calls. Up to 80 percent of all calls that an officer responds to may be service related. Some of these include the following:

- Searching for a lost child
- Medical calls
- Lost or abandoned pets
- Traffic control
- Assisting the homeless
- Civil matters such as landlord/tenant disputes

In addition to the everyday emergencies that police officers respond to when assisting the public, they also act as first responders. The police are often the first line of response to natural disasters and terrorist attacks, and lead rescue and recovery efforts for their communities.

As you can see, the roles and functions of law enforcement have become more complex over time. The age-old job of fighting and preventing crime will always be a cornerstone of police work, but the roles of the police will constantly change and evolve in response to the issues and demands of a changing society.

Societal needs are the driving force behind policing, and dictate police responses, attitudes, procedures, and changes in police culture. Let's examine some recent trends.

Antiterrorism has been an important issue, depending on the prevalence of national or local incidents. Police officers must stay vigilant to protect cities and communities from these acts, which goes hand-in-hand with the need for training and military-style equipment to combat and respond to such catastrophic incidents—even on the local level. These are necessities, but can often conflict with a society's perception of the police as too militant and aggressive. Police must work to balance this perception with the realities of their duty to protect.

Technology has most definitely shaped society's norms and behavior, and modern policing is no different. Of course, technology such as forensics and DNA have had a hugely beneficial impact on police and criminal investigations; however, there are other technological aspects that have also had an impact on policing.

Body cameras are another advancement that is gaining in popularity, and controversy. Pushback from police who are reluctant to wear them, differing opinions on when the cameras should be activated, and defining the legality of revealing recorded footage remain hot-button issues. As with anything else new to the technology field, procedures will continue to evolve.

Immigration is a particularly hot topic of conversation and controversy in today's society, and has ramifications for law enforcement as well. Issues facing police today include everything from learning how to work within communities that are non-English speaking to determining if an immigrant is legal or illegal and violated federal immigration laws. Also, cultural differences can make a simple police encounter more challenging because of potential differences in customs and traditions.

The use and perception of appropriate or excessive force by the police remains a hot-button issue. Close scrutiny by the public and media brings with it the possibility of civil unrest, as we have seen in many instances. This, in turn, potentially creates more distrust between the police and the community, and can erode the core of police community relations.

Occupational Characteristics

Police subculture contains many elements that make it unique. The first is called **working personality,** or the emotional and behavioral characteristics developed by members of a group in response to their work situation and environmental influences. The two main elements of working personality when it comes to police work are

1. Awareness of the threat of danger—learning to be suspicious of people and their behavior and always being on high alert.

2. The need to maintain personal authority. Police officers are constantly establishing their authority with the public, which at times affects their authority and power.

Another aspect of subculture can be found in **police morality**. Officers are placed in constant predicaments in which they must make quick decisions and determine right from wrong. As a result, police officers oftentimes develop a sense of high morality, which eases an officer's conscience during tense social interactions and dilemmas where they have to make quick and just decisions. A high morality also gives officers a sense of positivity about themselves as they work long hours and try to protect the public and keep communities safe.

Due to the nature of police work, it also creates a phenomenon called **police isolation.** Police isolation occurs when officers remove themselves from society, as they believe that the public is suspicious and hostile towards them. This is part of the subculture that currently exists in law enforcement. There are many reasons why this occurs, but one is that police often interact with society at the worst of times, like during crimes, injuries, and death, which can cause officers to pull away from society. Another isolating factor is the strange and long hours and irregular shifts within police culture.

Police isolation can lead officers to create more barriers with the public, as they naturally fall back within their own group or subculture. Officers often feel that the only people who truly understand them are other officers and family members. There are many types of stress that police officers face:

- **Work stress** that comes with law enforcement is part of the subculture that strengthens and increases internal police bonds. Law enforcement creates a large amount of stress that also results in high suicide rates, divorce, alcohol issues, and other related health conditions.

- **External stress** is produced by the threats and dangers of police work that officers may encounter on a regular basis.

- **Organizational stress** is created through the inner structure of police departments. Long hours, shift changes, and strict rules and procedures can contribute to this type of stress.

- **Personal stress** can occur when officers struggle to get along with peers and adjust their value systems.

- **Operational stress** results from dealing with the negative parts of society, which creates distrust in people whom officers encounter.

Now that you have a thorough overview of policing, let's turn our focus to the courts and how they operate.

THE COURT SYSTEM

This next section will detail the ins and outs of the U.S. court system—including its history, organization, and processes.

HISTORY OF THE COURT SYSTEM

Article III, Section 1 of the U.S. Constitution states:

> "The judicial powers of the United States shall be vested in one Superior Court and in such inferior courts as the Congress may from time to time ordain and establish."

Passed in 1789, The Judiciary Act created provisions for the Supreme Court. It also established that the court would consist of a Chief Justice and five Associate Justices. **John Jay** was the first Justice appointed by George Washington.

The Supreme Court had no control over the cases that went before them until 1891. It was then that the Justices began reviewing cases through certiorari. **Certiorari**, in legal terms, means *to make sure*, as in an appeal. In other words, it is a written order from the higher court asking the lower court for the records of a case for review. Colonies also created functioning courts. This combination of courts by the early colonials, and the creation of the federal court system through the U.S. Constitution, was the beginning foundation of our court system.

ORGANIZATION AND STRUCTURE

As we discussed earlier, the United States operates under a dual court system, which in essence establishes a federal and state system, unlike other countries that have a singular national court system. Each level will hear and preside over cases that fall into their legal jurisdictions. Federal courts will deal with crimes violating federal laws like drug trafficking, counterfeiting, kidnapping, and terrorist activities to name a few. On the state level, each state enforces its state constitution and laws. The majority of cases that are heard before the courts fall under the state level, as they enforce many more laws, including misdemeanors and minor violations.

The federal court system is comprised of 94 judicial districts that cover all federal laws. The location of the crime committed determines which district court covers the case. Within these 94 district courts, there are 12 regional circuits, which cover the U.S. Court of Appeals. If you wanted to appeal your case, it would be heard in the corresponding court of appeals within that district.

In addition to the 12 circuits, there are two appellate courts in Washington, D.C. The U.S. Supreme Court is the highest court in the land. It focuses on constitutional issues on both a state and federal level.

The states are set up on a similar basis, with some differences. On a state level, cases start in a trial court to determine guilt or innocence. Depending on the type of crime committed, a case could wind up in a **court of limited jurisdiction.** This trial court handles only misdemeanors and civil lawsuits for small amounts of money, which varies from state to state. On a state level, there are also **courts of general jurisdiction**, which hear felony cases and civil lawsuits, and impose prison sentences. In some states, general jurisdiction courts will also hear all types of criminal cases and violations including traffic cases. The next level is a **court of appeals**. These appellate courts only review judicial errors from the lower courts, and do not determine guilt or innocence. The last level is known as **courts of last resorts,** which are for final appeal. Sometimes the courts of last resorts are also known as the state Supreme Court, the court of appeals, or high court.

Whether state or federal, both systems start at a trial level court and then proceed upwards to a court of appeals and then to the highest court.

The judicial system is not only split between a federal and state level, but also between an adult and juvenile system. Let's take a closer look.

ADULT AND JUVENILE COURT SYSTEMS

For starters, the terminology is different for adults. An adult who is accused is known as a **defendant**, the accusatory court document is known as a **complaint**, and a hearing is called a **trial**. Trials in adult court are open to the public—you have a right to have a trial before your peers. During the trial, if one is found guilty he or she is sentenced with the main purpose of punishment in mind.

Juvenile courts, for the most part, completely differ from adult courts. However, there are some similarities, such as the right to an attorney, the right to cross-examine witnesses, protection from self-incrimination, notice of charges, and the need to be found guilty beyond a reasonable doubt. Let's look at some of the differences and how the juvenile system operates in contrast to the adult system.

In the juvenile system, the juvenile is referred to as the **minor**. Trial proceedings in juvenile court are called **adjudication hearings**, and the minor does not have the right to a public trial. Proceedings are behind closed doors to protect the minor's identity, and a judge will decide on guilt or innocence. There is no jury system because a juvenile's peers cannot judge him or her.

The ages for juvenile courts may vary from state to state, but can run between ages 10 to 16 and in some instances up to 18. However, juveniles may be tried as adults for serious violent offenses.

The juvenile courts do not use the terms *crimes* or *criminal acts*; they use **delinquent acts**. The courts are more lenient when it comes to the admissibility of evidence, and sentencing hearings are called **disposition hearings.** Once someone is found guilty, the purpose of the court is to keep the minor's best interests in mind and to seek rehabilitation—not punishment. The judges often use diversionary programs like probation, counseling, community service, and restitution.

PRETRIAL, TRIAL, AND POST-TRIAL PROCESSES

The criminal justice system is set in motion when a crime has been committed and the police begin an investigation. Following an arrest, the due process clause is attached to the offender as he or she moves through the court system.

As a case proceeds, the district attorney or prosecutor is in charge. During this pretrial phase, the prosecutor implements their policies when reviewing each case to help guide them in making legal decisions. These decisions can be seen in three phases. They are:

- **Legal sufficiency:** The prosecutor reviews the case and arrest to ensure that it meets the legal standard to pursue and move forward.
- **System efficiency:** Here, the prosecutor establishes policies to engage in speedy and early disposition of cases. Cases are screened, and some cases are plea bargained in exchange for a quick guilty plea to expedite the flow of cases.

- **Trial sufficiency:** The prosecutor determines if the case is strong enough and meets the legal standards to prosecute at trial and obtain a conviction. They review the police work, victims, and witnesses in order to proceed with a trial.

Prior to any trial, there are numerous steps that take place to protect the rights of the defendant and to determine if probable cause exists. This process works to ensure that the offender's constitutional rights are protected.

The first step in the process is the **initial appearance**. Initial appearance is when the offender is brought before the judge, within a reasonable amount of time, to be given formal notice of charges and information about their rights. At this point, the judge reviews the evidence to decide if the case can move forward. A bail hearing also takes place during this appearance. **Bail** is defined as a specific amount of money set by a judge to be paid as a condition of pretrial release to make sure that the accused will return to court.

The next step, especially for serious crimes, is a **preliminary hearing** with a judge, or a **grand jury** in front of a special jury. This process determines whether there is probable cause that a crime was committed and that the accused person committed it. This step does not determine guilt or innocence, but rather examines the legal standard of probable cause.

Once a judge or grand jury determines probable cause, the accused is processed to the next phase— arraignment. **Arraignment** takes place when the accused appears in court to hear the indictment or information that was produced in the previous phase. In other words, if probable cause was found against an individual, a document has to be produced by the prosecutor and filed in court. This is again for the accused to know what charges were filed against him or her in a preliminary hearing or grand jury. In a preliminary hearing, it is called an **information**, while a grand jury produces an **indictment**.

This sets the stage for the pretrial process. One of the many phases of the pretrial process is what is known as discovery. **Discovery** is the exchange of information between the prosecutor and the defense. The responsibility falls upon the prosecutor to relinquish evidence to the defense, to ensure both sides are on a level playing field during the trial. The prosecutor cannot surprise the defense at the last minute. This gives the defense adequate time to prepare a legal defense, once they receive the prosecutorial information through discovery.

Another pretrial step that takes place is known as a motion. A **motion** is basically a request to the court to do something or take action. There are all types of motions filed in a criminal case. One is a **motion to dismiss**, which is made if the defense feels an indictment or information has been completed incorrectly, or some sort of judicial error was made. This motion states that in the name of fundamental fairness, the court should dismiss the charges.

Another common form of motion is a **motion to suppress**. If the defense feels that any of the evidence in a case was obtained illegally under the Fourth Amendment, a motion will be filed before the court. The defendant will be allowed to testify before the judge. Based on the evidence, he or she will make a ruling about the admissibility of the evidence. Some of the evidence may be admissible and some of it may not be—the judge will determine this on a case-by-case basis.

The defense may also file a motion for a **change of venue**, which is where the trial will take place. If the defense feels they cannot get a fair trial at the jurisdiction where the crime occurred, the motion will be filed to request a new location. Factors that come into play when requesting a new venue include media coverage, community involvement, and any other public negativity surrounding the case. The judge will determine if the defendant can get a fair trial in the original jurisdiction.

In the beginning phase of the trial, a process takes place called a **voir dire**, which is the process of selecting a jury. This is where the prosecution and defense question prospective jurors and determine who will sit as jurors and alternates. The selection process also involves **peremptory challenge**, where each party is allowed a number of objections, without reason, to eliminate potential jurors.

Once the voir dire is completed and the jury is set, the trial will begin and the judge will give preliminary instructions to the jury. The judge will explain obligations, the law, and the presumption of innocence to the jury. **Opening statements** by both the prosecutor and defense then follow, which give both parties an opportunity to address the jury and explain the facts of the case.

The trial process in the United States is an **adversarial system**, wherein both parties argue for their side. After both parties present their cases and witnesses, the prosecutor can call rebuttal witnesses to disprove the defense, and then the defense is allowed to rebut the prosecutor's evidence.

The trial then progresses to the final stages, with **closing arguments** delivered by both sides. The attorneys address the jury once more, and present them with the facts of the case and the law. This gives both parties the opportunity to summarize their cases. When arguments are completed, the judge will give the jury final instructions on the law, the burden of proof, and the elements of the crime they're judging.

Then, the jury will be removed from the courtroom and begin their deliberations in an effort to reach a verdict. During deliberations, the jury has no contact with the outside world. When the jury has reached a verdict of guilt or innocence, they will return to court to read the verdict to the defendant. If the verdict is not guilty and the defendant is acquitted, the case is over and the accused is free to go. However, if the jury finds the defendant guilty then the sentencing phase is next.

Sentencing Issues and Trends

After a guilty verdict, the judge will determine a sentencing date. The date will be set some time in the future, in order to create a **Pre-Sentence Investigation Report (PSI)**. This report, led by the probation department, is created after interviewing the defendant and conducting an investigation of the defendant's past history, which includes criminal history, family, medical issues, and employment. The defendant is permitted to make a statement in the report, as well. Once all relevant background information is complete, a sentence recommendation will be given to the judge.

During the sentencing hearing, the judge will review the PSI and conduct a hearing to determine the sentence. Witnesses may be called, and both the defendant and victim can make statements. The **victim impact statement** allows the victim or family members to address the court, either in a written or verbal statement. The judge will then, under the sentencing guidelines, hand the defendant the appropriate sentence.

More than 2 million people are currently incarcerated in the U.S. prison system. This high number stems from the elevated levels of drug offenses and the consequences of the "get tough on crime" policies of the 1980s and 1990s. Currently, the federal prison population is growing, and half of the prison population is there for drug-related offenses.

Current sentencing trends have included some states abolishing mandatory penalties for drug offenses. More and more, courts are turning to alternative sentencing programs including community supervision, shock probation, drug courts, and treatment programs. Society is always looking for alternative methods for punishment and rehabilitation, as prison sentences can be very costly.

You should now have a solid overview of the courts and how they operate within the criminal justice system. Let's now turn our focus to corrections.

CORRECTIONS

This section covers all aspects of corrections: its history, the different systems used, and its evolution in a changing society.

History of Corrections

The American system of corrections, like other aspects of its criminal justice system, was derived from the English during the colonial period (1620–1776). In 1682, William Penn, the founder of Pennsylvania, adopted what was known as **The Great Law**, which was based on humane Quaker principles and emphasized hard labor in a house of corrections as punishment. Eventually, the colonies moved away from The Great Law, and jail time gave way to harsh physical punishments including whippings, branding, and mutilation.

After the American Revolution, theories regarding criminal punishment took another turn. The new theory of corrections believed that offenders could be reformed, which gave way to the birth of the **penitentiary**. Offenders were sent to penitentiaries for isolation from society, in order to reflect on their past behaviors, and hopefully to repent.

Pennsylvania opened the first penitentiary in 1790, based on the concept of **solitary confinement**. In 1819, New York was soon to follow with its first penitentiary located in Auburn. Here, inmates were held in isolation at night and worked with each other in complete silence during the day. They were issued prison striped uniforms.

In the 1800s, the **Reformatory Movement** emerged, and in 1876, Elmira, New York was home to the first reformatory prison. The Reformatory Movement emphasized training for prisoners, who were treated for what were perceived to be the social, biological, and psychological root causes of deviant behavior. Prisoners followed strict schedules that included work, academics, and vocational training.

There have always been debates about corrections and its role and purpose in society. Over time, corrections and its methods have changed according to society's needs and beliefs, but the main concept has never wavered—to protect society. Essentially, the system wants people to behave and conform to society's rules, laws, and norms, and criminal behavior is punished.

Purpose

The U.S. correctional system carries with it four goals:

- The first is **retribution**, which we covered earlier. This refers to the "eye for an eye" philosophy and calls for a deserved punishment that fits the crime.

- The second is **deterrence**, which is based on the belief that people's behavior can be controlled by the notion that criminal behavior will result in punishment. There are two types of deterrence: general deterrence, which is intended for society as a whole to prevent criminal behavior, and specific deterrence, which is targeted toward offenders with the hope that they will not commit any further criminal behavior.

- Next is **incapacitation**—the assumption that society can be protected from offenders by placing them in a correctional facility for a length of time. Execution falls under this umbrella, as well.

- Finally, **rehabilitation** is based on the notion of changing or restoring the offender to alter his future behavior and reform him as he returns to society. This is accomplished through education and vocational training.

The courts and correctional system have developed various forms of punishment and sentencing to fit the needs of society and the criminal justice system. With recent issues of prison overcrowding and a lack of resources for probationary services, counties and states have needed to make some changes to their sentencing guidelines and structures.

One of these changes is called **intermediate sanctions**, which are punishments that are not as severe or costly as prison sentences, but are more restrictive than regular or traditional probation. These sanctions can include monetary fines or forfeiture of illegally gained assets. They can also restrict one's freedom through home confinement, strict probation supervision, and community service. These sanctions are more effective when they are used in combination with each other. Additionally, these sanctions take into account the type of offense committed, the traits and attributes of the offender, and how best to serve the community.

Juvenile Correctional System

The regular adult prison system is relatively simple compared to the juvenile system. Adult prisons are intended for individuals 18 years and older and have fewer rehabilitative services than juvenile facilities. (Even though the juvenile system has more services than the adult system, there are more adult facilities in the form of jails and prisons.)

The juvenile correctional system contains many different correctional alternatives for the juvenile offender. As opposed to adult corrections, where the goal is punishment, the goal of the juvenile system is **rehabilitation**. Because of this goal, and the fact that the juvenile system has fewer institutional facilities, one alternative is juvenile probation. During probation, juveniles are closely supervised by probation officers and must follow strict rules and conditions, which are set by the juvenile court. These include drug-treatment programs and group counseling facilities. For these **community treatment alternatives**, the assumption is that the offender is not a danger to the community and will likely rehabilitate.

The juvenile system also contains **residential community treatment**. In residential treatment, a juvenile is placed in a nonsecure facility that is closely monitored by trained members. These treatment programs are composed in several different ways:

- **Group homes** are residences that are supervised by trained counselors who provide counseling, education, job training, and family living. The number of juveniles usually ranges from 12 to 15.

- **Foster care** is for juveniles who are orphans, or whose parents cannot provide care for them. The juvenile is placed in foster care with families to care and provide for them, with the intention of returning them to the community.

- **Family group homes** are simply a combination of group homes and foster care.

- **Rural programs** give juveniles the opportunity to work at forestry camps, ranches, and farms.

Other probationary programs include **Juvenile Intensive Probation Supervision (JIPS),** which is an alternative to incarceration. In JIPS, the juvenile is assigned to a probation officer with a very small caseload. These juveniles fall into a high-risk category and therefore receive close daily supervision by probation officers.

In **electronic monitoring**, another form of probation, the juvenile wears an electronic device and is monitored by the probation department. Movements are monitored, and limited to school, programs, court, and work, while the rest of the time is spent at home. Random visits and phone calls also ensure that the juvenile is home at appropriate times.

Capital Punishment

Let's now turn our focus to a discussion of capital punishment.

Capital punishment has almost always been a part of correctional history. It continues to be one of the most controversial topics in the criminal justice system. Capital punishment in the United States is still used and has been involved in many court cases, including cases adjudicated by the Supreme Court. Cases involving the death penalty often raise constitutional issues involving the Eighth Amendment, which forbids cruel and unusual punishment, as well as the Fourteenth Amendment clause of providing equality in justice.

The death penalty is used in federal, state, and military courts. Each state has the option of implementing the death penalty in its sentencing laws. As mentioned, the death penalty has been challenged many times based on its merits and constitutionality. Under the Eighth Amendment, the death penalty has been tested—not only with regard to execution of the offender, but also regarding different methods of execution.

A challenge that the U.S. Supreme Court faced in the past was based on lethal injection, particularly that lethal injections violated the Eighth Amendment. In 2008, the Supreme Court denied this claim and stated that lethal injection was not a violation of the Eighth Amendment.

One of the most famous cases involving capital punishment was *Furman v. Georgia*, in 1972. The Civil Rights movement had raised concerns about the death penalty—not only with regard to race, but also with regard to how the sentence was imposed. In this case, the U.S. Supreme Court banned the use of capital punishment. This case did not rule on the death penalty with regard to the Eighth Amendment, but rather from the standpoint of how it was applied to defendants. The Supreme Court determined that when courts applied the death penalty it was arbitrary and capricious, meaning there were no set laws or guidelines. There was no system in place, and sentencing was based on prosecutorial discretion, leading to a lot of disparity and questions of racial bias. In other words, the death penalty was chosen randomly as to when and to whom it was applied.

Following the Furman case, states that wanted to use the death penalty as a punishment needed to meet the Supreme Court criteria. These states implemented uniformity in death penalty cases for first-degree murder with aggravating circumstances.

Prison Organization

Let's review common terminology regarding incarceration.

Jails and **prisons** are probably the most misused terms in the correctional and criminal justice system. Like everything else in this system, these institutions are organized and structured. The first level of organization is **police booking** or holding cells, the first places offenders will pass through. Police use these facilities to detain offenders while they are being processed. Offenders will eventually be transported to larger facilities.

The next level is **jails**. Jails are used for multiple purposes. The primary purpose of jails is to hold defendants awaiting trial or who could not make bail. Also, if offenders are convicted of misdemeanor crimes, they would serve their time in local jails. Jails will also hold inmates for federal and state crimes who are waiting to be transported to the proper jurisdiction. Individuals with mental illnesses who are waiting to be transferred to a proper medical facility will also be housed in jails. The majority of inmates found in jails have not been convicted of any crimes, with the exception of misdemeanor offenses. Instead, these inmates are for the most part waiting to be charged, tried, or sentenced and transported to a proper facility or jurisdiction.

There are a few different types of jails. **Municipal jails** can be found in large cities like Los Angles and New York City, which are homes to the two largest city jails in the country. **County jails** are more common, in which the county will house and supervise the correctional facility located within its borders.

State prisons are correctional institutions that are used only for convicted offenders who are found guilty of felony crimes. Inmates who are sent to prison have been sentenced by the courts to serve a term of more than a year. State prisons can be broken down into certain categories, including male-only, female-only, and those for youth offenders convicted of serious crimes.

Prisons are also classified by the offense committed and the type of security provided:

- In **maximum security prisons**, the facility emphasizes security, with armed guards, towers, and restricted inmate movement. Here, there are fewer vocational and educational programs for rehabilitation.

- In a **medium security prison**, there is still a strong emphasis on security, but also opportunities for education, counseling, and other rehabilitation programs.

- Inmates in **minimum security prisons** may work in unsupervised locations outside the facility, such as prison farms, or take part in other rehabilitative programs, such as vocational and educational programs.

Federal prisons are used for all federal crimes, and are operated by the Bureau of Prisons. There are currently more than 100 federal correctional facilities, which are classified like state institutions into minimum, medium, and maximum security prisons.

Inmate Characteristics

Let's go over some facts about the current prison population in the United States:

- Presently, the prison population is approximately 92 percent male and 8 percent female.

- Approximately 26 percent of inmates are in the 20–29 age range, 31 percent are in the 30–39 age range, 23 percent are in the 40–49 age range, and 13 percent are in the 50–59 age range.

- African Americans make up 37 percent of the prison population, whites make up 32 percent, and Hispanics make up 22 percent.

Prison life poses many challenges for inmates, and subcultures within the system have a deep effect on their personalities, both during and after incarceration.

Prisoner violence, used for intimidation, power, and status, is common among inmates. Prison gangs are typically based on racial or ethnic backgrounds, and provide inmates with protection and a sense of belonging. Gangs create an atmosphere of violence and fear that can be found across many prison populations.

Along with inmate violence, which can shape people's attitudes and characteristics, sexual violence has an unfortunate presence in prison life. As a result of the prevalence of violent sexual acts in prison, the **Prison Rape Elimination Act** was signed into law in 2003. This law was designed to prevent violent sexual assaults among prisoners. However, because victim reporting of these assaults is sparse, it has been difficult to obtain accurate numbers, implement proper protections, and determine the law's effectiveness.

Issues and Trends

These issues and many more, including the accelerated decline in physical and mental health that takes place in correctional facilities, can cause extreme stress, depression, and other negative effects in inmates.

As mentioned previously, the correctional system and the pieces that comprise it are constantly changing. As new public policies develop, government officials must invest in correctional facilities to keep their communities safe. However, rising costs and the rampant issue of prison overcrowding may necessitate alternative methods for sentencing offenders. For example, in the juvenile system, the trend toward developing community-based residential facilities, rather than incarceration, continues to grow.

Another trend within correctional institutions is an ever-increasing influx of women (currently, the majority of incarcerated women are between the ages of 24 and 45, and half have racial or ethnic minority backgrounds). Approximately one-third of incarcerated women have been convicted of violent crimes.

As a result, corrections officials are now facing a new set of issues and challenges. Different facilities are needed for female inmates, with distinct programs to fulfill their needs. One of the most important issues female inmates face is childcare. Children who were cared for by a single-parent mother who is incarcerated are usually placed with relatives, friends, or in state foster care. Female inmates who are pregnant while incarcerated can be a challenge for institutions. Prisons are not traditionally structured for childcare, and the birth of a child by a female inmate raises many issues of concern. Typically, most states do not have family programs or facilities to keep the mother and child together. The average time that a female inmate spends with her newborn is three weeks, at which time the child is removed and placed with family members or social services.

Another trend in the correctional system over the last couple of decades has been the rise and popularity of private prisons—facilities that look similar to government-run prisons, but are operated by private, for-profit companies. These prisons house inmates from local, state, and federal governments for a fee. A private facility will charge, on average, $25 to $100 per day per inmate.

Prison privatization comes with many controversies. Advocates for privatization argue that it can reduce jail overcrowding, reduce staff costs, and save local and federal governments money. Supporters of these programs also claim that they can run these facilities more cheaply and efficiently than the states or federal government.

However, in order for private prisons to survive and make a profit, they must fill the facility with inmates and keep staffing and rehabilitative program costs down. Research has shown privately run prisons may not be that cost-effective or beneficial at all—both for inmates and for the criminal justice system. The debate on privatization will continue.

SUMMING IT UP

- A crime is an act committed in violation of established law. There are two types of crime: the first is **mala in se**, which are offenses that are immoral and considered wrong, like murder, rape, robbery, and assault. **Mala prohibita** crimes are offenses that are not necessarily inherently wrong, but are prohibited by law, such as gambling, prostitution, drug use, or traffic violations.

- U.S. crime is reported and tracked by the **Uniform Crime Reporting Program,** which establishes patterns and trends and breaks down crime by location, demographics, and other statistics.

- The **classical criminology** theory views criminal behavior as a conscious choice, which can be deterred by establishing predictable punishments. It also prioritizes quick punishment over severe punishment, and calls for humane prison systems as well.

- In the **utilitarian** philosophy of crime, philosophers believe that whether actions are morally right or morally wrong depends on the effects and results of the action, and that people will avoid crime to avoid pain and unpleasant consequences.

- The **positivist theory of criminology** suggests that crime is a result of an individual's sociological, biological, and psychological factors, and that the punishment should be tailored to fit the crime, rather than having a nonspecific set of general consequences for breaking the law. This view of criminality was supported further by psychologist William Sheldon's biological classification systems, psychologist Sigmund Freud's theory that a person's personality and behavior are controlled by early childhood influences, and Edwin Sutherland's sociological theory that criminal behavior comes from a person's personal influences in life.

- Other crime theories include the **control theory**, in which criminal behavior is caused by weakened social ties; the **labeling theory**, in which crime is a social construct instead of an individual act; and **anomie**, in which crime is a result of a breakdown in social rules and norms.

- The types of crime include **felonies** (major crimes punishable by incarceration for at least a year, and up to the death penalty), **misdemeanors** (minor crimes punishable by incarceration for a year or less), **visible crime** (street crime), **occupational crime** (crime of opportunity, like stealing from an employer), **organized crime** (criminal acts related to gambling, drugs, and prostitution committed by groups like drug cartels, the Mafia, etc.), **crimes without victims** (exchanges of illegal goods or services), **political crimes** (terrorist acts or crimes against the state), and **cybercrime** (crimes committed using computers or digital means).

- In crime reporting, the **dark figure of crime** is the difference between reported crimes and unreported crimes. It affects overall crime and reporting statistics. The FBI attempts to assess the dark figure of crime by conducting the annual National Crime Victimization Survey (NCVS) to determine the gap between reported **index crimes** (such as murder, arson, burglary, rape, and felony assaults) and crimes that go unreported.

- Factors that affect **juvenile delinquency** (criminal behavior by minors) include drug use, gang activity, and lack of economic or social resources. Gang activity in particular has increased, and includes more members from different age groups and different genders.

- The concept of codified laws goes back to the Hammurabi code, which was formed in 1750 B.C.E. Babylon and established the idea of punishing crimes. The code, which was based on the concept of "an eye for an eye," was the first to set legal standards for all forms of societal behavior, with varying penalties for crimes ranging from financial consequences to the death penalty.

- The American justice system developed out of the concept of English common law, and was refined and shaped by William Penn after the Revolutionary War. The U.S. Constitution further defined equal rights and legal protections for citizens.

- Due process, or fair treatment in all legal matters, is a fundamental concept of the American justice system. The Fifth Amendment to the Constitution outlines due process for American citizens, stating that no citizen will be deprived of life, liberty, or property without notice, or a chance to defend in court. Due process was applied to all states as well in the Fourteenth Amendment.

- The criminal justice system is made up of three main segments: law enforcement, the courts, and corrections. Law enforcement agencies include police on the state and local level as well as federal agencies under the jurisdictions of the Department of Justice and the Department of Homeland Security. The judicial branch includes all types of courts, including criminal, civil, small claims, bankruptcy, and family courts. The judicial branch functions as a **dual court system**, separating federal courts from state courts. The corrections system includes prisons, as well as probation and parole programs.

- In the **Political Era** of American policing (1840–1920), there were close relationships between police and political leaders in which both parties traded favors in exchange for loyalty.

- In the **Professional Model** era (1920–1970), a more progressive version of policing was meant to create more efficient local government and more resources for less fortunate people. To achieve these goals, the reformers tried to separate policing and politics, emphasized constant training for police professionals, and emphasized that laws should be enforced equally.

- In the **Community Policing** era (1970–present), policing moved away from direct crime fighting and closer to developing relationships between communities and the police as a way of increasing social service and reducing crime.

- A police **chain of command** is a structure that defines ranks and authority for all members of the department. The highest ranks are typically Commander, then Captain, then Lieutenant, then Sergeant, then Detective, then Police Officer, though this can vary depending on the police department. Line function officers are out in the field, while staff function officers typically work within the police department itself (such as clerks and administrative staff).

- As policing needs grow and change with society, the nature of policing has evolved as well. Antiterrorism has become a major focus of American police work. Advancements in technology (like sophisticated forensics, DNA, and body cameras) have also affected how police officers work and function in their communities. Immigration violations and excessive force are also current hot-button topics being debated when it comes to modern policing.

- **Subculture** is important to police work, because the police community is often closed and separate from most of society. Police subculture is often defined by the following characteristics: **working personality** (the characteristics developed by a group in response to their work and environment), **police morality** (relying on conscience to solve problems), and **police isolation** (working apart from society due to perceived hostility toward police).

- Although juvenile and adult courts have different terminology and are handled separately, both follow the same general trial processes. After a defendant or minor has been charged, the prosecutor determines whether there is sufficient evidence for a trial. Once a formal charge is made, a defendant has the option to make bail before the trial, and may be entitled to a preliminary hearing with a judge or grand jury to determine probable cause. Attorneys for both sides work on **discovery** and **motions** for court actions before the trial starts. After jury selection, the trial begins, and both the defense attorney and the prosecutor present evidence to the judge and jury. Once both attorneys give closing arguments for their respective cases, the jury deliberates and arrives at a verdict.

- After a guilty verdict, a defendant's sentence is determined separately. A **Pre-Sentence Investigation Report (PSI)** is compiled, taking factors into account like the defendant's history and circumstances, as well as statements from victims of the crime.

- The U.S. corrections system originated in England's common law, and has developed punishment and sentencing to support a set of four goals: **retribution** (punishment for crime), **deterrence** (discouraging future crime), **incapacitation** (taking offenders out of society), and **rehabilitation** (changing behavior). The juvenile prison system tends to focus on rehabilitation and alternative punishment and treatment programs that allow juveniles to re-enter society.

- **Capital punishment**, or the death penalty, is used in federal, state, and military courts, and can be implemented in laws at the state level. Capital punishment remains controversial due to constitutional debates over the cruel and unusual punishment outlined in the Eighth Amendment, as well as the Fourteenth Amendment clause ensuring justice applied equally.

- **Jails** are temporary holding facilities for defendants awaiting trial or hearings, defendants who could not make bail, or defendants serving misdemeanor sentences. **Prisons** are long-term correctional institutions that hold people convicted of felony crimes. Prisons are often divided by security level (maximum, medium, and minimum) or by demographic category (men's, women's, juvenile). **Federal prisons** hold people convicted of federal crimes.

CRIMINAL JUSTICE POST-TEST

Directions: Carefully read each of the following 60 questions. Choose the best answer to each question and fill in the corresponding circle on the answer sheet. The Answer Key and Explanations can be found following this post-test.

1. The majority of violent crimes that take place between an offender and a victim are
   A. interracial.
   B. biracial.
   C. unrelated to race.
   D. intraracial.

2. Crimes that are considered not necessarily wrong in and of themselves but are prohibited by law, such as drug offenses or prostitution, are called
   A. mala in se.
   B. mala prohibita.
   C. violations.
   D. morality crimes.

3. The criminologist who wrote *An Essay on Crimes and Punishments* and was a proponent of the classical criminology theory was
   A. Sigmund Freud.
   B. Edwin Sutherland.
   C. Cesare Lombroso.
   D. Cesare Beccaria.

4. The idea that criminal behavior stems from mental illness is known as
   A. XYY chromosome theory.
   B. labeling theory.
   C. psychological explanation.
   D. violent crime.

5. The theory that criminality stems from the broken ties between an individual and society is
   A. classical criminology.
   B. differential association.
   C. control theory.
   D. political crime.

6. Crimes that are committed from legal opportunities or businesses are called
   A. felonies.
   B. political crimes.
   C. organized crimes.
   D. occupational crimes.

7. Crimes that are considered street crimes and are most upsetting to the public are
   A. visible crimes.
   B. cybercrimes.
   C. white-collar crimes.
   D. misdemeanors.

8. The idea that some crimes occur and are never reported to the police is called
   A. UCR.
   B. crimes without victims.
   C. juvenile delinquency.
   D. the dark figure of crime.

9. An individual who has committed a criminal offense and falls under a particular age is known as a
   A. neglected child.
   B. dependent child.
   C. juvenile delinquent.
   D. recidivist.

10. One of the earliest criminal justice laws named after a ruler who dates back to Babylonian times (1750 B.C.E.) is known as
    A. Confucius' rules.
    B. Hammurabi code.
    C. Caesar's laws.
    D. Attila the Hun's laws.

11. Which term represents the theory of an "eye for an eye"?
    A. Restitution
    B. Due process
    C. Lex talionis
    D. Rehabilitation

12. The process that is founded on fair treatment in all legal matters and protects the rights of defendants, and also limits the powers of state and federal governments is called
    A. legislative process.
    B. equal protection.
    C. exclusionary rule.
    D. due process.

13. The double jeopardy clause states that
    A. people have the right to feel secure in their persons and houses.
    B. excessive bail is prohibited.
    C. a person cannot be subjected to prosecution more than once for the same offense in the same jurisdiction.
    D. individuals have the right to have legal representation.

14. The Fruit of the Poisonous Tree Doctrine can be found under which amendment?
    A. Second Amendment
    B. Fifth Amendment
    C. Fourth Amendment
    D. Fourteenth Amendment

15. Which amendment ensures an individual's protection from unreasonable searches and seizures from government agencies?
    A. Fourth Amendment
    B. Fourteenth Amendment
    C. Sixth Amendment
    D. Eighth Amendment

16. The Fourteenth Amendment states that
    A. the prosecution needs to establish mens rea.
    B. individuals are protected from self-incrimination.
    C. no warrants will be issued without probable cause.
    D. the due process clause is now binding to all the states.

17. When evidence is obtained from an illegal search and is not admissible in court, it is called
    A. adjudication.
    B. probable cause.
    C. the exclusionary rule.
    D. double jeopardy.

18. The agency within the criminal justice system that keeps the peace, maintains public order, and provides social services is
    A. victim services.
    B. the court system.
    C. corrections.
    D. law enforcement.

19. The agency within the criminal justice system that is the oldest segment in history and has the responsibility of punishment as well as rehabilitation is
    A. law enforcement.
    B. the judicial branch.
    C. family court.
    D. the correctional system.

20. Adjudication is the process that includes
    A. the standard to make an arrest.
    B. the standard to convict an individual in court.
    C. the process in which the courts determine guilt or innocence.
    D. the standard to determine a guilty state of mind.

21. The court system that the United States has is a
    A. one court system.
    B. Supreme Court.
    C. triple court system.
    D. dual court system.

22. Parole and probation fall under which system?
    A. The court system
    B. The correctional system
    C. Law enforcement
    D. They have their own separate systems.

23. Agencies such as the FBI and DEA are part of what system?
    A. Jurisdiction of courts
    B. Correctional agencies
    C. Law enforcement
    D. They are separate agencies unto themselves.

24. The status of the death penalty has been argued many times and has had many different outcomes in favor of it and against it. The debate of capital cases that have the death penalty as a punishment falls under which amendment?
    A. Eighth Amendment
    B. Fifth Amendment
    C. Fourth Amendment
    D. Sixth Amendment

25. Policing in America was based on what country's traditions?
    A. French
    B. Native American
    C. Canadian
    D. English

26. Sir Robert Peel created the first police force in London and had a four-part mandate that included
    A. creating a militia to maintain order.
    B. keeping the police and the community away from each other.
    C. reducing conflict between the police and the public.
    D. using as much force as possible to keep public order.

27. Policing can be broken down into different eras. Which era involved close ties and relationships between the police and political leaders?
    A. The Community Policing Era
    B. The Political Era
    C. The Professional Era
    D. The Crime Control Era

28. Which era was influenced by the Progressive movement, in which the reformers wanted the police to be well-trained and stay out of politics?
    A. Community Policing Era
    B. Political Era
    C. The 9/11 Era
    D. Professional Era

29. Police departments, like the military, have a hierarchy with ranks and a structure. That structure is called
    A. chain of command.
    B. management structure.
    C. mid-management supervision.
    D. rank organization.

post-test

30. The police serve the public and communities in many ways, including through sponsored police programs. An example of such a program is
   A. sharing investigative techniques with the public.
   B. assisting the police with traffic enforcement.
   C. D.A.R.E.
   D. having the police stay out of school activities and just leaving them to school officials.

31. Police subculture contains many unique elements. What are the two elements that determine the working personality of the police?
   A. Threat of danger and authority
   B. Isolation and stress
   C. Danger and isolation
   D. Authority and independence

32. A characteristic of police culture is known as police isolation. This occurs when police officers remove themselves from society because of
   A. programs in which the officer interacts with the public, like the ride along program.
   B. police interaction with society at the worst of times, such as crimes and death.
   C. programs like D.A.R.E.
   D. PALs for community residents.

33. There are various types of stressors that are unique to law enforcement. One type of stress is external stress, which includes
   A. suffering from depression and other health issues.
   B. lack of sleep due to unusual work shifts.
   C. threats of danger that accompany police work.
   D. stress from dealing with the negative aspects of society.

34. Stress that is related to working with negative aspects of a society, which causes distrust in people, is known as
   A. organizational stress.
   B. personal stress.
   C. operational stress.
   D. external stress.

35. Stress that is caused by adjusting your value system in the subculture of law enforcement and attempting to get along with your peers is known as
   A. personal stress.
   B. operational stress.
   C. organizational stress.
   D. external stress.

36. In today's modern policing there are new trends that are shaping police departments. These include
   A. DNA analysis for criminal investigations.
   B. body cameras.
   C. the use of technology such as forensics to process crime scenes.
   D. All of the above

37. The term *certiorari* refers to
   A. certification of a court case.
   B. satisfying legal standards.
   C. an order from a higher court asking the lower court for the records for review.
   D. dismissal of a case.

38. Who was the first justice appointed by George Washington?
   A. Franklin Roosevelt
   B. John Jay
   C. William Penn
   D. Thomas Jefferson

39. The United States has a state and federal court system. At the federal level, the courts are divided by district courts that cover federal crimes. How many federal districts are there?

A. 50

B. 75

C. 94

D. 100

40. The courts that handle felony cases and impose prison sentences are known as

A. courts of limited jurisdiction.

B. appeals courts.

C. courts of general jurisdiction.

D. family courts.

41. The Court of Appeals is responsible for

A. imposing sentencing.

B. determining parole eligibility.

C. determining probable cause.

D. reviewing judicial and procedural errors from the lower courts.

42. In the adult court system, the accusatory document that is filed in court is known as a(n)

A. voucher.

B. complaint.

C. indictment.

D. true bill.

43. In the juvenile court system, the juvenile is referred to as the

A. defendant.

B. delinquent.

C. juvenile offender.

D. minor.

44. In juvenile proceedings, the courts do not use the terms *crimes* or *criminal acts*. They are referred to as

A. delinquent acts.

B. offenses.

C. complaints.

D. charges.

45. In the judicial system, there are many components that make up court proceedings. After the offender has been processed by the police, the next step is

A. booking.

B. grand jury.

C. initial appearance.

D. arraignment.

46. The exchange of information between the prosecutor and the defense, in which the prosecutor relinquishes evidence to the defense to ensure a fair trial, is called

A. discovery.

B. motion.

C. grand jury.

D. information.

47. The United States has a trial process, which is known as

A. inquisitorial.

B. adversarial.

C. democratic.

D. federalist.

48. The United States currently has over 2 million people incarcerated. This number reflects the types of crimes and policies that were prevalent from the 1980s and 1990s; offenses from this specific time frame were predominantly

A. terrorism and immigration issues.

B. murders.

C. identity theft.

D. drug offenses and "get tough on crime."

post-test

49. The Great Law was based on humane Quaker principles and emphasized hard labor in a house of corrections. Who was the founder of the Great Law?
    A. John Jay
    B. George Washington
    C. William Penn
    D. Thomas Jefferson

50. In 1876, Elmira, New York built the first reformatory prison. The reformatory was based on
    A. treatment programs.
    B. treatment for social, biological, and psychological causes of deviant behavior.
    C. adhering to strict work schedules and vocational training.
    D. All of the above

51. Under the correctional system, rehabilitation is
    A. punishing the offender as severely as possible.
    B. punishment that fits the crime, as in "an eye for an eye."
    C. restoring the offender to change his or her future behavior in an effort to return to society positively.
    D. removing the offender from society for as long as possible.

52. Intermediate sanctions
    A. are punishments that are not as severe as prison.
    B. can include monetary fines and sanctions.
    C. include forfeiture of illegal assets and money.
    D. All of the above

53. What is the main goal of the juvenile correctional system?
    A. Rehabilitation
    B. Incarceration
    C. Punishment
    D. Retribution

54. The juvenile justice system is composed of residential treatment programs, which consist of
    A. securing juveniles in jail-like settings.
    B. detox centers for juveniles with drug addiction.
    C. placing juveniles in nonsecured facilities that are monitored by trained members.
    D. community service programs.

55. A probation program that puts a juvenile into a high-risk category and where he or she receives close daily supervision is
    A. parole.
    B. group home confinement.
    C. juvenile probation.
    D. Juvenile Intensive Probation Supervision (JIPS).

56. One of the most famous cases that involved the issue of capital punishment is
    A. *Terry v. Ohio.*
    B. *Furman v. Georgia.*
    C. *Gideon v. Wainwright.*
    D. *Chimel v. California.*

57. Jails are used for multiple purposes, such as
    A. detaining defendants awaiting trial.
    B. detaining defendants that could not make bail.
    C. detaining offenders convicted of misdemeanors.
    D. All of the above

58. The next level of incarceration after jail is
- **A.** a police booking facility.
- **B.** prison.
- **C.** community service.
- **D.** parole.

59. Prisons are classified into different levels. Medium security consists of
- **A.** fewer programs for rehabilitation and armed guards and towers.
- **B.** house arrest.
- **C.** unsupervised inmate work in locations outside the facility.
- **D.** a strong emphasis on security, but also education, counseling, and other programs.

60. When an individual is incarcerated, a person may exhibit certain characteristic traits. Prison violence may result and is part of the subculture that is used for many purposes, such as
- **A.** power.
- **B.** status.
- **C.** intimidation.
- **D.** All of the above

post-test

ANSWER KEY AND EXPLANATIONS

1. D	13. C	25. D	37. C	49. C
2. B	14. C	26. C	38. B	50. D
3. D	15. A	27. B	39. C	51. C
4. C	16. D	28. D	40. C	52. D
5. C	17. C	29. A	41. D	53. A
6. D	18. D	30. C	42. B	54. C
7. A	19. D	31. A	43. D	55. D
8. D	20. C	32. B	44. A	56. B
9. C	21. D	33. C	45. C	57. D
10. B	22. B	34. C	46. A	58. B
11. C	23. C	35. A	47. B	59. D
12. D	24. A	36. D	48. D	60. D

1. **The correct answer is D.** Intraracial crime is defined as the victim and offender being from the same race. The majority of crimes are committed between people of the same race. Choices A and B are incorrect because interracial means between different races and biracial concerns people of two races. Choice C is incorrect because statistics indicate that geography and race are key factors in offender/victim relationships.

2. **The correct answer is B.** Mala prohibita are offenses that are prohibited by law and are not wrong in and of themselves. Choice A is incorrect because mala in se offenses, like murder or rape, are considered naturally wrong. Choice C is incorrect because a violation is a prescribed punishment for a low-level offense. Choice D is incorrect because there are no crimes referred to as morality crimes.

3. **The correct answer is D.** Cesare Beccaria believed in the classical criminology theory, in which behavior stems from free will. Choice A is incorrect, as Sigmund Freud was a psychologist and theorized on the subconscious. Choice B is incorrect because Edwin Sutherland believed in a social theory

of criminal behavior. Choice C is incorrect because Cesare Lombroso believed in biological determinism.

4. **The correct answer is C.** Freud believed in deviant behavior stemming from psychological and personality disturbances. Choice A is incorrect because the XYY chromosome theory falls under the biological theory. Choice B is incorrect because the labeling theory believes that society creates deviance. Choice D is incorrect because violent crime is a category or type of crime, not an explanation.

5. **The correct answer is C.** Control theory is part of the social process theories, which state that if the bonds of family, church, and school are broken or weakened, this can cause criminality. Choice A is incorrect because classical criminology believes in personal responsibility and free will. Choice B is incorrect because differential association falls under the learning theory. Choice D is incorrect because political crime is a category of crime, not a theory.

6. **The correct answer is D.** Occupational crime is conducted through legal business

opportunities. A store clerk who steals merchandise from the store or a cashier who rings up false purchases to steal money are examples. Choice A is incorrect because a felony is defined by punishment of incarceration for more than 366 days. Choice B is incorrect because political crimes are crimes against the state or government. Choice C is incorrect because organized crime deals with acts that are already criminal such as gambling, prostitution, and drugs, and are usually found within enterprises like the mafia.

7. **The correct answer is A.** Visible crime is also known as street crime and includes murder, robbery, and assault. Choice B is incorrect because cybercrime involves the use of computers for illegal activity. Choice C is incorrect because white-collar crime is also known as occupational crime, not street crime. Choice D is incorrect because a misdemeanor is a punishment that can include incarceration for no more than 365 days.

8. **The correct answer is D.** The dark figure of crime is a dimension of crime that occurs but never is reported to the police. Choice A is incorrect because the UCR is the Uniform Crime Report that is generated by the FBI. Choice B is incorrect because "crimes without victims" is a crime category that consists of offenses such as drugs or prostitution and are typically moral issues. Choice C is incorrect because juvenile delinquency involves crimes that are committed by offenders under a certain age.

9. **The correct answer is C.** Juvenile delinquency includes an individual who has committed a crime and is under a certain age. Choice A is incorrect because a neglected child is a child who is receiving inadequate care by their parents. Choice B is incorrect because a dependent child is someone who

has no parent or guardian. Choice D is incorrect because a recidivist is someone who is a repeat offender.

10. **The correct answer is B.** Hammurabi was a Babylonian king who established laws to control human behavior and punish offenders through retribution. Choice A is incorrect because Confucius was a Chinese teacher and philosopher. Choice C is incorrect because Caesar was a general and politician for the Roman Republic. Choice D is incorrect because Attila the Hun was the leader of the Hunnic Empire, who wanted to destroy the Roman Empire.

11. **The correct answer is C.** Lex talionis falls under the notion of punishment and retribution. If you break someone's bone they would break your bone. Choice A is incorrect because restitution is the payment by the offender to the victim for any harm that was caused. Choice B is incorrect because it is based on legal fairness and treatment of all individuals. Choice D is incorrect because rehabilitation is the idea of restoring an offender back into society.

12. **The correct answer is D.** Due process guarantees judicial fairness and states that no person shall be deprived of life, liberty, or property, and as such protects all persons in the legal process. Choice A is incorrect because the legislative process takes place when laws are written and passed. Choice B is incorrect because equal protection is found within due process. Choice C is incorrect because the exclusionary rule applies to illegally obtained evidence.

13. **The correct answer is C.** A person cannot be subject to be tried more than once for the same offense in the same jurisdiction by the prosecutor. Choice A is incorrect because the right to be secured in persons and houses falls under the Fourth Amendment. Choice B is incorrect because excessive bail falls

under the Eighth Amendment. Choice D is incorrect because the right to legal counsel is in the Sixth Amendment.

14. **The correct answer is C.** The Fruit of the Poisonous Tree Doctrine is under the Fourth Amendment, as it deals with illegal evidence that is obtained during a search. Choice A is incorrect because the Second Amendment primarily deals with the right to bear arms. Choice B is incorrect because the Fifth Amendment is primarily about double jeopardy and self-incrimination. Choice D is incorrect because the Fourteenth Amendment includes the due process clause and fundamental fairness.

15. **The correct answer is A.** The Fourth Amendment protects people from unreasonable searches and seizures, and states that no warrants shall be issued without probable cause. Choice B is incorrect because the Fourteenth Amendment establishes fundamental fairness and the idea that all legal rights are binding to the States. Choice C is incorrect because the Sixth Amendment includes the right to counsel. Choice D is incorrect because the Eighth Amendment prohibits excessive bails, fines, and cruel and unusual punishment.

16. **The correct answer is D.** The Fourteenth Amendment incorporates all the other amendments, including the due process clause, and makes them binding to all the States. Choice A is incorrect because mens rea is not an amendment, but an element of a crime. Choice B is incorrect because protection of self-incrimination is in the Fifth Amendment. Choice C is incorrect because no warrants being issued without probable cause is in the Fourth Amendment.

17. **The correct answer is C.** The exclusionary rule states that any evidence obtained illegally will be excluded from court as inadmissible. Choice A is incorrect because

adjudication is the process to determine guilt or innocence. Choice B is incorrect because probable cause is the standard for an arrest. Choice D is incorrect because double jeopardy is subjecting someone to more than one prosecution for the same offense in the same jurisdiction.

18. **The correct answer is D.** Law enforcement is the primary agency within the criminal justice system that maintains public order, keeps the peace, provides social services, enforces the law, and apprehends violators. Choices A, B, and C are incorrect as they have different roles within the criminal justice system.

19. **The correct answer is D.** The correctional system is responsible for the welfare of the defendant and ensures that all sanctions are fulfilled. Corrections operates and manages jails and prisons while also providing rehabilitative services. Choices A and B are incorrect as they have other functions within the criminal justice system. Choice C is also incorrect as family court is limited to hearing cases of juvenile offender status.

20. **The correct answer is C.** Adjudication is the court process that determines if a person is guilty or not guilty. Choice A is incorrect because probable cause is the standard to make an arrest. Choice B is incorrect because beyond a reasonable doubt is the standard for conviction. Choice D is incorrect because a guilty state of mind is mens rea.

21. **The correct answer is D.** The United States works with a dual court system, at both the state level and national or federal level. Choices A, B, and C are all incorrect.

22. **The correct answer is B.** Probation and parole both fall under the correctional system, as probation is part of sentencing and individuals who are paroled are released from prison under strict guidelines and

supervision. Choices A, C, and D do not apply to corrections and are incorrect.

23. **The correct answer is C.** The FBI and DEA (Drug Enforcement Agency), are federal agencies, and they are part of the law enforcement system. Choices A and B are incorrect because those agencies are not part of either system. Choice D is incorrect because they may be separate agencies from each other, but both branches are law enforcement agencies.

24. **The correct answer is A.** The death penalty as a prescribed punishment for capital offenses falls under the purview of cruel and unusual punishment, which falls under the Eighth Amendment. Choice B is incorrect because the Fifth Amendment includes double jeopardy and self-incrimination. Choice C is incorrect because the Fourth Amendment deals with unreasonable searches and seizures. Choice D is incorrect because the Sixth Amendment is about the right to counsel and a speedy and public trial.

25. **The correct answer is D.** Policing, along with common law, was based on and founded from English tradition. Therefore, choices A, B, and C are all incorrect as they did not have any influence on American policing or laws.

26. **The correct answer is C.** Peel wanted to reduce conflict by having the police and community work with each other while creating a professional police force. Therefore, choices A, B, and D are all incorrect because they oppose the goals that Robert Peel wanted to accomplish.

27. **The correct answer is B.** The Political Era involved the police and government officials, such as mayors, having close working relationships and providing favors. Choice A is incorrect because community policing stresses a working relationship between the police and the community. Choice C is incorrect because the Professional Era occurred during the Progressive movement and involved getting politics out of policing and establishing a new type of police force. Choice D is incorrect because there is no specific Crime Control Era.

28. **The correct answer is D.** The Progressives were reformers who wanted to remove policing from politics and corruption and establish a well-trained, professional police force. Choices A and B are incorrect because those models do not incorporate these mandates. Choice C is incorrect because there has not been any specific 9/11 era formed as of yet.

29. **The correct answer is A.** The chain of command provides structure, defines ranks within the department including subordinates, and creates accountability and discipline. Choices B, C, and D are all incorrect because none of these terms exists or apply to rank and structure.

30. **The correct answer is C.** D.A.R.E. is a drug prevention program throughout educational and private sectors. Choice A is incorrect because the police may ask for the public's assistance; it does not share investigative techniques. Choice B is incorrect because this is strictly a police officer's role and duty. Choice D is incorrect because this is actually the opposite of what the police do, as they directly get involved in school activities to foster better relationships.

31. **The correct answer is A.** Danger and authority are the two key components that make up the working personality. Choices B, C, and D are all incorrect, as they do not comprise the correct elements of the working personality of the police force.

32. **The correct answer is B.** Police officers often find themselves isolated from the

community because of seeing people suffering from death, injuries, and other factors, and includes the tight subculture that is formed. Choices A, C, and D are actually the opposite of police isolation, as these programs are created to help bring the police and the community together.

33. **The correct answer is C.** External stress is often the result of facing threats and dangerous situations, which officers constantly face. Choice A is incorrect because health issues are a result of stress. Choice B is incorrect because lack of sleep due to shift work is organizational stress. Choice D is incorrect because it is the result of operational stress.

34. **The correct answer is C.** Operational stress is the result of distrust of people stemming from dealing with the negative side of society. Choice A is incorrect because organizational stress comes from the inner structure of work. Choice B is incorrect because personal stress occurs when trying to get along with your peers. Choice D is incorrect because external stress comes from the danger of police work.

35. **The correct answer is A.** Personal stress occurs when an individual is adjusting to the law enforcement subculture and reaches a conflict with their value system while trying to get along with their peers. Choices B, C, and D do not fit into this definition and are all incorrect.

36. **The correct answer is D.** Police departments have made large strides in implementing the use of technology, including computers and science, to become more professional and efficient.

37. **The correct answer is C.** Certiorari is a written order for a higher court to review the lower court records. Choices A, B, and D are all incorrect.

38. **The correct answer is B.** John Jay was a Founding Father, who wrote the Federalist Papers, and was the nation's first Chief Justice. Choices A, C, and D are all incorrect.

39. **The correct answer is C.** There are 94 federal court districts that cover federal crimes. This includes at least one district in each state, as well as the District of Columbia and Puerto Rico. Choices A, B, and D are all incorrect.

40. **The correct answer is C.** Courts of general jurisdiction hear all felony cases and have the legal authority to sentence individuals to prison. Choice A is incorrect because it hears misdemeanor cases. Choice B is incorrect because the appeals court reviews cases from the lower level courts. Choice D is incorrect because family court hears only family issues and juvenile offender cases.

41. **The correct answer is D.** Appellate courts do not determine guilt or innocence, but review for any judicial errors from the lower courts. Choice A is incorrect because trial courts impose sentencing. Choice B is incorrect because the parole board determines eligibility. Choice C is incorrect because the courts and prosecutors determine probable cause.

42. **The correct answer is B.** The accusatory instrument that is filed in adult court is known as the complaint. Choice A is incorrect because a voucher is a police receipt for property. Choice C is incorrect because an indictment is a grand jury proceeding. Choice D is incorrect because a true bill is the document that is produced from a grand jury.

43. **The correct answer is D.** In the juvenile court system, the juvenile is referred to as the minor. Choice A is incorrect because defendant is for an adult. Choices B and C

are incorrect because they refer to juvenile status.

44. **The correct answer is A.** The criminal acts are referred to as delinquent acts in the juvenile court system. Therefore, choices B, C, and D are all incorrect because the juvenile justice system does not use those terms.

45. **The correct answer is C.** Initial appearance is actually the first step of court proceedings, and occurs when the offender is brought before a judge for the first time to be given their formal notice of charges. Choice A is incorrect because booking is a police procedure and process. Choices B and D are incorrect because they take place later on in the judicial process.

46. **The correct answer is A.** The discovery process is the responsibility of the prosecutor to hand over evidence to the defense that will be introduced in court, so that the defense can prepare its case for a fair trial. Choices B, C, and D are all incorrect because they do not fit into the discovery process.

47. **The correct answer is B.** The adversarial process is one in which both parties argue for their sides as they present their cases and witnesses. Choice A is incorrect because an inquisitorial system is found in Europe, wherein the judge has an active role during the investigation. Choices C and D are both incorrect because they do not fall into the definition of an adversarial system.

48. **The correct answer is D.** Not only were drug offenses soaring during that time, but a new policy of getting tough on crime became the new way of thinking, both culturally and politically. Individuals who are still incarcerated from those times faced stiffer penalties as a result of those policies. Choices A, B, and C are all incorrect, even

though they are current issues facing the criminal justice system.

49. **The correct answer is C.** In 1682, William Penn, who was the founder of Pennsylvania, adopted The Great Law. Choices A, B, and D are all incorrect.

50. **The correct answer is D.** The Reformatory Movement began in the 1800s and emphasized treatment of prisoners to determine deviant behavior and rehabilitation.

51. **The correct answer is C.** Rehabilitation is the notion of restoring a person back to society through educational and vocational training. Choices A, B, and D are all incorrect, as they are part of other correctional goals.

52. **The correct answer is D.** Intermediate sanctions are more restrictive than probation and include all of the methods mentioned, and can work best in combination when they take into account the type of offense that was committed.

53. **The correct answer is A.** The juvenile justice system is designed for rehabilitation, and one of the main alternatives to incarceration is juvenile probation. Choices B, C, and D are all incorrect as they are not the goals of the juvenile system.

54. **The correct answer is C.** There are several types of residential treatment programs that are supervised by trained members. Choices A, B, and D are all incorrect as they are not part of any residential programs.

55. **The correct answer is D.** Juvenile Intensive Probation Supervision (JIPS) is designed as an alternative to incarceration; juveniles are assigned probation officers and receive strict supervision. Choice A is incorrect because parole is for adult prisoners being released from prison. Choice B is incorrect because group home confinement does not fit into juvenile probation. Choice C is incorrect

because juvenile probation is for juveniles who are not high risk.

56. **The correct answer is B.** In *Furman v. Georgia* in 1972, the U.S. Supreme Court banned the use of capital punishment. Choices A, C, and D are all incorrect, as they do not focus on capital punishment issues.

57. **The correct answer is D.** Jails are facilities that are used for all the reasons mentioned, as well as for holding inmates for federal and state crimes who are awaiting transportation.

58. **The correct answer is B.** Prisons are the next level of incarceration from jails; they are used for individuals convicted of felony crimes. Choice A is incorrect because police booking facilities are used after an individual is arrested. Choice C is incorrect because

community service is a sentence option after a conviction. Choice D is incorrect because parole is an early release from prison.

59. **The court answer is D.** Medium security consists of both armed security and rehabilitative services and programs. Choice A is incorrect because fewer programs and more security is seen at the maximum level. Choice B is incorrect because house arrest consists of a sentence classification in which the defendant is assigned to his or her home under supervision. Choice C is incorrect because this describes minimum security.

60. **The correct answer is D.** Prison violence is a characteristic that is found in prison facilities, and it forms subcultures. Violence is part of the existing subculture, not only inmate on inmate violence but inmate on officer violence as well.

Environmental Science

OVERVIEW

- Test Answer Sheets
- Environmental Science Diagnostic Test
- Answer Key and Explanations
- Diagnostic Test Assessment Grid
- Ecological Concepts
- Environmental Impacts
- Environmental Management and Conservation
- Social Processes and the Environment
- Environmental Science Post-test
- Answer Key and Explanations
- Summing It Up

The DSST® Environmental Science exam (formerly called *Environment and Humanity: The Race to Save the Planet* exam), is a multiple-choice exam designed to evaluate your knowledge in a specific area of physical science which includes ecological concepts (ecosystems, global ecology, and food chains and food webs), habitat destruction, environmental management and conservation, and social processes and the environment.

DIAGNOSTIC TEST ANSWER SHEET

1. Ⓐ Ⓑ Ⓒ Ⓓ   5. Ⓐ Ⓑ Ⓒ Ⓓ   9. Ⓐ Ⓑ Ⓒ Ⓓ   13. Ⓐ Ⓑ Ⓒ Ⓓ   17. Ⓐ Ⓑ Ⓒ Ⓓ

2. Ⓐ Ⓑ Ⓒ Ⓓ   6. Ⓐ Ⓑ Ⓒ Ⓓ   10. Ⓐ Ⓑ Ⓒ Ⓓ   14. Ⓐ Ⓑ Ⓒ Ⓓ   18. Ⓐ Ⓑ Ⓒ Ⓓ

3. Ⓐ Ⓑ Ⓒ Ⓓ   7. Ⓐ Ⓑ Ⓒ Ⓓ   11. Ⓐ Ⓑ Ⓒ Ⓓ   15. Ⓐ Ⓑ Ⓒ Ⓓ   19. Ⓐ Ⓑ Ⓒ Ⓓ

4. Ⓐ Ⓑ Ⓒ Ⓓ   8. Ⓐ Ⓑ Ⓒ Ⓓ   12. Ⓐ Ⓑ Ⓒ Ⓓ   16. Ⓐ Ⓑ Ⓒ Ⓓ   20. Ⓐ Ⓑ Ⓒ Ⓓ

POST-TEST ANSWER SHEET

1. Ⓐ Ⓑ Ⓒ Ⓓ   13. Ⓐ Ⓑ Ⓒ Ⓓ   25. Ⓐ Ⓑ Ⓒ Ⓓ   37. Ⓐ Ⓑ Ⓒ Ⓓ   49. Ⓐ Ⓑ Ⓒ Ⓓ

2. Ⓐ Ⓑ Ⓒ Ⓓ   14. Ⓐ Ⓑ Ⓒ Ⓓ   26. Ⓐ Ⓑ Ⓒ Ⓓ   38. Ⓐ Ⓑ Ⓒ Ⓓ   50. Ⓐ Ⓑ Ⓒ Ⓓ

3. Ⓐ Ⓑ Ⓒ Ⓓ   15. Ⓐ Ⓑ Ⓒ Ⓓ   27. Ⓐ Ⓑ Ⓒ Ⓓ   39. Ⓐ Ⓑ Ⓒ Ⓓ   51. Ⓐ Ⓑ Ⓒ Ⓓ

4. Ⓐ Ⓑ Ⓒ Ⓓ   16. Ⓐ Ⓑ Ⓒ Ⓓ   28. Ⓐ Ⓑ Ⓒ Ⓓ   40. Ⓐ Ⓑ Ⓒ Ⓓ   52. Ⓐ Ⓑ Ⓒ Ⓓ

5. Ⓐ Ⓑ Ⓒ Ⓓ   17. Ⓐ Ⓑ Ⓒ Ⓓ   29. Ⓐ Ⓑ Ⓒ Ⓓ   41. Ⓐ Ⓑ Ⓒ Ⓓ   53. Ⓐ Ⓑ Ⓒ Ⓓ

6. Ⓐ Ⓑ Ⓒ Ⓓ   18. Ⓐ Ⓑ Ⓒ Ⓓ   30. Ⓐ Ⓑ Ⓒ Ⓓ   42. Ⓐ Ⓑ Ⓒ Ⓓ   54. Ⓐ Ⓑ Ⓒ Ⓓ

7. Ⓐ Ⓑ Ⓒ Ⓓ   19. Ⓐ Ⓑ Ⓒ Ⓓ   31. Ⓐ Ⓑ Ⓒ Ⓓ   43. Ⓐ Ⓑ Ⓒ Ⓓ   55. Ⓐ Ⓑ Ⓒ Ⓓ

8. Ⓐ Ⓑ Ⓒ Ⓓ   20. Ⓐ Ⓑ Ⓒ Ⓓ   32. Ⓐ Ⓑ Ⓒ Ⓓ   44. Ⓐ Ⓑ Ⓒ Ⓓ   56. Ⓐ Ⓑ Ⓒ Ⓓ

9. Ⓐ Ⓑ Ⓒ Ⓓ   21. Ⓐ Ⓑ Ⓒ Ⓓ   33. Ⓐ Ⓑ Ⓒ Ⓓ   45. Ⓐ Ⓑ Ⓒ Ⓓ   57. Ⓐ Ⓑ Ⓒ Ⓓ

10. Ⓐ Ⓑ Ⓒ Ⓓ   22. Ⓐ Ⓑ Ⓒ Ⓓ   34. Ⓐ Ⓑ Ⓒ Ⓓ   46. Ⓐ Ⓑ Ⓒ Ⓓ   58. Ⓐ Ⓑ Ⓒ Ⓓ

11. Ⓐ Ⓑ Ⓒ Ⓓ   23. Ⓐ Ⓑ Ⓒ Ⓓ   35. Ⓐ Ⓑ Ⓒ Ⓓ   47. Ⓐ Ⓑ Ⓒ Ⓓ   59. Ⓐ Ⓑ Ⓒ Ⓓ

12. Ⓐ Ⓑ Ⓒ Ⓓ   24. Ⓐ Ⓑ Ⓒ Ⓓ   36. Ⓐ Ⓑ Ⓒ Ⓓ   48. Ⓐ Ⓑ Ⓒ Ⓓ   60. Ⓐ Ⓑ Ⓒ Ⓓ

answer sheet

ENVIRONMENTAL SCIENCE DIAGNOSTIC TEST

Directions: Carefully read each of the following 20 questions. Choose the best answer to each question and fill in the corresponding circle on the answer sheet. The Answer Key and Explanations can be found following this Diagnostic Test.

1. America's first environmental legislation was passed in response to what environmental issue?
   A. Water pollution
   B. Persistent pesticides
   C. The illegal wildlife trade
   D. Overfishing

2. Which process is a method used only in making ocean water suitable for drinking?
   A. Disinfecting
   B. Desalination
   C. Filtering
   D. Cleansing

3. What is one of the greatest benefits of high species diversity to an ecosystem?
   A. Diversity enhances the monetary value of an ecosystem.
   B. Diversity increases the stability of an ecosystem.
   C. Diversity increases the amount of energy available in an ecosystem.
   D. Diversity increases available habitats in an ecosystem.

4. All of the following are ways to combat air pollution from transportation EXCEPT:
   A. compact development.
   B. fuel efficiency standards.
   C. public parking.
   D. public transportation.

5. Which of the following terms describes how water is taken up into the atmosphere from a lake?
   A. Transpiration
   B. Evaporation
   C. Condensation
   D. Precipitation

6. What is it called when two individuals of the same species have different physical characteristics, and one is able to live long enough to reproduce and the other is not?
   A. Macroevolution
   B. Adaptation
   C. Natural selection
   D. Coevolution

7. Which of the following occupies the first trophic level?
   A. Consumers
   B. Carnivores
   C. Herbivores
   D. Producers

8. Industrial waste containing dioxins would be considered
   A. medical waste.
   B. hazardous waste.
   C. recyclable waste.
   D. solid waste.

9. The excessive growth of algae in a freshwater ecosystem is called
   A. water pollution.
   B. algaefication.
   C. eutrophication.
   D. deforestation.

10. Which of the following is an example of a species found in a pioneer community?
    A. Lichen
    B. Wildflowers
    C. Fungi
    D. Bacteria

11. The development of agriculture began with the concept of
    A. hunting and gathering.
    B. increasing food volume.
    C. manipulating plants and soil.
    D. clearing large plots of land.

12. In 1898, a Swedish scientist predicted that carbon dioxide emissions from excessive burning of fossil fuels could lead to
    A. the greenhouse effect.
    B. the Industrial Revolution.
    C. air pollution.
    D. global warming.

13. Which of the following is a possible way to protect rangelands from erosion and fire?
    A. Raise sheep instead of cattle.
    B. Rotate grazing areas.
    C. Plant fire-resistant vegetation.
    D. Only graze animals on steep slopes.

14. Which process removes large particles from wastewater?
    A. Primary sewage treatment
    B. Secondary sewage treatment
    C. Tertiary sewage treatment
    D. Quaternary sewage treatment

15. The first phase of population growth is often called the
    A. exponential phase.
    B. equilibrium phase.
    C. deceleration phase.
    D. lag phase.

16. What event was considered the first environmental justice action in the United States?
    A. The Flint water crisis
    B. The 1968 Memphis Sanitation Strike
    C. The Lacey Act
    D. The 1963 March on Washington

17. Which of the following is true of the Paris Agreement?
    A. It was signed in 2017.
    B. The United States is not a signatory.
    C. The agreement is voluntary.
    D. The agreement has strict enforcement mechanisms.

18. Which of the following is a type of volatile organic compound?
    A. Lead
    B. Sulfur dioxide
    C. Hydrocarbons
    D. Particulate matter

19. Designing industrial production methods with biological impacts in mind is called
    A. Industrial Revolution.
    B. industrial ecology.
    C. biological revolution.
    D. ecological diversity.

20. In 1970, Congress established
    A. Earth Day.
    B. the World Health Organization.
    C. the Environmental Protection Agency.
    D. Agenda 21.

ANSWER KEY AND EXPLANATIONS

1. C	5. B	9. C	13. B	17. D
2. B	6. C	10. A	14. A	18. C
3. B	7. D	11. C	15. D	19. B
4. C	8. B	12. D	16. B	20. C

1. **The correct answer is C.** America's first environmental law, the Lacey Act, prohibits trade in illegal animal, fish, or plants and was passed in response to an out-of-control poaching problem. Choice A was addressed much later by the Clean Water Act. Choice B is covered by a range of regulations overseen by the EPA. Choice D, overfishing, is addressed in the United States by a more recent law called the Magnuson-Stevens Fishery Conservation and Management Act.

2. **The correct answer is B.** The process of desalination is necessary to remove the salts from ocean water so that it can be used as a source of drinking water. Choice A is incorrect because all water sources are disinfected with chlorine, UV light, or ozone. Choice C is incorrect because filtering is a process that is performed on all drinking water supplies. Choice D is incorrect because all water is cleansed before it is safe for drinking.

3. **The correct answer is B.** More diverse ecosystems have more connections among organisms and are more resistant to disturbance. Choice A is incorrect since while increased value to humans might be a result of biodiversity, increased value is of no benefit to the ecosystem itself. Choice C is incorrect because the energy available will depend on the producers and access to sunlight or appropriate chemicals, not on diversity. Choice D is incorrect because more habitats generally lead to more diversity, not the other way around.

4. **The correct answer is C.** Public parking, or any other development that encourages driving, is not likely to have much effect on vehicle emissions. There may be a slight reduction since people do not have to circle for parking, but the effect will be small compared to the other choices. Choice A, compact development, reduces emissions by reducing the distances people need to drive. Choice B allows a car to go farther for the same amount of fuel, reducing emissions per trip. Choice D provides an efficient alternative to personal cars, reducing emissions.

5. **The correct answer is B.** Evaporation occurs in bodies of water as water on the surface is changed into water vapor, a gas, and released into the atmosphere. Choice A is incorrect because transpiration is the process by which plants lose water through the stomata in their leaves. This results in the release of water into the atmosphere, but through plants, not a body of water. Choice C is incorrect because condensation is the change from a gas to a liquid, and it involves water already in the atmosphere. Choice D is incorrect because precipitation comes from water already in the atmosphere that falls to the earth.

6. **The correct answer is C.** Natural selection, also referred to as survival of the fittest, occurs when one member of a species is able to survive and reproduce and another dies before reproducing. Choice A is incorrect because macroevolution refers to large-scale evolutionary changes over a long period of

time. Choice B is incorrect because adaptations are changes in an organism or species that don't affect their ability to survive and reproduce. Choice D is incorrect because coevolution is when two or more species interact and exert selective pressure on one another, which can lead to adaptations and evolutionary changes in both species.

7. **The correct answer is D.** Producers occupy the first trophic level and obtain energy from the sun. This energy is converted and some of it is passed on to other species at higher trophic levels. Choice A is incorrect because consumers occupy the second trophic level and above. Choice B is incorrect because carnivores occupy either the third or fourth trophic level. Choice C is incorrect because herbivores occupy the second trophic level.

8. **The correct answer is B.** Dioxins are toxic chemicals, and industrial waste containing dioxins is considered to be hazardous waste. Choice A is incorrect because dioxins are environmental pollutants and are not considered medical waste or biohazardous material. Choice C is incorrect because dioxins are not a recyclable material. Choice D is incorrect because dioxins are an organic chemical compound and are considered hazardous waste, not solid waste.

9. **The correct answer is C.** The excessive growth of algae and aquatic plants due to added nutrients in the water is called eutrophication. Choice A is incorrect because although nutrients can cause water pollution, the excessive growth of algae caused by added nutrients is more specifically called eutrophication. Choice B is incorrect because algaefication is not a term used by environmental scientists. The proper term for excessive algae growth is eutrophication. Choice D is incorrect because deforestation refers to activities that destroy forest environments, and does not refer to algae growth.

10. **The correct answer is A.** Lichens are a type of pioneer organism that establish themselves on rocks and contribute to the formation of a thin layer of soil, so other organisms can grow. Choice B is incorrect because wildflowers need soil to establish and grow. Choice C is incorrect because fungi need to grow on organic material. Choice D is incorrect because bacteria are introduced at later stages of succession.

11. **The correct answer is C.** The origin of agricultural practices began with the concept of manipulating plants and soil to grow desired crops. Choice A is incorrect because hunting and gathering of food came before the advent of agricultural practices. Choice B is incorrect because increasing food volume was a result of the Agricultural Revolution, not the beginning of it. Choice D is incorrect because clearing large plots of land and manipulating plants and soil were concepts that came after the advent of agriculture.

12. **The correct answer is D.** During the rise of the Industrial Revolution, Svante August Arrhenius warned that an increase in carbon dioxide could lead to an increase in Earth's temperatures, an effect that we refer to as global warming. Choices A, B, and C are incorrect because these aren't what Arrhenius warned against.

13. **The correct answer is B.** Rotating the areas where livestock graze will allow the plants to regrow before they are overgrazed. Choice A will not help since grazing too many livestock of any species will result in range destruction. Choice C is not a good solution since it is the grazing that increases fire risk in the first place. Choice D will not help since it does not reduce the number of animals grazed in a particular area, and may make things worse since slopes are more vulnerable to erosion than are flat areas.

14. **The correct answer is A.** The removal of large particles from sewage wastewater by

a process of filtering the water through screens takes place during primary sewage treatment. Choice B is incorrect because secondary sewage treatment involves the dissolving away of organic materials with microorganisms. Choice C is incorrect because tertiary sewage treatment involves the removal of inorganic nutrients such as nitrogen and phosphorus. Choice D is incorrect because there are only three sewage treatment steps, not four.

15. **The correct answer is D.** The first part of a population growth curve is often referred to as the lag phase because populations grow very slowly at first; the process of reproduction takes some time to get started. Choice A is incorrect because the exponential growth phase is the time of a high growth rate of a population. This usually follows the initial lag phase. Choice B is incorrect because the equilibrium phase occurs when a population is relatively stable, after the exponential growth phase. Choice C is incorrect because the deceleration phase is when the birth and death rates become equal and the population stops growing.

16. **The correct answer is B.** The 1968 Memphis Sanitation Strike combined civil rights and environmental activism and is considered to be the first environmental justice action in the United States. Choice A is incorrect since the Flint water crisis occurred in 2014, decades after activists first took notice of environmental justice issues. Choice C was an early act of legislation and was not connected to environmental justice. Choice D was a milestone in the civil rights movement but the environment was not one of the major concerns raised at the event.

17. **The correct answer is D.** The Paris Agreement, or Paris Accord, is a purely voluntary agreement that requires all signatory nations to devise their own means to reduce their greenhouse gas emissions. There is no provision to enforce the reduction target. Choice A is incorrect since the agreement was completed in 2016. Choice B is incorrect since the United States withdrew from the Paris Agreement in 2017. Choice C is incorrect since the agreement really is purely voluntary.

18. **The correct answer is C.** Volatile organic compounds are mostly composed of hydrogen and carbon atoms, and they are, therefore, called hydrocarbons. Choice A is incorrect because lead is not an organic compound. Choice B is incorrect because sulfur dioxide is not considered a hydrocarbon. Choice D is incorrect because particulate matter is a solid form of air pollution, not a volatile gaseous form.

19. **The correct answer is B.** During the mid-1990s, a concept called industrial ecology emerged, which aimed to integrate industry more closely with biology and limit ecological impacts. Choice A is incorrect because the Industrial Revolution marks the advent of the use of coal as a fuel source to power machinery used in the production of goods. Choice C is incorrect because there is no such thing as the biological revolution. Choice D is incorrect because ecological diversity concerns living organisms and ecosystems, not industrial production.

20. **The correct answer is C.** The Environmental Protection Agency (EPA) was established by the U.S. Congress in 1970. Choice A is incorrect because although the first Earth Day was held in 1970, it is not a government-sponsored organization. Choice B is incorrect because the World Health Organization (WHO) is an international organization that was established by the United Nations. Choice D is incorrect because Agenda 21 is a statement of principles for the management of global environmental issues.

DIAGNOSTIC TEST ASSESSMENT GRID

Now that you've completed the diagnostic test and read through the answer explanations, you can use your results to target your studying. Find the question numbers from the diagnostic test that you answered incorrectly and highlight or circle them below. Then focus extra attention on the sections within the chapter dealing with those topics.

Environmental Science		
Content Area	**Topic**	**Question #**
Ecological Concepts	• Ecosystems • Organism Relationship • Trophic Relationships • Energy flows and cycles • Biomes • Population biology • Evolution • Ecological succession	3, 5, 6, 7, 10, 15
Environmental Impacts	• Human population dynamics • Global climate change • Pollution—physical, chemical, and biological aspects • Agricultural • Industrial • Habit destruction • Land degradation	9, 12, 13, 18, 19
Environmental Management and Conservation	• Renewable and nonrenewable resources • Agricultural practices • Pesticides and pest control • Soil conservation and land use practices • Air pollution control • Water quality and supply • Wastewater treatment • Solid and hazardous waste • Environmental risk assessment	2, 4, 8, 11, 14

Environmental Science (continued)		
Content Area	**Topic**	**Question #**
Social Processes and the Environment	• Environmental justice • Policy, planning, and decision making • Global and environmental governance • Differing culture and societal values	1, 16, 17, 20

GET THE FACTS

To see the DSST® Environmental Science Fact Sheet, go to ***http://getcollegecredit.com/exam_fact_ sheets*** and click on the **Physical Science** tab. Scroll down and click the **Environmental Science** link.

ECOLOGICAL CONCEPTS

Approximately 30 percent of the questions on the DSST® Environmental Science exam will cover topics under the umbrella of ecological concepts. Ecology is the study of how organisms interact with one another and their nonliving surroundings. Ecologists study the ways in which organisms have adapted to their surroundings, how they make use of their surroundings, and how an area is altered by the presence and activities of organisms. When these interactions are examined at a global scale, it is called global ecology.

ECOSYSTEMS

Even though ecosystems are a complex network of interrelationships between organisms, all ecosystems have two main components:

- **Abiotic** factors are "nonliving" factors such as physical or chemical conditions within an environment. For example, in a salt marsh ecosystem, the abiotic factors would include climate, weather, water temperature, salinity, pH, soil composition, and oxygen content of the water and mud.

- **Biotic** factors are "living" factors, including all the living organisms within an ecosystem. In a salt marsh ecosystem, the biotic factors would include marsh grass, shrubs, and all plant life; fish, worms, insects, shellfish, crabs, and birds; and microorganisms such as bacteria and plankton.

Biotic factors can be organized into a hierarchy from the lowest level to the highest level:

1. **Organisms:** Individual life forms. For example, in a salt marsh, some organisms are marsh grass, flounder, and fiddler crabs.

2. **Species:** A population of organisms potentially capable of reproducing naturally among themselves to produce offspring that can also reproduce. All members of a species share similar behaviors, genetic structure, and appearance. For example, fiddler crabs are one species that inhabits salt marshes.

3. **Population:** A group of the same species living in the same geographic region at the same time. For example, the fiddler crabs living in a salt marsh in Maryland are a separate population from fiddler crabs living in a salt marsh in Delaware.

4. **Community:** All of the interacting populations of different species that live in a given area at the same time. In a salt marsh ecosystem, fiddler crabs, fish, birds, and plants all form a community.

Noting the above information, it is easy to see that an ecosystem is a community of different species that interact with one another and with surrounding abiotic factors. The interaction of both biotic and abiotic factors allows an ecosystem to respond to changes in the environment. When these interactions are examined at a global scale, it is called global ecology.

ORGANISM RELATIONSHIPS

Each species in an ecosystem has a specific role, or job, within the community. Examining the roles of species can help determine how they might interact. The functional role of each species in an ecosystem is its **niche**. A niche consists of all the physical, chemical, and biological conditions that a particular species requires in order to survive and reproduce within a given ecosystem. A description of an organism's niche always includes all the ways in which it affects other organisms and how it may modify its physical surroundings.

Ecologists have identified three general types of organism-to-organism interactions that take place in all ecosystems:

1. **Predation:** One organism, known as the predator, kills and eats another organism, known as the prey. The predator benefits from this relationship, and the prey is harmed. To succeed, predators have adapted several strategies, such as speed, stealth, or the ability to build a trap for their prey. At the same time, many prey species have adapted characteristics that help them to avoid predation. These characteristics include keen senses, the ability to camouflage, and the ability to remain motionless to avoid detection.

2. **Competition:** Within an ecosystem, many species compete for limited resources such as food, water, sunlight, and territory. Competition is classified as **intraspecific** if it occurs between members of the same species, and **interspecific** if it occurs between members of different species. Whichever organism is less harmed by the competition is the winner. One organism may win out over another by one of two ways:

   - In **interference**, one organism limits the access of another species to a resource.

   - In **exploitation**, two or more organisms have equal access to a resource, but one uses it more quickly and efficiently than the other.

The competitive exclusion principle states that no two species can occupy the same ecological niche in the same place at the same time. The more similar two species are, the fiercer their competition will become.

3. **Symbiosis**: A close, long-lasting physical relationship between two species. The two species are in close physical contact, and at least one of them derives some benefit from the relationship. There are three different categories of symbiotic relationships:

   - Parasitism: A relationship in which one organism, the parasite, lives in or on another organism, the host. The parasite generally derives nourishment from the host, and the host is harmed, or more rarely eventually killed, by the parasite.

   - Commensalism: A relationship between organisms in which one organism benefits and the other is not affected.

   - Mutualism: A relationship between organisms that is beneficial to both organisms. In many cases of mutualism, the species cannot live without each another.

BIODIVERSITY

Biodiversity is a term used to describe the diversity (variations) of genes, species, and ecosystems within a region. **Genetic diversity** is a term used to describe the number of different kinds of genes that are present in a given population. A high genetic diversity means there is a large amount of variation in structure and function among a population, and a low genetic diversity indicates that the population is almost all uniform in its traits. Genetic diversity is dependent on chromosomal mutations, migration of individuals or a population, sexual reproduction, population size, and selective breeding.

Species diversity is a measure of the number of various species within a given area. Some localities have high species diversity (a large number of species) and others have low species diversity. Factors that affect species diversity are the size of the area, human activities, and evolutionary and geological history of an area. Generally, but not always, the larger the area, the more species are present. A greater number of habitats in a given area will usually result in greater diversity.

Greater diversity means more connections among species and greater stability; more diverse ecosystems recover more quickly from disturbances such as natural disasters and are more resistant to damage from introduced non-native organisms.

Ecosystem diversity is a measure of the number of different kinds of ecosystems present in a given area. Even if areas appear to have general similarities (for example, all deserts have low rainfall), there are specific organisms that live in each ecosystem that create diversity.

TROPHIC RELATIONSHIPS

Ecologists divide organisms into four broad categories. Each level in the first two categories is known as a trophic level.

1. **Producers:** Organisms that are able to use sources of energy to make complex, organic molecules from simple inorganic substances in their environment. All other organisms rely on producers as a food source, either directly or indirectly. Producers are the first, or lowest trophic level.

2. **Consumers:** Organisms that require organic matter as a food source. They consume organic matter to obtain energy and organic materials that will help to build and maintain their own bodies. Consumers can be further divided based on what they eat:

   - Primary Consumers: These are organisms that eat producers and are also known as herbivores. Ecosystems generally have a large number of herbivores.

   - Secondary Consumers: These are organisms that eat other consumers and are also known as carnivores. Some carnivores primarily eat herbivores, while others consume carnivores and herbivores.

   - Tertiary Consumers: A carnivore that feeds on secondary consumers or below; these generally have few if any predators.

3. **Omnivores:** These include both producers (plants) and consumers (animals) in their diet. In trophic terms, omnivores feed at multiple trophic levels.

4. **Decomposers:** These are organisms, considered to be a type of consumer, that use nonliving, organic matter as a source of energy and material to build their bodies. When an organism sheds, excretes waste products, or dies, it provides a source of food for decomposers.

All ecosystems are stable, self-regulating units, but they are continually changing. The organisms within an ecosystem are continually growing, reproducing, dying, and decaying. Ecosystems must have a continuous input of energy to remain stable. This energy is usually provided by the sun, but there are unusual ecosystems in the deep sea where energy is derived from chemicals (chemosynthesis).

Producers occupy the first trophic level. Herbivores occupy the second trophic level. The third trophic level consists of carnivores that eat herbivores, and the fourth trophic level consists of carnivores that eat other carnivores.

Omnivores, parasites, and scavengers occupy a different trophic level depending on what they are eating at any given time. For example, if you eat a salad, you feed at the second trophic level;, and if you eat a steak, you feed at the third trophic level. Decomposers process food from all trophic levels.

FOOD CHAINS AND FOOD WEBS

A food chain describes the relationship of organisms in an ecosystem in terms of who eats whom. Members of a food chain occupy different trophic levels, and energy passes from one organism to another as they are eaten. For example, the leaves on a tree growing beside a lake would take energy from the sun and provide a food source for insects. These insects are a food source for spiders living in the tree. If a spider falls from the tree into the pond, it can then be eaten by a frog. In turn, this frog may be eaten by a bass that is then caught by a fisherman. In the next step of this food chain, the fish is then consumed by humans. The typical order in a five-step food chain is as follows:

producer → primary consumer → secondary consumer → tertiary consumer → decomposers

Because most consumers eat two or more types of organisms at different trophic levels, multiple food chains can overlap and intersect to form a food web. Complex food webs are more stable than simple food chains, but in this network of interactions, several organisms can be affected if one key organism is reduced in number.

ENERGY FLOWS AND CYCLES

Energy in an ecosystem is not static, it moves through the food chains and out through the food webs in a very specific direction. In almost all ecosystems, energy supplied by the sun is used to carry out **photosynthesis**—the chemical process by which water and carbon dioxide are converted into glucose and oxygen—by producers, e.g. plants, algae, or phytoplankton. Producers obtain energy from a source like the sun, and this energy is then passed through the producers to consumers and decomposers. The glucose is a sugar that is incorporated into the producer's body. Consumers that eat the plants transfer the plant, and the energy used to grow that plant, into their own bodies and so on up each trophic level. Each transfer of energy to another trophic level is called **trophic transfer.**

The available energy decreases as the trophic level increases; some energy is lost to the environment as heat with each trophic transfer. The decreasing amount of available energy at each level is known as the **energy pyramid**. When an organism dies, some of the energy it contained becomes part of the decomposer's body. The rest is returned to the ecosystem as **detritus**, a rich food source for plants and some animals.

NUTRIENT CYCLES

Nutrients also flow through ecosystems. As matter flows through an ecosystem, it gets recycled. Many chemicals that are important to sustain life and the growth of organisms cycle between organisms, the atmosphere, the oceans, and Earth's crust. These chemicals include carbon, nitrogen, oxygen, phosphorus, sulfur, and water. The cycles of these chemicals are called **biogeochemical cycles**. Biogeochemical cycles involve multiple ecosystems and have global effects.

Carbon Cycle: Carbon is the main element in all living organisms. It is also found in the atmosphere as carbon dioxide and in the oceans and rocks as carbonates. The carbon cycle includes processes and pathways that capture inorganic carbon-based molecules and convert them into organic carbon-based molecules that can be used by organisms. The same carbon atoms are used over and over. Carbon dioxide is fixed into plants and microorganisms through photosynthesis. Carbon passes through the food chains and webs as consumers eat. Fixed carbon in food and waste is broken down through respiration. Carbon from decomposing matter gets released back into soil. Carbon dioxide from the atmosphere moves into oceans. Sediment contains carbonate and compresses over time to form sedimentary rocks. Geological forces such as earthquakes and volcanoes return carbon from rocks back into the atmosphere. Human activity such as burning fossil fuels and raising farm animals like pigs and cattle also releases large quantities of carbon dioxide into the atmosphere.

Nitrogen Cycle: The major source of nitrogen is Earth's atmosphere. It is 78 percent nitrogen gas. Living organisms cannot utilize nitrogen gas, so it must first be converted to another chemical form, such a nitrates or nitrites. The chemical conversions in the nitrogen cycle are made by bacteria and other microorganisms. There are five important steps in the nitrogen cycle:

1. Nitrogen gas must be made into a chemically usable form by the process known as nitrogen fixation. Nitrogen-fixing bacteria can convert nitrogen gas from the atmosphere into ammonia, which contains nitrogen, in the soil. Nitrifying bacteria in the soil convert ammonia to nitrates and nitrates. This process is called **nitrification**.

2. Plants take up nitrates from the soil and incorporate them into amino acids. Animals eat the plants and incorporate the ingested nitrogen from plant amino acids into their own amino acids, proteins, nucleic acids, and other nitrogen-containing organic molecules. This process is called **assimilation**.

3. After animals and plants die, decomposers convert their nitrogen-containing organic molecules back into ammonia and return it to the soil. This process is called **ammonification**.

4. The ammonia can be used directly by many types of plants. Nitrifying bacteria in the soil are able to convert ammonia to nitrite and nitrate. Under conditions where oxygen is absent, denitrifying bacteria are able to convert nitrite to nitrogen gas. This process is called **denitrification**.

5. The nitrogen gas is eventually released back into the atmosphere, where it can then reenter the nitrogen cycle.

Phosphorus Cycle: Phosphorus is another element that is common to living organisms. It is present in many important biological molecules, such as DNA and cell membranes. Phosphorus containing ATP and ADP are important molecules for storing and utilizing energy in living organisms. Many enzymes require a phosphate group for activation or inactivation. Unlike carbon and nitrogen, phosphorus is not present in the atmosphere, so the phosphorus cycle is limited to soil and water. The major form of phosphorus is the mineral apatite, which is found in rocks and phosphate deposits. The weathering of phosphate rocks leaches phosphate into soil. Then plants take up phosphorus from the soil and incorporate it into their tissue. Animals eat the plants and take up the phosphate. When plants and animals die, decomposers release phosphate back into the soil. Animal excretion also contains phosphate that is released back into the soil.

Sulfur Cycle: Sulfur is important for the production of proteins because the amino acids cysteine and cystine contain sulfur. Sulfur is mainly found in rocks and soil as sulfate minerals. There is also sulfur in the atmosphere in the form of hydrogen sulfide. Weathering exposes sulfates from rocks, which are deposited into soil and aquatic ecosystems. Plants and other photosynthetic organisms take up and assimilate the sulfates into their tissue. Then animals eat plants and assimilate sulfates into their tissue. Death and decomposition of plants and animals convert organic sulfates into inorganic sulfates. Animal excretions also add sulfates to water and soil. Inorganic sulfates are then recycled. During decomposition in both soil and water, sulfates are converted into hydrogen sulfide gas that can escape into the atmosphere, water, soil, and marine sediment. Hydrogen sulfide gas can also come from volcanoes and power plant emissions.

Oxygen Cycle: Molecular oxygen is critical for all living things. It is a by-product of photosynthesis and a necessary reactant for cellular respiration. Biological and chemical processes help to recycle oxygen on Earth. The main supply of oxygen is our atmosphere. Oxygen cycles through the atmosphere, living organisms, and Earth's crust. Oxygen is removed from the atmosphere by chemically reacting with rocks and minerals exposed to weathering. Oxygen is also removed from the atmosphere through respiration of living organisms. Sunlight breaks down water into hydrogen and oxygen, and oxygen is released into the atmosphere. Photosynthesis also breaks down water into hydrogen and oxygen, releasing oxygen into the atmosphere.

Hydrologic Cycle: Water cycles between the atmosphere and Earth's surface and underground, and it exists in three states: solid, liquid, and gas. This cycle is primarily driven by the sun's energy. Water is stored in the atmosphere as water vapor (gas), on Earth's surface as a liquid (lakes, oceans, rivers, streams) or a solid (ice, glaciers), and in the ground as a liquid (groundwater) or a solid (ice in the form of permafrost). Energy from the sun is the source of power that drives the water cycle. Water can move among all these sites in six different ways:

1. Water moves from its liquid or solid state on Earth's surface to the atmosphere into its gaseous state through evaporation and sublimation.
2. Groundwater moves into the atmosphere through plants during the process of transpiration, a part of photosynthesis.
3. Thermal energy from the sun is absorbed by Earth's surface and snow and ice melt into liquid water. This water either flows into lakes, oceans, rivers, or streams or is absorbed as groundwater.
4. Energy released by water vapor in the atmosphere causes precipitation, and liquid water returns to Earth's surface.
5. Once on Earth's surface, water flows through porous surfaces and into liquid groundwater storage.
6. Liquid groundwater can also flow back to Earth's surface and into streams, lakes, rivers, and oceans.

Humans significantly impact the flow of all the biogeochemical cycles through the burning of fossil fuels, the conversions of natural ecosystems to agricultural land, agricultural runoff, and industrialization.

BIOMES

Biomes are terrestrial climax communities that have a wide geographic distribution. In general, the structure of ecosystems in a biome and the kinds of niches and habitats in those ecosystems are similar. However, it is important to recognize that although the concept of a biome is useful for discussing overall patterns and processes, different communities within a given type of biome show differences in the exact species present.

There are two major nonbiological factors that have an impact on the kind of community that develops in a given part of the world: precipitation pattern and temperature range. The aspects of precipitation that are most important are the total amount of precipitation per year, the form of precipitation (rain, snow, sleet), and its seasonal distribution. Temperature patterns vary greatly throughout regions of the world. Some regions, like tropical areas near the equator or areas near the poles, have a relatively consistent temperature throughout the year; other areas are more evenly divided between cold and warm temperatures. Each type of biome is dependent in large part on precipitation and temperature.

Desert

Deserts are one type of biome in which there are generally less than 25 centimeters of precipitation per year. The form of precipitation varies for each desert. Although deserts are typically thought to be hot and dry (Sahara and the desert of the Southwestern United States), there are some desert biomes in which temperatures are quite cool for a major part of the year (Gobi Desert and the deserts of the Northwestern United States) or even bitterly cold (Dry Valleys of Antarctica).

Many species populate a desert biome, but there are usually a low number of individuals of each species. In the past, humans had little impact on desert biomes in part because the hot, arid conditions did not allow for agriculture. Hunter-gatherer societies were most common in deserts. However, modern technology allows for water to be transported into deserts, cities have developed in some desert biomes, and there is also limited agriculture.

Grassland

Temperate grassland biomes such as prairies or steppes are widely distributed in temperate regions of Earth. Grasslands generally receive 25–75 centimeters of rain annually. In general, grassland biomes are windy with hot summers and cold winters. In many grassland biomes, fire is an important factor in releasing nutrients from dead plants into the soil and for preventing the invasion of trees. Between 60 and 90 percent of the vegetation is grass. Primary consumers eat the grasses, and there are often large herds of migratory animals such as bison living in grasslands. Carnivores also inhabit grasslands. Most of the moist grasslands throughout the world have been converted to agriculture. Drier grasslands have been converted to grazing for domestic grazers such as cattle, sheep, and goats. There is very little undisturbed grassland left.

Savanna

Savannas are found in tropical parts of Africa, South America, and Australia. They are characterized by extensive grasslands and occasional patches of trees. These biomes typically have a rainy season in which 50 to 150 centimeters of rain fall, followed by a drought period. Plants and animals time their reproductive activities to coincide with the rainy season, when food and water are more abundant. Savannas have been heavily impacted by agriculture. Farming is possible in moister regions, and animal grazing is found in drier regions. Irrigation is essential because of the long periods of drought.

Mediterranean Shrublands (Chaparral)

Mediterranean shrublands are located near oceans and are dominated by low shrubs. The climate varies from wet, cool winters to hot, dry summers. Rainfall is 40 to 100 centimeters per year. Vegetation is dominated by woody shrubs, and the types of animals vary widely. Very little shrubland exists that has not been impacted by humans. There are many major cities in this type of biome and also a large amount of agriculture.

Tropical Dry Forest

Tropical dry forests are heavily influenced by seasonal rainfall. This type of biome is found in parts of Central and South America, Australia, Africa, and Asia. Many tropical dry forests have monsoon seasons, and rainfall ranges from 50 to 200 centimeters. There are generally high human populations in tropical dry forests, and wood is harvested from them for fuel and building materials.

Tropical Rain Forest

Tropical rain forests are located near the equator in Central and South America, Africa, Southeast Asia, and some islands in the Caribbean Sea and Pacific Ocean. The temperature is warm and relatively constant, and it rains nearly every day, 200-500 centimeters a year. There is extensive vegetation, but soils are generally poor because all of the nutrients are taken up by plants. Tropical rain forests have a greater diversity of species than any other biome. Today, tropical rainforests are under intense pressure from logging and agricultural industries, although agriculture is generally not successful in the long term because of typically poor soil conditions.

Temperate Deciduous Forest

Temperate deciduous forests have changes of seasons, and trees lose their leaves in fall and regrow leaves in spring. This forest is typical in the eastern half of the United States, parts of South Central and Southeastern Canada, Southern Africa, and many areas of Europe and Asia. Winters are generally mild, and plants actively grow for about six months. There are generally 75 to 100 centimeters of precipitation per year distributed evenly. Each region of the world has certain species of trees and other organisms. Most of the temperate deciduous forests have been heavily impacted by human activity. Much has been cleared for agriculture and logging and to develop major population areas.

Taiga, Northern Coniferous Forest, or Boreal Forest

The evergreen coniferous forests found throughout Southern Canada, parts of Northern Europe, and Russia are known as taiga, northern coniferous forests, or boreal forests. These biomes have 30 to 85 centimeters of precipitation per year, and there is a great deal of snowmelt in spring contributing to humid climates. These regions have many lakes, ponds, and bogs, and conifers are the most common organisms in these biomes. Humans have a less severe impact on these biomes because of low population density. Logging and herding of reindeer are common activities.

Tundra

Tundra is the area north of taiga biomes. It is an extremely cold region with permanently frozen subsoil (permafrost), which means tundra is mostly full of short grasses and there are no trees. Tundra biomes experience ten months of winter. Less than 25 centimeters of precipitation fall each year, but summer months see generally wet soil conditions due to snowmelt. Water is not absorbed into the soil because of the permafrost subsoil layer. Therefore, many shallow ponds and waterlogged areas exist in summer. Also in summer months, there is a variety of small plants and swarms of insects that are a food source for migratory birds and waterfowl. Tundra is also home to a few hardy mammals such as reindeer and arctic hare. Many species of birds and large mammals migrate during summer months using the scattered patches of small communities known as alpine tundra. Very few people live in tundra biomes, but any damage to this ecosystem is slow to heal because of the very short growing season. Tundra land must be handled with care.

Aquatic Ecosystems

Aquatic ecosystems are shaped by the ability of the sun's energy to penetrate the water, the depth of the water, the nature of the bottom of the body of water, the water temperature, and the amount of salts dissolved in the water. Freshwater ecosystems have little dissolved salt, and marine ecosystems have a high salt content.

Oceans are defined as pelagic marine ecosystems and have many organisms that float or actively swim. **Plankton** are very small, sometimes microscopic organisms that are found in large numbers in oceans and large lakes and are an important food source for larger animals. **Zooplankton** are small animals (including larvae of larger organisms), while **phytoplankton** are microscopic plants or plant-like organisms that carry out photosynthesis. Phytoplankton, such as algae, live in the euphotic zone, the upper layers of the ocean where the sun's rays penetrate. The open ocean in the euphotic zone is known as the pelagic zone; closer to the coast, above the continental shelf is the neritic zone.

- **Benthic Marine Ecosystems:** Organisms that live on the bottom of oceans are part of benthic marine ecosystems (benthic systems are called littoral in shallow water near the coast). The substrate material on the ocean bottom is important in determining which species live in a particular benthic ecosystem. Temperature also has an impact on benthic ecosystems. An abyssal ecosystem is a benthic ecosystem that is situated in great depths of the ocean. No light reaches these ecosystems, so animals must depend on the fall of organic matter from the euphotic zone.

- **Coral Reef Ecosystems:** These are produced by coral animals that build up around themselves cup-shaped external skeletons. The skeletons of corals provide a surface upon which many other species live. Coral reef systems require warm water and are, therefore, found only near the equator.

- **Mangrove Swamp Ecosystems:** These are tropical forest ecosystems found in shallow waters near the shore of marine ecosystems and an adjacent landmass. These ecosystems are dominated by trees that can tolerate the high salt content of the water and excrete salt from their leaves. Seeds of these trees germinate on the tree itself, and then fall into the water and are buried in mud where they take root. These trees have extensive root systems that extend above water to take in oxygen. Mangroves are found in Southern Florida, the Caribbean, Southeast Asia, and Africa, as well as many other tropical and subtropical coasts.

- **Estuary Ecosystems:** An estuary is an ecosystem consisting of shallow water and a partially enclosed area where fresh water runs into the ocean. The salt content of water in estuaries changes with the tide and the inflow and outflow of the rivers. Organisms in this type of ecosystem have adapted to these changing conditions. An estuary is a productive ecosystem because the shallow regions allow light to penetrate the water, and rich nutrients are dumped from rivers into the basin of an estuary.

- **Freshwater Ecosystems:** These have a much lower salt content than marine ecosystems and have a large range of water temperature. Freshwater ecosystems consist of either relatively stationary water, such as lakes, ponds, or reservoirs, or moving water, such as streams or rivers. If a lake is deep enough, it has similar characteristics to an ocean ecosystem: There is a euphotic zone at the top, and there are many kinds of phytoplankton and zooplankton. Emergent plants grow near the shores and shallower regions of lakes. They are rooted to the bottom of the lakes and their leaves can float on the surface (water lily) or stick out above the water's surface (cattail). Submerged plants are rooted below the surface, but do not protrude above the surface (*Elodea* and *Chara*). The region of a lake with rooted vegetation is called the littoral zone, and the region where vegetation is not rooted is called the limnetic zone.

The productivity of a lake is dependent upon water temperature and depth. **Oligotrophic lakes** are deep, clear, cold and have a low nutrient content. There is low productivity in this type of lake. On the other hand, **eutrophic lakes** are shallow, murky, warm, and nutrient-rich. Productivity is higher in these lakes.

The dissolved oxygen content of water is also important to ecosystems. It determines the kind of organisms that inhabit a lake. When organic molecules enter water, bacteria and fungi break them down. The amount of oxygen used by these decomposers to break down a specific amount of organic matter is known as the **biochemical oxygen demand (BOD)**.

In streams and rivers, water is moving, so organisms like algae attach to rocks. The collection of algae and fungi in streams and rivers is called periphyton. Most streams are shallow, and light can penetrate to the bottom, but because the water is fast-moving, photosynthetic organisms do not accumulate enough essential nutrients for growth. Therefore, most streams are not very productive.

Most of the nutrients come from organic matter that falls into streams. In rivers, the water is deeper, and there is less light penetration. Organisms must rely on nutrients flowing in from streams. Rivers tend to be larger than streams with warmer, slower-moving water. Therefore, there is less oxygen in rivers, and frequently different species occupy rivers and streams.

Swamps and marshes delineate the transition from terrestrial ecosystems into freshwater aquatic ecosystems. Swamps are wetlands that contain trees that withstand the flooded conditions. Marshes are wetlands dominated by grasses and reeds.

Most freshwater ecosystems have been heavily impacted by human activity. Activity on land affects freshwater systems because there is runoff from land into lakes, rivers, and streams. Agricultural runoff, sewage, and trash affect freshwater ecosystems. Human impact on marine ecosystems comes in the form of overfishing, oil pollution from transportation, oil spills, and trash dumping.

POPULATION BIOLOGY

Population biology is a branch of environmental science that is concerned with characterizing the make-up and growth of populations and their impact on the environment and its organisms. A population is a group of individuals of one species that inhabits a given area. Population dynamics focus on the growth and limitations of a population and how that population interacts with its environment with respect to its growth and stability. Population genetics addresses the frequency and distribution of specific genes in a population and how these frequencies might change over time. Population genetics is also concerned with mutation rates within a given population. Different populations of the same species have different characteristics such as birthrate, mortality, sex ratio, age distribution, growth rate, migration rate, spatial distribution, and density. Demography describes the vital statistics of a given population.

Birthrate: The number of individuals added to a population over a particular time period, through reproduction of the species. Asexual reproduction is the process in which an organism such as bacteria divides to form new individuals. Sexual reproduction is the most common type of reproduction. Most species produce many more offspring than are needed to replace the parent generation. The birthrate in humans is usually described as the number of offspring produced by 1,000 individuals in a given year.

Death Rate or Mortality Rate: The number of deaths in a population over a given time period. For most species, mortality rates are high, but in humans it is relatively low. One way to study mortality is with a survivorship curve, which shows the proportion of individuals likely to survive at each age. The death rate in humans is referred to as the number of people in 1,000 that die per year. For a population to grow, the birthrate must exceed the death rate in a given year.

Sex Ratio: The relative number of males and females in a given population. The number of females has a bigger effect on the number of offspring produced in a population. However, the typical ratio approximates 1:1.

Age Distribution: The number of individuals in each age range in a population. Age distribution has a large influence on population growth rates. Among humans, different societies see vastly different age distributions. In general, a large reproductive population will cause future population growth.

Population Density: The number of organisms within a species in a given area. Movement from a densely populated region is called **dispersal**. Dispersal relieves overcrowding in a given area. The migration of individuals is referred to as **emigration**. Some organisms may leave their population to become members of a different population. This is called **migration**, or **immigration**. Biological ability to produce offspring is a species' biotic potential. Because most species have a high biotic potential, there is a natural tendency for populations to increase. In general, there is an exponential growth in populations for a given period. There is often a pattern of growth that includes the following:

- A lag phase in which the population grows more slowly
- An exponential growth phase
- A declaration phase in which population growth slows due to equal birth and death rates, which leads to
- A stabile equilibrium phase in which there is a stable population size

There are several main environmental factors that limit population size. Factors from outside a population are known as **extrinsic limiting factors**. Factors regulated within a population are called **intrinsic limiting factors**. As the population increases, density-dependent limiting factors are important. **Density-independent limiting factors** are influences that control population, but they are not dependent on limiting factors. Limiting factors can be divided into four main categories:

1. Availability of raw materials
2. Availability of energy
3. Accumulation of waste products
4. Interaction between organisms

The **carrying capacity** is the maximum population that can be sustained in a given area. The carrying capacity is determined by a set of limiting factors. Environmental changes such as forest fires or floods can change the carrying capacity of an area.

A given species has a particular reproduction strategy.

- **K-strategists** are organisms that tend to reach a stable population as the carrying capacity is reached. These species tend to occupy a stable environment and tend to be large organisms that have a long lifespan, produce few offspring, and expend a lot of energy to care for their offspring. These populations tend to be limited by density-dependent limiting factors.

- **R-strategists** tend to be small organisms that have a short lifespan, produce many offspring, do not reach the carrying capacity, and live in unstable environments. These organisms produce many offspring, but do not expend energy to care for them. These species tend to be limited by density-independent limiting factors.

In northern regions of the world, many species follow a population cycle in which periods of large populations are followed by periods of small populations. In general, this occurs because of the nature of ecosystems in this part of the world. Ecosystems are relatively simple with few organisms affecting one another.

NATURAL SELECTION AND EVOLUTION

Natural selection is the process that determines which individuals within a species will survive and reproduce, thereby passing their genes on to the next generation. Changes observed over time in the physical appearance or behavior of a species are due to the process of evolution. Individuals in a species who are best adapted to a certain environment will survive best and produce more offspring, thus changing the characteristics of a given species over a long period of time. Therefore, natural selection is the mechanism that causes the evolution of a species.

There are several factors involved in the process of natural selection. Individuals within a species have genetic variation; some of the variations are useful, and some are not. Organisms reproduce at such a rate that many more offspring are produced than are needed to replace the parent generation, but most of the offspring die. The excess number of offspring results in a shortage of food supplies and other resources.

However, because there is a genetic variation among individuals of a species, some have a greater chance of obtaining the necessary food and resources (or avoiding danger) and, therefore, are more likely to survive and reproduce. Over time, each generation is subjected to the same process of natural selection, so that the percentage of individuals with favorable variations will increase, and the number of individuals with unfavorable variations will decrease.

Therefore, over time, there is a considerable change in the type of species present and their characteristics. Some changes can take place in a few generations, whereas others have taken thousands or millions of years. The process of natural selection plays a key role in evolution, and through the study of fossil records, it is obvious to see that some new species evolve, while others die out.

- **Speciation** is the development of a new species from a previously existing species. In general, speciation occurs as two subpopulations adapt to different conditions and eventually are unable to interbreed because they are so different.

- **Polyploidy** is a condition in plants in which there is an increase in the number of chromosomes in the cells, and this can also lead to the development of a new species that cannot interbreed with the original species.

- **Extinction** is the loss of an entire species and is a common feature in evolutionary history. In general, extinction comes about due to changes in a species' environment or from human intervention.

- **Coevolution** is the idea that two or more species of organisms can influence the evolutionary path of the other. This is a common pattern since all organisms within an ecosystem influence one another.

SUCCESSION

Ecosystems respond to environmental challenges through succession. Succession is a series of recognizable and predictable changes over time to maintain the stability of the community. Succession occurs because the activities of a given species cause changes to the environment that make it suitable for other species. Succession proceeds until a stable climax community is reached.

There are two general types of succession:

1. **Primary succession** in new life is colonized in an environment that has a complete lack of life form and minimal water. Primary succession can occur in areas where volcanic activity wipes out life forms in an ecosystem. Primary succession takes a very long time to establish.

2. **Secondary succession** occurs when a portion of an ecosystem is disturbed by an event such as a forest fire. In this case, the area is eventually restored through succession, and it is a much more rapid process than primary succession because soil and water are usually already present.

Regardless of whether succession is primary or secondary, the process occurs in basically the same manner. First, new land is exposed. This land is either devoid of life (primary succession) or disturbed in some way (secondary succession). Next, pioneer species take root. Pioneer species are generally fast-growing plants that can thrive in exposed conditions and have a short lifespan.

Usually, lichen (an organism that includes both fungus and algae in a symbiotic relationship) or mosses begin to modify the ecosystem for the growth of other species. The collection of organisms at this stage is known as the **pioneer community**. Eventually, as a thin layer of soil is established, longer-lived plants are established. Each step in the sequence from the pioneer community to the climax community is a **successional**, or **seral stage**. The entire sequence of stages is known as a sere. At each seral stage, species either replace or coexist with previously existing species, and the ecosystem continues to be further modified at each stage, until the climax community is attained.

In a **climax community,** longer-living plants and animals are sustained by the environment. The difference between a climax community and a successional (seral) community is that climax communities maintain their diversity of species for a long time, and successional communities are temporary.

The organisms in a climax community maintain specialized niches, recycle nutrients, and maintain a relatively constant biomass, whereas successional communities do not. The general trend in succession is toward increasing complexity and efficiency.

With respect to aquatic ecosystems, with the exception of the oceans, most aquatic ecosystems are temporary. All aquatic systems receive a continuous input of soil and organic matter, and eventually bodies of water are filled in. This may take thousands of years, but it is a continual process. The successional stages of aquatic ecosystems are often called "wet meadow" stages and mark the transition of an aquatic community to a terrestrial community.

ENVIRONMENTAL IMPACTS

Approximately 25 percent of the questions on the DSST Environmental Science exam will cover topics dealing with environmental impacts. Let's review all the major concepts you will need to know for the exam.

HUMAN POPULATION DYNAMICS

Human population has been steadily increasing since the modern era, mostly because of the longer life span of populations. Developed countries have an increase in food production and better methods of controlling disease. All of this can be shared with the rest of the world, resulting in an improved quality of life overall. The world population is currently increasing at a rate of 1.12 percent annually, a slight decline from a decade ago.

At this rate, the world population is expected to reach 9.6 billion in 2050. Several factors must be taken into consideration to fully understand human population growth. Economic development plays a huge role in population growth; birthrates tend to be higher in developing countries, a combination of low childhood survival and lower access to family planning. More developed countries usually, have a relatively stable population growth, and less-developed countries do not.

Several factors interact to determine the impact of a society's population growth on the resources of a country. These factors include the following:

- Land
- Natural resources
- Size of a population
- Quantity of natural resources consumed
- Environmental damage caused by using resources

The relationship of all these factors can be expressed in the equation:

Impact on the Environment =

Population × Affluence × Damage Due to Technology

or (I = P × A × T)

Population density relates the size of a population to available resources. People in highly developed countries tend to have a greater impact on the environment because of technological development.

The **ecological footprint** of a population is a measure of the land and resources required to support the population and absorb its waste.

Demography is the study of human populations, their characteristics, and the consequences of growth. Demographers can predict future population growth by looking at biological factors, including the total fertility rate and age distribution. The total fertility rate is the average number of children a woman will bear in her lifetime. A total fertility rate of 2.1 is a replacement fertility rate whereby parents will be replaced by offspring when they die. If the number of births equals the number of deaths, there is zero population growth. Social factors that influence population growth are aspects like culture, traditions, and attitudes towards birth control. Women's rights have been determined to be a major factor; when women gain more influence over reproductive and economic decisions, birth rates tend to fall.

Political factors also influence human population growth. In many advanced economies such as Italy and Japan, the population is actually declining as birthrates have dropped below replacement level. As a result, some developed countries try to promote more births, whereas countries like China facing overpopulation have taken measures to control growth. Immigration also has an impact on the rate of growth in a population.

A human population often increases only if populations of other animals and plants decrease. When humans need food, they convert ecosystems into agricultural systems. In some cases, the long-term health of the environment is sacrificed to feed a population. Countries with the highest standard of living seem to have the lowest rate of population growth, and those with the lowest standard of living have the highest population growth rate.

This leads to the demographic transition model that occurs in four stages.

1. Initially, countries have a stable population with a high birthrate and death rate.
2. Improved economic and social conditions cause a decrease in the death rate, so there is a period of rapid population growth.
3. As countries develop an industrial economy, birthrates drop and population growth rates fall.
4. Eventually, birthrates and death rates are balanced again, but this time there is a low birthrate and low death rate.

GLOBAL CLIMATE CHANGE

The atmosphere is composed of 78.1 percent nitrogen, 20.9 percent oxygen, and 1 percent of a mixture of other gases, including carbon dioxide, methane, and water vapor. The atmosphere is composed of four layers: from the surface up to the edge of space they are troposphere, stratosphere, mesosphere, and the thermosphere.

Energy from the sun enters the atmosphere, but not all of that energy reaches Earth's surface. Clouds and gases high in the atmosphere reflect back about 25 percent of the sun's energy. Denser gas absorbs more energy, and gases are densest in the troposphere. Another 25 percent are absorbed by gases in the atmosphere, such as ozone, carbon dioxide, methane, and water vapor. These gases are known as greenhouse gases (GHGs). Of the 50 percent of the energy that reaches Earth's surface, some is reflected back into the atmosphere by rain, snow, ice, and sand. The rest is absorbed by Earth's surface.

The greenhouse effect is natural, and without our atmosphere to trap heat from the sun Earth would not be warm enough to sustain life. However, since the Industrial Revolution (discussed later in this chapter), human activities have added extra greenhouse gases into the atmosphere. Major human sources of greenhouse gases include burning of fossil fuels for industrial processes, power generation, and transportation; clearing and burning of forests;, and methane from livestock. There are natural sources of greenhouse gases as well, such as respiration and volcanic activity. The increased concentration of GHGs in the atmosphere increases the percentage of the sun's energy that is trapped by the atmosphere.

In 1898, Swedish scientist Svante Arrhenius calculated how much surface temperature might increase if atmospheric carbon dioxide increased. His work was built upon by Charles Keeling, whose work first linked increased anthropogenic carbon dioxide to observed temperature increases. So far, the average surface temperature has increased about 2° Fahrenheit since the 19th century, and human activities are believed to be responsible for most of that increase. There is a range of predictions about how much the global average temperature will continue to increase, depending on what actions are taken, and due to natural processes. The Intergovernmental Panel on Climate Change (IPCC) is tasked with processing the available data on climate change and producing regular reports on the subject.

The oceans have absorbed a large portion of excess CO_2 and heat, so ocean temperatures have increased and water chemistry is at risk of changing. The increased carbon dioxide forms a weak acid when mixed with seawater, a process called **ocean acidification**. Acidification may hinder marine organisms, such as coral, from properly forming shells or skeletons.

The possible outcomes of a global temperature increase, some of which have already been observed, will vary across the planet and will not be felt equally. Most of the hottest years have occurred since the year 2000, but not every single place on Earth has experienced record high temperatures. It is for this reason that the term global climate change is used instead of global warming; local weather continues to be highly variable.

At the moment, the greatest impacts are in the polar regions, where ice caps and sea ice cover have shrunk considerably. Glaciers at lower latitudes have also retreated. (Less ice means that less heat is reflected back into space, increasing the rate of change.) Some areas may see increased rainfall, while others may experience drought. Longer and more intense heat waves are likely, as are more intense storms. Species have begun to move around in search of their preferred temperature range; species that cannot easily move to cooler areas, particularly mountain species, are at risk of extinction. It is difficult to predict the exact timescale for these changes or to say exactly what will happen in any particular place.

Most researchers believe these changes to be inevitable unless either GHG emissions are drastically reduced or a way is found to remove excess GHGs from the atmosphere.

POLLUTION

Pollution is any matter or energy that has harmful effects when introduced into the environment. Pollution can enter the environment naturally, for example through a volcanic eruption, but humans are most often the source.

Physical Aspects of Pollution

Pollution can take almost any physical form—for example, solid waste like your household trash—but pollution can also be liquid or gas. Chemical pollution can settle into soil and remain there, forever unless the soil is decontaminated or excavated.

Pollution, generally gas or very small particles, that enters the air is called air pollution. Sources of outdoor air pollution include industrial output (smokestacks), engine emissions, power generation, accidental release from fossil fuel extraction, and fires, among others. Physical or atmospheric features, such as mountains or temperature inversions, can trap air pollution close to the ground, especially in populated areas. Indoor sources of air pollution may include cigarette smoke or radon, a naturally occurring radioactive gas.

Pollution that enters surface or ground water is water pollution. Water pollution is the result of population growth and industrial growth. A source of water pollution that is readily identifiable because it has a definite point where it enters the water is called a point source. Diffuse pollutants such as those that come from agricultural runoff, urban roadways, and rain are nonpoint sources of water pollution. Types of water pollution include municipal, agricultural, industrial, thermal, marine oil, and groundwater pollution.

Chemical Aspects of Pollution

There are several categories of air pollutants on Earth.

1. Primary air pollutants are released into the atmosphere in unmodified forms. These pollutants include carbon monoxide, volatile organic compounds (hydrocarbons), particulate matter, sulfur dioxide, and oxides of nitrogen.

2. Secondary air pollutants are primary pollutants that can interact with other compounds in the presence of sunlight to form new compounds such as ozone. **Photochemical smog**, a word formed by "smoke" and "fog," is a secondary pollutant formed when emissions combine and react in the atmosphere to form a dense, low-lying layer of air pollution.

3. The U.S. Environmental Protection Agency (EPA) has a category of air pollutants called criteria air pollutants. These include nitrogen dioxide, ozone, sulfur dioxide, particulate matter, carbon monoxide, and lead.

OZONE

Ozone is a molecule that consists of three oxygen atoms bound to one another. Ground-level ozone is an extremely reactive molecule that can cause irritation to respiratory tissue and damage to lungs.

Ozone is a secondary pollutant formed as a component of photochemical smog. However, there is also a necessary layer of ozone (the ozone layer) in the atmosphere that shields Earth from the harmful effects of ultraviolet (UV) radiation from the Sun. This ozone layer is slowly being depleted as a result of pollutants, especially chlorofluorocarbons (CFC), in the atmosphere. Less ozone in the upper atmosphere results in more UV light reaching Earth's surface. This can lead to increased risks of skin cancer, cataracts, and mutations.

The combination of sulfur dioxide or oxides of nitrogen with an oxidizing agent like ozone, hydroxide ions, or hydrogen peroxide, along with water, forms sulfuric and nitric acid in the atmosphere. Acid-forming particles are dissolved in rain, sleet, snow, and fog and can also be deposited as dry particles. All forms of precipitation that contain acid-forming particles are known as **acid rain**. The accumulation of acid-forming particles on a surface is known as acid deposition. Acid rain is a worldwide problem that stems from natural causes, such as vegetation, volcanoes, and lightning, as well as human activities, including burning of fossil fuels and the use of the internal combustion engine.

Water pollution can take many forms. Common water pollutants include oil or salt washed from road surfaces, pesticides, discarded medications, detergent, or raw sewage. One important category of water pollutants is the oxygen binders, substances that can remove oxygen from water. Ethylene glycol—antifreeze—has this property.

Agricultural runoff, e.g. fertilizer or animal waste, is another major source of water pollution. The excess nutrients, when washed into a body of water, promote high algae and plant growth. Eutrophication can result, or the surplus algae begins to die. Decomposition uses up the oxygen in the water. These oxygen-free areas are known as "dead zones." A large dead zone forms every year in the Gulf of Mexico near the mouth of the Mississippi River, caused by agricultural runoff washing out with the river.

BIOLOGICAL ASPECTS OF POLLUTION

Pollution may have a variety of biological impacts. Acid rain, for example, is suspected of causing the death of many forests, and it also causes damage to human-made structures, especially those made of limestone. Sulfuric acid converts limestone to gypsum, which then erodes away. There are also effects of acid rain on aquatic ecosystems, as evidenced in a progressive loss of organisms as the acidity of the water increases.

Some pollutants may be directly toxic to life; different substances are tested to determine the maximum allowable concentration in water before harm occurs to aquatic life. For pollutants that do not break down but linger in the environment, bioaccumulation is a problem. Small organisms consume small amounts of a pollutant; larger organisms eat many smaller organisms and accumulate all of the pollutants consumed by each of those small organisms. For example, higher and higher trophic levels feed on lower-level organisms, so the concentration of a pollutant accumulates and can be up to 2,000 times the original concentration in the highest trophic-level species, known as **biomagnification** or **bioaccumulation**.

Air pollution can settle into the ground or water, impacting soil or water chemistry, and impacting terrestrial and aquatic life. All forms of pollution can have health impacts on humans, but air pollution in particular is linked to numerous health concerns, including heart and respiratory disease. Children chronically exposed to air pollution are particularly at risk.

AGRICULTURAL IMPACTS OF POLLUTION

Early civilizations obtained food by hunting and gathering. The development of agriculture required domestication of wild plants into a controlled setting and greater control over land and soil. Food plants were manipulated through selective breeding to produce crops with greater nutrition and better taste (e.g. potatoes). Land had to be cleared to make way for crops and pastures for livestock.

The increase in yield of food grown allowed for an increase in populations (an increase in K for humans). With the advent of the Industrial Revolution, agriculture was also mechanized.

To operate effectively, new machines required large tracts of relatively flat land planted with a single crop, a practice known as **monoculture**. Although these methods produce abundant crops of food, the clearing of large tracts of land also leads to soil erosion and soil depleted of nutrients, which must be added back to the soil. Because of erosion problems, many farmers now use methods that reduce the time a field is left fallow.

Domestication of livestock has its own environmental concerns. Erosion also results from clearing forests to create space for animals, and overgrazing can damage fragile grasslands and ranges. A lot of viable land is required to grow feed for livestock, land that can't be used for other purposes.

INDUSTRIAL IMPACTS OF POLLUTION

The Industrial Revolution, beginning in the mid-1700s, was brought about by the use of coal as a major fuel source in England. It involved the invention of the steam engine and the development of machines to mass-produce goods. The steam engine also made large-scale coal mining possible. During the Industrial Revolution and afterwards, energy consumption increased, economies grew, and populations became more prosperous. An increase in coal use also caused an increase in air pollution, including a rapid increase in atmospheric CO_2 levels. Within the span of 200 years, energy consumption increased eightfold, and pollution became a serious problem in some countries. Industrialization made manufacturing much easier and cheaper, leading to a rise in disposable products (e.g., plastic bottles). Cheap, disposable manufactured goods led to a higher level of consumption, especially in wealthier nations, as well as increased resource use. The young science of industrial ecology, which aims to limit ecological impacts of industrial processes, may mitigate some of these environmental concerns.

Currently, the most rapid industrial development takes place in emerging nations. This development leads to a disproportionate amount of ecosystem degradation and loss of biodiversity in those countries. The damage to the environment in these nations can actually increase poverty instead of promoting wealth. Some economists believe that the ecological damage levels off when developing economies reach a suitable level of development.

HABITAT DESTRUCTION

To clear land for agriculture, farmers clear large tracts of forestland, a process called **deforestation**. Deforestation is mainly used for agricultural purposes, or to make room for human settlement. In some countries, forests are still cleared for wood to be used as a fuel source or for building materials. Even when only some of the trees are removed a forest can suffer damage. Removal of trees in tropical regions removes biomass, which contains most of the nutrients in the soil. The soil that is left is poor and not ideal for agriculture. In addition, deforestation leads to erosion of soil.

Deforestation causes carbon dioxide to stay in the atmosphere because there are fewer trees to take it in, which contributes to global warming. Evapotranspiration through the leaves of trees returns water to the atmosphere as part of the hydrologic cycle, but deforestation reduces this process and disrupts the hydrologic cycle. Deforestation also disrupts ecosystems and species that live in forests.

Patchwork clear-cutting, reforestation, and selective harvesting are methods used to try to avoid deforestation. When forests are left alone, they will grow back, but never to the same original state.

Habitats can also be destroyed in other ways. Waste disposal, especially improper disposal, can leave soil and land contaminated and even virtually destroyed. Excess use of motorized vehicles or even too much foot traffic can disrupt fragile landscapes, especially in desert or alpine systems. Wetlands and marshes can be dredged away to make room for shipping or they can be filled in, either to dispose of material or to make more room for development. Even something as small as mowing an old field can destroy natural habitat.

Mining, for fossil fuels or ore, also takes a toll on the environment.

- Coal or metals can be extracted by surface, or strip, mining, which involves removing the overburden material on top of a vein of coal to get to the coal below the surface. This method is efficient, but it disrupts the landscape. In the United States, regulations require that retired surface mines be replanted with vegetation, but habitat is rarely restored to its original condition.

- Underground mining extracts coal that is buried deep beneath Earth's surface. The method poses many safety concerns and health hazards for miners, but it doesn't disturb the above-ground landscape. However, underground mining still raises environmental issues such as subsidence, or sinking of the land, and the accumulation of large waste heaps. Mine waste, known as tailings, often contains toxic chemicals and disposal can cause extensive habitat damage, especially when sediment or toxins run into streams.

Marine habitats can be destroyed by illegal fishing techniques such as fishing with explosives, or damaged by legal but destructive techniques such as bottom trawling.

The excessive growth of algae and other aquatic plants in water with added nutrients is a process called **eutrophication**. When phosphates or nitrates are added to the surface of a body of water from sources such as organic waste from agriculture or industries, they can act as a fertilizer and cause excessive growth of algae. This undesirable algae growth can interfere with the use of the water. Also, as the algae dies, there is a decrease in oxygen levels in the water, and fish and other aquatic life die.

LAND DEGRADATION

Land, especially farm and rangeland, is a finite resource that can be lost if not properly cared for. Farmland is at risk of erosion; without the plants to hold the soil in place, soil can blow or wash away between crops under many farming methods. The nutrients in the soil can be used up if too many of the same crops (monoculture) are planted for too many years, without rotating in different crops to replenish the soil. Continuous farming, particularly monocultures, can eventually leave the soil unsuitable for farming.

Rangelands are vulnerable to overgrazing, especially in times of drought. Cattle and other livestock are often grazed in arid and semi-arid landscapes. If too many animals are allowed to feed before the plants can regrow, then erosion and fire risk increase. This problem is especially acute on publicly owned lands.

The conversion of dry, arid, or semiarid land into desert-like ecosystems is a process called **desertification**. Desertification is most prevalent in Northern Africa and parts of Asia where there is irregular or unpredictable rainfall. In many of these areas, there are populations of nomadic herders or subsistence farmers that are under pressure to provide food for their families, even at a cost to the environment. Overgrazing and over-farming lead to desertification in these areas.

ENVIRONMENTAL MANAGEMENT AND CONSERVATION

Environmental management and conservation involves a number of highly contentious political issues. Approximately 25 percent of the questions on the DSST Environmental Science exam will cover topics dealing with this topic.

NONRENEWABLE RESOURCES

Natural resources are those that humans can use for their own purposes, but that they cannot create. Soil, wind, and water are all examples of natural resources. A renewable resource can be formed or regenerated by natural processes, so that it is not used up. However, nonrenewable resources are not replaced by natural processes. Fossil fuels and mountain ranges are nonrenewable on a human timescale.

The energy sources most commonly used by industrialized nations are fossil fuels: oil, coal, and natural gas. They constitute 87 percent of the world's energy sources and are all nonrenewable resources, but that number is expected to decrease slowly. Humans are using up nonrenewable energy sources at a much faster rate than they can be replaced, which eventually will exhaust Earth's supply of these sources.

Coal mining and coal transport generates a lot of dust in the atmosphere, and there is also sulfur associated with coal that causes acid mine drainage and air pollution. Burning of coal causes acid deposition in the atmosphere, which is a cause of acid rain. The release of carbon dioxide from coal has become a greater concern with respect to the potential for global warming. Burning oil produces fewer emissions than coal but is still a major source of greenhouse gases and there are major problems associated with spills and leaks from oil pipelines.

In recent years, natural gas has become a greater source of energy for electricity production and heat, especially in the United States. As of 2017, natural gas was cheaper than oil, and produces fewer emissions when burned. However, methane leaking from wells, refineries, storage, and transportation of natural gas are serious concerns since methane is a potent greenhouse gas. A controversial method of extracting gas (and oil) called **hydraulic fracturing**, involves splitting open shale rock with water and chemicals, creating issues of wastewater disposal and air pollution from machinery. The practice has led to lower fuel prices but has also been banned in some countries and U.S. states.

RENEWABLE RESOURCES

As of 2015, only 13 percent of the world's power generation comes from non–fossil fuels. Of that, approximately 7 percent is from hydroelectric power, 4 percent is nuclear, and only 2 percent is from a combination of biomass, geothermal, wind, and solar energy.

- **Biomass** is used most in developing countries. All biomass is produced by green plants that convert sunlight into plant material through photosynthesis. Major types of biomass include wood, municipal and industrial wastes, agricultural crop residue, animal waste, and energy plantations. Plants such as sugar cane or corn may also be used to produce ethanol, an alternative fuel. The practice is controversial as it can drive up food prices. Using biomass fuels can create air pollution.

- **Hydroelectric power** relies on water to generate electricity. The construction of reservoirs, however, can cause environmental and social issues. One possible impact is that dams can cause flooding of land around them. Damming a river alters the natural flow and level of water in a river, and can impede the passage of migratory fish.

- **Tidal power** can also supply a renewable energy source, but this might result in negative impacts on shorelines. Currently, tidal generators are very costly.

- **Geothermal power** is linked to geologically active regions where thermal energy from Earth can reach the surface through thin layers of Earth's crust. Geothermal energy creates steam that contains hydrogen sulfide, which causes air pollution.

- **Wind power** is another source of energy, but it is dependent on the variability of winds. Places such as the Dakotas in the United States have the strongest winds, but because they are remote from large, energy-using population centers, there would be a loss in electricity if transferred to distant areas of the country. The moving blades of wind generators can pose a hazard to birds, depending on where the turbines are located. They can also produce noise that bothers nearby residents. More selective placement of wind farms and new technologies under development such as blade-free turbines may mitigate some of these concerns.

- **Solar energy** is a renewable energy source that can be collected through means of passive solar or active solar systems, but large solar farms can displace sensitive desert habitat.

- **Nuclear power** is generated when the heat from a controlled nuclear fission reaction is used to heat water and create steam, which is used to turn a turbine. Nuclear power produces very few emissions besides water vapor, but uranium fuel is a finite resource. The used fuel is highly toxic waste that is difficult to properly dispose, and nuclear accidents are rare but can be very serious. As a result, nuclear power has both renewable and non-renewable elements. Nuclear power remains controversial as an energy source.

AGRICULTURAL PRACTICES

The Green Revolution brought about the introduction of new varieties of plants and farming methods in the 1950s, '60s, and '70s. Both developed and developing countries benefited from the Green Revolution, and it has caused a significant increase in food production. The Green Revolution came about as a cooperative venture between Western countries to increase productivity and relieve hunger in Mexico and India. High-yield varieties of wheat were developed that were more resistant to pests and diseases. These new crops along with irrigation techniques and chemicals (fertilizers, pesticides, and herbicides) increased food production; however, many farmers in Mexico and India still remained poor.

Over time, more high-yield crops such as rice, sorghum, corn, and beans were introduced. Intensive farming methods to relieve hunger in Latin America and Asia were created. The Green Revolution has not been successful in parts of the world where the climate is arid and irrigation is not possible, such as sub-Saharan Africa. The Green Revolution also made crops more dependent on chemicals, which caused environmental concerns. The crop yield has increased as a result of the Green Revolution, but it has not solved the problems of world hunger.

The basic unit of agriculture is the farm, where farmers must clear land, plant seed, grow crops, and harvest them. Resources like land, water, soil, and seeds must be managed and conserved. There are several different types of agricultural methods practiced throughout the world.

- **Shifting agriculture** is practiced in many areas of the world where soil conditions are poor and human populations are low. It involves the cutting down and burning of trees in small area forests. Once the nutrients in the soil are depleted, the site is abandoned. In some parts of the world with poor soil conditions, such as tropical forests, this method is still used successfully.

- **Labor-intensive agriculture** is practiced in areas of the world with better soil conditions. It is still practiced in much of the world today, and it involves the extensive use of manual labor. This allows for low use of fossil fuels, but a lot of effort goes into an uncertain crop yield. In developing countries, the cost of manual labor is low compared to the cost of mechanized farming equipment.

- **Mechanized agriculture** developed after the beginning of the Industrial Revolution. This type of farming requires large tracts of mostly level land so the machines can operate, and the same crop is planted in large areas to maximize efficiency. In this type of farming, machines and fossil fuels have replaced human labor.

Fertilizers are used to increase crop yields. They can be valuable because they replace nutrients in the soil that are removed by plants. Macronutrients are the three primary soil nutrients: nitrogen, phosphorus, and potassium. Other micronutrients are also present in fertilizers (zinc, boron, manganese). Chemical fertilizers replace inorganic nutrients, but not organic materials in soil. The decomposition of organic matter returns organic nutrients to the soil.

Alternative agriculture methods include sustainable agriculture, which does not deplete soil, water wildlife, or human resources; organic agriculture, which prohibits the use of some pesticides and fertilizers; and other alternative agriculture practices that include all nontraditional methods such as hydroponics. Modern, more efficient irrigation methods such as trickle or drip irrigation, help conserve water by minimizing evaporation.

Precision agriculture is a technique of farming that addresses the concerns of conventional agricultural practices, such as fertilizer runoff in water supplies, pesticides accumulating in food chains, and groundwater contaminated by fertilizers. Computer technology allows farmers to vary the amount of fertilizers applied to different places in a crop. Thus, farmers use less chemicals overall more effectively.

PESTICIDES AND PEST CONTROL

In addition to fertilizers, modern mechanized farming practices require other chemicals such as pesticides, insecticides, fungicides, denticides, and herbicides. These chemicals can cause damage to the environment and many species. The use of persistent pesticides, such as DDT or toxaphene, has been mostly banned because of hazardous impacts on wildlife. These pesticides do not break down in the environment and remain a threat to food chains for many years. Non-persistent pesticides such as organophosphates break down fairly rapidly. Pesticides often end up in nearby water supplies where they can be hazardous to aquatic life.

Another problem with pesticides is that pest populations such as insects, weeds, rodents, and fungi can become resistant to the chemicals. Over 500 species of insects have developed resistance to pesticides. Most pesticides are not specific to a particular organism and end up killing beneficial species as well as harmful ones.

There are also health concerns to humans who either apply pesticides or ingest foods with pesticide residues. For most people, the most critical health problems are related to exposure to small quantities over a long period of time. Many pesticides cause mutations, cancer, and abnormal offspring in experimental animals. Despite this, pesticide use in many countries continues to increase because more food can be produced with the use of pesticides, fewer crops are lost to pests, and less money is lost by farmers.

A controversial modern method of pest control is genetic modification, where certain plants have been genetically altered to deter insects on their own. In many cases, such modifications have significantly reduced the use of insecticides. The effect of genetic modifications to reduce the need for herbicides have had less obvious results. Many consumers reject genetically modified organisms (GMOs) and some countries require products containing GMOs to be specially labeled.

SOIL CONSERVATION AND LAND USE PRACTICES

Erosion is the wearing away of soil by water, wind, or ice, which is a natural process that has been accelerated by agricultural methods. Soil erosion takes place everywhere in the world, but some areas are more exposed and have a higher degree of erosion than others. Erosion occurs mostly in regions where vegetation has been removed. Deforestation and desertification leave land open to erosion.

In order to maintain the proper soil and nutrients for crop growth, land converted to agricultural use must experience only minimal soil erosion. Therefore, many techniques are used to protect soil from eroding and to minimize the loss of topsoil. Some soil quality management components include enhancement of organic matter, avoidance of excess tillage, efficient management of pests and soil nutrients, prevention of soil compaction, coverage of the ground so soil is not exposed, and diversification of cropping systems.

Several land use practices can also help to control soil erosion.

- **Contour farming**, or tilling at right angles to the slope of the land, is a simple method of preventing soil erosion and is useful on gentle slopes. Each ridge produced at right angles to the slope acts as a dam to prevent water from running down the slope. Therefore, more water soaks into the soil and less soil is washed away.

- **Strip farming** helps prevent erosion on longer or steeper slopes. Strips of closely sown crops are alternated with strips of row crops. The closely sown crops such as hay or wheat slow down the flow of water, reducing soil erosion.

- **Terracing** is a method of preventing soil erosion on steep land. Terraces are constructed at right angles to the slope.

- **Waterways** are depressions of land on sloped ground where water collects. Instead of allowing the land to remain bare, it should be properly maintained with a sod covering. Then, the speed of water flow is reduced and erosion is decreased.

- **Windbreaks** should be established to stop wind from eroding soil. Windbreaks are plantings of trees or other plants that protect soil from wind.

Methods of tilling the land, such as reduced tillage and conservation tillage, also help to reduce the amount of soil erosion. There are several variations of conservation tillage, including mulch tillage, strip tillage, ridge tillage, and no-till farming.

AIR POLLUTION CONTROL

Because humans produce air pollution, it can be controlled by changes in human activity. Motor vehicles (including ships and airplanes) are the primary cause of air pollution, including CO_2, carbon monoxide, volatile organic compounds, and nitrogen oxides (NOx). Ozone is a secondary pollutant of motor vehicle use. Even though newer cars emit less nitrogen oxides, the mileage that people drive each year has increased, so NOx emissions have stayed the same. Almost all other air pollutants have been reduced significantly. Catalytic converters and an end to leaded gasoline also drastically improved air quality from automobile emissions. In an effort to reduce emissions in the United States, the mandatory fuel efficient standard for cars has slowly increased. Some manufacturers have introduced low or even zero emissions vehicles that rely partially or completely on electricity instead of fossil fuels.

Vehicle emissions can also be reduced through more compact development, improved mass transit, the increased cost of driving through tolls, or even direct bans on driving. Some Chinese cities only allow cars with even numbered license plates to drive some days and odd numbered plates to drive on other days as a way to lower the overall number of cars on the road.

Particulate matter emissions come from industrial activities, mining, farming, and the transfer of grain and coal. Improper land use is also a major source of airborne particulates, as is the burning of fossil fuels and wood. Technological fixes such as scrubbers are used by industries to trap particulate matter so it does not escape from smokestacks, but smaller particles that form sulfur dioxide and nitrogen oxides can still escape.

Power plant emissions of sulfur dioxide are also a cause of air pollution. Switching to the use of low-sulfur coal decreases emissions by about 66 percent. Switching to oil, natural gas, or nuclear fuels reduces emissions even more. It is also possible to reduce the sulfur in coal before it is used, but this process is costly and would drive up the cost of electricity. One benefit of these changes is a major reduction in acid rain.

Various policies aim to curb air pollution, such as regulations requiring natural gas refineries to reduce methane leakage.

DRINKING WATER QUALITY AND SUPPLY

Drinking water supplies in the United States come mainly from municipal sources. About 37 percent of municipal water comes from wells, and the rest is surface water contained in reservoirs. In rural areas, residents obtain water from private wells.

To ensure water quality safety, water is treated by the following processes: raw water is filtered through sand or other substrates to remove particulate matter; chemicals are added to remove dissolved particles; and water is disinfected with chlorine, ozone, or UV light to remove organisms. When fresh water is scarce, saltwater can be treated through desalination processes and made suitable for drinking.

WASTEWATER TREATMENT

Wastewater consists of storm water runoff, waste from industry, and domestic wastewater. Domestic waste consists primarily of organic matter from food preparation; garbage; washing clothes, dishes, and cars; and human waste. All wastewater must be cleaned before it is released, and, therefore, most municipalities and industries have wastewater treatment facilities.

Sewage treatment is classified as primary, secondary, and tertiary.

- **Primary** sewage treatment is a physical process that removes larger particles by filtering water through large screens and smaller particles by allowing them to settle out of the water as it sits in large tanks or lagoons. Water is removed from above the settled particles and is either released back into the environment or to another treatment stage.

- **Secondary** sewage treatment involves the holding of wastewater until all of the organic matter dissolved in the water is degraded by bacteria and other microorganisms. To promote the growth of microorganisms during this treatment stage, wastewater is mixed with highly oxygenated water, or it is aerated directly with a trickling filter system. Microorganisms eventually settle out of the water in the form of sewage sludge. Water and sludge are separated, and the water is disinfected, usually with chlorine, before it is released.

- **Tertiary** treatment involves techniques to remove inorganic nutrients such as phosphorus and nitrogen in the water that could potentially increase aquatic plant growth.

SOLID AND HAZARDOUS WASTE

Solid waste is garbage, sludge, refuse or any other discarded material resulting from industrial, agricultural, commercial mining, or municipal process. Solid waste can be solid, but it can also be liquid, semisolid, or even partially gaseous. Nations with high standards of living generally produce more solid waste than less developed nations.

There are several ways that humans dispose of solid waste. Landfills have been the primary means of solid waste disposal. Municipal solid waste landfills are constructed above impermeable clay layers lined with impermeable membranes. Each layer of garbage is covered with fresh soil to keep it from blowing away and to discourage scavengers. Contaminated water is trapped by leachate bottom layers. Decomposing waste does produce methane, which can be captured for use as an energy source.

Burning refuse in incinerators is another disposal method. Most incinerators are designed to capture thermal energy to make steam that is then used to produce electricity. Organic solid waste can be mulched or composted, and then reused in enriching soils or landscaping. Many municipalities now have composting facilities.

Hazardous wastes are by-products of certain industrial, business, or domestic activities that cannot be disposed of by normal measures. Waste is defined as hazardous if it causes or contributes to an increase in mortality or serious illness, or if it poses a serious threat to human health or the environment.

Hazardous waste ranges from waste containing dioxins and heavy metals to organic wastes. Hazardous waste can be liquid or in the form of batteries, computer parts, or CFL light bulbs.

Once a hazardous material has been identified, government agencies such as the Food and Drug Administration (FDA) and Occupational Safety and Health Administration (OSHA) determine acceptable exposure limits to the materials. Hazardous wastes can enter the environment, for example, by evaporating into the atmosphere or leaking through faulty pipes or improper disposal. Industries are now required to report the level of hazardous toxic waste released into the atmosphere.

Management of hazardous waste materials has become part of industrial processes, but the best way to deal with it is not to produce hazardous waste materials in the first place. The two most common methods of disposing of hazardous waste are incineration and land disposal, with land disposal being the primary disposal method.

Land disposal is carried out in four different ways:

1. Deep-well injection
2. Discharge of treated and untreated liquids into sewers or waterways
3. Placement of liquid or sludge in surface pits or lagoons
4. Storage of solid waste in specially designed landfills

RECYCLING AND RESOURCE RECOVERY

Recycling efforts, including composting of organic materials, vary around the world. As of 2015, the United States recycled about 34 percent of its waste; Germany had one of the highest rates at 62 percent. In the United States, container laws set in 1972 have provided an economic incentive to recycle. These laws include a two- to five-cent deposit on all recyclable beverage containers. This law reduced beverage container litter by almost 50 percent. Mandatory recycling laws are in effect in many cities and states. Municipalities often provide recycling containers and curbside recycling to assist residents.

Although recycling programs have been successful at reducing waste, there are some economic and technical problems associated with recycling. For example, plastics are recyclable, but each type of plastic requires different recycling methods, and, therefore, all plastics cannot be recycled together. Also, recycling of materials has produced an overabundance of those materials, especially in developing nations.

To help reduce waste, people can buy materials that last, have goods repaired instead of discarding them, buy items that are reusable or recyclable, buy beverages in reusable glass containers, take reusable lunchboxes instead of paper bags, use rechargeable batteries, reduce the use of disposable bags, separate recyclables from trash, recycle all recyclable materials, choose items with minimal packaging, compost organic materials, and use electronic sources as opposed to paper sources. Most effective of all, people can try to consume less overall.

ENVIRONMENTAL RISK ASSESSMENT

Risk to the environment from human activities can be determined through identifying potential hazards and the consequences of these hazards. The magnitude and probability of the consequences also need to be considered when assessing risk. Finally, there needs to be an evaluation of the risk, also known as **risk characterization**. A concept frequently used in environmental risk assessment is that of source-pathway-receptor. The pathway between a hazard (source) and a receptor (i.e., ecosystem) is investigated. If no pathway exists, then there is no risk to the environment. If a pathway links a source to a receptor, then the consequences need to be assessed.

SOCIAL PROCESSES AND THE ENVIRONMENT

Approximately 20 percent of the questions on the DSST Environmental Science exam will cover topics under the umbrella of social processes and the environment.

ENVIRONMENTAL JUSTICE

Environmental justice is the idea that everyone is entitled to a clean environment regardless of race, income, class, or any other factor. Environmental responsibilities and benefits should be shared equally among all people.

All too often, the burden of environmental hazards falls most heavily on low-income communities, often racial or ethnic minorities. Polluting factories or waste sites are more likely to be located in low-income areas. In the United States, rates of asthma are much higher among communities of color, a trend partially attributable to greater exposure to outdoor and indoor air pollution. Much of the world's electronics recycling and disposal takes place in developing nations in West Africa, where low-wage workers extract valuable components without proper safety procedures or equipment. Across the world, low-income areas often lack political influence to successfully advocate for a clean and safe environment.

The Memphis Sanitation Strike of 1968 is seen as the first major environmental justice action in the United States. The 2014 Flint Water Crisis, where the city of Flint, Michigan, endured excessive lead in their drinking water supply, is a recent environmental justice concern.

Today, most federal and state environmental agencies are aware of the environmental justice problem and have initiated procedures, policies, and working groups such as the National Environmental Justice Advisory Council (NEJAC) to try and address the disparity. Despite the awareness, environmental justice continues to be a major problem in the United States, and other countries.

POLICY, PLANNING, AND DECISION MAKING

In the United States, the turn of the 20th century marked the beginning of federal policy to protect and conserve the environment. The Lacey Act, enacted in 1900, is considered the first environmental law in the United States, and was passed in response to widespread poaching and illegal wildlife harvesting. The act prohibits trade in illegally taken fish, wildlife, or plant products. A major turning point in the conservation of open space was the designation of protected state and national parks beginning in the late 19th century.

The publication of Rachel Carson's *Silent Spring* is considered the beginning of the modern environmental movement. In 1970, with the advent of Earth Day and mounting public concern for the environment, the United States began to address some of the most obvious and pressing environmental problems. Over the last 45 years, important environmental laws, like the Clean Air Acts, Clean Water Acts, Resource Conservation and Recovery Act, Energy Policy Act, land use conservation acts and more, have helped to protect the environment, wildlife species, and human populations. Many of these laws have been amended multiple times.

One notable act is the Comprehensive Environmental Response, Compensation, and Liability Act of 1980, also known as the Superfund. This act's main purpose is to clean up abandoned or unmonitored hazardous waste sites, and where possible, identify the party responsible for polluting the site and have them pay for the cleanup. Abandoned site cleanups are paid for out of a trust fund established by the act.

The Endangered Species Act (ESA), signed in 1973, provides legal protection to threatened species including their habitat and ecosystems. Species are covered by the act after a review.

Until 1970, most federal agencies acted within their authority without considering the environment, but the National Environmental Policy Act (NEPA) was designed to institutionalize within the federal government a concern for the environment. As a result of NEPA, many states have instituted stronger state environmental policy acts (SEPA). States may set and enforce their own environmental laws in addition to any federal laws. Congress established the Environmental Protection Agency (EPA) in 1970. The EPA helps to shape environmental laws and controls the daily operations of industries and regulates the agencies authorized to protect the environment, often in concert with state regulators. Water quality standards (for non–drinking water), for example, are set by states, subject to EPA approval. The EPA also has direct control over several aspects of the environment, including the research and regulation of pesticides. Drinking water standards are also set directly by the EPA under the Safe Drinking Water Act.

GLOBAL ENVIRONMENTAL GOVERNANCE

Environmental concerns are a growing factor in international relations. Policies related to health, environmental, and natural resource concerns are beginning to enter the mainstream of political policies. There are many international institutions that address the global environment by gathering and evaluating environmental data, helping to develop international treaties, and providing funding and loans to developing countries.

Perhaps the most influential organization that has helped shape environmental policy is the United Nations (UN). The UN has 21 agencies that deal with environmental issues. Organizations formed under the UN include the UN Environment Programme (UNEP), the World Health Organization (WHO), the UN Development Programme (UNDP), and the Food and Agriculture Organization (FAO). However, some agencies fail to make significant progress because they are controlled by members with competing interests. Other institutions don't succeed because they are unable to address issues in their totality. For example, the World Bank can only address issues of air pollution and biodiversity for development projects that rely on funds from the World Bank.

Other organizations that influence environmental decisions are the Global Environment Facility (GEF) and the World Conservation Union (IUCN). All of these and other organizations have played a role in the following:

- Expanding the understanding of environmental issues
- Gathering and evaluating environmental data
- Developing international environmental treaties
- Providing funds for sustainable economic development in an attempt to reduce poverty
- Helping over 100 nations develop environmental laws and regulations

The International Organization for Standardization (ISO) was established in 1947 in Geneva to promote the development of voluntary standards for international trade. The ISO is a nongovernmental organization (NGO) that has developed over 10,000 standards that govern products. In the early 1990s, ISO began to work on standards for environmental management. These standards aim to do the following:

- Improve the understanding of the environmental impact of activities
- Have businesses comply with environmental regulations
- Prevent pollution
- Audit performance of businesses
- Set the standard of disclosing information about a business' environmental policy to the public

Despite tensions between domestic concerns, international relations, and environmental issues, there have been several successful international conventions and treaties that deal with the environment.

In 1987, the Montreal Protocol helped to start a decrease in CFCs in the atmosphere. The Earth Summit in 1992 aimed to develop better integration of national environmental goals with their economic goals. This summit led to the development of 27 principles to guide the behavior of nations toward better environmentally sustainable patterns; the adoption of Agenda 21; and a statement of principles for a global consensus on the management, conservation, and sustainable development of all types of forests. Later conferences have been less successful, with the major developing nations of China and India as well as the United States refusing to sign the Kyoto Protocol of 1997, while Canada withdrew in 2012. They Kyoto Protocol had some successes but did not succeed in lowering the global output of greenhouse emissions.

In 2016, 166 nations signed the Paris Agreement, where signing countries voluntarily agreed to each enact their own plan to reduce emissions to an increasingly low target. There was great flexibility in how a country might meet its emissions target, and there is no mechanism for enforcement or penalties if a target is not met. The United States withdrew from the agreement in 2017.

Like the Paris Agreement, most international environmental agreements are voluntary, in that countries must agree to participate. Most agreements are structured such that each individual participating nation has to set its own mechanisms and laws to meet the conditions of the agreement; the agreement does not replace national laws. Examples of international agreements structured this way are the 1995 Convention on Biological Diversity (CBD) or the Convention on International Trade in Endangered Species (CITES). In the case of CITES, several signatory nations do not have sufficient legal penalties to deter the illegal wildlife trade.

The world's oceans also provide areas of international cooperation. By the Law of the Sea, each coastal nation is allowed exclusive access to the waters up to 200 miles outwards from their coastline. The Law of the Sea treaty also provides guidelines for pollution prevention, marine research, and fisheries management, among others areas of international concern. Another example is the international ban on commercial whaling by the International Whaling Commission (IWC), enacted in 1986 and still in force despite several attempts to overturn it. There are also efforts to establish international marine protected areas (MPAs).

The European Union also works to maintain strict environmental standards for European countries. By 2000, more than 12 countries had adopted the policy of providing consumers with informational labels that enable them to be "green" consumers. Major corporations increasingly operate across national borders and have a major role to play in global conservation.

DIFFERING CULTURAL AND SOCIETAL VALUES

Many people, either within the same culture or in different cultures, differ in their views about the environment. People with widely different worldviews can examine the same data and arrive at different conclusions because they view the problem with different assumptions and values. Some environmental worldviews are human-centered, whereas others are life-centered.

According to the human-centered worldview, humans are the most important species and should manage Earth to their benefit, no matter how it might affect other species. Another human-centered view is the stewardship worldview, in which it is believed that humans have the responsibility to care for and manage the Earth. According to this view, we are borrowing resources from the Earth and have the ethical responsibility to leave the Earth in at least as good a condition as we now enjoy.

Those with a life-centered worldview believe we have an ethical responsibility—not just for humans, but for all species—not to degrade Earth's ecosystems, biodiversity, and biosphere.

Which worldview a person possesses is to a large extent personal, but economic development can play a role. Many developing countries, aware that other developing countries already spent decades or centuries degrading their environment to reach their current level of development, often feel that they should have the ability to take the same path and develop to a high level before worrying as much about environmental concerns. It is also more difficult to worry about broader environmental damage when immediate survival is a concern. Poverty can drive a human-centered view and sometimes contributes to more harmful development practices.

The message of environmentalism for the future should be one of hope. It calls for a commitment to overcoming today's challenges regarding the environment with respect to world population, pollution, energy sources, and food supplies. The environmental revolution that many environmental scientists hope to achieve in this century has the following components:

- A biodiversity protection revolution
- An efficiency revolution
- A sufficiency revolution
- An energy revolution
- A pollution prevention revolution
- A demographic revolution
- An economic and political revolution

SUMMING IT UP

- **Ecosystems** are a complex network of interrelationships between abiotic and biotic factors.

- A **community** consists of all interacting populations of various species living in a given area at the same time.

- There are three types of organisms in organism relationships: **predation**, **competition**, and **symbiosis**.

- There are three broad categories of organisms: **producers**, **consumers**, and **decomposers**.

- All organisms occupy one or more **trophic** levels, and available energy decreases as the trophic level increases.

- A **food chain** or **food web** describes the relationship of organisms within an ecosystem.

- **Biogeochemical cycling** is the process by which the most fit and best adapted members of a species survive and reproduce.

- **Succession** is a series of changes that ecosystems go through in order to maintain the stability of a community.

- **Biomes** are climax communities that are distributed around the world. In general, the structure of ecosystems within a given type of biome is similar.

- **Aquatic ecosystems** are shaped by the ability of the sun's energy to reach organisms below the water's surface, the depth to the bottom, the water's temperature, the amount of salts dissolved in the water, and the nature of the body of water.

- **Population biology** is concerned with the characterization of the make-up, growth, and impact of a population on the environment and its organisms.

- Earth's **atmosphere** is 78.1 percent nitrogen, 20.9 percent oxygen, and 1 percent other gases, including carbon dioxide, methane, and water vapor.

- There are four layers in Earth's atmosphere: **troposphere**, **stratosphere**, **mesosphere**, and **thermosphere**.

- **Human population growth** has a significant impact on the environment and a country's resources.

- **Developed** countries tend to have **low** rates of population growth, and **developing** countries tend to have **higher** rates of population growth.

- **Pollution** is a form of matter or energy that harms the environment.

- The **ozone layer** is necessary to block harmful UV light, but it is slowly being depleted by human activities.

- The **greenhouse effect** is necessary to keep Earth's temperature warm enough to sustain life. Since the Industrial Revolution, the concentration of **greenhouse gases** has increased in the atmosphere, increasing the amount of heat being absorbed. The increase in the Earth's surface temperature will have a variety of impacts on climate and local weather. The effects will not be identical across the planet.

- The **Industrial Revolution** brought about the use of coal as a fuel source and the advent of machines, both of which caused a significant increase in pollution.

- **The Agricultural Revolution** developed techniques of growing larger quantities of food, especially after the invention of mechanized farm equipment.

- Agricultural practices can lead to **deforestation** and **desertification**, especially in developing countries. Agricultural and industrial runoff can lead to the process of **eutrophication** in aquatic environments. Improper waste disposal can also destroy habitat.

- **Nonrenewable energy sources** constitute 86.5 percent of the world's energy consumption, and only 13.5 percent of our energy comes from renewable sources.

- **The Green Revolution** introduced new, faster growing and hardier plant varieties and improved farming methods. High yields were achieved through the use of chemical fertilizers, pesticides, and herbicides.

- Agricultural practices are dependent on soil type, land conditions, and economic conditions. **Fertilizers** increase crop yield, but they cause problems to the environment. **Pesticides** increase crop yield, but they are harmful to the environment and to humans and other species. **Alternative agricultural methods** aim to preserve the environment by using fewer or no chemicals.

- **Erosion** is a natural process, but some land use practices can accelerate erosion. Other practices help to control erosion.

- Human activity produces **air pollution**, but humans can help to control air pollution by changing activities and practices.

- **Water treatment techniques** are used to provide safe, clean drinking water and to clean up wastewater before it is released back into the environment. Solid and hazardous waste is disposed of in landfills or incinerated.

- **Recycling** helps to reduce the amount of solid waste, but there are some technical and economic problems associated with recycling.

- **Environmental justice** is the equal access to a clean and healthy environment regardless of income, race, creed, or any other factor. Low income, minority, and other marginalized communities often suffer the worst consequences from inadequate environmental protection. Governments are starting to address these concerns.

- **Environmental policy** consists of laws, rules, and regulations developed by government organizations to solve environmental problems. Both states and the federal government are involved.

- **International environmental policies** are established by the United Nations and other world organizations.

- People view environmental issues as **human-centered, stewardship-centered**, or **life-centered** issues.

ENVIRONMENTAL SCIENCE POST-TEST

Directions: Carefully read each of the following 60 questions. Choose the best answer to each question and fill in the corresponding circle on the answer sheet. The Answer Key and Explanations can be found following this post-test.

1. Which of the following is a predicted impact of global climate change?
   A. Greater sea ice cover at the North Pole
   B. Increased acid deposition
   C. More intense storms
   D. Ozone depletion

2. Which of the following is an essential practice in maintaining good soil quality for farming?
   A. Keeping the ground covered
   B. Keeping crops consistent
   C. Tilling the land frequently
   D. Compacting the soil

3. What would the population profile look like in a country in the first stage of the demographic transition?
   A. Many children, intermediate number of working-age adults, fewer elderly
   B. Many adults, fewer children, fewer elderly
   C. Few children, few working-age adults, many elderly
   D. Many adults, many children, more elderly

4. One consequence of introducing agricultural technology to a developing country is
   A. an increased carrying capacity.
   B. a decreased carrying capacity.
   C. a steady carrying capacity.
   D. no effect on carrying capacity.

5. Degradation of ecosystems and loss of bio-diversity in emerging nations is most often due to
   A. overgrowth of vegetation.
   B. development.
   C. flooding.
   D. poor soil quality.

6. Which of the following gases is thought to be a major contributor to the effect of global climate change?
   A. NO_2
   B. SO_2
   C. CO_2
   D. O_3

7. Where is secondary succession likely to occur?
   A. On a bare rock surface
   B. Land covered by floods
   C. Islands created by volcanoes
   D. A sandy beach

8. Mycorrhizal fungi live among plant roots, increasing nutrient and water access for the plants in exchange for carbohydrates. Such a relationship is best described as
   A. mutualism.
   B. commensalism.
   C. parasitism.
   D. competition.

9. Which of the following is an example of a life-centered worldview?
   A. Maintaining protected areas for wildlife
   B. Providing financial subsidies for industry
   C. Teaching sustainable development in schools
   D. Providing forested land free to farmers

10. Which of the following is generally true about soil erosion?
    A. The amount of topsoil remains relatively constant over long periods of time.
    B. Soil is eroding faster than it forms.
    C. There are no effective methods to prevent soil erosion.
    D. As soil erodes, new soil replaces it.

11. Which of the following is the correct order in a simple four-step food chain?
    A. Producer, tertiary consumer, secondary consumer, primary consumer
    B. Primary consumer, secondary consumer, tertiary consumer, producer
    C. Producer, primary consumer, secondary consumer, tertiary consumer
    D. Tertiary consumer, secondary consumer, primary consumer, producer

12. Which of the following is an example of a point source of water pollution?
    A. Urban street runoff
    B. A discharge pipe
    C. Acid rain
    D. Eroding stream banks

13. Which of the following is NOT an environmental justice issue?
    A. A new landfill placed in a lower-income community
    B. Exporting hazardous waste to a developing nation
    C. A new corporate headquarters located in an urban area
    D. Poor water quality in a predominantly minority area

14. The living components of an ecosystem are called
    A. biotic factors.
    B. abiotic factors.
    C. environmental factors.
    D. biosphere factors.

15. The ozone layer is a necessary part of the atmosphere protecting Earth's surface from
    A. meteors.
    B. air pollution.
    C. carbon monoxide.
    D. ultraviolet light.

16. What percent of the world's electrical power comes from nonrenewable energy sources and nuclear energy?
    A. 91 percent
    B. 87 percent
    C. 9 percent
    D. 4 percent

17. What is one potential consequence of unequal access to a clean environment?
    A. Nuclear accidents
    B. Declining availability of landfill space
    C. Dirty fuel power plants
    D. Higher rates of respiratory disease

18. Which phenomenon is necessary to keep Earth warm enough to sustain life?
    A. Biodiversity
    B. Global warming
    C. The greenhouse effect
    D. Depleting ozone layer

19. A primary goal of the Superfund is to
    A. clean up hazardous waste sites.
    B. apply certain requirements to storm water discharge.
    C. prohibit ocean dumping.
    D. gain control of point source pollution.

20. In a temperate deciduous forest, maple trees, birds, and squirrels all live in the same given area. All three species together make up a/an
    A. ecosystem.
    B. community.
    C. population.
    D. niche.

21. The total fertility rate of a population is the
    A. number of births and deaths.
    B. fertility rate necessary to replace a generation.
    C. number of children born to each woman in her lifetime.
    D. number of women of childbearing age.

22. Which of the following is an example of a persistent pesticide?
    A. DDT
    B. Diazinon
    C. Organophosphates
    D. Carbamates

23. What is one way that differing social views might make environmental protection decisions more difficult?
    A. People with opposing viewpoints cooperate easily.
    B. People with opposing viewpoints come to identical conclusions from the same information.
    C. People with opposing viewpoints always find common ground.
    D. People with opposing viewpoints can reach opposite conclusions using the same information.

24. Which of the following is NOT a feature of evolution?
    A. Limiting factors
    B. Extinction
    C. Genetic variation
    D. Natural selection

25. Which biome harbors the fewest species of plants?
    A. Tropical rainforest
    B. Tundra
    C. Wetlands
    D. Desert

26. In 1992, the Earth Summit aimed to develop a better integration of each country's environmental and
    A. ecological goals.
    B. biodiversity goals.
    C. economic goals.
    D. agricultural goals.

27. Which federal agency regulates the use of pesticides?
    A. Department of Agriculture
    B. Environmental Protection Agency
    C. National Institutes of Health
    D. Food and Drug Administration

post-test

28. Which of the following is an example of interspecific competition?
    A. Moss-tree
    B. Shark-remora
    C. Tapeworm-dog
    D. Hawk-owl

29. Which of the following are among the first organisms that may appear in secondary succession?
    A. Grasses
    B. Autotrophs
    C. Lichen
    D. Shrubs

30. Mass production contributed most to which major environmental concern?
    A. Habitat destruction
    B. Global climate change
    C. Solid waste
    D. Water pollution

31. Which fuel source can be produced from biomass materials that contain cellulose or starch?
    A. Carbon dioxide
    B. Coal
    C. Ethanol
    D. Oil

32. Improvements to the combustion engine have decreased which type of air pollution?
    A. Sulfur dioxide
    B. Volatile organic compounds
    C. Oxides of nitrogen
    D. Carbon monoxide

33. Which of the following is a possible difficulty of recycling plastics?
    A. It requires fossil fuels.
    B. It causes an increase in pollution.
    C. All types of plastic cannot be recycled by the same methods.
    D. Most municipalities do not recycle plastic.

34. Which of the following is NOT a source of acid deposition?
    A. Automobiles
    B. Trees
    C. Farm animals
    D. Factories

35. Which of the following statements most accurately describes the role of nitrifying-fixing bacteria in the nitrogen cycle?
    A. It converts ammonia to nitrites and nitrates.
    B. It converts nitrites to nitrogen gas.
    C. It incorporates nitrates into amino acid.
    D. It converts nitrogen gas into ammonia.

36. Which of the following is indicative of a high genetic diversity in a given population?
    A. Varied structures and abilities
    B. Uniform structures and abilities
    C. Highly evolved individuals
    D. Varied ecosystems

37. Which would be the best way to help permanently ensure environmental justice for a low-income community?
    A. Increase political representation
    B. Change zoning laws
    C. Provide free bottled water
    D. Retrofit old buildings

38. Organisms that obtain nutrition at all trophic levels are
    A. producers.
    B. carnivores.
    C. decomposers.
    D. herbivores.

39. The exploitation of minerals in oceans is controlled by the
    A. United Nations.
    B. Clean Water Act.
    C. Resource Conservation and Recovery Act.
    D. Law of the Sea.

40. Which of the following processes provides usable energy to producers?
    A. Photosynthesis
    B. Cellular respiration
    C. Digestion
    D. Osmosis

41. Which process of irrigation conserves the most water?
    A. Gravity-flow irrigation
    B. Flood irrigation
    C. Trickle irrigation
    D. Center-pivot irrigation

42. Which listed feature is the defining characteristic of a desert biome?
    A. High temperature
    B. Low biodiversity
    C. Sand dunes
    D. Low rainfall

43. Surface mining regulations require that land damaged from the effects of surface mining must be
    A. filled with topsoil when the mine is shut down.
    B. replanted with vegetation.
    C. converted to an artificial lake.
    D. cleaned and decontaminated.

44. What is the primary mechanism for setting standards for non-drinking water?
    A. The EPA sets all water quality standards.
    B. Standards are set only at the state level.
    C. The EPA approves each state's standards.
    D. Standards are set directly by an act of Congress.

45. Which of the following is an international organization that plays a major role in environmental conservation?
    A. CITES
    B. IUCN
    C. EPA
    D. UNICEF

46. Which act sets environmental policies at the state level?
    A. NEPA
    B. SEPA
    C. CERCLA
    D. CBD

47. Which of the following is a feature of sustainable agriculture?
    A. Planting multiple crops in the same field
    B. Use of fertilizers to increase crop growth
    C. Only planting in a field every other year
    D. Practicing monoculture

48. An endangered marine fish in coastal waters is protected by which law(s)?
    A. State law
    B. Marine Mammal Protection Act
    C. ESA
    D. Law of the Sea

49. Which of the following concepts is frequently used in environmental risk assessment?
    A. Pollution control
    B. Damage control
    C. Source-pathway-receptor
    D. Source-pathway-control

50. Two types of beetles live on the trunks of dead trees. Which best explains why brown beetles survive over green beetles in that situation?
    A. Green beetles taste better to birds.
    B. Brown beetles are less visible, so birds do not see them.
    C. Brown beetles reproduce faster than green beetles.
    D. It happens by chance.

51. The stewardship worldview of environmentalism maintains that
    A. we must consider our neighbors' well-being.
    B. we must care for all living creatures no matter how small.
    C. we have a responsibility to care for Earth so it is preserved for future generations.
    D. we are completely dependent on nature for our survival.

52. The first significant increase in atmospheric CO_2 levels is linked to
    A. the thinning ozone layer above Antarctica.
    B. the warming of ocean temperatures.
    C. an increase in vegetation on Earth.
    D. the Industrial Revolution.

53. Which scientific practice yields plants with desired traits?
    A. Mutation
    B. Selective crossbreeding
    C. Chemical enhancement
    D. Sustainable farming

54. Human populations can best be described as
    A. r-strategists.
    B. l-strategists.
    C. k-strategists.
    D. survivalists.

55. Which of the following describes the method of contour farming?
    A. Tilling only in a narrow region that is to receive seeds while all other soil is undisturbed
    B. Farming at right angles to a slope of land
    C. Diversifying crops planted in given area
    D. Leaving a ridge the previous year and planting the new crop in the ridge

56. What is one environmental problem that arose from the Agricultural Revolution?
    A. Soil erosion
    B. Air pollution
    C. Poor crop yield
    D. Increase in pests

57. Which of the following describes limiting factors?
    A. A factor that determines the fertility rate of an organism
    B. Always an intrinsic factor
    C. An environmental factor that determines size of a population
    D. Independent of the environment

58. The largest proportion of deforestation is caused by
    A. acid rain.
    B. drought.
    C. agricultural development.
    D. forest fires.

59. Which energy source can be obtained from a landfill?

- **A.** Ethane
- **B.** Hydrogen
- **C.** Methane
- **D.** Steam

60. In which area of the world listed below is desertification most prevalent?

- **A.** Western United States
- **B.** Northern Africa
- **C.** Eastern Europe
- **D.** Central America

post-test

ANSWER KEY AND EXPLANATIONS

1. C	13. C	25. B	37. A	49. C
2. A	14. A	26. C	38. C	50. B
3. A	15. D	27. B	39. D	51. C
4. A	16. A	28. D	40. A	52. D
5. B	17. D	29. A	41. C	53. B
6. C	18. C	30. C	42. D	54. C
7. B	19. A	31. C	43. B	55. B
8. A	20. B	32. D	44. C	56. A
9. A	21. C	33. C	45. B	57. C
10. B	22. A	34. C	46. B	58. C
11. C	23. D	35. A	47. A	59. C
12. B	24. A	36. A	48. C	60. B

1. **The correct answer is C.** Storms are predicted to increase in strength as a result of global climate change since there will be warmer ocean waters providing more energy to feed them. Note that it is difficult to link the strength of any given storm to climate change. Choice A is incorrect since ice cover is decreasing at the poles, not increasing. Choices B and D are incorrect since both acid deposition and ozone depletion are concerns that are mostly unrelated to greenhouse gases or climate change.

2. **The correct answer is A.** Bare soil is susceptible to wind and water erosion, so groundcover protects soil, provides habitats for larger soil organisms like earthworms, and can improve water availability to surrounding areas. Choice B is incorrect because the practice of crop rotation, rather than planting the same crop each year, is more beneficial to the soil. Choice C is incorrect because frequent tilling is actually damaging to soil and should be avoided. Choice D is incorrect because compaction reduces the amount of air, water, and space available to plant roots and soil organisms, so it should be avoided in order to maintain soil quality.

3. **The correct answer is A.** The first stage of the demographic transition is marked by high birthrates and high death rates. Such populations will have many young children but fewer elderly people. Choice B is characteristic of a country much later in the transition when birthrates have started to drop but the population has not yet begun to age. Choice C is a population in which birthrates have fallen below replacement level and adults are aging faster than more children are born. Choice D is a population in stage 2 of the transition, when birthrates are still high but death rates have fallen.

4. **The correct answer is A.** The carrying capacity within an environment can increase through advances in agricultural technology. Choice B is incorrect because the introduction of agricultural technology would increase, not decrease, the carrying capacity. Choice C is incorrect because there would be a continual increase in carrying capacity, not a leveling off. Choice D is incorrect because agricultural technology would affect the carrying capacity in a positive way.

5. **The correct answer is B.** Development, whether for industry or urban growth, in emerging nations can lead to loss of biodiversity and ecosystem degradation. Choice A is incorrect because an overgrowth of vegetation, even if it replaces native habitat, is still a typically better habitat than land that is built upon. Choice C is incorrect because flooding is not the major cause of loss of biodiversity or ecosystem degradation in emerging nations. Choice D is incorrect because poor soil quality is a possible consequence of industrial development.

6. **The correct answer is C.** Carbon dioxide (CO_2) is the most abundant of greenhouse gases, and it is thought to be a major contributor to global climate change. Choice A is incorrect because nitrous oxide, not nitrogen dioxide, is a greenhouse gas. Choice B is incorrect because sulfur dioxide is produced when fossil fuels are burned, and it is not a greenhouse gas. Choice D is incorrect because ozone is not a greenhouse gas, so it doesn't contribute to global climate change.

7. **The correct answer is B.** Secondary succession begins with the disturbance of an existing ecosystem. Floodwaters can cause heavy damage to ecosystems, providing an opening for new types of plant growth. Choices A, C, and D are not the best answers because these are all areas where there is likely a lack of organisms and primary succession would occur first.

8. **The correct answer is A.** The relationship is mutualistic when both species benefit from the relationship. Fungi and plant roots both benefit from the association. The fungus obtains organic materials from the plant roots, and the branched nature of the fungus assists the plant in obtaining nutrients from the soil. Choice B is incorrect because in this relationship only one organism benefits, while the other is unaffected. Choice C is incorrect because in this relationship, one organism obtains nourishment from a host organism, but in the process it may harm the host. Choice D is incorrect because the relationship doesn't represent a competition between the two species.

9. **The correct answer is A.** The life-centered view believes that there is an obligation to protect the biosphere and all the life in it; protected areas such as wildlife preserves would aid in that goal. Choices B and D are examples of a human-centered view. Choice C is an action that would be part of a stewardship view.

10. **The correct answer is B.** Every year, erosion carries away more topsoil than is formed; this occurs mostly because of agricultural practices that often leave soil unprotected from wind and water. Choice A is incorrect because some regions of the world lose significant amounts of soil over time. Choice C is incorrect because environmental scientists and conservationists work to reduce soil loss through many different soil conservation methods that have been effective in slowing the rate of erosion. Choice D is incorrect because soil erodes faster than it is replaced in nature.

11. **The correct answer is C.** The correct order of steps in a typical food chain is producer, primary consumer herbivore, secondary consumer omnivore or carnivore, tertiary consumer carnivore, and decomposer. Choices A, B, and D are incorrect because none of them represent the correct order of a typical food chain.

12. **The correct answer is B.** A discharge pipe is a point source of water pollution because the source of pollution is readily identified. Choices A, C, and D are incorrect because these are all examples of nonpoint sources of water pollution.

13. **The correct answer is C.** A corporate headquarters may be a boon to a local economy with minimal environmental impact. Such projects are usually sought out by municipal authorities and such development is not an environmental justice issue. Choices A, B, and D all involve conditions that might be hazardous to the environment or human health where the consequences are borne by a low-income or marginalized population.

14. **The correct answer is A.** Biotic factors are living organisms that interact with the environment. Choice B is incorrect because abiotic factors are nonliving components of an ecosystem; they are the matter, energy, and surrounding space that help to shape an environment. Choice C is incorrect because an environment encompasses all living and nonliving things interacting together. Choice D is incorrect because a biosphere is defined as the life zone of the Earth and includes all living organisms.

15. **The correct answer is D.** The ozone layer shields Earth from the harmful effects of ultraviolet light radiation. An intact ozone layer absorbs approximately 99 percent of ultraviolet (UV) light and prevents it from reaching Earth's surface. Choice A is incorrect because the ozone layer doesn't block meteor showers from reaching Earth. Choice B is incorrect because air pollution is found below the ozone layer of the atmosphere. Choice C is incorrect because carbon monoxide is a pollutant released into the atmosphere by activities on Earth's surface.

16. **The correct answer is A.** Nonrenewable fossil fuels and nuclear power provide 91 percent of the world's energy (87 percent fossil fuels, 4 percent nuclear). Choice B is incorrect because 87 percent of energy comes from nonrenewable energy sources alone. Choice C is incorrect because about 9 percent of the world's energy comes from renewable sources at this time, most of it hydroelectric. Choice D is incorrect because 4 percent of energy comes from nuclear energy alone.

17. **The correct answer is D.** Unequal access to a clean environment means some communities, usually low-income or minority communities, can experience more harm, such as respiratory disease from exposure to air pollution. Choice A, nuclear accidents, are an environmental justice issue if the accident only impacts certain populations. Choices B and C are not automatically problems that impact some communities more than others, but certainly they can be.

18. **The correct answer is C.** The greenhouse effect is necessary to sustain all life on Earth. Choice A is incorrect because although biodiversity *helps* to sustain a variety of life on Earth, it is not *necessary* to sustain all life. Choice B is incorrect because global warming can be harmful to life on Earth. Choice D is incorrect because the depleting ozone layer leads to global warming, not sustained life on Earth.

19. **The correct answer is A.** A primary goal of the Superfund Act is to clean up hazardous waste sites. Choice B is incorrect because it refers to a goal of the Water Quality Act. Choice C is incorrect because the prohibition against ocean dumping is a provision of the Marine Protection, Research, and Sanctuaries Act of 1988. Choice D is incorrect because it was the Clean Water Act of 1977 that first sought to gain control of point source pollution.

20. **The correct answer is B.** All the different populations living in a certain place make up a community. Choice A is incorrect because an ecosystem includes all living and nonliving things in an environment. Choice C is incorrect because each of the three species is a separate population. Different species

cannot be part of the same population. Choice D is incorrect because the role of each organism in a community is its niche.

21. **The correct answer is C.** The total fertility rate of a population is the number of children born to each woman in her lifetime. Choice A is incorrect because the number of births and deaths in a population is not the total fertility rate. Choice B is not correct because this describes the replacement fertility rate. Choice D is incorrect because the number of women of childbearing age doesn't reflect the total fertility rate.

22. **The correct answer is A.** DDT is a chlorinated hydrocarbon, which is a type of persistent pesticide. Choice B is incorrect because diazinon is a widely used nonpersistent pesticide. Choice C is incorrect because organophosphates are nonpersistent insecticides in that they decompose quickly into harmless by-products. Organophospates aren't species-specific and will kill all insects, whether they are harmful or beneficial. Choice D is incorrect because carbamates are nonpersistent pesticides that work by interfering with an insect's nervous system.

23. **The correct answer is D.** When people approach environmental problems from very different viewpoints, they can all view the same information but draw different conclusions about the right action to take. Since solving environmental problems usually requires consensus, different social or cultural values can make solving problems more difficult. Choice A is incorrect since generally different viewpoints make cooperation more difficult. Choice B is incorrect since frequently opposing perspectives reach opposing conclusions. Choice C is incorrect since while common ground often exists between opposing viewpoints, there is no guarantee that it will be found.

24. **The correct answer is A.** Limiting factors are not a component of evolution. In general, this term refers to factors in an ecosystem that limit its success. Choice B is incorrect because extinction is a common feature of evolution. Choice C is incorrect because genetic variability is necessary for evolution to occur. Choice D is incorrect because natural selection is an important part of evolution. Natural selection is the process in which the individuals of a species best able to survive and reproduce will pass on traits that will continue to be expressed in a species. This process leads to evolution of species.

25. **The correct answer is B.** Not very many species of plants can survive in the conditions of the tundra; there are no large plants, so an entire category of plants and the diversity it adds is missing from that biome. Choice A is incorrect because a tropical rainforest provides a warm, wet climate that is advantageous to producing multiple species of plants of all types resulting in an extremely high diversity. Choice C is incorrect because wetlands are a diverse environment with varying soil types that are conducive to plant diversity. Choice D is incorrect because despite their reputation, most deserts are far from barren and hold a great diversity of plant and animal life.

26. **The correct answer is C.** The Earth Summit aimed to integrate environmental and economic goals of countries so choices A, B, and D are incorrect.

27. **The correct answer is B.** The EPA researches and regulates pesticide use, although individual states also have a role in pesticide licensing and regulation. Choices A, C, and D are incorrect because researching and regulating pesticides is not the function of any of these agencies.

28. **The correct answer is D.** Hawks and owls are both predators that compete for the same prey, including mice and rabbits. Because hawks and owls are different species, this is called interspecific competition. Choice A is incorrect because moss and trees have a commensal relationship; some moss benefits by growing on the base of a tree, but the tree is not affected. Choice B is incorrect because the shark and the remora have a commensal relationship in which the remora benefits and the shark is unaffected. Choice C is incorrect because the tapeworm is a parasite to the dog, not a predator.

29. **The correct answer is A.** Since the damaged area still has intact soil, it would undergo secondary succession, and grass would be one of the first organisms to grow. Choice B is incorrect because autotrophic microorganisms would appear in an area where there are no life forms and no intact soil. Choice C is incorrect because lichen would be one of the first organisms to appear during primary succession. Choice D is incorrect because in secondary succession, shrubs would appear after grasses.

30. **The correct answer is C.** Mass production enabled the replacement of durable goods with inexpensive disposable products, such as plastic bags, and facilitated greater consumption. Many of these products end up in landfills or as litter. Choices A, B, and D are incorrect since while all of these increased as a result of the industrial revolution, all industries played a role, not just mass production.

31. **The correct answer is C.** Ethanol is an alcohol used as a fuel source; it is produced by the fermentation of sugar, starch, or cellulose. Choice A is incorrect because carbon dioxide is not a fuel source. Choice B is incorrect because coal is produced over time and under high pressure from decaying organic matter.

Choice D is incorrect because oil is a fuel source produced by oils released from the remains of marine organisms. Like coal, oil forms over a very long period of time.

32. **The correct answer is D.** Increased fuel efficiency and the use of catalytic converters have reduced carbon monoxide emissions. However, carbon monoxide pollution is still a problem because cars now drive greater distances and there are more cars on the road. Choices A, B, and C are incorrect because the level of all of these air pollutants is not affected by improvements in the combustion engine and catalytic converter.

33. **The correct answer is C.** Goods are manufactured using different types of plastic. All of these plastics need to be separated and recycled by different methods, which raises the price of recycling and might encourage disposal and waste instead of recycling. Choice A is incorrect because recycling doesn't require the use of fossil fuels. Choice B is incorrect because recycling can reduce air and water pollution. Choice D is incorrect because many municipalities have recycling programs.

34. **The correct answer is C.** Farm animals don't release any sulfur dioxide or oxides of nitrogen into the atmosphere. Choices A, B, and D are incorrect because they are all sources of acid deposition.

35. **The correct answer is A.** Nitrifying bacteria are able to convert ammonia in soil into nitrites and nitrates. Nitrogen-fixing bacteria are able to convert atmospheric nitrogen gas that enters the soil into ammonia that plants can use. Choice B is incorrect because denitrifying bacteria convert nitrites into nitrogen gas. Choice C is incorrect because the nitrates are taken up by plants and incorporated into amino acids. Choice D is incorrect because nitrogen-fixing bacteria are able to convert atmospheric nitrogen gas

answers post-test

that enters the soil into ammonia that plants can use.

36. **The correct answer is A.** High genetic diversity is a level of biodiversity in which there is a great variation in genetic material within a population; therefore, individuals will have varied structure and abilities. Choice B is incorrect because low genetic diversity yields a population that was more uniform in structure and ability. Choice C is incorrect because high genetic diversity indicates a variety of genes, but doesn't imply anything about the complexity of the organisms. Choice D is incorrect because a high genetic diversity doesn't imply varied ecosystems.

37. **The correct answer is A.** Reduced political influence is a major cause of environmental justice problems. Improving political representation to ensure that all communities have equal participation in the political process is one way to prevent future environmental problems. Choice B, changing zoning laws, might help, but only if the new laws make impactful development more difficult in affected neighborhoods. Unfortunately, zoning laws often perpetuate environmental injustice by limiting industrial development in marginalized areas. Choices C and D might help with immediate problems of dirty water or inefficient heat, but they are temporary solutions that will not permanently solve the problem of unequal access to a clean environment.

38. **The correct answer is C.** Decomposers are organisms that will feed off all other organisms within an ecosystem whenever those organisms shed, excrete waste, or die. Therefore, decomposers are capable of feeding off organisms at every trophic level. Choice A is incorrect because producers are plants and at the first trophic level. Choice B is incorrect because carnivores feed and occupy higher trophic levels only. Choice D is incorrect because herbivores occupy the second trophic level.

39. **The correct answer is D.** The Law of the Sea aims to create a legal mechanism for controlling the exploitation of mineral resources in open waters. Choice A is incorrect because the United Nations doesn't control the exploitation of minerals. Choice B, the Clean Water Act, regulates water pollution. Choice C is incorrect because the Resource Conservation and Recovery Act controls hazardous waste disposal.

40. **The correct answer is A.** During photosynthesis, carbon dioxide present in the atmosphere is taken in by plants and converted into glucose in a reaction powered by sunlight. Plants and animals—consumers—use the glucose as a source of energy. Choice B is incorrect because animals use the process of oxygen respiration to breathe and convert oxygen into carbon dioxide. Choice C. is not correct because the process of digestion doesn't occur in plants. Choice D is incorrect because osmosis doesn't play a role in providing an energy source.

41. **The correct answer is C.** Trickle, or drip, irrigation is a very efficient method in which 90 to 95 percent of the water reaches the crops. In this method, small flexible tubing is inserted at or below ground level, and small holes in the tubing deliver water to the plant roots. Choice A is incorrect because gravity-flow irrigation consists of unlined ditches filled with water; the water flows by gravity to the crops. Choice B is incorrect because flood irrigation includes large ditches filled with water similar to gravity-flow irrigation. Choice D is incorrect because center-pivot irrigation systems use center-pivot sprinklers that move in a circular motion to deliver water to crops, which uses a large amount of water.

42. The correct answer is D. Deserts are defined by the low amount of precipitation they receive. Although deserts are thought of as hot (choice A) it is not always the case and temperature does not define a desert. Biodiversity (choice B) varies from desert to desert, but is usually quite high. Choice C, sand dunes, are not found in all deserts.

43. The correct answer is B. The Surface Mining Control and Reclamation Act of 1977 required that all mining companies replant vegetation on land that was strip mined. Choice A is incorrect because the land doesn't only need to be covered with topsoil, but it must also have vegetation planted. Choice C is incorrect because there is no regulation specifying that strip-mined land be converted into lakes. Choice D is incorrect because the land doesn't need to be decontaminated.

44. The correct answer is C. Each state may set its own standards for non–drinking water, but the EPA must approve those standards. Choice A is incorrect since the EPA only directly sets standards for drinking water. Choice B is incorrect since each state is still subject to federal oversight. Choice D is incorrect since Congress empowered the EPA and the states to set and enforce water quality standards.

45. The correct answer is B. The International Union for the Conservation of Nature, or IUCN, is an international agency with the primary role of assessing the status of species and ecosystems and sharing advice about how to conserve them. Choice A, CITES, is an international agreement but is not an organization. Choice C, the EPA, is a U.S. Government Agency, not international. Choice D, UNICEF, is an international agency but its primary mandate is childrens' rights and well-being, not environmental issues.

46. The correct answer is B. SEPA stands for State Environmental Policy Acts. These vary from state to state but are often stronger than federal regulations. Choices A and C are both national. Choice D, CBD, is an international agreement.

47. The correct answer is A. In practices of sustainable agriculture, multiple crops are planted on the same plot and harvested at different times. Choice B is incorrect because sustainable agriculture doesn't promote the use of fertilizers or chemical pesticides. Choice C is incorrect because fields aren't left bare or unplanted. Choice D is incorrect because multiple crops are planted in one field.

48. The correct answer is C. Endangered species are protected by the ESA regardless of whether they inhabit state or federal territory, and ESA covers marine as well as terrestrial species. Choice A, state law, is incorrect for even though the fish inhabits state waters it is protected primarily by ESA if it is endangered. Choice B, the Marine Mammal Protection Act, does not apply to fish and is also not the primary law protecting endangered species. Choice D, the Law of the Sea, does not apply to coastal waters other than to designate each country's Exclusive Economic Zone.

49. The correct answer is C. A concept frequently used in environmental risk assessment is that of source-pathway-receptor. The pathway between a hazard source and a receptor is investigated. If no pathway exists, then there is no risk to the environment. If a pathway links a source to a receptor, then the consequences need to be assessed. Choice A is incorrect because pollution control is an action taken to reduce a risk, not assess one. Choice B is incorrect because damage control isn't a way to assess environmental risks. Choice D is incorrect because control of a hazard isn't a means of assessment, but a means of reducing risk.

50. **The correct answer is B.** Dead tree trunks are brown; a brown beetle will be better camouflaged against the trunks, and less visible to predators such as birds. Therefore, the brown beetle is less likely to be eaten and more likely to live long enough to reproduce. This process of natural selection favors the brown beetle over the green beetle. Choice A is incorrect because the taste of the beetles is no different. Choice C is incorrect because the reproduction rate is no different. Choice D is incorrect because natural selection doesn't happen by chance.

51. **The correct answer is C.** The stewardship worldview maintains that people have an ethical responsibility to be good stewards of Earth and need to manage it well for future generations. Choice A is incorrect because this human-centered worldview focuses on future generations. Choice B is incorrect because the stewardship worldview is a human-centered view of the environment. Choice D is incorrect because this isn't part of the stewardship worldview.

52. **The correct answer is D.** A rapid increase of CO_2 in the atmosphere was first observed during the Industrial Revolution when there was a significant increase in the amount of coal burned for energy. Choice A is incorrect because the thinning of the ozone layer over Antarctica may be the result of an increase in CO_2, but it is not the cause of an increase in CO_2. Choice B is incorrect because warmer ocean temperatures don't increase CO_2. Choice C is incorrect because there is less vegetation in many areas, not more.

53. **The correct answer is B.** Selective cross-breeding is a method in which scientists cross-pollinate plants with desired traits until they generate seeds that will grow plants with the target desired traits. Choice

A is incorrect because mutations wouldn't always produce desired traits. Choice C is incorrect because chemical enhancement isn't always a safe way to obtain plants with desired traits. Choice D is incorrect because sustainable farming is an agricultural practice of farming that doesn't use chemicals.

54. **The correct answer is C.** Humans can best be described as k-strategists because k-selected species have few offspring and spend a great deal of energy and time ensuring that their offspring survive to reproductive age. Choice A is incorrect because r-selected species have a large number of offspring and don't care for them after they are born. Choice B is incorrect because l-strategist is not a term relevant to population biology. Choice D is incorrect because survivalist is not a term used to describe human populations.

55. **The correct answer is B.** Contour farming involves tilling at right angles to the slope of the land. In this method, small ridges are created that help prevent water from running down the slope and eroding the soil. Choice A is incorrect because it describes strip tillage, which is a method that involves tilling only in the narrow strip that is to receive the seeds. The rest of the soil and any crop residue from the previous year are left undisturbed. Choice C is incorrect because it is describing the method of diversifying cropping systems, which helps supply the soil with a variety of nutrients. Choice D is incorrect because the method of leaving a ridge from the previous year is ridge tillage.

56. **The correct answer is A.** An increase in land developed for agricultural use has caused an increase in soil erosion. Choice B is incorrect because air pollution is not caused by agricultural land use. Choice C is incorrect because agricultural practices helped to increase crop yields. Choice D

is incorrect because the Agricultural Revolution didn't cause an increase in pests.

57. **The correct answer is C.** The limiting factor is a condition of an environment that determines the population size of a given organism. Choice A is incorrect because a limiting factor is an environmental influence on the population of an organism, but it doesn't affect fertility rate. Choice B is incorrect because a limiting factor is an extrinsic factor. Choice D is incorrect because the limiting factor is a condition within the environment.

58. **The correct answer is C.** Deforestation worldwide is largely due to the clearing of land for agricultural purposes. Choice A is incorrect because acid rain affects some forests, but most forests are cleared by human activity. Choice B is incorrect because drought is not a usual cause of deforestation. Choice D is incorrect because although forest fires are a cause of deforestation, more forests are cleared for agricultural purposes than affected by forest fires.

59. **The correct answer is C.** In a well-designed sanitary landfill, methane gas is trapped as it is released from the decomposing waste. It can then be used as an energy source. Choice A is incorrect because methane gas, not ethane, is obtained from landfills. Choice B is incorrect because hydrogen is not obtained from a landfill. Choice D is incorrect because steam is obtained from geothermal wells, not landfills.

60. **The correct answer is B.** Desertification occurs most often in regions such as Northern Africa because there is irregular and unpredictable rainfall. Choice A is incorrect because desertification is more prevalent in Northern Africa than the Western United States. Choice C is incorrect because desertification is not a particular problem in Eastern Europe. Choice D is incorrect because Central America receives heavy rainfall.

Fundamentals of Cybersecurity

OVERVIEW

The DSST® Fundamentals of Cybersecurity exam covers topics such as disaster recovery, operational and network security, authentication, authorization, access controls, application and systems security. This chapter provides a foundational knowledge of the subject, with a main focus on best practices and the major topics in the field of cybersecurity.

Chapter 10

answer sheet

DIAGNOSTIC TEST ANSWER SHEET

1. Ⓐ Ⓑ Ⓒ Ⓓ	5. Ⓐ Ⓑ Ⓒ Ⓓ	9. Ⓐ Ⓑ Ⓒ Ⓓ	13. Ⓐ Ⓑ Ⓒ Ⓓ	17. Ⓐ Ⓑ Ⓒ Ⓓ
2. Ⓐ Ⓑ Ⓒ Ⓓ	6. Ⓐ Ⓑ Ⓒ Ⓓ	10. Ⓐ Ⓑ Ⓒ Ⓓ	14. Ⓐ Ⓑ Ⓒ Ⓓ	18. Ⓐ Ⓑ Ⓒ Ⓓ
3. Ⓐ Ⓑ Ⓒ Ⓓ	7. Ⓐ Ⓑ Ⓒ Ⓓ	11. Ⓐ Ⓑ Ⓒ Ⓓ	15. Ⓐ Ⓑ Ⓒ Ⓓ	19. Ⓐ Ⓑ Ⓒ Ⓓ
4. Ⓐ Ⓑ Ⓒ Ⓓ	8. Ⓐ Ⓑ Ⓒ Ⓓ	12. Ⓐ Ⓑ Ⓒ Ⓓ	16. Ⓐ Ⓑ Ⓒ Ⓓ	20. Ⓐ Ⓑ Ⓒ Ⓓ

POST-TEST ANSWER SHEET

1. Ⓐ Ⓑ Ⓒ Ⓓ	13. Ⓐ Ⓑ Ⓒ Ⓓ	25. Ⓐ Ⓑ Ⓒ Ⓓ	37. Ⓐ Ⓑ Ⓒ Ⓓ	49. Ⓐ Ⓑ Ⓒ Ⓓ
2. Ⓐ Ⓑ Ⓒ Ⓓ	14. Ⓐ Ⓑ Ⓒ Ⓓ	26. Ⓐ Ⓑ Ⓒ Ⓓ	38. Ⓐ Ⓑ Ⓒ Ⓓ	50. Ⓐ Ⓑ Ⓒ Ⓓ
3. Ⓐ Ⓑ Ⓒ Ⓓ	15. Ⓐ Ⓑ Ⓒ Ⓓ	27. Ⓐ Ⓑ Ⓒ Ⓓ	39. Ⓐ Ⓑ Ⓒ Ⓓ	51. Ⓐ Ⓑ Ⓒ Ⓓ
4. Ⓐ Ⓑ Ⓒ Ⓓ	16. Ⓐ Ⓑ Ⓒ Ⓓ	28. Ⓐ Ⓑ Ⓒ Ⓓ	40. Ⓐ Ⓑ Ⓒ Ⓓ	52. Ⓐ Ⓑ Ⓒ Ⓓ
5. Ⓐ Ⓑ Ⓒ Ⓓ	17. Ⓐ Ⓑ Ⓒ Ⓓ	29. Ⓐ Ⓑ Ⓒ Ⓓ	41. Ⓐ Ⓑ Ⓒ Ⓓ	53. Ⓐ Ⓑ Ⓒ Ⓓ
6. Ⓐ Ⓑ Ⓒ Ⓓ	18. Ⓐ Ⓑ Ⓒ Ⓓ	30. Ⓐ Ⓑ Ⓒ Ⓓ	42. Ⓐ Ⓑ Ⓒ Ⓓ	54. Ⓐ Ⓑ Ⓒ Ⓓ
7. Ⓐ Ⓑ Ⓒ Ⓓ	19. Ⓐ Ⓑ Ⓒ Ⓓ	31. Ⓐ Ⓑ Ⓒ Ⓓ	43. Ⓐ Ⓑ Ⓒ Ⓓ	55. Ⓐ Ⓑ Ⓒ Ⓓ
8. Ⓐ Ⓑ Ⓒ Ⓓ	20. Ⓐ Ⓑ Ⓒ Ⓓ	32. Ⓐ Ⓑ Ⓒ Ⓓ	44. Ⓐ Ⓑ Ⓒ Ⓓ	56. Ⓐ Ⓑ Ⓒ Ⓓ
9. Ⓐ Ⓑ Ⓒ Ⓓ	21. Ⓐ Ⓑ Ⓒ Ⓓ	33. Ⓐ Ⓑ Ⓒ Ⓓ	45. Ⓐ Ⓑ Ⓒ Ⓓ	57. Ⓐ Ⓑ Ⓒ Ⓓ
10. Ⓐ Ⓑ Ⓒ Ⓓ	22. Ⓐ Ⓑ Ⓒ Ⓓ	34. Ⓐ Ⓑ Ⓒ Ⓓ	46. Ⓐ Ⓑ Ⓒ Ⓓ	58. Ⓐ Ⓑ Ⓒ Ⓓ
11. Ⓐ Ⓑ Ⓒ Ⓓ	23. Ⓐ Ⓑ Ⓒ Ⓓ	35. Ⓐ Ⓑ Ⓒ Ⓓ	47. Ⓐ Ⓑ Ⓒ Ⓓ	59. Ⓐ Ⓑ Ⓒ Ⓓ
12. Ⓐ Ⓑ Ⓒ Ⓓ	24. Ⓐ Ⓑ Ⓒ Ⓓ	36. Ⓐ Ⓑ Ⓒ Ⓓ	48. Ⓐ Ⓑ Ⓒ Ⓓ	60. Ⓐ Ⓑ Ⓒ Ⓓ

THE FUNDAMENTALS OF CYBERSECURITY DIAGNOSTIC TEST

Directions: Carefully read each of the following 20 questions. Choose the best answer to each question and fill in the corresponding circle on the answer sheet. The Answer Key and Explanations can be found following this Diagnostic Test.

1. Which of the following is most often used to create a secure VPN over an insecure medium?
   A. Secure Shell (SSH)
   B. Internet Protocol security (IPsec)
   C. Secure Sockets Layer (SSL)
   D. S-HTTP

2. The tool and technique for breaking into more systems, gaining further network access, or gaining access to more resources is
   A. exploitation.
   B. return.
   C. vendor announcement.
   D. full-disclosure list.

3. Which of the following involves an encryption algorithm, as well as a key to decipher it?
   A. Cryptography
   B. Antivirus
   C. Malware detection
   D. Security triad

4. The protection of information in electronic databases from unauthorized access, theft, or destruction is known as
   A. enterprise continuity.
   B. incident management.
   C. digital forensics.
   D. data security.

5. Which of the following terms refers to bringing key stakeholders together to determine necessary solutions based on laws, needs of the organization, and resources?
   A. Data classification
   B. Key management
   C. Collaboration
   D. Finding a solution

6. Which of the following is NOT part of the security triad?
   A. Confidentiality
   B. Integrity
   C. Availability
   D. Flexibility

7. Which of the following provides access to resources?
   A. Authentication
   B. Authorization
   C. Access controls
   D. Compliance

8. Which of the following involves securing and maintaining a secure environment—a well-developed process that starts with operational security policies establishing clear guidelines regarding what the operators should and should not do?
   A. Enterprise information
   B. Information architecture
   C. Technology architecture
   D. Security architecture

9. A specific method for identifying risks and threats is
   A. risk assessment.
   B. information architecture.
   C. technology architecture.
   D. security architecture.

10. The sustainability function of the cybersecurity process is
    A. operational security.
    B. security architecture.
    C. security implementation.
    D. access controls.

11. What is one of the frequently overlooked parts of a secure information system?
    A. Access controls
    B. Level of adaptability to change
    C. Information architecture
    D. Technology architecture

12. Which of the following encrypts individual messages that are transmitted over the Internet between clients and servers?
    A. Secure Shell
    B. Internet Protocol security
    C. Secure Sockets Layer
    D. S-HTTP

13. Which of the following are used for secure web communications for e-commerce, banking, and a number of other sensitive uses?
    A. Secure Shell
    B. Internet Protocol security
    C. Secure Sockets Layer
    D. S-HTTP

14. Which of the following involves network testing and recognizing and mitigating threats on a regular basis?
    A. Network security
    B. Operational security
    C. Vulnerability management
    D. Reconnaissance

15. Which of the following includes targeting IP addresses, targeting a website, performing business research, and Google hacking?
    A. Network security
    B. Operational security
    C. Vulnerability management
    D. Footprinting

16. Which of the following is established by aligning business, IT, software, hardware, network, human resources, operations, and projects processes with the overall security strategy of the organization?
    A. Enterprise information
    B. Information architecture
    C. Technology architecture
    D. Security architecture

17. Organizations use which of the following to help protect sensitive and secure equipment against environmental hazards?
    A. Exploitation
    B. Return
    C. Vendor announcements
    D. Environmental controls

18. Which of the following is the preservation of the ability to perform the essential functions required for operational effectiveness as it pertains to the continuity of the unit or organization?
    A. Enterprise continuity
    B. Incident management
    C. Digital forensics
    D. Data security

19. The process for determining whether a user attempting to gain access to a system is, in fact, the authorized holder of the appropriate credentials needed for access is called
   A. authentication.
   B. authorization.
   C. access controls.
   D. compliance.

20. Which of the following is an essential part of cybersecurity in information systems?
   A. Operational security
   B. Network security
   C. Access controls
   D. Enterprise information

ANSWER KEY AND EXPLANATIONS

1. B	5. C	9. A	13. C	17. D
2. A	6. D	10. A	14. C	18. A
3. A	7. B	11. B	15. D	19. A
4. D	8. D	12. D	16. A	20. B

1. **The correct answer is B.** IPsec is most often used to create a secure VPN over an insecure medium. Choice A is incorrect because a Secure Shell is a protocol developed in order to provide a secure method for accessing systems over an insecure medium. Choice C is incorrect because SSL is used for secure web communications for e-commerce, banking, and a number of other sensitive uses. Choice D is incorrect because S-HTTP encrypts individual messages that are transmitted over the Internet between clients and servers.

2. **The correct answer is A.** Exploitation describes the technique that attackers use for breaking into more systems, gaining further network access, or gaining access to more resources. Choice B is incorrect because return describes the actions an attacker takes to ensure he/she is able to return to the target unobstructed. Choice C is incorrect because vendor announcements are mailing lists announcing vulnerabilities, fixes, or any compensating actions that can be taken. Choice D is incorrect because full-disclosure lists are lists of vulnerabilities circulated among security professionals once all the necessary due diligence is complete.

3. **The correct answer is A.** The data security competency covers the important task of implementing and maintaining encryption. This is done through cryptography, which involves an encryption algorithm, as well as a key to decipher it. There are two types of keys: symmetric (secret) keys and asymmetric (public) keys. Choice B is incorrect because antivirus is software used to detect and remove viruses. Choice C is incorrect because malware detection is used to detect malware on the system. Choice D is incorrect because a security triad is the loss of confidentiality, loss of integrity, and loss of availability.

4. **The correct answer is D.** Data security is the protection of information in electronic databases from unauthorized access, theft, or destruction. Choice A is incorrect because enterprise continuity is the preservation of the ability to perform the essential functions required for operational effectiveness as it pertains to the continuity of the unit or organization. Choice B is incorrect because incident management governs the handling/reporting procedures for incidents related to IT management and security. Choice C is incorrect because digital forensics is the recovery of electronic information, often from devices that have been tampered with, destroyed, or compromised.

5. **The correct answer is C.** Collaboration is bringing key stakeholders together to determine necessary solutions based on laws, needs of the organization, and resources. Choice A is incorrect because data classification is the separation of data based on security needs of the organization. Choice B is incorrect because key management determines who will hold encryption keys, encryption key life-cycle management, and what the overall key management system

will look like. Choice D is incorrect because finding a solution is the process in which alternatives are weighed in order to find the best possible solution for the current environment.

6. **The correct answer is D.** The security triad consists of confidentiality, integrity, and availability. Choices A, B, and C are incorrect because they are part of the security triad.

7. **The correct answer is B.** The authorization process occurs after authentication, and it provides access to resources. Choice A is incorrect because authentication is the process of determining whether a user attempting to gain access to a system is, in fact, the authorized holder of the appropriate credentials needed for access. Choice C is incorrect because access controls are the controls used to determine which individuals can enter certain areas. Choice D is incorrect because compliance ensures that the authentication rules are followed.

8. **The correct answer is D.** Security architecture is the only choice that describes this process. Choice A is incorrect because enterprise information is established by aligning business, IT, software, hardware, network, human resources, operations, and projects processes with the overall security strategy of the organization. Choice B is incorrect because information architecture is the structural design of how information is shared. Choice C is incorrect because technology architecture is the process of bringing together the IT components of the system.

9. **The correct answer is A.** Risk assessment is a specific method for identifying risks and threats. Choice B is incorrect because information architecture is the structural design of how information is shared. Choice C is incorrect because technology architecture is the process of bringing together

the IT components of the system. Choice D is incorrect because security architecture involves securing and maintaining a secure environment.

10. **The correct answer is A.** Operational security is the sustainability function of the cybersecurity process. Choice B is incorrect because security architecture involves securing and maintaining a secure environment. Choice C is incorrect because security implementation is the process of implementing the cybersecurity processes. Choice D is incorrect because access controls are the controls used to determine which individuals can enter certain areas.

11. **The correct answer is B.** Level of adaptability to change is one of the frequently overlooked parts of a secure information system. Choice A is incorrect because access controls are the controls used to determine which individuals can enter certain areas. Choice C is incorrect because information architecture is the structural design of how information is shared. Choice D is incorrect because technology architecture is the process of bringing together the IT components of the system.

12. **The correct answer is D.** S-HTTP encrypts individual messages that are transmitted over the Internet between clients and servers. Choice A is incorrect because Secure Shell is a protocol developed in order to provide a secure method for accessing systems over an insecure medium. Choice B is incorrect because IPsec is most often used to create a secure VPN over an insecure medium. Choice C is incorrect because SSL is used for secure web communications for e-commerce, banking, and a number of other sensitive uses.

13. **The correct answer is C.** SSL is used for secure web communications for e-commerce, banking, and a number of other

sensitive uses. Choice A is incorrect because a Secure Shell is a protocol developed in order to provide a secure method for accessing systems over an insecure medium. Choice B is incorrect because IPsec is most often used to create a secure VPN over an insecure medium. Choice D is incorrect because S-HTTP encrypts individual messages that are transmitted over the Internet between clients and servers.

14. **The correct answer is C.** Vulnerability management involves network testing and recognizing and mitigating threats on a regular basis. Choice A is incorrect because network security is an essential part of cybersecurity in information systems. Choice B is incorrect because operational security is the sustainability function of the cybersecurity process. Choice D is incorrect because reconnaissance is the collection of publicly available information about a potential target.

15. **The correct answer is D.** Footprinting includes targeting IP addresses, targeting a website, performing business research, and Google hacking. Choice A is incorrect because network security is an essential part of cybersecurity in information systems. Choice B is incorrect because operational security is the sustainability function of the cybersecurity process. Choice C is incorrect because vulnerability management involves network testing and recognizing and mitigating threats on a regular basis.

16. **The correct answer is A.** Enterprise information is established by aligning business, IT, software, hardware, network, human resources, operations, and projects processes with the overall security strategy of the organization. Choice B is incorrect because information architecture is the structural design of how information is shared. Choice C is incorrect because technology architecture

is the process of bringing together the IT components of the system. Choice D is incorrect because security architecture involves securing and maintaining a secure environment.

17. **The correct answer is D.** Environmental controls help protect sensitive and secure equipment against environmental hazards. Choice A is incorrect because exploitation is the technique for breaking into more systems, gaining further network access, or gaining access to more resources. Choice B is incorrect because a return is the action an attacker takes to ensure he/she is able to return to the target unobstructed. Choice C is incorrect because vendor announcements are mailing lists announcing vulnerabilities, fixes, or any compensating actions.

18. **The correct answer is A.** Enterprise continuity is the preservation of the ability to perform the essential functions required for operational effectiveness as it pertains to the continuity of the unit or organization. Choice B is incorrect because incident management deals with the handling/reporting procedures for incidents relating to IT management and security. Choice C is incorrect because digital forensics is the recovery of electronic information, often from devices that have been tampered with, destroyed, or compromised. Choice D is incorrect because data security is the protection of information in electronic databases from unauthorized access, theft, or destruction.

19. **The correct answer is A.** Authentication is the process for determining whether a user attempting to gain access to a system is, in fact, the authorized holder of the appropriate credentials needed for access. Choice B is incorrect because the authorization process occurs after authentication, and provides access to resources. Choice C is incorrect because access controls are used to determine

which individuals can enter certain areas. Choice D is incorrect because compliance is the level at which the authentication rules are followed.

20. **The correct answer is B.** Network security is an essential part of cybersecurity in information systems. Choice A is incorrect because operational security is the sustainability function of the cybersecurity process. Choice C is incorrect because access controls are used to determine which individuals can enter certain areas. Choice D is incorrect because enterprise information is established by aligning business, IT, software, hardware, network, human resources, operations, and projects processes with the overall security strategy of the organization.

DIAGNOSTIC TEST ASSESSMENT GRID

Now that you've completed the diagnostic test and read through the answer explanations, you can use your results to target your studying. Find the question numbers from the diagnostic test that you answered incorrectly and highlight or circle them below. Then focus extra attention on the sections within the chapter dealing with those topics.

Cybersecurity		
Content Area	**Topic**	**Question #**
Applications and Systems Security	• Security triad • Accountability and non-repudiation • Fundamentals of cryptography • Security development life cycle • Best practices for migration from development environment to production • Antivirus protection and malware detection	3, 5, 6
Authentication, Authorization, and Access Controls	• Implementing authentication technologies • Authorization • Access controls	7, 19
Policies, Compliance, and Governance	• Security architecture • Risk assessment • Outsources process governance • Ethics and legal	8, 16, 9
Operational Security	• Securing and monitoring the production environment • Policies, standards, and procedures	10, 11
Network Security	• Protocols and services • Analysis tools and management • Infrastructure • Wireless	1, 12, 20, 13

Cybersecurity (continued)		
Vulnerability Management	• Testing the network • Recognizing and mitigating threats • Tools	2, 14, 15
Physical and Environmental Security	• Physical access controls and management • Environmental controls	17
Disaster Recovery and Business Continuity	• Fire backup, retention, offsite storage, archiving • Business impact analysis • Disaster recovery planning • Business continuity planning • Plan testing and maintenance	4, 18

GET THE FACTS

To see the DSST® Organizational Behavior Fact Sheet, go to *http://getcollegecredit.com/exam_fact_sheets* and click on the **Technology** tab. Scroll down and click the **Fundamentals of Cybersecurity** link. Here you will find suggestions for further study material and the ACE college credit recommendations for passing the test.

APPLICATIONS AND SYSTEMS SECURITY

First, let's focus on applications and systems security and gain some exposure to the Essential Body of Knowledge (EBK), the basics of encryption, and the communication of security concerns throughout the system development life cycle (SDLC). Approximately 15 percent of questions on the DSST Fundamentals of Cybersecurity exam will cover topics related to applications and systems security.

Applications and systems security begins with the security triad. The security triad is a model that was created to help organizations create policies for information security. The security triad model consists of availability, integrity, and confidentiality. These are the three most critical elements of information security. In terms of information security, confidentiality consists of the rules that will determine who has access to certain levels of information and also allows the organizations to limit the access. Integrity consists of the assurance that the information will be secured and will not be compromised internally or externally. Finally, availability relates to the reliable access to the information by only those individuals who have been authorized.

Best practices in information technology (IT) security are based on the Essential Body of Knowledge. The EBK is an umbrella framework, defining and outlining the competencies that are associated with IT work processes. The goal of the EBK is to establish a standard for concepts and terms in the IT profession.

There are 14 areas of common practice in the EBK regarding security:

1. **Data security**, which is the protection of information in electronic databases from unauthorized access, theft, or destruction.

2. **Digital forensics**, or the retrieval and recovery of electronic information, often from devices that have been tampered with, destroyed, or compromised.

3. **Enterprise continuity**—the preservation of the ability to perform the essential functions required for operational effectiveness as it pertains to the continuity of the unit or organization.

4. **Incident management**, or the process governing the handling/reporting procedures for incidents relating to IT management and security.

5. **IT security training and awareness**. This area of responsibility ensures that personnel are properly trained in necessary IT security concerns and functions, and that they are aware of the potential threats and issues that noncompliance with standards pose.

6. **IT systems operation and maintenance**. This responsibility deals with the development and carrying out of communications processes between security administrators and appropriate personnel. Development of collaboration processes with IT support and incident management are covered in this responsibility as well.

7. **Network security and telecommunications**. This area of responsibility covers the monitoring of operations professionals in the IT security realm. Personnel filling this role should be involved in the building and maintenance of the network security strategic plan.

8. **Personnel security**. This responsibility includes ensuring that human resources elements of the organization are adhering to all rules and regulations.

9. **Physical and environmental security**. This area of responsibility includes keeping the organization and its security assets safe in the event of natural disasters, or man-made disasters.

10. **Procurement** refers to obtaining or purchasing equipment for a specific information systems project.

11. **Regulatory and standards compliance**. This area of responsibility covers the adherence to applicable information security laws and regulations, as well as standards and policies.

12. **Risk management**. This area of responsibility covers the design, implementation, and control of a risk management process as it relates to information security assets.

13. **Strategic security management**, which broadly covers using sound strategic management principles to manage information security in the organization.

14. **System and application security**. This covers the security of systems as well as applications developed using the applications design process within the organization.

When bringing new services and applications into production, it is important to have the correct processes in place. The first step is to review the generic competencies that are provided in the EBK. These categories are used by security experts to define organizational security proficiencies, and they should be adapted to the needs of the project. This process is called tailoring.

EXECUTIVE AND SECURITY ROLES

There are three executive roles overseeing various functional events, classified as management, design, implementation, or evaluation events:

- The chief information officer, or CIO
- The chief information security officer, or CISO
- The IT security compliance officer

Based on that leadership structure, the next step is to assign roles to the personnel involved in the process based on the fourteen security roles established in the EBK.

First, there's the digital forensics professional. This is a highly specialized role, focused on the collection and analysis of digital evidence. Next, an IT security engineer typically serves as the architect of the IT security solution. In addition, an IT systems operations and maintenance professional maintains and operates the system on an ongoing basis. Finally, an IT security professional is the one who implements the system designed by the IT security engineer. It is common in smaller organizations for more than one of these roles to be filled by the same person.

ACCOUNTABILITY AND GOALS OF THE SECURITY SYSTEMS

The aim of the applications and systems security function is to identify and then eliminate defects in code that may be exploitable. This process should ensure that every instance of a piece of software or a developed system is developed, configured, and maintained in a trustworthy fashion. At the same time, this function ensures that each of these applications and/or systems is functioning and performing as designed.

These goals are accomplished by measuring outcomes against benchmarks, identifying and making smart judgments about risks, eliminating hidden problems through code inspection, aligning processes with best practices (such as the EBK), and ensuring optimal resource allocation.

BASIC STEPS TO AN ENCRYPTION STRATEGY

The public key infrastructure, or PKI, is the authority that issues and certifies both private and public keys as valid. This is essential for public-key encryption. There are seven basic steps to an encryption strategy.

- The first is collaboration, or bringing the key stakeholders together to determine the necessary solutions based on laws, needs of the organization, and resources.
- The second is data classification. This is where data is separated based on the security needs of the organization. Determinations are made at this stage about where information will be stored, who will have access, and what the process for provisioning and deprovisioning access will be.
- The third step is management. This determines who will hold encryption keys. It also deals with encryption key life cycle management and what the overall key management system will look like.

- Fourth is finding a solution. This is where the alternatives are weighed in order to find the best possible solution for the current environment.

- The fifth is access control. This step protects access using file permissions, passwords, and two-factor authentication. It is essential to do periodic audits of this information.

- The sixth are consequences—a fixed set of responsibilities and corrective measures for failing to meet those responsibilities. This protects an organization from potential compliance issues.

- Finally, we have SSL (secure sockets layer) decryption. This step allows professionals to have some level of transparency into secure processes since SSL encryption sometimes provides an exploitable wall for hackers.

SYSTEMS DEVELOPMENT LIFE CYCLE

Each step of the systems development life cycle (SDLC) offers opportunities to communicate security concerns. With security playing such a crucial role in systems development, is it essential that the process include many places where the communication of security concerns is both allowed and encouraged. Let's look at the major steps in the systems development life cycle and highlight possible opportunities for communicating those concerns as we view a much more detailed version of the process. While the basic steps of planning, analyzing, designing, implementing, and maintaining provide a good idea of what occurs in the SDLC, a more granular look at the core phases of systems design allows you to better view the process through the lens of the communication of security concerns.

In the **initiation phase** of the SDLC, the focus is on identifying a need or an opportunity. This serves as the genesis of the process, and it provides an opportunity to discuss possible security concerns from the outset. In this phase, a concept proposal is created. The concept proposal should place a focus on security, and it can certainly point to possible concerns as the rest of the process is developed and organized.

In the **system concept development phase**, the scope of the process is defined. A Systems Boundary Document is created and a cost/benefit analysis is performed. Risk management and feasibility studies are also done at this stage. During this stage, it is wise to consider specific security concerns as they relate to each of the documents and studies.

In the **planning phase**, a Project Management Plan is developed. This step is heavily focused on acquiring all the needed resources for the project. With that in mind, this serves as a good step to discuss resources that might be needed to deal with known and possible security concerns.

In the **requirements analysis phase**, the basic needs and requirements of the user are taken into consideration. This is the major focus for this phase, so it allows for a more comprehensive view of the user experience. This in turn provides an opportunity to consider security concerns as they relate to the end user. This is also the phase in which the Functional Requirements Document is generated. It should be highly detailed and comprehensive.

In the **design phase**, detailed requirements are converted into a fully formed and detailed Systems Design Document. While the key focus of this stage is to make sure the required functionality can be delivered, security concerns should be voiced and dealt with at this time, as well.

In the **development phase**, the completed design that was put together in the previous phases is compiled and combined, forming the beginnings of an information system. Databases are created and tested, and programs are refined. The systems environment is acquired and installed at this stage. A readiness review is conducted during this phase as well, and procurement activities are going on in the background. All these elements of the process provide small windows of opportunity for the communication of security concerns. The databases need to be secure, and readiness review needs to uncover possible security issues. Having security concerns on the front burner is essential during this phase.

In the **integration and testing phase**, the systems are developed and ready to be integrated for eventual end-user implementation. This stage focuses on making sure the system is conforming properly to all the requirements as they were specified and set out in the Functional Requirements Document in the requirements and analysis phase.

The **implementation phase** begins with final preparation for implementation. This includes ensuring all the elements of the system will work as planned and required in the production environment. This is also the principal stage that focuses on resolving problems that were uncovered and highlighted during the integration and test phases. This stage should be carefully monitored for the discovery of security issues.

In the **operations and maintenance phase**, the system is maintained and operated in a live production environment. This marks a turning point in the process as any tweaks and changes that are necessary at this point will need to be done in a live environment, taking into consideration the consequences of such changes on end users and the everyday business processes the system is supporting. Security concerns in this stage of the process may come from any number of stakeholders, including front-line employees, designers, vendors, and even customers. Having an organized conduit for security concern communication at this stage is more important than ever. Otherwise, valid security concerns could fall through the cracks as problems persist or even grow.

In the **disposition phase**, end-of-system activities are being conducted, and the system is preparing to be discontinued. It's likely at this phase that a new system has been developed to replace the current one, or that a system has simply done its ad hoc job for the organization and is no longer needed. Either way, heavy preparation of data for migration or archiving is performed during disposition. With so much migration and data motion necessary for this phase, the system is vulnerable to security issues. The communication of known concerns should be just as organized at this stage as it was in the previous one, as major security threats during disposition can be just as damaging here.

Data migration should be viewed as a vulnerable function for protected information. Just as money is transferred from bank to bank in armored trucks for safety, data must be properly safeguarded and encrypted during transfer.

AUTHENTICATION, AUTHORIZATION, AND ACCESS CONTROLS

Approximately 12 percent of questions on the DSST Fundamentals of Cybersecurity exam will cover topics related to authentication, authorization, and access controls. Access control is a core part of information security. Professionals must recognize that access control for physical space is implemented through the same identity, authentication, and authorization functions that are used to control electronic access control.

Consider the way you enter a controlled building. Often the security guard or officer checks your identification badge, then looks at you to verify that the picture on the badge matches the person he or she is verifying. A scan may be coordinated to ensure your credentials are active and that you are authorized to be given access to the building. This is the authentication process. First, we'll discuss implementing authentication technologies. Then, we'll discuss authorization and its phases and important elements.

AUTHENTICATION

Authentication is a process for determining whether a user attempting to gain access to a system is, in fact, the authorized holder of the appropriate credentials needed for access.

Authentication is often accomplished with passwords or passphrases, via a single sign-on (SSO), a system designed to allow access across multiple systems and platforms, a biometric authentication system, a digital certificate, or through public key infrastructure (or PKI) as we discussed in a previous section. Without user authentication, proper authorization cannot be determined for users of an information system, and the system is open to information security threats and data theft that can leave the organization exposed and vulnerable.

While no system is without its vulnerabilities, there are steps that can be taken to ensure the highest measure of security and protection of information systems through best practices and industry standard authentication processes and procedures. Let's discuss the three main factors for authentication upon which most authentication systems are built: something you know, something you have, and something you are. Let's break those three factors of authentication down and consider examples of each as well as appropriate uses for them in practice.

Something You Know

The first factor, something you know, establishes who you are based on something you know. Passwords are the most commonly used method of achieving this factor of authentication. Passwords can ensure trusted access to information systems as long as they are strong and secret.

Weak passwords create vulnerability at multiple levels of an otherwise secure information system, which is why many information security professionals are steering their organizations toward password policies that require stronger, more complex passwords. There is a line, however, between having a password that is strong enough to be secure, and so strong that the user has trouble remembering it. In cases where the user has trouble remembering a password, they might be tempted to keep it written down and on their person. This creates new vulnerabilities that defeat the purpose of strong passwords.

Let's review some of the best ways to require strong passwords that are still memorable. First, you should require at least one capital letter, as well as lowercase letters, in a password. Next, require at least one number as a part of the password. Finally, require at least one special character or symbol as a part of the password.

Let's look at a quick example. Consider a user named "Sally" who is using the following password for an information system. She generates the following as a possible password:

sampson

While the password is not Sally's real name, it is still more easily cracked than a more complex password. This sample password is only comprised of lowercase characters, and it is a name that could be included easily in a database of known possible passwords based on common language. Let's work on Sally's password together to strengthen it. First, we'll capitalize the word. This adds more complexity to the password. Next, we will change out a few of the letters for symbols that look almost like those letters. This helps Sally remember the password, because the letters are similar to the symbols, but it makes the password far more complex and less likely to be guessed or cracked. Finally, we will add a number to the password for one more level of complexity. Here is the new version of Sally's password.

S@mp$on8

Now Sally's password is much more complex and is still sayable so Sally can remember it by repeating it to herself … "Sampsonate."

Something You Have

The second factor, something you have, requires the user to verify authentication by producing or proving that he or she has something that proves authorized user status. Producing a valid identification token falls into this category. A swipe card is another example of this type of verification. Tokens can also be software installed on a specific device to authenticate a user based on his or her computer or mobile phone.

Facebook and other social networks use tokens to authenticate users regularly. When users access the platform from another device, they receive an e-mail at their authorized e-mail address to alert them of access from a device without a token. If the user approves, a token is issued to the new device and it becomes an authorized device on the account.

These systems could also be configured to deny access from devices with no token. This would prevent access, even with a password, if the attempted user is trying to log in from a device that has not been previously used for access.

Something You Are

The third factor, something you are, involves verifying actual physical characteristics (known as biometrics) to confirm the identity, and therefore the right to access systems, of an individual. This is, of course, the oldest form of authentication.

ALERT

Strong Password Requirements:

1. At least one capital letter, as well as lowercase letters

2. At least one number

3. At least one special character or symbol

Long before there were passwords of any kind, people were identified by their physical features. It should be noted that, prior to the existence of information systems as we know them today, tokens and passphrases were still commonly used as other factors of authentication.

Before we move on to authorization, let's discuss the trend toward ensuring tighter security through multifactor authentication. The use of multiple authentication factors can increase security by requiring more than one form of identity.

With recent hacks of information systems, two-factor authentication, or multifactor authentication, has been embraced across more and more applications. Social networks encourage users to use their mobile phones as a secondary factor after the password is correctly provided. The cell phone verification code via SMS text is another example of authentication through something you have. The verification code serves as a token, which is entered to prove that you have your mobile phone. Then, the process moves to authorization.

AUTHORIZATION

The authorization process occurs after authentication and provides access to resources. Once the user has proven his or her identity, the information system responds by going through the authorization process, wherein it determines the permissions and levels of access provided to the specific user. This releases only access to the authorized elements of an information system to which the user is entitled based on rights and permissions.

For example, when logging into Facebook, the user begins with the authentication process as we outlined before. Once the user is authenticated, Facebook's information system does not simply grant open access to the entire platform. Rather, it determines to which things the user has access. For instance, the user has access to his or her personal profile, including the permissions necessary to change a profile picture or add a status update.

However, that user does not have authorization to delete the profile picture of someone else or to add or delete items from another person's profile. This is an illustration that most clearly outlines the key differences between authentication and authorization.

The accountability principle is performed as the final step after authorization, ensuring that a proper record of the access has been recorded thereby leading to proper evaluation of the data security function. Without this necessary step, the essential paper trail cannot be preserved, and vulnerabilities would be much more difficult to detect and address.

Authentication and authorization are important when determining who is authorized to enter the systems or even to sign documents digitally. Non-repudiation provides the assurance that someone cannot deny something. This term is used in the ability to ensure that the individual who signed the contract or sent a communication cannot deny the authenticity of his/her signature because he/she has the authentication and authority to enter the system and conduct these practices.

POLICIES, COMPLIANCE, AND GOVERNANCE

Approximately 15 percent of questions on the DSST Fundamentals of Cybersecurity exam will ask about policies, compliance, and governance.

Any system is only as good as the strict governance that ensures it runs exactly as it was designed to run. At the same time, compliance with all the applicable procedures, directives, standards, policies, laws, and regulations is essential for effectiveness and security. No matter the quality of the security that is built into the architecture of the information system, the rules and procedures must be followed for it to be truly secure.

ENTERPRISE INFORMATION SECURITY ARCHITECTURE

Enterprise information security architecture, or EISA, is established by aligning business, IT, software, hardware, network, human resources, operations, and projects processes with the overall security strategy of the organization.

Security architecture, which was once silo-based and removed from the main service architecture of organizations, has since been repositioned as a core element of service architecture. The conglomeration of business architecture, information architecture, and technology architecture was previously known by the acronym BIT. Since the wide acceptance of security architecture as an essential fourth element to that model, the "s" was added to BIT and the model is now referred to as BITS:

> **B**usiness architecture
>
> **I**nformation architecture
>
> **T**echnology architecture
>
> **S**ecurity architecture

Security architecture plays an important role in adherence to legal requirements, which is why it belongs in this section on compliance and governance. If your security architectural framework helps you clarify the security risk posture of the organization and it adds value to your organizational security, it is built soundly and will play an effective role in operations. The security architecture should be rigid enough to provide protection, but flexible enough to grow with the organization so that it can add more value in the future. An ongoing review of the effectiveness and flexibility of the enterprise information security architecture will serve the organization well. A high-level overview of how the EISA weaves through the other parts of the BITS architecture will help you better understand how all the elements work together.

As we discussed before, security risks and threats should be identified in a well-designed security architecture as well as in the phases of the systems development life cycle, or SDLC. However, a specific method for identifying risks and threats is through threat assessment or risk assessment. Threat or risk assessments test the likelihood that a given threat or risk could occur, and they evaluate the degree of potential loss or harm that would result if it did. This allows the information security professional to use a standardized process for determining which threats and risks are imminent and dangerous to the organization.

There are many models for threat and risk assessment in use today. Some of those models are proprietary, and some are open source. However, most effective models are asking the same basic questions:

- What is it that needs to be protected?
- Who and/or what are the specific threats, vulnerabilities, or risks?
- What are the implications for the organization if the protected items become compromised?
- What is the true value to the organization of the protected information?

In order to determine the answers to these questions and conduct a proper assessment, it is important to fully understand the scope of the assessment. This lets the analyst know what exactly should be covered in the assessment.

After the scope is determined, data collection should be performed. This includes the current procedures to protect the information as well as any information about parts of the procedures that are missing or not being followed per regulations.

There are some great resources available, including *www.securityfocus.com*, which includes a searchable database of known vulnerabilities and relevant newsgroups for the information security analyst.

Next, the data is analyzed, as well as the underlying policies and procedures in order to gauge organizational compliance. Best practices should be at the heart of these policies and procedures. The analyst will then prepare a vulnerability analysis, which can be done with any number of helpful tools including SAIT, Whisker, or Nessus (vulnerability scanners). The analysis should give severity and exposure ratings to identified threats and risks. The higher the severity and exposure, the more important this issue is to deal with in the short run.

Next, a threat analysis is prepared, which details the types of threats, human and nonhuman (such as floods, lightning strikes, viruses, etc.) that could transpire. Finally, an analysis of acceptable risks should be performed and presented.

When outsourcing process governance, or any other element of organizational responsibility, understand that accountability for the outsourced processes remains with the organization. While it may be advisable to use the sources of a third-party firm with significant expertise in a certain domain, such as process governance, it is important to continue to monitor those elements and to retain the ultimate responsibility and accountability for those processes within the organization itself. Outsourcing in general requires specific governance, including service level agreements (SLA), monitoring, feedback, and reporting.

OPERATIONAL SECURITY

Operational security is the sustainability function of the cybersecurity process. It ensures round-the-clock protection of the assurance target. You will find that 10 percent of all questions on the DSST Fundamentals of Cybersecurity exam cover operational security topics. Note that operational security does not focus on one specific area of cybersecurity, but the ability of the entire organization to function.

KEY ELEMENTS TO OPERATIONAL SECURITY

There are three key elements to operational security, some of which we have already discussed:

1. security architecture
2. security implementation (of the architecture)
3. operation (of the implemented architecture)

Securing and maintaining a secure environment requires a well-developed process. This process starts with operational security policies that establish clear guidelines for the operators. The policies should set and define clear escalation paths and processes that are followed carefully when an operator steps outside the allowed process. These policies also serve as deterrents against purposeful misconfigurations of information security systems.

Another key element of operational security is a strong change management process. A frequently overlooked part of a secure information system is its level of adaptability to change. Monitoring of the operating systems, the hardware, and the configurations should be performed, logged, and evaluated regularly. Any changes to those crucial elements to the system should also be logged and stored.

OTHER ELEMENTS TO OPERATIONAL SECURITY

Other key elements to operational security are access control for network devices and authorization evaluation to ensure the minimum access required is provided to each user. Building dual control into the system is also key—network control and security control are both incredibly important, and should ideally never be handled by the same group. The monitoring process should also include active attempts to detect changes in the network. Configuration changes are a good example. Automation is a great way to work toward accomplishing and monitoring all these important elements of operational security.

CRITICAL THREATS TO CLOUD AND VIRTUALIZATION SECURITY

According to a report by the Cloud Security Alliance, there are nine critical threats to cloud and virtualization security. Ranked in order from most severe to least, they are as follows:

1. Data breaches, which deals with the unauthorized access of sensitive data
2. Data loss, which deals with the destruction of data
3. Account or service traffic hijacking, which deals with the loss of account proprietary information about account traffic and service traffic
4. Insecure interfaces and APIs, which link software together to allow them to cooperate
5. Denial of services, which deals with clients or other authorized users failing to be granted services they need to perform their required functions

NOTE

Key Elements to Operational Security:

- Access control for network devices
- Authorization evaluation to ensure minimum access required is provided to each user
- Building dual control into the system
- Including active attempts to detect changes in the network into the monitoring process

6. Malicious insiders, which involves attacks by users who may be authorized to use the systems, but are misusing them

7. Abuse of cloud services, including the overuse of allotted storage for non-work needs

8. Insufficient due diligence, which can lead to implementing the wrong solutions for the organization

9. Shared technology vulnerabilities, which deals with the risks involved in sharing technology among multiple entities (as in cloud computing)

SECURITY RISKS SURROUNDING VIRTUAL IT SYSTEMS

Many of the security concerns in traditional networks are also cloud and virtualization security concerns. However, a number of them are distinct to cloud and virtualization. Before an enterprise moves toward cloud-based and virtualization services, those in charge must consider the following three security risks surrounding virtual IT systems.

The first is **architectural**. This includes the layer between the physical hardware and the virtualized or cloud-based system that is running the IT services you are protecting. This is a potential attack target. Virtual machines (VMs) in one group of a network can attack VMs from another group, as an example.

The next is **hypervisor software.** This is the most critical piece of software in a virtual information technology system. If the hypervisor software has any vulnerabilities, it puts the entire VM at risk.

Finally, there's **configuration**. Since the virtual environment makes cloning images such an easy task, it is very easy to deploy new infrastructures. This can cause a configuration drift, which makes it very difficult to monitor the rapidly changing environment and invites possible risks to security.

Some additional risks to virtualization include VM sprawl, which is the proliferation of VMs that makes the accountability difficult or impossible; the high sensitivity of VM data; the security of dormant or offline VMs; the security of preconfigured VM images; the lack of visibility and control of virtual networks; the exhaustion of resources; the security of hypervisor software; and untenable risk due to cloud service provider APIs.

NETWORK SECURITY

Network security is an essential part of cybersecurity in information systems. Approximately 20 percent of all questions on the exam will cover network security topics. For this section, we will discuss specific protocols and services, the analysis and management of network security, and the network security infrastructure. We will explore best practices in network security based on the EBK, and we will discuss network security control policies.

WORK FUNCTIONS FOR MANAGEMENT OF NETWORK AND INFORMATION SECURITY

The EBK includes the following work functions for the management of the network and information security:

- taking into consideration goals/policies of enterprise to establish a network and information security program
- managing financial/IT resources to establish/maintain an effective network and information security program
- providing leadership to network and information security personnel
- presenting the scope of the network and information security program
- establishing effective communication between network and information security teams, as well as other important stakeholders
- establishing a program for monitoring/measuring performance of network and information security teams
- taking into account the appropriate network/IT based standards, laws, policies, directives, procedures, and regulations
- conducting network-based audits/reviews of management to ensure implementation of process improvement
- making appropriate changes/improvements as required

A shocking number of software currently in use to keep information confidential are not actual cryptosystems. Rather, they are regular applications that have had cryptographic protocols added to them. This is specifically characteristic of Internet protocols. Some experts claim that the Internet and its corresponding protocols were designed without any consideration for security, which was added as an afterthought.

Internet Protocol security (IPsec) and Secure Shell (SSH) are widely used to enable secure network communications across LANs, WANs, and the Internet. IPsec is used most often to create a secure virtual private network, or VPN, over an insecure medium like the Internet. SSH is used to secure remote logins. Note that both use encryption to ensure that the confidentiality and integrity of transmitted data is protected.

IPsec is a protocol framework, open-sourced in nature, which is used for the development of security systems. IPsec is in the TCP/IP protocol family. IPSec is used on IP-based networks to protect data integrity, the confidentiality of end users, and IP packet-level authenticity.

Secure Shell (SSH) is a protocol developed in order to provide a secure method for accessing systems over an insecure medium. The latest version of the protocol, SSH-2, offers a number of improved security features over its predecessor, SSH-1.

Secure Sockets Layer (SSL), and Secure Hypertext Transfer Protocol (S-HTTP) are used for secure web communications for e-commerce, banking, and a number of other sensitive uses.

Let's take a moment to discuss SSL and S-HTTP protocols. SSL is a protocol used for the encryption of public keys over secure channels on the Internet. SSL provides client authentication as well as

NOTE

IPsec

- Protocol framework
- Open-sourced
- In the TCP/IP protocol family
- Used on IP-based networks to protect data integrity, confidentiality of end users, and IP packet-level authenticity
- Used on LANs, WANs, and the Internet

NOTE

SSH

- Protocol developed in order to provide a secure method for accessing systems over an insecure medium
- SSH-2 offers a number of improved security features over SSH-1.

the encryption of data and server authentication. S-HTTP is an extended version of HTTP. It encrypts individual messages that are transmitted over the Internet between clients and servers. Using S-HTTP, information that passes between two computers via protected, secure virtual connection can be encrypted.

Several cryptosystems have now been reconfigured and adapted to function within the most widely used e-mail protocols. This has been done to incorporate a measure of security into a historically insecure communications vehicle.

S/MIME: SMTP/RFC 822, commonly called SMTP, was the first e-mail standard commonly used. This protocol has limitations and problems, such as the inability to send .exe files or binary objects. It also has issues handling character sets other than ASCII (7-bit). Such limitations have caused SMTP to be avoided by organizations needing stronger security as well as support for other character sets (international, for example).

PGP stands for Pretty Good Privacy. Developed by Phil Zimmermann, PGP is a hybrid cryptosystem. PGP combines a group of high quality cryptographic algorithms. It is the open-source standard for encryption as well as authentication of file storage and e-mail applications. PGP is available for many different platforms in desktop and commercial versions.

WIRELESS SECURITY

Wireless LAN networks (known commonly as Wi-Fi) are often assumed to be inherently insecure, even among those in the information technology industry. The wireless network interface of a device communicates with the access point via radio transmission. Without protection, the radio signals are susceptible to interception by wireless packet sniffers. To prevent interception of wireless communications, networks must adopt cryptographic security control.

Wired Equivalent Privacy, or WEP, is an 802.11-style network protocol, and an example of early protocols used with those specifications. Cryptographically, WEP is now considered weak as it cannot provide eavesdropping protection in a meaningful way. However, it provided security, for some time, in networks with low sensitivity. RC4 cipher streams are used by WEP. Each packet is encrypted using 64-bit keys.

Wi-Fi Protected Access, or WPA and WPA2, were created to resolve WEP's major issues. With a 128-bit size, WPA uses dynamic keys that are created and shared by authentication servers.

Public key infrastructure, which we discussed earlier, is a secure communication tool using software, protocols, encryption methodologies, third-party services, and legal agreements. PKI allows secure communication between users. Based on public key technology, PKI systems include certificate authorities (CAs) and digital certificates.

Using certificate authorities, registration authorities, certificate directories, management protocols, and policies and procedures, PKI solutions protect transmissions and receptions of secure information.

As part of a prudent approach to keeping an eye on networks, organizations should consider continuous monitoring and analysis programs that involve two key components: network monitoring software—for example, packet sniffers—and intrusion detection/prevention systems (IDPSs).

NOTE

SSL
- Used for encryption of public keys over secure channels on the Internet
- Provides client authentication and encryption of data and server authentication

NOTE

S-HTTP
- Extended version of HTTP
- Encrypts individual messages transmitted over the Internet between clients and servers

Packet sniffers (sometimes referred to as network sniffers) are programs, or devices, capable of viewing data as it moves along a network. Sniffers are sometimes used maliciously. For instance, people can use them for intercepting usernames and passwords, as well as other sensitive information.

To use sniffers effectively, operators need to grasp the basic structure of a network packet. If they do, security professionals can detect the type of traffic that is being transmitted, determine the sender and receiver, know the time of transmission, and even discover which applications are involved. This is called packet analysis. Packet analysis requires training on network packets, knowing RFC specifications, and training on spotting packets that raise suspicion.

Because of its universal use in UNIX/Linux systems, tcpdump is the standard in network sniffing. tcpdump is easiest to understand when you have practical examples to examine. Please take a few moments to view ***https://danielmiessler.com/study/tcpdump/*** for a helpful set of tcpdump examples, which will help you to better understand this topic and grasp this crucial area of network analysis.

INTRUSION DETECTION AND PREVENTION SYSTEMS (IDPS)

An important part of network management is network protection. Intrusion detection and prevention systems (IDPS) can help with that. IDPS data can help management with quality assurance, as well as continuous improvement. IDPS systems pick up attack-related information from successful compromise of outer network security architecture layers, firewalls for example. The information obtained by IDPS can be used for the identification and repair of network security architecture flaws (emergent and residual). This helps organizations increase incident response time as well as make additional continuous improvements.

IDPSs are host-based systems. They work together to protect the network. Network-based (or host-based) IDPS is primarily focused on the protection of network information assets. Let's spend a moment discussing the types of IDPS.

A network-based IDPS, or NIDPS, is placed on a computer appliance that is connected to an organization's network. It monitors network traffic on a specific segment, much like tcpdump, and looks for indications of attacks either still in progress or successfully completed. When activities occur that NIDPS is programmed to recognize as possible attacks, NIDPS sends notifications to network or security administrators.

Wireless IDPS systems provide monitoring and analysis of wireless network traffic. It looks for potential problems with wireless protocols. Products like Motorola's AirDefense, Fluke's AirMagnet, and the open-source Kismet have to be deployed physically around the protected site in order to monitor the broad range of wireless signals able to reach the facility.

IDPS systems that are network based reside on network segments, monitoring activities in that specific segment. But host-based IDPS reside on particular computers/service. These are typically known as the host, monitoring activity on that system alone.

IDPS technology uses a variety of detection methods to monitor and evaluate network traffic. Three methods dominate: the signature-based approach, the statistical-anomaly approach, and the stateful packet inspection approach.

Signature-based IDPS are preconfigured, attack patterns. They examine traffic for pattern matches of known signatures. The wide use of signature-based IDPS technology is primarily because of the number of attacks in which the attackers leave distinct, clear signatures.

Log file monitoring (LFM) IDPS are related to NIDPS. The system, which uses LFM, reviews server-generated log files, devices on the network, and other IDPS systems. These protocols look for signatures and patterns indicative of an imminent or recent attack.

Network infrastructure is comprised of the equipment (hardware), software, and services necessary to power and connect a network. Network hardware, network software, and network services make up network infrastructure:

- Network hardware includes routers, switches, and access points; fiber optic cable; and network interface cards.
- Network software includes operations and management software, computer and network operating systems, firewall software, and network security applications.
- Network services include T-1, DSL, or satellite; IP addressing services; and wireless protocols.

VULNERABILITY MANAGEMENT

Vulnerability management is our next topic, which comprises 15 percent of the questions on the exam. We have discussed risk assessment as well as threat assessment, but let's discuss network testing and recognizing and mitigating threats on a regular basis.

RECONNAISSANCE

Reconnaissance, fingerprinting, and vulnerability analysis tools are invaluable because they enable administrators to see what weaknesses potential attackers see.

Analysis and scanning tools tend to have distinct signatures. With that in mind, some Internet service providers (ISPs) keep tabs on those types of signatures in order to pull the access privileges from those using them. Administrators should work hard to earn a rapport with ISPs, and also to notify them any time they are planning to conduct a scan of the external network.

Let's discuss some of the most effective types of testing for networks and information systems. In the attack methodology, one preparatory element is the publicly available information about a potential target. The collection of this material is a process called reconnaissance. This is accomplished through perusing the Internet website or presence of the target. This is sometimes referred to as footprinting. One attack methodology includes the following key elements: targeting IP addresses, targeting a website, doing business research, and Google hacking.

After gathering publicly available information, the attacker will often communicate with the systems on the target network. This is the fingerprinting stage of the attack methodology, which is an exhaustive view of an organization's web presence, done with the purpose of identifying the services offered by the host. The following tools can aid in testing and preventing these types of attacks:

Network Testing Tools:

- **Firewall Analysis Tools**
- **Port Scanning Tools**
- **Wireless Security Tools**
- **Operating System Detection Tools**
- **Passive Vulnerability Scanners**
- **Active Vulnerability Scanners**
- **Fuzzers**

firewall analysis tools, port scanning tools, wireless security tools, operating system detection tools, passive vulnerability scanners, active vulnerability scanners, and fuzzers.

Once attackers gain intelligence on a target, network penetration begins. Typically, this is accomplished through a type of manual testing called penetration testing. There are also tools that automatically attempt to exploit vulnerabilities on a system.

When considered a part of the attack methodology, "exploitation" refers to the tools and techniques for breaking into more systems, gaining further network access, or gaining access to more resources. Netcat and packet sniffers are tools that can be used to find and prevent these vulnerabilities. When considered a part of the attack methodology, "return" refers to actions an attacker takes to ensure he or she is able to return to the target unobstructed. This could entail installing backdoors, installing bots, creating user accounts, or other actions.

Let's go a little deeper in this section and discuss the importance of vulnerability disclosure in order to get necessary assistance to information security professionals and provide the required information about threats, vulnerabilities, and attacks properly. This can aid the security professional in dealing with such threats and vulnerabilities. Understanding risks posed by a software vulnerability starts with the disclosure of the vulnerability by security researchers or by the software vendor. From there, the vulnerability assessment tools can start to look for the vulnerabilities and notify organizations when they exist.

There are three philosophical approaches to handling the disclosure of vulnerabilities: full disclosure, delayed disclosure, and responsible disclosure. Information security professionals should regularly consult public disclosure lists in order to remain informed about vulnerabilities.

The following documentation and sources should be consulted regularly to discover known and reported vulnerabilities and threats. First are vendor announcements. Most of the major vendors maintain mailing lists to announce vulnerabilities, fixes, or any compensating actions that can be taken (such as closing the network port associated with a vulnerable network service or disabling script execution in a vulnerable web browser).

Vendors tend to delay announcing vulnerabilities until they have had time to research them and develop a fix or identify compensating actions. This can create a window of vulnerability for organizations if the problem has been discovered elsewhere or disclosed to others. Once all the necessary due diligence is done, the vulnerability is disclosed via full-disclosure lists, which are circulated among security professionals. The SANS Institute, which hosts many respected network security conferences and offers various security certifications, also operates the Internet Storm Center, or ISC. The ISC's mission is to provide detection and analysis of network threats, assessments of their severity, and advice on how to counter them.

The Forum of Incident Response and Security Teams, or FIRST, is another organization that facilitates information sharing on the latest cyber-threats and attacks. Common Vulnerabilities and Exposures(CVE) is a public collection of information on security vulnerabilities and known exposures.

The United States Computer Emergency Response Team, or US-CERT, is a centralized collection and reporting facility that focuses on the tracking and dissemination of information about current computer security threats.

Finally, The National Vulnerability Database, or NVD, is the U.S. government repository of vulnerabilities, which includes CVE identifiers and alerts from the US-CERT on current threats, attacks, and vulnerabilities. The NVD allows searches in either direction (from CVE reference numbers to NVD reference numbers and vice versa).

PHYSICAL AND ENVIRONMENTAL SECURITY

Physical and environmental security topics, which comprise six percent of all exam questions, are essential to information system security. Regardless of the measures used to secure the network itself from intrusion, carelessness on-site or with end users can spell disaster and invite an attack. The following sections address physical access management, media management, and environmental controls.

PHYSICAL ACCESS MANAGEMENT

Physical access management is crucial to securing network and information technology facilities. Examples of physical access management procedures are as follows:

- locking the doors to server rooms with quality hardware locks
- including mantraps in case of intrusion—which automatically lock all external doors, trapping the intruder until security can be called
- using fencing around perimeter areas and a security gate or house if possible
- installing and using proximity readers to be alerted and to monitor individuals coming within a certain distance of sensitive areas
- using signs and guards to denote the security of the area
- using barricades to control access to the area by unauthorized vehicles
- using biometric security where possible to control access and ensure authentications of authorized entrants
- using alarms and motion detection in secure and sensitive areas

Some other important measures include keeping computer screens locked when walking away from them, even for just a moment or two, and using equipment to reduce the angle at which sensitive material can be viewed on a computer monitor. Choosing proper screen angles that face away from areas where viewing is possible is a good idea, as well, especially when entering sensitive authentication information such as passwords.

Media management is an important part of physical security. Not so many years ago, media management might be as simple as making a daily tap backup and carrying it to your home or another secure environment at the end of each day. Times have changed, though, and media is digital and easy to move around in large quantities.

The popularity of cloud-based media management has opened up a plethora of new options for information security professionals. Storage can be moved to redundant servers that are completely cloud based, or they can stick with off-site storage that is dedicated and secured 24 hours a day in many of the ways we will detail in the next section.

ENVIRONMENTAL SECURITY

Environmental controls help protect sensitive and secure equipment against environmental hazards. Some examples of environmental hazards to protect against are fire, flooding, electromagnetic interference, extreme heat and cold, and extreme pressure and humidity. You can protect against these environmental hazards by taking commonsense measures. Some of the best ways to protect against these specific hazards are:

- Install fire suppression systems to protect against fires in sensitive areas such as server rooms. Fire suppression systems that do not involve water are the best to use for sensitive electronics. A dry chemical suppression system would be the best method.

- Place equipment above the floor level for both circulation and prevention from minor flooding.

- Use electromagnetic interference, or EMI, shielding in sensitive areas to protect equipment like servers from electromagnetic waves that could endanger important information.

- Set up the server room, and any other sensitive areas with the extreme heat and cold of different equipment in mind. Hot aisles and cold aisles are typical, and special equipment is available to help prevent overheating or overcooling.

- Use environmental monitoring to protect against high pressure or high humidity. Also, dehumidifiers might be needed to remove excess humidity from the air around and in sensitive areas like server rooms.

As with any sensitive electronics, temperature controls are essential, and the equipment should never be allowed to go above or below the acceptable temperature levels specified by the manufacturers of the equipment.

DISASTER RECOVERY AND BUSINESS CONTINUITY

Approximately 10 percent of questions on the DSST Fundamentals of Cybersecurity exam will ask about disaster recovery and business continuity. No one wants to think about the worst-case scenario taking place, but it is important to have a disaster recovery plan and a business continuity plan in case of any disruptive events. These events could include a major catastrophe, such as a hurricane, or something as simple as a power outage. The key is to have a plan that will help the business to regain business practices as soon as possible. We will discuss backup and retention strategies of important documents, disaster recovery planning and business continuity planning, and plan testing and maintenance.

BACKUP AND RETENTION STRATEGIES

Having a strong document retention strategy is essential for all organizations in all industries. Document retention is important for legal and compliance reasons, legal obligations, auditing purposes, and business process improvements. The process can seem quite daunting, especially for organizations whose processes rely heavily on paper documents. The amount of business information has increased substantially in our electronic era. Such electronic documents as e-mails are now considered to be corporate records. There are three common mistakes that are found in document retention and within an organization's strategies.

The first failure is not having and enacting a retention policy. The retention policy should include what information is necessary for the organization today and in the future. The policy should include the documents, paper and electronic, that must be retained and indicate how long they should be retained. Employees should be trained on the policy and understand their role in the retention strategy of the organization. Policies should be written, enforced, and also tested through document audits regularly to ensure the policy is being followed. For example, if a bank is required to keep all loan files for five years, the bank needs to have a plan for where the loan files will be stored, who will maintain the list of files, and who will destroy the files after five years. These are all questions that the retention strategy should contain.

The second failure is lacking a solid backup system. It is important to have a retention strategy and to keep the required documentation. But what happens in case of a fire or a flood? What would happen to the documents, especially paper documents? Companies should frequently back up their entire systems for their electronic files and consider having servers at a different location to store the backed-up information. For paper documents, the organization may consider a third-party to store the documents or another off-site storage location. Once it has been determined the information is no longer needed, the company should use the retention plan and follow the instructions to purge the information. Many organizations have started using high-speed storage media. This process simplifies document retrieval and usually at a lower cost. Without a data repository in place, organizations are left with possible loss of information that could harm the business.

The third failure is the lack of automation in the retention strategy. With the enhancements of technology, much of the data backup process should be automated. However, organizations are often slow to make this change and struggle with automating the process. Without technology involved, the document retention strategy can take much longer and is subject to human error. With automated controls, the system automatically performs backups at scheduled times and also purges the information at specified times. Automation retention systems also provide the organizations with peace of mind. The systems are capable of having the following:

- An automation schedule
- Audit trails
- Purge requirements
- Document move requirements
- Procedures for control without employee involvement

Without human error, automation strategies provide consistency and rules to the retention process. This also follows the organization's governance plan and helps the organization to meet industry compliance requirements.

Many of the issues with document retention can be resolved by converting from paper processes to electronic processes. Large industries, such as hospitals and clinics, have discovered the benefits of electronic processes and have converted patient records to electronic records. Once an organization decides to make the change to electronic documentation, the organization should continually evaluate its systems to ensure that it meets all regulatory requirements.

Retention and backup systems are now considered two-fold. The first part is the technology and how technology will help to automate the processes. Once the hard part is done in terms of converting from paper to electronic, the organization will find that much of the remaining process is easier to manage. The second part is the human element. Employees will be trained to use the electronic system and to understand the guidelines and policies that are in place.

DISASTER RECOVERY PLANNING AND BUSINESS CONTINUITY PLANNING

Disaster recovery (DR) involves the plan for recovering access to hardware, data, software, and other systems that are needed to resume normal and critical business functions. The disaster recovery plan is used after a natural disaster or some other disaster that has caused a disruption in business operations. The disaster recovery plan should include how to overcome data, hardware, or software that has been damaged and destroyed and also how to determine the manpower needed to begin business operations again. For example, consider a hurricane. If the majority of the employees have evacuated, who is in charge of bringing the business back to operational status and how many employees will it take?

The disaster plan should have several different plans for possible scenarios. For example, some disasters might impact the data, software, and systems—such as a fire. The disaster plan should lay out how the organization will continue and where the employees will report to work if the building is destroyed. Other disasters might involve the systems and the employees, such as with an act of terrorism like we saw in the 9/11 attack in New York and Washington, D.C. The plans should be routinely updated and also adaptable to meet the situations that the organization may face.

Business continuity planning is the plan for how the organization will prepare for a disaster. Usually, top management and essential employees are involved in the business continuity plan. The plans should be detailed enough so everyone understands the process and how it will be implemented in the event of a disaster. The goal of the business continuity plan is to recover and restore the operations that are necessary to reopen the business. To ensure its effectiveness, the plan should continually be reviewed and also practiced.

The business continuity plan should help to protect the organization against future instances. A long-term shutdown of the business could lead to long-term issues, so it is essential for the organization to be back to operational status or critical operational status as quickly as possible. The ultimate goal of the plan is to expedite the processes to regain full operational status of the organization. The plan should include the critical operations that are needed, the essential personnel, and a business continuation plan.

PLAN TESTING AND MAINTENANCE

For the disaster recovery plan to succeed, it is important to test the plan and to ensure that the plan is feasible. In addition, the plan should be reviewed for any changes. For example, as the organization grows and changes, the plan should be revised to cover any areas that have been added and any key processes/operations that should be included in the recovery plan.

The testing of the disaster recovery plan also presents a chance for the organization to train the staff on their responsibilities and how the plan will work. The testing of the recovery plan will showcase any deficiencies and areas that need to be revised to ensure the success of the organization after a major disaster.

SUMMING IT UP

- Best practices in IT security are based on the information technology (IT) **Essential Body of Knowledge** (EBK).

- There are 14 areas of common practice in the EBK regarding security. These include data security, digital forensics, enterprise continuity, incident management, IT security training and awareness, IT systems operation and maintenance, network security and telecommunications, personnel security, physical and environmental security, procurement, regulatory and standards compliance, risk management, strategic security management, and systems and applications security.

- There are three executive roles overseeing various functional events, classified as management, design, implementation, or evaluation events. Those three executives are the **chief information officer (CIO), the information security officer, and the IT security compliance officer**.

- The aim of the application and system security function is to identify and then eliminate defects in code that may be exploitable.

- The **public key infrastructure (PKI)** is the authority that issues and certifies both private and public keys as valid. This is essential for public key encryption.

- There are 7 basic steps to an encryption strategy: collaboration, data classification, key management, finding a solution, access control, consequences, and SLL decryption.

- Each step of the system development life cycle (SDLC) offers opportunities to communicate security concerns.

- In the **initiation phase** of the SDLC, the focus is on identifying a need or an opportunity.

- In the **system concept development phase**, the scope of the process is defined.

- In the **planning phase**, a Project Management Plan is developed.

- In the **requirements analysis phase**, the basic needs and requirements of the user are taken into consideration.

- In the **design phase**, detailed requirements are converted into a fully formed and detailed Systems Design Document.

- In the **development phase**, the completed design that was put together in the previous phases is compiled and combined, forming the beginnings of an information system.

- In the **integration and testing phase**, the systems are developed and ready to be integrated for eventual end-user implementation.

- The **implementation phase** begins with final preparation for implementation.

- In the **operations and maintenance phase**, the system is maintained and operated in a live production environment.

- In the **disposition phase**, end-of-system activities are being conducted, and the system is preparing to be discontinued.

- **Access control** is a core part of information security. Professionals must recognize that access control for physical space is implemented through the same identity, authentication, and authorization functions that are used to control electronic access control.

- **Authentication** is a process for determining whether a user attempting to gain access to a system is, in fact, the authorized holder of the appropriate credentials needed for access.

- There are three main factors for authentication upon which most authentication systems are built: **something you know, something you have,** and **something you are**.

- The **authorization** process occurs after authentication, and provides access to resources.

- Any system is only as good as the strict governance that ensures it runs exactly as it was designed to run. At the same time, compliance with all the applicable procedures, directives, standards, policies, laws, and regulations is essential for effectiveness and security.

- **Enterprise information security architecture (EISA)** is established by aligning business, IT, software, hardware, network, human resources, operations, and projects processes with the overall security strategy of the organization.

- **Security architecture**, which was once silo-based and removed from the main service architecture of organizations, has since been repositioned as a core element of service architecture.

- **Operational security** is the sustainability function of the cybersecurity process. It ensures round-the-clock protection of the assurance target. Note that operational security does not focus on one specific area of cybersecurity, but the ability of the entire organization to function.

- There are three key elements to operational security: **security architecture, security implementation (of the architecture), and operation (of the implemented architecture).**

- Other key elements to operational security are access control for network devices and authorization evaluation to ensure the minimum access required is provided to each user.

- According to a report by the Cloud Security Alliance, there are nine critical threats to cloud and virtualization security. They include data breaches, data loss, account or service traffic hijacking, insecure interfaces and APIs, denial of service, malicious insiders, abuse of cloud services, insufficient due diligence, and shared technology vulnerabilities.

- Before an enterprise moves toward cloud-based and virtualization services, it must consider the following three security risks surrounding virtual IT systems: architectural threats, hypervisor software vulnerabilities, and configuration drift.

- **Network security** is an essential part of cybersecurity in information systems.

- **Internet Protocol security (IPsec)** and **Secure Shell (SSH)** are widely used to enable secure network communications across LANs, WANs, and the Internet.

- IPsec is a protocol framework, open-sourced in nature, used for development of security systems.

- SSH is protocol developed in order to provide a secure method for accessing systems over an insecure medium.

- **Secure Sockets Layer (SSL)** and **Secure Hypertext Transfer Protocol (S-HTTP)** are used for secure web communications for e-commerce, banking, and a number of other sensitive uses.

- **Wireless LAN networks** (known commonly as Wi-Fi) are often assumed to be inherently insecure, even among those in the information technology industry.

- An important part of network management is network protection. **Intrusion detection and prevention systems (IDPS)** can help with that.

- **Wireless IDPS** systems provide monitoring and analysis of wireless network traffic.

- **Reconnaissance, fingerprinting,** and **vulnerability analysis tools** are invaluable because they enable administrators to see what weaknesses potential attackers see.

- **Physical and environmental security** are essential to information system security. Regardless of the measures used to secure the network itself from intrusion, carelessness on-site or with end users can spell disaster and invite an attack.

- **Physical access management** is crucial to securing network and information technology facilities.

- **Media management** is an important part of physical security. Not so many years ago, media management might have been as simple as making a daily tap backup and carrying it to your home or another secure environment at the end of each day.

- **Environmental controls** help protect sensitive and secure equipment against environmental hazards.

- Having a strong **document retention strategy** is essential for all organizations in all industries. Document retention is important for legal and compliance reasons, legal obligations, auditing purposes, and business process improvements.

- **Disaster recovery (DR)** involves the plan for recovering access to hardware, data, software, and other systems that are needed to resume normal and critical business functions.

- **Business continuity planning** is the plan for how the organization will prepare for a disaster.

- For the **disaster recovery plan** to be successful, it is important to test the plan and to ensure that the plan is feasible.

FUNDAMENTALS OF CYBERSECURITY POST-TEST

Directions: Carefully read each of the following 60 questions. Choose the best answer to each question and fill in the corresponding circle on the answer sheet. The Answer Key and Explanations can be found following this post-test.

1. Which of the following reviews server-generated log files, devices on the network, and other IDPS systems to look for signatures and patterns indicative of an imminent or recent attack?
   A. Wireless IDPS
   B. Host-based IDPS
   C. Signature-based IDPS
   D. Log file monitor (LFM) IDPS

2. A frequently overlooked part of a secure information system is its
   A. access controls.
   B. level of adaptability to change.
   C. information architecture.
   D. technology architecture.

3. Which of the following involves an encryption algorithm, as well as a key to decipher it?
   A. Cryptography
   B. Antivirus
   C. Malware detection
   D. Security triad

4. Which of the following ensures a system is conforming properly to all requirements specified and set out in the Functional Requirements Document?
   A. Integration and testing
   B. Implementation
   C. Maintenance
   D. Disposition

5. Which of the following should be viewed as a vulnerable function for protected information?
   A. Data migration
   B. Disposition
   C. Development
   D. Access controls

6. The unauthorized access of sensitive data falls under
   A. data breaches.
   B. data loss.
   C. account hijacking.
   D. denial of service.

7. Which of the following brings the key stakeholders together to determine the necessary solutions based on laws, needs of the organization, and resources for the encryption strategy?
   A. Data classification
   B. Key management
   C. Collaboration
   D. Consequences

8. Which of the following provides access to resources?
   A. Authentication
   B. Authorization
   C. Access controls
   D. Compliance

9. Which of the following prevents overheating and overcooling?
    A. Electromagnetic interference
    B. Fire suppression system
    C. Temperature controls
    D. Humidifiers

10. Authentication is accomplished through all of the following EXCEPT
    A. passwords.
    B. digital certificates.
    C. public key infrastructure (PKI).
    D. a physical key.

11. Authentication involves how many main factors?
    A. One
    B. Two
    C. Three
    D. Four

12. Password-based authentication is not adequately strong security for systems that contain which of the following types of data?
    A. Sensitive
    B. General
    C. Secured
    D. Timely

13. Which of the following can ensure trusted access to information systems as long as they are strong and secret?
    A. Passwords
    B. Digital certificates
    C. PKI
    D. A physical key

14. Which of the following monitors activity on the host system alone?
    A. Wireless IDPS
    B. Host-based IDPS
    C. Signature-based IDPS
    D. Log file monitor (LFM) IDPS

15. Which of the following broadly covers using sound strategic management principles to manage information security in the organization?
    A. Environmental security
    B. Risk management
    C. Standards compliance
    D. Strategic security management

16. A WPA uses dynamic keys that are created and shared by authentication servers and a bit size of which of the following?
    A. 128-bit size
    B. 130-bit size
    C. 132-bit size
    D. 133-bit size

17. Which of the following is established by aligning business, IT, software, hardware, network, human resources, operations, and projects processes with the overall security strategy of the organization?
    A. Enterprise information
    B. Information architecture
    C. Technology architecture
    D. Security architecture

18. BITS stands for which of the following?
    A. Business architecture, information architecture, technology architecture, and security architecture
    B. Business architecture, information architecture, technology architecture, and service architecture
    C. Business architecture, infrastructure architecture, technology architecture, and security architecture
    D. Business architecture, information architecture, time architecture, and security architecture

19. Which of the following should be used for shielding in sensitive areas?
    A. Electromagnetic interference
    B. Fire suppression system
    C. Temperature controls
    D. Humidifiers

20. Which of the following is not part of the Security Triad?
    A. Confidentiality
    B. Integrity
    C. Availability
    D. Flexibility

21. EISA stands for which of the following?
    A. Enterprise information security architecture
    B. Enterprise information service architecture
    C. Exit information security architecture
    D. Enterprise index security architecture

22. The sustainability function of the cybersecurity process is
    A. operational security.
    B. security architecture.
    C. security implementation.
    D. access control.

23. Which of the following involves securing and maintaining a secure environment with operational security policies that establish clear guidelines regarding what the operators should and should not do?
    A. Enterprise information
    B. Information architecture
    C. Technology architecture
    D. Security architecture

24. Which of the following is a great way to work toward accomplishing and monitoring all the important elements of operational security?
    A. Automation
    B. Implementation
    C. Authorization
    D. Authentication

25. The protection of information in electronic databases from unauthorized access, theft, or destruction is known as
    A. enterprise continuity.
    B. incident management.
    C. digital forensics.
    D. data security.

26. Which of the following deals with the loss of proprietary information about account and service traffic?
    A. Data breaches
    B. Data loss
    C. Account hijacking
    D. Denial of service

27. Which of the following is an essential part of cybersecurity in information systems?
    A. Operational security
    B. Network security
    C. Access controls
    D. Enterprise information

28. Which of the following is the U.S. governmental repository of vulnerabilities?
    A. NVD
    B. US-CERT
    C. CVE
    D. FIRST

29. Outsourcing in general requires specific governance that includes all of the following EXCEPT
    A. service level agreements.
    B. monitoring.
    C. feedback.
    D. risk assessment.

30. Which of the following is most often used to create a secure VPN over an insecure medium?
    A. Secure Shell
    B. Internet Protocol security
    C. Secure Sockets Layer
    D. S-HTTP

31. Which of the following encrypts individual messages that are transmitted over the Internet between clients and servers?
    A. Secure Shell
    B. Internet Protocol security
    C. Secure Sockets Layer
    D. S-HTTP

32. Which of the following are used for secure web communications for e-commerce, banking, and a number of other sensitive uses?
    A. Secure Shell
    B. Internet Protocol security
    C. Secure Sockets Layer
    D. S-HTTP

33. A firewall is an example of which of the following?
    A. Risk assessment
    B. Information architecture
    C. Technology architecture
    D. Security architecture

34. Which of the following is used to secure remote logins?
    A. SSH
    B. IPsec
    C. SSL
    D. S-HTTP

35. Which of the following means "cannot deny?"
    A. Confidentiality
    B. Integrity
    C. Availability
    D. Non-repudiation

36. Which of the following provides client authentication and encryption of data and server authentication?
    A. SSH
    B. IPsec
    C. SSL
    D. S-HTTP

37. To prevent interception of wireless communications, networks must adopt which type of security control?
    A. Cryptographic
    B. Authentication
    C. Authorization
    D. Access controls

38. Which of the following is a specific method for identifying risks and threats?
    A. Risk assessment
    B. Information architecture
    C. Technology architecture
    D. Security architecture

39. Which of the following provide monitoring/analysis of wireless network traffic?
    A. Wireless IDPS
    B. Host-based IDPS
    C. Signature-based IDPS
    D. Log file monitor (LFM) IDPS

40. All of the following are tools for vulnerability management EXCEPT
   A. SAIT.
   B. Whisker.
   C. SARA.
   D. Nexis.

41. Which of the following involves network testing and recognizing and mitigating threats on a regular basis?
   A. Network security
   B. Operational security
   C. Vulnerability management
   D. Reconnaissance

42. Using an ID badge to enter a secured building is an example of which of the following?
   A. Security architecture
   B. Authorization
   C. Authentication
   D. Access controls

43. Which of the following includes targeting IP addresses, targeting a website, performing business research, and Google hacking?
   A. Network security
   B. Operational security
   C. Vulnerability management
   D. Footprinting

44. Which of the following terms refers to the tools and techniques for breaking into more systems, gaining further network access, or gaining access to more resources?
   A. Exploitation
   B. Return
   C. Vendor announcements
   D. Full-disclosure lists

45. The preservation of the ability to perform the essential functions required for operational effectiveness as it pertains to the continuity of the unit or organization falls under
   A. enterprise continuity.
   B. incident management.
   C. digital forensics.
   D. data security.

46. There are how many basic steps to an encryption system?
   A. Four
   B. Five
   C. Six
   D. Seven

47. Which of the following was once silo-based and removed from the main service architecture of organizations but has since been repositioned as a core element of service architecture?
   A. Risk assessment
   B. Information architecture
   C. Technology architecture
   D. Security architecture

48. Which of the following refers to the actions an attacker takes to ensure he or she is able to return to the target unobstructed?
   A. Exploitation
   B. Return
   C. Vendor announcements
   D. Full-disclosure lists

49. If a vulnerability is found, it may be necessary to install which of the following?
   A. Patch
   B. Policy
   C. Return
   D. Announcement

post-test

50. Which of the following provides detection and analysis of network threats, assessments of their severity, and advice on how to counter them?
    A. ISC
    B. FIRST
    C. Full-disclosure lists
    D. Vendor announcements

51. Which of the following ensures that a proper record of the access has been recorded to ensure proper evaluation of the data security function?
    A. Authorization
    B. Accountability
    C. Compliance
    D. Something you are

52. Which of the following facilitates information sharing on the latest cyber-threats and attacks?
    A. ISC
    B. FIRST
    C. Full-disclosure lists
    D. Vendor announcements

53. Which of the following help(s) protect sensitive and secure equipment against environmental hazards?
    A. Exploitation
    B. Return
    C. Vendor announcements
    D. Environmental controls

54. Which programs/devices (sometimes used maliciously) are capable of viewing data as it moves along networks?
    A. Data breaches
    B. Data losses
    C. Account hijackings
    D. Packet sniffers

55. Which of the following is an area of responsibility that includes keeping the organization and its security assets safe in the event of natural or manmade disasters?
    A. Environmental security
    B. Risk management
    C. Standards compliance
    D. Strategic security management

56. The verifying characteristic (known as biometrics) used to confirm the identity and the right to access systems is known as
    A. something you are.
    B. accountability.
    C. compliance.
    D. authorization.

57. There are three main elements to operational security. They include all of the following EXCEPT
    A. security architecture.
    B. security implementation (of the architecture).
    C. operation (of the implemented architecture).
    D. service architecture.

58. Which of the following involves changes necessary to be performed in a live environment?
    A. Integration and testing
    B. Implementation
    C. Maintenance
    D. Disposition

59. All of the following are philosophical approaches to handling the disclosure of vulnerabilities EXCEPT
    A. full disclosure.
    B. delayed disclosure.
    C. responsible disclosure.
    D. information disclosure.

60. Which of the following is a secure com-
    munication tool using software, protocols,
    encryption methodologies, third-party
    services, and legal agreements?
    A. Passwords
    B. Digital certificates
    C. Public key infrastructure (PKI)
    D. A physical key

post-test

ANSWER KEY AND EXPLANATIONS

1. D	**13.** A	**25.** D	**37.** A	**49.** A
2. B	**14.** B	**26.** C	**38.** A	**50.** A
3. A	**15.** D	**27.** B	**39.** A	**51.** B
4. A	**16.** A	**28.** A	**40.** D	**52.** B
5. A	**17.** A	**29.** D	**41.** C	**53.** D
6. A	**18.** A	**30.** B	**42.** C	**54.** D
7. C	**19.** A	**31.** D	**43.** D	**55.** A
8. B	**20.** D	**32.** C	**44.** A	**56.** A
9. C	**21.** A	**33.** D	**45.** A	**57.** D
10. D	**22.** A	**34.** A	**46.** D	**58.** C
11. C	**23.** D	**35.** D	**47.** D	**59.** D
12. A	**24.** A	**36.** C	**48.** B	**60.** C

1. **The correct answer is D.** Log file monitor IDPS review server-generated log files, devices on the network, and other IDPS systems to look for signatures and patterns indicative of an imminent or recent attack. Choice A is incorrect because wireless IDPS provides monitoring/analysis of wireless network traffic. Choice B is incorrect because host-based IDPS monitor activity on that (host) system alone. Choice C is incorrect because signature-based IDPS examine traffic for pattern matches of known signatures.

2. **The correct answer is B.** Level of adaptability to change is one of the frequently overlooked parts of a secure information system. Choice A is incorrect because access controls are used to determine which individuals can enter certain areas. Choice C is incorrect because information architecture is the structural design of how information is shared. Choice D is incorrect because technology architecture is the process of bringing together the IT components of the system.

3. **The correct answer is A.** The data security competency covers the important task of implementing and maintaining encryption. This is done through cryptography, which involves an encryption algorithm, as well as a key to decipher it. There are two types of keys: symmetric (secret) and asymmetric (public). Choice B is incorrect because anti-virus is software used to detect and remove viruses. Choice C is incorrect because malware detection is used to detect malware on the system. Choice D is incorrect because a security triad is the loss of confidentiality, loss of integrity, and loss of availability.

4. **The correct answer is A.** Integration and testing ensure a system is conforming properly to all requirements specified and set out in the Functional Requirements Document. Choice B is incorrect because implementation focuses on resolving problems uncovered and highlighted during the integration and test phases. Choice C is incorrect because maintenance involves changes performed in a live environment. Choice D is incorrect because disposition is when a system is at the end of its life.

5. **The correct answer is A.** Data migration should be viewed as a vulnerable function for protected information. Choice B is incorrect because disposition involves end-of-system activities for a system preparing to be discontinued. Choice C is incorrect because development is the completed design that is compiled and combined. Choice D is incorrect because access controls for physical space are implemented through the same identity, authentication, and authorization functions that are used to control electronic access control.

6. **The correct answer is A.** Data breaches deal with the unauthorized access of sensitive data. Choice B is incorrect because data loss deals with the destruction of data. Choice C is incorrect because account hijacking deals with the loss of proprietary information about account and service traffic. Choice D is incorrect because denial of service deals with clients or other authorized users failing to be granted services they need to perform their required functions.

7. **The correct answer is C.** Collaboration brings the key stakeholders together to determine the necessary solutions based on laws, needs of the organization, and resources for the encryption strategy. Choice A is incorrect because data classification is where data is separated based on the security needs of the organization. Choice B is incorrect because key management determines who will hold encryption keys, who manages the encryption key life cycle, and what the overall key management system will look like. Choice D is incorrect because consequences are a fixed set of responsibilities and corrective measures for failing to meet those responsibilities.

8. **The correct answer is B.** The authorization process occurs after authentication and provides access to resources. Choice

A is incorrect because authentication is the process for determining whether a user attempting to gain access to a system is, in fact, the authorized holder of the appropriate credentials needed for access. Choice C is incorrect because access controls are used to determine which individuals can enter certain areas. Choice D is incorrect because compliance is the level at which the authentication rules are followed.

9. **The correct answer is C.** Temperature controls help prevent overheating or overcooling. Choice A is incorrect because electromagnetic interference is used for shielding in sensitive areas. Choice B is incorrect because fire suppression systems protect against fires in sensitive areas such as server rooms. Choice D is incorrect because humidifiers remove excess humidity from the air around, and in, sensitive areas like server rooms.

10. **The correct answer is D.** A physical key is not an example of how authentication is accomplished. Choices A, B, and C are all incorrect because they are all ways to ensure authentication.

11. **The correct answer is C.** Authentication involves three main factors: something you know; something you have, and something you are.

12. **The correct answer is A.** Password-based authentication is not adequately strong security for systems that contain sensitive data.

13. **The correct answer is A.** Passwords can ensure trusted access to information systems as long as they are strong and secret. Choice B is incorrect because digital certificates are sent along with documents. Choice C is incorrect because PKI involves physical access. Choice D is incorrect because a physical key is not part of cybersecurity.

14. **The correct answer is B.** Host-based IDPS systems monitor activity on that (host) system alone. Choice A is incorrect because wireless IDPS provide monitoring/analysis of wireless network traffic. Choice C is incorrect because signature-based IDPS systems examine traffic for pattern matches of known signatures. Choice D is incorrect because a log file monitor IDPS reviews server-generated log files, devices on the network, and other IDPS systems to look for signatures and patterns indicative of an imminent or recent attack.

15. **The correct answer is D.** Strategic security management broadly covers using sound strategic management principles to manage information security in the organization. Choice A is incorrect because environmental security includes keeping the organization and its security assets safe in the event of natural or manmade disasters. Choice B is incorrect because risk management covers the design, implementation, and control of risk management processes as they relate to information security assets. Choice C is incorrect because standards compliance covers the adherence to applicable information, security laws and regulations, as well as standards and policies.

16. **The correct answer is A.** With a 128-bit size, a WPA uses dynamic keys that are created and shared by authentication servers so choices B, C, and D are incorrect.

17. **The correct answer is A.** Enterprise information is established by aligning business, IT, software, hardware, network, human resources, operations, and projects processes with the overall security strategy of the organization. Choice B is incorrect because information architecture is the structural design of how information is shared. Choice C is incorrect because technology architecture is the process of bringing together the IT components of the system. Choice D is incorrect because security architecture involves a well-developed process that starts with operational security policies that establish clear guidelines regarding what the operators should and should not do.

18. **The correct answer is A.** BITS stands for business architecture, information architecture, technology architecture, and security architecture.

19. **The correct answer is A.** Electromagnetic interference is used for shielding in sensitive areas. Choice B is incorrect because fire suppression systems protect against fires in sensitive areas such as server rooms. Choice C is incorrect because temperature controls help prevent overheating or overcooling. Choice D is incorrect because humidifiers remove excess humidity from the air around, and in, sensitive areas like server rooms.

20. **The correct answer is D.** The security triad consists of confidentiality, integrity, and availability. Choice A is incorrect because it is part of the security triad. Choice B is incorrect because it is part of the security triad. Choice C is incorrect because it is part of the security triad.

21. **The correct answer is A.** EISA stands for enterprise information security architecture.

22. **The correct answer is A.** Operational security is the sustainability function of the cybersecurity process. Choice B is incorrect because security architecture requires a well-developed process that starts with operational security policies that establish clear guidelines regarding what the operators should and should not do. Choice C is incorrect because security implementation is the process of implementing the cybersecurity processes. Choice D is incorrect because access controls determine which individuals can enter certain areas.

23. **The correct answer is D.** Security architecture involves securing and maintaining a secure environment with operational security policies that establish clear guidelines regarding what the operators should and should not do. Choice A is incorrect because enterprise information is established by aligning business, IT, software, hardware, network, human resources, operations, and projects processes with the overall security strategy of the organization. Choice B is incorrect because information architecture is the structural design of how information is shared. Choice C is incorrect because technology architecture is the process of bringing together the IT components of the system.

24. **The correct answer is A.** Automation works toward accomplishing and monitoring all these important elements of operational security. Choice B is incorrect because implementation involves starting the processes within the organization. Choice C is incorrect because authorization involves deciding who will have authority. Choice D is incorrect because authentication is the process of determining the identity of the authorized individual.

25. **The correct answer is D.** Data security is the protection of information in electronic databases from unauthorized access, theft, or destruction. Choice A is incorrect because enterprise continuity is the preservation of the ability to perform the essential functions required for operational effectiveness as it pertains to the continuity of the unit or organization. Choice B is incorrect because incident management governs the handling/reporting procedures for incidents relating to IT management and security. Choice C is incorrect because digital forensics is the recovery of electronic information, often from devices that have been tampered with, destroyed, or compromised.

26. **The correct answer is C.** Account hijacking deals with the loss of proprietary information about account and service traffic. Choice A is incorrect because data breaches deal with the unauthorized access of sensitive data. Choice B is incorrect because data loss deals with the destruction of data. Choice D is incorrect because denial of service deals with clients or other authorized users failing to be granted services they need to perform their required functions.

27. **The correct answer is B.** Network security is an essential part of cybersecurity in information systems. Choice A is incorrect because operational security is the sustainability function of the cybersecurity process. Choice C is incorrect because access controls are used to determine which individuals can enter certain areas. Choice D is incorrect because enterprise information is established by aligning business, IT, software, hardware, network, human resources, operations, and projects processes with the overall security strategy of the organization.

28. **The correct answer is A.** NVD is the U.S. governmental repository of vulnerabilities; this includes CVE identifiers and alerts from the US-CERT on current threats, attacks, and vulnerabilities. Choice B is incorrect because US-CERT is a centralized collection and reporting facility that focuses on the tracking and dissemination of information about current computer security threats. Choice C is incorrect because CVE is a public collection of information on security vulnerabilities and known exposures. Choice D is incorrect because FIRST facilitates information sharing on the latest cyber-threats and attacks.

29. **The correct answer is D.** Risk assessment is not a part of the specific governance requirements for outsourcing. Choices A,

B, and C are all incorrect because they are specific requirements for outsourcing.

30. **The correct answer is B.** IPsec is most often used to create a secure VPN over an insecure medium. Choice A is incorrect because a Secure Shell is a protocol developed in order to provide a secure method for accessing systems over an insecure medium. Choice C is incorrect because SSLs are used for secure web communications for e-commerce, banking, and a number of other sensitive uses. Choice D is incorrect because S-HTTP encrypts individual messages that are transmitted over the Internet between clients and servers.

31. **The correct answer is D.** S-HTTP encrypts individual messages that are transmitted over the Internet between clients and servers. Choice A is incorrect because a Secure Shell is a protocol developed in order to provide a secure method for accessing systems over an insecure medium. Choice B is incorrect because IPsec is most often used to create a secure VPN over an insecure medium. Choice C is incorrect because SSLs are used for secure web communications for e-commerce, banking, and a number of other sensitive uses.

32. **The correct answer is C.** SSLs are used for secure web communications for e-commerce, banking, and a number of other sensitive uses. Choice A is incorrect because a Secure Shell is a protocol developed in order to provide a secure method for accessing systems over an insecure medium. Choice B is incorrect because IPsec is most often used to create a secure VPN over an insecure medium. Choice D is incorrect because S-HTTP encrypts individual messages that are transmitted over the Internet between clients and servers.

33. **The correct answer is D.** A firewall is a type of security architecture. Choices A, B, and C are incorrect.

34. **The correct answer is A.** SSH is used to secure remote logins. Choice B is incorrect because IPsec is used most often used to create a secure virtual private network, or VPN, over an insecure medium like the Internet. Choice C is incorrect because SSL is used for encryption of public keys over secure channels on the Internet. Choice D is incorrect because S-HTTP encrypts individual messages transmitted over the Internet between clients and servers.

35. **The correct answer is D.** Non-repudiation means "cannot deny" and is used to send letters and other e-documents so the receiver cannot deny they received them. Choices A, B, and C are incorrect because they are a part of the security triad.

36. **The correct answer is C.** SSL provides client authentication and encryption of data and server authentication. Choice A is incorrect because SSH is used to secure remote logins. Choice B is incorrect because IPsec is used most often to create a secure virtual private network, or VPN, over an insecure medium like the Internet. Choice D is incorrect because S-HTTP encrypts individual messages transmitted over the Internet between clients and servers.

37. **The correct answer is A.** To prevent interception of wireless communications, networks must adopt cryptographic security control. Choice B is incorrect because authentication is the process for determining whether a user attempting to gain access to a system is, in fact, the authorized holder of the appropriate credentials needed for access. Choice C is incorrect because the authorization process occurs after authentication, and it provides access to resources. Choice D is incorrect because access controls are

used to determine which individuals can enter certain areas.

38. **The correct answer is A.** Risk assessment is a specific method for identifying risks and threats. Choice B is incorrect because information architecture is the structural design of how information is shared. Choice C is incorrect because technology architecture is the process of bringing together the IT components of the system. Choice D is incorrect because security architecture involves securing and maintaining a secure environment requires through operational security policies that establish clear guidelines regarding what the operators should and should not do.

39. **The correct answer is A.** Wireless IDPS provides monitoring/analysis of wireless network traffic. Choice B is incorrect because host-based IDPS monitors activity on that (host) system alone. Choice C is incorrect because signature-based IDPS examines traffic for pattern matches of known signatures. Choice D is incorrect because log file monitor IDPS reviews server-generated log files, devices on the network, and other IDPS systems to look for signatures and patterns indicative of an imminent or recent attack.

40. **The correct answer is D.** Nexis is not a tool that is used for vulnerability management. Choices A, B, and C are incorrect because SAIT, Whisker, and SARA are tools used for vulnerability management.

41. **The correct answer is C.** Vulnerability management involves network testing and recognizing and mitigating threats on a regular basis. Choice A is incorrect because network security is an essential part of cybersecurity in information systems. Choice B is incorrect because operational security is the sustainability function of the cybersecurity process. Choice D is incorrect because reconnaissance is the collection of publicly available information about a potential target.

42. **The correct answer is C.** The authentication process would involve using an ID badge to enter a secured building. Choice A is incorrect because security architecture involves securing and maintaining a secure environment through operational security policies that establish clear guidelines regarding what the operators should and should not do. Choice B is incorrect because authorization involves identifying who has the authority to enter. Choice D is incorrect because access controls are used to determine which individuals can enter certain areas.

43. **The correct answer is D.** Footprinting includes targeting IP addresses, targeting a website, performing business research, and Google hacking. Choice A is incorrect because network security is an essential part of cybersecurity in information systems. Choice B is incorrect because operational security is the sustainability function of the cybersecurity process. Choice C is incorrect because vulnerability management involves network testing and recognizing and mitigating threats on a regular basis.

44. **The correct answer is A.** Exploitation refers to the tools and techniques for breaking into more systems, gaining further network access, or gaining access to more resources. Choice B is incorrect because a return is the action an attacker takes to ensure he/she is able to return to the target unobstructed. Choice C is incorrect because vendor announcements are mailing lists announcing vulnerabilities, fixes, or any compensating actions that can be taken. Choice D is incorrect because full-disclosure lists of vulnerabilities are circulated among security professionals once all the necessary due diligence is done.

45. **The correct answer is A.** Enterprise continuity is the preservation of the ability to perform the essential functions required for operational effectiveness as it pertains to the continuity of the unit or organization. Choice B is incorrect because incident management is the governing of the handling/reporting procedures for incidents relating to IT management and security. Choice C is incorrect because digital forensics is the recovery of electronic information, often from devices that have been tampered with, destroyed, or compromised. Choice D is incorrect because data security is the protection of information in electronic databases from unauthorized access, theft, or destruction.

46. **The correct answer is D.** There are seven basic steps to an encryption system. Choices A, B, and C all list the incorrect number of steps.

47. **The correct answer is D.** Security architecture was once silo-based and removed from the main service architecture of organizations, but has since been repositioned as a core element of service architecture. Choice A is incorrect because risk assessment is a specific method for identifying risks and threats. Choice B is incorrect because information architecture is the structural design of how information is shared. Choice C is incorrect because technology architecture is the process of bringing together the IT components of the system.

48. **The correct answer is B.** A return is the action an attacker takes to ensure he/she is able to return to the target unobstructed. Choice A is incorrect because exploitation covers the tools and techniques for breaking into more systems, gaining further network access, or gaining access to more resources. Choice C is incorrect because vendor announcements are mailing lists announcing vulnerabilities, fixes, or any compensating actions that can be taken. Choice D is incorrect because full-disclosure lists of vulnerabilities are circulated among security professionals once all the necessary due diligence is done.

49. **The correct answer is A.** If a vulnerability is found, a patch should be installed to fix the issue and to eliminate the threat. Choice B is incorrect because policies are made to determine how the vulnerabilities are found. Choice C is incorrect because returns are not used to fix vulnerabilities. Choice D is incorrect because announcements would be used after the patch has been installed to inform the users of the fix.

50. **The correct answer is A.** ISC provides detection and analysis of network threats, assessments of their severity, and advice on how to counter them. Choice B is incorrect because FIRST facilitates information sharing on the latest cyber-threats and attacks. Choice C is incorrect because full disclosure lists of vulnerabilities are circulated among security professionals once all the necessary due diligence is done. Choice D is incorrect because vendor announcements are mailing lists announcing vulnerabilities, fixes, or any compensating actions that can be taken.

51. **The correct answer is B.** Accountability ensures that a proper record of the access has been recorded for proper evaluation of the data security function. Choice A is incorrect because authorization provides access to resources. Choice C is incorrect because compliance is the strict governance that ensures it runs exactly as it was designed to run. Choice D is incorrect because something you are is a verifying physical characteristic (known as biometrics) to confirm the identity and the right to access systems.

52. **The correct answer is B.** FIRST facilitates information sharing on the latest cyber-threats and attacks. Choice A is incorrect because ISC provides detection and analysis of network threats, assessments of their severity, and advice on how to counter them. Choice C is incorrect because full disclosure lists of vulnerabilities circulate among security professionals once all the necessary due diligence is done. Choice D is incorrect because vendor announcements are mailing lists announcing vulnerabilities, fixes, or any compensating actions that can be taken.

53. **The correct answer is D.** Environmental controls help protect sensitive and secure equipment against environmental hazards. Choice A is incorrect because exploitation covers the tools and techniques for breaking into more systems, gaining further network access, or gaining access to more resources. Choice B is incorrect because a return is the action an attacker takes to ensure he/she is able to return to the target unobstructed. Choice C is incorrect because vendor announcements are mailing lists announcing vulnerabilities, fixes, or any compensating actions that can be taken.

54. **The correct answer is D.** Packet sniffers are programs/devices capable of viewing data as it moves along a network and are sometimes used maliciously. Choice A is incorrect because data breaches deal with the unauthorized access of sensitive data. Choice B is incorrect because data loss deals with the destruction of data. Choice C is incorrect because account hijacking deals with the loss of proprietary information about account and service traffic.

55. **The correct answer is A.** Environmental security is an area of responsibility includes keeping the organization and its security assets safe in the event of natural or manmade disasters. Choice B is incorrect because risk management covers the design, implementation, and control of risk management processes as they relate to information security assets. Choice C is incorrect because standards compliance covers the adherence to applicable information, security laws and regulations, as well as standards and policies. Choice D is incorrect because strategic security management broadly covers using sound strategic management principles to manage information security in the organization.

56. **The correct answer is A.** Something you are is a verifying physical characteristic (known as biometrics) to confirm the identity and the right to access systems. Choice B is incorrect because accountability ensures that a proper record of the access has been recorded for proper evaluation of the data security function. Choice C is incorrect because compliance is the strict governance that ensures it runs exactly as it was designed to run. Choice D is incorrect because authorization provides access to resources.

57. **The correct answer is D.** Service architecture is not one of the three main elements of operational security. The main elements include security architecture (choice A), security implementation (choice B), and operation of the implemented architecture (choice C).

58. **The correct answer is C.** Maintenance involves making necessary changes in a live environment. Choice A is incorrect because integration and testing ensure a system is conforming properly to all requirements specified and set out in the Functional Requirements Document. Choice B is incorrect because implementation focuses on resolving problems uncovered and highlighted during the integration and test phases. Choice D is incorrect because

disposition is when a system is ready to be ended.

59. **The correct answer is D.** Information is not one of the three philosophical approaches to handling the disclosure of vulnerabilities. Choices A, B, and C are all incorrect because they are approaches to handling the disclosure of vulnerabilities.

60. **The correct answer is C.** Public key infrastructure is a secure communication tool using software, protocols, encryption methodologies, third-party services, and legal agreements. Choice A is incorrect because passwords can ensure trusted access to information systems as long as they are strong and secret. Choice B is incorrect because digital certificates are sent along with documents. Choice D is incorrect because a physical key is not part of cybersecurity.

answers post-test

Introduction to Law Enforcement

OVERVIEW

- **Test Answer Sheets**
- **Introduction to Law Enforcement Diagnostic Test**
- **Answer Key and Explanations**
- **Diagnostic Test Assessment Grid**
- **History of Law Enforcement**
- **Overview of the U.S. Criminal Justice System and Processes**
- **Law Enforcement Systems in the United States**
- **Law Enforcement Organization, Management, and Issues**
- **Criminal and Constitutional Law and Precedents**
- **Summing It Up**
- **Introduction to Law Enforcement Post-Test**
- **Answer Key and Explanations**

This chapter includes the basic information covered in an Introduction to Law Enforcement college course. Topics discussed include the history of law enforcement, the criminal justice process, the law enforcement system in the United States, law enforcement organization and management, and criminal and constitutional law and precedents.

Chapter 11

DIAGNOSTIC TEST ANSWER SHEET

1. Ⓐ Ⓑ Ⓒ Ⓓ   5. Ⓐ Ⓑ Ⓒ Ⓓ   9. Ⓐ Ⓑ Ⓒ Ⓓ   13. Ⓐ Ⓑ Ⓒ Ⓓ   17. Ⓐ Ⓑ Ⓒ Ⓓ
2. Ⓐ Ⓑ Ⓒ Ⓓ   6. Ⓐ Ⓑ Ⓒ Ⓓ   10. Ⓐ Ⓑ Ⓒ Ⓓ   14. Ⓐ Ⓑ Ⓒ Ⓓ   18. Ⓐ Ⓑ Ⓒ Ⓓ
3. Ⓐ Ⓑ Ⓒ Ⓓ   7. Ⓐ Ⓑ Ⓒ Ⓓ   11. Ⓐ Ⓑ Ⓒ Ⓓ   15. Ⓐ Ⓑ Ⓒ Ⓓ   19. Ⓐ Ⓑ Ⓒ Ⓓ
4. Ⓐ Ⓑ Ⓒ Ⓓ   8. Ⓐ Ⓑ Ⓒ Ⓓ   12. Ⓐ Ⓑ Ⓒ Ⓓ   16. Ⓐ Ⓑ Ⓒ Ⓓ   20. Ⓐ Ⓑ Ⓒ Ⓓ

POST-TEST ANSWER SHEET

1. Ⓐ Ⓑ Ⓒ Ⓓ   13. Ⓐ Ⓑ Ⓒ Ⓓ   25. Ⓐ Ⓑ Ⓒ Ⓓ   37. Ⓐ Ⓑ Ⓒ Ⓓ   49. Ⓐ Ⓑ Ⓒ Ⓓ
2. Ⓐ Ⓑ Ⓒ Ⓓ   14. Ⓐ Ⓑ Ⓒ Ⓓ   26. Ⓐ Ⓑ Ⓒ Ⓓ   38. Ⓐ Ⓑ Ⓒ Ⓓ   50. Ⓐ Ⓑ Ⓒ Ⓓ
3. Ⓐ Ⓑ Ⓒ Ⓓ   15. Ⓐ Ⓑ Ⓒ Ⓓ   27. Ⓐ Ⓑ Ⓒ Ⓓ   39. Ⓐ Ⓑ Ⓒ Ⓓ   51. Ⓐ Ⓑ Ⓒ Ⓓ
4. Ⓐ Ⓑ Ⓒ Ⓓ   16. Ⓐ Ⓑ Ⓒ Ⓓ   28. Ⓐ Ⓑ Ⓒ Ⓓ   40. Ⓐ Ⓑ Ⓒ Ⓓ   52. Ⓐ Ⓑ Ⓒ Ⓓ
5. Ⓐ Ⓑ Ⓒ Ⓓ   17. Ⓐ Ⓑ Ⓒ Ⓓ   29. Ⓐ Ⓑ Ⓒ Ⓓ   41. Ⓐ Ⓑ Ⓒ Ⓓ   53. Ⓐ Ⓑ Ⓒ Ⓓ
6. Ⓐ Ⓑ Ⓒ Ⓓ   18. Ⓐ Ⓑ Ⓒ Ⓓ   30. Ⓐ Ⓑ Ⓒ Ⓓ   42. Ⓐ Ⓑ Ⓒ Ⓓ   54. Ⓐ Ⓑ Ⓒ Ⓓ
7. Ⓐ Ⓑ Ⓒ Ⓓ   19. Ⓐ Ⓑ Ⓒ Ⓓ   31. Ⓐ Ⓑ Ⓒ Ⓓ   43. Ⓐ Ⓑ Ⓒ Ⓓ   55. Ⓐ Ⓑ Ⓒ Ⓓ
8. Ⓐ Ⓑ Ⓒ Ⓓ   20. Ⓐ Ⓑ Ⓒ Ⓓ   32. Ⓐ Ⓑ Ⓒ Ⓓ   44. Ⓐ Ⓑ Ⓒ Ⓓ   56. Ⓐ Ⓑ Ⓒ Ⓓ
9. Ⓐ Ⓑ Ⓒ Ⓓ   21. Ⓐ Ⓑ Ⓒ Ⓓ   33. Ⓐ Ⓑ Ⓒ Ⓓ   45. Ⓐ Ⓑ Ⓒ Ⓓ   57. Ⓐ Ⓑ Ⓒ Ⓓ
10. Ⓐ Ⓑ Ⓒ Ⓓ   22. Ⓐ Ⓑ Ⓒ Ⓓ   34. Ⓐ Ⓑ Ⓒ Ⓓ   46. Ⓐ Ⓑ Ⓒ Ⓓ   58. Ⓐ Ⓑ Ⓒ Ⓓ
11. Ⓐ Ⓑ Ⓒ Ⓓ   23. Ⓐ Ⓑ Ⓒ Ⓓ   35. Ⓐ Ⓑ Ⓒ Ⓓ   47. Ⓐ Ⓑ Ⓒ Ⓓ   59. Ⓐ Ⓑ Ⓒ Ⓓ
12. Ⓐ Ⓑ Ⓒ Ⓓ   24. Ⓐ Ⓑ Ⓒ Ⓓ   36. Ⓐ Ⓑ Ⓒ Ⓓ   48. Ⓐ Ⓑ Ⓒ Ⓓ   60. Ⓐ Ⓑ Ⓒ Ⓓ

answer sheet

INTRODUCTION TO LAW ENFORCEMENT DIAGNOSTIC TEST

Directions: Carefully read each of the following 20 questions. Choose the best answer to each question and fill in the corresponding circle on the answer sheet. The Answer Key and Explanations can be found following this Diagnostic Test.

1. Robert Peel created the first police force in 1829 in what city?
   A. New York
   B. Manchester
   C. London
   D. Chicago

2. Modern policing deals with quality of life (QOL) issues and assumes that disorder creates fear and that deviant behavior is representative of the community not caring. This theory is known as
   A. aggressive policing.
   B. broken windows.
   C. police inactivity.
   D. collective efficacy.

3. Police responsibilities include
   A. conducting routine investigations.
   B. organizing public functions such as parades and picnics.
   C. responding to medical calls, fires, and other emergencies and disasters.
   D. All of the above

4. The person who advocates for a defendant is
   A. the judge.
   B. the jury.
   C. the defense attorney.
   D. the prosecutor.

5. As a reflection of society's needs, there are many courts besides the criminal court. Which of the following is a type of court?
   A. Bankruptcy court
   B. Civil court
   C. Smalls claims court
   D. All of the above

6. The term *adjudication* in criminal court refers to
   A. making a plea bargain.
   B. determining an individual's guilt or innocence.
   C. sentencing a guilty party.
   D. dismissing the charges.

7. At the federal level for law enforcement, there are two main branches. They are
   A. judicial and legislative.
   B. executive and judicial.
   C. Department of Justice and Department of Homeland Security.
   D. FEMA and the Department of Defense.

8. Which law enforcement agency is responsible for protecting the governor?
   A. Local police force
   B. State police
   C. Secret Service
   D. Private security firms

9. The largest municipal law enforcement department is the
   A. LAPD.
   B. Chicago PD.
   C. Baltimore PD.
   D. NYPD.

10. Police departments have a strict structure and hierarchy called
    A. rank structure.
    B. manager levels.
    C. chain of command.
    D. supervisors/subordinates.

11. Which officer interacts with the public on a daily basis?
    A. Staff function officer
    B. Line function officer
    C. Detective
    D. Desk officer

12. There are many challenges that police officers face in today's society, and one of the biggest challenges is
    A. how to respond to crimes faster.
    B. what type of uniforms the department should issue.
    C. how to build trust and cooperation with the community.
    D. issuing traffic summonses for revenue.

13. What city experienced massive protest and an anti-police movement in recent times?
    A. Los Angeles
    B. Chicago
    C. Ferguson
    D. Detroit

14. What type of encounter do police engage in with the community during routine patrols?
    A. Traffic enforcement
    B. Medical calls
    C. Gunshot victims
    D. Police ride-alongs

15. Making arrests, determining right from wrong, and experiencing internal conflict can result in
    A. working personality.
    B. resentment of police work.
    C. empathy.
    D. high morality.

16. External stress for a police officer is produced by
    A. divorce and alcohol.
    B. threats and dangers that officers may encounter.
    C. adjusting to a different value system.
    D. distrusting people that the police encounter.

17. As technology advances in society, so does law enforcement. Development and improvement of nonlethal devices in law enforcement can be found in
    A. Tasers and stun guns.
    B. rubber bullets and bean bag guns.
    C. OC (pepper) spray and spike strips.
    D. All of the above

18. In 1791, the Founding Fathers adopted the first 10 Amendments. They were called
    A. Constitutional law.
    B. the Bill of Rights.
    C. the Declaration of Independence.
    D. Amendment Rights.

19. The Fourth Amendment
   A. establishes the right for people to be secured in their person and houses against unreasonable searches and seizures.
   B. asserts that any person shall not be compelled to be a witness against himself.
   C. guarantees the right to a speedy and public trial.
   D. prohibits cruel and unusual punishment.

20. The right to counsel and the right to a speedy and public trial are covered under what amendment?
   A. The Second Amendment
   B. The Sixth Amendment
   C. The Fifth Amendment
   D. The Fourth Amendment

diagnostic test

ANSWER KEY AND EXPLANATIONS

1. C	**5.** D	**9.** D	**13.** C	**17.** D
2. B	**6.** B	**10.** C	**14.** A	**18.** B
3. D	**7.** C	**11.** B	**15.** D	**19.** A
4. C	**8.** B	**12.** C	**16.** B	**20.** B

1. **The correct answer is C.** Robert Peel created the first London police force, which was modeled for future police departments. Therefore, choices A, B, and D are all incorrect.

2. **The correct answer is B.** Broken windows theory represents a community that does not care as a result of local abandonment, which then creates fear and disorderly behavior. Therefore, choices A, C, and D are all incorrect.

3. **The correct answer is D.** The police have many responsibilities, such as the ones listed here. Other responsibilities include crime prevention, safety awareness programs, and traffic enforcement, to name a few.

4. **The correct answer is C.** The defense attorney is an advocate for his or her client and ensures that his or her client's rights are enforced and not violated. Choices A, B, and D are incorrect because they have different responsibilities in the courtroom.

5. **The correct answer is D.** As a result of the complexities of society, the courts of today have various roles and responsibilities to help enforce society's rules and behavior.

6. **The correct answer is B.** *Adjudication* means resolving disputes in a court of law and, applied to criminal court, simply means the process to determine the defendant's guilt or innocence. Therefore, choices A, C, and D are all incorrect.

7. **The correct answer is C.** Federal law enforcement has two main branches that enforce federal laws—the Department of Justice and the Department of Homeland Security. Choices A, B, and D are all incorrect, as they are not law enforcement branches or are agencies that fall under the purview of these branches.

8. **The correct answer is B.** The state police is the main agency that is assigned to the protection of the state's governor. Therefore, choices A, C, and D are all incorrect.

9. **The correct answer is D.** The NYPD is the largest municipal police department in the country. Therefore, choices A, B, and C are all incorrect.

10. **The correct answer is C.** The chain of command provides structure that defines ranks and creates accountability, discipline, and control. Therefore, choices A, B, and D are all incorrect.

11. **The correct answer is B.** The line function officer interacts the most with the public as a result of daily patrol operations. Choice A is incorrect because staff supports the patrol function. Choice C is incorrect because detectives are limited as to when they engage with the public, usually in solving crimes. Choice D is incorrect because the desk officer works inside the precinct running inside operations.

12. **The correct answer is C.** Building trust and cooperation with the community is of major concern and responsibility for police

departments. Building relationships will foster better cooperation and understanding between the community's needs and the duties of the local police department. Choice A is incorrect because police will always respond to crimes rapidly. Choice B is incorrect because uniforms do not rise to the level of community relations. Choice D is incorrect because issuing summons is done for public safety.

13. **The correct answer is C.** After the shooting of Michael Brown by a police officer in Ferguson, protests and riots erupted, sparking a campaign against the police nationwide. As a result of many factors in the case, relations between the police and community eroded. Choices A, B, and D all have some history of police protests and riots, but the most recent one occurred in Ferguson.

14. **The correct answer is A.** Traffic enforcement is one of the most common ways in which people interact with the police. During this encounter, the officer must exhibit courtesy and professionalism, even when issuing a summons. Choice B is incorrect because even though medical calls are common, traffic enforcement is part of routine patrol duties. Choices C and D are incorrect because they do not fit in with a high rate of police encounters.

15. **The correct answer is D.** The subculture of police work creates a high sense of morality to help the officer cope with dilemmas and conflicts and to help ease the officer's conscience. Choice A is incorrect because working personality contains elements that shape an officer's personality. Choice B is incorrect because making arrests and determining right from wrong may not result in resentment but can be a fulfilling part of the job. Choice C is incorrect because officers may not develop empathy for making arrests

and other situations that the officer may encounter.

16. **The correct answer is B.** External stress is a result of the dangers and threats that officers may face. Choices A, C, and D do not fit the description of external stress.

17. **The correct answer is D.** The development of nonlethal devices has been an important issue in law enforcement. Besides nonlethal devices, the advancement in computers and forensic science has been extremely beneficial in law enforcement.

18. **The correct answer is B.** The first 10 Amendments are known as the Bill of Rights. They include the First Amendment of free speech, freedom of religion, and the right to assemble peacefully. Therefore, choices A, C, and D are all incorrect.

19. **The correct answer is A.** The Fourth Amendment protects people against unreasonable searches and seizures by the government. Choice B is incorrect because it applies to the Fifth Amendment. Choice C is incorrect because it applies to the Sixth Amendment. Choice D is incorrect because it applies to the Eighth Amendment.

20. **The correct answer is B.** The Sixth Amendment includes the right to counsel, the right to a speedy and public trial, and the right to confront witnesses. Choice A is incorrect because it establishes the right to bear arms. Choice C is incorrect because it refers to double jeopardy. Choice D is incorrect because it refers to unreasonable searches and seizures.

DIAGNOSTIC TEST ASSESSMENT GRID

Now that you've completed the diagnostic test and read through the answer explanations, you can use your results to target your studying. Find the question numbers from the diagnostic test that you answered incorrectly and highlight or circle them below. Then focus extra attention on the sections within the chapter dealing with those topics.

Introduction to Law Enforcement		
Content Area	Topic	Question #
History of Law Enforcement	• Pre-Colonial heritage and colonial heritage • 1800s and 1900s • Contemporary (2000) • Contributions of theorists and practitioners	1, 2
Overview of the United States Criminal Justice System and Process	• Role of police • Role of prosecutors • Role of defense • Role of court • Role of corrections • Measurement of crime	3, 4, 5, 6
Law Enforcement Systems in the United States	• Federal • State • Local • Special district police agencies	7, 8, 9

Introduction to Law Enforcement (continued)		
Content Area	**Topic**	**Question #**
Law Enforcement Organization, Management, and Issues	Operations 1. Infrastructure and hierarchy 2. Line 3. Staff Community relations and policing Police issues 1. Image, professionalism and subculture 2. Police ethics and discretion 3. Future policing and technology 4. Law enforcement/public focus and priorities Women and other minorities in policing	10, 11, 12, 13, 14, 15, 16, 17
Criminal and Constitutional Law and Precedents	The Constitution and Bill of Rights Supreme Court case law Federal and local laws and ordinances	18, 19, 20

GET THE FACTS

To see the DSST® Introduction to Law Enforcement Fact Sheet, go to ***http://getcollegecredit.com/ exam_fact_sheets*** and click on the **Introduction to Law Enforcement** tab. Scroll down and click the **Introduction to Law Enforcement** link. Here you will find suggestions for further study material and the ACE college credit recommendations for passing the test.

HISTORY OF LAW ENFORCEMENT

Law enforcement, as with most aspects of our laws, court system, and political structures can be traced back to English tradition. Our system is based on the model established by the founding father of policing, **Sir Robert Peel**, who in 1829 created the first London police force. As a result, officers were called "bobbies," after him. Peel's philosophies comprise much of modern policing today.

Peel had a four-part mandate, which is still prevalent in today's policing. His goals were to prevent crime without repressive force or use of the military; maintain public order by nonviolent means; reduce conflict between the police and public; and show efficiency through the absence of crime.

American policing can be broken down into the following three historical periods.

THE POLITICAL ERA

The **Political** era took place between 1840 and 1920. In this era, there were close ties and relationships between police and political leaders. The police were loyal to the mayors and their political parties—in other words, the police helped keep local politicians in power and were paid, and received favors, for their work and loyalty.

In 1845, New York City created the first full-time paid police force. Because this era was filled with corruption, positions and ranks were often the result of payoffs. For example, becoming a New York City police captain cost $10,000. Besides power, that rank came with a lot of extra benefits and payoffs. However, this system couldn't last, as the corruption became too much and reformers were eager to change the relationship between police and politicians. This led to the second era of policing.

THE PROFESSIONAL MODEL

The **Professional Model**, from 1920 through 1970, moved away from corruption as the progressive movement began to influence policing. The progressives were primarily made up of upper middle class and educated individuals. Their goals were to create a more efficient government and to have more support services for those less fortunate in society. These reformers wanted the police and the police departments to become more professional. However, in order for this to happen there were certain elements the reformers needed to establish.

First, they wanted police to stay out of politics; reformers felt the police should be neutral when it came to political leaders. This is true today, as police departments do not endorse candidates for office.

Next, they wanted the police to be well trained. Training is a major component for professional policing. Training never ends for law enforcement—it is a constant reminder that as a society becomes more complex and evolves, policing has to keep pace and reflect those changes and the evolving needs of society. There was also a great call for police departments to use new technology, both day-to-day and in training. This, of course, continues today—as technology advances, law enforcement must constantly train in the latest weapons, nonlethal weapons, computers, and technology, among other new developments.

The reformers also wanted assurance that all laws would be enforced equally, with the main task of the police being to fight crime.

COMMUNITY POLICING

In the early 1970s, policing moved away from traditional crime fighting as its sole mission and moved toward incorporating services for the community; thus, the next era was referred to as **Community Policing**.

Police did not want to isolate the communities they served, and worked towards strengthening relationships between communities and police. This is not to say that the police stopped enforcing the law—rather, they expanded their roles to include more social service calls. With fragile relations between the police and some of our communities in today's society, community policing is as important as ever in an effort to help bridge the gap.

As the era of community policing continues, some criminologists suggest that a new model of policing should be established. As a result of 9/11 and other terrorist attacks, the next era might be labeled Homeland Security. Time will tell what the next official era and its components will become in our ever-changing world.

THEORIES OF LAW ENFORCEMENT

Contemporary policing, which includes the core tenets of community policing philosophy, is based on the premise of **problem-oriented policing**, sometimes called **community and problem oriented policing (CPOP)**. This entails a shift in focus from a reactive response to a proactive one in order to solve problems. It also focuses on **quality of life (QOL)** issues, which pay more attention to the needs of communities. Police giving more focus to nonemergency matters creates more public accountability, while also including input from the citizens in the communities that they serve.

Contemporary community policing works from a national model, known as the **S-A-R-A**, or **SARA model**:

> **S** is for scanning, which involves identifying the problem concerning the public and police.
>
> **A** is for analysis, which involves learning the problem's causes, determining how frequently and under what conditions the problem occurs, and locating resources for assistance.
>
> **R** is for response—acting to alleviate the problem, outlining a response plan, mapping out specific goals, and carrying out the plan.
>
> **A** is for assessment—determining whether the response worked (Were the goals achieved?), collecting data, determining sustainability for the plan, and conducting an ongoing assessment for the problem.

Another issue under modern policing is the **broken windows** theory. This theory assumes that disorder creates fear and that disorderly behavior is representative of a community not caring. Metaphorically speaking, the rundown building with the broken windows represents a community that does not care; as a result, fear and disorder are created and people in the community feel that they have been abandoned by the police and political leaders.

Under the policing portion of this theory, in order to clean up the QOL issues and address certain low-level crimes the police must focus on the smaller issues. This is turn works toward fixing and solving the bigger problems. Once these issues get addressed and QOL begins to improve in the community, people start to believe in it again. So, if that broken down building gets fixed up, it is representative of the community showing that it cares about living standards, and the people will in turn care more.

There are many theories that attempt to explain deviant behavior and the causes of crime. One prominent theorist is **Jeffrey Reiman**. Reiman is from the Marxist camp and school of thought. Reiman's theory seeks to reduce crime by reducing poverty. He believes in establishing social and economic justice by changing the course of capitalism.

Cesare Beccaria was a criminologist from the 18th century who believed in **Classical Criminology**. Beccaria wrote a famous book entitled *An Essay on Crimes and Punishment*, which essentially states that behavior stems from free will and people are accountable for their behavior. He believes that criminal behavior is a rational choice; people choose to commit crimes after weighing the pros and cons of a particular scenario, and that fear of punishment keeps people in check.

Another theory of deviant behavior came from **Edwin Sutherland**, who wrote about social process theories of criminality in the early part of the 20th century. Sutherland was also a proponent of the learning theory, which states that criminal behavior is learned through interactions with others, such as family and friends.

Emile Durkheim and **Robert Merton** believed in a theory called anomie. **Anomie** is defined as a breakdown in, and disappearance of, the rules of social behavior. When the rules and norms that guide behavior are weakened or disappear, then deviant behavior is the result.

Now we're going to take a closer look at the U.S. criminal justice system.

OVERVIEW OF THE U.S. CRIMINAL JUSTICE SYSTEM AND PROCESSES

The role of the police officer has changed dramatically over time, and will most likely keep changing as a reflection of an ever-evolving society. That being said, there are still responsibilities of the police that remain the same. The old motto of "to protect and serve" still holds true today. Let's examine what this actually means, alongside an overview of the criminal justice system in the United States and how it operates.

POLICE

Let's start by exploring some of the day-to-day responsibilities of the police. On TV and in the movies, the police are portrayed as tough people who fight crime and get into shootings and car chases. However, approximately **80 percent of police calls are service related**. This means that, for the most part, these calls are noncrime related.

Some of these service calls entail assisting everyday citizens in times of crisis and emergency—everything from a lost child to medical calls and vehicle accidents, as well as rescues from fires and other natural disasters. The term **first responders** is a title given to police for responding to these types of calls.

Traffic related issues are another day-to-day component for police departments in the United States. Here, responsibilities include enforcing traffic laws with citations, setting up DWI checkpoints, responding to vehicle accidents, and facilitating traffic accident reconstruction investigations.

Preserving life is always the first responsibility of the police. However, the concept of "to protect and serve" goes much further. Police investigate crimes, conducting investigations that are both routine and complex. They also conduct crime scene searches, in which an officer's duty is to protect and preserve the crime scene first (unless there is a person's life at stake), interview witnesses, and conduct interrogations of suspects.

The community aspect of policing plays a vital role in today's society. Besides the community policing we discussed earlier, police are involved with local schools, and address crime prevention techniques with local residents and businesses. They also conduct driver safety awareness programs and drug prevention programs.

The police are also responsible for organizing security at public functions like parades, concerts, outside festivals, or anywhere a public gathering is taking place. They provide safety and protection at public gatherings like demonstrations and protests, which can pose challenges. Balancing the rights of free speech and lawful assembly, all while protecting the people and the community, can be a difficult job for the police. For example, imagine a police officer assigned to a protest. On one side of the street are angry people protesting for abortion rights; on the other side of the street are angry people protesting for the right-to-life movement. Not only does it become challenging to protect everyone's safety, but the police officer also has to remain neutral and cannot let his or her own emotions get in the way.

PROSECUTORS

The role of the **prosecutor**, which includes district attorneys (DAs), encompasses many functions and responsibilities within the criminal justice system. Prosecutors are official officers of the court, and thereby must perform their duties in a legal and ethical manner. Prosecutors are responsible for prosecuting all crimes within their jurisdictions. For the most part, local prosecutors are elected officials and need to be aware of public opinion as well, which at times can turn the office into a political arena.

Prosecutors not only try defendants to obtain convictions, but also to get justice— for the victims and for the people they represent. This is why they are known as the peoples' attorneys. Their duties also include reviewing and prosecuting juvenile cases, and in some jurisdictions, they might have oversight regarding traffic violations.

Prosecutors also review police reports and the arrests police make, and form relationships with police, judges, defense attorneys, and political leaders. Prosecutors also need to have the skills and ability to work with victims and witnesses in each and every case. They are responsible for ensuring that arrests meet the legal standard and requirement for prosecution within the court system.

It is because of these powers vested in the prosecutor's office that they can govern and rule on each case that comes before them. In other words, the DA's office has the most discretion and power within the criminal justice system. These attorneys can decide to prosecute, decline prosecution, upgrade or downgrade charges as they see fit, or drop charges and cases at any time.

DEFENSE

Defense attorneys, like prosecutors, are officers of the court, and also seek justice. However, these attorneys have different and distinct roles. A defendant needs to share the truth with his or her attorney, which includes whether or not he or she committed the crime. It is up to the defense attorney to represent his or her client to the best of his or her ability, regardless of the defendant's innocence.

Under lawyer/client privilege, the defense attorney is barred from revealing any statements made in confidence by a client. All of this takes place prior to appearing in the courtroom. The defense attorney needs to assess the case and give his or her legal advice to the client. It is very important that the defendant not hold anything back from his or her attorney, so that the attorney can put together the best defense possible. The attorney reviews the case to make sure the police acted, and continue to act, properly and within the guidelines of the law, while ensuring that there is probable cause and a **prima facie** (Latin for "at first view") case exists against his client.

It is not the defense attorney's job to determine the guilt or innocence of her client, but it is her job to be an advocate for her client throughout the criminal justice process. This includes advising the client at every step of the way as to the best course of action. In some cases, that may result in a plea bargain. During this phase, the defense attorney makes sure that she gets the best deal possible for her client, by working and negotiating with the prosecutor and ultimately getting approval by the judge.

It is common knowledge that the defense attorney attempts to put doubt in the minds of the jury in a trial case, in an effort to receive a not guilty verdict. It is also an important function of the defense attorney to ensure that his client's constitutional rights are not violated by anyone and that **due process**, or fair treatment within the court system, is achieved.

Many defense attorneys represent individuals who cannot afford an attorney on their own—these clients are called **indigents**, which include the majority of clients that public defenders represent.

COURT

Courts have many functions in today's society. Their main role is to enforce society's rules and help guide behavior. Besides criminal courts, there are many types of courts and they all have a role in keeping order in society. These include family and juvenile court; civil court, which handles matters of contracts, lawsuits, and business disputes; surrogate courts; bankruptcy courts; tax courts; and small claims courts.

You are probably most familiar with criminal courts. Their main function is to ensure that due process is being applied justly and fairly, in accordance with the Constitution, in criminal cases. The term **adjudication** is often used within the court system. Adjudication is defined as resolving disputes and issues in a court of law. When adjudication is applied in a criminal law setting, it merely means that we are determining an individual's criminal guilt or innocence.

Whether we are in the federal court system or the state court system, in the United States we have an adversarial process. The **adversarial process** is the process in which lawyers for both sides represent their clients and present arguments and evidence in order to seek the truth.

CORRECTIONS

Corrections represents a very important part of our criminal justice system. Corrections refers to any discipline given to offenders after they have been convicted but it can also be applied to any accused defendants. What is the role of corrections in society? In the word *corrections* we see the word *correct*, meaning to change people's behavior to conform to society's values, rules, and laws. Corrections can be viewed as the management and punishment of people who have been convicted of a criminal offense for the protection of the community and society as a whole.

Besides incarceration, some of the more common forms of corrections can be found via probation and parole. The **three P's—prison, probation, and parole**—may control the correctional system, but there are many other forms of corrections and punishment. Corrections, like police work, is ever changing, in an effort to reflect the needs of society.

CRIME

Measuring crime statistics is an extremely valuable component of the criminal justice system. Data can show us national trends in crime. As we follow local crime statistics, we can see if crime is on the rise or decline and what categories are increasing or decreasing. Crime reporting is also a very useful tool for crime detection and follow-up investigations. The criminal justice system thrives on crime reports and statistics. So, the question remains, how is crime reported and measured?

Before we get into reporting techniques, let's expand upon a key concept: the **dark figure of crime**. The dark figure of crime refers to the dimension of crime that is never reported to the police. This is not to say that the crime never took place; rather, it was just never reported or recorded. It does not matter what the crime is, or how big or small—people will have many different reasons for not reporting it to the police.

If someone breaks into a car and steals some old papers, it may not be worth the person's time to report it. Unfortunately, for a more serious crime like rape, the victim may feel ashamed or responsible and may not want to face what might arise when reporting this crime.

When a crime report is completed and processed, it becomes part of the **National Incident-Based Reporting System**, or **NIBRS**. In this report, the police officer describes each offense that was committed during the crime. For example, if someone is robbed at gunpoint and also assaulted, the robbery is the most severe charge; but the assault and weapons charge is key and must be noted, as well.

National crime reports are published and generated every year. These reports are called **Uniform Crime Reports,** or **UCR**. They are compiled and generated by the FBI. All police departments, including local, state, federal, and tribal departments, have to report their yearly statistics to the FBI. In turn, the FBI studies and analyzes these statistics and publishes these reports to the public. These reports are broken down into categories for statistical purposes, which helps law enforcement to follow trends and patterns in crime.

Most crimes reported to the FBI are placed into categories. These categories, called **index crimes**, include murder, burglary, rape, grand larceny, robbery, grand larceny (auto), felony assaults, and arson.

The UCR is extremely helpful and accurate, but because of the dark figure of crime, it may be an incomplete picture of crime trends. In order to close the gap between the UCR and the dark figure of crime, the United States Department of Justice created the **National Crime Victimization Survey (NCVS)** in 1972. The Department of Justice uses the Bureau of Justice Statistics to send out surveys two times a year to determine the number and types of crimes and victims that went unreported, in addition to reported incidents.

Now let's turn our focus to law enforcement systems in the United States, including the terminology and organizations you should know.

LAW ENFORCEMENT SYSTEMS IN THE UNITED STATES

Law enforcement can be broken down to local, state, and federal levels. Each level enforces the laws that fall under its **jurisdiction** (the geographical location or area where a law enforcement department has control). In addition, each level can be broken down further into the various agencies that comprise this complex network.

FEDERAL

Let's start at the federal level. Each agency is designed to enforce the particular laws authorized by the Constitution, Congress, and the executive branch of the federal government. Within the federal layer of law enforcement there are two main branches; each branch oversees a number of different agencies that enforce specific federal laws.

The two main branches of federal law enforcement are the **Department of Justice**, or **DOJ**, and the **Department of Homeland Security**, or **DHS**. Prior to 9/11, the DOJ was the largest branch for federal law enforcement. In 2002, after the events of 9/11, President George W. Bush signed an executive order that restructured and realigned the departments and agencies that fall under them. The agencies that are now assigned to the DOJ are the Federal Bureau of Investigation; the Federal Bureau of Prisons; the Bureau of Alcohol, Tobacco, Firearms, and Explosives; and the Drug Enforcement Administration. The DHS is now considered the largest branch with the most federal officers assigned to its agencies. These agencies include Customs and Border Protection, the Federal Emergency Management Agency, Immigration and Custom Enforcement, the Transportation Safety Administration, the U.S. Coast Guard, and the U.S. Secret Service.

STATE

State police, while enforcing state laws, take on various roles and responsibilities that vary from state to state. However, just like any law enforcement agency, these officers are duty bound in enforcing state laws, mainly with traffic laws on highways, interstates, and expressways. Another primary responsibility of state police, besides traffic enforcement, is to protect state capitals and assign security and protection for state governors. State police can support smaller departments with investigations through the use of technology and forensics, as well as support training and academy classes for smaller jurisdictions that cannot provide for themselves.

LOCAL

There are more than 12,000 local police departments in the United States, serving a wide range of municipalities: cities, towns, villages, counties, and more. Local governments have the ability and power to create their own police departments. From the New York City Police Department, the largest in the country, to small departments that may consist of only two or three individuals, local police departments enforce the laws of the jurisdiction they serve.

When police departments exercise their jurisdictional powers, they have the authority and power to arrest, conduct searches and seizures, and enact all the other powers vested in them. This may include, but is not limited to, enforcing traffic regulations and laws, investigating crimes, responding to emergencies as first responders, and maintaining public order. Once out of their jurisdiction, they may not carry the same legal powers.

SPECIAL AGENCIES

Another category of law enforcement is known as **special police** or district police agencies. These agencies have limited jurisdiction in a geographical sense, as well as in the realm of police power. They include airport police, transit police, college or university police, housing police, game wardens, sanitation police, and environmental police.

While they may also conduct criminal investigations and have the authority to make arrests, special police are limited as to where they are assigned to and trained. Some of their training may be less involved and rigorous than traditional police, and some can be more specialized. For example, airport and transportation hubs have their own unique challenges for law enforcement, and game wardens have different laws that empower them. These are just a few examples of specialized departments that may carry specialized training.

LAW ENFORCEMENT ORGANIZATION, MANAGEMENT, AND ISSUES

Now that we've covered the systems, let's look at how each is organized and the issues they face on a daily basis.

OPERATIONS

The structure of modern-day police departments can be traced back to Sir Robert Peel. During his construction of the London police force, he realized that the military could not police the streets and communities for numerous reasons. However, during the transition from a military force to a police force, Peel realized that even though the military could not effectively patrol the streets, the police department should model itself structurally like the military to be most effective. As a result of this, we often refer to the police as a paramilitary organization.

As in the military, police departments have hierarchies that resemble military ranks. There may be differences between the two institutions, but there is no doubt that there is rank structure within police departments. This hierarchy is also called a **chain of command**. The chain of command provides structure that defines ranks and authority over subordinates. This structure creates accountability, discipline, and control. Another term that may be used to describe police structure is **command and control**.

A common rank structure in policing (in order from lowest ranked to highest ranked) is as follows:

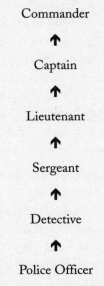

Commander

↑

Captain

↑

Lieutenant

↑

Sergeant

↑

Detective

↑

Police Officer

After the rank of captain, titles and structure may vary depending on the particular police department.

Line function refers to the officers who are on the street or in the field performing their duties. They are involved in operations that include patrol, investigation, and traffic enforcement. The line function officer is the person who interacts with the public on a daily basis.

The **staff function** supports the line function, allowing them to operate effectively. These functions can include clerks, the administrative staff in a precinct, and even the motor division that repairs patrol cars.

There is a large list of support functions that are required in order to keep departments functioning properly. For example, the computer repairs division, or IT, maintains the computers and terminals within a department.

COMMUNITY RELATIONS AND POLICING

In light of recent events, policing has become ever more difficult and the relationship between police and the communities where they serve may be at an all-time low. As a result of some high-profile incidents and past negative history between the police and the public, confidence and trust have been eroding for a long time. Building confidence and trust on both sides is a challenging task. The community and the police must work together to rebuild the trust and cooperation between them. Solving crimes may help, as a community with trust in its police force will assist it with information when available. It can also help relieve any tensions if an incident takes place between the police and an individual. Cooperation helps promote safety for both sides—the police and the public.

Today's societies have changed and become more complex and multicultural, which presents major potential challenges for policing and can contribute to ever-growing tensions between communities and the police. This can have serious negative consequences on community safety. In light of negative police encounters, and with the recent spate of anti-police marches and demonstrations, what mechanisms can repair the trust and confidence between the police and the communities that they serve?

First, the police should acknowledge the challenges they are facing within their communities and explore possible tactics to resolve specific conflicts. They should create clear channels of communication with their communities, so productive discussions can occur; these dialogues can explore historical tensions, how the police are perceived, and the challenges of trying to change the community's perception of them. Sometimes, part of the problem is that the community fails to realize what the main objectives are for the local police. In these discussions, police should stress that they are out there working to keep the community safe and protected. They should discuss various methods used and explain *why* they are used, but be open to change. Police must also communicate the idea that while some practices may be unpopular, some are necessary in order to save lives and keep people safe.

Second, police must be transparent and accountable. Transparency might be one of the most important issues in improving police/community relations. This can take on several meanings. First, it can mean exactly what we mentioned before, discussing challenges and the methods and strategies that are being used by the department. Police should try to be transparent with community leaders and members about the types of enforcement used and the goals behind each. Topics can include but are not limited to: the types of crimes they are enforcing, quality of life issues they aim to improve, and ideas for how to best serve and protect their communities.

Transparency can also mean that a police department should release as much information as possible when a police incident occurs. However, the police should make it known that it can only release so much without jeopardizing an investigation. As information is being gathered, the police will need to determine what should be released to the public and what cannot due to the open investigation. This can be a tricky balancing act, but it is important—releasing information right away to the public, so they are not misinformed and led by misinformation, can help prevent adverse relations with their communities.

There have been examples of critical police incidents wherein the police have not been transparent with the public, which led to greater distrust between the two. Such events further divide the police and the community, and can become difficult to repair.

POLICE ISSUES

Police departments should also work to reduce all bias. It is strongly recommended that officers at all levels receive training on diversity, bias, and multicultural issues. Many cities and towns have communities with a variety of racial and ethnic backgrounds and cultures, and it is important for officers to be able to communicate effectively with all individuals. This training can start at the recruit level, and continue through service training for seasoned officers. Officers who receive this training can help break the cycle of bias and stereotypes.

Police should closely collaborate with their communities. It is important for the police to make themselves known in their communities and to their residents. Many people avoid interacting with the police outside of an enforcement or emergency scenario. This can result in people developing negative associations with the police. Finding opportunities to interact with community members in a nonenforcement context can help to reduce bias on the part of community members and police officers. Also, getting to know community residents helps both groups to break down personal barriers and overcome stereotypes. This can also be accomplished through community-oriented policing. Improved relations will help close the gap between police and the community.

Image

Police should also promote community-building programs. When there are positive interactions between the police and the community, it helps to build trust and form a close-knit working relationship between the two. This helps to reduce tensions and potential conflicts with the police, and in turn helps in solving and reducing crime. When the police see themselves as part of the community, instead of outsiders, this fosters positive results and improves police community relations. This can be accomplished through various police-sponsored programs, which include the Police Athletic League, ride alongs, police-involved school activities, and police-led community events. Other activities that the police can sponsor are parades, picnics, holiday parties, and sporting events. Social media is another great tool for the police to get out their messages and promote community relations.

Police departments should work to promote internal diversity. Police agencies need to understand that diversity within their departments is critical. However, diversity is not always an easy task to accomplish. Recruiting and convincing young people in the community to pursue a career in law enforcement can be difficult. Police agencies need to reach out to their communities to try and put an end to the negative stereotypes of law enforcement, and show how it can be a positive career path in which younger members of the community can give back and make positive changes. Along with proactive recruitment, there should be a fair and open process for promotions and career path advancement. As this happens, hopefully the public will see a positive diversity throughout their police departments and feel that they are reflective of their communities.

Professionalism

Police departments across the nation can also form better community relationships by improving their level of professionalism. Improved public relations through professionalism can occur simply by practicing courtesy on a daily basis. **Courtesy** is a cornerstone of good policing, and should be an integral part of a police officer's duties and functions. By being courteous, not only does the police officer represent the department respectably, but he or she also has a better chance of gaining the respect of the public. Courtesy must be extended to all citizens in order to create trust between the police and the community. Treating people with kindness and respect will foster a positive attitude and create a professional image for an officer and his or her department.

When officers conduct themselves in a professional manner, they should avoid certain practices that could potentially take away from a sense of courtesy and professionalism. First, they should not have an overbearing attitude towards the public—even in tense situations, police should remain respectful and calm. Police officers should also try not to use a rough tone of voice. Yes, there may be times where the officer's tone of voice needs to be rough or controlling, but it should not be the default setting.

Police should not routinely practice unnecessary rough treatment of suspects and prisoners—only necessary force should be used. They should also avoid showing any apathy while on duty—all people and situations must be treated with respect and seriousness. Apathy can also extend to an unkempt appearance and dirty or messy uniform—both must be avoided. A courteous and professional officer looks and behaves professionally at all times.

Even with all the negative attention the police receive, national Gallup polls show the public still has a generally positive impression of the police overall. However, impressions vary by neighborhood and community. In a low-crime area, the image of the police is probably more favorable, in contrast to a community with a higher crime rate where the overall image of the local police might be less positive. This can be the result of numerous factors, including poor police-community relations.

Subculture

Police work is one of a few institutions that not only strives for, but depends on, an exclusive subculture. By definition, a **subculture** is a group whose members have a shared set of beliefs, values, and attitudes. The police world is a closed and oftentimes unfamiliar one, and is largely separated from the rest of society. Like the military, it goes through its own training process to shape the minds, thoughts, values, and attitudes of its members. This process transforms recruits into the officers they will need to be to handle the rigorous job of law enforcement. Officers develop shared values that affect their views of human behavior and their roles in society. The process reinforces the notion that police officers are responsible for each other's safety and well-being.

Police subculture contains many elements that make it unique. The first is called **working personality**, the emotional and behavioral characteristics developed by members of a group in response to their work situation and environmental influences. The two main elements of working personality when it comes to police work are: 1) an awareness of the threat of danger—learning to be suspicious of people and their behavior and always being on high alert; and 2) the need to maintain personal authority. Police officers are constantly establishing their authority with the public.

Another key aspect of police subculture can be found in **police morality**. Officers are placed in constant predicaments in which they must make quick decisions. As a result, police officers oftentimes develop a sense of high morality. Developing this sense of high morality serves to ease an officer's conscience during tense interactions and dilemmas where they have to make quick and just decisions. A high morality also serves to give officers a sense of positivity about themselves as they work long hours to protect the public and keep communities safe.

Due to the unique and challenging nature of police work, a phenomenon known as **police isolation** can emerge. Police isolation results when officers remove themselves from society, often due to the belief that the public is suspicious and hostile towards them, which is often a part of the subculture that exists in law enforcement. There are many reasons why this occurs. Police often interact with society at the worst of times, like during crimes, injuries, and death, which can cause officers to pull away from society. Police culture keeps police within themselves due to the type of work they do, as well as the long hours and irregular shifts. Social bonds are enforced by police family members as well.

Police isolation can lead officers to create more barriers with the public, as they naturally fall back within their own group or subculture. Officers often feel that the only people who truly understand them are other officers and family members.

There are many types of stress that police officers face:

Work stress that comes with law enforcement is part of the subculture that strengthens and increases internal police bonds. Law enforcement creates a large amount of stress that also results in high suicide rates, divorce, alcohol issues, and other related health conditions.

External stress is produced by the threats and dangers of police work that officers may encounter on a regular basis.

Organizational stress is created through the inner structure of police departments. Long hours, shift changes, and strict rules and procedures can contribute to this type of stress.

Personal stress can occur when officers struggle to get along with peers and adjust their value systems.

Operational stress results from dealing with the negative parts of society, which creates distrust in people whom officers encounter.

Police Ethics and Discretion

Law enforcement and society place a great emphasis on ethics, integrity, and fighting corruption. These ethical standards cannot be comprised. When we talk about ethics in law enforcement, there are a few distinct characteristics worth noting. First, **ethics** are a set of morals and ideas that help us decide what is right from wrong. What is distinct about ethics in law enforcement is that something can be legal but also be unethical, and sometimes the law must determine the fine line between unethical and illegal. At times, these lines can be blurred and interpreted differently. It must be noted that the vast majority of police officers perform their duties at the highest standards possible, both ethically and legally.

Corruption can be defined as an act involving the misuse of authority for some personal gain. There are different levels of corruption that may occur in law enforcement. The most common form of corruption involves what are called **grass eaters**. Here, the officer accepts payoffs that might come their way. These are typically more passive acts. For example, traffic stops are part of the police work routine, and accepting money for not issuing a ticket falls into this category. Another example is not writing a parking summons in front of a store if given benefits from that store.

Meat eaters are officers who misuse their power for personal gain. This is more of an aggressive form of corruption, and can involve criminal activity such as selling illegal drugs or being part of a drug organization.

There are other ethical pitfalls that exist for police officers, such as misuse of authority. This can include a large range of behaviors, such as an inappropriate use of force, racial profiling, and giving certain favors to people while denying others the same treatment.

There are ways that law enforcement typically deals with these ethical and illegal situations, in an effort to restore trust and confidence back to the community. Police department issues involving corruption and misconduct are handled by an **internal affairs** unit. It investigates illegal activities and allegations against officers, as well as misconduct. These allegations may not be illegal, and can include violations of policies and procedures.

Law enforcement officers are empowered with the use of discretion. **Discretion** is seen as the ability to act and make decisions based on one's judgment and conscience, and it must be utilized within the framework of the rules and laws. It is used throughout police work, and carries a lot of weight and responsibility. The reason that officers exercise a lot of discretion is because human behavior is complex, and decisions involving rules and laws may require some flexibility in particular situations. For example, when an officer conducts a car stop for a vehicle violation, he or she is enforcing the vehicle and traffic laws of the state and can issue a citation to the motorist. However, the officer, using the discretion and power he or she holds, does not have to issue that ticket—a simple warning may suffice depending on the situation.

Future Policing and Technology

Let's talk now about how policing continues to evolve within an ever-changing society.

Policing, over the course of time and history, has been largely preventative in the way that police respond to crimes and calls for help. Even though the police still conduct rapid responses to crimes and incidents, new research shows that additional police strategies can be developed and used to combat crime and other issues in the community, including shifting patrol tactics, using directed patrol, concentrating on hot spots, and maintaining a focus on community policing.

Furthermore, as technology constantly advances in society, law enforcement evolves in an effort to take advantage of new innovations. Technological advances in law enforcement includes the development and improvement of nonlethal devices such as Tasers, stun guns, OC (pepper) spray, rubber bullets, beanbag guns, and spike strips.

Obviously, the use of computers is another key advancement. Name checks, DMV checks, arrest records, and background information are all shared in this new age of technology and information sharing. Databases containing fingerprint history and DNA matches are increasing in size and becoming more crucial for effective investigation. DNA has revolutionized law enforcement and the field of forensic science. Not only does it help solve crimes and lead to the arrest of suspects, it also can help investigators eliminate potential suspects.

Scientific innovations have helped law enforcement with processing crime scenes in a more effective and professional manner. Examining ballistics, latent fingerprints, and blood splatter are just some of the technological achievements in law enforcement. A **GIS**, or **geographic information system**, now helps many police departments map out problem locations and the nature and frequency of crimes committed there. There are also gunshot detection programs, which include computer reports that can help determine the location of gunshots.

Patrol cars and the mobile digital computers officers utilize are becoming more advanced. The sharing of information among local and federal authorities has increased, helping to prevent and detect terrorist acts. Body cameras are another advancement gaining in popularity. As technology changes the way law enforcement operates, the legal limits and ramifications of using any new innovation must always be considered and addressed.

Law Enforcement, Public Focus, and Priorities

Despite its evolution, law enforcement priorities and goals throughout history have generally stayed the same: to serve and protect the public, enforce the law, and stay vigilant in fighting crime. However, as society changes and becomes more complex, law enforcement priorities within these paradigms may evolve.

Throughout history, law enforcement's priorities have been a reflection of the times in which they exist. For instance, the crack epidemic in the 1980s and early 1990s, which led to a surge in drug use and gang wars within inner cities, was at one point a major priority for law enforcement. Today's priorities remain largely the same regarding crime and social services, but we are seeing an expanding role for modern police departments nationwide, including an increased focus and resources on terrorism and homeland security issues.

Women and other Minorities in Policing

In today's society, police agencies across the nation are making strides to become more diversified. Even though the field as a whole may be behind regarding equal representation of certain communities, police departments have put a tremendous amount of resources towards recruiting both women and minorities into law enforcement.

The percentage of female officers rose from 1.5 in 1970 to 12 percent in 2007. That may not seem like a lot, but taking into account both small and large departments, it is a significant increase—and this is a continuing trend. That said, women face many difficulties breaking subculture barriers. And though the growth of women in law enforcement continues to be on the rise, there are still some discrepancies when it comes to men and women in police departments. For instance, in larger agencies, women hold less than 10 percent of supervisory roles and only about seven percent of top or upper command positions, including ranks of captain or higher.

Over the past few decades, as women integrated into law enforcement, subcultures needed to be realigned. The process has not been an easy transition. In years past, women were not allowed on patrol, were referred to as "matrons," and were assigned only to working in jails with women and children. Today, the idea that women could not handle the daily rigors of policing has, for the most part, disappeared. These notions have largely been dispelled over time, as women continue to perform their duties valiantly and courageously. Research has found that men and women can both perform police duties in a similarly effective fashion. However, women oftentimes are forced to confront a variety of doubts and questions, such as: Can women handle situations that require force? Does training or equipment need to be altered for female officers? Will assigning men and women as partners on patrol cause any problems?

Like women, minorities have historically faced a number of issues as they enter into the field of law enforcement—most notably bias and racism. Statistics now reveal that 40 percent of police officers in larger departments are represented by minorities; African Americans represent approximately 12 percent of officers in all local departments, and Hispanics represent approximately 10 percent of officers in police agencies.

Police departments are also actively recruiting new officers from other ethnic backgrounds, including Asians and Pacific Islanders. As police agencies increase their recruitment efforts to better represent the diverse communities they serve, it is hoped that community relations will continue to improve over time.

Next, let's take a closer look at criminal and constitutional law and precedents.

CRIMINAL AND CONSTITUTIONAL LAW AND PRECEDENTS

THE CONSTITUTION AND BILL OF RIGHTS

The U.S. Constitution provides people certain inalienable rights including life and liberty. It also gives Congress and the president certain powers to run the country effectively. Let's look into the rights it bestows and how law enforcement is involved.

The Constitution was ratified in 1788. In 1791, the founding fathers adapted the first 10 Amendments, called the **Bill of Rights**, to protect citizen's rights, which are vital to our democracy. Let's look at some of the amendments it contains.

> **The First Amendment** states that Congress shall make no law respecting an establishment of religion, or prohibiting free speech, the press, the right of the people to assemble peacefully, or the right to petition the government regarding grievances.

> **The Second Amendment** states that a well-regulated militia to protect the State and the right of the people to keep and bear arms shall not be infringed upon.

Among the remaining amendments, there are a select few that deal with the criminal justice system. However, to fully understand these amendments we first must examine the **Fourteenth Amendment**. This amendment was ratified in 1868, and had wider ramifications for years to come. The Fourteenth Amendment states:

> *"...no State shall deprive any person of life, liberty or property without due process of law, or deny to any person within its jurisdiction the equal protection of the laws."*

In essence, what took place within the court system was that the due process clause was not clearly defined, and was at times not applicable to all or certain types of criminal cases. It was also not always clear which rights applied, and when. The courts implemented a fairness test, which was applied on a case-by-case basis. So, the Fourteenth Amendment stood alone, and could not be equally applied to all state officials on an equal basis. In other words, the individual state would determine what was fair during a specific criminal proceeding. This left a huge gap for interpretation regarding how to handle and proceed with criminal cases.

SUPREME COURT CASE LAW

In 1953, the U.S. Supreme Court passed a ruling that applied the Fourteenth Amendment to the Bill of Rights through a process called **incorporation**. What the court decided was that elements of other Amendments (including the Fourth, Fifth, Sixth, and Eighth Amendments) were now connected to the due process clause, and binding to all the states. This meant that amendments that protected people's rights were no longer up to states' interpretation anymore—all criminal cases proceeding through the justice system (whether federal, state, or local) had to be conducted in a consistent manner and apply the Bill of Rights equally to all suspects and defendants.

Let's examine a few of the other amendments in the Bill of Rights that have a direct result on the criminal justice system.

The Fourth Amendment states that the right of the people to be secure in their persons, houses, papers, and effects against unreasonable searches and seizures shall not be violated, and no warrants shall be issued but upon probable cause. This amendment protects the people from unreasonable searches and seizures, and limits the actions of law enforcement and government during criminal activity. The Fourth Amendment does give way to certain exceptions of police search and seizure under specific cases. However, if the courts determine that the police acted unfairly or violated the Fourth Amendment clause and evidence was illegally seized, it would fall under the exclusionary rule and can be excluded at trial.

The **exclusionary rule** is applied when illegally obtained evidence during searches and seizures must be excluded from trial. In other words, the evidence is not admissible at trial. This is also known as the "fruit of the poisonous tree" doctrine—any evidence (the fruit) seized illegally (poisonous tree) is not admissible in a court of law.

However, the Fourth Amendment does come with certain exceptions that allow law enforcement officers to conduct warrantless searches. Let's examine some of these.

The **search incident to lawful arrest** (SILA) states that after an officer makes a lawful arrest, the officer has the right to search the person: including his or her pockets, clothes, bags, and so on. If anything is recovered during this search, it is added on the original charge, or it can be evidence that connects them to the crime.

The **plain view doctrine** states that police do not need a warrant to examine and seize any contraband or evidence that is open and in view at a location where they are legally permitted to be. So, if the police are legally at a house, and drugs or guns are left in the open and they see it, the officers can seize the contraband and make arrests.

Auto exception, the Carroll doctrine, states that officers can search a vehicle if there is a connection between a crime and the vehicle or the people in the vehicle. The plain view doctrine can also be applied here. If the police see drugs or a gun on the floor or in the back seat, they can search the vehicle.

The concept of **consent** states that if you voluntarily give the officer consent or permission, they can search you or whatever location you permit.

During an **emergency or exigent circumstances**, an officer can enter a location without a warrant if he or she believes there is a threat of harm to the public or destruction of evidence.

Stop, Question, and Frisk states that if an officer believes someone is committing, or is about to commit a crime, he or she may stop the individual and conduct a pat down if suspicion of dangerous criminal activity is taking place. The decision regarding the legality of this action comes from the court case *Terry v. Ohio*, and such stops are also known as **Terry stops**.

Hot pursuit refers to foot pursuits. During the course of a pursuit, an officer can lawfully enter a constitutionally protected area without a warrant to effect an arrest. However, if an officer loses sight of the target and pursuit stops, a warrant may be needed.

Inventory usually refers to vehicles—when a vehicle is taken into police custody an inventory search must be conducted. During the course of the inventory search, whatever the police find is fair game.

What needs to be stressed here is that due to certain circumstances, these are such things as warrantless searches. However, once an officer has finished the immediate search and wants to continue it for whatever reason, law enforcement must obtain a warrant.

Another consideration that must be taken into account is that not every search is going to result in an arrest. If an officer conducts a lawful warrantless search based on reasonable suspicion and does not make an arrest, the officer does not violate anyone's Fourth Amendment Constitutional rights.

There are other instances in which a person may voluntarily give up their Fourth Amendment rights. For example, to board a plane, you voluntarily get searched and screened, thereby temporarily giving up your right to be searched without a warrant. The same thing often occurs while crossing a national border or even going to large venues like sporting events and parades, where bag checks are routinely conducted.

The **Fifth Amendment** states that any person cannot be subject for the same offense to be twice put in jeopardy of life or limb, nor shall he or she be compelled to be a witness against himself or herself in any criminal case. This amendment protects the public from what is called **double jeopardy**. It prohibits prosecutors from subjecting a person to prosecution more than once in the same jurisdiction for the same offense—they get one try to convict the accused. The Fifth Amendment also addresses self-incrimination, which simply means that the state cannot force someone to answer questions about themselves that may reveal a criminal act.

The **Sixth Amendment** includes the right to counsel and to a speedy and public trial, the right to confront witnesses, and the right to an impartial jury. This amendment ensures that there are no closed proceedings—all criminal trials must be fair and open. It protects the accused from excessive government powers during a criminal proceeding. You have the right to have legal representation protecting your rights and to cross-examine your accusers and witnesses against you.

The **Eighth Amendment** states that excessive bail shall not be required, nor excessive fines imposed, nor cruel and unusual punishment inflicted. Although this amendment prohibits excessive bail, this language is open to interpretation, and often differs depending on the accused crime. Certain crimes, like murder and rape, may require that no bail is set, and the accused be remanded back to jail. Such a ruling must be deemed reasonable, depending upon the circumstances set before the court and judge.

Cruel and unusual punishment is subject to interpretation and open for debate, as the death penalty can be applied to capital cases. The death penalty has been an issue that has been contested from state to state right up to the Supreme Court.

There have been a large number of U.S. Supreme Court decisions that have been ruled on and have become legal case law. Let's review some of the most important cases that are associated with criminal matters.

The first case to review is *Mapp v. Ohio*. This landmark decision found a violation of the Fourth Amendment due to unreasonable search and seizure. During an encounter with the police, Dollree Mapp, working in an illegal gambling racket, was alleged to be hiding a suspect in a bombing incident. When the police kicked in the door, they forced their way in and showed her a piece of paper claiming it was a warrant. During the search for the bombing suspect, Mapp snatched the papers from the police and became belligerent and was subsequently arrested. In the course of the search, the police discovered pornographic material. After being found guilty, Mapp appealed to the Supreme Court, claiming her Fourth Amendment rights were violated. The Supreme Court agreed and overturned her conviction, stating that the exclusionary rule must be applied to the states, and that the Fourth Amendment must be incorporated not only to federal courts, but to the states as well.

Another historical case, which we briefly mentioned before when discussing stop and frisk, is *Terry v. Ohio*. In this case, an officer observed three suspicious individuals walking up and down the street and looking into store windows while having a discussion. A detective who observed them approached the suspects, questioned them, and proceeded to pat down one of the men, named Terry. During this frisk, the detective discovered a pistol. He then patted down the other two and recovered another revolver. All three suspects were placed under arrest. It was Terry's argument that the detective violated his Fourth Amendment rights of unreasonable search and seizure. The courts rejected this argument, stating that the officer had grounds for the stop, as the men were acting suspiciously. Therefore, the stop and frisk was legal and justified based on their suspicious behavior.

The next case to review is *Miranda v. Arizona*. This case deals with the Fifth Amendment right to avoid self-incrimination and the Sixth Amendment right to counsel. Miranda was arrested for the kidnapping and rape of an 18-year-old woman. After Phoenix police officers arrested Miranda, he was then interrogated for two hours, during which time he signed a typed confession. However, during the interrogation, Miranda was never told of his right to counsel, nor his right to remain silent. Miranda's lawyer argued to the Supreme Court that the statements were not voluntarily given and that Miranda was not afforded his due process right to counsel and to avoid self-incrimination. The Supreme Court overruled the initial conviction based on the improperly obtained confession (Miranda was retried in the lower courts and was subsequently found guilty). As a result of this ruling, suspects now need to be made aware of their right to remain silent and right to counsel.

This next case is *Gideon v. Wainwright*. This landmark case dealt with the Sixth Amendment. Gideon was arrested for an alleged burglary of a pool room. During his arrest and appearance in court, Gideon proclaimed that he was not afforded representation by counsel, and his Sixth Amendment rights were being violated. The Florida court explained to Gideon that he was not entitled to counsel because the law did not provide the state the right to assign counsel, unless it is a capital case. Since this clearly was not a capital case, Gideon was not represented and was eventually convicted. While in jail, Gideon continued his appeal all the way to the Supreme Court, stating that his Sixth Amendment rights were violated. The Supreme Court unanimously sided with Gideon, stating that all indigent defendants charged with serious crimes, under the Fourteenth Amendment, are entitled to counsel. This eventually expanded to all crimes and police interrogation. Gideon was later acquitted in a subsequent trial with a lawyer.

The next case, *Tennessee v. Garner*, involves the use of deadly physical force, which falls under the Fourth Amendment (regarding seizing a suspect). Garner, a 15-year-old, was fleeing from a burglary when officers gave chase and pursued him. When Garner tried to climb over a fence an officer shot him, in accordance with Tennessee law stating that police are allowed to shoot a suspect who is fleeing from a serious crime. Garner died later that night. This case eventually made its way to the Supreme Court, and the court stated that under the Fourth Amendment deadly force cannot be used against an unarmed fleeing suspect, unless the officer has probable cause to believe the suspect poses a threat of death or serious injury to the officer or another person.

FEDERAL AND LOCAL LAWS AND ORDINANCES

Let's conclude this chapter with an overview of the three levels of law: federal laws, state laws, and local laws or ordinances.

Federal laws apply to every person in the United States. The Constitution does not define federal crimes except for treason and sedition, as federal laws originate from Congress (the process begins with the U.S. House of Representatives, then the Senate, and then the final bill is signed into law by the president). Federal laws include crimes like terrorism, any type of WMD (weapons of mass destruction), illegal immigration, and drug and human trafficking. Other laws that can be passed and enforced are done so by **Presidential Executive Orders**—these are directives by the president that instruct officers and agencies to execute specific guidelines.

State laws and their constitutions cannot nullify any rights that are guaranteed by the U.S. Constitution, but it can add to rights not covered by the U.S. Constitution. State laws come from state constitutions and state criminal codes. These laws are written by the state legislature and signed by the governor.

Most states have the same or similar criminal laws and codes, as state criminal law must uphold the rights guaranteed by the U.S. Constitution, and because consensus of state law from state to state can benefit the public as well as the police. All persons within a state are subject to the laws of that state, regardless of whether or not they are residents of that state. The most common laws found in a state's penal codes involve murders, assaults, rapes, robberies, burglaries, larcenies, drug offenses, and weapons.

The sources of **local laws or ordinances** are a city or town's local leaders and mayor or town counsel, and usually cover violations and other minor infractions. These laws and ordinances usually involve less than misdemeanor-level crimes, and address behaviors that do not rise up to the level of state law. For instance, a town may have ordinances for things like park violations, trespassing after dark, or driving while using a cell phone. One city even has an ordinance against wearing sagging pants. These violations, for the most part, carry no real jail time and are punishable by fines.

This concludes our review of the topics you should know to succeed on your DSST Introduction to Law Enforcement exam. Good luck!

SUMMING IT UP

- Modern policing is credited to **Sir Robert Peel**, who created the first London police force in 1829. His four-part mandate is still used in today's policing: preventing crime without military force; maintaining public order without violence; reducing conflict between the police and the public; and showing efficiency by reducing crime.

- In the **Political** era of American policing (1840–1920), there were close relationships between police and political leaders in which both parties traded favors in exchange for loyalty.

- In the **Professional Model** era (1920–1970), a more progressive version of policing was meant to create more efficient local government and more resources for less fortunate people. To achieve these goals, the reformers tried to separate policing and politics, emphasized constant training for police professionals, and emphasized that laws should be enforced equally.

- In the **Community Policing** era (1970–present), policing moved away from direct crime fighting and closer to developing relationships between communities and the police as a way of increasing social services and reducing crime.

- Contemporary policing is based on **problem-oriented policing**, or **community and problem oriented policing (CPOP)**. In this premise, police focus on taking proactive steps to prevent or solve a problem, instead of reacting to a problem that has already occurred. This kind of policing works on a national model called the **SARA Model**, in which police **scan** to identify a problem, **analyze** the causes and patterns of a problem, **respond** to alleviate a problem or come up with specific plans, and **assess** the success of the resolution, collect data, determine sustainability for the future, and conduct ongoing research as necessary.

- In the **broken windows** theory of policing, police focus on cleaning up quality of life (QOL) issues as a way of using small fixes to resolve bigger crime problems.

- Other theories focus on the sources of crime. **Jeffrey Reiman**'s theory suggests that social and economic justice can reduce crime by reducing poverty. **Cesare Beccaria**'s Classical Criminology theory states that people choose to commit crimes, and that fear of punishment can reduce crime. **Edwin Sutherland**'s social process theories suggest that criminal behavior is learned. **Emile Durkheim** and **Robert Merton**'s anomie theory suggests that crime rises as social behavior rule and norms are weakened.

- Everyday duties of American police include service calls (which make up 80 percent of police calls), assisting in emergency situations as first responders, traffic issues, investigating crimes, working with the community, and organizing security for public events.

- **Prosecutors**, also known as the people's attorneys, are court officials who are responsible for prosecuting all crimes in their jurisdictions. They work with the police, judges, defense attorneys, and politicians. They typically have the most power in the criminal justice system, because they have the power to prosecute, as well as change or drop charges at any time.

- **Defense attorneys** are officers of the court who defend clients who are charged with crimes. They work with judges and prosecutors to ensure that their clients receive **due process** (fair treatment). Many defense attorneys are hired by clients, but public defenders work with clients who cannot afford an attorney on their own.

- The main function of courts is to **adjudicate**, or enforce laws and guide behavior. Different types of courts include criminal court, family and juvenile court, civil court, surrogate courts, bankruptcy courts, tax courts, and small claims courts. In the United States, both federal and state courts function in an **adversarial process**, in which lawyers represent different sides of a case, and present arguments and evidence accordingly.

- The **corrections** system manages and punishes people who have been convicted of criminal offenses. The system is currently characterized by **three P's—prison, probation, and parole.**

- Crime statistics are an essential part of the criminal justice system. Crime reports are collected as part of the National Incident-Based Reporting System (NIBRS), and annual crime statistics are published every year in the FBI's Uniform Crime Reports (UCR). The National Crime Victimization Survey (NCVS) collects data about crime to determine the difference between reported crimes and the dark figure of crime (crimes that go unreported).

- At the federal level, the Department of Justice (DOJ) and the Department of Homeland Security (DHS) are the largest branches of law enforcement. The DOJ manages the FBI; the Federal Bureau of Prisons; the Bureau of Alcohol, Tobacco, Firearms, and Explosives; and the Drug Enforcement Administration. DHS manages Customs and Border Protection, the Federal Emergency Management Agency, Immigration and Customs Enforcement, the Transportation Safety Administration, the U.S. Coast Guard, and the U.S. Secret Service.

- At the state level, police enforce state laws, including traffic laws on state roadways, protecting state capitals and governors, and investigating crimes using technology and forensics.

- At the local or municipal, level police departments enforce laws in their own jurisdictions, or municipalities. These police arrest, conduct searches and seizures, enforce traffic regulations and laws, investigate crimes, act as emergency first responders, and maintain public safety and order. In addition to local police, special district police agencies have power over specific areas, like airports, public transportation, college campuses, or outdoor parks.

- A police **chain of command** is a structure that defines ranks and authority for all members of the department. The highest ranks are typically commander, then captain, then lieutenant, then sergeant, then detective, then police officer, though this can vary depending on the police department. Line function officers are out in the field, while staff function officers typically work within the police department itself (as clerks and administrative staff).

- Police can address tensions between their departments and the community by acknowledging any communication challenges they have, as well as conflicts; by being transparent and accountable to the community; by reducing bias; and by working closely with the community not only on policing, but also on community-building. Factors like courtesy and fair treatment can also be used to improve relationships and impressions among the community.

- **Subculture** is important to police work, because the police community is often closed and separate from most of society. Police subculture is often defined by the following characteristics: **working personality** (the characteristics developed by a group in response to their work and environment), **police morality** (relying on conscience to solve problems), and **police isolation** (working apart from society due to perceived hostility toward police).

- Police corruption comes in two different forms: grass eaters (who accept bribes or payoffs in exchange for favorable outcomes) and meat eaters (who misuse their power for personal gain). Corruption is typically investigated and handled by internal affairs departments.

- Several amendments in the Constitution's Bill of Rights govern police behavior and law enforcement powers. The **First Amendment** protects citizens' rights to free speech, freedom of religion, freedom to assemble, and freedom to petition the government. The **Second Amendment** protects citizens' rights to bear arms. **The Fourth Amendment** protects citizens from unreasonable search and seizure. The **Fifth Amendment** protects citizens from having to incriminate themselves at trial. The **Sixth Amendment** guarantees citizens the right to a fair and speedy trial. The **Eighth Amendment** states that excessive bail shall not be required.

- Additionally, there are doctrines that further govern police searches. The exclusionary rule prevents illegally obtained evidence from being used in a trial. The search incident to lawful arrest (SILA) allows police officers to search someone who has been lawfully arrested. The plain view doctrine states that police do not need a warrant to examine or seize any contraband that is out in the open. The auto exception, or the Carroll doctrine, allows police to search a vehicle if there is a connection between a specific crime and the people in the vehicle. Otherwise, searches require consent and a warrant, unless there are emergency circumstances.

- Legal cases have defined legal precedent for arrests and investigations. *Terry v. Ohio* determined that officers have the right to stop and frisk based on probable cause. *Miranda v. Arizona* guaranteed that suspects would be advised of their legal rights upon arrest. *Gideon v. Wainwright* guaranteed that a defendant who couldn't afford an attorney would be given a free one. *Tennessee v. Garner* determined that deadly force cannot be used against an unarmed suspect, unless there is immediate threat to the officer.

- Federal laws, which originate from Congress, apply to every person in the United States. State laws apply to residents of the state, and they cannot nullify federal laws. Local laws cover lower level infractions and misdemeanors and are enforced on the town or city level.

INTRODUCTION TO LAW ENFORCEMENT POST-TEST

Directions: Carefully read each of the following 60 questions. Choose the best answer to each question and fill in the corresponding circle on the answer sheet. The Answer Key and Explanations can be found following this post-test.

1. In 1845, New York City created the first full-time paid police force. As a result of the corruption-filled era of policing at that time, it cost $10,000 to become a police captain. What era was this?
   A. Professional era
   B. Political era
   C. Community policing era
   D. Modern era

2. Contemporary policing consists of police community relations. A national model that represents this is called SARA, which stands for
   A. Search, Assess, Rescue, Assignment.
   B. Search, Assign, Respond, After Action Report.
   C. Scan, Assign, Report, Assess.
   D. Scanning, Analysis, Response, Assessment.

3. Robert Merton believed in a theory called *anomie*, which states that
   A. deviant behavior is criminogenic.
   B. deviant behavior is taught at a young age.
   C. deviant behavior is a result of the rules and norms of society disappearing.
   D. deviant behavior is of free choice.

4. The theorist who believes that deviant behavior can be solved through economic justice and reducing poverty is
   A. Reiman.
   B. Merton.
   C. Beccaria.
   D. Lombroso.

5. There are many components of the criminal justice system. The organization that goes by the motto "to protect and serve" falls under
   A. the role of the prosecutor.
   B. the court system.
   C. the role of the police.
   D. the role of corrections.

6. One of the most difficult jobs the police may encounter on a regular basis is
   A. testifying in court.
   B. issuing a summons.
   C. balancing First Amendment rights of free speech with lawful assembly.
   D. wearing heavy equipment on a daily basis.

7. The person who is responsible for seeking justice within his or her jurisdiction is the
   A. prosecutor.
   B. judge.
   C. police officer.
   D. mayor.

8. The role of the prosecutor is to
   A. work with the police and review arrest reports.
   B. make sure arrests meet legal standards.
   C. form working relationships with judges, defense attorneys, victims, and political leaders.
   D. All of the above

9 . In the criminal justice system, who has the
most discretion?
A. Police
B. Judge
C. Prosecutor
D. Supreme Court

10. An indigent is
A. a juvenile.
B. a victim.
C. a person who is representing himself
or herself.
D. a person who cannot afford his or her
own attorney.

11. The defense attorney is barred from revealing
any statements made to him by his client.
This is called
A. discretion.
B. lawyer/client privilege.
C. discovery.
D. a motion.

12. The role of the defense attorney is to
A. refuse to plea bargain.
B. petition the court for a lighter
sentence.
C. receive a not guilty verdict and
protect the client's constitutional
rights.
D. review the case for probable cause.

13. The U.S. court system is based on an adversarial process, which is when
A. the judge and the jury are working
against each other.
B. the prosecutor and judge face off
against each other.
C. the prosecutors and defense attorneys
represent their sides through arguments and evidence.
D. the defense and the judge argue
against each other.

14. The role of corrections in society is to
A. determine a person's guilt or
innocence.
B. determine probable cause.
C. assist police in conducting
investigations.
D. manage and punish convicted
offenders.

15. A common form of corrections in today's
society is
A. prison.
B. probation.
C. parole.
D. All of the above

16. The notion that a dimension of crime occurs
and is never reported to the police is known
as
A. victimless crimes.
B. the dark figure of crime.
C. National Crime Victimization Survey
(NCVS).
D. Uniform Crime Report (UCR).

17. Crime reports that are generated every year
by the FBI are known as
A. Uniform Crime Report (UCR).
B. National Crime Victimization Survey
(NCVS).
C. National Incident-Based Reporting
System (NIBRS).
D. the dark figure of crime.

18. The UCR measures crimes from various
categories including
A. drug offenses.
B. shoplifting.
C. burglary.
D. terrorist threats.

19. After 9/11, President Bush signed an executive order restructuring departments and agencies that fall under them. As a result, which department is the largest federal law enforcement department?
    A. Department of Justice (DOJ)
    B. FBI
    C. Department of Homeland Security (DHS)
    D. FEMA

20. The agencies assigned to the DOJ are
    A. FEMA and the DEA.
    B. U.S. Customs and Border Protection and the U.S. Secret Service.
    C. the Transportation Security Administration and the FBI.
    D. the FBI and the Bureau of Alcohol, Tobacco, Firearms, and Explosives (ATF).

21. The agencies assigned to the DHS are
    A. the FBI and the DEA.
    B. Immigration and Customs Enforcement (ICE) and the U.S. Secret Service.
    C. FEMA and the Federal Bureau of Prisons.
    D. the U.S. Coast Guard and the DEA.

22. Which agency supplements local officers for smaller towns that may not have their own police forces?
    A. The neighboring town's police department
    B. Contract security guards
    C. State police
    D. Neighborhood watches

23. The state police is responsible for
    A. traffic enforcement on highways, interstates, and expressways.
    B. protection of the state's capital.
    C. security protection of the state's governor.
    D. All of the above

24. Locally operated law enforcement agencies are known as
    A. municipal police departments.
    B. state police.
    C. federal officers.
    D. specialized police forces.

25. Police departments that work in a limited jurisdiction but may carry different sorts of power are called
    A. federal agencies.
    B. private contractors.
    C. special district police agencies.
    D. local police departments.

26. Special police agencies, or district police agencies, include
    A. airport police.
    B. game wardens.
    C. transit police.
    D. All of the above

27. Cities and towns have the ability and power to create their own police departments. Local laws are enforced within their own jurisdictional territory. They are known as
    A. special district police.
    B. local law enforcement municipalities.
    C. federal agencies.
    D. neighborhood patrol.

28. Robert Peel wanted to model police departments after what organization?
    A. The military
    B. Other large-city police departments
    C. Neighborhood watch programs
    D. There was no model from which to choose.

post-test

29. A common rank structure in police departments that goes from the bottom to top in order is
    A. captain/lieutenant/commander.
    B. lieutenant/police officer/captain.
    C. police officer/sergeant/lieutenant.
    D. commander/sergeant/police officer.

30. Line officers are involved in operations that consist of
    A. patrol.
    B. traffic enforcement.
    C. investigations.
    D. All of the above

31. For line function officers to operate and perform their regular patrol duties, they are supported by
    A. specialty units.
    B. the detective bureau.
    C. staff function officers.
    D. the hierarchy structure.

32. Staff function officers help support patrol officers to function on a daily basis. These include
    A. clerks and administrative duties.
    B. motor divisions to keep the patrol cars functioning.
    C. computer divisions and gunsmiths for weapons repair.
    D. All of the above

33. Police departments today have many important responsibilities. One of the main concerns and responsibilities of the police is
    A. establishing neighborhood watches.
    B. building community relations.
    C. limiting media coverage of police incidents.
    D. establishing contracts with the department and police unions.

34. For the police to function better, they should have policies regarding
    A. being transparent and accountable.
    B. solving crimes without outside assistance.
    C. maintaining fewer communications with the public.
    D. implementing strategies without the community's concerns.

35. One way that the police can be transparent with the community is by
    A. talking about the types of crimes they are enforcing, including traffic summonses.
    B. disregarding what the community thinks.
    C. giving detailed information when investigating a crime.
    D. releasing contract information between the department and the police union.

36. Another way to promote police community relations is by
    A. arresting more people.
    B. issuing more parking summonses to help the flow of traffic.
    C. keeping communications to the public minimal.
    D. promoting activities like picnics, parades, and holiday parties.

37. A police-sponsored program that helps with community relations is
    A. the Police Athletic League (PAL).
    B. a police ride-along.
    C. a school activity such as DARE.
    D. All of the above

38. Another effective means in building community relations and trust is to
- **A.** hire people from the military.
- **B.** promote diversity.
- **C.** show the community arrest numbers to prove efficiency.
- **D.** discuss police budgets at community meetings.

39. The latest national Gallup Poll shows that the public has what view of police officers?
- **A.** A negative image
- **B.** No opinion of the police
- **C.** A positive image
- **D.** The opinion that the police are necessary but have too much power

40. There are many ways that the police can help police relations within the community. What can the force, particularly a patrol officer, do to help with community relations?
- **A.** Arrest as many people as possible
- **B.** Issue traffic summonses
- **C.** Keep his or her distance from the public
- **D.** Use courtesy and professionalism when dealing with the public

41. For police officers to act in a professional manner, they must avoid certain types of behavior, including
- **A.** using a rough tone of voice, unless under certain circumstances.
- **B.** unnecessary rough treatment of suspects and prisoners.
- **C.** having an unkempt appearance with a sloppy or dirty uniform.
- **D.** All of the above

42. Beliefs, values, and attitudes that are shown by members of a group are called
- **A.** socialization.
- **B.** professionalism.
- **C.** subculture.
- **D.** morals.

43. The threat of danger from police work and keeping one's own authority is exhibited in what is known as
- **A.** socialization.
- **B.** working personality.
- **C.** subculture.
- **D.** stress.

44. A result of police work, working long irregular shifts, and the police subculture is a phenomena known as
- **A.** depression.
- **B.** lethargy.
- **C.** police isolation.
- **D.** a career path.

45. Police isolationism occurs as a result of
- **A.** social bonds that are enforced by police families.
- **B.** police interacting with society at the worst of times, such as during crimes and death.
- **C.** officers keeping to themselves and their own kind due to the type of work they perform.
- **D.** All of the above

46. There are various types of stress that are a result of police work. One type of stress that is created through the inner structure from working long hours and shift changes is called
- **A.** external stress.
- **B.** operational stress.
- **C.** personal stress.
- **D.** organizational stress.

47. Morals and values that help police distinguish right from wrong are known as
- **A.** ethics.
- **B.** policies.
- **C.** procedures.
- **D.** supervisory instruction.

post-test

48. Police work can lead to different forms of corruption. The most common form of corruption is known as
    A. meat eaters.
    B. on the take.
    C. grass eaters.
    D. midnight raiders.

49. Which unit/person investigates corruption and misconduct for law enforcement?
    A. Police commander
    B. Internal affairs
    C. Federal prosecutors
    D. District attorney

50. Women in law enforcement have made great strides in recent times; however, when they first arrived in law enforcement, they were referred to as
    A. policewomen.
    B. police ladies.
    C. matrons.
    D. police girls.

51. Blacks and Hispanics were two minority groups that broke the barriers into law enforcement. What is the percentage of minorities in today's large police departments?
    A. 8 percent
    B. 40 percent
    C. 60 percent
    D. 20 percent

52. The Fourteenth Amendment covers
    A. freedom of speech.
    B. the right to bear arms.
    C. the right to life, liberty, and property.
    D. the right to counsel.

53. Under the Fourth Amendment, there are a number of exceptions for a warrantless search. The exception that allows an officer to examine and seize contraband or evidence that is in view of the officer is known as
    A. consent.
    B. stop, question, frisk.
    C. the auto exception.
    D. the plain view doctrine.

54. When evidence is obtained illegally during a search and is not admissible in a court of law, it is known as
    A. the exclusionary rule.
    B. a search incident to lawful arrest.
    C. consent.
    D. the auto exception.

55. The auto exception allows officers to search a vehicle without a warrant if there is a nexus between a crime and the vehicle or people in the vehicle. This is called
    A. consent.
    B. exigent circumstances.
    C. the Carroll doctrine.
    D. hot pursuit.

56. The landmark case that falls under the Fourteenth Amendment against unreasonable searches and seizures is found in
    A. *Mapp v. Ohio.*
    B. *Gideon v. Wainwright.*
    C. *Miranda v. Arizona.*
    D. *Tennessee v. Garner.*

57. Under the exception to the Fourth Amendment, stop, question, and frisk allows an officer to stop someone, question him or her without a warrant, and conduct a pat down if necessary. This falls under what case law?
    A. *Miranda v. Arizona*
    B. *Mapp v. Ohio*
    C. *Terry v. Ohio*
    D. *Gideon v. Wainwright*

58. Which case involves the use of deadly physical force?
    A. *Mapp v. Ohio*
    B. *Miranda v. Arizona*
    C. *Terry v. Ohio*
    D. *Tennessee v. Garner*

59. Laws regarding federal crimes originate from
    A. state legislatures.
    B. Congress.
    C. the president.
    D. the Supreme Court.

60. State laws are written and passed by the
    A. legislature and the governor.
    B. city council and the mayor.
    C. Congress and the president.
    D. legislature and judges.

ANSWER KEY AND EXPLANATIONS

1. B	13. C	25. C	37. D	49. B
2. D	14. D	26. D	38. B	50. C
3. C	15. D	27. B	39. C	51. B
4. A	16. B	28. A	40. D	52. C
5. C	17. A	29. C	41. D	53. D
6. C	18. C	30. D	42. C	54. A
7. A	19. C	31. C	43. B	55. C
8. D	20. D	32. D	44. C	56. A
9. C	21. B	33. B	45. D	57. C
10. D	22. C	34. A	46. D	58. D
11. B	23. D	35. A	47. A	59. B
12. C	24. A	36. D	48. C	60. A

1. **The correct answer is B.** The Political era took place from 1840–1920 and contained close ties to local politicians and police departments. This era was filled with corruption as a result of those relationships. Choices A and C are incorrect because they moved away from political ties, and choice D is incorrect because there is no Modern era model.

2. **The correct answer is D.** SARA stands for Scanning—ID the problem, Analysis—learn the causes of the problem, Response—formulate a response plan to carry out, Assessment—determine if the plan worked. Choices A, B, and C are all incorrect.

3. **The correct answer is C.** Merton and Durkheim both were proponents of anomie, believing that when there is a breakdown and disappearance of society's rules, deviant behavior results. Choices A, B, and D are incorrect because they all fall into different theories of deviant behavior.

4. **The correct answer is A.** Jeffery Reiman believed the causation of crime was based on economic disadvantages and that crime can be eradicated through economic equality.

Choice B is incorrect because Merton believed in anomie. Choice C is incorrect because Beccaria believed in free will and choice. Choice D is incorrect because Lombroso believed in the biological theories of deviant behavior.

5. **The correct answer is C.** One role of the police is summarized by the motto "to protect and serve." Choices A, B, and D are incorrect because they serve the criminal justice system in a different capacity.

6. **The correct answer is C.** During times of protests and demonstrations, police must balance people's rights to free speech and assembly with protecting the community from lawlessness and violence. Choice A is incorrect because testifying in court may be nerve wracking but is not the most difficult job. Choice B is incorrect because issuing a summons is part of routine patrol. Choice D is incorrect because even though wearing police equipment may be uncomfortable, it is not a difficult part of the job.

7. **The correct answer is A.** The prosecutor has the responsibility of seeking justice by discovering the truth and prosecuting the

case to ensure a conviction. Choices B, C, and D are all incorrect as they all have different roles and responsibilities.

8. **The correct answer is D.** The prosecutor forms many working relationships, including dealing with the police, victims, and witnesses to seek the truth and present the case in court.

9. **The correct answer is C.** Prosecutors have the most discretion, as they decide on the case (including all final charges), prosecute the case in a trial or plea bargain, or dismiss the case entirely. Choices A, B, and D are all incorrect, even though they may have limited discretion.

10. **The correct answer is D.** Defense counsels usually represent indigents in the criminal justice system, as a majority of defendants are represented by public defenders. Choice A is incorrect because a juvenile may be indigent but is referred to as a *minor* in family court. Choices B and C are incorrect because they do not fit the definition of *indigent*.

11. **The correct answer is B.** The lawyer/client privilege act bars defense attorneys from revealing anything their clients tell them in confidence. This includes if a client states that he or she committed the offense. Defense lawyers have a legal obligation to their clients to ensure their rights are not violated. Choices A, C, and D are all incorrect.

12. **The correct answer is C.** The defense counsel's responsibility is to try to put doubt into the jury's mind for an acquittal, as well as to protect the client's constitutional rights. Choice A is incorrect because the defense counsel is part of the plea bargain negotiation. Choice B is incorrect because upon conviction the defense counsel will suggest a lighter or more lenient sentence on behalf of his or her client. Choice D

is incorrect because the defense counsel reviews everything about the case, just as the prosecutor does.

13. **The correct answer is C.** In criminal court, both the prosecutor and the defense face each other to best represent each side. Our judicial system is based on both lawyers in any courtroom facing each other as adversaries. Choices A, B, and D are all incorrect because the roles are not adversarial by nature.

14. **The correct answer is D.** The role of corrections is to "correct" people's behavior to conform to society's rules and laws, as well as to punish convicted offenders and protect society. Choices A, B, and C are all incorrect because they are not the role or responsibility of corrections.

15. **The correct answer is D.** Even though the three P's, prison, probation, and parole, are the most common and recognizable forms of corrections, there are numerous other forms, such as house arrest, community service, and restitution. Corrections, like other parts of the criminal justice system, keeps changing to reflect the needs of society.

16. **The correct answer is B.** The dark figure of crime occurs when crime takes place but is never reported to the police. Choice A is incorrect because victimless crimes is a crime category that may include drug or prostitution offenses. Choice C is incorrect because the NCVS is a self-generated survey or report to help identify crime victims. Choice D is incorrect because the UCR is generated by the FBI as a statistical report.

17. **The correct answer is A.** The UCR is generated by the FBI as a yearly statistical crime report that is provided to the FBI by all local, state, federal, and tribal departments. Choices B, C, and D are all incorrect because even though they are part of the process of measuring crime, they are not part of the UCR.

18. **The correct answer is C.** Burglary is considered an index crime. Even though the UCR is a comprehensive crime report, index crimes are murder, rape, robbery, felony assault, burglary, grand larceny, grand larceny auto, and arson. Therefore, A, B, and D are all incorrect.

19. **The correct answer is C.** Prior to the executive order, the DOJ was the largest department. After 9/11 restructuring, the DHS became the largest federal law enforcement department. Choices A, B, and D are all incorrect.

20. **The correct answer is D.** Both the FBI and ATF fall under the jurisdiction of the Department of Justice. Choices A, B, and C are all incorrect because some agencies may be under the DHS, as in FEMA, the Secret Service, and U.S. Customs and Border Protection.

21. **The correct answer is B.** Both ICE and the U.S. Secret Service fall under the jurisdiction of the Department of Homeland Security. Choices A, C, and D are all incorrect because some agencies may be under the DOJ, as in the FBI, DEA, and Federal Bureau of Prisons.

22. **The correct answer is C.** The state police helps support local towns without their own police forces and acts as the lead agency for any criminal investigation. Therefore, choices A, B, and D are all incorrect.

23. **The correct answer is D.** The state police has the responsibility of enforcing state traffic laws as well as protecting the state's capital and governor.

24. **The correct answer is A.** Local law enforcement agencies that are responsible for their jurisdiction in cities or towns are known as municipal police departments. Therefore, choices B, C, and D are all incorrect.

25. **The correct answer is C.** Special district police agencies carry power that is used in their assigned districts to enforce the laws and rules within their geographical boundaries. Choice A is incorrect because federal agencies is too broad of an answer, as special police agencies may exist on a federal or state level. Choice B is incorrect because private contractors do not have police powers. Choice D is incorrect because local municipalities or municipal police departments may not be trained in specialized law enforcement fields.

26. **The correct answer is D.** District police agencies can be found in many departments (e.g., sanitation police, university police, and environmental police) and they offer specialized training.

27. **The correct answer is B.** Local police departments and municipalities enforce all laws, including local ordinances within their jurisdictional boundaries. If a smaller town does not have its own police department, it will be aided and supplemented by state authorities. Therefore, choices A, C, and D are all incorrect.

28. **The correct answer is A.** Robert Peel modeled the police after the military to have a hierarchy and an infrastructure for discipline and organization. This is why police departments are known as paramilitary organizations. Therefore, choices B, C, and D are all incorrect.

29. **The correct answer is C.** Generally speaking, the rank structure starts with the police officer. Detectives follow but they may not be considered a rank but rather an assignment or unit. Some police departments may use corporal, but the next level is sergeant, lieutenant, and then captain. After captain, departments may carry different levels and titles.

30. **The correct answer is D.** Line function officers are involved in all related patrol functions and operations.

31. **The correct answer is C.** Staff function officers operate on many levels, all contributing to support the patrol function officers. Choice A is incorrect because specialty units help supplement the needs of patrol. Choice B is incorrect because detectives are responsible for investigating and solving criminal cases. Choice D is incorrect because it does not apply to this.

32. **The correct answer is D.** Staff function officers are a large part of police operations, as they are responsible for keeping patrol up and running on a daily basis.

33. **The correct answer is B.** Modern police departments take on many roles and responsibilities. Besides responding to crimes, traffic enforcement, and service calls, police departments are continuously working with the community to build better relationships and partnerships. Therefore, choices A, C, and D are all incorrect.

34. **The correct answer is A.** The police should be transparent and accountable to the community it serves. This can help reduce tensions and future conflicts, while helping to promote better cooperation within the community. Therefore, choices B, C, and D are all incorrect.

35. **The correct answer is A.** To build a better relationship with the community, transparency is important. Informing community leaders on goals of the police department and its type of enforcement may help create a better understanding. This does not mean that the community will always agree with the police, but at least policing is not done in secrecy. Choice B is incorrect because it does not help with community relations. Choice C is incorrect because the police

cannot share certain vital information from the investigation. Choice D is incorrect because some information may be open to the public but it may not be a major issue for community relations.

36. **The correct answer is D.** Police departments should, and often do, sponsor such events and support the community during these events. These types of events help to break down the barriers between the police and the community. Choices A and B are incorrect because they may be looked upon negatively by the public. Choice C is incorrect because the police want to keep the lines of communication open with the public.

37. **The correct answer is D.** Police departments promote all of these programs and more to foster and build stronger community relationships. These programs are vital to both the community and the police.

38. **The correct answer is B.** Promoting diversity and recruiting can be a difficult challenge for the police department. The police may have negative images that can hurt them in recruiting people from different ethnic backgrounds. The police need to show that it is a positive career and that they can make a difference. Choices A, C, and D are all incorrect.

39. **The correct answer is C.** The national Gallup Poll reveals that the majority of the population view the police in a positive light for the job they do protecting the communities. This is not to say that there are no negative opinions of the police. Choices A, B, and D are all incorrect.

40. **The correct answer is D.** Police officers should be trained that courtesy and professionalism are part of their duties when dealing with the public. Courtesy as a daily part of patrol will help the police image. Choices A and B are incorrect because even

though they may be part of the officer's duties, they do not always promote a positive image. Choice C is incorrect because it alienates the community from the police.

41. **The correct answer is D.** Police officers in many ways need to avoid unprofessional behavior. Avoiding particular mannerisms, attitudes, and behavior can help promote a positive image of the police.

42. **The correct answer is C.** A subculture is defined as a group that shares beliefs, values, and attitudes. Police work has a strong subculture that is unlike other institutions and that transforms a person in the law enforcement field. Therefore, choices A, B, and D are all incorrect.

43. **The correct answer is B.** Working personality is part of the subculture and socialization that transforms an individual into a police officer in response to threats and danger. Choices A, C, and D are all incorrect, as they may be part of working personality but do not complete the definition or traits that comprise law enforcement working personality.

44. **The correct answer is C.** Police isolation occurs when officers remove themselves, and try not to interact with, the rest of society because they feel the public is hostile toward them. This is also a part of the subculture that exists within law enforcement. Choices A, B, and D are all incorrect as they do not fit into the definition of police isolationism.

45. **The correct answer is D.** Police isolation occurs because the police mainly feel comfortable around each other and withdraw from society. This can lead to more barriers between the police and the public as distrust grows.

46. **The correct answer is D.** Organizational stress is from the inner structure of law enforcement that consists of strict rules and procedures. Choice A is incorrect because external stress is produced by threat and dangers. Choice B is incorrect because operational stress is from dealing with the negative side of society. Choice C is incorrect because personal stress deals with getting along with peers.

47. **The correct answer is A.** Ethics is a set of morals and values that help distinguish right from wrong. The police face many ethical dilemmas every day during their patrol duties. Choices B and C are incorrect because they guide police officers on how to handle certain situations and what rules to follow. Choice D is incorrect because it does not fit the definition of police ethics.

48. **The correct answer is C.** Grass eaters is the most common form of corruption that occurs from the routines of police work. These acts may include payoffs on traffic stops and summonses. Choice A is incorrect because meat eaters are more involved in criminal acts. Choices B and D are incorrect because the terms do not apply.

49. **The correct answer is B.** Internal affairs is a unit that investigates illegal activities, misconduct, and allegations against officers. Misconduct does not necessarily denote illegal activities but may include violations of policies and procedures. Choice A is incorrect because police commanders will not necessarily conduct criminal investigations against officers. Choices C and D are incorrect because prosecutors and district attorneys may investigate officers for illegal activities but they do not investigate misconduct.

50. **The correct answer is C.** Women were routinely referred to as *matrons*, as they were assigned to duties such as working in jails with women and children. Therefore, choices A, B, and D are all incorrect.

post-test

51. **The correct answer is B.** Approximately 40 percent of police officers are minorities in large police departments. Additionally, police departments are becoming more multicultural as larger numbers of people from varying ethnic backgrounds are entering the field. Therefore, choices A, C, and D are all incorrect.

52. **The correct answer is C.** The Fourteenth Amendment grants everyone due process rights when being accused of a criminal offense. Choice A is incorrect because freedom of speech is found in the First Amendment. Choice B is incorrect because the right to bear arms is found in the Second Amendment. Choice D is incorrect because the right to counsel is in the Sixth Amendment.

53. **The correct answer is D.** The plain view doctrine states that any evidence or contraband that is open in view of the officer may be examined and seized. Choices A, B, and C are all incorrect because they do not fit into the plain view doctrine category.

54. **The correct answer is A.** The exclusionary rule falls under the Fourth Amendment, in which any evidence obtained through an illegal search and seizure is not admissible at trial. Choices B, C, and D are all incorrect because they are exceptions to the Fourth Amendment known as warrantless searches.

55. **The correct answer is C.** The Carroll doctrine allows the officer to search a vehicle without a warrant. Choice A is incorrect because consent means that an individual gives the officer permission to conduct a search. Choice B is incorrect because exigent circumstances allow an officer to enter a location under an emergency. Choice D is incorrect because the officers are allowed to go into locations without a warrant during pursuit of a suspect.

56. **The correct answer is A.** *Mapp v. Ohio* is one of the most famous cases under the Fourth Amendment, in which the police were searching for evidence, entered the house illegally without a warrant, and discovered pornographic material. The evidence was deemed inadmissible. Choices B, C, and D are incorrect because they are all unrelated to the Fourth Amendment.

57. **The correct answer is C.** In *Terry v. Ohio*, an officer observed suspicious individuals, stopped them, conducted a pat down, and recovered some firearms. These are known as Terry stops. The court ruled that the police had the right to stop and frisk the suspects. Choices A, B, and D are all incorrect, as they do not apply to *Terry v. Ohio*.

58. **The correct answer is D.** *Tennessee v. Garner* is the case law that establishes use of force guidelines for police departments and actually falls under the purview of the Fourth Amendment. Choices A, B, and C are all incorrect because they do not apply to the use of force.

59. **The correct answer is B.** Congress writes the laws that define federal crimes. Once it passes both houses in Congress, it goes to the president to sign into law or veto. Choices A, C, and D are all incorrect because they do not write federal laws.

60. **The correct answer is A.** State laws are written by the state legislature and signed into law by the governor. Choice B is incorrect because city council and the mayor are responsible for city and local ordinances. Choice C is incorrect because Congress and the president are responsible for federal laws. Choice D is incorrect because judges cannot sign a bill into law.

The Civil War and Reconstruction

OVERVIEW

Understanding key people and places, as well as analyzing events and actions, are important to being successful on the DSST Civil War and Reconstruction exam. In this chapter, we'll cover all key exam concepts, including pre-secession and causes of the war, secession, Fort Sumter, major battles, the political climate, the assassination of Abraham Lincoln, the end of the Confederacy, and Reconstruction.

Chapter 12

answer sheet

DIAGNOSTIC TEST ANSWER SHEET

1. Ⓐ Ⓑ Ⓒ Ⓓ 5. Ⓐ Ⓑ Ⓒ Ⓓ 9. Ⓐ Ⓑ Ⓒ Ⓓ 13. Ⓐ Ⓑ Ⓒ Ⓓ 17. Ⓐ Ⓑ Ⓒ Ⓓ

2. Ⓐ Ⓑ Ⓒ Ⓓ 6. Ⓐ Ⓑ Ⓒ Ⓓ 10. Ⓐ Ⓑ Ⓒ Ⓓ 14. Ⓐ Ⓑ Ⓒ Ⓓ 18. Ⓐ Ⓑ Ⓒ Ⓓ

3. Ⓐ Ⓑ Ⓒ Ⓓ 7. Ⓐ Ⓑ Ⓒ Ⓓ 11. Ⓐ Ⓑ Ⓒ Ⓓ 15. Ⓐ Ⓑ Ⓒ Ⓓ 19. Ⓐ Ⓑ Ⓒ Ⓓ

4. Ⓐ Ⓑ Ⓒ Ⓓ 8. Ⓐ Ⓑ Ⓒ Ⓓ 12. Ⓐ Ⓑ Ⓒ Ⓓ 16. Ⓐ Ⓑ Ⓒ Ⓓ 20. Ⓐ Ⓑ Ⓒ Ⓓ

POST-TEST ANSWER SHEET

1. Ⓐ Ⓑ Ⓒ Ⓓ 13. Ⓐ Ⓑ Ⓒ Ⓓ 25. Ⓐ Ⓑ Ⓒ Ⓓ 37. Ⓐ Ⓑ Ⓒ Ⓓ 49. Ⓐ Ⓑ Ⓒ Ⓓ

2. Ⓐ Ⓑ Ⓒ Ⓓ 14. Ⓐ Ⓑ Ⓒ Ⓓ 26. Ⓐ Ⓑ Ⓒ Ⓓ 38. Ⓐ Ⓑ Ⓒ Ⓓ 50. Ⓐ Ⓑ Ⓒ Ⓓ

3. Ⓐ Ⓑ Ⓒ Ⓓ 15. Ⓐ Ⓑ Ⓒ Ⓓ 27. Ⓐ Ⓑ Ⓒ Ⓓ 39. Ⓐ Ⓑ Ⓒ Ⓓ 51. Ⓐ Ⓑ Ⓒ Ⓓ

4. Ⓐ Ⓑ Ⓒ Ⓓ 16. Ⓐ Ⓑ Ⓒ Ⓓ 28. Ⓐ Ⓑ Ⓒ Ⓓ 40. Ⓐ Ⓑ Ⓒ Ⓓ 52. Ⓐ Ⓑ Ⓒ Ⓓ

5. Ⓐ Ⓑ Ⓒ Ⓓ 17. Ⓐ Ⓑ Ⓒ Ⓓ 29. Ⓐ Ⓑ Ⓒ Ⓓ 41. Ⓐ Ⓑ Ⓒ Ⓓ 53. Ⓐ Ⓑ Ⓒ Ⓓ

6. Ⓐ Ⓑ Ⓒ Ⓓ 18. Ⓐ Ⓑ Ⓒ Ⓓ 30. Ⓐ Ⓑ Ⓒ Ⓓ 42. Ⓐ Ⓑ Ⓒ Ⓓ 54. Ⓐ Ⓑ Ⓒ Ⓓ

7. Ⓐ Ⓑ Ⓒ Ⓓ 19. Ⓐ Ⓑ Ⓒ Ⓓ 31. Ⓐ Ⓑ Ⓒ Ⓓ 43. Ⓐ Ⓑ Ⓒ Ⓓ 55. Ⓐ Ⓑ Ⓒ Ⓓ

8. Ⓐ Ⓑ Ⓒ Ⓓ 20. Ⓐ Ⓑ Ⓒ Ⓓ 32. Ⓐ Ⓑ Ⓒ Ⓓ 44. Ⓐ Ⓑ Ⓒ Ⓓ 56. Ⓐ Ⓑ Ⓒ Ⓓ

9. Ⓐ Ⓑ Ⓒ Ⓓ 21. Ⓐ Ⓑ Ⓒ Ⓓ 33. Ⓐ Ⓑ Ⓒ Ⓓ 45. Ⓐ Ⓑ Ⓒ Ⓓ 57. Ⓐ Ⓑ Ⓒ Ⓓ

10. Ⓐ Ⓑ Ⓒ Ⓓ 22. Ⓐ Ⓑ Ⓒ Ⓓ 34. Ⓐ Ⓑ Ⓒ Ⓓ 46. Ⓐ Ⓑ Ⓒ Ⓓ 58. Ⓐ Ⓑ Ⓒ Ⓓ

11. Ⓐ Ⓑ Ⓒ Ⓓ 23. Ⓐ Ⓑ Ⓒ Ⓓ 35. Ⓐ Ⓑ Ⓒ Ⓓ 47. Ⓐ Ⓑ Ⓒ Ⓓ 59. Ⓐ Ⓑ Ⓒ Ⓓ

12. Ⓐ Ⓑ Ⓒ Ⓓ 24. Ⓐ Ⓑ Ⓒ Ⓓ 36. Ⓐ Ⓑ Ⓒ Ⓓ 48. Ⓐ Ⓑ Ⓒ Ⓓ 60. Ⓐ Ⓑ Ⓒ Ⓓ

THE CIVIL WAR AND RECONSTRUCTION DIAGNOSTIC TEST

> **Directions:** Carefully read each of the following 20 questions. Choose the best answer to each question and fill in the corresponding circle on the answer sheet. The Answer Key and Explanations can be found following this Diagnostic Test.

1. Popular sovereignty was established by which of the following?
   A. Missouri Compromise
   B. Kansas-Nebraska Act
   C. Dred Scott decision
   D. Republican Party

2. *The Liberator* was most notable for what reason?
   A. It was the most famous train on the Underground Railroad.
   B. It was the nickname for Abraham Lincoln, after he issued the Emancipation Proclamation.
   C. It was the first American ironclad.
   D. It was an anti-slavery publication founded by William Lloyd Garrison.

3. How did the plantation system hurt the voting strength of the South?
   A. Because the plantations were so spread out but took up so much land there was room for fewer people in the South.
   B. Slaves were still counted at three-fifths for voting, so smaller plantations did not have as many votes as large plantations.
   C. Plantation owners rarely voted because their political power in local government was done primarily through illegal means.
   D. Each plantation only counted as one vote regardless of the number of men on it.

4. Why was Lincoln's election a catalyst for southern secession?
   A. Lincoln had campaigned on a hard platform of banning slavery.
   B. Lincoln believed in breaking up large southern plantations.
   C. Lincoln had won the election without a single southern vote.
   D. Lincoln promised to go to war with the South if elected.

5. What major advantage did the Confederacy have at the start of the Civil War?
   A. The Confederacy had a larger population.
   B. The Confederacy had European aid.
   C. The Confederacy was fighting a defensive war.
   D. The Confederacy held a majority of the country's railroads.

6. Which battle allowed President Lincoln to issue the Emancipation Proclamation?
   A. Second Battle of Bull Run
   B. Antietam
   C. Gettysburg
   D. Appomattox

7. The Emancipation Proclamation proclaimed slaves to be
   A. free in all Union states.
   B. free in all border states.
   C. free in all Confederate states.
   D. free in all states.

8. Which general took control of the Union in their campaign for the West in 1862?
   A. George B. McClellan
   B. Ambrose Burnside
   C. Ulysses S. Grant
   D. William T. Sherman

9. How did the battle of the *Monitor* versus *Merrimac* mark a turning point?
   A. It was the end of wooden ships with naval warfare being replaced by ironclads.
   B. The Confederate victory brought European aid to their cause.
   C. The Union victory allowed President Lincoln to be reelected.
   D. The Union defeat led to a call to institute the draft.

10. New opportunities arose for women during the Civil War including the ability to take part in which field?
    A. Military officers
    B. Nurses
    C. Plantation owners
    D. Government office employees

11. How did African American soldiers face prejudice during the war?
    A. Former slaves were forced to take a loyalty oath to the Union before serving.
    B. Escaped slaves were not allowed to fight for the Union.
    C. African American generals were given the lowest number of troops to command.
    D. African Americans were segregated into all black units.

12. The Battle of Gettysburg's effect on the war was which of the following?
    A. The Confederate victory prolonged the war and forced the Union to institute the draft.
    B. The Confederate loss left Lee to retreat and the South never regained the offensive.
    C. The Union victory led to the Emancipation Proclamation.
    D. The Union loss forced Lincoln to publicly shame his generals and replace them.

13. How did Massachusetts' 54th Regiment change the course of the Civil War in 1863?
    A. Their victory in the western campaign pushed Confederate forces away from the Mississippi River.
    B. Their surprise invasion of southern Pennsylvania on Union forces led to the greatest causalities of the war.
    C. The regiment was the first all-black union in the war.
    D. The regiment was the first to employ a black general with white soldiers.

14. Who ran against Abraham Lincoln in the election of 1864?
    A. Former General George McClellan
    B. Former slave Frederick Douglass
    C. Confederate President Jefferson Davis
    D. War Democrat Andrew Johnson

15. Sherman's victory in Atlanta was significant for what reason?
    A. Confederate hopes for European aid ended.
    B. Confederate morale and volunteers increased dramatically.
    C. It secured the Mississippi River and New Orleans port for the Union.
    D. It secured Lincoln's reelection in 1864.

16. General Grant's western campaigns in 1864 were successful due to his strategy of
    A. attrition.
    B. using black soldiers.
    C. guerilla warfare.
    D. blockades.

17. What Union victory at the end of the Civil War was important because it destroyed the symbolic center of the Confederacy?
    A. Vicksburg
    B. Richmond
    C. Gettysburg
    D. Appomattox

18. How would Lincoln's Reconstruction plan be described as compared to Congress' plan?
    A. Lincoln's was harsher to the Confederacy than that of Congress.
    B. Lincoln's was similar to that of Congress.
    C. Lincoln's was more lenient than that of Congress.
    D. Lincoln did not have a plan as he was assassinated.

19. Congressional Reconstruction was dominated by which political party?
    A. Republicans
    B. Democrats
    C. Whigs
    D. Southern plantation owners

20. Reconstruction in the South was characterized by which of the following?
    A. Failure to transition to a new, industrialized, and socially equitable society.
    B. Continued economic success and a new, diversified labor force.
    C. Favorable decisions made between former Confederate and Union leaders to increase the infrastructure of the South.
    D. Increased participation and economic success for former slaves.

ANSWER KEY AND EXPLANATIONS

1. B	5. C	9. A	13. C	17. B
2. D	6. B	10. B	14. A	18. C
3. A	7. C	11. D	15. D	19. A
4. C	8. C	12. B	16. A	20. A

1. **The correct answer is B.** The Kansas-Nebraska act divided the territories into two parts and allowed each to decide whether to allow slavery or not. This idea of allowing people to vote on expanding slavery or not is known as popular sovereignty. Choice A is incorrect because the Missouri Compromise created a specific line in which slavery could not expand. Choice C is incorrect because this case, while allowing slavery to spread, did not allow the people to vote on the decision. Choice D is incorrect because the Republican Party opposed the idea of popular sovereignty when proposed by Democrat Stephen A. Douglas.

2. **The correct answer is D.** *The Liberator* was an anti-slavery newspaper published by known abolitionist William Lloyd Garrison. The paper was in existence for almost 30 years and continually pushed for an immediate and absolute end to slavery. Choices A, B, and C are incorrect because *The Liberator* was a newspaper.

3. **The correct answer is A.** The size of plantations made it difficult for many to be in a given area, which lowered the population capabilities and number of voters in the south. There were more people living in the North because more could fit. Choice B is incorrect because counting slaves actually gave southerners more strength than without. However, the statement that large plantations were at an advantage is not relevant to the prompt. Choice C is incorrect because there is no evidence for

this statement to be true; while many were involved in politics a good number did so legally and also voted often. Choice D is incorrect because it is false; votes were based on people not plantations.

4. **The correct answer is C.** Abraham Lincoln was not elected by a popular vote but carried all but one free state in the North, winning the electoral vote. No electoral vote from the South went to Lincoln yet he was able to become the 16th President. Choices A, B, and D are incorrect because they are all false statements. Lincoln ran on platforms that were the opposite of all the incorrect choices.

5. **The correct answer is C.** The Civil War was fought primarily on southern soil, with the Union needing to take the offensive and have a decisive win to end the battle. The Confederacy was able to fight a defensive war, on its own soil, that needed only to end in a draw for secession to hold. Choices A, B, and D are all incorrect as they are all false statements. The Confederacy had fewer people, no foreign aid (only a hope for one), and fewer railroads.

6. **The correct answer is B.** The draw encouraged Lincoln while keeping European aid from reaching the Confederate Army. Lincoln used the battle as a way to shift the focus of the war onto slavery. Choice A is incorrect because the Union took a loss at both battles of Bull Run. Choice C is incorrect because Gettysburg came after

the proclamation was announced. Choice D is incorrect because it was not a battle.

7. **The correct answer is C.** The Proclamation declared all slaves in states of "rebellion" to be "then, thenceforward, and forever free." However, as Lincoln was not president of the Confederate states, the Proclamation freed little to no slaves. Choices A, B, and D are incorrect because the Proclamation did not declare slaves to be free in any of these places.

8. **The correct answer is C.** President Lincoln changed generals many times but finally found one that would continually defeat the Confederates in Ulysses Grant. Grant was in charge of gaining New Orleans and the Mississippi River in 1862 before being selected to control all the Union Army by 1864. Choices A, B, and D are incorrect because they were not generals in charge of the Western campaign. McClellan and Burnside were, at one point, each head of the Union Army (with Burnside replacing McClellan in 1862) and Sherman was placed under Grant's command.

9. **The correct answer is A.** This was the last time wooden ships were used in maritime battle. Ironclads would become the primary ships for naval battle moving forward as they were less vulnerable than wooden ships. Choice B is incorrect because European aid never came to the Confederacy. Choice C is incorrect because Lincoln was not reelected until 1864 and the battle was in 1862. Choice D is incorrect because a draft was not instituted after the battle.

10. **The correct answer is B.** Men had only been doctors and nurses prior to the Civil War. However, women stepped in to fill their roles, as they did in other sectors, when so many men were off fighting. Choice A is incorrect because women could not serve as military officers. Choice C is

incorrect; although many women did take over farms and plantations because of the battles, becoming a planation owner was not a new opportunity (just perhaps a more likely one than it had been before). Choice D is incorrect because women could not run for political office.

11. **The correct answer is D.** The 54th Massachusetts was an example of an all-black regiment that was created during the Civil War. African Americans could fight, but not with whites. This is a practice that would continue into the 1950s in American wars. Choice A is incorrect as there was no oath required. Choice B is incorrect because escaped slaves could and did fight for the Union. Choice C is incorrect because there were no African American generals.

12. **The correct answer is B.** The victory included more than 50,000 casualties over three days. After the unsuccessful charge by George Pickett left a crucial part of the Confederate Army destroyed, Lee was forced to retreat to Virginia. Choice A is incorrect because the Union was victorious. Choice C is incorrect because the Proclamation had been issued months prior after the Battle of Antietam. Choice D is incorrect because the Union was victorious.

13. **The correct answer is C.** The use of black troops, while segregated, marked a turning point in the war and American history. The 54th took a group of all black soldiers into battle under a white general and gained the nickname "Army of Freedom." Choice A is incorrect because the regiment did not fight in the battle for the Mississippi River in the west. Choice B is incorrect because the regiment did not fight for the Confederates. Choice D is incorrect because the regiment was all black with a white general (there were no black generals during the Civil War).

14. **The correct answer is A.** McClellan had been the head of the Union Army on more than one occasion and ran against Lincoln, on a platform of making peace with the Confederates. Choices B, C, and D are incorrect because they were not opponents of Lincoln in the election.

15. **The correct answer is D.** Sherman's victory in Atlanta and "March to the Sea" employed a total war tactic that destroyed the Confederate's remaining infrastructure and broke the spirit of its soldiers. Choice A is incorrect because European aid had long been avoided due to Union victories. Choice B is incorrect because Confederate morale was destroyed by the Union victory. Choice C is incorrect because both the Mississippi River and New Orleans had been secured years prior by General Grant.

16. **The correct answer is A.** Grant believed in wearing down his enemy and destroying their lines of supply until they surrendered. He continued to drag out battles for months and eventually reduced Lee's army. Choice B is incorrect because black soldiers alone were not enough to help win in the Western campaigns. Choice C is incorrect because Grant did not use this type of fighting. Choice D is incorrect because blockades were not possible in Western territories.

17. **The correct answer is B.** The victory at Richmond was symbolic because it served as the Confederate capital and heart of their country. The defeat marked the unofficial end to the war, as many saw no need to continue. Choices A, C, and D are incorrect because they were not symbolically relevant to the Confederate cause.

18. **The correct answer is C.** Lincoln proposed the ten percent plan, which allowed more Confederate states to re-enter the Union, and more quickly. Choice A is incorrect because Congress's plan was more harsh, requiring fifty percent to Lincoln's ten percent of Confederates having to pledge loyalty to the Union for reentry. Choice B is incorrect because the plans were different—Lincoln's plan was ten percent compared to Congress's fifty percent. Choice D is incorrect because Lincoln had begun to develop a plan as early as 1863.

19. **The correct answer is A.** Known as "Radical Republicans," the party of Lincoln had control of Congress and after Lincoln's death controlled the Reconstruction process. Choices B, C, and D are incorrect because they were not the controlling political parties.

20. **The correct answer is A.** Much of the South remained stuck in pre-Civil War times, with industrialization halted by a lack of (or damaged) infrastructure with Jim Crow laws and sharecropping that attempted to continue racism against African Americans. Choice B is incorrect because economic success from cotton production decreased as the labor forced remained similar to what it was before war with sharecropping. Choice C is incorrect because many decisions made were not favorable towards the South, with the planter aristocracy remaining in place and little attempt to industrialize happening. Choice D is incorrect because former slaves saw little economic success in the South in the years following the war.

answers diagnostic test

DIAGNOSTIC TEST ASSESSMENT GRID

Now that you've completed the diagnostic test and read through the answer explanations, you can use your results to target your studying. Find the question numbers from the diagnostic test that you answered incorrectly and highlight or circle them below. Then focus extra attention on the sections within the chapter dealing with those topics.

Civil War and Reconstruction		
Content Area	Topic	Question #
Causes of the war	• United States society in the mid-nineteenth century • Slavery • Anti-slavery and abolition movement • Westward expansion of free and slave territory • John Brown's raid on Harper's Ferry • Political situation in 1860	1, 2, 3
1861	• Secession • Formation of confederacy • Fort Sumter • Lincoln's call for volunteers • First Manassas (Bull Run) • Union Army versus Confederate Army • Lincoln versus Davis leadership	4, 5
1862	• Southern strategy • War in the East • War in the West • Major battles • Emancipation Proclamation	6, 7, 8, 9
1863	• Casualties • Role of women in the war • Black Americans and the war • Major battles	10, 11, 12, 13

Civil War and Reconstruction (continued)		
1864	• Political situation • War in the West • War in the East	14, 15, 16
1865	• Sherman's Carolina Campaign • Fall of Richmond • Lee's surrender • Assassination of Lincoln • End of the Confederacy • Cost of the war	17
Reconstruction	• Presidential reconstruction plans • Southern response • Congressional reconstruction plans • Military reconstruction • End of reconstruction	18, 19, 20

GET THE FACTS

To see the DSST® The Civil War and Reconstruction Fact Sheet, go to ***http://getcollegecredit.com/ exam_fact_sheets*** and click on the **Social Sciences** tab. Scroll down and click **The Civil War and Reconstruction** link. Here you will find suggestions for further study material and the ACE college credit recommendations for passing the test.

CAUSES OF THE WAR

UNITED STATES IN THE MID-NINETEENTH CENTURY

As the first half of the nineteenth century wore on, there were compromises made and politicians did their best to skate around major divisive issues, including the issue of slavery. By mid-century, the country had changed, and a greater focus was put on democracy, territorial expansion, and the future of the nation—these changes would lead to a divide that could not be quickly healed.

Industrialization

By the 1840s, the United States looked very different depending on where you lived. In the South, you could still find plantations and farmland reaching across the region but land was running out, and planting cotton was demanding on the soil. The North had begun transitioning into an industrial society, with factories replacing cottage industries and the transportation revolution evolving from canals to railroads.

The railroads connected the north to the west, and allowed for grains and foods to travel back and forth. This relationship helped grow the market economy of the United States, as well as created more interdependence between the regions.

Inside of northern factories, laborers were competing for jobs with new immigrants arriving from Europe. Tensions developed, as many of the lower-skilled positions were given to immigrants because they were willing to take less pay, leading to a nativist movement within the region (and the creation of such political parties as the Know-Nothings). Urbanization was taking over this part of the country, and the industrial growth led to a more diversified economy that would become a large strength for the Union during the Civil War.

The plantation system established in the South had little room for railroads or urban development; **King Cotton** had taken over both the South and the United States economy, and the region hungered for more land to grow cotton instead of a desire to industrialize. Because of the massive amount of land required for plantation life, the South had a smaller workforce but a larger role in the economy. By the start of the Civil War, the cotton industry would account for almost 57 percent of the United States' exports, so many in the region were eager for new farmable land. Most people living in the region were not plantation owners, however, and instead worked as small farmers or subsistence farmers. The South did benefit from the new technology created by industrialization, and sent much of its cotton to northern factories while also taking advantage of new advancements in farming tools.

During the **antebellum period**, many reforms were taking place that changed the course of American society. One of the greatest reforms was known as the **Second Great Awakening**, a series of religious revivals that attempted to counter the rationalism and Puritan teachings of the previous decades. Much like the politics of the time, religion had become diverse and open to new groups and ideas. The movement itself saw many forms and groups, including the Baptists, Methodists, and Mormons, with a focus on the democratization of American society. Perhaps the greatest impact of the Second Great Awakening, however, was its influence on abolition and the war on slavery. With a renewed focus on religion, many in the North began to speak out against the sins of slavery and adopted a moral argument for ending the practice.

The United States' population had more than doubled during the early half of the nineteenth century and it would double again leading into the 1850s. Birthrates were high during this period but immigration from European countries was also a key contributing factor. With the addition of new technology, manufacturing, transportation, and commercial agriculture the United States saw people living longer and enjoying more opportunities. Not only did wages increases, so too did the need for labor, leading to a higher standard of living and national economy.

TIP

King Cotton was the belief that economy and politically, cotton was king in southern society.

TIP

Antebellum period is a term used to describe the period before the Civil War.

The North continued to hold a population advantage due to compact living arrangements created by the new industrial centers. Factory life was more appealing to immigrants coming to America, as it did not require owning land, which helped to increase the number of people living in the northeast.

The South was fairly spread out, with almost 9 million of the nation's 23 million people living on small farms and larger plantations. Of those people, more than one-third were enslaved Africans who were forced into bondage as opposed to about 250,000 free African Americans found in the North (there were also about 250,000 free African Americans in the South).

Another key difference between the regions was their views on tariffs, as those in the North saw high tariffs as a way to protect American industries at the cost of southern profits. This issue would be raised time and again (most famously in the battle over the **Tariff of 1828**, otherwise known as the **Tariff of Abominations**), and had a large effect on creating the tension that would lead to the Civil War. Those in the south were at constant conflict with the raising of tariffs.

Slavery

Slavery had become synonymous with wealth in the south following the introduction of Eli Whitney's cotton gin in 1793. Although most people in the South did not actually own slaves, a degree of one's wealth and power was measured in land and slaves. Because there was a strict racial hierarchy in both the north and south, as well as an economic advantage to the practice, many people turned a blind eye to the practice for much of the early nineteenth century. However, as the North began to industrialize and manufacturing increased, many in the north no longer saw the economic necessity for slavery.

Also, with the aforementioned Second Great Awakening putting a greater emphasis on religion and democracy, **abolitionists** began to raise the question that had been previously ignored by the United States Constitution and politicians. Men like **John C. Calhoun** spoke out about slavery, referring to it as a "necessary evil." The North had been reaping the benefits of cotton production and the Union was economically strong because of it (a notion that southerners believed was validated by the **Panic of 1857**). There had historically been an unsaid agreement that slavery benefited both regions of the country for some time, and the South was prepared to defend its pro-slavery labor conditions.

Anti-Slavery and Abolition Movement

Slave owners started to shift their defense of slavery away from being just economically beneficial to using religion, race, and standard of living as support for their "peculiar institution." Slave owners used scripture from the Bible to justify both slavery and racism against African Americans. They also looked to pseudo-science to falsely "prove" that Africans were better suited for slavery and even argued that conditions were better for slaves than those working in northern factories.

By mid-century, abolitionists began to speak out more, and two camps developed: **gradual abolitionists** and **immediate abolitionists**. Gradual abolitionists believed that slavery should be ended over time and allowed to die its own death, whereas immediate abolitionists wanted an abrupt end to slavery.

Abolitionists saw slavery as a sin and many, such as **William Lloyd Garrison**, took to new mediums to speak out against it. Garrison, a white abolitionist, began publishing an anti-slavery newspaper

TIP

The United States Constitution did not mention the practice of slavery in America specifically; it did ban the use of the slave trade after 1808 and created the *Three-Fifths Compromise* for representation.

entitled *The Liberator*. The paper called for the immediate, and sometimes radical, abolition of slavery and would remain in publication for over 30 years.

Another voice in the movement came from a former slave, **Frederick Douglass**, who published his anti-slavery newspaper, *The North Star*. Perhaps the biggest attack on slavery would come from an unlikely place—a woman living in Connecticut.

Harriet Beecher Stowe wrote a fictional account of an African American slave that would eventually become the second-best-selling book of the century, just behind the Bible. The book, *Uncle Tom's Cabin*, created an even deeper divide between North and South and became a major factor in the rise of the abolitionist movement. The book appalled southerners, who saw it as highly inaccurate and using falsities to further the abolitionist cause.

Finally, an economic attack on the institution of slavery would be seen in **Hinton Rowan Helper's** book, *The Impending Crisis of the South*. This was a different approach towards fighting slavery, and used the economy and industrialization as reasons why slavery was hurting the South.

Slaves looking to escape bondage would find allies in members of the **Underground Railroad**, a network of safe houses and secret passages that helped them find their way to the North or even Canada. This was extremely dangerous, and many abolitionists as well as slaves endangered their lives by participating. However, the work of people like **Harriet Tubman**, among others, was vital to securing freedom for many slaves.

Overall, the abolitionist movement took many forms, as there was no "right" way to defeat slavery. Back to Africa movements, political parties, and violence were all attempts to end the southern practice, but initially had little to no success. The thirst for more land consumed slave owners, who looked for more ways to profit from cotton, and the United States government was happy to oblige as **Manifest Destiny** dominated the country's agenda for the foreseeable future.

Westward Expansion of Free and Slave Territory

In 1820, the country was faced with a dilemma when the Missouri territory applied for statehood. The United States was at a perfect balance of free and slave states; Missouri entering would offset that balance and shift political power to the South. **Henry Clay** engineered the **Missouri Compromise**, a compromise between the regions that allowed Missouri to enter as a slave state, Maine as a free state, and, most importantly, created a system for the future by making the 36°30' N line a dividing mark. Any state entering the Union *above* the line would be free (except for Missouri) and any *below* a slave state. This important compromise helped keep the country together for over thirty years and many politicians saw it as sacred. All that would eventually change, as cotton became even more vital to the southern economy.

The Mexican War

The ideas of Manifest Destiny and western fever had taken over much of America by mid-century, with **James K. Polk's** election in 1844 a prime example of its popularity. When the dark horse candidate was elected on a platform of expansion, thanks primarily to voters from the south and west, America pressed firmly forward on fulfilling its Manifest Destiny.

TIP

Peculiar institution was a term used to describe the southern system of slavery.

ALERT

The Missouri Compromise was held sacred by many (including Abraham Lincoln) as the only thing keeping the Union together.

After a brief spat with Great Britain over Oregon, Polk turned his attention to California. First, Polk attempted to buy the land from the Mexican government while also negotiating the Texas border, but was turned away. In response, he sent **General Zachary Taylor** and his army to the Rio Grande border. Tensions were high and fighting broke out, leaving 11 Americans dead. This event led Polk to declare war on Mexico, with a large majority in Congress approving the measure (although there were doubters, such as **Whig party** members, which included a young Abraham Lincoln, who declared that the decision to go to war was based on "spot resolutions").

It was a relatively short war, but its effects had great consequences in the United States, specifically regarding slavery. **David Wilmot**, a Pennsylvania Congressmen, proposed that all territories acquired as part of the **Treaty of Guadalupe Hidalgo** (1848) not permit slavery. The measure was defeated in the Senate, and what to do with the territory would be settled by the **Compromise of 1850**. Once again, Henry Clay came to the rescue, as the line created by the Missouri Compromise would cut directly through California, which wished to remain free. Clay's proposal included the following:

- admit California as a free state (adding to the North's political power)
- allow slavery to be decided by popular sovereignty in both Utah and New Mexico
- settle the Texas border dispute by paying the Mexican government $10 million
- ban the slave trade in the District of Columbia
- adopt and enforce a new, stricter Fugitive Slave Law (which was rarely enforced in the north, upsetting southerners)

The Kansas-Nebraska Act

In 1854, the Kansas and Nebraska territories were ready to apply for statehood and both saw the economic benefits of being open to slavery. **Senator Stephen A. Douglas** also looked to benefit from the territories when he proposed the **Kansas-Nebraska Act** to Congress. Douglas, who had presidential aspirations, needed southern approval to build a railroad through the central United States. To win over southern votes, he proposed that **popular sovereignty** be used to decide the slavery question in both territories. By effectively removing the line created by the Missouri Compromise, slavery could now spread into northern territories. When the bill passed, political outrage and citizen violence broke out in the territories—and even inside the walls of Congress.

People on both sides of the argument, pro-slavery and anti-slavery, flocked into the territories, hoping to swing the vote to their sides. Fighting broke out between them, leading to bloodshed and violence (termed **Bleeding Kansas**). The conflict grew so large that rifles, known as **Beecher's bibles** (after *Uncle Tom's Cabin* author Harriet Beecher Stowe), were even shipped with books to supply the anti-slavery forces in the fight.

This violence would last almost two years, and even make its way into Congress as **Preston Brooks** caned **Massachusetts Senator Charles Sumner** on the Senate floor in an act that defended the institution of slavery. In reaction to the situation created by the Kansas-Nebraska Act, a partnership of different, smaller political parties joined together to form the **Republican Party**. With the goal of stopping the spread of slavery across the country, Republicans would grow stronger as more people

TIP
Manifest Destiny was a term coined by John O'Sullivan, which stated that it was America's mission, or destiny, to expand from the Atlantic Ocean to the Pacific Ocean.

ALERT
The *Wilmot Proviso* reinforced the idea that slavery was a dividing and controversial issue. The failure of the act proved that the South was unwilling to relent on the practice.

began to oppose the peculiar institution. However, this strength was found almost exclusively in the North.

The Dred Scott Decision

The final blow to the Missouri Compromise would come in 1857 via a Supreme Court decision made by **Chief Justice Roger Taney**. The case involved a slave, **Dred Scott**, who had been moved to the free territory of Wisconsin before returning to Missouri two years later. Scott argued that this made him free and sued, resulting in a Supreme Court case. Chief Justice Taney ruled against Scott, citing the Fifth Amendment of the Constitution (Taney claimed slaves were property, not citizens). The decision effectively ruled the Missouri Compromise unconstitutional and made all parts of the country open to slavery. This only heightened tensions between regions, and southerners were excited to end the question forever as well as open new territories to the institution. The decision would be hotly discussed and disputed, including during the Lincoln-Douglas debates for the Illinois Senate seat in 1858 (won by **Stephen A. Douglas**).

John Brown's Raid on Harper's Ferry

John Brown had been no stranger to violence in his abolitionist mission, as he took part in the fighting of Bleeding Kansas. After the Dred Scott decision, Brown attempted to arm slaves in Virginia in his greatest example of radical abolitionism. Federal troops ended his attempt after only two days, and Brown was hung for treason. The country was firmly divided over this event. Southerners pointed to Brown's radical activities as proof the North would do anything, including use violence, to end slavery. Northern abolitionists saw John Brown as a martyr for their cause, even as many others in the region spoke out against his use of violence. The events of the 1850s only further cemented what many in the country had feared: war would be the only answer to the question of slavery.

1860

In 1860, the country saw four candidates running for the White House, with three drawing votes from each other's bases. Northern Democrats hoped to run **Stephen A. Douglas**, but he wasn't popular in the South, leading to **John C. Breckinridge** being nominated as well. The Constitutional Party's **John Bell** and the Republican candidate, **Abraham Lincoln**, challenged both Democratic Party nominees.

The results of the election mirrored the events of the country to that point; the North voted for Lincoln and he carried every free state. Breckinridge and Bell held the South, and Douglas received 12 electoral votes, meaning that due to the population advantage in the North, Abraham Lincoln was elected the 16th president without obtaining a single southern vote.

This confirmed what the South had long feared—no matter what they did they were still at a political disadvantage and their voices would go unheard. A last-ditch effort was made to calm the fears of southern slave owners by **Senator John Crittenden**, but to no avail (the **Crittenden Compromise** sought to restore the Missouri Compromise line). Following Lincoln's election, South Carolina voted to secede from the Union with seven states leaving before he had even taken office. Citing

ALERT

The Kansas-Nebraska Act is a key catalyst in the onset of the Civil War. It made the Missouri Compromise mute, it created the Republican Party, it caused massive violence, and it would be cause for such events as the Lincoln-Douglas debates.

TIP

Popular sovereignty permitted the citizens of a territory to vote whether to allow slavery or not.

the **Virginia and Kentucky Resolutions** as support for their decision to protect states' rights, the president-elect addressed preserving the Union during his first inaugural address:

> *"I am loath to close. We are not enemies, but friends. We must not be enemies. Though passion may have strained it must not break our bonds of affection. The mystic chords of memory, stretching from every battlefield and patriot grave to every living heart and hearthstone all over this broad land, will yet swell the chorus of the Union, when again touched, as surely they will be, by the better angels of our nature."*

1861

After the election of Abraham Lincoln, with no electoral votes coming from the South, the president faced a crossroads in dealing with the **secession** of South Carolina and other southern states. As the Confederate States of America created their own constitution (one similar to the United States' but with provisions on tariffs and slavery) under President Jefferson Davis, Union President Lincoln faced a tough decision in regards to a federal fort in Charleston, South Carolina. **Fort Sumter** was in desperate need of supplies but had been blocked by southern forces. Lincoln had to decide: would he send reinforcements and risk starting a conflict or would he let the troops suffer? The president formally announced he would send supplies and provisions to the fort, placing the burden of what to do next onto South Carolina. The response was thundering, literally, as South Carolina fired its guns on the fort. The Civil War had begun.

THE START OF WAR

The original enlistment for Union troops was only 90 days, as Lincoln was optimistic that his army would easily defeat their Confederate brothers. The Union Army had many advantages, including a much larger population and a strong navy that dominated the waters during the war. Economically, the Union had control of the banking centers, factories, and railroads, and their provisions and weapons were never in danger of being in short supply. Perhaps the greatest strength for the Union would be their president; Abraham Lincoln would display his leadership skills throughout the war. Although there were struggles with his leadership style, including his tireless control of every decision (as evidenced by his shuffling of generals), Lincoln showed great vision and strength. His ability to retain the border states through martial law (and later the **Emancipation Proclamation**) was not without criticism, but overall he was seen as a strong and legitimate president.

Jefferson Davis, on the other hand, seemed ill-equipped for the position of president. Perhaps his biggest challenge had nothing to do with him, but rather the position of the Confederate states. Secession had been based on the idea of states' rights, so any attempt to create a stronger central government in the South during the war was met with resistance. Davis had little to give in terms of military leadership and the Confederate states lacked supplies, money, and a navy; instead, they placed much of their hope on using cotton exports to bring foreign support to their side. What turned out to be the greatest advantages for the Confederate states, however, were their dedication to the cause and their generals. The South had a cause they were fighting for, and they had the best-trained generals leading the charge on their own land. Many of the generals leading the South, including

TIP

Thomas Jefferson and James Madison wrote the Virginia and Kentucky Resolutions in response to the Alien and Sedition Acts of 1798. They stated states had the right to declare federal law unconstitutional.

TIP

After the events at Fort Sumter, four more states joined the Confederacy including the state of Virginia. Richmond would become the capital of the Confederate States of America.

Robert E. Lee, had graduated from West Point and fought in the Mexican-American War. This experience, coupled with the ability to fight a defensive war on home soil, gave the South hope that they could hold out long enough for the Union to tire of the war.

Comparison of Union and Confederacy, 1860–1864			
	Year	**Union**	**Confederacy**
Population	1860	22,100,000	9,100,000
	1864	28,800,000	3,000,000
Free	1860	21,700,000	5,600,000
Slave	1860	400,000	3,500,000
	1864	negligible	1,900,000
Soldiers	1860–1864	2,100,000	1,064,000
Railroad miles	1860	21,800	8,000
	1864	29, 100	negligible
Manufacturers	1860	90%	10%
	1864	98%	negligible
Arms production	1860	97%	3%
	1864	98%	negligible
Cotton bales	1860	negligible	4,500,000
	1864	300,000	negligible
Exports	1860	30%	70%
	1864	98%	negligible

First Manassas (Bull Run)

Most believed the war would be a quick exercise in northern dominance, including many in the South. The first major battle of the war was fought in Virginia near **Bull Run Creek** at **Manassas Junction.** Here, it was the leadership of a Confederate general, **Thomas "Stonewall" Jackson,** that made the difference. This battle all but ended the chances for a swift Union victory and a loud boom from the Confederate drum was sounded. The South had proven their abilities not only to the Union, but also to itself. Confidence was high in the South following the battle, as the rebel yell of the Confederacy was born. Lincoln's call for 1 million new volunteers after the battle was a wake-up call to those in the North who had been overconfident the war would end quickly. It would also lead to a major reorganization of the army, which included dividing troops between the Eastern and Western theaters, removing several generals, and Lincoln taking even greater control of military operations.

1862

SOUTHERN STRATEGY

By the start of 1862, the Confederacy was in a better position than the Union as their morale was high, they had been victorious in various battles in Virginia, and they were succeeding in continuing a war that no one in the North really wanted to fight. The original southern strategy was simply to wait the North out until they tired of war and simply let the Confederacy leave the Union. The Confederate Army did not actually have to win the war, only protect their land—it was the North that was fighting to save the Union.

President Jefferson Davis himself believed the best strategy for the Confederacy was simply to "survive." However, as victories mounted, General Lee led his army into enemy territory hoping to gain an even greater advantage: support from Great Britain and more importantly, their navy. Most of the South's cotton exports had been purchased by Britain and the Confederacy thought they could leverage those exports into foreign aid. But a victory in enemy territory would most assuredly prove to Europe that the Confederacy was a legitimate threat to defeat the Union, weakening it in the process.

MAJOR BATTLES

Unfortunately for the Confederacy, the victory they so desperately needed did not come and the consequences would forever end their chances of gaining foreign support. The battle at **Antietam** would not only go down as the single bloodiest day of the war, with over 22,000 soldiers injured or killed, but the Union "victory" (which actually was a military draw) would keep foreign powers from supporting and supplying the Confederacy.

Great Britain had found a new source of importing cotton (from India and Egypt), and they were more concerned with President Lincoln's newly announced **Emancipation Proclamation**, which put the focus of the war squarely on slavery. The Union did, however, miss a great opportunity to pursue the retreating General Lee into the Shenandoah Valley, prompting the president to make a change in Union command.

Following the battle at Antietam, Lincoln would replace **George B. McClellan** as general of the Union in the east with **Ambrose Burnside**, primarily because he believed McClellan was too cautious. Burnside, however, would never be labeled as cautious and immediately led a disastrous attack on the Confederacy at **Fredericksburg**. The Union suffered heavy casualties, and the event highlighted the fact that the war had no end in sight. The Confederacy continued to push deep into Union territory, as the **Peninsular Campaign** under Union General McClellan proved unsuccessful. Confederate General "Stonewall" Jackson secured much of Tennessee, and by the end of 1862 the Confederacy was closer to the Union capital than their own capital of Richmond.

Perhaps the only bright spot for the Union in the Eastern theater would be at sea, as their superior navy was able to provide an effective blockade on southern ports. The Union successfully countered a Confederate **ironclad**, the *Merrimac*, with their own ironclad, the *Monitor*, in a battle that was the first of its kind. Prior to the *Merrimac*, ships had been constructed of wood for speed, but after this

TIP

An ironclad was a ship made of and protected by iron instead of wood.

Chapter 12: The Civil War and Reconstruction

battle naval engagement would never be the same, as ironclads easily tore through their wooden counterparts. The Union blockade would remain intact and the Confederacy would continue to struggle to obtain supplies from their ports.

The Union had better success in their western campaigns under General Ulysses S. Grant. Their goal was to gain control of the Mississippi River and the port at New Orleans as part of their **Anaconda Plan**. U.S. Navy ships under **David G. Farragut** were able to take the port, while Grant's men led a charge towards Tennessee at both **Chattanooga** and **Shiloh**. These battles were bloody, terrible, and ended in victories for the Union that would upset Confederate holdings. However, both battles proved to the armies that the war would continue to drag on—with growing casualties.

EMANCIPATION PROCLAMATION

In 1862, President Lincoln realized the war could no longer continue simply as one to "save the Union." Northerners began to tire of the war and volunteers were down, but more importantly morale in the field was waning. He was also receiving pressure from more radical members of his party to take a stance on slavery.

Lincoln was weary of losing the important border states, where slavery was still in practice, so he had resisted calls for emancipation. With the military draw at Antietam, Lincoln saw his chance to change the course of the war and give the Union a greater purpose for fighting. On January 1, 1863 President Lincoln officially issued the Emancipation Proclamation, which freed all enslaved people in the rebellious states.

While the declaration had no legal effect on the war (Confederate states ignored the proclamation as Lincoln was not their commander-in-chief), the morale of the Union was immediately improved and the border states were able to keep their slaves. Soldiers now had a moral purpose for fighting the war, and freed slaves were now permitted to fight for the Union. The proclamation also kept Great Britain's government (which had already banned slavery) from officially recognizing the Confederacy due to pressure from its citizens.

1863

The turning point in the war would come in 1863, when Confederate confidence and morale came crashing down. Heavy casualties, the influx of new African American soldiers to the North, and difficulty providing provisions for their soldiers would finally catch up with the Confederacy. 1863 was not only a turning point for the war, but also for the society that took part in it.

WAR AND SOCIETY

Following the Emancipation Proclamation given by President Lincoln in January of 1863, almost 200,000 African Americans came to serve in the Union Army. **Freedmen**, as they were known, had escaped the perils of slavery and the South to come and fight for the Union in an attempt to right the social wrongs of the peculiar institution. These added soldiers helped the Union gain an even greater advantage on the battlefield.

TIP

The Anaconda Plan was the Union strategy for victory in the Civil War that attempted to blockade the southern ports, to cut off supplies to the Confederacy.

TIP

The Emancipation Proclamation was issued in September of 1862 and ordered that all enslaved people in the rebellious states would be free. It is important to remember that Lincoln was *not* president of the Confederate, or rebellious, states; thus, his words did not free any slaves.

Master the™ DSST® Exams, Volume II

However, after joining the northern cause they still faced discrimination, as there was still racism present above the Mason-Dixon line. African American soldiers were segregated into all-black units, had only white commanders, and initially earned less pay for their service. They would find more support in western campaigns under General Grant (something that would not be forgotten during his election for president in 1868), but in general they saw less action than white units.

The most famous example were the 1,000 men of the Massachusetts 54th, who fought most famously in the **Battle of Fort Wagner** under **General Robert Gould Shaw**. They helped to rescue white troops and proved their bravery as the **Army of Freedom**. Overall, over 37,000 soldiers died in battle, including some who signed up and fought for the Confederacy.

The decision to turn the Civil War into a campaign against slavery was not popular among everyone in the North, as proven by the **draft riots** that broke out in New York City during July of 1863. Some whites, primarily Irish Americans, were upset that the poor were being sent to die in a war for African Americans. African Americans, along with wealthy whites, were attacked during the riots, which led to property damage and the deaths of over 100 people. The violence proved that racism continued to exist even in the North and that not everyone was pleased with the course the war had taken.

TIP

During the Civil War a drafted soldier could pay a "substitute" $300 to take his place in the army.

ROLE OF WOMEN IN THE WAR

Women, too, had a place in the war as men needed support both on the battlefield and back home. In the south, women took over the family farms and continued to take care of the fields; the North saw women working in factories. The greatest impact women would have on the Civil War, however, would be found directly on the battlefield. Inspired by women like **Florence Nightingale**, whose work in England encouraged the likes of **Dorothea Dix** and **Clara Barton**, the medical profession in America was forever changed.

The **Sanitary Commission** was created in 1861 to provide medical care for troops, while other women helped wherever they could. Women took on the roles of military nurses, tending to injured soldiers on and off the battlefield. While medicine itself was not always effective (and in fact sometimes more deadly than the wounds created by war), the introduction of women as nurses was a bright spot for the profession ,even though they had very little medical training. Barton, specifically, took her experiences from the battlefield and began the **American Red Cross** after the war. The war, along with the rights given to African Americans after it ended, would also be a catalyst for the **Women's Rights Movement**.

MAJOR BATTLES

1863 was also a turning point in the war because of the number of casualties that resulted from the numerous battles. No loss was more devastating to the Confederacy than that of "Stonewall" Jackson during the **Battle of Chancellorsville**, at the hands of his own troops no less. Union troops, under **General Hooker**, were forced to retreat (while losing over 14,000 soldiers), but not before taking the lives of over 10,000 Confederate soldiers. This battle would soon have another war-changing consequence, when General Lee decided to make a push towards Washington D.C.

Over 50,000 men died during the three-day clash at **Gettysburg** as Lee led his troops into Pennsylvania. The **Battle of Gettysburg** is perhaps the most famous Civil War battle, due to its bloodshed and President Lincoln's famous speech afterwards. The Confederacy had hoped a victory at Gettysburg would turn the war back in their favor while also forcing the Union to finally end the war. General Lee's army in northern Virginia, flanked by **James Longstreet** and **George Pickett**, made would what would be their greatest challenge to the Union Army in the Eastern theater. President Lincoln had decided that the Union would make its stand at Gettysburg and by the second day the **Army of the Potomac** would hold its ground. On the third day, Pickett led a fatal charge directly into Union lines, which devastated the Confederacy, both militarily and psychologically. Lee and his troops were pushed back as a result of the battle, and never regained the offensive or the confidence they had when the year began.

TIP

Attrition means the act of gradually reducing the strength or effectiveness of someone or something through sustained attack or pressure.

In the Western theater, General Grant of the Union Army was continuing his successful push to control the Mississippi at the **Battle of Vicksburg**. This would be the start of Grant's strategy of **attrition**, which would become the key to his victories moving forward. The Union general surrounded and starved the city for almost a year, resulting in full control of the Mississippi River for Lincoln's forces and the position of general-in-chief of all Union armies for Grant.

1864

As another year of war passed, so too did the passion for fighting for some in the North. With an election coming and no end to the war (or the casualties) in sight, many looked to an alternative to lead the Union. Those in the Confederacy looked to the election with great attention and hope, as selection of a former Union general for United States president might be their best chance at having their own country.

POLITICAL SITUATION

It seemed that everything was stacking up against Abraham Lincoln in 1864, as the economy, the number of casualties, and political support were all moving in the wrong direction. The effects of emancipation had worn off and it was replaced with war fatigue on numerous fronts, which were not confined simply to the battlefield.

Economically, the war was having a huge financial cost, which forced Congress to pass the **Morrill Tariff** as well as the **first income tax** in an effort to raise needed funds. These attempts to raise money would not be enough however, and the Union resorted to printing paper money, known as **greenbacks**, to help the war effort. Because this legal tender could not be redeemed in gold, the North would see inflation hit incredible peaks (it would also lead to a rise in "shoddy millionaires" who became rich selling poorly made products to the Union Army), even with an established Treasury Department in place.

Workers did not see much in terms of wage increases but the North did see a large increase in manufacturing. There were also great benefits to the war that would not be seen until well after its conclusion, including the **Homestead Act**, **Morrill Land Grant Act**, and **Pacific Railway Act**. However, the North continued to struggle with the continuing war as the number of deaths grew to numbers never seen before, or again.

Cities and families looked vastly different as so many men left to fight, and part of the toll would be expressed politically. Northern Democrats saw a split within their party based on ideas of war and peace as **Copperheads**, or **Peace Democrats**, started a greater push to end the war. While their primary motive focused on "King Lincoln" and his war on slavery, many were drawn to the idea of ending a war that caused so much death and destruction to society. Volunteerism declined and, as the draft riots proved, support for the war was waning. This division would be fully seen as the next presidential election began to take shape.

The Confederacy faced many disadvantages from the start, as their very existence clashed with vital elements of government survival. The Confederate government also struggled to find ways to pay for the war, as many of its citizens had little money (the wealth of most plantation owners was based on their farms, not actual currency), resulting in the need to print money. This inevitably led to inflation, and by 1863 life would only get worse when a food shortage hit the women working the southern farms.

The situation was worse for Confederate soldiers, as they had little rations, supplies, or even clothing, which left many to resort to picking up after the dead in battles. Perhaps the greatest harm to the Confederacy came from what was initially a perceived strength: their ports. The Union Navy was much stronger than that of the Confederacy, and their Anaconda Plan had been successful in controlling both the Mississippi and many important southern ports. The Union blockade had borne fruitful results, keeping Confederate supplies from reaching their men. The Confederacy had been left to support itself with no outside help or provisions, leaving their only realistic chance for a victory the northern election of 1864.

TIP

The *Homestead Act* helped to settle the Great Plains; the *Morrill Land Grant Act* helped create land for colleges; the *Pacific Railway Act* authorized the transcontinental railroad.

PRESIDENTIAL ELECTION IN THE NORTH

Lincoln ran for reelection in 1864 but made some noticeable changes that included a new party name and vice president. The Republican Party had established itself ten years earlier, disputing the Kansas-Nebraska Act and the expansion of slavery. But as the war continued on, and many in the North began to question why they continued to fight (and lose countless bodies), Lincoln needed to find a way to unite his party while growing his support base.

Republicans renamed their party the **Unionist party** and selected War Democrat **Andrew Johnson** as his vice president in an attempt to combat the growing strength of the Copper Democrats. Running against Lincoln was a familiar face, former General George B. McClellan, who had a strong platform of making peace and ending the war. Many in the North, including Lincoln himself, thought McClellan had a strong chance of winning and those in the Confederacy saw it as their last hope. However, it would be the events that led up to the election, specifically the campaign of **William T. Sherman**, that changed not only the election but the war itself.

THE RISE OF MODERN WARFARE

At the start of the Civil War, traditional military practices were still being used, as many of the generals had trained at West Point. Focusing on a limited war and battles, fighting with muskets, and attacking in close-order formations seemed the basic plan for war in 1861. However, as technology improved and the war dragged on, the war would transition into one of attrition in an attempt to kill as many men as possible.

This was made easier with the advent of deadlier weapons such as the rifle (which was more accurate at close range, could be used to identify targets at longer ranges, and could inflict more damage). The rifle would end up being a key advantage for the Union, as the Confederacy could not match the production or speed in which they produced it in the North. Minié balls were also introduced, a cylindrical bullet with a hollow base that expanded when fired, inflicting more damage to soldiers and increasing casualties. Additionally, cannons were used in new defensive ways, to take down bullets and also to shoot down lines of attackers. With all of the new destruction created by technology, strategies had to adapt, and generals began changing how they approached battles.

WAR IN THE WEST

President Lincoln's greatest hope for being reelected in 1864 was a string of decisive victories, which supported the Union's decision to continue with the war. Those victories would come courtesy of William T. Sherman, Grant's replacement as general in charge of the west. Sherman had a different vision for the war and his 100,000 men who followed him on campaign across the Confederacy. Destroying and burning everything in his path, Sherman gave a new meaning to the term "total war." His scorched-earth approach not only destroyed the homes, farms, cities, and infrastructure of the South but its effects would be felt for years to come (Sherman even told his men to bend the rail lines so they could not be used to transport supplies to the Confederates, effectively stunting their ability to advance their economy).

Not only did Sherman's men destroy everything in their path, they also destroyed what morale the Confederacy had left. When Sherman took **Atlanta** in September of 1864, the Confederates evacuated the city, and watched the flames rise as they left. This victory, coupled with another naval success by **Admiral Farragut** at **Mobile Bay**, was more than enough to secure reelection for Lincoln. The writing was on the wall; the Union was closing in on victory.

WAR IN THE EAST

By 1864, Grant had left his post in the west to take over the Union Army, marching directly towards Lee in the east. His first major test was at the **Battle of the Wilderness**—as was usual for Grant, casualties were high and the fight resulted in a draw. It was what Grant did next, however, that showed Lincoln had finally picked his head general correctly.

Grant followed the Confederate Army into Virginia before making, in his own words, his only regret, at **Cold Harbor**. As fires broke out, casualties rose even higher because his men could not escape the flames, and when it was all said and done over 13,000 Union soldiers were lost (compared to 2,500 Confederates). Although he was upset at the result, Grant did not waver and he continued

TIP

Another major change in the Civil War was medicine, as many soldiers actually died from disease or infections sustained by poor treatment on the battlefield. Amputation and gangrene were common, as was contamination.

TIP

The capture of Atlanta was followed by Sherman's March to the Sea, which included a conquest in Savannah before moving into South and North Carolina.

deeper into Virginia, racking up more deaths and a new nickname—the butcher. Lee and the Army of northern Virginia had been effectively reduced by the constant total war efforts of Grant, and was pushed back to their capital at Richmond. The war was nearing its end.

1865

The final year of the war saw a swift and dramatic turn following the successes of Union Generals Grant and Sherman. The Confederacy had seen far-reaching losses on the battlefield, in production, and, most importantly, to its morale. Many within the South saw it as only a matter of time before the Union was restored under the newly reelected Abraham Lincoln. As the Thirteenth Amendment was passed by the Senate at the start of the year, the Confederacy also knew that slavery would be no more, leaving the Confederacy to pick up the pieces scattered by Sherman's march to the sea.

THE FALL OF THE CONFEDERACY

Sherman had successfully liberated prisoners at **Andersonville**, the infamous southern prison camp, in late 1864, and then captured the important **Port of Savannah** while escaped slaves joined his march. He resumed fighting in the new year by marching north through the Carolinas, continuing his campaign of total war. Burning everything in his path, Sherman did not let his men forget which state was the first to call for secession from the Union, and South Carolina was nothing but ashes by the time his army reached the North Carolina border. Sherman was sure to leave nothing untouched, including businesses, homes, and even the capital of Columbia. The destruction would remain in the minds of many following the war, leading to resentment and bitterness.

Fall of Richmond

While Sherman was heading up the east coast, Ulysses S. Grant had forced the Army of Northern Virginia into retreat. Losing control of **Petersburg** and its accompanying railroad, Lee and the Confederacy had essentially given their capital of Richmond to the Union. All of the Confederate leaders, including government officials and President Jefferson Davis, left the city and took their records and valuables. As the Union arrived, they were greeted not by soldiers but by angry southern white men who had gathered to burn the city in anger.

Before long, Lee would be forced to surrender in Virginia at **Appomattox Court House** within the Wilmer McLean home. His men had no supplies and were dangerously close to starvation, and as a sign of peace General Grant allowed them to return home (even allowing them to keep their horses and giving them rations). Although President Davis attempted to keep the war alive, it was painfully obvious to everyone else that this was the end of the Confederacy.

COSTS OF THE WAR

The Civil War would go down as the deadliest war in American history, with over 800,000 casualties before the Union was restored. The South was a shell of its former self—their entire economic institution of slavery had been dismantled, its infrastructure was destroyed and burned to the ground, and

TIP

The Army of northern Virginia was the primary fighting unit of the Confederate Army in the east, under command of General Robert E. Lee.

its government was now at the mercy of Northern Republicans. The North had more people, more industry and technology (including rail access), and, most importantly, more power.

The costs of the war were great on both sides, but the cost of losing was even greater for the Confederacy. It would take over 20 years for the South's economy and infrastructure to recover from the war, and it took even longer for its population to recover. Their political structure would also face changes in light of the newly-found freedom and citizenship of African Americans (however, there would be very few southern Democrats elected to the oval office over the next century).

Casualties and Losses in the Civil War	
North (Union)	**South (Confederacy)**
110,000+ killed in action/died of wounds	94,000+ killed in action/died of wounds
230,000+ accident/disease deaths	26,000–31,000 died in Union prisons
25,000–30,000 died in Confederate prisons	290,000+ total dead
365,000+ total dead	137,000+ wounded
282,000+ wounded	436,658 captured
181,193 captured	
Total: 828,000+ casualties	**Total: 864,000+ casualties**

50,000 free civilians dead

80,000+ slaves dead

Total: 785,000–1,000,000+ dead

While the country mourned its lost sons and brothers, President Lincoln began to piece together his plans for restoring the Union, known as **Reconstruction**. Lincoln had always believed the South could never *legally* leave the Union; thus, they never *actually* left in his mind. He was piecing together a way to heal the nation from the Confederate "rebellion" when **John Wilkes Booth**, a Confederate sympathizer and former actor, shot and killed the president at **Ford's Theater** on April 14, 1865. The assassination of Abraham Lincoln would change the course of Reconstruction, as a Democratic vice president from Tennessee was left to clash with Radical Republicans.

RECONSTRUCTION

The period following the Civil War saw a divided nation attempting to heal from the wounds of a devastating war, as well as the death of their president. The Union was whole in theory but far from it in practice, as both sides of the conflict faced rebuilding after a devastating war.

For the South, it would be more difficult; much of the fighting had taken place on their soil and, especially after Sherman's March, civilization would need to catch up to the industrial world of the North. Not only did the South need to recover physically, but politically as well, as Congress was dominated by Radical Republicans who wished to punish the South. African Americans had also been given the right to vote and few would forget the Democrats' role in starting the conflict as Republicans were "waving the bloody shirt" before each election. As African Americans faced a new day following the **Reconstruction Amendments**, the South would eventually return to many of its prewar practices, if only under another name.

PRESIDENTIAL RECONSTRUCTION PLANS

As early as 1863, before Lincoln was assassinated, he had begun to formulate a plan that would allow the South back into the Union. As stated previously, Lincoln did not believe the South had actually left the Union (he believed in **contract theory** over **compact theory**), and instead saw them in a state of "rebellion." The president knew it was important to return the Union to whole as quickly as possible and did not believe the people within a rebellious state should be punished for what their government officials had done (but he did believe strongly that those officials should not regain power).

Lincoln's plan for Reconstruction was called the **Proclamation of Amnesty and Reconstruction**, or the **ten percent plan**, because when ten percent of a rebellious states' voter population took a loyalty oath their state government could be returned. Under this plan, most Confederates would be given a pardon by taking this oath and accepting the **Thirteenth Amendment** (acceptance would also have to be part of the state constitution).

Republicans in Congress contested this plan, and the **Wade-Davis Bill** was introduced the next year in an attempt to challenge the leniency of the president's proposal. The **Wade-Davis Bill** required 50 percent of the state population to take a loyal pledge and refused to allow any Confederate to vote on the bill, for fear power would return to previous leaders. Lincoln refused to sign the bill however, and when Congress was away the president used a **pocket veto** to stop the bill.

Everything would change after Lincoln's death, however, as former War Democrat Andrew Johnson attempted to implement his plans for Reconstruction. The Tennessean faced challenges from his cabinet and the Republican Party in Congress for his plan's leniency. Although similar to Lincoln's ten percent plan, President Johnson made use of a pardon that would eventually allow many of the planter aristocrats who ruled the South before the war back into power. The president's plan took away the right to vote and hold office from all former leaders and government officials of the Confederacy, as well as those with over $20,000 in taxable property. Because of Johnson's use of the pardon, by the end of his first year the South's political lineup looked eerily similar to pre-secession.

CONGRESSIONAL RECONSTRUCTION PLANS

During the war, the North saw a large shift towards Republican power as the Democrats were blamed for slavery and the Civil War ("waving the bloody shirt"). With a larger population and an ability to work with the president to determine how to readmit the Confederate states, the Republican Party did everything it could to protect its political power.

A group within the Republican Party, including **Senator Charles Sumner** of Massachusetts and **Senator Thaddeus Stevens** of Pennsylvania, pushed to give African Americans more civil rights following the war. The goal was not only to help African Americans, especially in the South, but to

Waving the bloody shirt was a political slogan used during Reconstruction, blaming Democrats for the Civil War and its bloodshed.

Compact theory was the belief that the states had formed a compact in creating the United States, and therefore could nullify their agreement. *Contract theory* was the belief that the people, not the states, formed the Union.

A *pocket veto* is an indirect veto of a legislative bill by the president or a governor by retaining the bill unsigned until it is too late for it to be dealt with during a legislative session.

strengthen the Republican base in the region as well. It was clear that few within the South supported the Republican platform, but the passage of the **Fifteenth Amendment** would increase the voting population to include African Americans, who would most assuredly vote Republican.

The *Radical Republicans*, as they were labeled, saw their opportunity to push a stronger civil rights agenda, while punishing the South, following Lincoln's assassination. Congressional leaders butted heads with Lincoln's successor, President Johnson, but had the ability to go around him on many issues.

The greatest achievement would be the passage of the Reconstruction Amendments, the **Thirteenth, Fourteenth, and Fifteenth Amendments**. These were the first steps in granting African Americans freedom, rights, and suffrage (while also being catalysts for a stronger Women's Rights Movement). These amendments were part of a Congressional plan that included a rejection of President Johnson's plan for Reconstruction.

- The Thirteenth Amendment ended slavery in the United States.
- The Fourteenth Amendment granted citizenship to African Americans by declaring that all persons born or naturalized in the United States were citizens.
- It also forced states to respect the rights of citizens and provide them with "equal protection" and "due process of the law."
- Finally, it disqualified former Confederate leaders from holding state or federal offices while renouncing the debt of their defeated governments.
- The Fifteenth Amendment granted suffrage to African American males by prohibiting any state from denying a citizen's right to vote "on account of race, color, or previous condition of servitude."

Congress followed up their rejection of the president's plan with a tremendous victory in the 1866 elections. Johnson toured the country in an attempt to attack Republican candidates, in the hope that they would lose their seats in Congress. However, the "swing around the circle" tour backfired, and not only did more Republicans win, creating majorities in both the House and Senate, but the president was large relegated to a bystander role in governing. The Radical Republicans were able to override his numerous vetoes to create three **Reconstruction Acts** in 1867.

- The former Confederate South was divided into five military districts, each placed under control of the Union Army.
- Readmission to the Union would now require not only ratification of the Thirteenth Amendment, but also the Fourteenth Amendment.
- State constitutions had to place guarantees for all citizens to be franchised, regardless of race.

The military-focused Reconstruction placed an army general as governor of the region and attempted to secure the newly-minted rights of African Americans—the South was placed under martial law, with troops remaining in the region, until each state reached Reconstruction requirements. During this time, Congress also passed the **Tenure of Office Act**, which prohibited the president from removing a federal official or military commander without Senate approval. This was an obvious attempt by Republicans to keep President Johnson, a Democrat, from removing key Radical Republicans from the cabinet he inherited from President Lincoln. A key member of that cabinet was **Secretary of War Edwin Stanton**, the man in charge of southern military governments.

ALERT

Radical Republicans benefited politically from allowing freedmen to vote while also removing democratic opponents.

TIP

The terms *franchise* and *suffrage* refer to giving a person the right to vote.

Johnson was well aware of the true motivations behind the act, and he tested its merits by promptly firing Stanton. The House would bring impeachment articles against Johnson in 1868, and the trial ended with Johnson remaining president by one vote (it was obvious to all that the act and trial were politically charged and not constitutionally based). Johnson would remain powerless for the remainder of his term, and Union war hero Ulysses S. Grant would be nominated and then elected president in 1868. The Republican president would owe much of his victory to large support from the African American voting population.

THE SOUTHERN RESPONSE

While all of the Reconstruction requirements were officially met, the harsh reality saw few actually being followed, as many in the South found ways to continue to push racism and segregation. **Black Codes, sharecropping**, and **Jim Crow laws** all crept into southern society while Congressional leaders turned their attention to the economy in the North.

Black Codes developed as states began to restrict the rights of freemen. These codes had devastating consequences on African Americans and seemed to place them into positions of economic disadvantage. Black codes included the following:

- African Americans were not allowed to testify against whites in court.
- African Americans could not rent or borrow money to buy land, leading many to having to resort to signing work contracts, known as **sharecropping**.

Sharecropping was a new form of slavery in many ways. Following the war, most African Americans in the South could not read or write and only knew one job: working with crops. Because they had no money, homes, or employment they looked to what they knew—a field that had recently lost almost all of its workforce. Sharecropping allowed a worker (black or white) to plant and farm on someone's land. In exchange for use of the land, the sharecropper would then repay the landowner in crops. Most of these workers also needed money for the crops, food, or homes so they would exchange even more of what they yielded to the landowners. As the system continued it began to replicate a key element of slavery: dependency.

Jim Crow laws were attempts by southern states to legally deny African Americans the right to vote (which was now guaranteed by the Fifteenth Amendment), while also segregating them (most often a violation of their Fourteenth Amendment rights). In southern states, laws were passed that became voting "qualifiers," such as the following:

- **Poll taxes:** Any citizen wishing to vote had to pay a poll tax, or fee. While this was effective in stopping many African American voters, it also denied many poor whites the ability to vote.
- **Literacy tests:** Any citizen wishing to vote had to pass a literacy test, which was designed to stop freemen from voting. Again, however, many poor and illiterate whites were also disenfranchised.
- **Grandfather clause:** This was the most effective way of disenfranchising African American voters, as only those whose grandfathers had been able to vote could also vote. While

almost no African Americans could navigate this clause and keep the right to vote, many poor whites could.

SEGREGATION

The Fourteenth Amendment required that all people born or naturalized in the United States were to be given due process as citizens. This meant that African Americans were to be given the same rights as whites, but in the south this ceased to be the case, especially after the landmark 1898 U.S. Supreme Court case *Plessy v. Ferguson*. The decision in this case ruled that citizens could be separated as long as they received equal services or amenities. This legalized the ability of the South to create two separate societies—one black and one white. There were separate schools, and later separate water fountains and dining areas. The biggest issue with this ruling (as was the case with much of Reconstruction) was the lack of enforcement. Once troops left the South there were few reasons for the ruling to be followed, leading African Americans to face greater challenges with less support and resources. The ruling would later be overturned in 1954, by Brown v. Board of Education of Topeka Kansas.

As governments in the South essentially restored the old ways of the past while "legally" oppressing African Americans, there was another challenge they faced in obtaining their rights. Racism and anger following the Confederate loss had caused new terrorist societies to form.

One such group was the KKK, or **Ku Klux Klan**, composed mostly of lower class white males who attempted to use violence and fear tactics to keep African Americans from voting, among other things. These groups wore all white with hoods and used torches to light their way. The KKK used many different tactics to oppress African Americans, including lynching in public and hanging. The KKK not only disliked African Americans, they also hated anything they felt challenged white power or kept white males from taking their "proper" place in society (including women's rights, prohibition, and any non-Catholic religious denomination). The focus on African Americans was much more apparent, however, following the increase of federal rights during Reconstruction, as KKK members believed African Americans were threatening their job opportunities and livelihoods.

In an attempt to combat all the discrimination and disadvantages African Americans were facing, Congress created the **Freedmen's Bureau** (Bureau of Refugees, Freedmen, and Abandoned Lands). This agency included the first unemployment and welfare offices and was often the only place where African Americans could find assistance following the war.

The Freedmen's Bureau gave food, shelter, medical aid, and education to freedmen. As many had no formal schooling, this would become important toward helping them become literate while also providing a chance to escape the South for job opportunities elsewhere. Some African Americans tried to move north for factory jobs or west in hopes of taking advantage of the Homestead lands offered by the federal government. Overall, the majority was forced to stay in the South and work as sharecroppers, however, as the Bureau received little support (especially from President Johnson, who used his veto power against it) and ceased to exist after 1870.

Other attempts were made to politically assist African Americans, such as the **Civil Rights Act** of 1875, but there was little support or enforcement and politicians would begin to move their attention

TIP

The term "freemen" was used to describe former slaves who were now free in the Union.

towards a different focus. There would be no new civil rights legislation introduced to Congress until the 1950s.

There were some notable political successes for African Americans, including two southern African Americans being elected to the Senate (**Blanche K. Bruce** and **Hiram Revels**) and a few being elected to the House of Representatives. However, the majority of Congressmen remained white and the combination of African Americans and Radical Republicans who moved from the North would cause much anger in the South. Nicknames were created for two such groups—scalawags and carpetbaggers.

A scalawag was the name given to southern Republicans, while northerners who came to the South, most likely looking to make a profit, were called carpetbaggers and deemed corrupt. These derogatory terms reinforced the divide in the South, which was not only based on race but also political gain.

THE END OF RECONSTRUCTION

When President Grant took office, his administration quickly made Reconstruction its focus (amidst a myriad of scandals). **Redeemers**, or southern conservatives, had gained control of the South's government and many in the North had grown tired of the Radical Republicans' mission in favor of a focus on the growing northern economy. Redeemers brought back many elements of the previous South, including a hatred for taxes, a stronger focus on states' rights, and, most devastating for Reconstruction, white supremacy.

Democrats retook control of southern states and by 1876 they created a battle for the office of president. **Samuel J. Tilden** of New York received a victory in the popular vote but missed winning the Electoral College by one single vote. The Republican Party nominated **Rutherford B. Hayes** of Ohio and, due to their majority in Congress, was awarded a series of disputed Electoral College votes that kept Tilden from winning. The resulting compromise gave the Republican Party the White House, but at the cost of ending Reconstruction as Hayes removed the remaining federal troops from the South (Hayes also agreed to build a southern transcontinental railroad).

As historians look back on Reconstruction they do so with a divided view. On one hand, the federal government not only reintegrated the South following the Civil War but also rebuilt its economy and infrastructure into a powerhouse that would be realized during the Gilded Age. Furthermore, African Americans were given rights in federal amendments that would not only define them as citizens and give them suffrage, but also served as inspirations for future generations, such as was seen in the Women's Rights Movement.

However, the record is murkier when discussing the ability of African Americans to obtain and use those rights as well as the deepening racial divide. Generations continued to see segregation, discrimination, and racial tension as emblematic of the failure of Reconstruction to address the real problems.

SUMMING IT UP

- **Industrialization** changed the North, replacing traditional cottage industries and creating new transportation methods such as canals and railroads, which would ultimately connect the north and the west. The growing markets and increasing urbanization led to the expansion and diversification of the economy, which would help support the Union during the Civil War.

- While the North was becoming more industrial, the South was growing its economy around plantations—particularly in the cotton industry. **King Cotton**, or the belief that cotton was the "king" of the southern economy, came to account for more than half of U.S. exports by the start of the Civil War.

- In the **antebellum period** (before the Civil War), the U.S. population had increased greatly through higher birth and immigration rates, as well as increased lifespans and better quality of life. The increased population also increased wages and the demand for labor.

- The North and the South began to differ in significant ways economically, with the North favoring high tariffs to protect American industries, and the South opposing the limits these tariffs placed on southern profits. This would become a contributing cause of the Civil War.

- Slavery also became a point of opposition for the North and South, as the North moved away from slavery and toward industrialization while the southern economy depended heavily on the agricultural labor provided by slaves.

- The **abolitionist**, or anti-slavery, movement arose from the Second Great Awakening and its emphasis on religion and democracy. Publications such as **Frederick Douglass's** anti-slavery newspaper, *The North Star*, and **Harriet Beecher Stowe's** book, *Uncle Tom's Cabin*, helped the movement gain momentum. At the same time, members of the **Underground Railroad** were working to help slaves escape their bondage and move to free regions in the North and Canada.

- In 1820, the **Missouri Compromise** allowed Missouri to enter the United States as a slave state and Maine as a free state, to help maintain the balance between free and slave states. It would also create a dividing line for future states: states above the line would be free states (except Missouri), and states below the line would be slave states.

- As part of the resolution to the **Mexican War**, the United States adopted the **Compromise of 1850**, which admitted California as a free state, allowed Utah and New Mexico to decide slavery by popular sovereignty (popular vote), settled the Texas border dispute by paying $10 million, banned the slave trade in the District of Columbia, and created a stronger **Fugitive Slave Law**. Later, the **Kansas-Nebraska Act** would allow Kansas and Nebraska to decide slavery via popular sovereignty, removing the dividing line set by earlier compromises. This would be a major contributing factor of the Civil War.

- In the election of 1860, Republican **Abraham Lincoln** defeated Democrats **Stephen A. Douglas** and **John C. Breckinridge**, and Constitutional Party member **John Bell**. Lincoln was elected without a single southern vote, further increasing tensions between the North and the South.

- The Civil War officially began with the **secession** of the southern states, led by South Carolina. The newly formed **Confederate States of America** created their own Constitution, set their capital as Richmond, Virginia, and elected **Jefferson Davis** as their president. The war got underway when Union President Lincoln attempted to send supplies to South Carolina's Fort Sumter, which was under a blockade by the southern military.

- **The Battle of First Manassas** (a.k.a. Bull Run) showed that the war would not be the quick northern victory that many expected, with Confederate generals like **Thomas "Stonewall" Jackson** showing military strength. Other significant battles in 1862 included **Antietam**, which was the single deadliest day of the war (22,000 soldiers injured or killed); **Fredericksburg**, during which the Union suffered heavy losses; and the battle between ironclad ships *Merrimac* and *Monitor*, which was the first battle of its kind and ensured that the Union's blockade of supplies to the South would remain intact.

- In January 1863, Lincoln issued the **Emancipation Proclamation** as a way to resolve pressure from the slavery debate and change the focus of the fighting. The proclamation freed all enslaved people in the southern states. While the proclamation was not legally recognized in the Confederate states and thus did not technically free any slaves at the time, it improved morale in the Union states, and allowed freed slaves to enlist in the Union Army. More than 200,000 of these freed slaves would eventually serve in the Union Army.

- The **Battle of Gettysburg** proved to be a turning point in the war, due to heavy losses that stopped the Confederate Army's momentum. More than 50,000 Union and Confederate soldiers died at Gettysburg, and after the battle General Robert E. Lee's army had lost their offensive edge.

- By 1864, support for the war was declining in the North as well, and the costs of the war had led to an economic crisis that required Congress to pass the **Morrill Tariff** and the **first U.S. income tax**.

- **General William T. Sherman's** successful capturing of Atlanta provided the support Lincoln needed to win reelection in 1864, and showed that the war was coming to an end for the Confederate Army. Additional losses in the east to **General Ulysses S. Grant's** Union Army essentially pushed General Lee's army in Northern Virginia back to their capital.

- The Confederate armies ultimately fell in 1865, forcing General Lee to surrender to Grant's Union forces at **Appomatox Court House**, Virginia.

- After the war, the southern economy was at a major disadvantage to the industrialized North, with slavery dismantled and many plantations destroyed. It would take more than 20 years for the southern economy to recover from the Civil War.

- Lincoln's **Reconstruction** plans were meant to restore the Union, and bring the South back into the fold politically. The course of the Reconstruction plans changed when Lincoln was assassinated by **John Wilkes Booth**, a Confederate sympathizer. New President Andrew Johnson implemented his own plans for Reconstruction, which included taking political and voting rights from the Confederacy's leaders, government officials, and financial backers. However, Johnson also implemented pardons that negated the consequences for many southern political figures.

- Congressional Reconstruction plans included an aggressive civil rights agenda from the Radical Republicans. The **Thirteenth, Fourteenth,** and **Fifteenth Amendments** to the

Constitution gave freedom, rights, and suffrage to African Americans. Congress also created the **Reconstruction Acts** in 1867, which divided the South into military districts, required Confederate states to accept the Thirteenth and Fourteenth Amendments in order to be accepted back into the Union, and called for all citizens to have the right to vote.

- Reconstruction measures were not popular in the South, and many states implemented policies that continued racism and segregation. The **Black Codes** adopted by southern states restricted African Americans from testifying against white people in court, and prevented them from borrowing money for land, which led to **sharecropping** (planting on someone else's land in exchange for crops) and former slaves' continued dependence on wealthy landowners. Additionally, **Jim Crow laws** attempted to prevent African Americans from voting by instituting **poll taxes**, **literacy tests**, and the **Grandfather Clause** (in which one could only vote if his grandfather had been able to vote—an impossibility for anyone whose grandfather had been a slave). The divisions were deepened with segregation, which claimed to create "separate but equal" services and facilities for African Americans and white people.

- Although the Union was technically whole in this postwar period, the Reconstruction period failed to address the larger issues of the divide between the Union states and the former Confederate states.

THE CIVIL WAR AND RECONSTRUCTION POST-TEST

Directions: Carefully read each of the following 60 questions. Choose the best answer to each question and fill in the corresponding circle on the answer sheet. The Answer Key and Explanations can be found following this post-test.

1. The Republican Party platform of the 1850s was centered around the belief that
   A. slavery should be banned in all territories and ended as a practice.
   B. slavery should be banned in new territories but remain where it was.
   C. slavery should be allowed in new territories but only with a vote of popular sovereignty.
   D. slavery should be allowed in all territories but slaves only counted as three-fifths in voting.

2. John Brown's raid on Harper's Ferry had which of the following effects?
   A. It frightened northern abolitionists, and they unilaterally rejected Brown's motives.
   B. It frightened southern whites because the use of violence was attributed as a northern attack on the institution of slavery.
   C. It united abolitionists in their cause and was a major turning point in how they attempted to affect change.
   D. It forced the North to condemn Brown's actions and attempt to reconcile with the South following the incident.

3. Which is true about southern society in the mid-19th century?
   A. The southern economy was extremely diverse.
   B. Rich plantation owners had little political influence or power.
   C. A majority of southerners did not own slaves or large amounts of land.
   D. Many African Americans held political offices or positions.

4. The Compromise of 1850 was extremely controversial because it declared a stricter what?
   A. Separation of church and state
   B. Fugitive Slave Law
   C. Tariff
   D. Homestead Act

5. The Wilmot Proviso was significant because it attempted to do which of the following?
   A. Ban slavery in all territories in the United States.
   B. Ban slavery in all territories acquired from the Mexican War.
   C. Ban slavery in all territories above the Mason-Dixon line.
   D. Ban slavery in all territories that didn't allow for popular sovereignty.

6. Which factor is the most likely reason for Lincoln's victory in 1860?
   A. The Democratic Party votes were divided among multiple candidates.
   B. Lincoln ran on a platform of allowing slavery to remain but not expand into new territories.
   C. The southern cotton economy had begun to shrink and the region was beginning to industrialize.
   D. Abolitionist messages were reaching far more people and it showed in the final vote.

7. Why did the northeast and midwest develop an economic partnership?
   A. The expansion of the railroad linked the regions while allowing fast and cheap transportation.
   B. The use of canals allowed for more trade along rivers such as the Mississippi.
   C. The northeast's desire for grains coupled with the midwest's growing capabilities created a likely pair.
   D. The refusal of the South to produce anything other than cotton made the North look elsewhere for trade.

8. Harriet Beecher Stowe enflamed the abolitionist debate with what book?
   A. *The Liberator*
   B. *The Impending Crisis of the South*
   C. *Uncle Tom's Cabin*
   D. *The North Star*

9. The Dred Scott decision was important for which of the following reasons?
   A. It created the idea of popular sovereignty, which allowed citizens to vote on the progress of slavery in a territory.
   B. It allowed slavery to move into any territory, regardless of the Missouri Compromise.
   C. It freed all slaves in Confederate territory.
   D. It formally legalized South Carolina's nullification of federal law.

10. Mid-nineteenth century America would best be described how?
    A. Politically and religiously diverse
    B. Economically and socially sluggish
    C. Territorially and diplomatically stagnant
    D. Demonstrating racial and gender equality

11. Which of the following examples would be the best evidence of Abraham Lincoln's leadership style during the early years of the Civil War?
    A. Lincoln's proclamation of emancipation to increase morale for the Union
    B. Lincoln's institution of the draft for more soldiers
    C. Lincoln's decision to allow the border states to retain slaves
    D. Lincoln's constant changing of generals and leaders because of ineffective results

12. Which document would those in South Carolina reference as evidence that their decision to secede was just and legal?
    A. The Missouri Compromise
    B. The Kansas-Nebraska Act
    C. The Virginia and Kentucky Resolutions
    D. The Dred Scott decision

13. How did the Union view the Civil War at its start?
    A. The North saw the war as a battle over slavery.
    B. The North saw the war as a battle to preserve the Union.
    C. The North saw the war as unwinnable.
    D. The North saw the war as legal and understandable.

14. Which of the following would be a military strength for the Confederacy over the Union?
    A. Banking and capital
    B. Military leaders
    C. African American soldiers
    D. Factories

15. Why was the First Battle of Bull Run (Manassas) so important?
    A. It set the tone and proved the illusion of a short war to be false.
    B. It allowed African American soldiers to fight in combat for the Union for the first time.
    C. It allowed Abraham Lincoln to announce the end of slavery after the Union victory.
    D. Four more southern states, including Virginia, seceded after the Confederate victory.

16. What was Lincoln's goal at Fort Sumter?
    A. To give up the fort as an act of peace
    B. To surrender the fort in an effort to prevent war
    C. To send provisions of food to troops
    D. To attack the Confederacy in hopes of a quick war

17. The Confederacy's economic strategy during the Civil War centered on the belief that
    A. the North needed the capital created by the sale of cotton.
    B. European demand for cotton would lead to foreign aid.
    C. the use of a blockade of shipping would undercut northern merchants.
    D. northern factories would go bankrupt without cotton for clothing production.

18. The battle of Antietam was significant for the Confederacy for what reason?
    A. The Union removed General McClellan, a Confederate and peace sympathizer.
    B. The battle failed to gain European aid and open recognition from foreign powers.
    C. A large number of slaves had escaped to the North prior to the battle.
    D. Lee's weakened army wasn't able to retreat, forcing excessive casualties.

19. The battle at Fredericksburg was devastating for the Union due to which General's reckless strategies?
    A. George McClellan
    B. Ambrose Burnside
    C. Ulysses Grant
    D. "Stonewall" Jackson

20. What boosted the Union morale in 1862?
    A. The decisive victory at Gettysburg
    B. The Emancipation Proclamation
    C. The capture of the Confederate capital at Richmond
    D. The promotion of Ulysses S. Grant to head of the Union Army

21. Northern soldiers were diverted from their attack on Richmond in 1862 for what reason?
    A. To address the gains of "Stonewall" Jackson in Tennessee that included capture of food and supplies
    B. To address the loss of the Union capital of Washington D.C. to General Lee
    C. To support the Union blockade of southern ports such as Charleston
    D. To hear the Emancipation Proclamation given by President Lincoln

22. The southern strategy would best be described as?
    A. Strongly offensive and aggressive
    B. Patient and defensive
    C. The Anaconda Plan
    D. Total war

23. The Emancipation Proclamation was careful not to upset which group?
    A. Republicans
    B. Democrats
    C. Border states
    D. Abolitionists

24. Where was the Confederate military most vulnerable in 1862?
    A. In military leadership, where many generals were inexperienced or young
    B. Within the morale of its people, where many southerners questioned the war
    C. In the east, as their capital and major cities were under Union barrage
    D. At sea, where the Union Navy won many important battles

25. The single bloodiest day of the war was fought in 1862 where?
    A. Antietam
    B. Bull Run
    C. Vicksburg
    D. Gettysburg

26. What was the Confederate Army under command of General Robert E. Lee known as?
    A. Massachusetts 54th
    B. Confederate Nation of Soldiers
    C. Army of Northern Virginia
    D. Richmond Rough Riders

27. Why was the battle of Vicksburg significant for the course of the war?
    A. The Confederacy secured control of the western front following their victory.
    B. The Union marched from Vicksburg to the sea, burning everything in its path.
    C. The Confederacy had taken the offensive only to lose its greatest casualities.
    D. The Union secured control of the Mississippi River.

28. Where were African Americans most welcomed for combat during the Civil War?
    A. In Confederate regiments fighting for the South
    B. In Union units with other white soldiers
    C. In western regiments under General Grant
    D. They were not welcomed

29. How did the toll of the war and the shift to a war over slavery impact the North in 1863?
    A. With victories mounting more volunteers joined the Union Army.
    B. Riots broke out over the draft, resulting in the death of many African Americans in New York.
    C. Economic hardship and failure to monetize led to cutbacks in Union supplies.
    D. Large rallies and support for Lincoln led him to run unopposed in 1864.

30. Which of the following statements is false about the casualities of the Civil War?
    A. New strategies of formations and military tactics led to many lives being taken.
    B. New military technology found in weapons was deadlier than war had ever seen.
    C. Poor medical techniques and infection led to higher death rates.
    D. A shift to a war of attrition meant more focus on wounding and killing the enemy.

31. Which of these women made notable contributions on the Civil War battlefield in the area of nursing?
    A. Elizabeth Cady Stanton
    B. Clara Barton
    C. Florence Nightingale
    D. Susan B. Anthony

32. What factor led most to the Confederate's casualty rates being higher than that of the Union's?
    A. The Confederate Army had more men, which meant more men to lose.
    B. The war was fought primarily in the South, which mean more southerners were exposed to war.
    C. The Union focused on utter destruction and a strategy of no retreat, as opposed to the patience and thoughtfulness of the Confederacy.
    D. Production of rifles was slower and the materials for rifles were more difficult to procure.

33. What was the most devastating result of the battle at Chancellorsville in 1863?
    A. The Union victory led to over 10,000 Confederate dead.
    B. The Union loss led Lincoln to replace General Hooker with General Meade.
    C. "Stonewall" Jackson was accidentally shot by his own troops and died.
    D. A Confederate plan to invade the North no longer made sense after the loss.

34. 1863 was the high point for which of the following?
    A. Union morale
    B. Confederate confidence
    C. Freedmen
    D. Women

35. What general was most famous for his "charge" at Gettysburg?
    A. Grant
    B. Lee
    C. Jackson
    D. Pickett

36. 1863 saw the greatest northern victories in what two cities?
    A. Chancellorsville and Shiloh
    B. Gettysburg and Vicksburg
    C. Antietam and Appomattox
    D. Manassas and Bull Run

37. How did women and African Americans alter the course of the war?
    A. They added more support on the battlefield for both sides.
    B. They allowed the war to become about equal rights instead of states' rights.
    C. They were able to fight for the Union, creating a distinct advantage in the number of troops.
    D. They began to vote, which allowed them to influence political decisions.

38. What was different about Grant's approach following the Battle of the Wilderness?
    A. He retreated to higher ground found in the northwest.
    B. He used new weapons such as the Minié ball.
    C. He used new tactical formations.
    D. He pursued Lee after the battle and into Virginia.

39. What 1864 battle was Grant's greatest regret?
    A. Battle of the Wilderness
    B. Cold Harbor
    C. West Point
    D. Fort Sumter

post-test

40. What became the Confederacy's greatest hope in 1864?
   A. Pursuing Grant into Washington D.C. and taking the Union capital
   B. Protecting Richmond and awaiting European aid to arrive
   C. McClellan winning the election over Lincoln
   D. Draft riots in the North over emancipation

41. What general did Grant leave behind to secure the west in his absence in 1864?
   A. Hooker
   B. Burnside
   C. Meade
   D. Sherman

42. Which is false regarding how new technology, such as rifles, changed the course of the war?
   A. Close order formations were now more fatal and had to be replaced.
   B. Firepower was more accurate and deadly.
   C. Generals began wearing privates' uniforms to be protected.
   D. Rifles could be used to shoot down other bullets or cannon balls as a defensive tool.

43. Sherman's total war was significant for years even after the war. Why?
   A. It destroyed the infrastructure and rail lines of the South.
   B. There were more casualties in his wake than at any other period in the war.
   C. The victories forced the South to surrender the Confederate capital of Virginia.
   D. The United States has used the strategy in every other war they have fought.

44. What was the name of the southern prison camp liberated by the Union in 1864?
   A. Andersonville
   B. Cold Harbor
   C. Charleston
   D. Appomattox

45. What was the name of the Union strategy that isolated the South using blockades?
   A. The Anaconda Plan
   B. Scorched-earth
   C. March to the Sea
   D. Attrition

46. Which battle, led by Union Admiral David Farragut, helped to deprive the Confederacy of badly needed supplies in 1864?
   A. New Orleans
   B. Atlanta
   C. Potomac
   D. Mobile Bay

47. General Sherman's Carolina Campaign would best be described as what type of war?
   A. War of attrition
   B. Total war
   C. Guerrilla warfare
   D. Patient war

48. General Lee and the Confederacy met where to surrender to the Union?
   A. Appomattox Court House
   B. Richmond, Virginia
   C. Ford's Theater
   D. Gettysburg

49. Who was the man who killed Abraham Lincoln?
   A. Robert E. Lee
   B. George B. McClellan
   C. John Wilkes Booth
   D. George Pickett

50. How was the Confederate Army treated after its surrender to General Grant?

 A. Harshly as soldiers were stripped of clothing, weapons, horses, and mules.

 B. Humanely, as soldiers were given rations and allowed to keep their horses.

 C. Indifferently, as Grant tended to his own troops and ignored the Confederates.

 D. As traitors; any Confederate was immediately put on trial for treason.

51. Which amendment to the Constitution afforded citizenship to African Americans?

 A. Thirteenth Amendment

 B. Fourteenth Amendment

 C. Fifteenth Amendment

 D. Emancipation Proclamation

52. The southern governments of 1865 (under President Johnson) were

 A. extremely different from the pre-war governments; African Americans were afforded many rights and ex-Confederates no longer held office.

 B. moderately different from the pre-war governments; new constitutions gave African Americans many rights but ex-Confederate leaders were reelected.

 C. similar to the pre-war governments; new state constitutions failed to address voting rights for African Americans and many ex-Confederates returned to Congress.

 D. nonexistent compared to the pre-war governments; southern governments were stripped of all powers and not an official part of the Union.

53. The Reconstruction Acts of 1867 did which of the following?

 A. Officially accepted the Confederate states back into the Union

 B. Impeached President Johnson

 C. Gave African Americans the right of citizenship and the right to vote

 D. Placed the South into five districts under military occupation

54. What term was given to northerners who went to the South after the Civil War?

 A. Scalawags

 B. Carpetbaggers

 C. Freedmen

 D. Sharecroppers

55. What was the greatest success of the Freedmen's Bureau?

 A. Obtaining the right of citizenship for African Americans

 B. Protecting the right to vote for African Americans

 C. Supplying the opportunity for education for African Americans

 D. Creating a Civil Rights Act (1875) for African Americans

56. Which group would be known by the term "radicals" during Reconstruction due to their belief in obtaining full rights for former slaves in the South?

 A. Democrats

 B. Republicans

 C. Freedmen

 D. Abolitionists

post-test

57. The withdrawal of federal troops and subsequent "end" to Reconstruction was brought about by which of the following events?
   A. The assassination of Abraham Lincoln
   B. The impeachment of Andrew Johnson
   C. The creation of the Reconstruction Acts of 1867
   D. The election of Rutherford B. Hayes

58. The impeachment of President Johnson was focused on Johnson's attempt to do what?
   A. Allow the Confederate states back into the Union before ratifying the Thirteenth Amendment
   B. Allow Confederate leaders to return to Congress and positions of power in the South
   C. Remove Republican members of his cabinet without the approval of the Senate
   D. Remove Federal troops from military zones in the South after the election of 1876

59. How would one describe the Civil Rights Act of 1875?
   A. Poorly enforced and supported
   B. Revolutionary and inventive
   C. Positive and effective
   D. Wasteful and corrupt

60. How would one best describe the legacy of Reconstruction?
   A. Successful, as many African Americans obtained greater rights and opportunities
   B. Successful, as the South was seamlessly integrated into the Union and extended new opportunities to those oppressed prior to the Civil War
   C. A failure due to the lingering effects of racial discrimination, sharecropping, and the return of Confederate leaders to Congress
   D. A failure due to the lack of infrastructure improvements in the South and lack of suffrage amendments

ANSWER KEY AND EXPLANATIONS

1. B	13. B	25. A	37. A	49. C
2. B	14. B	26. C	38. D	50. B
3. C	15. A	27. D	39. B	51. B
4. B	16. C	28. C	40. C	52. C
5. B	17. B	29. B	41. D	53. D
6. A	18. B	30. A	42. D	54. B
7. A	19. B	31. B	43. A	55. C
8. C	20. B	32. D	44. A	56. B
9. B	21. A	33. C	45. A	57. D
10. A	22. B	34. B	46. D	58. C
11. D	23. C	35. D	47. B	59. A
12. C	24. D	36. B	48. A	60. C

1. **The correct answer is B.** The Republican Party was not in favor of slavery expanding but believed that by simply containing it, it would slowly end itself. Choice A is incorrect because the Republican Party understood that slavery needed to remain in some places and believed it would eventually die out. Choice C is incorrect because the Republican Party did not support the idea of popular sovereignty as it gave slavery the opportunity to expand. Choice D is incorrect because the Republican Party did not want slavery to expand into new territories.

2. **The correct answer is B.** John Brown's raid was used as a form of propaganda in the South and portrayed as an act every northerner wished to partake in. Southerners condemned the act and were afraid more were to come especially after Brown received martyrdom in some areas of the North. Choice A is incorrect because Brown was seen as a martyr in abolitionist areas of the North. Choice C is incorrect because many abolitionists were still against Brown's tactics and the use of violence. Choice D is incorrect because while there was a short

"cooling" period between regions, the North did not reject Brown's actions outright.

3. **The correct answer is C.** The majority of people living in the South did not own slaves and had very little land, and many actually worked on the land for other, larger plantation owners. Choice A is incorrect because the economy was dependent on one crop, cotton. Choice B is incorrect because rich plantation owners dominated southern politics. Choice D is incorrect because few to no African Americans participated in southern politics prior to the Civil War.

4. **The correct answer is B.** The Fugitive Slave Law was added to the Compromise of 1850 in order to persuade southerners to accept the loss of California. However, many in the North refused to accept the law or enforce it. Choices A, C, and D are incorrect because they were not part of the Compromise of 1850.

5. **The correct answer is B.** David Wilmot proposed that all territory acquired as part of the Mexican War should be free territory only. The Wilmot Proviso did not pass and

answers post-test

instead the Compromise of 1850 was passed. Choices A, C, and D are incorrect because they are not part of the proposal made by David Wilmot.

6. **The correct answer is A.** The Democratic Party had two candidates, including Stephen A. Douglas and John C. Breckinridge, and the Constitutional Union candidate was John Bell. With the southern Democratic votes going to Breckinridge and the Northern Democratic votes going to Douglas, Lincoln had a unified Northern Republican Party behind him. Choice B is incorrect because while it correctly identifies Lincoln's platform, the South did not vote for him thus it was not a reason for his victory. Choice C is incorrect because it is false; the southern economy was very strong in 1860. Choice D is incorrect because there were still numerous places in the South that refused to accept an abolitionist message.

7. **The correct answer is A.** The creation of the railroad connected the northeast to the midwest, allowing a partnership of trade to develop. Because it would become America's largest industry the railroad also replaced river routes as the primary form of transportation. Choice B is incorrect because canals were no longer used as much as they had been before and the northeast was not connected via the Mississippi River. Choice C is incorrect because while there was a partnership based on grain, it was not directly why the partnership developed. Those in the northeast still had access to some grains but the use of the railroads made trade with the midwest more practical. Choice D is incorrect because there was still plenty of trade between the regions due to cotton.

8. **The correct answer is C.** Stowe's work, *Uncle Tom's Cabin*, divided the nation as northerners took it to be a literal account of what slavery was like; southerners saw it

as pure propaganda created by a northerner who had never seen slavery in the South. The book became more popular than any other book in the United States after the Bible. Choices A, B, and D are incorrect because they were not written by Stowe.

9. **The correct answer is B.** The Supreme Court under Roger Taney cited the Fifth Amendment to declare slaves property, not people, thus allowing them to travel anywhere their masters' desired while making the Missouri Compromise unconstitutional. Choices A, C, and D are incorrect because they were not included in the court ruling.

10. **The correct answer is A.** By 1850, more Americans had a say in politics and shared their different opinions on slavery. At the same time, there were more religious offerings as the Second Great Awakening created a democratic view on religion. Choice B is incorrect as the economy was indeed growing especially the market for cotton. Choice C is incorrect as America was territorially growing through Manifest Destiny. Choice D is incorrect as the country was still far from racial and gender equality.

11. **The correct answer is D.** The constant shifting of generals and leadership is best evidence for the struggles Lincoln faced as a leader. Until Sherman's March to the Sea there was no guarantee that Lincoln would serve a second term and many saw these early changes as poor leadership. Choices A, B, and C are incorrect because, although all are true actions of President Lincoln, they came later in his term and were not characteristic of his early leadership style.

12. **The correct answer is C.** The Virginia and Kentucky Resolutions, created during the Alien and Sedition Acts, were used twice by South Carolina (during the nullification crisis in the 1830s and again in the 1860s) as support for states being able to nullify

federal law. Choices A, B, and D would not be cited as evidence for secession, as they are related specifically to slavery, not states rights. Choice A is incorrect because the Missouri Compromise created a line in which slavery was legal. Choice B is incorrect because the Kansas-Nebraska Act put slavery up to a vote via popular sovereignty. Choice D is incorrect because the decision allowed slavery to move anywhere in the United States.

13. **The correct answer is B.** The Union under Abraham Lincoln declared the war to be fought over saving the country, not slavery (Lincoln even admitted that if he could save the union without freeing any slaves, he would). The goal was to have the Confederacy reenter the Union first and then deal with slavery afterwards. Choice A is incorrect because the Union did not fight to end slavery early in the war (as proven by the border states retaining slavery after the Emancipation Proclamation). Choice C is incorrect because the Union believed the war would be won easily and quickly. Choice D is incorrect because Lincoln did believe the South had the legal right to secede and after the war his Reconstruction plan after the war supports this.

14. **The correct answer is B.** The Confederate generals were vastly superior to those in the Union, specifically Lee and Jackson. Many from the South had trained at West Point and had battle experience from the Mexican War. Choices A, C, and D are incorrect because they were Union advantages.

15. **The correct answer is A.** The Confederate victory showed northerners that the South would not go quietly and that the war would continue for a long time. Choice B is incorrect because African Americans did not fight for the Union in this battle. Choice C is incorrect because Lincoln made no such announcement after the military loss. Choice D is incorrect because all southern states had seceded prior to the battle.

16. **The correct answer is C.** Lincoln declared that he would not send weapons to the troops at Fort Sumter but he would not let them to starve. He placed the decision for war on the Confederates as he was only attempting to supply his troops with provisions. Choices A and B are incorrect because Lincoln refused to surrender the fort. Choice D is incorrect because Lincoln did not wish to attack but instead prevent any war by sending only food.

17. **The correct answer is B.** The Confederacy believed that European countries such as Great Britain would come to their aid in an effort to preserve the cotton trade. However, other countries such as India began selling cotton and the Confederacy no longer held a monopoly that could be used over Europe. Choices A and D are incorrect because the North had diversified its economy and was not dependent on cotton for use in its factories. Choice C is incorrect because the North attempted to blockade the South, not the other way around, as the Confederate Navy was extremely weak.

18. **The correct answer is B.** The Union victory (and subsequent decision to make the war about slavery) kept European powers from joining the fight. The recent banning of slavery in places such as Great Britain coupled with the Confederate loss was enough to keep foreign nations from entering into a conflict against the North. Choice A is incorrect because although McClellan was removed after the battle, McClellan was not a Confederate sympathizer and had yet to promote the idea of peace with the South. Choice C is incorrect because slaves escaping wasn't uncommon and was not a very significant factor in this particular

battle. Choice D is incorrect because Lee was able to retreat.

19. **The correct answer is B.** Burnside had replaced the more cautious McClellan and led the army wildly into battle at Fredericksburg with a full frontal assault, causing casualties and another Union loss. Choices A and C are incorrect because they were Union generals, but not in command at Fredericksburg. Choice D is incorrect because Jackson was a Confederate general.

20. **The correct answer is B.** The Emancipation Proclamation changed the course of the war for the Union, giving soldiers a new reason to fight and increasing the number of volunteers due to the newly formed direction of the war: ending slavery. Choice A is incorrect because the Union did not have a decisive win at Gettysburg in 1862. Choice C is incorrect because Richmond was not captured in 1862. Choice D is incorrect because Grant had yet to be promoted.

21. **The correct answer is A.** The success of "Stonewall" Jackson in Tennessee forced the Union to redirect troops to the west in an effort to address the heavy losses of food and supplies. Choice B is incorrect because Lee did not capture Washington, D.C. Choice C is incorrect because the Union troops did not change course to help with the blockade. Choice D is incorrect because the address was not given publically.

22. **The correct answer is B.** The Confederate Army was able to fight on their own turf and advance when necessary; they used a strategy that was patient and opportunistic while more defensive in nature. Choices A, C, and D are incorrect because they better describes the Union strategy.

23. **The correct answer is C.** The border states remained in the Union and were an integral part of its success, providing food.

By only "freeing" slaves in the rebellious states, Lincoln was able to maintain those border states that still had a use for slavery. Choice A is incorrect because Lincoln was a member of the Republican Party and many asked for a harsher stance on slavery. Choice B is incorrect because many Democrats (who were found primarily in the South) were upset. Choice D is incorrect because abolitionists were happy with the first step and asked for a greater stance on slavery.

24. **The correct answer is D.** The Confederate Navy was weak and no match for the Union Navy; this was a main reason they had hoped for European aid. Choice A is incorrect because one of the strongest Confederate advantages was their leadership. Choice B is incorrect because many in the South believed more strongly in the war than their northern counterparts. Choice C is incorrect because in 1862 the Confederate Army was very strong in the east and they held their important cities.

25. **The correct answer is A.** The battle of Antietam saw more blood in a single day than any other battle in the Civil War, with over 20,000 men dead or wounded. While other battles would have higher totals, none would be from a single day of fighting. Choices B, C, and D are incorrect because they did not have as many dead or wounded in a single day of battle.

26. **The correct answer is C.** The troops under Robert E. Lee came directly from the center of the Confederacy in Virginia, fighting as the primary regiment of the South. Choice A is incorrect because this was the name of the all-African-American regiment of the Union. Choices B and D are incorrect because there were no regiments with these names.

27. **The correct answer is D.** The Union victory gave them control of the most important

river in the country and an important strategic region of the war, securing the west for the Union. Choice A is incorrect because the Confederacy did not win nor did it control the West. Choice B is incorrect because the March to the Sea came later in the war. Choice C is incorrect because both statements are false.

28. **The correct answer is C.** General Grant supported the use of African American troops and encouraged the use in the west (this would later be a reason he was elected president). Choice A is incorrect because African Americans were not welcomed by the South in regiments until late in the war. Choice B is incorrect because African American soldiers were kept segregated from white soldiers. Choice D is incorrect because the Union did allow African Americans in the war in their own regiments.

29. **The correct answer is B.** The Emancipation Proclamation changed the Civil War to a battle over ending slavery. Coupled with the length and high number of casualties, many in the North became tired and upset with the course of the war. When President Lincoln instituted a draft that seemed to target lower-class citizens (substitutes could be bought by the rich), riots broke out near the New York draft offices over the issue. Choice A is incorrect because the need for a draft proved volunteers were not increasing. Choice C is incorrect because the Union had instituted a monetary system and stabilized its economic situation during this period of the war. Choice D is incorrect because Lincoln was not widely supported and faced a difficult election period.

30. **The correct answer is A.** Old strategies and tactics continued deep into the Civil War, with front formations leading to more deaths when facing the new, more deadly

technology of the war. Choices B, C, and D are all true statements about the war.

31. **The correct answer is B.** Clara Barton, later known for her work with the American Red Cross, created a name for herself during the war by tending to soldiers on the battlefield. Choices A and D are incorrect because they fought for women's suffrage but had no role in the Civil War. Choice C is incorrect because, although she was an inspiration for many women during the war, Nightingale was from Europe and had no direct contribution during the war.

32. **The correct answer is D.** The Confederacy often had to resort to taking weapons off the dead because they lacked the production and materials to create enough supply for its troops. Choice A is incorrect because the Confederacy had fewer men than the Union. Choice B is incorrect because, although the war was indeed fought mostly in the South, there were still fewer Confederate soldiers than Union soldiers in the war. Choice C is incorrect because the Union did focus on these tactics, but often at the expense of its own soldiers not the Confederates.

33. **The correct answer is C.** Jackson's death, a week after being shot accidentally by his own troops, was devastating to the Confederates because he was one of the strongest, if not the strongest, generals they had after Lee. The Confederates never recovered from losing Jackson. Choice A is incorrect because although 10,000 died on the Confederate side, that was not as big of a blow as the death of Jackson (also, the Union did not win the battle). Choice B is incorrect because although Hooker was replaced by Meade, this move was did not have a large impact on the war or the Confederates. Choice D is incorrect because the Confederates would indeed

begin plans to invade the North after their victory.

34. **The correct answer is B.** The Confederate Army was advancing through Pennsylvania and Union fear was growing at the start of 1863. The continual changing of generals by Lincoln coupled with victories by Lee's army put Washington D.C. in his crosshairs. Choice A is incorrect because Union morale was sinking until the victory at Gettysburg turned the tide. Choice C is incorrect because slavery still existed in the country and freedmen (freed slaves) were still facing segregation and discrimination. Choice D is incorrect because women had been involved in many battles throughout the war as nurses, but 1863 was not a significant change in their position.

35. **The correct answer is D.** Pickett's charge on the heart of the Union's lines at Gettysburg was not only unsuccessful but led half of his 14,000 troops to their deaths. Choices A, B, and C are incorrect because they did not lead a historically memorable charge at Gettysburg.

36. **The correct answer is B.** The Union victories at Gettysburg and Vicksburg turned the tide of the war, leading the Confederacy to retreat while losing more men and supplies. This would be considered the beginning of the end for the Confederate States. Choice A is incorrect because the Union was not victorious at Chancellorsville. Choice C is incorrect because Antietam was in 1862 and Appomattox was not a battle. Choice D is incorrect because they are the same battle, fought in 1862.

37. **The correct answer is A.** The inclusion of women as nurses and African Americans as soldiers changed the course of the war, creating more and better support for both sides. Choice B is incorrect because the war never became about equal rights for either group. Choice C is incorrect because the Union already had an advantage in population and number of troops so just their inclusion alone did not change the course of the war. Choice D is incorrect because neither group could vote during the war.

38. **The correct answer is D.** The Union and its generals had rarely followed the Confederates into southern territory after a retreat. In 1864, Grant continually pursued and pushed Lee back in an all-out furious attack that resulted in high casualties. Choice A is incorrect because there was no Union retreat. Choice B is incorrect because new weapons had been used throughout the war. Choice C is incorrect because new formations were rarely if ever used during the war, which led to more casualties because of the new technology.

39. **The correct answer is B.** The Battle at Cold Harbor saw Grant obtain a new nickname, the Butcher. With high casualties that resulted from a full-on assault that was coupled with fires his men could not retreat from, Grant believed this to be the only battle he regretted. Choice A is incorrect because it was a decisive victory for Grant. Choice C is incorrect because it is a military school, not a battle. Choice D is incorrect because Grant was not involved in the first shots of the Civil War at Fort Sumter.

40. **The correct answer is C.** By 1864, the only hope remaining for the Confederate States would be peace, and former Union General George McClellan ran on a platform of peace if he won. For a time it looked as though he would win, with many in the North tiring of the war and unhappy with its number of casualties. Choices A, B, and D are incorrect because all these events had passed and no longer seemed viable options for Confederate victory.

41. **The correct answer is D.** William T. Sherman was Grant's most trusted general and placed in charge of securing the West while he pursued Lee. Choices A, B, and C are incorrect because they were not left in command by Grant.

42. **The correct answer is D.** Cannons, not rifles, were used as defensive tools during the Civil War. While rifles became more accurate, they were still used as offensive tools. Choices A, B, and C are incorrect because they are all true of modern warfare during the Civil War.

43. **The correct answer is A.** The South was placed almost 20 years behind the North in terms of infrastructure and economy following the war, with a big reason being Sherman's scorched-earth tactics that destroyed the South and its railways (Sherman's men bent the lines behind them as they marched to the sea). Choice B is incorrect because other battles had more casualties; Sherman's greatest destruction came to the land and homes, not people. Choice C is incorrect because Sherman did not march to the Confederate capital. Choice D is incorrect because this strategy has not been used in every battle since.

44. **The correct answer is A.** Andersonville was a notorious southern prison camp that saw deplorable conditions and barely any rations for captured Union soldiers. Choices B, C, and D are incorrect because they were not prison camps.

45. **The correct answer is A.** The Anaconda Plan was a two-part process that included taking control of the Mississippi River and implementing a blockade on Confederate ports to cut off its supplies. By 1864, the plan had been successful and Confederate troops were in dire need of supplies. Choices B and C are incorrect because scorched-earth was how Sherman handled his march to the sea,

burning everything in his wake. Choice D is incorrect because attrition was the constant wearing down of an opponent; while it was part of the Union strategy, it did not specifically isolate the South.

46. **The correct answer is D.** The Union Navy was sure to uphold the blockade on southern ships, stopping important shipments from arriving to reinforce the Confederates at Mobile Bay. Choices A, B, and C are incorrect because they were not naval battles that supported the blockade in 1864.

47. **The correct answer is B.** Sherman marched through Carolina with a goal to attack Lee's army and never let secession be an option again. He burned everything in sight with no regard for anything in his path. Choice A is incorrect because the march was not focused on wearing down the enemy, but destroying it. Choice C is incorrect because Sherman's march was not hidden and continued to destroy resources head-on with all of his troops. Choice D is incorrect because Sherman pushed through the region quickly without pause.

48. **The correct answer is A.** Generals Grant and Lee met at Appomattox in the McLean House where the Confederates officially surrendered to the Union. Choice B is incorrect because it is not as specific as choice A. Choice C and D are incorrect because General Lee did not surrender at these places.

49. **The correct answer is C.** The assassination of President Lincoln took place at Ford's Theater when John Wilkes Booth, former actor and Confederate sympathizer, shot him. Choices A, B, and D are incorrect because they were not the assassin.

50. **The correct answer is B.** Grant allowed for a respectful surrender that had a happy effect on the troops. Allowing the Confederates

to keep their horses and mules would give them a chance to better plant their crops the following year. Choices A, C, and D are incorrect because they are false statements that didn't happen.

51. **The correct answer is B.** The Fourteenth Amendment states, "All persons born or naturalized in the United States and subject to the jurisdiction thereof, are citizens of the United States and of the State wherein they reside. No State shall make or enforce any law which shall abridge the privileges or immunities of citizens of the United States; nor shall any State deprive any person of life, liberty, or property, without due process of law; nor deny to any person within its jurisdiction the equal protection of the laws." Choice A is incorrect because this amendment ended slavery. Choice C is incorrect because this amendment gave African Americans the right to vote. Choice D is incorrect because it was not an amendment and only freed slaves in rebellious states during the war.

52. **The correct answer is C.** The South was easily able to return to the Union under President Johnson and many former Confederate leaders took back their positions of power in politics. States, while having to ratify the Thirteenth amendment, did not support or endorse African Americans voting in their constitutions (while doing nothing to curb Jim Crow laws). Choice A is incorrect because African Americans struggled to practice their rights under governments that included former Confederate leaders. Choice B is incorrect because new state constitutions did not support African American rights and did more to confine them than help. Choice D is incorrect because southern governments regained powers relatively quickly and rejoined the Union.

53. **The correct answer is D.** The act declared the governments recognized by Johnson inoperative while dividing them into five military districts, each with military supervision. Choices A, B, and C are incorrect because they were not part of the Reconstruction Act of 1867.

54. **The correct answer is B.** *Carpetbagger* was a derogatory term given to a person from the North who moved to the South attempting to make profit off the war-torn area. Choice A is incorrect because it was a term given to a southerner who supported the Republicans in the North. Choice C is incorrect because it was a term for freed slaves. Choice D is incorrect because it was a term for freed slaves or poor whites who worked on plantations after the war, using their labor as trade for wages and housing.

55. **The correct answer is C.** The Freedmen's Bureau was an agency created to help freed slaves, African Americans, and poor whites. It was most successful in creating a welfare-like system that gave African Americans a place to become educated, job skills, and even a place to stay. While it was underfunded by the federal government and ended relatively quickly, it still helped many freed slaves and African Americans learn to read and write. Choice A is incorrect because that right was obtained by the Thirteenth Amendment. Choice B is incorrect because the Freedmen's Bureau was not able to protect this right in the South as Jim Crow laws and violence often stopped African Americans from voting. Choice D is incorrect because the Freedmen's Bureau was not responsible for this act being created.

56. **The correct answer is B.** Republicans were known as "radicals" because of their stance on rights for African Americans. Choices A, C, and D are incorrect because they were

not described by the term "radical" during Reconstruction.

57. **The correct answer is D.** The election of 1876 saw a compromise that gave Republicans control of the presidency (Rutherford B. Hayes) in exchange for removing troops from the South. Choices A, B, and C are incorrect because they were not the reason federal troops left the South.

58. **The correct answer is C.** Johnson, a War Democrat, had come into office after Lincoln's election and wanted to place members into his own cabinet. When he attempted to remove his war secretary, he was in violation of the Tenure of Office Act. Choice A is incorrect because all states ratified the amendment before reentering the Union. Choice B is incorrect because even though Johnson allowed this to happen it was not in violation of any law. Choice D is incorrect because Johnson was not in office during this period.

59. **The correct answer is A.** The Civil Rights Act of 1875 would be the last time until the 1950s the federal government attempted to procure the rights of African Americans. The act itself saw little enforcement in the South, from southern governments or the federal government. Choice B is incorrect because the act attempted to continue the rights created in the Thirteenth, Fourteenth, and Fifteenth Amendments and took no new steps to securing rights for African Americans. Choice C is incorrect because

the act was just the opposite. Choice D is incorrect because there was no corruption with the act, only a lack of enforcement.

60. **The correct answer is C.** While some improvements were made in areas such as infrastructure and federal legislation, discrimination by Jim Crow laws and sharecropping remained in the South following the war. Many African Americans continued to struggle to gain equality and many white leaders from before the war returned to positions of power. Choice A is incorrect because while African Americans did gain more rights and even political office, the majority struggled to practice those rights in the South. Choice B is incorrect because there were many struggles with bringing the South back into the Union and equality was not found for many after it. Choice D is incorrect because there were some improvements to infrastructure and a voting amendment was indeed passed (Fifteenth Amendment) even though it was not often followed.

answers post-test

NOTES

NOTES